To Mickey
Your are
a peace
maker
Just Be peace
enjoy
Soga

# Jeshua's Song

## By the Saga-Oracle

### Iva Deane GeMMell

*Jeshua was born,*
*When there was more day than night,*
*He is the sun,*
*He is the light.*
*MiryAmah was born,*
*When there was more night than day,*
*She is the moon,*
*She shows the way.*
(Magdalene's Well, page 75)

All rights reserved. No part of this book shall be reproduced or transmitted in any form or by any means, electronic, mechanical, magnetic, photographic including photocopying, recording or by any information storage and retrieval system, without prior written permission of the publisher. No patent liability is assumed with respect to the use of the information contained herein. Although every precaution has been taken in the preparation of this book, the publisher and author assume no responsibility for errors or omissions. Neither is any liability assumed for damages resulting from the use of the information contained herein.

Copyright © 2011 by Iva Deane GeMMell

ISBN 0-7414-6543-4

Printed in the United States of America

This is a work of fiction. Names, characters, places, and incidents either are the product of the author's imagination or are used fictitiously. Any resemblance to actual events or locales or persons, living or dead, is entirely coincidental.

Published June 2011

INFINITY PUBLISHING
1094 New DeHaven Street, Suite 100
West Conshohocken, PA 19428-2713
Toll-free (877) BUY BOOK
Local Phone (610) 941-9999
Fax (610) 941-9959
Info@buybooksontheweb.com
www.buybooksontheweb.com

# ACKNOWLEDGEMENTS

This book is possible only because of a network of special people who offered their energy so the project could be completed. Your love was the fuel I ran on.

Sincere thanks go out to Karl and Bev Karlskin, my first spiritual teachers, now passed on into the nonphysical and no doubt, still assisting many find a path to peace. They helped me see that being 'mystical' was not abnormal, rather, simply a state of being sensitive and aware. I feel your presence and know you helped with this book, too. I will never forget you.

Thank you, Cindy Dort, healer of body, mind and soul, for introducing me to Karl and Bev, and your lifelong friendship. I can't possibly count the times you have been there for me. I am grateful you have carried on Karl and Bev's legacy and expanded and perfected your own healing ministry, as well. It's important.

Thanks to Rhonda Birirtz whose inquisitive mind stimulated so many in-depth conversations throughout the years and who was an early motivation for me to 'listen' to Jeshua's story. I loved our partnership in *Magdalene's Well*, and wish you the best as you continue on to follow your dream.

Shawna Dockery and Amy Jones, your encouragement as I asked you to review an original rough copy of *Jeshua's Song*, inspired me to finish this project, and I thank you both. Amy, you reminded me that the story was more important than the struggle it took to get the words formatted into something readable. I needed to hear that. Shawna, your call as you finished the book was soothing to my soul, and music to my ears. In so many ways you have held my hand and given me loving strength to carry on.

Edi Land, the angels surely sent you. I will always remember the day you dropped by at Mystic Beads when I was doing readings.

You said you liked to do punctuation and if I needed help to call. I called. Your commitment to your promise encouraged me and reminded me that *Jeshua's Song* was a promise I made, too.

Also, thanks to Jessica and Phil Falcone for inviting me to your lovely home for tea, and your suggestion of the computer grammar check program. How you managed to get me out of the computer chair I was glued to for weeks, I will never know. That cup of tea, delightful company and suggestion gave me a double-check option and made this book easier to edit, and eased my anxiety.

Also a deep heartfelt thanks to Beth McKechnie, for your friendship and constant encouragement, especially reading, *Jeshua's Song,* even as high school teaching drained your energy. Your suggestions were right on target. I'm grateful that you saved a little of that precious energy to help me. The follow-up discussions of the chapters helped me see through the reader's eyes. Your remarks were confirmations I needed to hear.

Thanks, to my friend Larry Ford, who took months out of his life to help me. Your willingness to take over cooking, cleaning and animal chores, along with holding down your own job is appreciated beyond words. When life's frustrations and sorrows seemed to drown me you brought the life boat. You are a wonder.

Thanks to my kids, Deana Carnes, Robin Ballard, Tony Suddon, and Joe Suddon, for your patience with an obsessed mother and your encouragement during some difficult times. You and your families are my greatest treasure.

Also, thanks Tony for being the perfect model for the cover of this book. Your eyes look deeper, and see more than anyone I know.

In addition, thanks Joe for a letter you wrote to me years ago when you were just a young boy. I recently rediscovered it in an old book. It proved written words matter far beyond the moment they are composed.

Deana, thanks for the Sunday morning calls and the patient ears as I sorted my frustrations. Your wisdom always refreshed me.

Robin, thanks for taking two weeks out of your life to escort me around Scotland. And for all the other times you have hung out with your mom and made me feel loved and appreciated.

Kate Monroe, my cousin, who is more like a sister, thank you for your love and support, even after all the lost years. You, and your husband Elmer, are proof that unconditional love is the greatest motivation ever. To that magic formula you added 'wisdom' and 'yes,' that helped me stay on track.

Hazel Crosbie, your encouragement has opened more doors in my life in a multitude of ways than I could ever list. Thank you for being the final proofreader of *Jeshua's Song* and offering your insightful feedback. Your life experiences and background in world religions made you the perfect critic, as I completed this mission. Your friendship and love mean the world to me.

Finally, thanks and appreciation to the voices I have heard my entire life–the loving guardians–who have always given me love and compassion, and steered my life down the right paths.

How do I thank MiryAmah and Jeshua, who I was sure, were too holy to ever ask the likes of me to tell their life stories? They taught me that we are all 'holy' and our life has many perspectives. When things felt overwhelming, or circumstances were totally distracting, I clearly heard Jeshua say, "Don't give up on me now!" I realize now he also meant, "Don't give up on myself either."

# CONTENTS

| | |
|---|---|
| The Decision | (1) |
| Soul Song | (8) |
| Emergence | (16) |
| Master Child | (27) |
| My First Spiritual Journey | (37) |
| The Mountain People Welcome Me | (44) |
| Animal Teachers | (50) |
| Going Home | (64) |
| Goodbye Again | (73) |
| The Herbalist Apprentice | (81) |
| The Healer | (91) |
| Healing Outreach | (102) |
| The Sacred Bowl | (116) |
| The Wisdom Well | (124) |
| The Christopher | (129) |
| Visiting The Temple Elders | (134) |
| A Difficult Farewell | (145) |
| The Blue Egg Of Destiny | (153) |
| Madness | (163) |
| What You Seek, Seeks You | (175) |
| The Alchemist's Apprentice | (186) |
| The Saga Of The Ancients | (206) |
| Wandering With My Cousin John | (232) |

| | |
|---|---|
| The Gift Of The Red Robe | (253) |
| Song Of The Sea | (267) |
| Peter, Oh Peter, My Rock | (279) |
| Divine Union And The Sparrows | (297) |
| A Sabbath Day Healing | (313) |
| Mother's Surprise | (328) |
| The Crown I Did Not Want | (337) |
| Death Of A Messiah | (351) |
| The Healing Skull Of Mu | (374) |
| The Great Gift | (394) |
| Bi-Locating To My Beloveds | (407) |
| The Faraway Land | (424) |
| The Gifts Of The Sea-Goddess | (446) |
| 'Fisher One' | (459) |
| Lily Of The Lake | (473) |
| They Know Not What They Do | (484) |
| Home To Heal | (501) |
| Love Has To Let Go | (514) |
| The Little Queen | (526) |
| Holy Communion | (549) |
| Over Land And Sea | (565) |
| The Path Of Peace | (583) |
| Precious Innocence; Lost, Then Found | (599) |
| Take Me Home, Jeshua, Take Me Home | (614) |

# PROLOGUE

*Jeshua's Song* is the story of the sacred masculine told through the voice of Jesus, or Jeshua as I have come to know him. It is the sequel to *Magdalene's Well*[1], the story of the sacred feminine, published in 2004, in which Mary of Magdala, the wife of Jeshua ben Joseph, shared her life story. The first draft of *Magdalene's Well* was completed in three short months, about the same time that *The da Vinci Code* by Dan Brown appeared on the literary scene. *Magdalene's Well* was not inspired by Brown's popular work of fiction nor was the tale changed in any way due to his work; even so, there were many similarities between the two books.

*Jeshua's Song*, like *Magdalene's Well* was not researched or charted, it simply was a story that came through me. I'm not a biblical scholar and don't consider this a biblical tale. In the case of *Magdalene's Well* the narrative first came through like a flood, and then it was given to my dear friend Rhose. Between the two of us the tale was recorded. We didn't intend to seek out a subject and write a book. Yet, we knew that the sacred feminine was present in this account, which we were unexpectedly asked to share. Hearing the voice of Mary Magdalene caused me to question my sanity, which included a visit to a counselor. My father had just passed on as well, and I thought I might be 'losing it!' My counselor, believing I had somehow tapped into the archetype of Mary Magdalene, urged me to carry on with the project saying, "See where it takes you."

*Magdalene's Well* is the feminine perspective. Nevertheless, people kept asking for the sacred masculine perspective, too. That's when Jeshua asked to be heard. Mary Magdalene caused me to seek a psychiatrist's couch, but Jeshua nearly put me over the edge. I felt totally unworthy of listening to him. I had to put skepticism aside and revert to my days as a journalist and simply agree to the assignment; just write down what I heard and visualized, as best I could.

---

[1] Saga-Rhose, *Magdalene's Well*, 2004, Infinity Publishing, Haverford, PA

Rhose inspired the name of the sequel, *Jeshua' Song*. A very appropriate title, too, since Jeshua speaks of how all creation leaves a trail of light and sound.

While the tale came through in sequence–in this type of writing mode, which is a constant flow–it was much like my journalist days when I tried to keep up with people telling me their interesting stories and my notes ran into each other. Grammar, order, punctuation, all came in later. I had to move past questioning the source. I realized that the story was more important than whether it was fictional or actual. I noticed the subject of 'self-worth' was a struggle for Jeshua, too. I had to move beyond the need to prove the fascinating tale I was hearing. Thus, I'm not sure if this book is a parable, an alternate reality[2], actual fact, or a product of my imagination. I just recorded what I saw and heard. Even so, I'm quite sure I couldn't have imagined this fantastic tale and the unique twists and turns Jeshua's interesting and inspiring life-experience took.

As the movie-like tale unfolded a chapter at a time, it seemed mere moments had passed once the day's passage was seen, heard and recorded. Actually, it was usually eight to ten hours later, quite the opposite effect I felt as Mary Magdalene shared her story. Back then, it felt like hours had passed as each chapter was done for the day, when it was really only minutes. Her chapters averaging about an hour, compared to Jeshua's all day sessions. In this type of consciousness flow[3] writing, time and logic don't apply as they normally would, except the story followed Jeshua's life sequence, from before birth, until after his death.

I attended a workshop for learning styles when I transferred from teaching college art to working for an outreach program for at-risk children. I discovered that consciousness flow writing was a rare, but natural way, of learning and communication for some people.

---

[2] The concept that many versions of the universe unfold at the same time

[3] A way of writing which is like a "flowing experience." In art it is called "in the zone". The sense of time and place disappears and the experience is dreamlike, and feels like one is carried by a current

# The Saga-Oracle

As I learned to work with such students, I finally understood my own writing and art style. Once the words, or art, (I use the process in both situations) are allowed free-flow, the next step is to prepare and share. In this totally-unplanned flowing process, it can be overwhelming when preparing the written narrative, due to this process. The constant flow of words, as the tale plays out, results in sentences being inverted, chained, stated and restated several different ways, often with old and new vernacular mixed together like a tangled web. Nevertheless, the story was there, whole and complete, even if additional explanation and footnotes were added in later drafts. I found it especially helpful to look up the meaning of individual's names Jeshua referenced. In each case, the names always fit perfectly with the spirit and personality of the person he mentioned. If I thought clarification important again, I repeated some footnotes, so that readers didn't have to find the original reference in previous pages.

As I headed into preparation to share this tale, a dream-like memory of each chapter triggered a flashback of the entire episode. I became caught up in the story I barely remembered, due to the trance-like mode it originally came through.

Years ago I accepted I am an oracle[4]. I don't claim to be spouting messages from the gods, but often words, art images, and messages just automatically came through me, and through word of mouth, messages traveled far and wide. Former President Clinton and the Dalai Lama both wrote notes of thanks regarding oracle messages they received. Mostly, everyday people requested and received messages and found the answers they were seeking within them. As I grew in my own awareness, so did my understanding of my natural abilities as a storyteller, or a 'saga.' Being the message-bearer isn't my chosen occupation; it is just who I am.

---

[4] Oracles were thought to be portals through which the gods spoke directly to man. In this sense they were different from seers (*manteis*, μάντεις) who interpreted signs sent by the gods through bird signs, animal entrails, and other various methods.

As a child this ability wasn't understood, especially since it is a flowing process. To my family, when I was in the flow, I was spouting things they didn't want to hear, and probably weren't ready to face, or I was chatting away with my invisible friends. I was told to "shut up" so many times, that my little brother's first words were "shut up." Even though I was an extremely shy child, I forced myself to come out of my shell and took up the teaching profession. I found that as a teacher, often whatever was needed, to help students understand the subject I taught, just came through, if I entered the flow. Naturally, I didn't share my technique openly, due to the 'strangeness' of the process. After half the college where I taught (and a good number of people from the community) asked for messages I finally put self-judgment aside, and became comfortable in the process. In teaching, as in journalism, I told the story and moved on. Since I didn't create the message, I wasn't attached to it, and simply released it to whoever made the request. I later learned that was what oracles did.

In that spirit, I listened to the voice of Jeshua tell the story of his life in his own way, from his personal emotional perspective; how he felt as he moved through that sojourn. Always, love and compassion were the common thread. Still, insecurities nearly paralyzed me, even as the story fascinated me, because I truly believe, the voice I heard was Jesus (Jeshua). My personal parameters of possibility expanded. As unattached as I am from ownership of creating this story, I am still in awe that Jeshua would trust me with such a tender, revealing tale. I knew the message was more important than the process, and I continued on with the encouragement of friends.

I suggest to the reader, simply read the story. Don't try to fit it into the framework of history or dogma. It's not meant to threaten your religion or philosophy. After you are finished reading this tale, I believe you will know 'Jeshua the man' and appreciate the side of him that most have never considered, his humanity and his humility. Perhaps we will never know if Jeshua's life is fact or fiction. Perhaps we don't need to know.

# THE DECISION
## Chapter One

The Galactic Council, an overseeing body of high masters and mastras[5], convened in order to call forth the spirit essence of individual souls, which had volunteered for a grand mission upon the blue planet[6]. The council appeared in forms of beings from many sojourns within the galactic territory of their keep. They sat patiently waiting and hoping that what they planned would manifest through these brave volunteers they summoned. The summoned group was, after all, among the volunteers in an earlier project in a time and place when gods of old used the blue planet for a resource and its people as slaves. Then too, it was evident that the energetic balance of the physicality upon Tara[7] (planet Earth) was showing tilt. Those were the early days of this era. However, since then there have been adjustments made to give the beings of this playing field a chance to develop, free of enslavement.

Again, the planet was showing signs of energetic imbalance even more drastic than before. If this tilt was left unaddressed, the project would collapse. The council is ever determined to be successful in bringing divine energetic balance to physicality and the odds were good that the same group would offer to assist in this great and grand project at such a critical point. The genetic coding was, after all, beginning to show a presence. The peace code (gene)[8] could not be denied, yet still remained un-awakened in most individuals.

As the immense portal of the Council Chambers opened wide, the first soul to be interviewed was ushered in. A sweet feminine soul entered and none more gentle or appropriate could have been found. "Mary One," a council mastra said, "Greetings and

---

[5] Feminine version of master
[6] Earth
[7] An ancient name for the Blue Planet, "Earth"
[8] DNA code

welcome once again to the chambers of the Universal Order of Overseers[9]."

"I am honored," Mary said in her unassuming way, as she slipped to her knees. She was currently incarnated and appeared in the form of the human body she presently occupied now, about 15-years-old. Mary always was humbled to be summoned by the overseers. Even though this was not her first time, her memories of such times were merely dream-echoes in her physically awake time. She couldn't imagine why she was here in the Galactic chambers once again.

Gently smiling, the mastra reassured Mary, saying, "Arise, dear one, for we are the ones honored." The galactic overseer looked human in form, but she gave the impression as being without weight or mass. She had the essence of a human body, yet it was much different in form, more elongated with a graceful flowing quality. The external surface of the mastra seemed to shimmer and flow with ever-changing hues of blue, ranging from aqua to turquoise then sapphire. The catalyst for the flowing color-change, much like the waters of the Caribbean, affected her speech with words that washed in and out like the tide. Her melodious voice caused her to appear to move and speak as if in response to some inner-liquid symphony, that orchestrated every thought and movement.

"Will you play a role in the upcoming drama about to manifest in the Tara-land experiential place?[10]" the mastra asked. "All that will be asked of you is unconditional love and ultimate trust. However, that will be most difficult in many ways," the mastra explained. "Seemingly, this is a simple plan; but to implement it means that challenge, along with the deepest sorrow imaginable, will be met. There is not one of us, on this council of thirteen beings here, who could accomplish this as it should unfold. We

---

[9] Beings who oversee the evolution of consciousness as it plays out in physicality

[10] The earth place to experiment in evolution of consciousness at the physical level

can't hold the depth of compassionate courage that is the makeup of your very soul, dear one."

The familiar setting of the council chambers was room-like. Mary remembered being here before. There was no visible ceiling and the council sat in a semi-circle, where the guest was able to step forth and face all at once. The floor gave the illusion of everything floating in space, because of the clear crystal it was made from. The council sat at a curved table and chairs that were reminiscent of translucent marble with a slight pink tinge. There were great doors that swung effortlessly and seemingly dissolved as they silently opened. Still there was complete awareness of all in the room whenever they opened or closed. Monumental columns of stone appeared to neither support, nor be supported by anything, and only added to the presence of the beautiful space. Mary remembered, the enormous room always felt open, even when the doors were closed.

Mary raised her eyes to face the entire council of thirteen. She looked long and deeply into their eyes, one at a time. She knew them well and had stood in this very spot before. As she collected her feelings and thoughts, tears began to flow because she was overcome with emotion. Being already incarnated into a society upon the planet, she knew that the attitudes had critically tilted the respect and love for the feminine to an all-time low. Within the attitude of those she lived among, she was not nearly important enough for the honor she now was offered. But she knew, before she entered this lifetime, that this moment might come to pass. At least she knew there would be those asked to bring forth masters and mastras in the physical realm. As Mary was a mastra herself, she also understood it was usually those in the higher vibratory category who were expected to carry the burden of parenting, or mentoring, to insure success. Those sent would plant seeds of balance to shift the energetic playing field back to its Divine stability, or Onement. Knowing that it would be a burden, still she gladly accepted the request out of love for all creation. The depth of her compassionate love was such that no other soul could hold the vibration of love as she could and she knew this ability was greatly needed.

After visually scanning all thirteen council members, Mary simply nodded her head and moved aside near one of the vast columns in the room. At that moment a council elder called Joseph forth. He immediately came through the portal of the galactic chambers and walked towards the council, looking old and tired. He walked forward slowly, with awe and reverence for the group he approached. All he said was, "Why me?" as he bowed his head. The council members in unison said, "Why not?"

"Mary is so young in this life experience," Joseph stated out of concern.

"She will need the protection and the wisdom of an elder to get through that which we ask of her," said one of the council members. "Do you wish to take this task upon your already-tired shoulders?" He paused, so Joseph could think about the request. The spokesperson, finally with all due sympathy said, "We know that your heart is heavy from the recent departure of your beloved wife, Enlina, or Sara, as she was known to others."

Enlina was the priestess name of Joseph's first wife and his heart always associated that name with her, even though others knew her as Sara. "She waits at the door, blessed one. She still walks in spirit with you and she will speak to you, if that would make this decision easier. If you agree to undertake this task, we want you to know that the women will suffer far more than the men," one of the mastras on the council said.

"How is that so, mastras and masters?" Joseph asked, as he glanced toward the door, where the spokesman said Enlina awaited. When Joseph saw Enlina, she nodded her head, put her hands into a prayer position and blew a kiss towards him, then dissolved. A tear gently rolled down his cheek.

"The corruption of attitudes defile and defame women, because they have an inner strength and wisdom that can't be taken from them, even as there will be an attempt to deify the male players in this drama," the council mastra explained. "There are several possibilities to the outcome of this project, including total failure. We don't know if it will be successful, but we must carry on, nonetheless. We hope to plant seeds that one day will insure that thoughts that exclude, will change and move into an attitude of inclusiveness. We need a father-protector who is totally unselfish, who can love so deeply that expectations are not the measure of his love. Your lineage carries the codes necessary for the child, who will be the way-shower for the path of peace. We know you can do this, for you have already shown repeatedly, lifetime after lifetime, that you have the ability to love beyond logic and reason, while still holding the sword ready to fight for those in your keep. Are you ready to accept another mission of such magnitude?"

Again, Joseph scanned the entire group of thirteen, looking deep into their eyes. That is the way of the soul, to communicate through a look of inner knowing. All understood that he had accepted, because if he had not, he would have looked away, rather than directly at them. The council all nodded in agreement and Joseph stepped away, to stand alongside beautiful, gentle Mary, where he reached out to take her hand.

It was then my turn to enter the chambers. I floated in, not so physically solid as Mary and Joseph, since I had not yet incarnated into this time and space, and wasn't being summoned from the place of weight and mass in the $3^{rd}$ dimension of physicality. I was still in the ethers, or in the inner-dimensional realms. Specifically the 'odd' dimensions are places of experience and growth, while the 'even' ones are meeting places or transition places between the physical and the non-physical. However, 'between dimensions' is a place of spirit at rest or in preparation, where soul groups' true home is located. I was much more prepared for this meeting, because I had already attended several pre-meetings in which the task was discussed, viewed and reviewed. Having already volunteered, I was about to meet those who would parent me, if they agreed to the task.

A master spokesman greeted me with heartfelt enthusiasm. "A delight to see that you have not reconsidered and postponed this sojourn, beloved one," he said. "You already know the ones called Mary and Joseph from several incarnations in which you have had good experiences with them, dear Jeshua[11]? It was at your request that we have asked them to join us."

"I know and love them with all my heart and soul," I replied. "I would be honored to be their son and to represent son-ship, or 'sun-ship', of the Divine. There has been a forgetting that all, each and everyone within all creation, are sons and daughters of that which they know as God and it is my utmost desire to help humanity remember their 'sun-ship'."

"Yes, Jeshua, that is the mission, to remind those that have forgotten, that the sun is the star that holds the key (or intent) of physical life on this planet, as do suns in other places of such experience as we have discussed and studied at length. Thus it represents the life-giving force of the creator and all that it affects. All are children; watched, protected and allowed sufficient freedom to grow and learn within the opportunity. They remain ever under the authority of the mighty suns through the duality of nature. Being of a spherical shape, even the sun has dual polarity. This life-giving force has both positive and negative polarities (masculine and feminine), just as all creation does within its energetic core. Some within humanity understand this concept, but the masses have no idea of the energy which spins and twines within their physical bodies and within all creation upon the planet, in order to allow this biological life experience to be successful. Every being has an 'inner sun', which is their physical energetic core. Most humans don't realize how their thoughts and beliefs affect their bodies. They get lost and focus on fear, and can't feel the warmth from their own inner-core sun."

"Are you ready to face fear? It is the plan that you will have to be a way-shower of love, not a warrior of fear, and we assure you the playing field will not be fair. You will be at every disadvantage, but you will be a power that will start a great wave of good change in this stagnant arena that we target. There is no dishonor, if you decide that you would rather not partake of this task. We have

---

[11] The Hebrew name for Yeheshua (Yeshua) in a shortened version, known to the Western world as "Jesus"

others who would consider the undertaking, but we believe you are best suited, Jeshua. What is your final decision on this?"

A great wave of emotion flooded through me. I knew I would not decline this request, but I needed the one I loved beyond measure at my side. "I can't accomplish this without my beloved other," I said as I looked down at the crystallized floor.

"Why do you downcast your eyes, Jeshua? We know this and that is why we have picked you; because in picking you we have also picked your counterpart. Let us bring her to the forefront, for she is here and ready to put forth her decision, as well."

Gracefully, MiryAmah[12] approached me; lovely to behold, she moved naturally into my embrace. "In this task I shall come in a bit later," she said, "but I intend to walk with you in this mission, my beloved—every step of the way, if I can. It has been said many a time but never have I felt it so strongly that 'together we can change the world.' I am with you, dearest heart, as I always am," MiryAmah whispered.

We turned to face the council and accepted the mission by looking long and deep, into the eyes of each council member. As we met their eyes, one-by-one they nodded their heads and folded their hands, with their fingers tips pressed together and touching their mouth. Then they opened their hands and blew a sacred breath toward us.

The master who was recording the session said, "It is done then. You, Jeshua, shall come forth then, on the summer solstice when the sun holds reign. You, dear MiryAmah, shall come forth at a later date, when the moon holds reign and night is longest. Together, you are the 'yin and the yang', as the eastern territories would describe wholeness. You will demonstrate Oneness and inclusiveness. We all pray this mission will be a success and we hope suffering will not be overwhelming for you or those involved. No matter what you experience, know that you are in a state of grace and the angelic ones are ever nearby. Take comfort in this, but also realize that these angelic ones cannot interfere in

---

[12] Mary Magdalene

the mission, even as they help hold it on track and remind you of the divinity of your efforts within this incarnation."

"Now, spend some time with Joseph and Mary. You have much to discuss. We have already met with MiryAmah's volunteer parents, who also await you. It is time to celebrate the decision."

# SOUL SONG
## Chapter Two

It is a pleasure to have the opportunity to tell how my life story 'felt', as Jesus, or Jeshua ben Joseph. Records seldom deal with the emotional feelings of my physical lifetime; yet only the experiencing soul knows the depth of it. The Akashic Records[13] record life sojourns as a song, comprised of light and sound that dance together as experience unfolds. Just as grand symphonies have a variety of harmonies and disharmonies, so too does each lifetime. In fact, to look at a soul experience on the ley-lines[14] of the 'Divine cloak of God'[15], or Akashic Records, the sounds and lights are beyond imagination, all interplaying at once. These symphonies are precious and guarded by angels, who will not allow such beauty and magnitude to be shared with the unworthy, or shall I say 'the un-ready'. To access someone else's soul song, permission must be granted by their guides and the guardian angels of the records. Some believe they are entering the Akashic records and accessing other people's information, but in reality, they are entering the "foggy zone" that surrounds the real Akashic records. This zone is comprised of intentions unrealized, attitudes and perception not in accord with the actual truth of the record, and any number of other mistaken and misplaced attitudes that try to attach to the trail of truth. While never diminishing the true

---

[13] The record of all action and reaction written upon energetic lines comprised of light and sound that twine and interlace with each other like a web
[14] An energetic grid that carries the vibrations of all action and reaction
[15] The ley-line web that records all experience and spreads out through all creation like a vibrating cloak

symphony, the foggy zone is a poor substitute for a 'soul song', which is beyond description in its beauty and harmony and beyond the fog. Each soul's records chain and link lifetime to lifetime, like a never-ending story.

To plan a life experience in the physical, one must review their soul records. It is a wonderful experience, and souls find that they are much more beautiful than they ever imagined. They also discover places of disharmony at a personal level and realize where they should focus their attention to achieve balance and divinity. Disharmony means, 'not in tune, or not moving' and/or 'not in the light.' Souls all seek 'enlightenment' and 'attunement', which are the compositional aspects of their 'soul song', comprised of the golden cord of light and the silver cord of sound. Thus, visiting one's Akashic Record is integral in incarnational decisions and the impact that lifetime might have as an individual soul and at the greater group consciousness level.

As the decision was made for my life experience as Jesus (later known as Jeshua, which is my true soul name), I reviewed my own record and could see evidence of my progression of consciousness, or evolution. I also noticed the places in my experience that needed correction at the karmic level. I had my share of struggles and challenges, too, and each lifetime, one works through many issues.

Before I met with the Galactic Emergence Council,[16] I had already attended my own soul symphony, and it was beautiful to behold. That may sound boastful of me to say, but I assure you that your own soul song is the most beautiful song you will ever hear and see. It is evidence of your relationship with the 'Wonder of Wonders', the Creator of all of this opportunity called 'physicality' as well as all other experiencing modalities. It confirms your unique soul mission, for you belong to groups of individual souls working on aspects of evolution, much like instruments that interact in a grand symphony. All your soul songs together create the Divine Harmony of God.

---

[16] The council that prepares souls to enter physicality again

Many wonder why they were born. The answer is, to add their soul song to this majestic symphony of the Divine. To do so one must interact with all creation and especially with those who are part and parcel of your intended purpose, your own brilliant musical section. As you add more incarnations, experiences and discoveries your soul song expands and so does the entire symphony. If only you had eyes to see and ears to hear the beauty of that which you contribute to in the most divine way.

As I examined my Akasha record, I realized that my soul song always involved a mission of awareness of divinity, especially as it relates to the 'positive and negative'[17] energetic frequencies. Think of the electrical system that you use and still don't fully understand. This may help you see, within your minds and hearts, that of which I speak. Even as I understood the scope of my soul mission, I realized that the other part of me, the negative energetic aspect (my feminine counterpart) had to be an equal player in this mission of divine recognition, at an inner level, but even more at the external level. There was a time when it was no longer beneficial for the sake of evolution (which is moving towards the realization of divinity) for beings, or creative aspects of the Divine, to be physically oriented in outer expression as both positive and negative, even as they were always internally both energies. It was decided that the two polarities of your soul's Onement[18] would separate and be as help mates (complements and complete-ments)[19] to the other, especially in the human form as genders. This arrangement would ensure that there could be total understanding of how God is completely and perfectly reflected within each aspect of creation and within the close relationships of those God-particles incarnate. Energy is the essence of the Divine, and it is two distinct energetic modes that make Onement, just as your electrical devices need the positive and the negative charges equally to carry current. Two unseen, but real forces combining in perfection, both active and receptive, are your essence and the mirror image of God within you.

---

[17] Energy that is active and reactive, or goes out and receives.
[18] The perfect balance of positive/negative, masculine/feminine, light/dark, active/receptive
[19] The essence of duality in that one part completes the other

A soul typically reviews their soul song within the Hall of Review, which is a grand cavern-like structure, that looks like a crystalline geode. The floor is reflective, even as the walls and ceilings and multiple levels reveal a multitude of facets with many points and shapes, all shimmering the colors of the rainbow. This is a semi-physical place, for it is the physical from whence one comes after physical transition, or in the case of review for rebirth, it is the physical that calls you back. The hall helps the soul feel the mass of weight and solidness as they transition to or from physicality. It is the grand theatre you have always remembered and often visited in your dreams.

My beloved MiryAmah joined me as I reviewed my soul song, and she reviewed hers as well, for she would follow me into physicality, after she had helped me hold the vibrational cord steady during my early years. Some would call her my Twin Flame,[20] or true Soul Mate, and it is true that she and I are 'One,' just as you are also 'One' with your beloved other. Usually one will enter evolution within the physical realm, while the other anchors them within the ethereal domain, holding the vibrational cord of intention steady. In some cases, if the evolutional level is sufficient, there is an opportunity to incarnate together. However, that is always a difficult situation, because what one feels and experiences, so too does the other. Such a situation can be overwhelming and often the mission fails when this technique is attempted. Not only the bliss, but the pain is experienced full measure. Without the anchor in the heavenly realm to help bear the burden, there is a great potential of overwhelming the spirits of those involved.

Even so, this time we had an entire fleet of angels and guardians with us, due to the importance of our mission. There were a few others like us, who were peace code activators, coming through as well. Along with the code activation, some of us were to be living

---

[20] The other part of you. The one who holds the same energy but in opposite polarity

## Jeshua's Song

examples of how the masculine and the feminine (positive and negative) interact in the Divine Dance of Evolution.[21]

The tilting of attitudes of the human species upon this earth-plane didn't reflect the delicate balance of Divine Creational Intention at the time of our review and mission. The 'Dance of Life' was not beautiful as God designed it to be. To understand how energy works within your own reflective body-physical and all creation is to know God. The discovery of this Divine plan is a major reason for free-will within the physical arena which Tara offers. There were forces in place that were stopping the discovery, through enforcing fear instead of nurturing love and divine discovery, and they were obstructing the evolution of consciousness.

You are all God-particles, with none more or less precious than the other. You were created so that God could experience discovery. While God knows all God cannot experience discovery without you and all aspects of creation sent out to find their way home again.[22] You were sent forth to reconnect the little particles to the Whole once again through evolution (discovery). That pleases and completes God and is known as 'Onement,' your ultimate goal. That means that sometimes you have to discover what is 'not', in order to discover what 'is.' However, to stay stuck, or choose the 'not' and ignore the true lesson is to invite suffering into your lives, as free will allows you to 'reap what you sow'. When I say 'you,' I include myself and my beloved as well, for we are all part of the same family, all sons and daughters of the Divine. Being such, we cannot discover our divinity if we honor only half of our beingness[23]. The polarity of positive and negative is within all creation. Balancing these energies is ever an ongoing effort, so that every action and reaction can be evaluated, as understanding of divinity plays out.

Humanity is at a critical point in self-discovery, for if a man cannot love and honor his beloved wife and mother, he doesn't

---

[21] how the energies, the positive and negative, interact
[22] God knows all, but within the creation of the God fragments, that knowing is latent and must be discovered.
[23] The divine soul within all its modes

love himself, thus can't know the kingdom of heaven. The Heaven I speak of is the state of 'reflecting God, therefore knowing your own divinity.' This is true at a group level as well as a personal level. Group attitudes echo out into society as they form countries and biological racial groups. Groups hold a personality or 'collective spirit,' which is the reflective composite consciousness of those within the assemblage.

At the time of my soul song review, there was great concern in many areas of the planet, due to the unfortunate events that occurred as life-forms interacted within this plane. The situation was partly due to previous relations, where co-creators[24] eons before had not sorted out their own energetic balance issues, especially as it related to genders. As lords, they passed the attitudes of imbalance on to those they oversaw. The mind-set then implanted a bad seed, that accepted fear and rejected peace.[25] I will come to this issue later in my tale. However, remember all co-creators have a responsibility to that which they co-create, and you are a co-creator, too. This, in essence, is the basis of the Universal Law of Karma.

You don't create 'soul,' or 'spirit', for that is the stuff of God. You create vehicles for soul to use, as you seek to understand the laws of creation and practice discovery. These vehicles, no matter what they are, animate or inanimate, attract appropriate beings who wish to evolve and discover through the opportunity. The earth plane is an opportunity place for learning co-creation, with many chances to bring balance into your lives and into that which you create. Fear is non-movement. There are times when it is important to stop and take account of what is about to transpire, but it has become used as a tool to control evolution. Those in power stopped the main-stream from discovering their own divinity as individuals to hold fast control and ensure enslavement, using fear as their main tool. This situation was originally allowed to run its course for the sake of learning, until it threatened the

---

[24] Explained further in chapter twenty-two, "Saga of the Ancients"
[25] Referring to genetically altered humans whose physical vehicles were designed to produce slaves to do hard labor for those claiming to be gods and not willing to do their own difficult physical work

balance of the entire galaxy. The galaxy is a group of beings, too, or entities, and these stars, planets, orbs and all who co-exist within, upon, and around the great void also have a mission of Divine Discovery. What happens at the microcosm[26] level also happens at the macrocosm[27] level.

Since humanity became the most aware species upon Tara, you hold the responsibility, not the superiority, for the safekeeping of this experiencing place in your keep. At the time of my beloved's and my review of our soul songs, at the request of the Galactic Council for this realm, it was apparent that web records of experience were beginning to dim and stop the lovely ebb and flow of its natural rhythms in many places upon and within Tara. Upon inspection of the web, it was seen that the area of the Middle East was of the greatest concern, even while there were other pockets of stagnation as well, due to energetic imbalance and antiforce[28] stopping the movement of evolution there, too. The other places would be addressed at a later time by another team. Those of us who were sent in had reached the mastra/master state, which meant that we had evolved to the point that we understood the balance within ourselves and within all creation. We were experts of energy movement, at a personal level and in a relationship sense, which included personal associations, social arenas, and especially with God. We were sent in order to do some fine-tuning.

We knew that we would have to honor the laws of physicality and somehow remember from early on our task. A babe usually passes through the channel of forgetting in order to enter the physical experience with a clean slate. The newborns typically go through stages of 'fully knowing' as infants, and then gradually forgetting as they grow older. During the so-called 'pretending' stage in early childhood, they practice manifesting and interacting with the unseen ones, but eventually forget so that the slate clears with no regrets from past lifetimes for the mission at hand. With the help

---

[26] Smallest possible component

[27] Largest possible component

[28] Anti "against" movement, collective force of fear that does not want evolution of consciousness

of their guides, one day, something is triggered and intuitive remembrances occur or they simply 'feel' their soul-intention. This begins the process of working towards their divine task at the instinctive level. The plan of having both MiryAmah and I in the physical, with a brief period of anchoring between our emerging births, we understood would be a challenging time. We had to exhibit awareness at an early age. Those who birthed and nurtured us needed confirmation that, indeed, we were mastra and master, to ensure that we would be encouraged in our soul mission.

Usually mastra/master souls volunteer to incarnate for the purpose of bringing opportunity for unconditional love and compassion through bodies you might term 'limited'. However, for this mission we had to occupy more normal physical and mental vehicles to demonstrate the energetic polarities working as they were intended, in unrestricted physical circumstances. We were to plant attitude-changing seeds within the masses, who were greatly confused as to their worth and purpose in the physical experience. That required that we appear fully present in our bodies and minds, to plant the seeds we wished to manifest. The unconditional love that physically and mentally challenged individuals offered was no less important; but for this balancing project, we required a physical vehicle less restricting and more independent.

As we listened to our soul songs, MiryAmah and I knew that this would be a sweet/sad experience at the most profound level, but well worth the effort. We loved all creation and willingly offered ourselves for the project, even though we knew we would suffer for the cause of energetic perfection. All mastras and masters hold great love for creation, and they offer themselves for your sake and all divinity. They never desire to be exalted for their offering. Their suffering is balanced with great joy, which is the most Divine of emotions, and the greatest reward imaginable.

As I prepared for the conception ritual, I heard my soul song loud and clear. It gave me courage to enter the sacred womb of my mother. I would practice moving in and out of physicality through the first four months in the womb. When I was totally certain of my decision, the quickening would occur and my sweet child-mother would feel me moving about in the sacred chamber, assuring her that all was well.

To help me in this difficult vibrational shift into the physical, a twin in the same membrane sack of divine water would accompany me. If this double birthing had come to pass, this other would be my identical twin, but that was not the purpose this time. It was my beloved MiryAmah there with me for the first six moons, helping me and finally retreating and allowing my little body a chance to absorb the vehicle of her physicality into my own for the sake of our mission later to unfold. I needed an extra energetic boost to come forth this time, for my vibrational level was so refined that it was difficult for me, in the last three months within my mother's womb, to hold my own without the energy MiryAmah had offered through her twin body which I absorbed. I knew that we were not really separated, and I accepted this sacred offering in the spirit it was given; as all babies do, I took what I needed. Mother Mary sensed and mourned this lost one, even as she knew that all was in Divine Order. When the time was appointed, on the longest day of the year, I came forth.

# EMERGENCE
## Chapter Three

As I remember the time of my emergence, I remember most the great hope and expectation of the Galactic Council, that this experiment would somehow cause a change in the tilted attitudal balance of this planet of experience. Since the time of quickening,[29] I had been spending most of my time within the newly forming physical vehicle, snuggled inside my beloved mother Mary's womb. I practiced movement and discovered my physical body, including sucking my own thumb. No one could have asked for a better mother. Mother knew me fully present from the time of her first knowledge of my intentional emergence through her divine body, and she always loved me tenderly and completely.

---

[29] About 4 months into the gestation period during my mother's pregnancy

## The Saga-Oracle

I remember most the lullabies, she would sing to me, as I rocked in her comfortable womb. My mother made songs up as she went about her daily routine, and they were always words of cheer and appreciation for our relationship. I enjoyed the gentle rocking motion of her body and could hear her sweet voice singing to me throughout her day, which kept me quite content. I also liked the touch of my parents, both father and mother, as they put their hands upon my mother's swollen belly and spoke encouraging words to me. It helped develop and prepare me for this journey into physicality. Babies are much more aware than most believe. Even though the process of birth is called the 'forgetting channel', the process is not instant and unfolds slowly. Babies forget what has been and what is eternally true at a conscious level, as they discover words and pay attention to the outer world surrounding them. This helps them focus on this lifetime opportunity, to rediscover what they already knew coming in. Some keep some remembrance intact. My plan was to remember as much as possible for the sake of my intentional mission, so that I could make the best use of my time in this sojourn.

There is much a babe can sense about the mother, while still rocking within the incubation chamber. I knew my mother was concerned for what others might think, since her pregnancy was not the usual. She 'knew' my father as any bride would, but only after a dream where angelic beings came to her, to confirm the importance of the divine plan. A dream angel caused great passion and confusion, for the angel triggered my mother's desire in preparation for the sacred seed that would contain my soul/spirit for this journey. My parent's first intimacy was fruitful; however, it was also unplanned and spontaneous, during the time that couplings were planned carefully. My mother's passion, triggered by the dream, surprised my father who was much older and more experienced, and he didn't expect such desire from a young inexperienced woman.

I remember heaving sobs of confusion, as my mother told my father Joseph that she believed she was somehow unfaithful to him, because she had dreamed of being intimate with an angelic being, yet had awakened in his arms. I could feel his withdrawal from her as he heard this news, and I felt the sincere dread within my young mother, as she wondered if she had sealed her and my doom by being so honest. She was young and not yet wise, she believed, in the ways of man-woman communication. It was her nature not to hide anything from her beloved, but the customs of the time didn't separate dreams from reality in action, and Joseph could have chosen to banish her as unfaithful.

The next day the song she tried to sing after this confession wasn't joyful, and it didn't sooth her or me. During the night, the angels came to speak with my father and told him not to fear, that this child was fully his, and they had come to open the channels of passion within my scared, but ever-faithful mother, so the intended seed would have an open channel to the Divine Womb.

"We didn't violate your wife, dear Joseph," they said. "We only triggered the extreme desire of the female for the male she faithfully loves, because this child must spring forth from great love. It was not the dream that impregnated this dear bride of yours, but her passionate embracing of you during the dream. She saw you as an angel. She had been worried about how you felt about her as your wife, dear one. She hadn't yet come to you as such, because she felt that your heart was still with your first beloved wife, now in spirit. She wasn't sure if her love could fill that void. By bringing her into a state of passion for the divine within you, even as she envisioned you in her dream as angelic, her blockage to conception was dissolved. Indeed, dear Joseph, this is your son and one to be proud of, and you will dream more dreams as the full measure of this mission is remembered. You are an important player in this divine drama, and your cooperation was given forthwith at the highest soul level. Now wake up and bring your young wife into your arms. She needs to know that you love her, as she does you."

During my incubation period, there was never again a time of sorrow between my parents. My mother truly loved her elder husband with all her heart. When she had to leave him to help an older cousin during her pregnancy (after many years of believing she was barren) mother deeply missed my father, and I could feel her separation sorrow. The child of my mother's cousin was important within this mission, too, and he would be a forerunner for me. Should I falter, or my physical life end, John would be the back-up plan.

The time was getting close to my emerging. Mother Mary, being of the priestess sect, would have loved to birth me in the traditional woman's way within an emergence temple; however, Herod's Roman agenda was to keep the power of the woman subdued. He outlawed all women's rituals, because he knew that within these rites women sealed their power, and he didn't want them to know the truth of their natural strength. The birthing traditions were the most powerful of the rituals that women conducted and if a woman was found to be birthing in the old priestess way[30], both she and her child were killed.

Another concern to my parents was that under Roman rule, the census (which Herod conducted to satisfy his lifestyle, ambitions and responsibility to the Emperor) was scheduled for the same time I would emerge. Herod ordered all men to register at the place of their birthing, so that the taxes could be figured and levied; taxes that would make the leaders comfortable, but would devastate the everyday people. I have always deplored the idea of taxes, and maybe this is the root cause of my feeling; for my mother and father were poor but hardworking people and they worried about how they would pay such a price just to 'be'. They were troubled more about the journey to father's birth-city, since I was soon to be born.

I remember the rocking motion of my mother, as she rode upon a gentle donkey. My father carefully lifted her up to the position of sitting sideways upon this little, but strong beast's back, and we began our journey to Bethlehem, the place of my father's birth. Because the donkey's body supported my mother, and since I was still very much a part of her physical being, I could converse at a soul/thought level with this little beast of burden, as our bodies were pressed together. I learned that this animal was relieved to be at our service and that the previous owner was guilty of exceedingly inhumane treatment. He didn't feed her well, she told

---

[30] With women present and mother and father working together in a natural way to bring the child forth without fear

me, nor would he limit the loads she carried. He constantly whipped her. Her coat held many scars and was dull and matted, instead of shiny and healthy, due to ill treatment by this first master. Father had happened upon her one day just before we departed, she told me. As we trotted along, conversing mind to mind, she said she was faltering that day, under too great a load. She fell to the ground, and her master kicked and whipped her. My father, who was walking by, noticed the situation and yelled, "Leave that poor donkey alone, you brute!" The donkey's master, none too pleased to be spoken to in such a manner, said he would kill her, because she was of no use to him, and he found a large rock to crush her skull, right there in the street.

Father grabbed his arm, stopping him and calmly said, "I would like to purchase this animal, for I have need of a donkey." The cruel master laughed, realizing that he would get some money if he played this out to his best interest, and waited for the next question.

"What is your price?" father said.

The cruel one gave a price one would pay for ten such animals. Father laughed and said, "You must think me a fool," and began to pretend to walk away. The little donkey told me that she feared that was the end of her.

But greed won out. Father knew it would, and the man said, "What will you pay me for this wretch?"

"I have but one shekel, and if it is good enough to pay the temple taxes, it should be good enough to purchase a donkey, that, as you said, is a worthless wretch."

Thinking for a moment, the cruel one finally said, "Sold. Pick up your donkey tonight."

Father was already unlashing the burden from the poor donkey's back and said, "No! I'll take my charge now, and you shall be gone, or I will have your hide." Not willing to bear the burden he expected from his overworked donkey, nor tempt fate and have father follow up on his threat, the man took the highly-prized silver shekel and left, leaving his load there in the road.

Father helped the little beast to its feet and spoke with it on his way back to the place where mother waited. They walked slowly, because the donkey was wobbly. Father said to the donkey, "I hope you can carry my beloved wife, heavy with a child." He worried, for he didn't have any more shekels to buy another beast of burden, should the animal not have the required strength. The gentle donkey began to walk with more spring in its step, understanding the task at hand, and that it would be one of love and devotion. It was determined to be up for it. The little donkey had dreamed of being a servant of love, and being respected and protected. Animals have dreams, too, it told me, as I rocked along there in my mother's womb upon its back.

The donkey told me that when father arrived home with his new beast of burden, mother didn't even consider that this animal was not perfect. She did, however, realize that it was in need of nourishment, and she quickly found food for her. Within the week, all was prepared for the journey, and 'Little One' (the pet name mother had given this little steed) was much improved. The journey would take several days, due to the condition of my mother, so full of me. Little One was gentle in her pace and sure in her step, as she carried my beloved mother and me down the road to Bethlehem, following patiently behind father. There was no discomfort for anyone, including the faithful donkey.

The records say that my family traveled by day and slept at night; but that isn't true, because it was the height of the summer season and the sun was so hot, that it was very uncomfortable to travel under the scorching rays of the sun. Furthermore, the route from Nazareth to Bethlehem, which went toward Egypt, was not safe with the roadway peppered by those who would kill for as little as a drink of water or a mouthful of food, because they were afraid that they would perish, unless they took what they needed. Also, they rather enjoyed being the ones feared in this game of lack. For the most part, we traveled quietly by night and found a safe place to sleep in the daytime.

Our first stop was along the Sea of Galilee, where we found shelter within the home of relatives of father's first wife, Enlina. The family was quite taken with my mother and loved her from first sight. She had that effect on everyone and everything. I remember her heart beating quite fast as she prepared herself to meet Enlina's family. She still worried that father would find her a poor replacement for his first beloved wife, and that Enlina's family would agree. She had little to dread from them, however. They welcomed her straight away and even fed and bedded down Little One with their own well-loved family donkey.

Shortly after our arrival the family offered a pre-birth ceremony, that pleased my mother and eased her fear of this unknown moment. Father's former mother-in-law was trained in the old priestess ways. She asked father if she could take this little mother to meet her women's group, who were gathering that very evening in her courtyard. She made no mention of what type of ceremony she planned, however. Father sounded a little worried as he granted permission, because we usually would rest during the daylight hours and depart sometime in the dark of the night, and he wasn't quite sure what his former mother-in-law had in mind. Permission was granted though, and mother and I were whisked off to someplace that smelled and felt wonderful from my inner-perspective. As it turned out, we were taken to the home's central courtyard. It was more than a mere courtyard when the women were present though–it was a ritual place.

After our formal introductions, Enlina's mother had sent news to her group of twelve women to come and bless a child shortly to come forth. She could plainly see that my emergence was not far off. The women all knew what to bring, upon getting the message from the little girl runners, since they had been summoned before for the same secret ceremony. The ritual required sacred sound, smells, textures and colors; all so that the senses within the babe would fully awaken. Each had items that they regularly used for this purpose, thus no coordination was necessary, and they arrived with appropriate tools in hand.

## The Saga-Oracle

Mother knew immediately when she entered the courtyard that this was a priestess circle, and she sighed with a sense of relief. "Oh, dear ones," she said, "You are the answer to my prayers."

Enlina's mother said, "I knew the minute I saw you that you were one of us, and even if you weren't, we still would have gathered to do the blessing ritual for you and this babe you bring forth." With that said, the ceremony began and father was kept busy with the men, so as not to interfere with 'woman's work'.

My mother was taken inside a centrally located red tent that the others had quickly constructed for this ritual anointment. She was gently stripped of her robes, which were immediately taken to be laundered in lavender water and dried. Then she was laid out upon a soft reclining cushion, covered by a silken coverlet, while outside the other women played the flute, cymbals and lyre. They were singing a song of welcome, and I felt so ready to come forth and play with them, I literally tried to dance in the womb that cocooned me; however, the time was not yet ripe. My mother was given a tea laced with wine to relax her that tasted sweet and soothing. The silken scarf was removed, and she was rubbed head to toe with ointments. They used olive-based oils of jasmine and frankincense (from the bark of the Boswellia tree from Arabia and Africa, and a precious substance kept secretly by the priestesses). The power of the jasmine flower and bark of frankincense was called forth. This symbolized that I would represent the delicate beauty of a tiny flower (a beautiful babe), which would be the basis for a mighty tree (my legacy). Mother sighed in pleasure at their loving and nourishing attention. Then, through her eyes I could see bright rainbow colors in a cloth the priestesses brought forth. Mother was soothed by the vibrations of this rainbow robe that was carefully draped over her nude body, for it felt so calming. Its texture was velvet-like and I sensed the softness of it, and Enlina's mother said, "Soft like a newborn babe."

Mother emerged from the red tent wrapped in the rainbow garment, and father was brought forth. "I had forgotten this ritual," he said to his former mother-in-law as he immediately understood what she had been up to. "I am pleased that you accept my new bride and myself, and have blessed our family-to-be with your tradition." He then kissed Enlina's mother on each cheek, with tears flowing freely, as both remembered the same rituals for each of his other children, done in the identical way here in her home.

His former mother-in-law composed herself after a cry and said, "What this sweet child sees in you, old man, I will never understand. However, I do know that you will be good to her and respect that she is priestess-ordained. Go in peace then, and do not cheat Herod out of his hard earned taxes–hard-earned by you that is."

We departed later that evening under cover of darkness and spent some pleasant nights walking beneath the star canopy. We had only one brief episode in which danger seemed eminent, but for some odd reason, those who felt so ominous mellowed when they saw the condition of my mother, having stumbled onto our camp, and they left us unharmed.

We arrived in Bethlehem after a week of traveling and went to an inn, the place where travelers stayed. Well-to-do travelers rented a room above the animal quarters, and the place was already bustling with those coming for the census count. Poor travelers, such as we, slept together in the hay barns. We were told that there was no room for us, however. One of the inn helpers noticing our situation took pity on us. He was the keeper of the animals for the inn, and he directed us to a cave not far away that was also used to house animals in the winter months. "It's a quiet place," he said, "and this time of the year, it's not used much." He had noticed my tired mother as she sat upon Little One, so huge with me by now, and thought of his own wife and how he would feel if she was in a similar situation.

He directed us, saying, "The cave is not far. Go past the sheep pastures where the shepherd's guard their flocks and look east away from the sun. By this time of the day, the dusk light shines on the entrance to a cave and you will find a path leading to it. I think it will serve your need." We gratefully followed his directions; as we walked past the boys and men tending the sheep, they watched us but didn't question where we were going. They used this cave from time to time, but during the hot season they preferred to sleep under the stars.

Father and mother found the empty grotto and set about making it comfortable. Father gently helped mother down from her perch upon Little One, assuring her that he would prepare the lodgings. She, of course, ignored him and began to gather straw and place it in an animal manger. He thought she was probably preparing a place for Little One to feed, and he shook his head. "Women," he mumbled, "think they are limitless in strength, until they drop from exhaustion." Tomorrow, the plan was to travel into the city of Bethlehem to be counted in the census and pay the tax, as was the law.

Mother was becoming very uncomfortable and father made a bed of straw for her to lie upon. No sooner had she lain down, she began to feel me preparing to come forth. She was afraid and with fear came pain. I actually knew full well the moment and place to emerge, as all incoming souls do. It had been pre-planned that I would be in this area, at this time, for this emerging, and I couldn't wait a moment longer. Night was now upon us, and Father made a little fire and hurried to a nearby spring to fill our water vessel. All the while he prayed for the safety of his wife and new babe. His other children were assisted at birth by a mid-wife. In his long life, he had seen many women die in childbirth, and Mary was so young, he thought with remorse.

While he was gone, as best she could, my mother prepared herself for this emergence. She was anxious, with no priestesses present to help her and this was, after all, her firstborn. She had saved a tea given to her by Enlina's mother. Upon father's return, she asked if he would prepare it for her. He felt overwhelmed and nervously began to do as she requested.

He thought, 'What was I thinking in taking such a young bride and bringing her so far from her people at a time like this?' The light from the cave opening dimmed, and he instinctively stepped in front of my mother as a protective barrier. A shepherd appeared at the entrance, with a woman by his side. He said that the stars were speaking to him this night, and he was told to bring his spouse who was a mid-wife, to the cave. He admitted that he had watched the procession of the little family, as they moved past his flock a little earlier, but hadn't noticed that a child was due. His little wife bowed and asked if she could be of service to us. My father Joseph sighed in relief and said as he looked towards the heavens, "Blessed be! You have heard my prayers."

The shepherd's wife quickly moved towards my mother, who was beginning to moan, moving about, trying to ease the pain in her lower back. When the midwife took off her cape, lo and behold, she was attired in the garb of the priestess. Mary thanked Holy Mother God, and father took his rightful place, to catch the emerging infant. The tea began to relax mother and the soothing, confident voice of the mid-wife allowed the process to unfold without further ado. The shepherd went back to his sheep and the remaining three–mother, father and the midwife–brought me forth, with little pain and much joy.

I passed through the channel of forgetting, determined not to forget so much this time, as the season changed from the longest day, moving towards the equinox, or equalized day. I was born at 11:11 am on 'Summers Day'[31]. My mother and I were cleaned and the afterbirth was properly preserved, to be used in sacred rituals. A small portion of it would be preserved, and enclosed in a sacred packet, that I would wear upon my body for the rest of my days. The packet would also hold a piece of my mother's and father's hair, along with my own silky soft baby hair, true to the way of the priestess birthing ritual. All these items were intended to guide and protect my physical life journey. Mother held me close and my father kissed us both upon the sacred spot at the top of our heads. Mother put me to her breast for first milk, so important to my survival.

Soon there were other shepherds standing at the entrance to the grotto. They had also read the stars and felt that something wonderful was about to happen and made the connection of seeing the little family traverse the sheep pastures earlier. These gentle herders spent many hours studying the skies and could read the

---

[31] Summer Solstice

starry nights as well as any astrologer could. They could sense important moments, and they said they could hear a harmony that seemed divine on this very night; my soul song. My birth was as holy as any other emergence of a babe, for every birth is divine. There is a glorious song sung at all births and the sensitive shepherds, who spent much time alone, were aware of the sounds of nature and heard the song of my soul, as I came back into the physical realm. They simply were visiting to say, 'Welcome to this world.' One shepherd laid a tiny newborn lamb in the manger next to me for warmth. Both the lamb and I needed warming. He said, "Every babe is a blessing, are they not?" and mother and father quietly smiled and nodded.

"What will you name this child?" the mid-wife asked. "I must conduct the name-blessing properly and welcome this soul into the world."

"Yeheshua[32]" mother Mary answered, "Little, sweet Yeheshua"– (later to be translated to Jesus or Jeshua, depending on the language). However, my name of endearment was simply 'Esa,' which my mother had called me, since before I emerged.

The mid-wife picked me up and held me high above her head. Looking skyward, she said, "Take nourishment and thrive, little Yeheshua, for your journey begins, and our hope is great."

# MASTER CHILD
Chapter Four

My early childhood years were blessed in many ways. I thank my beloved parents who showed me perfection in parenting and

---

[32] A common Hebrew/Aramaic name symbolically connected to the 5-point pentagon, each point representing "Yod, Hey, Shin, Vau & Hoy" meaning "..*the word made fresh*..." and also the code of the mystical Divine Masculine. See teachings of the Rosicrucian's for more extensive explanation

unconditional love for that blessing. It was apparent since my birth, that I was a different child than the norm. I don't tell you this to brag about my capabilities; rather, I tell you this so that you will understand, that masters also reincarnate. They are advanced beings in development and communication and not anymore blessed or beloved than any of you. Often, those deemed by you simple and limited, are the physical vehicles they choose, as I have already told you. I assure you that those who take the bodies of the supposed simple ones are not simple at all. Their task is to offer an opportunity for unconditional love, a difficult goal, and only advanced masters are up to that task.

I, however, had agreed to work on the Divine Balance Project; thus I had to have no physical or mental limitations within this sojourn. So being, I began to speak in sentences as soon as my vocal cords would support such communication. My forgetting was not yet closing the doorway to my Akasha memories, and it never fully closed to the extent that is normally evident among children. At first I knew at the level of feeling that I had an important mission. Even as a small aware baby, I had confidence in myself. I visualized 'saving the world', much as your action heroes play in the mind of children now; only I was not a warrior, rather I was a leader.

Before we left Bethlehem, where the Magi had found us through astrological observations, there was unrest due to Herod being unnerved by the rumors of their visit. It was thought that the legendary Magi were seeking a newborn king. The tall dignified Magi always claimed attention and respect, and it's not often that they appeared in the region, so many people were discussing the event. Herod, an ego-driven cruel overseer-king, under orders from the occupying Romans, had to keep a close eye on the region and had spies constantly monitoring the populace. When they brought him the news of the Magi's visit, Herod nearly went insane, taking the rumors seriously. He knew the Magi wouldn't make an appearance, unless something important brought them forth from the far-lands.

It has long been wondered, if the Magi's homeland was originally Arabia. Actually, they were of the watchers, or guardians, and their true home was a faraway planet, another place within another dimension. Those working on the Tara project, however, often took up residence in the Far East and some were counselors to the legendary Queen of Sheba[33]. Being guardians and guides, they frequently were found within the courts of those with balanced and focused intents, where their work wouldn't be restricted. The Magi were aware of my destiny before I consciously remembered it. I experienced a degree of forgetting, so that I could be fully present in childhood. I later learned that many innocent boy babes were murdered as cruel Herod sought to eliminate anyone threatening his power. He felt my presence, not in a holy sense, but as a threat to his authority and control over the people. He intended to snuff out any risk to his seat of authority.

I wasn't destined to be a king in the way that some interpreted, as a power holder. I was to be a leader, which to the guardians meant 'king' or 'queen.'

When the mistaken idea was apparent and the danger eminent, my family and I were whisked off to the land of the pharaoh for safekeeping. There we were protected by some of the same watchers, only this time they kept a lower profile.

My first words were spoken one morning to my beloved mother in exile in Egypt. I remember practicing talking to Little One, who was still lovingly serving us. Often, a child talks to animals first. They are good teachers and even better listeners. Once I could form words, I listened carefully for the key words in the Aramaic language spoken by my parents. I picked up a fair amount of the Egyptian language, too. I was three or four months old upon my speaking debut. We were still staying in our temporary home at Tahpanhes,[34] when I announced to my mother, "I love you, dear one!"

She turned around and looked at me with eyes wide in disbelief. I was lying on a blanket by the stream, where the women washed their clothes. The waterway eventually fed into the mighty Nile

---

[33] The Queen of Sheba may have referred to the title of the Queen Mother of Nubia when acting as the chief astronomer or high priestess of a star-venerating religion that was centered in Africa, with satellite centers in Arabia, Asia, and Europe
[34] Also known as Daphnae, an ancient fortress town

River that supported and nourished this land. Mother had a pile of wet cleaned clothes lying beside her, as she stooped on another rock. She was dipping garments into the water, to wash them. Upon hearing these words, she nearly fell into the stream. Then in her wide-eyed wonder, she looked to see who among the other women was talking to her in such a tiny voice.

One of the women thought my mother had uttered the words to her, and replied, "I love you, too, dear Mary." My mother stopped her washing and approached me; I was positioned on a nearby flat rock, in a reclining position, since my back muscles couldn't yet support me. My eyes were locked upon hers, and I was delighted that I had gained her attention.

She looked closely into my smiling face and said, "Surely, dear sweet son of mine, that tiny voice couldn't be yours?"

I repeated myself and wiggled from head to toe. I was delighted to be able to communicate through spoken word with this gentle mother of mine. My tiny body could hardly contain the joy I felt.

Quickly leaving her wash, mother scooped me up, thinking that the others may imagine me bewitched, should they realize I was speaking complete thoughts, and rushed home. The woman, who thought mother had uttered the words of love to her, brought the wash to our house and asked if all was well. Mother told her I was looking ill and made excuses for her hasty departure. In the privacy of our abode, she asked me a question again, just to be sure she was not going soft in the head.

I replied, "I listen and I learn, mama." I was not one for baby talk about nothing. In the beginning, most of my uttering's were questions, simple pronouncements, or statements about love. My father was clearly shaken, at the spectacle of me blabbering away, now that I knew I could. I greeted him in words of love that evening, when he came home and his eyes grew round, too. He was startled that such a little one could speak in clear sentences, as well as love greetings. He remembered the dream of the angels when he had worried about my parentage, and spoke of it to my mother.

"Surely we are blessed," he exclaimed. "Our family is somehow part of a Divine Plan, Mary, as we dreamed and hoped it would be." Mother agreed by a simple nod, and he further said, "We have long been preparing for this possibility within our group of Nazarites.[35] This is proof of our success, as we hoped." Looking at my mother with love and sadness at the same time, he continued, "We must speak with the council and let them know our master child has announced himself with love."

From that point on, all our dreams were extremely vivid and communication between our heavenly guides was forthcoming and clear. We officially began our special project in the evolution of consciousness. One day, my father took me to speak with the council. I remained silent. They looked at me, then back to my father, and I could read their thoughts. They were wondering if my father was going senile. Even though they believed the possibility of master children coming forth, my early speaking abilities were, nevertheless, hard for them to accept. I was still a tiny babe after all.

Father pleaded, "Speak to the council, son, for they think I have lost my senses."

I slowly looked at each of the council members, mindful of when I met with the council before I was born, and finally said, "You see me, but you don't know me." That was all that was needed to impress them. The amazement of the council members fed my pleasure. As a baby I found extreme joy in astounding the big people.

There was a strict concept of religion and purpose already in place in the land of my birth, along with a more fractured Roman pantheon of gods. The populace of the region was often confused, as they tried to live with the unconsciously merged concepts. The ideologies had been skewed toward male dominance of power and control for a long time. Priests were the source of enlightenment and spiritual progress in this arena. Those such as my father,

---

[35] This was a splinter group of the Essenes who leaned toward total equality of the genders, seeing them the reflection of the Sacred Masculine and the Sacred Feminine, both creating a ONEMENT

however, who was a Nazarite Essene, dared to believe that consciousness could evolve at a personal level. They were considered a threat to the status quo of society. Even among our group of exiles, many of the Essene brothers and sisters were not advanced enough in their thinking, to handle a young babe having a conversation in sentences. Anything out of the norm was suspicious. I had to learn to remain silent in the company of others, unless mother or father gave the nod of approval. However, it was rare that I would speak in public, for Herod had his spies everywhere, since he was still uneasy about the rumors of my birth. He was never sure if the murder of infant boys had cleared the threat. Father took a great chance in presenting me to the village council, and my reluctance to speak was because I already knew that not all the council members were in accord.

I was full of conversation, when alone with my parents though. Usually questions were my format, including, "Why can the butterfly fly and not me, mother?" or "Why can father go to the council gatherings and not you, mother?" or "If Little One is our friend and helper, how can it be that we own her?" Sometimes I would say, "Why are you thinking I am unsafe, mother?" and she realized that I was reading her mind, too. One day I told my father not to worry, for he could die if he chose, and I would be safe, at least until I was grown. Then he knew that his mind had no doors to me either.

By the time I was three, I was openly conversing about a multitude of subjects, with everyone close to the family. More than a few thought I was demented. It didn't occur to me not to talk to birds and plants, along with people, and I openly chatted with all these friends constantly. It was as if I was in love with my own voice, as any child experiences if given the chance. I was exploring my mind, perceptions, hopes and desires, through verbalizing in a constant flow of chatter day and night. All life around was food for thought, which led to discussion.

We, and many others of our people, were in exile near Alexandria, Egypt, a rich and interesting place for anyone, especially an inquisitive boy child. One day word reached our community that Herod had died and left his kingdom to his two sons, splitting the territory in two segments. In and around the large port city, news traveled fast, since many people traded within this hub city. Herod wanted his sons, whom he saw as extensions of himself, to hold power. However, his favored son was not the wisest or strongest and that worried Herod. He decided that splitting the kingdom was his only option, since he knew his sons would hate the one that inherited the throne. This solution would provide both brothers with a throne of power. They would have to cooperate, instead of undermine each other, Herod surmised.

Father decided it was time to return to our home in the south of Galilee, after hearing the news of Herod's death, since it didn't appear that his sons would carry on the quest to find a would-be king, being busy establishing their own seats of power. We traveled back the same route we had come, using the inland pathways, avoiding Judea, where the more evil of Herod's two sons held reign. To me, this was a great adventure. I drove the people of the caravan crazy with my constant questions, since I was now free to speak to almost anyone. Many of those in exile traveled together back to our homelands, and I constantly talked to anyone who would listen.

My mother worried because she couldn't keep track of me. I often escaped her and wandered at will, even though I was yet a small toddler. She finally told me, that if I ever became lost, to look for the women who had a little dove embroidered on the edge of their robe sleeve; to speak only a few words, but tell them I am the child of Joseph and Mary, in need of assistance. They would help me, she said. She cautioned me to be careful who I spoke to, nonetheless, for there were those who would not find little boy's questions welcome. My poor mother did all she could, to protect and watch over me, but I was so quick-minded and interested in everything, I was a handful. If I had not been a young self-centered child, I would've noticed that she didn't look well. In fact, she was often sick and nauseated, which worried father. I was a self-absorbed child, involved in discovering the world around me; right from my first steps at seven months of age, I realized no limitations and more than once I had been rescued. My mother told me I had an entire fleet of guardian angels working double duty.

That statement only spurred a rather lengthy barrage of questions about angels. "What are angels, mother?" "Are they the shiny ones I see at night by my sleeping place?" "Does everyone have them and can everyone see them?" and on, and on. Patiently, mother always listened to every word I uttered and answered ever query completely, thus she was my first teacher.

One day I fell into a river, slightly downstream from where the clothes were being washed on a short stop-over on our journey. As I floated down to the bottom of the deep swift river, I noticed a huge fish. Having no fear I just held my breath and naturally copied this interesting creature's motion, and swam around it, as it swam around me. When I could no longer hold my breath the fish did a rather odd thing, but at the time it seemed quite natural to me; it gave me a mouth-to-mouth fish kiss and blew air into my tiny body. I locked onto its lips and siphoned the air like a babe on a nipple-bottle. It was quite the wonderful game to me, so I kept swimming and exchanging breath with the fish, until it pushed me to the surface, where I heard my mother running along the river banks, screaming as the current was carrying me downstream. The fish, along with several others, pushed me towards the shore. As we approached a shallow area, mother ran into the water to retrieve me, sobbing and scooping me up from the water's edge. The large river fish leaped out of the water, as my mother took me and swam on with the others that helped push me. That was the first time I saw my mother in anguished tears. Her weeping moved me so, that I vowed to never again cause her sorrow. A promise, I wouldn't be able to honor.

As my mother composed herself, but before she could ask me why I scared her, I asked, "Do we eat fish, mother?"

"Yes, we do sometimes," she sobbed, wondering why I was not screaming in terror.

I looked back at the water, to see my new-found friend leap high again over the surface of the water and replied, "Not nice to treat friends like that." Later I learned why we had to consume each other in order to survive in the physical realm, but I was young and still sought simple truths and this was a more complex teaching for a later time.

As the caravan continued on towards our homeland, I sensed my parents were concerned for my safety, and I overheard the caravan master say I was such a pest. He said I should be tied to our donkey, Little One.

I thought, yes, that would be a good idea, and she and I could just escape and adventure together. Little One and I were great pals and tied together or not, we would have a grand time of it, I thought. Our donkey became a babysitter for me. If I wasn't already on her back and began to wander, she would gently grab my garments with her teeth and pull me back to the road. It caused some talk among the travelers; that little boy being nipped on the seat of his robe by the donkey and drug back in line. Some of the women made jokes and asked mother if she would rent Little One out for their children. Little One was like a big sister to me, having always been there since my birth, thus I found no offence as she kept watch over me. I was an energetic child with an overactive imagination. Today children like me are labeled ADHD[36] and considered handicapped. This type of energy is seldom a disorder, but rather a difference and an inconvenience to those who prefer everyone conform to a norm. As it was, the women did concoct teas for me from time to time, so that I would get a night's rest. Seeing all the new places along the caravan road excited me to the point I couldn't sleep for fear, I might miss something.

When we reached the home of father's former in-laws, we had a fond welcome. I was allowed to speak with the family and enjoyed being the center of attention. We didn't stay long, however, and soon departed for a small nearby hamlet, where father had a house. We would settle there, and many of those who were in exile with us did as well. Our family grew and thrived for years in this little community. Soon my brother James joined us, and I shared the devoted family attention. My baby brother grew at a faster rate than I, and we seemed more like twins, when seen together, even though I was three years older than him.

---

[36] Attention Deficit Hyperactivity Disorder

## Jeshua's Song

My father spent more and more time with the council of Essenes, once we returned and mother was meeting with a women's council, too, along with chasing after two little children. My parents were open with each other about the meetings they attended and were constantly comparing the lessons and concerns among their groups. They had a deep abiding relationship and were the best of friends. By this time, both the men's and women's groups had recognized that I was a master child. As such, I would have to be merged into the secret master-child network that would take me away for long periods of time for training and safety.

My mother worried and fretted, when it was clear I had to depart. "I have enjoyed this child for such a short time," she lamented. "I don't know how I can allow him to leave so young!" she said, yet she knew that it was in divine order that I must go. I was being sent to the far-land to school with the mountain people, the monks, both men and women, who lived high in the Himalayas. It was a safe place, they assured me, as I resisted the idea. I still felt safest near my parents and didn't want to leave. The monks had sent for me, already knowing of my need for their training. It was a rare occurrence for them to contact us, and the eldest of our council knew that they didn't beacon, unless there was a tremendous need and divine plan. I might be away for one to five years for this first segment of master training, my parents reluctantly told me. I cried at the thought of it.

On my departure day, I was placed aboard a huge camel's back, by a caravan drover. As excited as I was to go for a camel ride–a new experience for me–when I looked back at my parents, I saw my mother cry again. I leaned down and reached for her, held by my heels by the camel drover who kept me from falling, and I embraced mother in my little arms as long as I could. It felt like rocks had settled into my belly, and my throat began to close. I remember feeling the tears of my mother and my own mix. My father was being supported by some of the other elders, as his sorrow sapped his strength. My little brother James, in father's arms, held on to his robe, as if he could support father. I felt great sorrow and guilt, at being the source of their grieving. Looking backward at my father's face, as the camel moved away, I feared that I might never see him again. My heart was heavy, but my determination to cooperate was stronger. As he and I locked eyes, he realized that I knew his days were numbered and his knees buckled. It was a difficult day for a boy of five years of age.

# MY FIRST SPIRITUAL JOURNEY
## Chapter Five

The journey to the land of the far mountains must have taken weeks, but to me, inquisitive and full of wonder, it seemed but a short time. I constantly thought of my sweet parents and the possibility that I might not see my father, or heaven forbid, my mother again. As for my inner feeling about my father, I wasn't sure I was ready for him to take leave of me. I already felt a power to alter my reality and knew I was creating my circumstances even at the young age of 5-solar-cycles.[37] I hadn't yet learned that opposing cooperative intentions[38] would temper my confidence in co-creational considerations, and I might not always get what I desired.

There was a funny sort of fellow in command of my safety, and he kept an eye on me at all times. He noticed that I spoke with the camels, the birds and any animal that crossed my path. The fact that they listened to me, was exhilarating in itself. He didn't speak to me, or anyone, and I never heard his name spoken, but he watched me constantly. He looked rather small and square in build, with a dark completion and slightly slanted eyes, and had the strength of a mighty bull. I called him my 'silent friend' and tried to pull him into friendly conversation, but to no avail. He tended to all my needs and wouldn't let others approach me. This caused some suspicion among those in the caravan, not understanding such a concern for a mere child. We switched caravans often and, with many new travelers coming and going throughout our journey, their opinions weren't a problem. None

---

[37] 5 years

[38] When a group of beings have the same intention thus it becomes more likely to manifest

dared to approach me, or they would be pushed away and the chastising face of my protector would leave no question as to his intention. It was a bit lonely, yet the silent one had a sweet way of comforting me by laying his hand on the crown of my head and smiling down at me. He had a sense of when my heart ached and his touch was always a comfort. I grew to love him, but yearned to speak to another person who would speak back. I was a very verbal child and loved having an audience, at least one that responded to my constant questing. The camels, and later the yak, some dogs, birds and other wild animals, did speak to me in a mind-to-mind way. Without their interesting conversation, I believe I would have gone quite mad on that long passage.

One of my constant friends for most of the trip was a raven, which did amusing back flips as it flew. One day, my raven friend turned into a giant white bear. This occurred rather suddenly because one of the travelers, who had determined that I was being isolated because I was holding treasure–a treasure that he wished to unburden me of–lay in wait to attack me. He hid behind a rock along the path one morning, when my silent guard was preoccupied with my bundle of blankets and supplies that were slipping from their rigging on our pack animal. My guardian was trying to tie them to a yak that didn't want to cooperate that day, so it was requiring some attention. I remember observing the situation and then telling the yak that I would be grateful if he would cooperate. He settled down, changing his yak-mind, and cooperated. In the meantime, I walked near the rock where the traveler lay awaiting his chance to accost me. Flip, as I called my raven friend, was on my shoulder. Suddenly in a flash of brilliant light he transformed into a huge white bear, jumped in front of me and pounced on something. The bear's prey was writhing and screaming, quite a spectacle. After a moment, I realized that it was a man this bear was attacking.

My guardian came at a dead run, pulled his sword to pierce the white bear, when I held his hand back, screaming, "No! The bear is protecting me. That man tried to attack me." The white bear instantly transformed back into the raven, flew off to a rocky perch and made such a ruckus, cawing and flapping its wings indignantly that others began to take notice. Lying there in the trail, dazed and looking quite shameful, the man couldn't explain his behavior in attacking a small boy. Nor need he do so, for both my guardian, and I already knew his intent, as did all those near us. He was immediately tied, draped over a yak, and both were turned loose upon the mountain trail, which was the way of crime punishment of the caravan.

"What shall become of this one?" I asked my silent guard. He shrugged his shoulders. The yak turned back, and bawled at me in his yak-voice, and told me that he would dump his stinking burden soon enough and return when he could. That was the first time I felt any danger in my life. I knew that threats might occur due to this special duty I was in preparation for, but in this case, it was pure greed that fed the menace.

We traveled for days and days. The terrain became harder to navigate and the feeling of going higher and higher was noticeable. The weather went from hot to very cold, with no middle zone, as we ascended the mountains. We were either putting on blankets or stripping them off and comfort eluded us. Soon the trail became most difficult to see, much less pass. The travelers and pack animals were being left at mountain villages, a few at a time, as we passed through them, until, at last, it was just me and my silent friend and one large warm, hairy wondrous yak, trudging up and up the treacherous mountain trail. I had noticed thick blankets being picked up at the last village. These blankets were woven of heavy wool and smelled like a yak, so I surmised that the long hair of this friendly beast of burden was used in the making of the heavy wraps. I had seen old women pulling the long hairs from the animals and spinning it, as we moved through villages. I also saw the rolls of spun hair by looms, where younger women were making cloth from it.

Silently, my guardian gave me one of the blankets, then another, then another and eventually set me upon the warm back of the huge yak, and I stayed comfortable, even as I felt crushed by the weight of the heavy spun material. Snow fell in great white abundance. I had never seen snow before and asked constantly what this beautiful white stuff was, but the silent one never answered me. I stuck my tongue out and tasted it, but found that my tongue near froze, so decided maybe I shouldn't explore that part of the cold white stuff of the mountains.

"Yak," I said, quite out loud so that my guardian could hear and know of my frustration at not being conversed with, "Are you the only one who will speak with me? Am I being punished for speaking too much, do you think?"

The yak grunted and groaned as he kept trudging onward and upward, but I could translate those sounds into answers with the mind-to-mind technique. "Apparently there is some reason your kind is not speaking to you, little one," he said. "I don't have a feeling of punishment with this though, for it seems more of a test of strength or some other odd reason. It's difficult for us animals that serve the humans, to understand their thinking. We see the images of thoughts quite clearly and sense intentions as well, but sometimes they don't match the action. What I do see, dear child, is an old ancient one conversing with you soon. Maybe your conversation is being saved for this important one." Animals can be quite prophetic I had discovered.

"I hope you're right," I said to the yak, "because I am tired of hearing my own voice and want to hear the music of another human talking to me soon, before I forget how to have a conversation with my own kind."

At that point, we stopped and my guardian pulled out a container of an oily substance smelling of animal tallow, herbs and smoke, which had a buttery consistency. He began slathering this stuff all over my face and hands and eventually my feet. I made funny faces, for it was most unpleasant to smell, yet, I noticed that where it touched my skin, I felt a warm tingling sensation. He helped me down from the warm back of the yak, and then turned it around, sending it back down the trail the way we had come. Most of our provisions still dangling from the harness, the yak familiar with such requests, turned obediently, trudging in reverse down along the trail.

My guardian took my hand and looked at me with a look of serious concern and then looked down over the edge of the trail we now stood upon. The snow was coming down hard, and the wind swirled making it nearly impossible to see. With the wind picking up even more, being on a mountainside hearing howling wind was unpleasant and a bit scary for a little fellow like me. The snow cleared for a moment, and I could see a drop off that seemed endless. I felt a rush of adrenalin, since this was indeed an unstable position, and I had no urge to go near the cliff's edge. My silent guardian took my hand in his and moved forward onto a narrow ledge stepping slowly and carefully along this precarious rim. He pulled me along behind him, and we inched along the thin foothold barely deep enough for my tiny feet to stand upon, much less his man-sized bare feet. However, he carefully placed each footfall and moved along the edge, pulling me behind him. He stopped a short distance along our slim path and looked at me; I knew he wanted me to step with exactly the same confidence as he had shown so expertly. I also knew that if I didn't follow his direction, I could easily die and surely never see my loved ones again in this lifetime. It was thus, in a frigid blinding snow storm, we two snow-covered white figures, one larger and one quite small, inched along a jagged mountain ledge for hours and hours. The warmth of the buttery salve kept my feet, hands and face warm, but I was beginning to feel very chilled, and my chest was so tight, I couldn't get my breath. My guardian didn't put much salve on himself, because he had saved what was left for such a moment for me. His face looked like frozen ice, and I feared for his safety. He stopped, and carefully pulled the salve container from his blanket covering, reached into the jar and smeared the last of it on my heart and stomach. It warmed me immediately and I felt tremendous gratitude, as I took a deep breath of lifegiving air, be it frigid and stinging my lungs with each gulp. Then he held his hand on his own heart, wiping the remaining small amounts of salve upon him, and we proceeded on. Just when I thought the ledge trail had ended my guardian suddenly fell backward into an unseen crevice. Since he held my hand, I tumbled with him into the hidden fissure in the cliff rock.

We fell deep down, into a black hole in total darkness. As we fell, my guardian pulled me close to him, wrapping himself around me, making a protective ball of his body. We fell into the depths of the unknown, bouncing off hard rock walls, with me incased by him as he sought to protect me. The giant ball of man and child finally abruptly stopped after a long descent. My guardian was completely still, I wondered if he survived. Thankfully, I felt his warm breath ever so slightly warming my cheek, and he moaned from extreme pain.

We unfolded in the darkness, him moaning and me sobbing. I was but a little boy and tears came appropriately easy. I clung to my guardian. It was so black and cold within this dark hole. I was terrified. He pushed me, still sobbing, up onto his back and seemed to want me to ride him as I would ride a donkey. I complied, for what else could I do, knowing that this was not a game, but a direct command for the sake of survival. I did say, however, not expecting a reply, "Where are we and what happened?" I sobbed and rode upon the guardian's broad back, inching our way somewhere in the dark. At the same time, wanting so badly to be embraced in my mother's warm protective loving arms, I may have uttered something like, "I want my mommy."

As my guardian's strong body crawled forward on hands and knees, feeling his way, we somehow made progress. I remember a point where we could have chosen several directions. He took one–for reasons unknown to me–and we moved onward on those mighty torn knees, which I knew were being badly bruised and ripped. I could feel his pain and smell the blood from his wounds. Lying upon his back, I hugged him tightly; clinging to his neck, for just hearing his breathing comforted me. I could not imagine being alone in such a place and I felt gratitude for his company and comfort in this cold, deep, dark place. We continued for a long time, and I began to sense that the strength of my silent friend was giving out. His breathing became labored and his painful moans grew louder. I could hear gurgling sounds coming from deep inside him, and it sounded haunting. Not knowing what else to do, I did what I saw my parents do so many times; I prayed with every ounce of determination and strength I could muster. In a whisper, I said, "Please, in the name of all that is holy, good and knowing, save this silent guardian, for he thinks only of me and not for himself, and he is more worthy of mercy than I am."

At that exact moment, the darkness was filled with light. I blinked, for the brilliance blinded me as much as the darkness had. While my eyes adjusted to the light, my guardian lifted me carefully from his body, setting me aside with tender care even as he suffered. When my eyes adjusted, I saw tears running down his cheeks and his mouth was wide open, mouthing a silent 'thank you' prayer. He had no tongue. His mouth was a hole with some teeth missing but only a stub where his tongue should have been. I could hear the silent words as clearly as if he spoke them normally. He kept mouthing, 'thank you,' repeatedly. As I began to look around wondering where the light came from, I saw an old man holding a walking staff that had a small crystal skull at the very top. He was standing a short distance in a tunnel, at a higher point than we were. The source of light radiated from the crystal skull on his staff. His beard was long and pure white, as was his hair. His eyes were curiously white too, seeing but not seeing, and they appeared to glow. The light coming from the crystal at the top his staff shimmered with reflective rainbows, which bounced around the space like dancing light beings. The eyes that could, or maybe could not see, looked at me, and I felt warm love fill me up.

"The first lesson is a success, dear child," the ancient one said, in an old gravelly voice. "Elmira[39]," he said, looking at my guardian, "you have done well by bringing me this little one and for that I shall heal your wounds and dissolve your pain." My guardian's name, finally revealed to me, I thought. Elmira smiled with relief upon hearing that news and the old one made a sweep with his arm, inviting us to follow him as he turned and walked deeper into the now visible tunnel. We arose and followed. Elmira, regaining some strength, found his stance and took my hand. We moved along behind the brightly lit old man, who walked through a winding tunnel, lit only by his staff's skull.

---

[39] Jeshua's guardian's name which means "princess". It is likely that it meant "guardian of the princess" in Arabic.

# THE MOUNTAIN PEOPLE WELCOME ME
Chapter Six

Elmira and I walked behind the wise one, so ancient I couldn't imagine his age, with complete confidence that he would take us to safety. Soon we arrived at a portal in our path with a great stone archway that was blocked by a huge boulder. Our way-shower gently pushed it aside with little effort, no doubt knowing a secret to moving this guardian of the gate. Beyond the portal, we found sunshine and grass, and I heard birds singing. Our sage friend noticed my astonishment and smiled with satisfaction as he led us forth.

We traversed a well trodden trail and arrived at a grove of ancient trees where many of the singing birds perched. The trees had trunks, which met the ground again and again, making each tree seem as if a forest unto itself. We entered this grove of forest-trees and twined our way onward, until we arrived at one that had an entranceway within its many tangles. Entering the twisted root opening, we traveled a time in an underground passageway, until we began to ascend upward on a winding stairway that must have pierced into a mountain. I noticed along this stairway, that there were many intersections with a multitude of choices of direction, but we always took the upward route.

Finally, we arrived at a simple cave room, which had an opening in its rock wall that was an overlook out to the mountains. It wasn't the view of the sunny place we just left, but rather the rugged snow-covered Himalayan mountain range which had challenged us as we moved along the narrow ledge not so long ago. The wind whipped and the snow swirled in great spirals outside the window portal; however, we didn't feel the biting cold that we experienced outside on the ledge, nor did we find the thin air hard to breathe, though the window had no glass or curtain keeping the harsh elements out. I later learned that the elder put a climate barrier, much like an invisible window pane, in this overlook portal.

As we entered the room, the old sage invited us by a gesture to sit down on folded yak-hair blankets, rich chocolate brown in color and quite comfortable, lying on the floor. We immediately sat in expectancy of what might come next. Our rescuer sat on an identical mat and spoke again. He had not said a word since our first greeting. His voice was clear and almost musical this time, quite unlike the echoed gravelly voice we heard within the cave tunnel where he found us. As it turned out, the sound of his voice depended on the space he spoke within. Evidently, this cave chamber afforded a more musical quality, while the deep tunnel, he rescued us from made his voice seem rougher.

He looked somewhat amused, as if he could read my mind and said, "Welcome to my humble abode, dear ones. You arrived right on time; however, your journey was quite stressful if I am correct." Both Elmira and I nodded wondering how much he knew. Then the old one said, "Tell me of your journey."

Being such an enthusiastic young one at the time, I jumped right in with every detail of the expedition, including my interaction with my animal friends (not necessarily in the order of events as they played out). I especially dwelled upon the times that Elmira had protected me, and my frustration at his silence, thinking that he didn't like me and found his task unpleasant. "I wish I had understood that his tongue had been taken," I said, "then I wouldn't have felt as if he didn't want to speak with me." Elmira sat silently and listened to the conversation, along with the old sage. He showed no hint of exasperation at my rendition of our journey, or my frustration due to his silence.

The ancient asked, "When did you stop thinking about your own safety and switched to be concerned about Elmira's, child?"

"It was in the dark, dear elder," I said. "I could smell the blood from Elmira's knees and being on his back, I could feel his heart attempting to overcome his pain. I also could feel the fear he felt in his desire to keep me safe. I knew that he would die for me if it came to that choice. I felt so grateful to him–a man with such a loving and loyal heart–that my entire being was taken over with the love of this guardian. I desired more than anything that he be safe, thus I simply asked it to be so." My descriptions flowed out, with all due detail.

The ancient one silently nodded and sat for a while in deep thought. He finally said, "Do you always get what you ask, little one?"

The question put me into a moment of silence and deep thought, too. "I'm not sure, dear elder, for there are times when I don't get my wishes granted, and times when I do. It seems that when my wish is from a certain place within my heart, it always seems to be so. At such times, I see it like a weaver connecting one thread to another, and I know that the entire cloth is really 'One'. Somehow there is a rip in this cloth that needs mending," I explained, hoping that I had not strayed too far from the subject. I couldn't think of a better way to convey my answer. I continued, "It's like the one in need, is a thread in this God-fabric, and I simply ask that it be reconnected to the divine cloth, because it is important; linked to many others, and part of the Oneness of the special Divine Cloak[40]." I had watched my mother and other women spin and weave in the evenings and early morning hours, so this metaphor was the best I could come up with. I often day-dreamed and saw how everyday tasks could be seen as a reflection of greater truths. As a boy, there was a constant magical coded world ever speaking to me.

"Give me an example, of when your wish was granted," the elder one said.

"Once when I was very small I fell into the river, and I knew that I couldn't yet swim well enough to keep from being swallowed by the water. I wasn't afraid and simply held my breath, waiting to see what happened when one drowned. Yet, within my mind's eye in that fleeting moment, I could see how many people would be affected by my leaving. I saw the consequence this would have on my mother and knew that she would grieve herself to death, always regretting taking her eyes off me as a babe so unaware of

---

[40] All experience, also called the Akashic Records, intertwined into what some refer to as the "The Cloak of God"

danger. I knew, too, that my father and mother had made a promise to bring me forth and raise me up for a divine mission. I'm still unsure of what that mission is," I clarified. "I realized dying would break an important link in a garment of love and affect many others. Dying wasn't scary to me, but living was a fulfillment of a promise that I knew I had to keep. At that moment, I asked to stay so that sorrow wouldn't visit my dear sweet mother, nor my father, or any others that loved me; you might say, I made a request, and it was granted. That was when the fish came to me; a really big fish!" The ancient one and Elmira chuckled a bit, because my eyes got huge when I related how big my fish saviors were.

"The men in our village said big fish lived in the river, but never would these big ones take the fisherman's hook. One of those mighty fish swam toward me, after I fell in. I was deep under the water and the fish spoke to me with its mind. He reminded me of you, ancient one. I could tell by just looking into his eyes, he was old and wise, too. He told me 'be not afraid', and he gave me air by kissing me. Soon this fish, and others like him, had me safely ashore in the shallow water, where my mother came and scooped me up, weeping hard, yet extremely happy to see me breathing on my own."

"Hmmm," the elder one uttered. "It's important for you to contemplate how your magic works and why. Now Elmira, what have you to say about your adventure?"

"But he can't speak, elder," I said. "He has no tongue!"

The elder smiled and so did Elmira, who awkwardly, but in a clear enough voice began to speak slowly and told of his adventure, never even asking how it was that he could once again physically talk. It was the one and only time in my life that I heard him speak vocally. He told of losing his tongue, so he could not reveal the secrets of a long-ago master, who had kept treasures in secret places and did things that were literally 'unspeakable'. When his usefulness was done, he spoke of finally being cast aside after having his tongue cut-away to insure his silence. He became a wandering beggar until he came to the village of the Nazarites.

"They were good people," Elmira said. "They took me in and healed my festering wounds. I stayed with them, gained strength and eventually attempted to repay my debt for their loving compassion, by being a guardian of the most expert kind. I was quiet and effective in this duty, because my eyes and ears became quite keen, even as my voice was no longer there, one sense having gained from the loss of another."

Elmira said, "One day, the Nazarites asked me to honor them by guarding a most dear treasure. I was a bit confused, because I had never known these gentle people to desire precious things, nor establish any kind of wealth in their society. I expected to see treasure like my old master had–silver, gold, gems, jewelry and such–but this treasure was a small talkative child," and he nodded to indicate me. "I loved this lad from first sight," he mentioned, glancing over towards me. "I realized that there must be those who would be a threat to this child, since the gentle ones considered him a treasure." Thinking for a moment he commented, "But I knew they considered all the children as such and this confused me. Even so, I would do anything for the compassionate people who showed me pity and healed me, body and soul, and especially for this child I have grown to love."

As he continued his story, I noticed he had an odd accent, and I wondered where he called home. "The Nazarites have many enemies, since their way of thinking is different from the norm where they live, and they hold every woman and man sacred, and especially the children. They have an ability to foresee the future, and I sensed this child was destined to be a force of good for all creation. Why else would they send him away to safety?"

Finally, he said, "I never knew how to show my love, other than loyalty. I would gladly give my life for this boy's sake, and for the sake of those who have entrusted him to my safekeeping." He looked at me with a loving gaze and went on to say, "Yet when things seemed so dire, all he thought about was my well-being." He dropped his head, saying, "I'm not worthy."

The ancient one sat a moment taking his time to answer, reviewing carefully what he heard. Finally, he said, "This self-judgment of worthiness is the root of all evil, because it denies divinity from the very core of your being and dims your soul light." He looked at both Elmira and I and continued on saying, "The Divine Creator of All That Is, all consciousness, and all not yet conscious of itself, deemed you worthy to experience this physicality, yet you would allow others to dim your soul light and diminish your worthiness. How is it that you give up so easily on yourself? You were chosen to be the guardian for this wee one, because you are worthy, Elmira. You were saved from the brink of death, due to his understanding of that worth, as he cried out for your sake."

Then he quickly changed the subject. "You'll stay awhile here among the sages and the sagas of the high mountains. When the time is right, we'll send you back through the underground passages, down the caravan trails to your people, the Nazarites. You shall be proof of the success of your lessons and go on to do many noble missions for those you dearly love, because you both are worthy of the tasks asked of you.

At that point, the ancient one arose and bid us to do the same. He said he would see to our hunger, since we still experienced that desire. We went forth from his chambers and eventually arrived at a place where others (elders, children, men, women and all sorts of beings) were enjoying a meal in a large cavern hall. Many languages were spoken, yet everyone understood each other. Food was present in abundance; food I never imagined. Seated at a low table and offered a bowl of something that looked delicious, I eagerly took a bite. The taste was beyond description in flavor, texture and color. I was informed it was wild vegetables and mushrooms from the mountain meadows and some berries as well. They also had bread on every low table–flat bread and fluffy yeast breads–which, due to my exhaustion, filled me to the point that I nodded off to sleep, there at the shared meal.

When I awoke, I was in a small cave chamber, upon a yak mat, covered by a blanket of bright colors and above me was a small portal looking out to the snow-covered high mountains. I looked out into the snowy scenery, not feeling cold, but feeling lonely for my parents, my friends, and my world as I knew it. I wondered how long I would be in this strange, but friendly and fascinating place. I also wondered if I would ever be up to the task that was expected of me. Then I did what comes naturally to children and sensitive ones of such a tender age, I cried. I sobbed huge tears that streaked down my cheeks and tasted salty and wet. I felt something warm lean against me and was startled to see a hairy silvery-colored animal, almost like a dog, snuggling against my side. I learned later it was a mountain wolf. It simply laid its head in my lap and sighed, and I felt better and once again fell asleep.

# ANIMAL TEACHERS
Chapter Seven

As children often do with animals, the wolf and I became fast friends. I later learned from one of my mountain teachers, that this wolf was rescued as a tiny pup. I formed a friendship with the care-keeper of the children, who shared the story.

She told me, "This pup's mother had frozen when she was moving her babies to safety, due to a traveling human wandering near her den. She didn't like his energy," she said. "The wanderer saw the mother wolf as she moved her last pup to the new safer den. She was exhausted, yet determined to hide her babies. He slung a rock at her that normally she would have easily avoided. Due to her exhaustion, the rock found its target, and she took a direct hit to the head. Still somehow she moved on, wounded and in terrible pain, with streaks of blood staining her beautiful fur. The wanderer didn't even care enough to inspect the damage done to her. Stoning animals was just fun and games for him. She collapsed before she reached her new den, and pushed her pup under her body to protect and keep it warm."

I asked, "How did you know how this played out? Did someone witness this awful thing?"

"No, a messenger just found the wee one under the frozen body of his mother, on a path between villages. The warmth of her body saved him," the storyteller told me. "They were found with the

# The Saga-Oracle

she-wolf curled up around her beloved pup, protecting him even as she had physically departed."

I was fascinated and urged my teacher to continue. "The mother wolf died on one of our mountain trails, in a blizzard that had caused everything to go pure white, making the path barely visible. She and her pup were as white as the snow that was covering everything. The messenger, who regularly is sent from the secret valley to bring news of the lower lands to the mountain sage, nearly stumbled over the frozen body of the mother wolf as he returned during the storm. When he examined this lump, which he knew shouldn't be there; he discovered the poor creature and heard whimpers. Knowing the animal he inspected was frozen solid; he carefully turned her body over and found the tiny pup under her, barely alive. He quickly built a sling out of his cape and put the dead mother and whimpering baby into it. He pulled it along behind him sensing that was best, believing that the pup might muster the will to live with his mother nearby."

Storytellers always fascinated me and my quick mind would try to jump ahead of what they were saying. I asked, "How is it you know all the details of this tale."

I thought she was ignoring my question as she continued. "Upon arriving at the mountain sage's cave, the messenger related the news and the situation he encountered. The sage laid his hands upon the frozen mother wolf's head and communicated with this ice-covered one," my storyteller explained. "After that, the sage's assistants were instructed to go back down the trail to a well known petrified tree. Then, go due north one-hundred paces to the face of an outcropped rock. Under this rock, near some freshly dug ground, they would find the new den and four more wolf pups. The master instructed the rescuers to bring the litter of pups to him. He had made a promise to this she-wolf, that he would raise her family for her. This released her, so that she could move to the inner-dimension in peace." I could picture the entire tale as the saga teacher remembered it. "It was the master sage who told me," she said. "When he touched the soul of the dead mother wolf, he accessed her memory, which was best to completely understand the situation and honor her last request, as well as attend to the unfinished commitment she fully intended to honor with her babies. The sage could see her spirit, and he saw her pacing around him and her baby. He knew she couldn't move on until she felt sure that her family would survive."

Animal stories were most interesting for me, as they are for all children, but also these tales were expert teaching tools. During the time I spent in the mountains, my wolf companion never left my side and somehow was not named either. It simply was my friend and constant companion. I began to learn the vocal language of wolves, as he told me that he was taught wolf-speak from the mountain sage, not having the opportunity to learn from his mother. He also told me that his brothers and sisters went back to the wild when they were of age, as promised, but that he had chosen to remain with the mountain people, to repay them for their kindness and compassion.

I began my lessons the day after my arrival in the high mountains. Elmira was always somewhere nearby, just far enough from my new wolf friend to feel comfortable. Elmira never learned how to be at ease with the animal kingdom. He couldn't hear their inner-voices as many children and I did. He was raised in the desert where the animals co-habit with humans, but seldom formed relationships, other than master and slave. The non-domesticated animals were often dangerous snakes and lizards and were feared. He tolerated animals, but rarely approached them or spoke to them, as I did.

I emerged from my cave room that first morning, feeling an overwhelming desire to go back to the mountain sage's quarters. I intuitively headed into the maze of tunnels followed by my white wolf companion who was followed by Elmira, who walked a respectable distance not sure if this animal might be dangerous, but keeping an eye on the situation, nevertheless. I arrived by inner-guidance at the portal of the mountain sage's cave. He stood awaiting me and ushered me into his room, looking very satisfied that I had heard his silent call.

After formalities and some butter tea, which warmed and stimulated me in a most invigorating way, I met my first teacher,

Lehya[41], who stepped out of the face of the rock right there in the master's chambers. Such magic kept me constantly excited and helped to keep my homesickness at bay. This rock person looked like a hooded sage, but the material of her cloak was the very rock that she just emerged from, now animated and filled with energy and motion. I would learn to talk to rocks and the ground itself from her. As Lehya said, "We rock people have much to teach you, and important secrets to share as well."

To a child, everything is possible; thus everything is achievable and experienced at many levels. I had no trouble walking away with a rock person. I was excited to begin my lessons with this fascinating teacher. My first lesson was to learn the basic properties of the different substances. I spent many days collecting specimens and identifying what they were comprised of, along with their proper names. Lehya taught me the appropriate manner of asking permission to take a sample. As we approached a translucent green rock formation one morning (or any source I might sample), she instructed, "You ask the mother rock, or mother-earth place, for a small piece of her and tell her truthfully why you want this portion of her body." I learned to respect creation in all its modalities in that simple way, and I began to understand the 'ask and ye shall receive' concept at its most basic level. I also discovered that the very ground I walked upon was a part of a being's body, and that I should always respect other physical vehicles, no matter what they were comprised from, along with their spirit.

I gained much knowledge from the rocks, and the earth that surrounded them, during my time with Leyha. I discovered they grew like me, and that they had a 'knowing' of who was near them and what their intentions were. They kept secrets within their mass–secrets that were astonishing and some that were not so great. They absorbed the history of whatever happened around them. The 'not so wonderful' secrets were always the result of disrespect and disconnection between beings and nature. The rocks and the earth bore silent witness to this unbalanced reaction

---

[41] A form of the name 'Leia'. Also the name of an herb that "smells like horses"

to life. They could also absorb energetic vibrations and conduct them elsewhere, when bidden to do so, as crystals were well equipped to do. They could cleanse anti-energy or anti-actions that were destructive, or as you often term–evil. You might call this episode my 'Stoneology' or 'Earthology' class[42].

When I mastered the concepts that taught to me to communicate with stone and earth beings, I went on to my 'Wind and Water Class'. The two were combined because they, like stone and earth, supported each other. The wind is the way the water moves its energy about, both above and below the surface. The water is like liquid energy, that evaporates as its currents constantly ebb and flow, releasing the energy to the ethers as vapor. Cycles, or energy in motion, are often symbolized by the infinity sign which looks like the Arabic number 8 lying on its side (∞). This symbol shows how cycles crisscross within recycling movement. The symbol of the 8 is also connected to the ancient adage 'as above, so below'. Once one learns how energy moves, the key to all creation is unlocked. In my first lesson in this class, I learned that the wind, along with Mother Earth's gravity, kept water in motion making evolution possible. Through constant movement, substances integrate, merge and offer myriad ways to experience physicality. This has been referred to as 'primordial soup' by some, since it refers to all the floating life organisms in water, that combine into greater more complex organisms, all opportunities for experiencing physicality.

My wind teacher was birdlike and one of the last remaining bird-tribe[43] beings. She actually had hollow bones and wings that folded under extra long arms. I was among a small group of students, but because of the way the class was conducted, we often had lessons one-on-one. Children learn best, through direct experience. Our bird teacher, who never gave us a formal name, taught us to merge with her at the mind-soul level. In that way, we became one with her. I must admit, I found this an extremely

---

[42] The study of the soul and physical properties of stone and earth

[43] Ancient legends speak of spirit helpers who were extraterrestrial bird people

interesting way of learning, which offered us an entirely new perspective.

Once we merged with the winged-one, one at a time, we would ride the wind above the great sea. This demonstrated how the energy above the water moved in waves, just as the water below did; only on invisible currents of air. We glided on the airwaves, lifted and supported by the outstretched wings of the wind-rider, with whom we were one. The energy that held us up is similar to the negative ions that develop after an electrical storm, which causes everything to be crystal clear due to high electromagnetic charge. The ability to sense and see becomes extremely enhanced at such times. We could see the wind from that newly-taught perspective, and we could ride the waves of each breath of the impressive breeze, even as we couldn't really see the path of the wind, but gave ourselves up to the flow it afforded.

The bird teacher, still very much in control of its flying body which it offered us, would wait until the moment when we understood the air current concept, and then it would dive deep into the water, which was quite a thrill and surprise to us. Once under the surface we would compare the ionic nature of this liquid arena as well, which was closer to your positive energetic charge, where everything mingles together. We understood then that within this watery realm, due to the energies above and below the surface, there was ability for many organisms to swim and mingle. As they co-habited and co-existed, they also co-created in this immense bowl of divine soup. That often meant that they consumed each other, which was my first lesson in how energy holds its vibration within a system of merging from one organism to another. My teacher pointed out, that as I merged the energy of the mountain carrots into my own system after a meal, I was now myself but expanded (carrot and person). I learned what we consume, we become; and what we become, we assumed expanded responsibility to. Thus, those that ate the gazelle would have a part of them that is the gazelle. That meant that they may have to learn to face fear and know when to flee the threat of danger; not standing to fight, rather knowing when to depart in a hurry for the sake of survival. Furthermore, it meant not shirking responsibility, but rather being part of it, and so forth. These wonderful lessons were a perfect way to learn Onement. Flying on waves of wind and swimming in the deep water gave us the experience, instead of an abstract theory, and those kinds of lessons are unforgettable.

We even experienced the bird eating a fish, feeling the entire process of digestion and integration of the fish energy into the bird body. A wave of satisfaction took the form of gratitude, following the gulping down of this fish. Our bird teacher explained, it helped the spirit of the fish return to its place of origin, to await another chance to be a fish, or if it was ready, to experience another type of physicality. A part of its fish spirit also merged with the bird that ate it. Once this area was fully explored, and our teacher was satisfied that we had learned the essence of the lesson, we moved on to our next class and a new teacher; some of us went in one direction and some went toward another; sometimes within a group and occasionally as a single student, depending on how we understood and integrated the previous lesson.

My next class was 'The Animal Realm'. My faithful white wolf companion became integral in the learning of these lessons. My new teacher was a high mountain wolf as well, and was a saga.[44] If it were not for my mind-to-mind conversations with my companion, and wolf vocal lessons during my resting time, I surely wouldn't have believed my eyes and ears in this class.

I, along with my two traveling companions–my wolf-friend and Elmira trailing behind–walked along a mountain trail with only intuition to guide us. We came upon a huge she-wolf sitting, waiting for our arrival, on a large boulder along the mountain path, and I knew my lesson began here. I kept looking for a person to appear, to take control of the class. This majestic silver-gray wolf just watched me, cocking her head this way and that, as if in wonder of what this people-pup was expecting or thinking. I tried mind-to-mind communication with her, but got nowhere. I looked back at my wolf friend who telepathically urged me to be patient, assuring me that I would be talking to this animal soon enough. Finally, as I seemed a bit confused and anxious, the she-wolf

---

[44] Female counterpart to 'sage', or 'wise one'

# The Saga-Oracle

spoke out loud to me in my own language. My expression had to have been dramatic, with my mouth gaping open in astonishment. My first lesson with this teacher was that wolves not only laugh, but have a great sense of humor. The saga-wolf spoke to me in my own Aramaic language and her face contorted as she formed the words. The wolf grimaced as she spoke, but with an unmistakable sound of humor, as her breath sucked in with a wheezing sound and pushed out with a grumbling vibration in rapid repetitive gasps, leaving no doubt that this was not a hostile moment. It was a sight to see, for a young fellow like me. I felt laughter well up through the depths of me, at the sight of this unexpected spectacle. I laughed until tears of merriment trailed down my face, and the wolf just kept making the ridiculous sounds as she laughed, too. We both rolled around on the ground, kicking our feet, making it even funnier.

"You make me laugh, wee one," the wolf finally said. "Never have I seen such a look of surprise on any creature's face. Surely, you have spoken in the language of my kind. How is it, you think we can't master your language, if we so choose?"

"I dunno," I muttered. "I just haven't seen one such as you do it before, and it looks, well, kinda funny."

"Your kind looks funny to me, too, when they attempt to howl; but let us agree that talking wolves and surprised people-pups are quite the funny lot. Shall we be about our lessons?"

"Are you my teacher?" I asked, glad that I didn't try to impress her with my wolf-howling abilities.

She replied, "Who better to learn animal-speak from? Bring your companion and follow me. I know this white one, and once he has his mind made up, there will be no changing it. He's not about to let you venture too far from him as long as you're in the high mountain place. Now move along, all of you, for I assume that Elmira will follow as well, once he has his wits back about him, since he is equally determined to keep his promise of guardianship."

She knew us, I thought. Indeed, these mountains were a magical place.

Her pronouncement ushered us forward into a procession out across the middle highland. She led, with myself behind her, the white one behind me, and at a respectable distance, but still near enough to protect me, Elmira, trudged along behind, shaking his head and muttering something about how no one would ever believe this mission he had agreed to assist.

Our first expedition was to the valley we had traveled through to the master's cave when I initially arrived, where the sun shines and the birds sang all the time. "Soon enough," she-wolf said, "we shall explore the outer regions, but for now we will begin by learning to converse with those that live in the secret valley. They are a cheerful lot so you will get some happy-talk from them."

Indeed that was true–I learned to sing like a bird, croak like frogs, chirp like the crickets, and talk wolf, which still made 'She', (my teacher's name) and my white wolf companion chuckle remembering how surprised I was that they could talk human. I also learned to talk deer, yak, squirrel, rat, cat, and so on. Many animals shared the special valley with the mountain people and there was a firm friendship and cooperative spirit among them.

Once you can talk to animals, you understand that they aren't different from us. They just don't worry as much. They know how to live in the moment. Since I was still a small child, this living in the moment wasn't hard for me. The animals warned me that as I grew into my adult years, I would probably develop the 'worry factor,' as they called it. The animals had noticed, the older you become as a human the more you dwell on what might yet come, and you miss the wonder of the 'now' moment. They also understood that the more humans worried, the more they reflected on the past, too. The animals couldn't fathom why humans would choose to worry. They wisely noticed that sometimes, if the human's consciousness was expanded enough, they realized that they created their 'now moment', and they took more notice of it.

# The Saga-Oracle

Humans, they said, are so caught up in the future and past that they can't appreciate the 'Eternal Now'[45].

The yak told me, "In this constant worry, you miss the great smells, tastes and opportunities that Mother Nature has presented on her plate of earthly delights. You forget the greatest key to all meaningful physicality, living in the moment." I found the yaks to be sage-like and dedicated animals, and I hadn't forgotten the one that delivered me to the mountain pass so comfortably.

We soon explored the outer mountain ranges. She-wolf had Elmira and I bundle up and bring along the warming salve, since this would be a difficult trek. I could sense Elmira was reluctant to go back out into the treacherous frozen unknown. His concern for me was apparent upon his worried face.

She-wolf said, "See what I mean. Look at Elmira. See the worry lines upon his face? Notice how his heart beats faster and his hands grip his staff, to the point that they nearly merge with it." Checking carefully to see if I made the observation, she went on, "This is what worry does," looking very sternly at my guardian. "Now, Elmira, you shall not experience the wonder of the snow and see the crown jewels of Tara in the ice formations, much less notice the beauty of the trail." He looked chastised. "Though you will be safe on this journey, you can't relax and enjoy it as your wee charge does." I was seldom called by my name. I was usually called 'wee one' or 'lad'. Elmira struggled to release the worry, but he just couldn't forget all the dangers that might threaten his promised mission to keep me safe.

I was determined to experience this lesson within the 'now' moment and didn't miss much on the trail to the high den of the snow leopard. Just getting there was an integral part of my lesson –the journey to the destination. We moved along treacherous trails to the snow covered cliffs. My first animal conference was with the mighty feline of the high mountains, whom I didn't see until I was standing right next to her. Since the wolf is usually a pack

---

[45] The only place to experience what you have manifested. The past is a memory, the future a hope or plan

animal and the leopard a solitary one, I didn't know that they tolerated each other. There seemed to be no hesitation, as she-wolf, my teacher, approached the leopard's den. The great cat emerged, sniffed noses with She, and looked at me. Such a magnificent creature, I thought, as white as the snow, with spots that resemble shadows sprinkled across her beautiful winter coat. Because she blended so well with the snow, I didn't notice her as we first approached. She must have been reclining in the mouth of her den. I didn't even see her at first when my wolf teacher sniffed noses with the leopard, until she spoke to me from under the overhanging rock. I thought the snow bank itself was coming to life and talking to me. Then I saw the long tail swish back and forth, as cats do when thinking cat thoughts. The huge cat lived high in the thin air of the rock faces on the apex of the rocky cliffs but hunted, she told me, at lower levels where she was more successful. Even as she said this I thought I sensed her sizing me up as the guest of honor 'as her next meal.'

I found her quite beautiful and very wise and soon learned the basic sounds of her language and how to utter them. At that point, we practiced having a conversation within cat language, a language which involved body language as well as sound. Cats are very fluid communicators and their bodies speak as loud as their words. The leopard told me how she had to eat flesh to fulfill her mission, and that she wouldn't hesitate to eat me, if she had the opportunity to do so. Her head swayed from side-to-side as she spoke.

Astonished, I said, "You would eat me? I wouldn't eat you."

"Of course not," she meowed in the snow leopard's low crumbly voice. "It is not your mission to eat me, after all, is it? You don't need snow leopard cat merged into your being, but I could use a good people-pup like yourself, for it would help me understand why humans kill my kind for fur and throw our flesh away." She then turned her back to me and looked over her shoulder saying, "I shall refrain from partaking of your flesh this time, because I respect She," nodding toward the she-wolf. "I understand that you are here to learn for your own mission and speaking leopard is a part of it. Hopefully, you might teach your kind to respect us more appropriately."

I replied, "Yes," and added, "I would much rather learn to speak leopard, then become a part of a leopard by being consumed." That answer must have pleased her because she began to purr loudly and squeezed her beautiful eyes. The lesson proceeded. I learned that the purr is a song. It can be a song of contentment, and usually is, but it also could be a song of deep distress. Leopards have a death song, which they sing as they die. I learned what each roar meant, how to call a mate, how to warn the prey that I'm hungry, and if they don't choose to be my next meal, they had better move on fast. What greater lessons a boy could learn, I couldn't imagine. All humans have a warrior protector within, as well as a peacemaker. and the leopard helped me understand that balance. After spending some time with the snow leopard, I realized that She, my wolf teacher, had left, but Elmira and my companion wolf friend were still with me, patiently watching from a distance. When the lesson was finished, I rejoined them. Guided and protected by my two devoted guardians, I returned to the safety of the cave chambers. I chatted non-stop all the way back along the snowy path, remarking on how amazing the snow leopard was, as both of my guardians patiently listened.

My last lessons were how to understand my own kind's thoughts, and when to move into a person's mind to read their, often-confusing, musings. I wish I could share the lesson. but this is a guarded teaching. I will expand on it at a more appropriate time. The mountain sage himself was my teacher for this important segment. "You are a quick learner," he said. "I thought it would take you years to learn the lessons arranged for you among the high mountain peaks and its hidden valleys. However, you learned in a fraction of the time expected and have only been here three sun cycles[46]. Your people were right to honor our request to take you on as an intern. You are as gifted as they said, and I sincerely hope your gifts will be well received, when you are ready to fulfill your mission."

---

[46] Three years

It seemed as if the three year time was just three weeks, and I asked why that was so. My wise sage teacher said, time was experienced differently in this enchanted valley and surrounding mountains, much like it would be in other dimensional warps[47], such as the land of the fairy folk.

Noticing that his remark captured my curiosity, he explained, "The place that elementals call home is even more enchanting and could be difficult to integrate into your understandings." He looked at me intently and explained, "There will come a counterpart for you, wee one, who will know well of this fairy place, for she will be training within this realm. She'll fill you in on this magical, but dangerous, place of elemental beings." Evidently, he could see future possibilities, too, I realized. He then said, "Just know that you have your part to learn, and she has her part. If the mission unfolds as planned, you will be drawn together sooner or later to become One in intention and One in Spirit," he explained. "I know that she will come into your life. I don't know how or when, just that she will, and you know it, too."

Having no desire to play grown-up with the girls yet, and sensing that was what he meant, I said, "Are you talking about a girl?" It wasn't that I didn't like them, but I just couldn't see myself hanging out with them. As a small boy, they seemed to be interested in different things than I was. I wanted to explore, and they wanted to mother all things, including the earth herself. I wanted to ride the wind, and they wanted to smell the flowers and experience mother earth's beauty. Forgetting my worry lesson, I said, "Am I to share my life with a girl, someday? What if she doesn't like the same things I do?"

"It may not seem to excite you now," the mountain sage said, "because you are having a grand time exploring and discovering the elements of Tara, the earth planet, and the space she floats within, but I assure you that your counterpart will fulfill your heart's desire. She has adventures to share with you that you will find fascinating. One day you will share your lessons with her, too. It is the way of it, and how the counterparts of energy, being

---

[47] Dimensions within dimensions

different yet alike, complement and complete each other, merging and creating a Divine Union."

I thought about what the sage was saying and 'not saying' about the elementals. I wondered about the mysterious one who would have the chance to explore that magical realm and my mind took me to my early baby days. I could remember all the way back to my birthing, which I was told not to talk about, because it was rare that one would hold such a memory, and might cause suspicion. To be so gifted would be feared, my parents said, and I might be pushed out of the social arena and branded a demon. I thought it would be great to share some of those precious memories with someone. Maybe this girl would be good for me after all.

I recalled that most stories mother told me, reminded me of this fairy realm the sage mentioned. "Are those stories of my babyhood real?" I asked him. "Is that what you are trying to tell me then, dear sage teacher? My mother was not just amusing me with made-up tales?"

"There is truth to the stories as they intermingle with imagination, to entertain and teach lessons, yes, that's true. Things that adults no longer trust as truth, or things that they don't want to face as such, are often kept within the childhood tales. It keeps them in the safest place of all, within innocence! Do you understand, child?"

I thought for a moment and realized, that by the very fact that the adults didn't believe the endless possibilities they shared as stories to entertain their children, the truth was secretly safe and always present in the minds of all people, who, after all, were once wise, open-minded children themselves, who lived in the 'now'. The tales were not feared then, thus not censored, or sealed away to be forgotten. "A great idea!" I proclaimed. "Wish I had thought of it."

The sage answered, "You did" and winked at me. "Now it's time for you to go home. Your family awaits your arrival, and your father needs to see you, before he leaves on a journey to his soul home."

"But, he is home, isn't he?"

"Your real home is not upon Tara, young one, or in a place, or within a time, but rather it is outside of dimension and totally within energy at the purest level. You will learn more about this from your next teacher. Now sleep well and say your good-bye to the white one as you do your evening talk, for he'll miss you, wee one, and his heart will be heavy upon your departure."

"Can't I take him with me?" I asked.

The sage just shook his head. "There are places you must go where he can't. That would break his heart. He must stay here."

My eyes began to tear up, and I mumbled, "I will now leave in sadness, for I can't stand hurting anyone or anything, especially my wolf friend, who has been such a comfort to me." My head seemed to crash into my chest for the sadness drained me.

The sage reached out, put his ancient hand on my shoulder and said, "Then, if I promise to keep this white one at my own feet for all his days, shall that give you the opportunity to move on in joy, dear heart?"

I always felt peaceful and happy at this great sage's feet, where I often sat to listen and learn, and I knew that this would be a perfect solution to my dilemma. At the prospect of such an arrangement, my head moved back upward, and my eyes answered before my voice did. "Yes!" I almost shouted with tears of joy now washing my cheeks, "Surely he wouldn't miss me so much, with you to look after him."

The sage chuckled and said, "Or rather, he will look after me!" He said, "Then so it is. Tomorrow morning you will depart."

# GOING HOME
## Chapter Eight

I didn't want to leave the high mountain place, yet down deep within me–where a child keeps their great love for their parents–there was a painful emptiness. I missed my family, especially my mother and father. Unconditional love resides within a deep inner-place and always holds the hope of a perfect relationship. I was lucky in this life to have two parents who adored me. Their separation from me was as sorrowful to them as it was for me.

I remembered leaving them three short years ago, when my heart was so deep in sorrow. My heart was heavy again, and I felt an urgency to return home. I knew something was wrong there, something so important that I was being pulled back to my family before the intended span of time and lessons unfolded. Thus I felt a desire to be quickly on my way, even though I wished to stay.

Since the moment of departure was not a joyful exit, it was kept quiet and private, with only the master sage and my white wolf companion (my ever faithful guardian in this mountain realm) seeing my guardian Elmira and me off.

The passage itself took about three months. It was not the joyful discovery experience of my previous journey to the high mountains. I couldn't shake the sense of something amiss at home, thus the urgency outweighed the desire of discovery along the byways. Elmira and I left the enchanted valley in the high place, traveling in reverse, except we followed an underground tunnel to the base of the mountain instead of chancing the precarious ledge again. Little by little we joined up with others, and the caravan grew in size, as the passes and paths widened at lower elevations. Ultimately, we joined a caravan heading toward the desert we had to cross to get home. There were others with us who seemed familiar to me on our journey. They walked near, but didn't converse with us, as we mixed quietly among the travelers.

We arrived in my homeland, dusty and tired in the dark hours of early morning, unannounced yet expected. My mother was priestess-trained, even though she kept that early training quiet these days, for fear of endangering our family. She knew her child was near, and was uneasy the entire day and couldn't settle into sleep that night. The Romans had succeeded in squelching the priestess customs by shear brutality and often murder, resulting in the women hiding their priestess ways. Even so, she had been on edge all day, but kept her intuitional feelings to herself fearing she may be wrong this time. However, she chanced doing some secret priestess divining, and her suspicions were confirmed.

In the darkness of the early morning, I could hear her before I saw her. A moaning cry came out of the dark, followed by a more joyful shriek. She emerged from the night about a mile from my family home, running with arms open wide like a giant dark bird, piercing the night's womb. She ran directly to me, even though no one was carrying torches, since it was decided that for the sake of safety it was best not to draw attention to those who would dare walk in the dark. Mother just knew my position among the quiet travelers and came straight to me.

We had left the main caravan at dusk, because they stopped for night rest, and we wanted to travel on to our destination with little attention. We were only a few in numbers now. Still, some had traveled the entire way with Elmira and me. I never noticed when they showed up or when they left us, after I rejoined my mother. At the first piercing sound coming out of the dark, Elmira, ever on guard, took out his long knife. He soon realized it was my dear mother, put the knife back in its scabbard, and stepped aside revealing me. I was 8-years-old now, taller and more mature than the 5-year-old child who had left three years previously.

Mother swept me up into her arms and twirled me around and around; how she managed since she was a small woman, and I was a half-grown child, I can only account to passionate love. Soon we were both soaked with tears of joy. "My baby, my baby boy!" she kept saying, repeatedly. If it wasn't that I was so happy, I might have been embarrassed with my mother twirling me like a little one.

I kept saying, "Mother, dear mother," for words can't adequately convey how it felt to be reunited.

She simply took my hand, and we walked in silence ahead of the guardian group, with only Elmira in front keeping an eye on the path to my home. The others eventually vanished. I didn't notice since I was only aware of my mother's hand in mine and the fact that I was going home.

As we entered our dwelling, mother whispered a "shish," putting her fingers to her lips to convey the universal message for quiet. We stepped across the threshold, pushing away the lambskin door covering, and I felt a rush of gratitude to be home again. All were sleeping in our humble, wonderfully-appreciated abode. She took me to her favorite sitting place, and we simply sat and held each other in silence, until the dawn woke the rest of the family.

There were more present in the household than I remembered. Mother had dozed off in her exhausted bliss, since she had been awake and alert for most of the night, sensing my return. My little sister Jemima,[48] a delightful girl, still a toddler, awakened first and approached me. She toddled to me and stood gazing with a most peaceful pleasant look upon her little face. I knew instantly that she was my sister, even though we hadn't met before. She reminded me of Mother. I wondered as I gazed back at her, what the renaming of this dear peaceful soul would be one day when she came of age. It was the custom to give a child a new name about age thirteen. To me, she seemed like the bird of peace, 'the white dove', and even her complexion was pale in places. I later learned that she had the sign of the dove from birth. You would understand this as albinism[49]. It can be total or partial. My dear sister Jemima was a partial albino in that she had patches of white skin, one blue eye and one brown eye. Often such children had a white mark somewhere on their body that resembled a dove in flight. As this dove-child reached up and touched my face with her tiny index finger, I noticed the dove shape in the palm of her hand. From that moment on she was always my 'little dove'. She simply said, "Emanuel[50]," as her sweet baby eyes made contact with my eyes. I thought, 'what a sweet thing for this little one to say to her brother, who she had never before seen.' To consider me 'God's Beloved' at such a young age seemed angelic to me.

My mother woke, as did the others, including my father and someone I didn't know. The little home had people sleeping

---

[48] Hebrew name meaning "Dove"
[49] Latin word meaning "white". An inherited genetic condition with partial or complete absence of pigment in skin
[50] Emanual means "beloved of God" or "God is with us"

everywhere in its two tiny rooms. The stranger turned out to be a helper for my father, who was not well. The family looked at mother and me, wrapped up in each other's arms, with disbelief at first, then great joy. They also looked at Jemima in total amazement, since she was a shy child and this surprising morning, she had not only spoken her first word, which had wakened them, but acted like she had known me from birth.

My mother's smile lit up the room. Jemima pointed at me and said, "Emanuel," again. No one had referred to me by this name previously. They must have wondered why little shy Jemima would call me such. Maybe she was saving her first words for me. Since I had spoken so young our parents had feared Jemima had not received the gift of speech. She was about 2-years-old, and had not uttered one word or sound, until now. 'What a homecoming gift indeed!' I thought, as I began to understand the significance of the moment. Not only did our family find me wrapped up in mother's arms unexpectedly, they also never anticipated hearing the voice of their youngest sibling, little Jemima. The two miracles lightened a heaviness I sensed within the home.

I realized my father was not in the same good physical health as I had last seen him. The stranger, Gladori[51], a very elderly healer-woman, was at father's side helping him rise and come to me. He could hardly walk and sagged heavily against the spindly, but strong, old woman. Mother wanted to assist, but it was clearly understood that Gladori was there for that purpose, and my mother respected her dedication to her duty. Even so, I met father halfway across the dirt floor which spanned the small room and threw my arms around him in a most childlike greeting. I didn't feel the need to be as formal as would be expected of a son of eight years. It wasn't as if I hadn't learned the proper way to behave when approaching adults; it was just that I didn't care much about formalities at that moment. I wanted to be close to my dear father and feel his body reconnecting to mine. That superseded official procedures of greeting.

---

[51] Old variant of Gladys. Gaelic in origin meaning "Delicate Flower"

When I held him, he felt awfully thin and frail. His body had changed drastically since I last saw him on my departure day. He had frequently been mistaken for my grandfather when we were together before I left, because he was much older than my mother. To me, he was ageless and the strongest, bravest man I knew. I hadn't considered (not unusual for a child of my age) what happened to the physical body as one moved on in years. I felt immediately that the energy within my father was slipping away. I wanted to energize him somehow. I cried, not tears of joy, but tears of frustration. I hadn't yet learned how to give healing energy to others intentionally. Right now, I wanted to focus all my intentions on filling my father up with life-force, so he could be strong again.

I had felt a healing essence go out from me from time to time; once to a tiny bird that fell from its nest and broke its wing, and another time, to Elmira when he had broken his toe trying to keep up with me on one of my adventures. Even so, the healing was not an intentional thing. It just happened out of love and concern. When I saw pain on Elmira's face that day, I didn't want him to suffer, especially since he was retrieving me from a rocky ledge I was exploring, against his wishes. Of course, I held the same love and concern for my father as I clung to his frail body, but in this situation, I couldn't seem to summon the healing. I sobbed and felt the greatest grief at the realization.

"I feared this," my mother said. "The child would know the extent of his father's condition without our telling him." She came to me and wrapped her arms around both father and me. Gladori, who gently assisted father, sat him down on a sitting bench, because he couldn't stand any longer. She lowered him tenderly. He looked as if he would break apart, trembling and moving with the utmost effort to find comfort.

"What has happened to father?" I demanded to know as I looked at mother and back to father. It didn't take any special talent of perception to see how he had declined physically since I last saw him.

"He is preparing to go home again, to the place of pure love and within the heart of God," mother said.

"But isn't his home here with us?" I cried. "And why does he have to be sick to go on this journey?" I insisted. I hadn't had lessons in dying yet, so it didn't dawn on me that he might be ready for that transition.

"I'm not sick, son, just worn out," he explained. "I had a great life and have known joys and overcome some challenges which I feared I would never surmount. I have sons and daughters from my previous family, who are your sisters and brothers. I am blessed by two sons and a lovely little girl and also a son yet to come in my second family." We all looked surprised to hear this news, especially my mother. He looked at her and explained, "I sense this son, yet don't know how this shall be." Mother looked at father in a most puzzled way, for she knew she was not with child, yet she knew father also held strong intuition. He was usually not wrong about such things.

Father then asked Gladori to leave us for a while, and she gracefully said she would come when, and if, he called. Mother smiled at Gladori in thanks, for understanding the request and honoring it. She touched Gladori's hand as she departed and even though the death-watcher would normally never leave her charge until the crossing was complete, this situation warranted a shift in plans.

We three sat upon the bench, side-by-side, silently pleased at being together for a moment as we gathered ourselves from the emotional drama that had just played out. Little Jemima stood in the doorway with the sheepskin drape pulled back and watched us, allowing us time to discuss what she could feel we needed. A wise child, I thought, as I looked at her silhouette, dark and graceful with the sun shining behind her. The other family members had followed Gladori out the door as well, knowing that father, mother and I needed some private time to catch up.

Finally father said, "I have no right to ask for more time upon this physical plane. I have been given so much from our Dear Maker, and my life has been rich and rewarding. I have had two wives dear to my heart, both in their own unique way, and both priestess-trained, which to me, being of the mystery school myself, is a great honor. My life thus was more fulfilled than most men." It was difficult for him to talk, but I could see he was not finished. Mother and I patiently waited for him to catch his breath and carry on.

"The children I have been honored to father are the light of my life, and the great mysteries of my wives have been the stuff that makes life interesting and full of endless possibilities. Yet here I am at death's door, graced by the presence of my little Esa, whom I had to give up so early for the sake of the greater good. Still I want more. How can I be so ungrateful?" He put his face into his old hands and cried.

Mother reached across me, took father's hands from his face and held them, saying, "You have never been ungrateful, dear heart, and you have never asked for something that was not of Divine Order, thus there must be a reason for this yearning."

"I truly wish this to be so, my dear wife," father replied. "I feel ungrateful in wishing for more. I have already been abundantly granted so much. Nevertheless, it seems that I have asked for more time without intentional thought," he whispered tenderly as he looked towards me.

I sat between them, watching my parents comfort each other and tried to understand father's feelings. My 8-year-old mind, even though I had an advanced intellect and master training, nevertheless was still innocent and direct. I blurted out, "Father, I wish you back. I need a brother and I need you."

He looked at me with a somewhat amused expression and said, "You do?"

"Yes," I answered. "I need a father for awhile more, too, and mother needs some more little girls. The elders say that a woman must have a husband to have children. I think I must have wished you to stay. Did I do the wrong thing, father? The sage told me once, when they found the wolf mother who had babies that she was hiding from danger, but she had frozen and died, to wish her back was not in Divine Order. So the sage made a deal with her, he promised he would take her babies, raise them and keep them safe. One became my protector. But father, I don't want someone to take your place yet. I want you to be my protector. Is that selfish of me?"

Father swept me up in his arms and arose from the sitting bench. Holding me in his arms, he twirled around much as mother had done on the dark path earlier. I felt his energy dramatically strengthen with each spin. I noticed my mother sitting on the bench, watching us in amazement. I was laughing and squealing as children do, when their fathers are twirling them. Within the joyful moment, I hadn't realized how much stronger my beloved father had become in a near instant. Gladori ran back through the door, hearing all the commotion and stood with the same look of astonishment upon her face. Then father stopped and looked surprised too, not even out of breath after all the physical exertion. Truly, a miracle had happened and none of us cared how; we just appreciated that father's condition had improved and his energy level was instantly rejuvenated through some miracle.

"I believe the boy's wish has healed you, dear heart," my mother said, as she rose and embraced father. We danced around the room in glee. Finally, we stopped and mother looked at Gladori saying, "This will have to be kept between us, or our child will not be safe, as you well know, dear friend."

Gladori then said, "I believe we were wrong, when we said Joseph's time to leave approached (knowing full well that the death-watchers seldom made such mistakes). He was just feeling a bit low due to some dis-ease.[52] It's time for me to attend to other important matters, and I hope I won't need to see this family again for a long time." She walked away looking much frailer and older than my dear father did.

Mother looked down at me and said, "Why is it that this child amazes me and scares me just as much?" She continued, with a

---

[52] A way of seeing illness as an effect of misaligned energy, out of "ease", which would represent energy out of alignment (disease)

worried look on her face, "The miracle of this master child constantly manifests so naturally, yet it is the very reason we can't keep him close to us. Those who would witness his talents would not understand them and would destroy him. What they don't understand they hate." Her eyes closed and her head dropped, and I felt that somehow I had hurt my parents by wishing for too much. She and father gently set me down on the bench once again. I felt full of shame for who I was and for wanting too much.

My father got down on his knees and, looking straight into my eyes, said, "We will have our time together, son. I promise you. At second initiation, when you're 13- years-old, I shall insist that you be with this family, including me, so that you can learn the way of the council of mysteries. You are learning so much from your teachers already. But I will insist that your mother and I be your last young-years teachers, before you are launched into your master mission." Sensing my worry about my wish, he said, "Your wishes and your very essence blesses all creation, son. Don't ever apologize for being who you are."

# GOODBYE AGAIN
Chapter Nine

It may seem my childhood was perfect, magical and set apart from the normal frustrations and challenges of family life. True, it was somewhat different in our particular spiritual community; however, all children's young years, if given the chance, are magical and perfect in many ways. My family knew that some such as I would emerge to bring the message of peace back to the forefront, if we were supported and developed to that point. The Nazarites had a plan for protection and development of such children. I was only one of the several who came through, but most didn't survive. Either they were too fragile for the crass, violent, judgmental atmosphere, or they were revealed and disappeared mysteriously from the fold, never to be heard of again. There were those who feared us; a sad response, since we were bringing the essence of nonjudgmental love to their doorsteps and the hope of the future was our mission.

For that reason, I didn't get to spend much time with my parents as a young child and again faced separation, when my heart wanted to stay under their loving wings.

Father's health immediately improved. I could see strength and the glow of life increase with each passing hour. My little sister, Jemima, after calling me 'Emanuel,' never stopped talking and became quite communicative within our family unit. She chattered constantly, like a brook un-dammed gushing forth. Jemima had deep understandings, even at her young age. Had she not been a girl, she would have been hidden and educated elsewhere. Sadly, even in the Nazarite society, there was some confusion about how mastras[53] fit into the scheme of things. The social order, for the most part, believed that women always assumed a supportive role. At least little Jemima and James, my brother would remain close to our parents. Father had promised that I would be with him at my second initiation nearly seven years away. That seemed like a long time to my child mind, and I dreaded the separation.

I left in the night, before those of the village could equate my father's healing with my presence. My father was one of the elders on the high council, but nevertheless, he didn't trust everyone. Too many of the special children turned up missing. Father had his suspicions, that there might be some from the outside communities that infiltrated our society because we were secretive about our beliefs. Those who thought differently from the norm were usually squelched. Our branch of Nazarites was under suspicion, because we were not afraid enough. Violence, or intimidation, is how fear holds its power. The only other member of the council father trusted completely was the high elder priest, Jacobite, so old none could remember when he wasn't sitting in the leader position.

Jacobite arrived at our humble home the morning of Father's healing and saw firsthand the improvement in his condition. He knew that I had been summoned and had arrived, since it was actually he who had conveyed the message for my return. He had wanted to give me a chance to say good-bye to my father.

---

[53] Female Masters

Jacobite asked, "Your condition changed after contact with your son, Joseph?" knowing the answer already. "This is confirmation that we were not wrong about the potential of this child. You realize that by his very gift, he is a threat to many who would fear his power to heal." He knew that my parents had already thought of this, as evidenced by my mother asking Gladori not to mention what had occurred in our humble home earlier. "Those threatened by such wonder are like wounds that want to fester and go putrid," the elder explained. "They say they want a healing, and their wounded attitudes and flesh often appear to heal on the surface, but deep down, inside themselves, they fester and only feel alive in their pain." As he spoke, he had a look of compassionate concern on his face, because he understood the situation in our little family. He continued on saying, "This is true among us and especially in the outer society as you both know." He looked at his bare feet, kicked up a little dust from the dirt floor, and said what he wished he could have avoided. "Are you prepared to send this master child back to safer realms?"

Father nodded and I noticed huge tears rolling down his face. Mother, as if denying hearing the inevitable, was not with us at that moment; she was busy preparing a hot drink for the elder, putting off the pain. Jacobite looked towards me and then back to Father. I knew that he understood the bond that was strained by this arrangement. I cried, too, for in our community tears were allowed to run their course, never to be kept at bay. Sorrow and joy were evident in such watery emotions. This time, however, joy seemed far away.

When mother entered the room, she looked at the tear-streaked faces of father and me, then noticed the sad face of Jacobite. She knew the decision had not gone the way she hoped, yet was fully aware that a mother's desire might not be possible. She dropped the hot drink vessel she carried and slumped to the floor, crying, "Oh no!" She had hoped she could somehow keep me close to the home hearth.

"How is it that a miracle can bring such joy and sorrow at the same time?" she cried into her hands, which covered her face. She seemed as if melted upon the floor in the wetness of the spilled drink. Father and I went to her side. We sat on the floor alongside her and wrapped her in our arms. We were so closely entwined, that our heartbeats felt like drums, pacing a song of sorrow.

Jacobite tenderly went to mother and stooped down to the floor, where she had collapsed. As we were still sitting enfolded in each other's arms, he embraced us silently and wept, too.

"Sometimes, I wish I were not born!" I cried, and then proclaimed, "My coming has been too difficult for my parents." Jacobite looked into my eyes, with the compassionate gaze for which he was well known, and I knew how much this affected him, too. This man understood the depths of others' feelings. When they hurt, he hurt.

Hearing what I said, both mother and father gasped. Father stood up, and lifted mother and me from the floor. He seated us on the bench, and then knelt down in front of it, so he could look directly in our eyes, as was the custom of the Nazarites when speaking heart-to-heart, and said, "That's not true, son."

Jacobite said to me, "You are the hope of us all. Should you not have been born, we would have no chance for Divine Unity."

Taking my sad face in his hands, father said, "Son, your mother and I wanted you more than life itself. We knew a special child would come through us, because of our great desire to help all creation live within love instead of being prisoners of the doctrine of fear. We diligently trained for the task of parenting the likes of you. You came through a channel of pure love. That was the intent of our council, but especially your sweet mother's and my intention. Had you not been born, our great love for each other and all creation wouldn't be fulfilled. You are a child conceived within a loving union and supported by a devoted community. We can't imagine life without you. You are our joy, our hope and our evidence of Divine Love manifest. Please, never wish that you weren't born. The sorrow we feel is nothing compared to the joy that you bring us and, no doubt, the joy you will bring to many others along the way.

# The Saga-Oracle

My mother hugged me close and said, "My son. I have known you forever, and I find happiness and fulfillment in being your mother. I take comfort in this, even as I must be about my other divine duties. I forever hold you near and dear to my heart. As your father just said, the sorrow is nothing compared to the joy of your son-ship, which I know I must share with the world and all creation." She lifted my face and kissed me right on the mouth! That was seldom done between a mother and child, and I knew that our relationship went far beyond our physical kinship, for I could feel her spirit merge with my own as the innocent kiss conveyed her sacred breath. Even then, I knew, deep down in my young heart, that mother and I had shared many sojourns. That intimate kiss reminded me, that she birthed me and was the first to love me unconditionally.

"I'm sorry mother. I hate to hurt you and father," I said, as I looked over to my father, noticing that Jacobite had departed leaving us to our private moment.

Father said wistfully, "It's not you that hurt us, son. It's the mind-set of those who are so fearful that they would destroy the divine messengers of God, rather than climb out of the snake-pits they create in their minds. To send you to safety, and to further learning, is but a twinge, compared to the pain of knowing the danger, should you stay. We will have to schedule a lifetime in which we can enjoy your childhood as it should be enjoyed," he said, with a slight chuckle to lighten up the moment. "If only those fearful ones could feel the joy of children, then they would believe in love, instead of giving their energy to fear. It's the children who will lead them back to Divine Love. Children place no conditions on their parents, at least naturally that's the case," father said, "even as they expect their parents to fulfill their physical needs. It is usually the parents who place conditions upon the children. They teach them to bargain for love and the lesson they offer is fear-based. Parents too often threaten not to love them, unless they enrich the family in some way," father said with sadness. "They miss the real richness the children offer in abundance."

Mother said, "That thinking is crazy. All children enrich their parents and all creation just by being born." Father nodded his head in affirmation. I knew then that, indeed, I did enhance their lives more than I hurt them, with my special problems of awareness.

Elmira was summoned and he was instantly there ready to take up his guardianship. I suspect he held guard very close to our residence, ever watching over me as he pledged he would. I left again that night.

Elmira was given directions verbally by Jacobite as to our next connecting point. I didn't know where I would go, but I knew it would be a long way from the societies that surrounded my homeland, and sadly, even from our Nazarite community. I tried to get back into a sense of adventure, but I felt depressed as Elmira and I, together left in the dark of the night again.

Just before dawn, we found the appointed caravan. This one was comprised of Samaritans, those often misunderstood people of the desert. They were scorned by most of the Hebrews, because they didn't follow the doctrine of the temple laws of the land, or the Hebrew way. They had their own way of being, which didn't exclude anyone from their hospitality. I once saw a Samaritan boy stop and pick up an injured vulture, which was stoned by someone in another passing caravan as it fed on a dead animal by the wayside. To the Hebrews, the vulture was considered 'unclean,' never to be touched or pitied. The boy spoke softly to the bird in vulture-speak. Now that I had been further trained in animal-speak, I recognized the various species' language forms and understood what was being said.

The Samaritan boy told the bird that he would bind its wounded wing and set the broken bone, but it would have to ride the wind current and rest on the high air waves longer for now. He told the bird that it would have to give healing time, before it returned to glean and clean the roadside of unfortunate animals that had perished there. The vulture settled down and allowed the boy to tend its wounds. It smelled foul and its appearance was repulsive, but the boy didn't seem to notice the putrid smell and the rotten particles of flesh, hanging from its feet and feathers.

# The Saga-Oracle

I observed the caravan master stopping the procession and simply saying, "It's time to take a break, I believe," and all waited for this process to unfold. When the bird was tended and some herbs administered to the wound, as well as fed to the mighty winged one, it flew off into the depths of the azure sky, struggling as it gained altitude. However, it managed to go higher and higher as the boy recommended. Everyone watched as it pierced the sky, finally finding an updraft, and simply glided like a kite with little wing effort, there high above us. There was no comment from anyone; just acceptance and relief that this wayside bird had been assisted and was on its way to recovery.

A woman (maybe his mother) approached the boy and began cleansing him. She didn't scold him for touching an unclean thing. She simply washed him in a solution made of spring water and some herbs that she carried in a bag at her waistband. When she finished, we moved on again with little discussion of the incident. I saw many acts of kindness as we traveled with this group, and wondered what laws of the land people thought the Samaritans violated, for surely the greater law is to hold compassion for all creation.

We quietly traveled about a week, off to the side of the travelers, with little or no communication with them. I was lonely and sad, and wished I could befriend some of the children. They kept their distance however, because they thought I was Elmira's slave-boy. They seemed to hold enough contempt for that supposed situation to keep separate from us, yet stayed ever watchful. They had been asked to keep us safe without knowing why, and they were honorable people who kept their word. I noticed many facial expressions of concern, along with puzzlement, for if I was indeed Elmira's slave, he didn't seem to treat me badly. I'm sure they took that into consideration. The Samaritans were what you might term 'standoffish' of situations that were not in accordance with their mind-set, as most people would be. Even so, I had no doubt that I would be treated as kindly as the vulture, should I need their compassionate attention. It was a delicate situation, and my bodyguard held a perfect balance that insured isolation, yet protection.

The Samarian caravan was comprised of many donkeys with colorful bundles piled high and tightly strapped upon their backs. There were also cattle, sheep, goats and about twenty people we traveled with. I noticed even the animals were quiet. I remembered my trek with the camels when I was younger, when I mind-read their mental conversations. They were more communicative and conversed with one another about many things, especially about awkward humans. The animals on this trek were not so mindfully chatty, yet they were content. This observation interested me; I desperately wanted to understand everyone, including animals, all nature (trees and stone), and all that revealed its consciousness to me. Since my three years with the mountain people, I was much more aware now, than on my first journey. I saw a resemblance of personality between the Samaritans and their animals, and knew that a quiet group-consciousness united them.

One day we came to a split in the trail. The caravan went one way and we went the other, no goodbyes, no discussion, simply a quiet separation. The boy I had seen earlier, however, had another bird friend who had flown down to perch and ride on his shoulder. This time a raven was conversing and enjoying the company of the boy. As we parted paths, he turned and looked at Elmira, and whispered something to the raven. It flew from his shoulder and came our way. Elmira watched the bird circle us, then land on a nearby rock. My guardian looked at the silent boy, who nodded. Elmira, who understood the language of silence, knew the boy was sending his friend to be with us. My guardian acknowledged the gesture with his own silent nod. I nodded, too, and we proceeded on to an unknown destination, accompanied by the raven.

I knew we would follow directions, link by link, until we arrived somewhere. I wondered if the flipping raven shape-shifter, who had protected me before, was the raven the boy sent with us. We never found out. The bird just stayed nearby and once in a while, it would ride on my shoulder as it did the Samaritan boy's. Then one day it flew off to pursue other bird adventures.

# THE HERBALIST APPRENTICE
## Chapter Ten

That fork in the road, when Elmira and I just walked a different direction from the Samaritans without a word spoken, reminded me of my life. It seemed like I had come to the point in my life that I had to accept that sometimes I had to take a side road and split off from those I would rather stay in step with. Elmira, my silent guardian, either had detailed instructions accompanied by an excellent memory, or he was trained in receiving bearings from someplace within his mind and heart. Our journey took us here and there for nearly a year, before we finally arrived at the humble house of Yasma, the healer.

Yasma lived in a huge city full of beautiful buildings; however, many smaller abodes surrounded the magnificent mansions. Yasma's neighborhood consisted of tumbled-down shacks, made from anything the people could find, laid out as far as the eye could see, below the towering fortress walls of the grander buildings.

I had never seen so many people in one place in my entire life. We found our way down a side street of ramshackle dwellings, which seemed unloved and uncared for. Elmira walked with a purpose to one shabby dwelling in particular and, upon arrival, he just stood there before the doorway, which was simply an opening draped with a ragged cloth. Immediately, the cloth was pulled back and in the humble portal stood a very old man. He had so many wrinkles, that I couldn't see his eyes until he opened them. He stood there with a mere loincloth covering his lower body. He was bent with age and looked older than anyone I had ever met, even Jacobite, who I thought was ancient. The dust of the earth was embedded upon him from head to toe. He could have been a clay sculpture standing there, but I could see him breathing and, eventually, he opened his eyes. I was relieved to see that he had them, right where they should be, but hidden in the folds of old flesh. "I am

## Jeshua's Song

Yasma,[54]" the old man simply said. Elmira bowed to him and, in thought language, said a word I had not heard before, "Nameste'.[55]" I was improving my mind-to-mind skills with Elmira. This was the first time he allowed me to listen to a conversation with someone else. The greeting was unusual for my guardian, who was typically private about his thoughts. The old one looked down toward me, and I imitated my guardian, only verbally, bowed with folded hands as I saw Elmira do, saying, "Nameste'," myself.

"I am Yasma", the old man said again. "Welcome to my humble home, child." He was speaking in my Aramaic language. Then he whispered, "The god in me welcomes the god in you, as well." Elmira stepped aside and took his usual position near the doorway, after peeking into the little home to make sure all was well. I stepped into a different world that day; one that I could not have imagined existing.

I was about nine years of age by this time and in many societies, I would be considered a young adult. Here, in this far eastern place, that was true as well. Yasma pointed to a ragged cloth in the corner of his space and said, "That's your bed, child." He then pointed to another cloth lying on the bare floor in the opposite corner and said, "And this is my bed. That is all you need to know of this abode for now. It's your home, for a while."

He took my hand and we exited the place, into a busy dusty street with many people scurrying in every direction, carrying all kinds of things, including children. People often had vessels on their heads, huge full bags over their shoulders and so forth. They were talking and shouting at the same time. Donkeys brayed under burdens that seemed larger than the little animals. Hump-shouldered cattle roamed the streets at will, under no supervision and bearing no burdens, all intermingling with the endless crowd

---

[54] Derives from name Jasmine, or city in Azerbaijan, derived from the Arabic intermediary; also Yasmin, which is also used in Hebrew

[55] The Hindi gesture Namaste' represents the belief that there is a Divine spark within each of us that is located in the heart chakra

of people. To me, it was colorless and confusing. Even though Elmira and I had just come through these streets, it seemed even more overwhelming as I was pulled along by Yasma. The comfort of having Elmira ever near helped me cope. Thinking of him, I looked back over my shoulder to Yasma's doorway, but he was gone, now melted into the crowd, too. I searched for my friend and guardian in the confusion that Yasma led me into. All I saw were masses of people and animals that were shapes that just emerged from the dusty pathway, and then melted again with the crowd, ultimately disappearing into a cloud of dust. I felt pangs of dread and insecurity in this strange place, without Elmira by my side. We walked in silence, dodging and snaking our way through the endless crowd. Yasma held my hand, dragging me along, pulling me with more force than I would expect from an old one. I had a feeling that my guardian was close, but couldn't separate that feeling from wishful thinking.

Soon we came to a market street, and Yasma took me to a place of interesting smells. There were dried plants and oils in bottles everywhere within this tiny open-front store. It seemed chaotic to me; but to the herbalist it was perfectly organized. I watched him find what he needed for a customer, who was trying to describe her condition by pointing to her belly. Once she left, Yasma said, "Okhamu, I have brought you an apprentice." He spoke the native tongue of the land, but I got the idea by the universal body language, which the old Tibetans had taught me. Yasma then looked at me and said in Aramaic, "I will see you when your day is done here," and he walked away.

I looked at Okhamu and back to Yasma. I was unfamiliar with them both and this strange city seemed huge to me. I didn't know where I was, why I was here, or if I had been abandoned. I couldn't even sense Elmira near anymore.

"Don't just stand there with your mouth hanging open, boy, we have work to do", Okhamu shouted in my language. He threw a broom at me. Pointing to the dusty floor, which was actually just packed down dirt, he said, "Get that loose dirt out of here before it spoils my herbs and don't make a cloud of dust doing it." He turned and went back to what he was doing when I arrived, grinding something in a stone bowl, using a hand-shaped stone as a grinder. Only this time there was no customer conversing with him. He was simply on task, doing what he does in this shop of herbs.

I swept all day and if I happened to raise too much dust, Okhamu would shout at me and scold me for my lack of ability to even sweep. Day dissolved into night and still the street seemed busy; but now I was seeing more colorful garments on some of the women. Since all I did was sweep and sweep, my attention began to reach out into the crowd for the sake of keeping my mind occupied, thus passing the time easier. I heard these ladies talking and laughing, and saw them approach men from time to time. The men looked pleased to be approached, but didn't have a look of respect upon their faces as they watched the women move on, or as some of them went away with one of the men. The body language of lust was a new one for me. I was truly naive about society's judgmental attitudes.

Okhamu saw me watching the women and said, "What are you looking at, boy? The ladies of the night wouldn't be interested in you yet." Then he laughed and finally began to close his small street shop. When he was done, he simply walked away, not even looking my way.

I stood there on the street and yelled to him as he began to enter the dusty night crowd of people. "How do I get home?" I asked.

He turned and yelled back, "That's a good question, boy," and he moved into the crowd leaving me alone and confused.

I had been protected all my life and had come to believe that I was special enough to be carefully watched over. What could this be? Why would I travel nearly a year under careful guard, only to be abandoned in the dirty streets of some unknown city? Where was Elmira now? I stood there and cried. After all, I was still a child, even if on the edge of adulthood as some cultures considered.

I don't know how long I wallowed in self-pity, before I began to hear child voices discussing something and giggling. I looked up to see a band of dirty-faced children, looking at me and no doubt thinking I was pretty pathetically funny. I couldn't understand what they were saying, but I knew they were not sympathizing by their body language; rather they were finding me vulnerable and odd enough for a good laugh. I surmised that, since I couldn't understand their language, I would try to use a form of animal-speak, or mind-to-mind, to converse with them. When I attempted this type of communication stating my situation, their eyes lit up, and they heard my plea. The tallest boy looked at the others, and he thought, "He knows our secret language." The others nodded and looked back at me, all bright-eyed. "Then you are one of us, strange lad, even if you look funny," he answered via mind-speak. With that statement he came over, brushed the tears from my cheeks, put his arm around my shoulder and walked me back to the others, who all embraced me. I can't describe the relief and joy of this moment, of being lost, then found, by kindred spirits. We walked back into the streets arm in arm, together going someplace unknown, but at least I no longer felt alone, even as I thought, "Where are you, Elmira?"

I learned that this group consisted of lost or abandoned children. They lived in the streets and had several safe havens they constructed out of discarded junk, in locations here and there about the streets, hidden in the alleys and under rubble no one bothered to remove. There were other such 'crews,' as well; some were friendly and some weren't, but it seemed that if you were one of the crews then you were more secure. Children alone were often abused by the low-life types, which preyed on those they found vulnerable. It was a sad situation, but I noticed that there were also those, whose hearts went out to the children. I often saw the women of the bright colors take in the very young abandoned ones. My friends said they were well treated.

My crew taught me the street language and shared with me all that they had, which wasn't much. They survived by any means possible, and couldn't understand why I would honor my duty to Okhamu. Even so, I returned each day to sweep, and patiently waited for my herbal lessons to begin. They wanted to teach me the fine art of stealing from the wealthy without them even knowing, or how to befriend someone only to slip their wallets when the opportunity afforded. I understood why they lived this way, but I also knew I couldn't take advantage of others, because trust was one of my greatest passions, and I couldn't betray anyone by breaking it. Thus, I held to my principles, and the others finally gave up trying to teach me the way of the streets.

I was sure Okhamu trusted that I would be his apprentice and honor what I was directed to do by Yasma. I just showed up at his shop early every morning, ready to sweep again. He never said much to me about where I spent my nights, but did disapprove of the company I kept, since the crew would bring me to his store each morning and pick me up every evening. One of the rare times he spoke, he said, "Yasma keeps a respectable place for you, and you choose these vagabonds to live with."

By now, I was speaking the local language better; however, I seldom spoke in Okhamu's presence. He was surprised when I responded in his language, "I try to find Yasma every night, when you give me leave. Do you know how I can find him?"

"You can find him in your heart, boy," he said, in a softer tone of voice than usual.

"There seems to be no place in his heart for me, since he left me with the likes of you, who only will teach me to sweep and replace dirt with dirt repeatedly, day in and day out," I responded.

Okhamu looked at me and said, "You haven't asked for more."

"You mean I have to ask?" I said with surprise.

"Ask and it shall be given!" he replied, with a wise expression upon his face.

"Then I ask. Instruct me, teacher of herbs."

"Now, that is more like it," he said, "but what is it you ask?" He wanted me to be more specific in my request.

"I ask to know of the herbs, teacher?"

He looked toward me saying, "Put that broom down and get over here. I'll be happy to show you some secrets that the plants would share with our sorry kind, lad."

Thus, began my first lesson in herbology.[56] As I progressed, I was allowed to make some of the mixtures and, finally, Okhamu trusted me enough to permit me to fill orders for seekers of health and well being. This was way more interesting than sweeping dirt from dirt, a never-ending chore. It dawned on me once while I was doing the constant sweeping, that there probably was a lesson therein, but it took me awhile simply to ask for more.

My friends, whom Okhamu didn't trust around the storefront, became protectors of the place and Okhamu was astounded that they could be honorable. He noticed them shielding the shop and running off those who would steal if given a chance. One day, when he was watching them, I asked, "How is it, teacher that these children were abandoned and left to survive on their own, and people hate and distrust them so?"

He seemed to be thinking about the question, and replied, "I guess I didn't think of it like that, lad. They just seemed like pests to us shopkeepers, since there are so many who would steal to survive. We never thought of why they were abandoned."

I asked, "Would you steal to survive?"

"I get your point," he murmured. Then he said, "They honor you, to the extent that they keep my shop safe from those who I have previously had so much trouble from. They have become my little guardians. Maybe it's time I repay my debt." He walked out of the shop without explanation, knowing full well that, in his absence, I would carry on with business and that my friends would not break his trust. The bridge of confidence had been established. I felt honored to have been part of its building.

He returned a short time later, with his arms full of food. He had so much food, he could barely carry it all. He went to work creating a feast for some important people, I thought. I only ate

---

[56] Study of herbs and herb combinations for various uses

bread and rice most days, and some cheese, if I was lucky to get it. I usually got this from my friends. I learned not to ask how they got their food, since it was not how they got it, but that they shared it, which mattered in my present state of survival.

As I worked, I watched Okhamu spread a tattered blanket upon the dusty floor. He eventually stood up to look at it and shook his head, clearly not satisfied. Considering his personality, I was not about to get into his head and read his thoughts, since I didn't feel I should go there until I was invited, thus wondered what he was doing. He was a complicated man, and I was afraid to check out his thinking process and possibly trigger his short temper. Shaking his head, indicating this cloth would not do, he snatched up the ragged blanket from under the food he had just placed on it, and found a bright colored cloth instead, that he pulled from an ornate chest he used for a sitting stool. He spread this beautiful fabric upon the dusty ground and carefully laid the food out once again.

"Are you expecting royal guests," I asked.

"Yes," he replied. "Call your friends forth from their guardian posts, lad, for we have a feast to enjoy."

I looked at him, then down at the beautifully-arranged offerings, and instantly thought my mind-to-mind message to my crew, who immediately appeared with smiles on their faces. They cautiously entered the store, and Okhamu pointed to the feast, and said, "Sit and enjoy." At first, we just stared at him and at the food, for this seemed bizarre and unbelievable. He bowed to us and wouldn't settle himself, until each and everyone was comfortably seated upon that beautiful cloth, which held food beyond our wildest dreams. Some things we had tasted, if we found rare scraps or when one of the crew had 'mysteriously' appeared with a tidbit; but most of the feast's offerings, we had never seen nor tasted before.

About then a customer arrived, one who was a regular and of high caste, and often had a huge order. The man impatiently looked at the street kids sitting on the brightly-colored cloth, eating the feast. Okhamu said, "Can't you see that we have taken a break to celebrate here? Join us, or leave us; for now, the only business I conduct is enjoying my friends."

The customer looked at the vagabond children and myself, with a look of disbelief upon his well-shaven face, and said, "Okhamu, are you losing your senses? All I see are urchins, throw-away children; and if their parents didn't want them, why would you befriend them?"

"I befriend them, because they are my greatest teachers, as they are yours, too. Join us, or reject the gift of their presence and miss the chance of a lifetime," the herbalist said with conviction. The smallest of my crew, a little girl, approached the man. Such a child was rare in the streets since little girls suffered worse fates than boys when abandoned, and were quickly taken by those who would use and abuse them. She was taken in by our gang and disguised as one of the boys, to keep her safe from that fate. She extended her dirty little hand to this astonished, well-dressed customer. We all knew that this was a powerful, deciding moment. Would he take the child's hand or would he reject it? I hoped with all my heart that he would see past the dirt, past the circumstance, and into the heart of this little girl, who in her short 4 or 5 years had grown so wise. He did! Taking her hand, he seated himself with us, and we all partook of the feast so heart-fully presented. We even invited some of the street women to our table on the humble floor. This was a departure from the normal custom of men and women eating separately, and at first they declined, until our little one beckoned them to join us, as she did with our first guest. She was hard to resist, or maybe they sensed that already a female was partaking of the feast, because the group of three women of the night joined us in our unexpected celebration and found a seat upon the blanket of many colors.

Okhamu told them that if they were good enough to lay with men, they were also good enough to dine with them. I didn't understand that statement, but even the littlest one in my group did, for she looked down for a moment, almost in shame and nearly revealed her secret, that she was a little girl and not a street boy. Our crew knew that, of course, but it was a secret they all knew they must keep as long as they could for the child's safety.

## Jeshua's Song

Many customers came and went during our meal; but not a one could entice Okhamu from his pleasure of being host at his special celebration. He remarked that he had never enjoyed a feast more, and I saw a side of the man that was hidden from most during his daily living. The little one asked him if he had children. He said he used to, but his family had all died in a terrible epidemic. He asked her and the others if they wanted to be his family. They, of course, thought he was kidding. I wasn't so sure.

When our guests finally left, and I was helping Okhamu clean up, he said to me, "I have taught you all I can about the herbs. You know how to mix and prepare them for the health and well-being of those in need. It's time for you to go home now, lad. I have enjoyed your company immensely."

I replied, "Home–where's that?"

"Yasma has awaited your return long enough, lad," he said, as he nodded toward the shop door, as if to get me going in that direction.

"But, I can't find him," I desperately replied, worried that I would be abandoned again and looking about for my crew, which usually waited for me. They were not to be seen, however, having already disappeared back into streets. I felt the fear of the unknown welling up inside of me.

"You haven't really tried to find him, now have you," Okhamu answered. "Move along. Go home now." It seemed that he was sweeping me out, like I was the dust on the floor on which we had just feasted.

"Can that desolate little place Yasma lives be my home?" I questioned.

"It can and it is. You haven't looked deep enough within that so-called 'desolate place,' have you, lad. Maybe it's time you did. Go home!"

"But what if I can't find it?" I half cried. "You will!" He said.

# THE HEALER
Chapter Eleven

I felt lost again. So many times, I felt lost, and then I would find myself once again. I never missed my family more than when Okhamu had insistently said, "Go home!" I desperately wanted to go home to my parents. However, I knew that was not exactly what he meant. I yearned for the smells of my mother's cooking and cleaning, the feel of my father's beard and many other delights of memory that represented home to me. That's always the desire of the child after all; to have parents who love and protect them, guiding every step of their growing years. Half of my desire was granted and for that I am ever grateful.

My crew, those who adopted me into their midst in this strange faraway city, didn't have a family to go home to. A couple of them had been orphaned, so did have some memory, or idea of a loving parent, but most had simply been turned out to survive on their own for other convenient reasons. The lucky ones, sadly, were the little girl babies who were drowned shortly after birth because the parents couldn't afford more than one daughter's dowry later in life. The custom sprang from hardships within the family, such as poverty or relationship problems, coupled with the cultural attitudes in which a son was deemed a success and a daughter a failure. It was the father or elder son who could choose to discard the others, and sometimes the father's mother made the decision. As I walked alone in the streets, not sensing my crew or my guardian with me, I felt the deepest loneliness. I didn't know that Elmira had not given up his task. He was ever close by, watching and guarding, still on duty, just not revealing himself. I also didn't know that my crew, as well, were making sure my path was safe. Much considerate kindness is never revealed and goes unnoticed.

I walked along the streets, not knowing or caring where I went. My intuition must have taken over, for in no time I found myself back at the portal of Yasma's humble home. This time, however, there were many people sitting around outside his doorway. People in physical distress I noticed, since they looked lame and ill and their eyes seemed to hold a look of desperation within their depths. I carefully picked my way through the crowd and peeked into the doorway. I saw Yasma laying his hands upon a woman's swollen belly. I remembered that when I first saw the herbalist, he, too, was tending a woman in pregnancy. The women suffered within the most sacred of conditions, I thought.

Yasma said to the woman, "Fear not, dear one. This child shall be born on time and in perfection, for your heart has paved the way, and your intention is pure. Rejoice!" The woman then rose up and silently offered Yasma a loaf of flatbread, which he gracefully accepted. He added it to a pile of such offerings, and she quietly left, as another seeker came forth. Yasma noticed me as the other seeker entered and asked the next patient for a moment before his healing session. The man graciously agreed, though he probably had been waiting hours already, judging by the crowd outside Yasma's doorway.

"Welcome home, lad," Yasma said, with joy written all over his ancient wrinkled face.

"I'm not sure if it is home, but I'm here again," I replied almost defiantly.

"You have completed your apprenticeship in herbs and medicinals, no doubt," he said without reaction to my attitude. "I'm grateful that you finally came home. I have many in need of assistance today." He waved me to come closer to him, saying, "Come forth, lad, and give me a hand."

I moved closer and noticed the man who awaited attention had an extremely crooked arm. "Healed wrong," Yasma said. "When he was but a child, it was broken, due to him being put to hard work too soon." Yasma showed me where the bone had snapped and how it lost its way, because it wasn't set back to the pattern of the skeletal structure properly. "It's all a matter of finding the divine pattern, you see," he said, "and then getting the wayward energy back into the proper pathway, or within the divine pattern." He continued to explain what caused the arm to heal wrong, saying, "You see, when energy loses its way, it splits and divides itself, and often can't reunite; thus it finds another path that isn't in accordance with the divine plan. Scar is a veil that creates isolation to the part that is lost. It does this to isolate and keep safe the damaged area; but actually what happens in many cases is that it keeps the other part of the energy from finding and reuniting once again. Thus it becomes an affliction. This condition affects the physical body, but even worse the thinking. Thinking is a shape-shifter," he added. I looked puzzled by that statement, so Yasma explained, "You will see, lad, how the mind shapes the body." He went back to his explanation, saying, "The man's arm has lost its polarity, its connection to its own counterpart energy. The physical body must be in line and 'One' with the Divine. That can only be achieved when the body is energetically balanced."

He stopped to see if I was following what he was trying to convey. Satisfied, he went on, saying, "Some say a demon lives in his arm, and they feel that the poor man is tainted, because he houses such a monster. In reality, it doesn't matter what shape his arm is in, as long as he keeps his heart equally balanced through right thinking and attitudes. Then compassion rules," Yasma explained. "Those who believe in demons causing the condition promote such nonsense, because they are afraid that they might one day be maimed and fear is judgmental. Thus they make the victim deserving of the misery, because all they know is fear and its harsh form of blame."

Yasma was clearly opening up to me now. I forgot my frustrations, since my attention was focused on the healing energy he was demonstrating and explaining.

He finally laid his hands on the patient's arm and closed his eyes. Intensity of purpose was evident upon his old face. A light appeared that traveled down through the ceiling into the top of Yasma's head, continuing down through both of his hands and into the arm of the afflicted one. I could sense that, although the energy came into Yasma's head in Onement, it split into two factions, one a sender[57] and one a receiver,[58] as it traveled down his arms, only to reunite once again within the arm of the suffering man. It was clear that this misshapen arm was painful. The energy

---

[57] Positive
[58] Negative

then appeared once again, only this time it came up through the floor of the humble hut splitting sooner and going through each of Yasma's legs and finally merging along with the other energy within the afflicted arm. What I saw next amazed me, since I had never seen light and sound healing before. The misshaped arm began to vibrate, not erratically, but in a most harmonic fluid fashion. It had a sound as well, that seemed like the purr of a mighty cat at an extremely low pitch. It was a stretched out humming of sorts, however with more definition than a cat's purr. It sounded like "Ommmmmmmmmm" to me, with the last part drawn out and trailing the beginning, reverberating out around the man. I had never heard sound emit from a body appendage prior to this session. The afflicted man's flesh absorbed the light, even as more and more came through Yasma's hands; I wondered how much of this powerful energy a body could tolerate. Then the arm began to reshape. I could see the bone align itself under the skin. The crookedness, little by little, became straight and the knobbiness became smooth as the sound faded. The skin took on a tone of health and instantly the glow of wellness beamed through the entire man, still young enough to have many tasks yet to fulfill upon his path. His face lit up, as Yasma slowly withdrew his hands. The grateful man embraced Yasma with two equally perfect arms and wept in gratitude. He felt and rubbed his healed arm as if trying to absorb the reality of the healing.

"How can I ever repay you?" he asked Yasma. Before Yasma could answer, the man said, "Ask for anything, and it shall be given; for each breath I take, from this day forward throughout my life, I will give thanks to you, dear healer, and I offer you my faithful allegiance."

"I don't want thanks for just doing my work," Yasma replied, in a low soothing tone. "I only ask that you hold compassion within all that you do and never allow a child to suffer what you have suffered, dear man, which was neglect. Neglect is the demon that would waste the gifts of God, who has planted seeds of divinity in every single aspect of creation. To neglect a child is like a gardener having sewn a garden he doesn't visit, doesn't protect, doesn't tend nor honor, after he has planted the seed of hope. Then this neglectful farmer one day says, 'Why doesn't my garden grow and grace me with its gifts divine?'" Yasma was certainly verbal today, I thought, and wondered if he always healed and offered a life lesson, too. He continued on, saying, "Those who would neglect the divine garden (child in this case), would also blame the 'stupid garden' for not being abundant."

I envisioned this man as a neglected child, full of potential, yet a withered arm due to neglect had been keeping him from his bountiful destiny. I knew this story was important to the healed man, to insure his healing would extend to his soul. Yasma's tale of the Divine Gardener showed me that parables, or stories, made it easier for people to absorb the truth.

The man looked around the sparse room, noticing the two ragged blankets lying on the floor and little else in the one-room abode. The same two rags I had seen upon my first glimpse of this humble place, still in the same corners. He asked if he could work on the space for the healer. "I could make a fine door and maybe a table and I certainly could make you a proper bed, dear elder, to make you more comfortable. Please allow me to be of service and repay you for this miracle you have accomplished."

"I have everything I could possibly want," Yasma said. "I have abundance beyond measure, and I'm truly grateful for this humble home and my warm blanket. If you feel a need to offer repayment, I would ask that you return today after I have seen the last of today's seekers. I have a task for you to do then, my friend. All this bread, food and other offerings that seekers give from the heart, thus I gratefully accept, must be distributed. I request that you find those who are in need and give them a blessing by sharing this abundance. You will find the greatest need in the streets where the homeless wander, and you may find it in the palace where the heart is lost. You will have to put aside your attitudes of worthiness, dear man, for all are God's creation and all are worthy, no matter what cast or station they hold in this lifetime."

Yasma continued, saying, "Don't think that I want you bragging about your healing, for that isn't my doing. You allowed this healing and you arranged for this moment of divine energetic exchange within your own mind and heart by showing up at my door. I was simply the conduit. You will forget how this happened very quickly, which is as it should be. It's my hope that in seeking out the lost and hungry and offering them the food and gifts of love, you will remember how perfect the pattern of creation truly is and how it looks and sounds when it vibrates with love."

The man bowed his head, saying he would wait until the last seeker had left and vowed to keep his promise of fulfilling any request of the healer. He departed and took a position of rest nearby, patiently waiting for his task.

The next person brought in an urn of cold water. Yasma gratefully took it and said to me, "They just seem to know what I need." He handed me the urn first, saying, "Here, share this water with me, lad and quench your thirst, for the day will be long and the body needs to be replenished." I drank the sweet water and thought I had never tasted better. My depression began to dissolve. After my thirst was quenched, he tipped the urn himself and gratefully drank the refreshing water.

The day was long indeed. Yasma worked until early nightfall. After he had seen the last of the seekers, as promised, the man with the now strong-and-healed arm came forth quietly and gathered the day's payments. Yasma only kept one loaf of flatbread for him and me to share. Yasma told the still-grateful man to make sure he allowed himself at least a loaf of bread or a salted fish. "You must be willing to see your own need as worthy, dear man," he said, "before you can truly see another's great need." Yasma bowed and said, "Namaste." After the man departed, Yasma took a candle from the top of the doorway where a little ledge afforded a place to keep it. He had some flint stones there and quickly made fire by gathering the dust from the floor and cracking the stones within the various fibers of dust he found. He lit the candle from the small fire he created.

He bid me to join him, sitting cross-legged upon the floor where he had laid the bread, right in the dirt and dust. He said a brief prayer of gratitude over the bread, and then looked at me, so I gave thanks as well. We ate in silence, as the sun dipped finally into the total darkness of the night. We had only one small candle to light our simple meal of bread, but such a wonderful taste it held. I could tell Yasma was exhausted, from the way he sighed and groaned.

He finally said to me, "You are a healer. lad. I could tell when you first came to my doorway not so long ago. It beams from you. For those of us with like vibration, it is evident and comforting to see and feel another in tune with us. We love to be around those like ourselves," he said, with a slight chuckle. "Isn't that right?" Not waiting for my reply, he went on. "That's why I sent you to Okhamu's shop, so that you could understand how Mother Earth offers gifts for the sake of healing. Father Sky also is a healer, dear one, and you will see how they work together for the same cause, within all creation and within all attunements. Father Sky, or that force that is 'out there,' heals through light in the form of light energy. The herbs that incubate and grow from the dark womb of the earth heal through the void, the dark realms governed by the feminine hum of Tara, Mother Earth, who offers the Divine Sound vibrations. Healing is accomplished through both sound and light," he explained. "The sound waves are ingested into the body or inhaled, and in some cases, just absorbed. That's done through herbs and other natural substances that Tara offers. The wounds are dressed and the bodies internalize the energy of the plant, stone, bone, or concoction best for the ailment; thus the herbs are the Divine Mother's gift of attunement. It could be said that Mother Earth *attunes* and Father Sky *enlightens*. Neither is best, and neither is complete without the other. It is ever the dance of light and sound, which courses through all creation and blends to achieve Divine Balance. The light must ultimately be internalized as well to fulfill the pattern; and the herb must grow into the light of the day to mature enough to offer its magic. It is ever a natural cycle of these two energies pulling toward each other and merging, then reemerging separately to dance again and again, offering perfection within creation," Yasma explained.

Then he said, "So now that you have come home, shall we begin working with your talents of healing?"

"I fear I am not all that talented," I said and looked downward, away from the old one's eyes that pierced right through my soul even in this dimly lit room. I felt unworthy and knew I was not all that grateful for this opportunity.

"I suppose your father's recovery was just a stroke of luck then, lad, is that true? The reason you went home was to heal the man. The reason you had to leave and come here was because you healed him. Your talents are natural and your ability holds no bounds. To ignore them is to neglect the holy gift sent through you. It would be the divine seed in the garden untended and thus lost to its good purpose. Don't you see?"

I simply shook my head 'no.' I was falling into depression again and missed my true home so much that my heart wanted to drop out of my chest right here on the piece of flatbread, that I couldn't bring myself to finish eating, due to the self pity I was feeling.

Yasma said, "I can't heal your heart, lad. Your body maybe, but only you can heal your heart. Your parents suffer more than you know, having to give you up so young. They have accepted a great burden in being portals for a master child such as you. Make no mistake; you are a master who has volunteered to pass through the tunnel of forgetting for the sake of all creation. It's the birthing process that helps a baby enter the joy of growing and learning. If they remembered all their past experiences within their conscious thoughts, they would be so overwhelmed, that joy would be sacrificed. It would be a heavy burden to know what has already passed, because then what is yet to come would probably be missed, along with the wonder of 'now.' Master or not, you had to forget, so that you can remember, bit by bit as you are ready. Forgetting is your chance to discover your true identity once again and that's found in the 'now' moments. Every soul must do that over and over, until they know beyond a doubt that they are Divine. You are a master, which means you know this already. There are many masters present, that bless all creation," he remarked. "However, most are unrecognized. Sadly, there are also many who would harm the masters, instead of honoring their leadership. Those who would harm the likes of you, and others like you, only think they are secure in the power struggle of the 'greed-of-need' they worship. You masters threaten the very illusion of all of that. When masters come near those within such walls of false security, systems collapse and fear dissolves."

I said, "How can you be sure I'm a master, Yasma?" I didn't feel any different than anyone else and had heard this description of me before, but was not convinced I was up to the expectations it encompassed.

"It's in your eyes, lad. It's difficult to hold the gaze of a master for long and not be profoundly changed. Too often such ones as you are brutally blinded on purpose, by those who fear becoming aware of the responsibility of every breath they take and, equally, every action they do, if they look into such a gaze. It's true, that often the dams in evolution of consciousness can only be broken by masters, and that's why you are called in, you see?"

I redirected our conversation to a thought I had been pondering. I asked, "Why didn't you let the man whose arm was healed make you a bed, Yasma? Indeed you are getting up there in age. Having a good night's sleep would benefit you and make your days easier," I said. "Surely you are worthy."

He looked at me and I saw that he was a master as well, for his gaze held the compassion of the deepest truth therein. He said, "But lad, I am comfortable. I have everything I need here. I have a place out of the sun and wind to sleep within, and to use as a healing temple. I have a perfectly good blanket to keep me warm and people bring me food. The only thing I have that I don't need, is the other blanket that I reserved for you when you came home again. What more could I want?"

At that remark, he could see the tears rise in my eyes, for they gleamed in the candlelight. "It feels like I don't have a home, Yasma," I said. "If I'm a master, I'm one without a home." I was still feeling sorry for myself and feeling unworthy of the status that Yasma would grant me.

"Ah! The lesson of the home is a great one, lad. It's not a place after all, rather it's a position in time where one finds oneself and realizes that, 'yes,' this is where I am centered, where I am supposed to be at this time and in this space." I still felt tearful, as he continued. "Within the peace that is married to divine intention, we find our true home. It's a place where your heart finds its purpose and where your mind agrees that this is divine and this is mine to do! That's when the intention decides to enter action, balanced and determined to move into one's soul mission." I tried to understand what he was sharing, because I knew from listening to him all day that he was a wisdom-keeper.

Yasma continued on, "How did you feel today as you were helping the seekers in this place of healing, lad?" He seemed to be looking right into my heart with his question. It was my heart that responded to the situations as they played out this long day, not my head, which was still in a state of confusion and depression due to homesickness.

I thought for a moment, and then said, "I felt relief for the seekers, because I knew it was most likely they would be healed. Most did leave better for the visit, didn't they, Yasma? Even so, I didn't do anything but help you, when you requested. You did the actual healing."

Focusing on a part of my answer, Yasma said, "Why do you feel that not all were healed, lad? Your question belies your realization that healing is not always possible."

I replied, "Some didn't want to be healed, Yasma. I noticed it right away. They were either sent here, or they changed their mind. It seemed to me that they desired to hold tight to their pain instead of give it up." That puzzled me and I guess my brow must have wrinkled up a bit, as I struggled with the possibility. Yasma put his hand upon my forehead, and I felt a release of tension immediately. What peaceful, lovely hands, I thought.

"That's quite true, lad," Yasma said. "For a healing to be accomplished, it must follow upon the trail of self-acceptance. One must love oneself enough to risk change. To be ill, or in a state of 'dis-ease', the body and mind conform to a distorted pattern. Sadly, many feel safer in the misery they know, afraid of the harmony they have forgotten. As you surmised about the man with the misshapen arm, now his responsibility is much greater, isn't it? He is stronger and his strength will be used and maybe even abused. As a healer you can only do so much, and you can't hold responsibility for what a being chooses, once they are in balance again."

"I never thought of that part of healing," I replied.

Yasma said, "I could tell from the healing episode, that he desires to be a great warrior who would protect by killing, if necessary. If I had asked him to go out and kill every last one of the seekers still waiting, his loyalty and his gratitude to me would have been sufficient for him to do so, without a second thought. By sending him on a mercy mission, I'm hoping his heart will be opened and his desire to defeat will merge into a desire to harmonize and hold peace, rather than to fight for the sake of what he terms 'right'. If he goes on to be a great destroyer of people and places, I can't hold the responsibility for his actions."

As if he could read my mind and the next question I would pose, he said, "Yes, if that happened, the healing enabled him to abuse others, you could say. At the same time, it enabled him to see further and to go deeper into compassion, because it was compassion that held the light true to its course as it moved into his crooked bones. It was the choice of compassion that merged the two energies successfully. Compassion kept pain from entering the body, as the bones found their original perfect pattern. It will be compassion that will open his heart as well, and I believe he will benefit from this task he has agreed to do, as those he chooses will also. Each day, I ask someone to accomplish this task of disbursement of the abundant payments I have received for doing my work. It is spinning the energy; the give and the take spin out and return in like measure."

"Now, lad, it's time for us to say our night prayers and retire. Tomorrow we will take our healing on the road and visit some who can't come to us." He snuffed out the candle, murmuring a thanksgiving for the meal we had just enjoyed. In the darkness, he went to his sleeping place, still mumbling words of thanksgiving and asking for another day to do more healing. I sat there in the dark, wondering how many times I would be just left to figure things out for myself. Now, I thought, I must remember where that other rag of a blanket lay and find my way to it with no light and no direction from my new healing teacher.

Eventually, I did what Elmira had done so long ago, there in the dark caves when he put me on his back and crawled on hands and knees feeling his way; I slowly crawled and felt my way in the dark. Just remembering that time brought back the echo, of how much I wanted Elmira to be safe and not in pain anymore. I was thinking of that when my hand touched something that felt smoother than anything I had ever been privileged to touch. It was as soft as the most exquisite velvet that the elders wore on festive occasions in my Nazarite village. I pulled the material close to my face and rubbed it on my cheek. It smelled fresh, like a flower covered in morning dew. I wondered how this wonder of wonders came to be here, and how I hadn't noticed it before the daylight dipped below the horizon. I wrapped myself in the wonderful cloth, and it covered me totally. I fell into a most pleasant sleep.

# HEALING OUTREACH
Chapter Twelve

I awoke the next morning within a dream of being wrapped in the finest soft blanket, smelling of fragrances soothing and so much like the rare flowers of the high mountains during the warmer seasons. I stretched and softly moaned with pleasure as I heard Yasma moving about already in the early pre-dawn hours. It was the time of awakening, just before the light pierces the new day. Yasma was humming. He moved in my direction, stooped down and petted my head, like one would stroke an animal they were fond of. This didn't offend me, for I knew petting to be a human action that was the closest to unconditional love. The animals felt they had taught us humans such compassion gestures, and maybe they had. "Arise, lad," Yasma said, as he stroked my head.

Taking to my feet, I asked Yasma what we would do this dawning day. "We shall go to those who can't come to us, but first we must do the morning prayers and invoke the unseen protectors and guides, and you shall join me," he announced matter-of-factly.

Reluctantly, I took the precious blanket that had afforded my body such a pleasant night's sleep. As I grasped the silky warm material to pull it from my appreciative torso, I noticed it was the same rag of a blanket I had seen in the corner, from my first introduction to Yasma. I must have looked rather surprised, for Yasma laughed and said, "Interesting, how appreciation can alter one's perception, isn't it, lad?"

He beckoned me to his side and hand-in-hand; we went to a nearby well and drew up a bucket of refreshing water. He slowly did a cleansing ritual I hadn't seen done before. He dipped both his hands into the bucket and thanked the water for its refreshment and healing. Then taking the container of water into his old wrinkled and gnarled hands, he poured it over his head, saying, "Cleanse from my head any thoughts un-divine, so that I may be an instrument of peace and healing this day." He let the water slowly flow down his nearly bald head over his face. When it had found its path to his eyes, he bathed them, saying, "Cleanse my vision so I only perceive divinity within my sight." Then he took more water and drank it, saying, "Cleanse my mouth, so I speak only divine words. Allow the cleansing to course through my body, so that I may have another day to assist my brothers and sisters in their path towards love." Finally he disrobed–which meant taking off the scant loincloth covering–and stood there nude without reservation and cleansed his body. Making sure that he washed his heart area, he said, "Cleanse my heart, so that I can come to all with a clean, clear compassion for their needs." He turned to me as I stood watching and asked, "Would you do me a rare honor, for I have never brought anyone to my morning ritual in the past. I have never had the honor of having my back washed."

How could I resist him? The look of such peace on that lovely old wise face was enough for him to bid anything of me, and I wondered how could I have ever doubted his intentions towards me?

"I would be honored, master," I sincerely answered.

"No, lad, I assure you. The honor is mine," he humbly said, as he turned around so his back could be attended to.

I noticed that his back was crooked and places seemed to be red and aggravated. He never complained, so I had thought he must be in perfect health under that layer of dust on his body, but I could tell that he possibly neglected his own health for the sake of others.

"How is it, dear teacher," I said, "that you can heal others, when you are so clearly in pain and discomfort yourself?"

"I get like this because I sometimes take on too much of other's conditions," he replied. "It's nothing," he assured me.

"How do I bathe your back?" I asked, not sure how to honor his request as he desired.

"Do it your way, lad," he said.

"I don't have a way," I almost pleaded, because I felt a bit out of my league here, with this master teacher patiently waiting for the small favor he requested.

"Make it up as you go then, lad, for everyone must find their own path, their own way, and their own rituals as they move through their life's mission."

Ok, I thought. I brought up a fresh bucket of water, began talking to the water and asked it to bless my dear teacher with cleansing and healing. I dipped my hands into the water, which seemed conscious, alive and full of energy to the point that it glowed. I closed my eyes and visualized Yasma's back receiving this sacred substance, totally in accordance with God's will, to the point that perfection would find its path. I remembered the healing I first witnessed upon returning to Yasma's humble home. I was thinking, I'm a long way from that capability, yet I still visualized the light-energy marrying the earth's sound-energy. Doing so, I began at the top of Yasma's spine and slowly massaged in a spiral fashion, first one direction then another, all the way to the lowest point of his back. As I moved, I visualized the light and the sound twining and moving as my hand directed. My eyes were so focused, or maybe closed, I didn't notice the sun break the horizon as this ritual unfolded. I was so intensely involved with the act of washing and blessing Yasma's back, that I entered a light trance, until I heard him moan, which brought my attention back to his physical presence. The sunlight was spreading a warm glow over the area I had just worked on. It looked different in the morning light, I noticed. In dimmer light, it looked so distorted and reddened. Now Yasma's back looked fresh and fully straight and perfect.

Yasma turned around and murmured, "Oh, if I could only keep you with me throughout my days; I'm sure I would be around another hundred years. You're a healer, lad, and though I may soon depart from this plane of existence, I shall do so knowing that there are those who will do even more than I have ever hoped to accomplish."

I replied, "I bet you have accomplished a lot in your entire years, master, and surely I couldn't do as much as you have, to bring healing and love back into people's lives."

"Don't bet on it," he said with a wink. "You have no idea how much you can, and will, accomplish in your short life."

That statement caused me to think and wonder out loud, "My short life? Will I then die soon, master?" I asked.

"Don't worry yourself," he whispered, "for you will have three lifetimes in one." Then he chuckled quietly at my obvious bewilderment to his answer.

"You will see, lad," he said. Then he asked if he could be honored to wash my back as soon as I was ready, nodding toward the well. "You'll find healing at the well, lad. One day, you will also find great love and devotion waiting for you there. As you quench your thirst at such a place, remember that there is a loving spirit that resides within the depths. These life-giving wells are memory reservoirs, as well as refreshing and cleansing places. Do your morning ritual," he suggested, "and if you don't already have one, make one up." He walked a short distance away and seated himself cross-legged with his back to me, re-wrapping his loin cloth as he walked. He closed his eyes and entered a deep meditation.

When I was done with my cleansing and prayers, I stood fully unclothed, knowing that this was not embarrassing to Yasma, for his naked body didn't offend me either. I said, "I'm ready, master." He silently rose, came to me and washed my back, and it felt wonderful. Only my mother's touch seemed more soothing to me and maybe the hugs of my father as well. It's hard to describe the sensation, but it was truly divine. Yasma finished and asked if I needed time to meditate, or would I like to do a walking meditation as we moved into the day's work. I replied that walking would be nice, and we departed. I loved walking meditations and had enjoyed them on many long journeys, when such opportunities afforded themselves. It made my days flow easier. I followed quietly, doing my gratitude prayers and wondering what the day would offer.

We arrived at a grand house inside a high-walled compound just outside of the ramshackle city, as the morning sun was at full brilliance. The place was exquisite, to say the least, being surrounded by a tall wall that had vividly-colored mosaics embedded into its pristine white adobe surface. The mosaics depicted dancing girls, also creatures I hadn't yet encountered, like a human with an elephant head, and snakes and such. The fascinating images didn't trouble me. However, I wondered why we were honored to see all the grandeur upon entering the palatial compound. I thought that maybe we would be tending to a servant of this place, as we headed to a small gate at the rear of the wall and rang a bell. The long cord dangling for visitors was even ornate, and we pulled it to announce our arrival. Yasma clanged the bell in a definite pattern, three distinct clangs followed by silence then three rapid clangs. Very quickly, the small doorway was opened and a smiling, yet concerned, maid bid us enter, saying to Yasma, "Follow me, master," taking no notice of me.

If one's eyes can become exhausted from over-stimulation, certainly mine were, as we entered another doorway and traversed the hallways of the grand place. The beauty and bright colors of the structure astounded me. It was like a maze, and I remember remarking at how impressive this place was. The maid, finally acknowledging my presence, said, "This is nothing but the servant's hallways. You should see the hallways of those we serve. We can only be in those areas if on duty for our masters." I couldn't imagine how anything could be more beautiful. That feeling lasted only a moment longer, however; for the maid forthwith took us through a doorway hidden behind a large brightly-colored tapestry, which had an image of a unicorn on it. Later I asked Yasma why that mighty white horse had a horn on its head. He told me there were places that coexisted with ours, which had the most marvelous beings. The unicorn was beloved there and remembered by many, who were privileged to travel among these expanded dimensions in their dreams or otherwise.

"I want to go there," I whispered, to no one in particular.

We entered a dark narrow hallway, lit by tiny torches behind the tapestry. It appeared to be cut from bedrock. We went higher and higher, with steps rising time and again within the narrow winding dark hallway we traversed, finally reaching another doorway. At this portal the maid knocked, using the same pattern that Yasma had used with the bell–three distinct knocks, followed by three rapid knocks. Immediately, the door opened and we entered a beautiful room. My visual senses were blasted to new heights in the awe of it. Gold, red, and brilliant blues bombarded me; but in spite of the beauty, there was a sense of foreboding therein. Yasma didn't seem to notice anything. He was only focused on a huge carved bed, adorned to the point of being visually overwhelming. Surrounding this majestic bed chamber were many maids, attending someone who was moaning and thrashing about. Then I heard a baby cry.

One of the maids said to Yasma, "Thank you, master, for I didn't know what to do." She explained that the attending mid-wife was taken to be punished by the master of the house. "He holds her responsible for the state his favorite wife is in, since she brought forth this firstborn son. He has had many daughters," she explained, "but never has one of his wives given him a son until now and as much as he wants this babe, he wants this young wife more."

Yasma took in the situation and asked if we were secure, for the moment. He was assured that for a short time, we were safe, since the master had said he couldn't bear to see his young wife suffer and had left in haste. Yasma then asked the attending maids to strip the covers from the youthful mother and to strip her as well. At first they looked at him with astonishment at such a request. He said, "Do you think this old man has need of lustful thoughts or actions at this stage of my life?" They were thinking this over, when he said, "We'll save her life, if you can put your fears aside for just a few moments."

The first maid, obviously the superior, said, "Girls, I sent for Yasma, because I know that he is a healer like no other, and I trust him completely. I have seen his abilities, and I know that he can help. Trust him for just a moment, for the sake of our beloved mistress." They then did as requested and soon the young woman, still wracked with pain and bleeding profusely, was upon a bare sheet, with only towels to soak up the vast flow of blood gushing forth from her nude body.

I noticed Yasma place one hand on the top of her head and call down the light. He then boldly placed his other hand right between the legs of this poor young mother in pain, and brought in the sound from that location. His hand was soon covered with blood, and the maids were beside themselves at seeing this. I recognized a moment of need, and I asked them if the babe was well. Their attention was so focused upon their mistress; they were deaf to the cries of the newborn son.

I took the hand of the maid most in distress and said, "Your mistress needs you to quiet her baby now. She can't heal, if she thinks her baby is in distress." As I walked her toward the cradle where the baby had been placed, a couple of the other maids also followed me. I looked back at Yasma, who still held the little mother with a hand on her head and the other at the birth portal. I could see the energies of light and sound uniting, as I redirected my attention to the little newborn. I touched the crying infant, and he stopped wailing. Within his sobs, he began to fix his eyes on my own. I talked to him in thought language and assured him that his mother was in good hands with the master healer, Yasma. He shifted his gaze to the maids, and I sensed that he wondered if he should trust them. He already trusted me, because we had talked in the language of spirit. I assured him that these maids would spoil and amuse him, if only he allowed them the chance, and he gave his first smile to the little maid who was most afraid. Her attention was immediately shifted by his sweet smile and her fears dissolved into joy, as she reached to pick him up from his cradle.

By this time, his mother was no longer moaning or struggling in pain. I heard Yasma tell the maids helping him, "Finally, we have the sacred placenta coming forth, which nourished this babe until the mother's milk could take over. Put it in a bowl of cool water and keep it safe until, your master releases the mid-wife. She will know what to do with it, since there are important reasons to preserve this substance. The child and the mid-wife will be glad for its preservation," he assured them. They quietly nodded, amazed and were so glad for their mistress's improvement, that should they be bidden to do so, they would have tried to pull down the moon.

"Now bring the babe, since the last stage of this healing can only be accomplished by this gifted son." The little maid, now not possessed by fear, wouldn't give up her charge to anyone else, and she brought the babe forth and handed him to his mother, who immediately put him to her breast. He began to suckle enthusiastically, with no prompting or urging. Yasma smiled and wiped his bloody hands on an available towel, and we all looked at the nude mother nursing her naked newborn son and saw a most beautiful and perfect sight.

At that moment, we heard a great commotion outside the main doorway, and we were ushered quite quickly out the way we had come in. Before we got far from the location, I could hear the sound of a man's voice saying, "Oh, my God, you have forgiven me and brought back my beloved," and then I heard this man weep and summon the midwife, from wherever he had sent her.

Quite quickly we were back in the street and walking away from the palatial home. Yasma smiled. I couldn't help but ask him what he was thinking. He was still covered in the mother's birth blood.

"I'm thinking how wonderful motherhood is and how much our poor mothers suffer, just so that we can come forth," he replied.

"I don't think I would be a good mother, Yasma," I said. "Surely I would perish in such an act as bringing a child forth from my body."

This made my master teacher laugh even more. "You probably have lived as a woman and had many children, dear lad; for to become a master you would have had to experience all life forms in both the positive and negative (masculine and feminine) forms, I assure you. However, since you are remembering and re-learning as you move through this mission, I tell you that bringing a child forth doesn't have to be as painful and as bloody, as what you just witnessed. That young wife was afraid of the process, because she was not allowed to learn from those who would teach her the way of it, her own womenfolk. She was denied women's companionship, due to her husband's insecurity about her safety. He loved her to the point of keeping her prisoner, and she was cut off from her sisters, with only the attending maids who didn't dare to share their 'knowing' with her. Luckily, for her, there was the overseeing maid who knew of my work and sent for us, risking her own life in the process. Love will move through fear if allowed to do so, dear lad. You will come to know that on many occasions, even when fear threatens you and your work. Always remember; Love is the only thing that can dissolve fear."

We moved on through the day, visiting many elderly, crippled and poor individuals and even some tinier babies. We finally ended up at a place of isolation, where the ones with the body sores lived. This colony of lepers was at the outermost side of the city from the grand house we began our day. No doubt, so they didn't have to see the ugliness, desperation and sorrow of those who were banished there. It was, for the most part, simply a huge natural hole in the ground, which had walls of rock in which various caves, some deep and some just mere shallow impressions, dotted the rocky faces and offered shelter to the lepers. Before we came this far however, we had been warned to go no further by a sign with an odd image painted on it. The image was a circle with two dots for eyes and a down-turned arc for a mouth. I remarked on the oddity of the sign. Yasma said it meant that if you went further, you would be very unhappy. Even as he explained, we never missed a step. I wondered why we didn't heed the warning, but by now, after yesterday and this morning with what I saw and heard, I trusted Yasma completely.

Once within the colony, the joy on the resident's faces commanded my attention. I was eager to learn and perceive all I could, from this master who people loved so dearly. The lepers knew when Yasma came, one could be chosen, to be healed and if that one was pure of heart and mind and soulfully ready, the healing would be total and someone could be free of this horrible prison of a place. They had weeks to make the choice, since Yasma's visits were regular but far apart. I wondered how they could be sure they had chosen well. Yasma explained that if the chosen one was conflicted, or had intentions that were not of the best for all concerned, their healing would be incomplete. In that situation, Yasma further told me, they would stay within the colony, until they were ready to be healed. This, he said, would happen without his assistance, depending on the person involved; or the person may be lucky enough to meet another healer someday and have a chance to get it right that time.

I could see a large number of sad miserable beings in the compound, and I asked how they made the final selection. "Oh that!" exclaimed Yasma. "It's a lesson in itself, for there is great debate as to who is worthy and who isn't, until they realize that they all are worthy." The elders who have grasped this in previous choosing, often let the newcomers go through the process so that they arrive at the same conclusion on their own, thus respecting the discovery more completely."

I pondered this, asking, "Then, how do they finally choose?"

"Usually by lottery of those they think are ready, which comes to a vote; or in some cases they just know that one is ready to be released from suffering and the vote is unanimous."

Continuing my inquisition, I asked, "How can they make a mistake and present one who isn't yet ready, then?"

Yasma, nodding, as if expecting my barrage of questions said, "Because even in such a case, they 'know' that sometimes the healing takes time and an increment of steps to overcome the fear of being whole, or the fear of not being perfect in physicality. You see, some will be so angry at the condition, that they haven't yet made peace with it; and it won't go away until they resolve it to peace. So, no matter who is chosen, it is the right choice after all."

We finally reached the place where Yasma said he liked to do his healing, because it was the most visible to everyone–almost a natural theater. It was near the center of the valley and situated in such a way, that both sound and light were amplified. There, expectantly waiting was a small group of lepers with a very old woman in their arms, whose sores seeped and looked extremely raw. They laid her gently on a natural rock shaped like an elevated table. Once she was safely placed, they backed away with respect to us, who didn't have the body sores. They didn't want to infect us with their misery.

There were many who were silently perched like birds, in various higher places among the rocks and walls, attentively watching closely. They obviously had all agreed to this selection and desperately needed to see a miracle, so that they could hold hope in their hearts for themselves as well.

The woman seemed as old as Yasma, maybe older. He knew her as he approached, and I could see that the two were friends before this meeting. She reached for him and said, "Old man, why would you waste your time healing this old woman?" He hugged her and she pulled away slightly, out of fear, or habit, that her touch would harm him.

## The Saga-Oracle

Yasma gently pulled her back to his embrace and said, "Don't fear a friend, dear Gladia,[59] I can't harm you, and you can't harm me, because we don't fear each other, and we are so old that not even dis-ease wants us." They then closely embraced and held each other for a long time, and he whispered something into her ear. She sobbed and kissed his cheek. Through her tears and sobs she said, "There are so many others more worthy than me. Why they chose me, I shall never know."

Yasma smiled and pulled back, to look into her eyes with a look of passionate tenderness. I could sense a great love between the two and wondered if they were lovers once. He said, "Obviously. you have wonders yet to perform, my dear, and it must be that you have something to accomplish outside of this valley of tears."

"Whatever it is, I will willingly participate, but I hope one day to be released from this old body that no longer can support the feelings I have, when I see the likes of you," she replied in such a sweet voice, almost the voice of a maiden. Then she whispered (due to the acoustics of the place we could even hear the whisperings), "Another life, another time, I shall share my passion and desire with you, my beloved," and she kissed Yasma full on the mouth deeply and with the same intensity that I often saw my parents, in the privacy of our home, do as well. Her mouth was surrounded by ugly sores, yet Yasma never hesitated and seemed to melt into the deep and passionate kiss, entwined in her old frail arms and she in his. They didn't hear or see the others cheering and raising a joyful ruckus, due to being so lost within the embrace and the moment. Love is fascinating. whether you are within it or witness to it.

In spite of all the noise and cheering, they didn't hurry this reunion. Yasma, ever the good teacher, turned to me and told me that when he first saw his beloved Gladia, she had lost a child and was cast from the house of her husband. It was he, who rescued

---

[59] Female form of 'Gladiator,' but means 'glad' in the female form, which is the direct opposite of the male, who has to fight to death so that others can cheer. Gladia means ;fight to live;

her. This caught me off guard, and I asked, "You were not her husband, then?"

"No, lad. I was too young and too poor to be chosen for her, and they chose someone who loved her beauty and neglected her soul." As he remembered, his eyes took on a faraway cast that only fond memories can create. "When she lost the newborn baby boy, she was cast out by her chosen husband and his family, as unfit to be among his wives and concubines." Gladia watched Yasma remembering their meeting, with a smile of confirmation on her peaceful face. "Her family was shamed and her husband knew his only option was to turn her out in the streets, which he did, still bleeding as the mistress was this morning." He was in deep sorrowful thought and continued, "Oh! If only I had the knowledge then, that I used this morning, maybe I could have saved her from a life of suffering and barrenness." She continued to watch him tell the tale and he went on, saying, "It was her destiny to be a healer of the street women however, and it was she that ultimately taught me the technique I used this morning. But most of all, Gladia taught me to love to the depths of my heart," he stressed as he lovingly looked at her. Through his entire explanation, the old leper woman lay peacefully and patiently, watching him, too.

The cheering and the noise arose again from the onlookers, who brought us all back to the intention of the moment and the healing ritual began. An instant hush took over the perched leper watchers. Yasma began his work. The light and the sound were brought from the four directions this time; north, south, east, and west, as well as pulled down from the sky and brought up from the earth. Yasma didn't disrobe Gladia, but laid his hands here and there upon her tattered robes. Her arms, face and part of her legs were visible, however, due to the aged material that was literally falling apart. At these revealed places, the onlookers could see the angry red sores began to immediately lose their redness and size. Within only a few minutes, Gladia's skin was clear and healthy-looking. The watchers were silently appreciative and knew that she was healed. She sensed her healing, too, without looking at her body and said, "Now, Yasma, don't go smoothing out my wrinkles. I worked hard to get them and definitely don't want to look like a maiden, now that I have left that behind me. Heaven forbid; being a maiden is not easy."

He just laughed and said, "Now why would I smooth out your lovely wisdom lines, dear heart, and chance that you wouldn't find my craggy old face appealing?"

After an attunement in which Yasma anointed Gladia with an oil essence on the top of the head, at the bottom of the lower lip, and at the navel area, and finally at the bottom of each foot, the healing ritual was done, and the love offering was officially brought to us. This time it was a walking stick for Yasma. It was carved with lovely animals on its naturally-gnarly and adequately shaped surface. "Yasma loves the animals," one of the presenters said to me, noticing my interest. "So we hoped he would love this gift and, for once, keep something. We all worked on it," he said.

Yasma took the cane and admired it, saying, "Now, why would I need a walking stick such as this?" yet it was plainly understood that he was pleased and wouldn't be passing along this grateful gift.

Gladia said, "You need it–to beat off all your lady admirers, of course," and she laughed and rose from her healing place. The two walked away together, with Yasma leaning on the walking stick, which was clearly making his stride easier. I wasn't sure what I was to do now, and I felt a hand hold me back from following.

One of the elders present said, "Give them time alone child. When they're ready, they'll be back. Then Gladia will rest awhile in the transition cave. When she is sure her healing is accomplished, she will go out among the people again."

I thought about this and asked how long she had been with the lepers. "A long time, and she blessed many here with her healing gifts. She came to us with no sign of leprosy," he said with a look of deep appreciation for the sacrifice she chose. "She has a great mission yet to attend to, out among the others and we all know it and honor it."

I noticed day was sinking into the night again and wondered how we would find our way home. I was directed to the path we had used to enter this place, and told someone was waiting for me, which I assumed was Yasma. I wondered why he had returned so soon. I expected his visit with Gladia would last much longer.

I walked along, thinking that no matter how old and decrepit a person seemed, they had stories to tell of passion, love, journeys and challenges. I thought I might just ask Yasma some of those questions on our way home.

I was deep in such thought, when I saw a shadow on the path ahead. The form looked familiar, but definitely was not the frail Yasma. Then I made the connection. "Elmira," I yelled, "where have you been?" and ran to him. It seemed such a long time, since I last had seen him, when, in fact, it had only been a few weeks. He swept me up in his arms and hugged me, until I thought I would break. Both of us cried tears of joy at this reunion. Tears flowed easily in my arena of experience. I loved this guardian of mine, who had not abandoned me after all, and my heart was pleased to take his hand and move on down the path of my life journey once again.

# THE SACRED BOWL
Chapter Thirteen

Time is relevant to so many factors. For instance, there are times when a day seems like a year and, quite the opposite as well, when a year seems only a mere day. So it was when I found my beloved Elmira waiting for me on the path. Though I had never really been that far from him, it felt to me like eons of time had passed. Probably, because I thought I was abandoned, since I had last seen him a few weeks previously.

That feeling of abandonment was one of my major lessons throughout my early life. I finally realized that you can only abandon yourself. There's no guarantee that souls traveling through physicality will be united in creation's evolutionary dance, and if they do find each other, there is no telling how long before they separate and follow other paths. Even soul mates dance together, then separately, as they move through the stages of experiencing. Of course, within their hearts the twin-soul flame, or the part of yourself that has split for the cause of evolution, is always therein; for what one experiences, so too, does the other, but you alone must walk the path wherever it winds and twines.

Upon seeing my beloved guardian, I was overjoyed, as he was, too. As it turned out, he was not all that far from me and knew of my actions and movement from place to place, probably hidden somewhere near and watching. I could tell by our reunion that he was uneasy about being out of my conscious presence.

As we began to walk away, I asked of Yasma. "Shouldn't we wait for him?" Elmira just shook his head 'no', and moved on. Traveling with a non-speaking guardian has it challenges, but by now I could sense most of the quiet internal conversation he was willing to share with me in mind-to-mind talk. Eventually, I noticed I could hear his voice inside my head quite clearly. I would practice asking him 'yes' or 'no' questions. He would answer with the appropriate head nod or sway. This offered me a wonderful opportunity, because I began to experiment with distance mind-talk. I would lag behind him several steps, experimenting to see if his voice weakened, which it didn't. He would often warn me not to stray too far behind, or my mind message would be more than just a test. Even as I was trailing further behind, he was always totally aware of my location. I began to wonder if he had eyes in the back of his head! Being amazed and amused with the ability to expand communication with my friend, I asked Elmira if he always knew what was on my mind. His mind-talk reply was, "Only when it is expedient to do so." He respected my privacy, he reassured me. That was a relief. Boys my age can fantasize about almost anything; many things we don't wish to share with others.

Thus began my 'quiet training,' and I didn't speak for nearly a year. At least, I didn't speak with my vocal cords. Rather, I held a constant chattering questing mode within my head. There were times when Elmira asked me to meditate in the quiet-zone for a

117

while, because he was getting a headache from all the mind chatter.

I wondered where we would go this time as we left the leper colony. My life, by the age of around nine years, was like a big adventure, having seen so much already. It's hard to pin my exact age down, since until one's thirteenth year, the time of the second naming and dedication to God ceremony, such passages as birthdays went by without notice. Added to that, due to the complexity and richness of time, it's hard to explain how I experienced time. It wasn't linear for me, rather more like a zone. I would compare this to the various time zones around the planet. When something happens within the night in one zone, even though the other zone may be in daylight, it still happens at the same moment no matter what the light or clock records.

We didn't stop at any shelters that first night, or for many nights. We simply continued down a dusty road, stopping at night to sleep like the homeless. I wasn't sure Elmira knew where we were going. As the thought passed through my mind, he shook his head 'no.'

I thought, 'Great! If Elmira, my guardian doesn't know where we're going, how do we ever find our way to where we're supposed to be?'

Elmira just shrugged his shoulders again.

After a couple of days, we began to get hungry. We had no money or means of providing for our needs, nor had we been taken in by anyone, so there were few options open. We kept to ourselves and often would leave the path if we saw people approaching, since Elmira was still concerned for my safety and kept us isolated.

However, on the third day of our traveling, I happened to see a very skinny man sitting on the side of the path in the hot sun. He looked like an ancient statue. He sat crossed-legged, bare except for a loin cloth much like the one Yasma wore, and he was bald and wrinkled from head to toe, too. At first I thought it was Yasma. The man sat with his eyes closed and looked like he had been there for a long time. I walked over to him and looked closely, since I wasn't sure if this was an actual man or a statue, again reminiscent of Yasma. When I determined it was, in fact, a real man, I checked to see if he was breathing, and I couldn't detect breath. I looked back at Elmira, and he shrugged his shoulders again, answering the unspoken question.

The dusty man sat with a wooden bowl in front of him. It had a couple coins in it. I thought, 'What will a dead man need of coins?' But still, I would never have helped myself to what I knew was not mine, nor did I think that was an option. I was just 'mind-sorting' the situation. I decided to take a moment and pray for the safe journey of his soul, who I was nearly certain, had passed on. I sat cross-legged in front of him and began my mind-talk mantra, that phrase that gets me centered and ready to be quiet and receptive to divine guidance. The high mountain sages taught me this was the first stage of prayer. Everyone has their own mantra, they told me, one that is attuned to their particular soul.

As I entered this quiet-zone I saw the sage more clearly. He smiled and greeted me in that non-physical place, saying, "Hello, little one." I was small for my age and appeared years younger than my actual age.

I returned the greeting with the inner voice, asking when he had passed from the physical, and he laughed at me–not in a degrading way, but in a way full of mirth and fun. "I'm not dead, little one, nor am I just a dusty bump in the road," he said. "I'm simply in my receptive mode so that I can be of assistance to such as you, who travel the dusty path alone."

"I'm not alone," I clarified. "I have my guardian," nodding towards Elmira, who was a short distance away watching me and everything else as well—ever on duty. Even in this non-physical dimension I was still partly in the third dimensional world, only it was not as dense, and it was like an alternate dimension, a spiritual/mental place.

"That's true, young man, and your friend shines as brightly as you do yourself, thus, child-man, you are blessed." In this zone we were conversing within, we could see energy more easily and color waves danced around everything.

I had never been called 'child-man' before and wondered if I had lost track of time more than I thought. It was just a couple of days, since I left Yasma, and surely I couldn't have grown to a man in that short time. My growth was a concern for me, because I feared that I would never attain a man's stature. The physical stage of these middle child years is naturally a place of transition. I wanted to get on with it and not be stuck in the little kid stage.

As this crossed my mind, my dusty friend chuckled again. "You have the wisdom of a child and the experience and maturity of a man already. That's why I see you as a child-man," he replied, there in the quiet-zone.

"Am I dead, too, now?" I asked, for I noticed that my hunger pains had ceased to bother me.

"No, you are quite alive and well within the physical realm. You just are not experiencing the illusion of the body vehicle in this zone, so you are more in the spiritual body which thrives on the nourishment of love," he told me.

"Can I then forget about food and shelter and stay in my spiritual body most of the time?" This seemed to be the perfect place and the intensity of light and sound in the zone was appealing. Everything that surrounded me in this realm was more brilliant, because I could see the God Essence of everything. Although it was the same place as the third dimensional space we occupied, it was crystal clear and the natural sounds were like a symphony of greatest perfection. I had never experienced it so intensely in my meditations before. I wanted to stay.

He looked at me carefully, before he replied. "You could, but you won't, because you must be within the arena you came to change and improve, and that means you must feel all the effects of physicality, pleasant and not so pleasant."

## The Saga-Oracle

I was disappointed. The thought of survival out there in the land of need seemed to daunt me. I was still a boy after all. I longed for my parents to fulfill such needs of survival, or if they couldn't, have a qualified adult in their place. Elmira comforted me, but he was prone to disappearing from time to time.

The dusty one looked into my heart and soul, as these thoughts coursed through my head. He had compassionate wisdom in his eyes. Always the wisdom was reflected in the eyes, I had noticed. He then looked down at his bowl and told me about it.

"This, child, is a begging bowl, some say." His dusty hands cupped the bowl, as he brought it up to his chest. I wasn't sure if I was still in the quiet-zone or back in the physical. After a pause, he went on to say, "But it really is a holy receptacle of the utmost importance. It is a physical symbol of the body in many ways. It doesn't have to be filled, but because it has a space for 'fulfillment,' it invites filling. Those who answer the invitation it offers, as it sits here before me, think they are offering a blessing to God, or whoever carries such a sacred vessel; but actually they don't realize that when they put something into the bowl, whatever they offer is magnified many times over in blessings for themselves, filling the Holy Grail[60] within them. It is good they don't realize this truth, for if they did it wouldn't work so well, since logical judgment would stop the process," he explained.

I was clearly concerned at that statement and said, "Do you mean that now that you have told me this secret, I can never put anything into a begging bowl, I mean, Sacred Bowl?"

"Maybe so," he answered. Then he said "Maybe not so. Wouldn't you help one such as me, even if you knew there was nothing in the effort for yourself?"

"Of course," I said, "I would be pleased to help you, but I have nothing to put in your bowl, and thus I can't even do that for you." At this my heart seemed to feel heavy, and yes, even in the spirit-

---

[60] Symbol of the receptacle of the soul

body you can feel such things, and possibly you feel them more intensely.

He looked at me and smiled a wise smile of knowing. Then he said, "Don't you know what you have given this beggar alongside the dusty road, youngster? You have filled this bowl to overflowing."

I couldn't think of a thing of value that I could have given this stranger, so I just thought, "No, I guess I don't know what I have given you, my friend."

"You have given me the greatest gift of my life, young brilliant one," he replied in a voice now coming forth in a singsong fashion, "for I have waited all my life for you to pass this way. I knew you would be the only one that would sit on the dusty ground and come to me as you have done, through the doorway of the heart; entering the chamber of my soul, where you would overflow my fulfillment bowl with love." Then he asked, "Why did you stop, child, and come to me?"

"Because I didn't know if you were alive or dead," I replied. "If you were alive, I wanted to see if I could help you. If you were dead, I wanted to help you find your way to the afterlife, to the true home of us all as my teachers have taught me."

"In other words, child, you came to me of pure unconditional love and compassion. Certainly there is nothing this dusty old man can do for you, or so you may have thought," he answered.

I thought about this and said, "I didn't think about it. I just reacted at seeing you here by the road, all covered with dust, all by yourself and alone."

"Hmmm," he murmured. "You did think about the coins in my bowl as I remember, but never a thought about what they could do for you in your situation, only in wonderment as to how they could be used in my circumstance. Isn't that true?"

"I guess I did think of that. I am sorry if I have offended you, for I certainly wouldn't take advantage of you, poor man," I answered.

"You would never take advantage of anyone, child, for your soul is to loving. I knew that from the first moment, I saw you coming down the path. Even though my eyes were closed and my body still, my soul was totally awake and aware. Nevertheless, don't think of me as a poor man, for I'm wealthy beyond measure, as you yourself are, too, my child. Many adore you already and many more will love you, once they meet or hear of you. You are a way-shower, sent at a time of great need. You are a gift to all creation. Be patient and learn as much as you can, so that you will know exactly what is needed in every situation and be ready to enter these places of the heart, that need healing at all levels of involvement. A rich man I am, and you are richer by far, for you have developed your loving nature enough to do more than I could ever do."

"I don't know about that," I said, "but I hope that one day (every child's wish), my parents will be glad I was born."

"All creation is glad you were born," my dusty friend said. "I know it's a bit late, but may I give you a gift to celebrate that birth?" He looked deeply into my eyes until I thought he had become me and I, he.

I simply nodded my head in the affirmative, and he began to physically move about, exiting the quiet-zone and opening his long-closed eyes. He stretched his frail body, as he unwound his legs and moved his arms. This brought me to my physical body as well, and I immediately felt the hunger pains again; but his gaze was compelling, so I enjoyed this mind-communication for a while more. It was hard for me to move, after just sitting a little time. It must have been tremendously difficult for the old one to move after so long sitting, but he didn't complain. He simply rose and handed me the bowl with the coins.

Still in my silent mode, I thought, "But I can't take your coins and your sacred bowl."

He spoke physically, clearing his raspy throat first, saying, "It has been years, since I took this position and used these vocal cords, so pardon me if they sound rusty." He then went on to say in his gravelly voice, "I would be honored if you would take this gift I have waited long to give you. I knew that you had made a decision to come forth into physicality, and I also knew that one day you would cross my path. I don't know how I knew; I just knew. Your passing by, is your gift to me; finding me and pausing for a moment is the most important moment in my life. Such love and compassion cannot be repaid, only accepted as the blessing it truly is. I wish to share this with you. I have waited to give you my sacred bowl, and I assure you it will 'fulfill' all your needs, starting with the two coins therein."

He handed me the bowl. I took it. I looked upon it with awe, for I knew the simple wooden vessel was holy. The old man bowed, turned and walked away on wobbly frail legs that held him up quite adequately. He paused, turned and said, "Namaste', my friend, Namaste'."

I replied, "May the god in me honor the god in you as well, great teacher." He disappeared into a cloud of dust. I watched to see if he emerged from the dusty cloud, but I saw him no more.

## THE WISDOM WELL
Chapter Fourteen

It was indeed over a year before I spoke verbally again with anyone. Elmira and I wandered in places I never imagined existing, with only our sacred bowl to provide us with the necessities of life. People put things in it, without being asked. Other times, things just appeared in it—sometimes coins which we gave away, but often it was food or maybe a bit of cloth that appeared. I found that not much is necessary in physicality, for my needs were few, as were Elmira's. We never starved or felt deprived. We discovered the blessings of the land and tasted the offerings of plants along our path, too. We enjoyed drinking from small natural springs along the way. There is no sweeter drink, I assure you, than the nectar of Mother Earth. Often the women, on their way to the wells, would put something into our sacred bowl; nuts, fruit and various vegetables that they could spare. I just nodded, smiled my appreciation and thanked them within the mind-talk I was perfecting. They smiled back, knowing my gratitude.

One early dawn day we passed by the well. I initially saw it through the mists quietly awaiting the women, who would shortly come for its precious water. It felt good to be here first, before anyone else, not to ensure that I would be able to quench my thirst–surely wells didn't run dry all that often–but because it felt so peaceful. I sat on the well wall and drew the bucket of water up, slipping down to the ground with my back leaning on the well wall. I felt at peace, as the morning began to dawn, and the fog burned off. There was such a difference between the cool of the night and the arid intense heat of the day, that a mist would often develop, and it was soothing. The dawn smelled fresh and earthy. The sweet-tasting water satisfied. Elmira refreshed himself as well, and walked away as he often did at this early hour. He had a way of saying his daily prayers within his head and, knowing that I could mind-talk, I think it was his way of asking for privacy as he prayed and meditated. I was more peaceful after many months of wandering, and my chatting mind wasn't as intrusive, as when I first discovered this form of communication. Still, there were times Elmira needed some privacy for personal sacred moments, and I did, too. I would rest here and watch the dawning day begin and enjoy the moment. That was often the way I prayed, just being in the moment with total peace.

I laid my head back upon the stone wall of the well and heard it speak to me. At first, I thought I was hearing one of my animal friends mind-speak, and I looked around for the source of the voice. It was definitely the inner-voice communication I heard. The voice was fresh and crisp and the well soon clarified who was doing the talking, informing me that all creation (whether created by humans, animals, or any entity, for that matter) held consciousness, or awareness of self, so why was I so surprised that it could speak to me?"

There in the purple, pink and blue light of the dawning morning, I jumped back and looked at the well wall; and then carefully stretched my neck out and looked down into the well's depths, with obvious consternation, and asked, "How can this be so, for surely only God can create consciousness, and you were made by man's hands?"

The well then laughed, which rippled and splashed its waters a bit, and a voice that seemed to echo from its greatest depths, replied, "Of course, little one, God created consciousness. But all creation is co-creating containers for that consciousness to utilize constantly. That's how it works. Can't you see the obvious?"

I pondered this, made a pile of sand and asked the well then, if there was awareness within this pile of sand I just created; partly, to test the voice and the theory it was presenting to me at the same time.

A small different voice said, "You made me, and I am here for as long as you desire, or as long as I desire, whichever comes first."

Now the sand was talking to me! I looked to see if Elmira was done with his morning prayers, wondering if he was a witness to me losing my mind. The well chuckled again and caused some more splashing. It told me to play pretend with the pile of sand. I looked at the pile of sand I kicked up and back at the well, peering again down deep into it, not quite ready to believe I was talking to an object made by the hands of man and wondering if I was dreaming. A clear bell-like voice echoing off the walls, said, "Pretend that this little pile of sand you just made here beside me is a castle. You have heard about such places, haven't you?"

I certainly did know how to pretend, being still in the years where all sorts of imaginations flourished, so I said, "Sure, I've seen a palace or two, and I can pretend that this little pile of sand is such a place." I was always ready to imagine.

Just as most children can do, I entered imagination easily, and before my eyes, the little sand hill began to grow and take a majestic sand castle shape. It had wonderful places within its palace walls that only a child could imagine, like a courtyard that was full of apple trees, so the children could climb them and eat the fruit. Olive trees, as well, grew in tangles, so that children could make secret pathways through them and play for hours. There were rooms for elders, cooks and animals of the court, too. Of course, present was a throne room, which had a small throne for a child who would hold reign. In my mind, the children held rule in this magical place. I imagined colored tapestries that hung on the walls, and they appeared with all sorts of animals I loved, including a unicorn brightly woven, similar to the one I had seen with Yasma. I picked up pebbles and made grand places for people to sit upon; they became ornate seats full of fine jewels and softest cushions. I imagined lots of food for everyone, spread out on a round table, where no one was lesser or more worthy when seated. I had a great time imagining and, as fast as I could imagine, it materialized.

I walked about my castle and wondered how I could share this wonderful place with my beloved family. Immediately, my parents, brothers and sisters appeared and joined me in my fabulous creational abode. My joy at seeing them was as real to me, as the breath I take to sustain physical existence. I pinched myself to see if I was in a dream, for surely I must be. I knew that I was a wanderer now with no need of all this grandeur, but I was having such a wonderful time imagining and manifesting, I couldn't bring myself to stop just yet. I wanted my family to see the courtyard with the apple and olive trees so led them there through the maze of hallways, which I had imagined such a place would need. As I entered the courtyard, I noticed the well, in the middle of the trees. I didn't remember adding it to my vision, but nevertheless, I was grateful that it was there. My family was moving about inspecting the wonder of the place; I sat on the edge of the well and lovingly watched them, as they appreciated what I had created.

Then, I heard the well speak again. "Have you met the spirit of the castle yet?" it asked.

"This place has a spirit?" I questioned back.

"You made the place, so the spirit came, that's true, lad," the well replied.

While I was thinking this over, my family came and said they loved what I had created, but they missed our humble home. They told me they must be going now, so that they could feel the comfort of our little two-room abode that, they were sure, missed them, too. I waved goodbye to my loved ones and noticed my sacred bowl sitting on the rim of the well. I said to the well, "I don't need this palace. I just imagined it, because it was fun. Even so, now if I unimagine it, what will happen to the spirit of the castle? Will it die?" I asked worried that I had created a responsibility I wasn't ready to hold.

"It will wait for another child to make a grand sand castle, or some other imaginative creation. It will have many opportunities to experience being a house, or a castle, or maybe even a sand dragon, I assure you," the well answered. "You have no obligation to that which decides to fill your creative cup, but at the same time you have responsibility for it." I wasn't quite sure what the well meant and knew I would have to think about how that would be so for awhile. "But you do have a responsibility to realize all creation is divine and has a divine purpose," the well said, which helped me begin to understand. "Today the purpose of the little pile of sand was to teach you the power of imagination and how that power is the basis of all creation. Dust will return to dust, but it will have enjoyed all sorts of opportunities along the way, filling imagination cups. Everything is made of God stuff, and that stuff rearranges itself in many forms and then plays within the form, even as it forms the form, you see."

"How is it that a well knows so much?" I asked.

"Because of the company I keep," the well said. "The women gather here and when they have finished with talking about their needs, pains and sorrows, they move into possibilities and 'knowings'. One can learn a lot, being a well."

"My palace must be unimagined now," I told the well, "because I don't need it. It made me happy to create it, and I loved seeing my family again, but all I need is the sacred bowl, right now, and another drink of your sweet water." At that pronouncement I brought the water pail up again and quenched my thirst. When I set it down on the ledge, I no longer saw a castle, just a little pile of sand.

It was nearly full light by this time and Elmira came walking toward me, with a smile on his face. His prayers must have gone well, I thought.

I thanked the well and we moved on. We had no destination and no worries, except that I could sense Elmira thought I could use a bath sometime soon. We headed towards a small stream, where we heard early-morning chatter from some women, who were bathing little children therein.

I found a place downstream that was quiet and away from the others. I entered the water and thanked it for its cooling cleansing of my body. I looked at Elmira and said out loud, "The silence is over, my friend. It's time to walk towards home, for there is a family I love and a humble house that serves us well, waiting for me to return." He nodded his head and I stepped from the water, clean and refreshed. I dressed in my robe, and we headed into the rising sun, instinctively knowing that was the way home. The twining stream eventually had to be crossed; so we watched for the path that appeared on both sides and headed towards the morning light.

# THE CHRISTOPHER
Chapter Fifteen

With my announcement to Elmira at the stream, that it was time to go home, I took my authority for the first time. Until then, it was he who decided where we went. Elmira, I remember, looked at me with an expression of wonder and expectation, as if he was waiting for this day.

We found the place where the path crossed the stream, and we waded into the water. Each step, however, seemed more and more difficult, as the stream began to rise, and the water began rushing forth, engulfing us as we were about halfway across. I could sense Elmira wondering if there was a flash flood upstream. Yet, the skies didn't indicate a storm. Before long the water was so high and rushing, that I began to lose my footing. Elmira picked me up, put me on his shoulder, and began to walk toward the opposite shore, which was closer.

I was approaching 10 years of age, but still a small child. My growth spurt hadn't yet visited me, and while my mind was maturing, my body was in no hurry. We had to fight the current as the water rapidly got deeper. As I sat high on Elmira's shoulders, I sensed a physical struggle for him, who I had always believed stronger than anyone I had ever met. I was suddenly a heavy load. It didn't make sense. I had seen this strong guardian of mine lift and throw rocks, which weighed much more than I, on countless occasions just for fun. I began feeling heaviness within myself as well, which was difficult to explain, having never encountered such a feeling before. It was as if I couldn't help Elmira or myself, because my arms and legs were made of lead. Even my head seemed too heavy to balance, there on my own shoulders. I lay my head down upon Elmira's, and I could feel him strain under this unexplained weight. I couldn't imagine why all this rushing water and weight descended upon us.

Elmira sank to his knees, which left only part of my body and his head above water. I clung to him for dear life. He struggled, but was determined to keep me safe. I couldn't read his thoughts, for the moment was too chaotic, and I feared we both would drown. He finally rose to his feet once again, lifting me out of the water and gasping for air with every ounce of strength he could muster. His determination was his reserve strength, and we ultimately made our way to the shoreline we intended to reach. As Elmira made the final step, perhaps the most difficult, he gasped and groaned, contorting his face as he finally lifted his foot to the shore. At that precise moment, everything changed back to calm and quiet. The stream was normal, not gushing, as it was as we entered on the other side.

Elmira and I looked back and wondered what happened. He carefully removed me from his shoulder and set me on the ground. Then we heard a pleasant voice say, "It's a heavy load you carried, Elmira; yet the load from this day forward will be much greater for the one you bear so bravely."

We turned our heads toward the voice and saw an old woman dressed in red robes, sitting on a large boulder. She had a beautiful face, which barely peeked out of the hood of her robe. It was an old face, with lines and the effects of age apparent, which enhanced rather than detracted from her luminance. She waited for us to compose ourselves and respond to her straight-forward statement.

I informed her that Elmira couldn't speak physically. Then I said, "Yes, we were heavy—so heavy, did you see, dear elder? If you did, do you know why this happened?" I had already had so many lessons from the elders; I expected that she would surely know.

She smiled and replied, "I indeed saw what happened, and I have a good idea why. Your guardian was not the heavy one, child. It was you and his devotion to you was the only reason he could bear the burden you presented."

"Oh my!" I whispered, realizing the enormity of the task asked of Elmira. I finally said, "I don't want to be a burden."

The old woman nodded her head and replied, "I know. You're destined to bear many burdens for others, as you move down the road of your important life journey into your soul mission. I assure you that you are not considered a burden, nor will that ever be the case. This guardian has proven to be a true 'Christopher', or one who bears the 'Christ'," she said, as she nodded towards Elmira.

Following her gaze towards Elmira, I looked back to the lady in red and asked, "What is a 'Christopher' and a 'Christ,' beautiful lady?"

"Well, let's start with the Christ part," she replied. "To be a Christ means that one has become fully aware of their relationship to the nameless Source of all Creation; the one many refer to as God.

This Christ is then usually referred to as a 'master,' or if they have incarnated as a female they are called a 'mastra,' but for the most part, the mastras go unrecognized." She went on, saying, "Unfortunately, most of the true masters go unrecognized as well." I begged her to tell me more, so she continued, "Masters and mastras, because they are so aware of their true divine relationship to God, often take on great missions for the good of All That Is. That greater good is always connected to the knowledge of 'Onement' with the grand Mysterious Creator. These souls give more, because they are more aware of their divinity and their true relationship with the original divine intention. They understand that evolution, or soul growth, is always moving towards the Source. They help keep all creation on course, so that each particle of God can once again become 'One' with God."

I thought about the Christ beings and asked if there were many of these souls upon the 'physical playing field', as one of my early teachers called this life we experienced.

She rolled her eyes a bit, almost like there was something I wasn't getting. "They are rare indeed, these true masters," she said in a low voice, staring into my eyes to the point that I thought she was diving into my soul and merging with me, much like the dusty man did who gave me the sacred bowl. Then she began to speak again, which brought me out of the reverie, and said, "As for the 'Christopher,' this refers to the equally rare individual who has volunteered to incarnate for the sake of a Christ on the appointed Divine Mission. The Christopher is always a guardian, and their devotion is immeasurable. Without their devotion, the mission often fails," she emphasized.

"Do you mean that my Elmira is a 'Christopher'?" I asked in amazement.

"That's right, child," she said looking at me with a hint of laughter on her lovely ancient face.

"Who is the Christ that Elmira then guards?" I asked, still not understanding the full scope of the conversation, ignoring the obvious.

## The Saga-Oracle

The lady looked down at her feet and slowly slipped off her rock-seat. She walked over to me, laid both her hands on my shoulders and kneeled down so that we were face-to-face, for she was a very tall woman. She took that dive into my eyes again, and I felt the warmth of her presence within me. She spoke in a very quiet voice, saying, "Go home, Christ child, for your mother misses you. Your father longs to hold you near and dear, too. His days in this world are short."

I closed my eyes visualizing my father and mother. I could see sadness in their hearts and knew that it was partly loneliness for me; the same loneliness I felt for them as well. I must have kept my eyes closed for a while, because when I finally opened them, the lady in red was gone and Elmira was now sitting upon the rock watching me. His face was peaceful and his attitude, as always, loving. This time, however, I realized that he was awaiting my instructions. Something indeed had shifted and I began to feel responsibility to my personal authority. I knew, I alone would decide what I should do, and when I would do it, from this point forward. In a way, in the same instant, I mourned the loss of my childhood, where others were responsible for my well-being. Even when I was with the street children, there had been those who looked out for me. Now, I sensed, that would no longer be the case.

Taking my responsibility, I easily slipped into the role of directing our journey and again announced to Elmira, "It's time to move towards home," and we began to moving in the direction of my homeland. I instinctively knew which way to go. We had walked quite a distance, when the rest of the communication with the ancient wise woman came back to me. She had called me 'Christ child.' Surely, I thought, she must be wrong, for I couldn't be a master. I had a difficult time accepting the confirmation, I probably knew at the soul level, was true. I still rejected the idea that I was somehow a master already; after all, they were my teachers. I could accept that, yet my conscious mind was not ready to go further.

I had no doubt that Elmira was worthy of being a 'Christopher,' however, and I felt honored that he took time for the likes of me, when he was such an important guardian.

I couldn't wait to be home again. The thought of reunion with my loved ones made my steps cover ground with more ease than ever before. As I realized that my feet were gliding easily, and the path seemed smoother, I noticed Elmira and I both were bobbing along in an odd rhythm like joyful children.

# VISITING THE TEMPLE ELDERS
Chapter Sixteen

My childhood might seem as a fairy-tale, but remember that children don't know the limits that adults have placed on physicality. They naturally see the fairy-folk, and much of what is not believed, as real in their life experience. Some call this childhood period my 'lost years', but they weren't lost to me, only to many of those who would later claim they knew me in the records of time. I believe that to truly know someone, you must understand the child within them. If you could see how they traveled through their early molding years, you would understand them from a broader perspective. Since my early years were spent away from my homeland, there weren't many from that region that really knew me, in a true sense. The record keepers have glossed over my young childhood, and tend to idealize and generalize my early-on experiences to their standards of understanding. They also idealized my parents' memory, especially my mother. They shaped our family as their political and social minds thought best. They decided that nothing remarkable, in those early years, happened in our family, other than the moment of my birth. All that they could envision, thus taught as truth, was a quiet bliss, in a perfect family setting.

My mother was, and still is, a sweet soul and perfect as every soul is. My father Joseph was in all ways my real earthly father, yet we were brothers; as my beloved mother was my sister, too, in the bigger picture, since we are all children of God. The mistaken concepts that surround this 'Supreme Creational Being' many call 'God' are the root of most misunderstandings and judgment. Those who would separate beings into categories, some worthy and some not, have a concept of a God that they shape to fit their mode of thinking. Spirituality formed into religion creates many opportunities for leaders to 'control', rather than lead, through coloring the truth to suit their agendas. I didn't want to create a new religion. I just wanted to bring some awareness into the one I was born to. But that would come later. As I walked toward home I was thinking of spiritual ideas and sorting what I had learned in my few short years in this sojourn. I wasn't yet sure what the scope of my responsibility would be.

My early childhood training was a natural process, and not part of a larger group or class, or even tied to a particular religion; thus the concepts I learned, I integrated into self-understandings. That was the intent of those who nurtured me. Thanks to great master teachers, I had a fully-active open mind and a compassionate heart. Without these two equalizing factors, I wouldn't have been able to walk along and ponder the spiritual issues as I did. I would have asked a priest and taken his word as God's word.

I believe that the most important lesson of all creation is the simple concept of 'ONE'. It was almost too simple to grasp, I realized, as I pondered this great question. Some call the ONE I speak of as 'All That Is'. Some describe the ONE as 'First Prime Creator'. Most indigenous people don't try to explain the Supreme Being at all, just referring to this ONE as the 'Great Mystery'. I have found walking was the best way to do deep thinking. I was sorting out the wisdom my master teachers had shared, along with things I always knew.

Humans forever ponder the big question of how did we come to be? The other beings, animal kingdom and such, just accept themselves and explore the moment in time they incarnated within. Even so, I'm human after all, even if many believe otherwise. Thus, I let my mind wander within the 'why' question in my walking trance. In my mind's eye, I could see a huge ball of brilliant light. I saw it expand and explode with little parts of the brilliant light filling the dark void, but even as the explosion took place the brilliant source was never diminished, with each spark still part of the luminous ball of light. I reflected on why God would create this way. I realized that the very act of creation is God discovering Divine Self through parts of the ONE sent out to experience all sorts of situations, and still find the God therein. That is the essence of ONEMENT, which many of my teachers mentioned. As I walked along, it was like puzzle pieces falling into place. All my teachers had given me pieces of the mystery, but it was far from complete and I was seeing the larger picture merge piece by piece in my long walk.

I was entering my tenth year, when I decided to go home; though by the time I arrived home, I would be in my eleventh year. I consider this the beginning of my responsibility phase. I was more aware than most children my age would normally be, and already my purpose was weighing heavily upon my mind. Always advanced in my mental development, it was the teaching of the masters that made me so reflective at such a young age. Whether they realize it or not, children pass through the 11-year-portal[61] of responsibility. I was no different than any other child, just stepping up to the portal with a lot more preparation than most and a little sooner, being, 'almost' 11-years-old.

There are many ways to read the road signs of one's life. Often those that do so are criticized for reading too much into too little. Criticism is a way that antiforce holds back natural evolution. Your entire sojourn is mapped out, in terms of possible routes; you might take to your soul-goal. Those routes have many signs along the way. The number 11 is one such sign and always representative of a portal, or a doorway, that lies between the two upright pillars[62] (11). It's always a transition place. Even as you enter a building going from the outside in, or from one room to the other, the two uprights of the doorways offer a portal so you can

---

[61] This is the age the children begin to realize right from wrong, and their compassionate heart awakens 11 is always a portal and like a doorway, it offers entrance to a new space and place

[62] Symbolic of equalized energetic modes-masculine/feminine. Often the two pillars are present in temples and sacred spaces to indicate the sacred portal.

transition into a different space. This principle is repeated in nature, too, repeatedly. At the age of 11, one usually soulfully walks through the pillars of life experience and begins to sense their soul-mission. True, there are sweet souls who agree to come for a brief period, sometimes, for one reason or another, they just change their mind and depart at a younger age. They, too, have a soul mission, but what I reference is related to those who have come to mature into adulthood. Age 11, then, is the point when life changes. It is a point of passage into the responsibility of life at all levels.

I grasped my responsibility quite naturally, when I told Elmira we were going home, even though I hadn't yet walked through the 11-year-portal. It wasn't a conscious decision, rather a spontaneous reaction to my own inner guidance.

Children are well-balanced individuals energy-wise, in that they don't determine one energy modality over another when they move through their early years, unless forced to do so by their parents. They may be acting feminine and be introspective, exploring the inner realms, or practicing nurturing and such; or they may explore their masculine, external action-based modes for a while, which naturally includes learning to be a protector, and other active pursuits. For the most part, at first nothing is expected of them. Then little by little their parents instill upon the children their own attitudes and priorities, which all too often, teach the child to separate their identity into being 'boyish' or 'girlish'. If they don't meet their parents' expectations, they are often considered failures, and the children suffer their entire lifetime due to that judgment. Frequently, that suffering reverberates out and affects others as well.

The old saying, 'Separate the wheat from the chaff,' is symbolic of how social attitudes place judgment on all aspects of life. In families, this way of thinking caused separation and judgment, especially regarding their children who suffered an inner-separation. As I compared families' attitudes to this old adage, I visualized the two parts of the same plant. The wheat became separated into worthy and less worthy (wheat and chaff). In the case of children, the boys were seen as the wheat and the girls as the chaff. As I thought about this, walking along toward home, I visualized the chaff part of the wheat. It may not be the part you want to bake bread with (the grain), but it is no less worthy, for it supported the grain, sprouting, growing first and without it, bread couldn't be made. I could visualize more vibrantly within the mode of metaphor, and I was struggling with the very thing I came to change–attitudes.

I continued on thinking about the wheat. For the most part, the task relegated to the chaff is: first sprouting, then support the growth, and then producing the grain. When that duty is done, it becomes bedding for animals and people, or roofing material, or mixed in with the mud to make stronger adobe walls for homes and temples. It had so many uses, after it had 'birthed and dropped its holy seed,' that I wondered why the old adage of separation referenced it. The saying commonly meant 'separate good from bad,' but obviously that wasn't true in most places they applied this so-called wisdom. I wondered why the richness of the chaff was not recognized and respected as much as the grain. Thinking like this became the basis of my parables later in life, as I realized the power of words and symbols, and how people use and abuse them.

I couldn't get this idea of 'wheat' and 'chaff' out of my mind. It kept coming back again and again, when I thought I had mulled it over completely. The act of non-resistance that meditation offers is like a river undammed. It must flow. So I thought more about the metaphor of wheat. The chaff was quietly supportive, I surmised. It was mainly thought of as something to stuff mattresses or bed animals down with, after producing the treasured 'seed'. That stimulated my mind to explore the modes of 'night-sleeping' and 'awake-walking'. Sleeping is a time of feminine dominance,[63] just as the actively-awake time is thought of as masculine dominance;[64] but that doesn't mean women are just sleepers and only men are walkers in the light of the day, even if some attitudes are rooted in that corrupted view. The idea, that the feminine is passive and asleep, and the masculine is active, I found, was often

---

[63] A receptive mode
[64] A active mode

beneath the surface in most communities, and the root to suppressing women. When it is understood that every being ever created (animate and inanimate) has both masculine and feminine energies (positive and negative), and naturally shifts from being introspective to extrospective,[65] as they move through their experience of physicality, dissolves bias attitudes.

Metaphors, or stories, began to make truth easier to sort and understand, as I walked and meditated. The divine plan echoed in all creation, I realized. Even so, I noticed that the most humble of animals and people carried the greatest burdens, like the little over-laden donkeys and countless other animals used for heavy work. Children and women seemed burdened in many ways, as well. I thought about why that would be so. Was its God's will or man's will?

Elmira and I finally arrived in my homeland, which some refer to as 'the holy land'. It was holy to many, because it was the site of early civilization. Such a place has an ingrained vibrational energy that invites those within it to either rise to great heights, soul-wise, or likewise, sink very low. This place of my birth offered both opportunities in abundance. It's not a place of moderation, rather a place of extremes, as it still is.

I reached my home, a Nazarite village, which was somewhat set apart from the other towns in the area, due to the difference in mind-set of those in the sect. I walked into the village unrecognized. People looked my way with little concern; no doubt the energy that surrounded me was similar to theirs. Unconsciously, soul-to-soul, no one goes unrecognized, and my presence, which was in harmony with their own, didn't disturb anyone. Elmira had changed, too. He wasn't as stocky in build as he once was, now leaner and looking smaller due to the way we had lived for the past six years. We walked along the road that passed the temple, where the elders gathered each day to converse and discuss God, who they believed they knew well. I could hear the murmurs of a discussion, going on within the walls of the temple building.

---

[65] Looking outside oneself

*Jeshua's Song*

I noticed a few women, patiently sitting outside the ornate carved temple doors, like lotus flowers on the ground, quietly waiting for someone or something. I stopped, stooped down and asked one wise-looking elder woman, why she was not within sharing her wisdom.

"I'm not permitted to be present," she said, in an exasperated voice, as if I should know this, for heaven's sake. "This place is far too sacred for the likes of me," she replied. I noticed a slight twinkling smirk of irony cross her wise old face.

"How can it be that those within these walls seek wisdom, when she sits right here at the doorstep of the temple unrecognized," I asked. I wasn't trying to charm her. I simply was being honest and hadn't yet developed the ability of tact.

The old woman's face lit up, and her eyes danced at this statement. "The village, I regret to say, due to the closeness of the outer world, has caught the disease of corrupted attitudes of exclusion, dear boy." She then looked away, telling me in her body language that the conversation was done. It must have been painful for her to think of the exclusion she was subjected to.

I looked up at Elmira, and he indicated that he was as confused as I was about the situation. I hadn't expected to find this attitude in my own village.

I rose and said to Elmira, "I need a few moments, before I go home, dear friend," and I entered the portal of the temple.

Upon my entrance into the inner sanctum, the men stopped their conversation, realizing that there was a stranger in their midst. They paused, because once they had convened, they seldom had anyone dare to enter the sacred inner-sanctuary, much less a mere boy.

I nodded as my eyes met theirs and asked permission to join them. Astounded that a boy would be so bold and ask such a thing caused some irritability among them. However, the leader who I recognized from long ago–the same man who had sent me away–was present, looking much older, but still holding authority within this group. He sat towards the back and watched the debate, more than entered it. He recognized me, but said nothing about knowing who I was. However, he spoke, which in itself commanded attention; since he never bothered to speak, unless there was something profoundly important to say. "Let the lad have his say," he said. "After all, it took courage to boldly enter and ask for acceptance." After some haggling, they agreed that I could join them, just this once, and took up their conversation where they left off, ignoring me, the little uninvited listener.

While I am indeed a good listener, I am also good at seeing through smoke screens. This place was smoky indeed. They were discussing how man and earth are related, and how man is superior, and earth and all creation is there for his purpose. That was a bit much for me. I didn't understand how the elder one, so wise and yet looking so tired, could sit there and allow the conversation to continue such a ridiculous concept. What I didn't yet understand was that true leaders often permit those they lead to take side roads, so they know where the dead ends are. Unfortunately, this group was getting quite comfortable heading toward a dead end.

I am a spontaneous individual, even though I can remain quiet for a long time–as I demonstrated in my silent year–I just spoke up, saying, "Excuse me," several times, trying to get those present to allow me a comment. Finally, the old elder, who had heard me the first time, again spoke to the others, who were oblivious to my request, saying, "Let the boy speak!" He actually shouted, and it was understood that this was not a request, but a demand. Several of the men huffed and puffed with self-importance. They were clearly aggravated at such an interruption, but because they respected their leader, they looked my way and had an expression of, 'Oh well, get on with it, so we can get back to our important conversation.'

I smiled, accepting the opportunity and asked them, "Why don't you bring in the one who is best able to answer the question of the relationship of earth to man?" They looked back and forth at each other, thinking that all the experts were already present.

I went on to explain, "The wise old woman, who sits at the doorstep of this temple, could answer that question in a heartbeat, yet you would take the entire day and argue the point, trying to get your conclusion to fit your attitude." To say that remark didn't meet with approval is an understatement. The men repeated over and over that a woman would just cause disruption with her silly ideas.

I couldn't believe that my village people, who were supposed to be well-balanced in attitudes and relationship with all creation, were so close-minded. I wasn't ready to give up and went into the lesson of the balance of the energies within creation, much like what I had been thinking along the path home, but I explained even more. It never dawned on me that a mere 11-year-old boy probably shouldn't be offering lessons to the priests. It was close to the summer solstice when I visited the temple and there's no doubt that entering the temple was my actual 11-year-portal of passage into responsibility. I didn't give it much thought, but as I reminisce, I know that I officially entered into my accountability that day.

My lessons, as a very young child in the high mountain place, along with my parents' teachings, were my philosophical foundation. As I spoke, I kept referring to the earth as 'Mother' or 'Tara,'[66] which is the high mountain peoples' word for 'Mother of All'. That at first confused the elders. Once they accepted that there are many ways to refer to the same thing, they seemed to follow my train of thought, even as they struggled with the importance of the 'Mother of All' concept. I had to use stories to illustrate what they couldn't grasp, as I tried to explain my thoughts to them. It felt like only a short time within the chambers had passed, yet it had been hours, and the sun was setting. Finally finishing my perspective, just before I left, the old wise-woman was at last invited into the sanctuary and asked to explain the relationship between man and earth previously discussed. I thought, at least progress was accomplished in this deep conversation, and they were allowing a woman's voice to be heard.

---

[66] To the Tibetans "Tara" is the mother of all Goddesses

She simply said, "Earth is our Mother; sky our Father. We are the children, yet we are all one creation, which expands far beyond what we know as earth and sky. Creation will give of itself, or take for itself, that which it needs to find its 'Onement'. We as humans will take what we need from the earth. She will take what she needs from us, too, as all beings must. What is taken must always be respected, and only taken after permission is granted from the giver, be it Mother Earth or any of the beings, she shares herself with. To take without permission is a terrible act of aggression and disrespect, which ultimately destroys both the taker and the giver. Likewise, the other side of the coin, my dear gentlemen, is that humans must give to those who need, just as our Earth Mother gives of her bounty, her gardens, her mountains and her waters to us. Our Father, the sky, gives as well; he gives breath; he gives sky water (condensation or rain) so that our thirst is quenched, and of course, he gives us the light we need to grow and thrive within. He gives the sun a place to be and shine its life-giving warmth down upon us, too. It is always an equally-respectful give-and-take Divine Dance," she said. "Achieving that balance is the sacrifice and blessing of all creation." She paused, to see if they were following her. I wasn't sure they were, because people often only heard what they wanted to hear. However, she continued on, "God created the scale of justice, not to be tilted, but to be level and equal. When the balance is not honored, it is cause for great sadness for the ONE and all It's aspects. Thus Divine Justice is not served, and the Divine Intention is not achieved. If justice doesn't find its balance, then Divine Respect isn't offered, nor holy gifts appreciated. God is not a destroyer," she said with conviction, as she looked at everyone in the room. "God is a Creator." At this, she folded her hands in the prayerful position saying, "May the God in me honor the God in you," and she departed. I thought, "Wow! She knows the prayer of the mastras."

The elder leader was almost overcome with emotion at hearing her wise words, but I don't think the others had accepted the message. They sat as if dazed and didn't have much to say. Then I heard a commotion outside of the temple and heard my mother's sweet voice, frantically screaming, "I don't care if women aren't allowed in the temple, Joseph. I know my child is in there, and I shall find him now!" She burst forth into the dark inner-chambers, which were draped in rich tapestries floor to ceiling, and found me calmly sitting there in the midst of the elders. She ran to me and threw her arms around me, sobbing great tears of joy and relief. My father followed her. I noticed his face was not dry either, as he carefully kneeled down, too. He took me in his frail old arms along with my mother. I believe it is impossible for anyone not to be moved by a reunion of parents and child so long separated. I could feel everyone rejoicing and recognition began to dawn on most of those present, that this was Joseph and Mary's little boy, who was sent away, now returned.

That meeting of the elders was much different than ever before, I like to think. Each took away some degree of expanded wisdom. It was not my doing, however. I was just being me, asking questions and offering my 11-year-old opinion. It was the wise-woman who knew the answer to the question they posed, and shared it. The great rejoicing love of my parents opened the councils' heart portal; so instead of the message going to their heads, only to swim to the point of drowning and being lost again in a sea of mistaken logic, it took root in some of the elders' hearts. When the head rules the heart, compassion is lost and the essence of the truth of God disappears in the fog. Some of the fog had been lifted, and I was delighted.

My family and I rose and left. My sister and brother had heard that my parents were in the temple. We lived in a small community, and news traveled fast. They ran to the holy meeting place, too. People had heard my mother shouting my name, as she ran through the village, as well. The fact that she had entered the temple, without asking special permission, was enough to cause a stir among the village people and the news traveled like a tidal wave.

My family missed me as much as I missed them. My parents, brother, sister and I walked home very slowly. Father was too frail to walk fast. Through all the emotion, my mother reached her hand out to Elmira and pulled him along with us. He was as much a member of this family, as any of us.

# A DIFFICULT FAREWELL
## Chapter Seventeen

I loved being home again. Elmira seemed to drift off from my life, after my visit to the temple in the village. I thought I could see his shadow from time to time, but wasn't sure if it was simply wishful thinking again. He had been my constant companion for most of my life, even though there were times when he kept a low profile, and I wondered if he was nearby. The thought occurred that he might still be watching. I often hoped that was the case, for I missed his silent reassuring presence and preferred to believe he was somewhere ever on guard, still being a Christopher, though I wasn't certain I was worthy of a Christopher's keep.

At my first family meal after my return home, we were seated on the floor of our home before a slightly elevated table, which was our customary way of taking meals. We were all excited and everyone wanted to talk at once. My father, looking frail in his elder years, was showing the effects of aging. He seemed smaller to me, or maybe I was just bigger. He was still active within the Nazarite council of the village. My mother, now more mature, for she was so young at my birth, was ever beautiful to my adoring eyes. How she loved all of her children so completely and unconditionally was amazing. There was never a doubt from anyone of us, that she loved us totally. My brother James was about the same size as myself upon my return home. I was told that the villagers often thought he was me, and in order to keep my presence safely private, those presumptions were allowed to play out as they would. He didn't mind, he told me. I watched him closely when he spoke of such times, to see if that 'robe of mine' he wore from time to time, when he allowed people to think I was he, bothered him; after all, he was James, and I was Jesus, or Esa, as my parents called me. I could see no sorrow or aggravation within him, as we allowed confused identities.

My sister was still a delightful sprite and a great comfort to my mother. All she wanted was to walk in Mother's footsteps, literally. Little did I know that she was already being groomed to follow in the priestess-tradition. All the advanced training, that we children were given, was kept private, and we had no idea of what the others were learning, nor did we inquire. We simply accepted that our parents would do what was best for each child, according to their talents and interests.

My half-brother and sisters also attended that first meal, but didn't bring their spouses or children; they respected the need I might have for an intimate reunion with my immediate family. Needless to say, it was a great homecoming for me and a time I will never forget, especially when Joseph[67], my elder half-brother, came in, scooped me up in his arms and whispered his greeting of "welcome home, little master." He must have been emotionally moved, because he got tears in my ear. Mother laughed so hard, I thought she would fall over. When my brother Joseph called me master, I thought of the sage along the path, who gave me the sacred bowl. He had called me a master, too. And the old priestess by the raging water had hinted at such a thing, as well. I had never been told in my years away, that this was the case for sure, even as the word 'master' slipped into the conversation from time to time, so I was confused. It's something you must discover for yourself. However, I knew, since my visit to the Nazarite temple, that something greater than myself came through as I spoke with the priests. It was as if my mouth belonged to me, but the words came from a sacred place. It was a powerful feeling, but not a feeling of power. Even the deep thinking along the path home seemed like it was something sacred flowing through me, to ponder and sort. I had mentally and heart-fully processed the concepts as they popped into my head, due to my experiences with my teachers. The distance melted away, as I walked and meditated. Now I know I was being prepared for responsibility to my soul-mission as rabbi, the teacher, later.

I felt only love and acceptance from my family. The elderly high priest, who had sent me away years ago, came to visit us a few days later. My parents were concerned, because James and I looked so much alike. They worried that if we were seen together, how could he be me, or I he? They mentioned their concern to

---

[67] Later to be known as Joseph of Arimathea and often confused as Jeshua's uncle

Jacobite and asked advice, because James had allowed many to think that he was me. Confusion was a two-edged sword. One side disconnected judgmental assumption; the other side invited it. If James and I appeared together now, we feared it might invite the speculation we would rather avoid.

"Well," Jacobite said, as he approached me and got down on his knees to be more at my level, "our little sage is home and so mature for such a small one, eh?" I wasn't all that tall yet, and I was a bit sensitive about it. He embraced me and kissed the top of my head, which was the customary greeting by those who were of our inner-circle of friends, family and protectors. I felt blessed.

"Hail, high priest," I said with a smile, looking at his wise old face. He didn't stay kneeling long and rose, since it was hard to stay in that position in his advanced years. "Can I finally stay home with my family now?" I asked, as I helped him to his feet, hoping not to be sent away once more and knowing full well, that this man might have summoned me through mind-speak, and his directive could just as easily send me away again.

He gazed down at me, appeared to be thinking deeply and said, "We'll see, lad. We'll see." Then he looked at my parents and the expression on their faces showed their great need and desire to have me with them in the family home.

Father said, "Isn't there some way we can keep our son near and safe? I fear I'm not long to be in this world. I need my beloved wife and children with me now, close by, so I can leave in peace." He hung his head and said, "I'm such a needy soul, and I apologize for my lack of courage and commitment."

The elder high priest just smiled, patted father on the shoulder and said, "I wish there were more like you, dear friend. Your courage and commitment are so far beyond what most could muster. I assure you–you are not needy or lacking of anything." As father looked at the priest, Jacobite said, "I'll see what I can do."

In the Nazarite village, the high priest was the one with the last word on everything; yet he was not a dictator, usually allowing the council to decide most matters of importance, and he simply monitored them. However, some decisions and intentions were kept within an extremely limited circle of people, especially pertaining to the emerging masters and mastras, which proved successful, even as the outcome was yet to be determined. I say the outcome was yet to be determined, because even though the intentional children emerged, their reception was less than divinely greeted. Children like me seemed to be a threat, mostly to those in the outer villages, who followed a strict religious dogma, or those that governed as regents for the Romans. They didn't want change. They wanted to control the situation within their realm for the sake of their own agendas. Anyone who would shake their towers-of-power was a threat to their false perception of security. They felt secure by keeping the populace overpowered within a state of fear; they could be controlled that way, for ignorance and fear easily became a way to reinforce slavery. Sadly, the prison they knew within the state of fear they perceived in their minds, was safer than the freedom they didn't know. The overpowered became pawns in the fear-structure system and were as much of a threat to the gifted children as their masters were, having been convinced that to agree with fear was their security.

Thus, most of the special children disappeared. Some were sent to safe havens. Some went away from home one day never to return, or were mysteriously taken from their beds in the night. Many were blinded and maimed to the point that they became mentally altered, for remember, it was the eyes that pierced the soul and exposed internal corrupted attitudes. Those warped attitudes were inner-demons in control of minds, which closed off compassionate hearts. It was evident that even within our enlightened village; there were some who weren't as loyal to the cause of balance, as they led others to believe. The goal of equality, united by love, may sound idealistic, but why not aspire to such an ideal? If you can imagine it, you can achieve it, my mountain masters and the old healer had taught me. The controllers (those who ruled by fear) taught that it was human nature to sin. They taught that procreation was a sin to bear, too, which shaped legends to conform to the fear agenda. Our Nazarite sect originally believed in Divine Balance, and that all creation, including humans, are naturally blessed and good. It was what they did with that goodness (God-ness) that mattered. To that end, they planned for the masters and the mastras to come through and plant the seeds of love and peace, so that goodness, not evil, would prevail.

I didn't realize that I was nearly the last survivor of the so-called 'special children,' born through the intentional actions of those within the project. Even so, I was beginning to understand, that my purpose in this life was destined to be far-reaching and important. Jacobite, after conferring with my parents, decided to wait and see what people assumed when they saw me out and about with James and the family. After hearing me at the temple, I think he wanted to personally watch me for a while and see how I progressed among those I was called into this world to help.

I began the rapid growth spell that sneaks up on boys about my age, and my physical body began to reshape and change. Within a few short months, I became a head taller than James, yet we were the same size when we first appeared together this time home and many assumed we were twins. Later, it was understood, that I was the older brother and most thought that I was living with Joseph of Arimathea, my elder half-brother, all these years. He lived in another village and far enough away, that the people who would have noticed my absence, seldom saw one another. We didn't fill in the blanks for them; rather we just went about our business of being the sons we were born to be. This went on for several wonderful months, with my family enjoying each other and filling me in on family news that happened while I was gone. I didn't talk about my experiences at first, thinking that some of the occurrences were a bit much for even my family to believe. Instead, I slipped into my habit of telling a simple story, yet including enough details to bring life into the tale. This proved to be the best way to share the essence of my journey and bring forth the teaching I wished to share. However, I kept many of my teachings private for now, because I was just fitting those puzzle pieces together.

It was apparent that father was getting weaker and weaker. Father soon needed support to walk. He walked to the council meetings each night when his group met, supported by James and me. He said, when he had to be carried, he was done with his work therein.

## Jeshua's Song

That day arrived too soon for all of us. Father couldn't rise one morning and sent for us, including his first family children and their families as well. It took most of the day for all to arrive. As twilight approached, we were all present, quiet and supportive. We gathered around, where he was lying on his sleeping mat in our humble home's second room. We filled the space to capacity. He spoke to us in a weak whisper.

"My family and children," he said, looking at each of us separately. "I have sent for you out of a greedy need for myself. Please forgive this old man. I am soon to travel to my true heavenly home, and I want to see you just one more time, through these physical eyes, before my transition." We quietly began to weep, hearing what we dreaded to hear, yet knowing for a while now, that the time was close. He said, "Don't weep for me, beloveds. I have had a good life. My only regret is that you may have to suffer somehow for the changes we advance, through our beliefs and behaviors, as Nazarite Essenes. Even so, I know for sure, that you and your children will suffer more, if changes are not forthcoming. I have been lucky in my life and love you all equally with all my heart. I love my sons and my daughters in the same way. You are not less or more worthy, due to your birth choices, nor due to gender or birth order, and certainly not due to your mothers," he stressed. "I love both of my wives with all my heart."

Mother Mary was clearly devastated as she stood nearby, listening and watching her husband, so frail and elderly, while she still looked incredibly young. You could see the love and appreciation in her eyes, as she gazed down upon my father, lying there on his death-bed on the floor surrounded by his family.

We were all quiet, knowing that father had things to say and that his strength was waning. The time was short; nevertheless, we all dreaded the moment, even as we respected it.

"You will have to play games, children, as you protect each other. You may have to keep your relationship confusing to outsiders. Know that one within our midst could change the world for the better. However, I fear the world doesn't want to be changed. I'm

## The Saga-Oracle

not talking about our beloved Mother Earth, Tara, when I say 'world'. I speak of those that hold the reins of power upon this lovely planet,[68] thus it is the space and place Tara hosts us within, I speak of. The world is dominated by those who are controlled by blind fear; they, in turn, control through it as well, and they will kill you before they will let you take off their blinders."

He asked to see us individually, looked at me and said, "Stay, Esa, my beloved son. You are the way-shower." The others quietly left us alone. He had to gather strength to continue with what he wanted to say. "You are the hope of all creation. You must find your counterpart, just as I found your sweet mother, and together you will show the way by being a perfect example of balance in the physical." He went on whispering, "The energy of the masculine and feminine must merge, through love and knowledge of being equally worthy. Even our Nazarite group knows this, but can't practice it in the open, for fear of our wives and daughters being stoned and defiled. The fear of the feminine is the greatest source of greed and corruption known. She, the Sacred Feminine, is dishonored, even, as 'She' is the only divine portal into this physical realm. Before you were born, Esa, your mother and I volunteered to 'intend' to offer a portal for a master to come to work on this project, as did others of like-mind. To my knowledge, you are the only one left, able to fulfill the mission, from our original plan. You will surely suffer greatly, as you try to help the blind see. For this, I grieve. I'm not sure I can give such a precious one as you up for sacrifice, while still in the flesh. Before I go, I want you to know that, even as your mother and I knew you could create castles out of sand that are grand to the point of astounding us, we know more so, that you can create castles within hearts far grander." That was the first mention of my experience by the wisdom well. I hadn't shared that episode with anyone. My parents' involvement in my life was more far-reaching than I had guessed. "Know, dear son, that I leave now, not to be away from you, but so that I can be closer to you."

---

[68] The Essenes knew that Mother Earth was a planet, as did the Magi and understood that other planets existed

## Jeshua's Song

I was broken-hearted and felt myself wilting down upon the deathbed of my beloved father. Leaning over him, I said, "I don't want you to go. I can heal you again," and threw my arms around the now-shrunken body that seemed like a small bag of bones. "Father," I cried, "let me try to bring your body back to health, and you can stay with us. I can't bear to lose you. I just got home."

He looked into my eyes and whispered, "I can't bear to be here in the physical, where you must suffer. I'm too old for that kind of sorrow. In my soul-body, I'll see past the suffering, and maybe be of more help to you. I promise to be a guide to you and to meet you, when you step through the veil I now approach as I leave this old body behind. Let me go, child, as you must. I ask for your blessing, little master."

"How can I bless you, father?" I asked. "I'm no master. I'm not worthy to be one, and if I was, I would make you whole once again, so you could enjoy your family for a long time to come."

Father looked at me and said, "Master,"–I didn't grasp his statement–"Master," he said again. I looked and nodded my head to acknowledge that I heard him. "Master, I am not worthy to be your father, yet you have chosen me. You will free me from this life I no longer can tolerate; because if you were not a master, you would not understand that I must be free. If you were simply an entity with advanced knowledge of healing, you would heal me whether I liked it or not. It would fulfill you to do so–even if that healing would keep me in this prison of a body a while longer. Your urge to heal would be stronger than your wisdom to concede. But you are a true master, and you know that you must let me go."

Knowing he was right, I buried my head in his shoulder and cried my sorrow; for the last time, I melted into his gentle arms.

I'm not sure if the others heard all of this or not. I was too caught up in the emotional conversational moment to notice and his voice was a mere whisper. I remember kissing my father's cheek and being led away, while the others visited one at a time, and also emerged from the deathbed with sorrowful tears streaming down their cheeks. Finally, he was left alone with our mother, who I could hear weeping for a while, then she fell silent. We waited outside our little abode doorway for a long time, listening to the silence, holding each other, all wishing we didn't have to say goodbye to the one who had been such a loving father to us. Even so, we knew that he wished to go now and in his various roles, as father, husband and leader in our community, he had given full measure.

Finally, my brother Joseph said, "I think I'd better check on our parents." He slipped back through the doorway, and then reappeared again almost immediately. He had a slight smile on his face and whispered "shush," as he put his finger up to his lips, and indicated that we should follow him. We quietly followed and found our mother and father together under the blankets on the mat, wrapped in each other's arms in a loving embrace, like parents do in private tender moments. Mother was sleeping now, for we could see the gentle rise and fall of her body as she peacefully rested. Father was sleeping as well, but his body no longer rose and fell with the breath of physical life. He left this world in mother's arms. Later she told us that he was greeted by Enlina, his first wife, whom mother saw clearly, as she came to help our father across the threshold of death. She was grateful that someone he loved so dearly came for him. Mother never held jealousy or uncertainty regarding this beloved first wife of father's. Enlina's family had treated her, as if she was their own daughter, when she came to their door just before my birth. As we gazed down on our two parents, we knew our life was forever changed. Our silence, as we allowed her to rest, confirmed that we honored their marriage and their divine love. We waited quietly so that she could rest as long as she desired, one more time, in the arms of her beloved husband.

# THE BLUE EGG OF DESTINY
Chapter Eighteen

After my father passed on, our lives changed drastically. We no longer had the same privileges we once enjoyed, when father held a seat on the council. It surprised us that, before the new day dawned, after father's passing, there were those who made it known that things now changed. Some on the council resented father, thinking his ideas of equality and respect for the women too dangerous to entertain. The hatred for the sacred feminine was like a demon that devoured men's minds and closed their hearts, their own sacred feminine-center. It had spread like a disease, and sadly, it was infecting our community.

This infection caused a return to some old rules from long ago that were restrictive and unfair. Widows didn't have the same rights as married women, even in our supposed forward-thinking peaceful sect and our poor mother was told that she could not go to the well, until the wives and maidens had taken their water first. I wondered how anyone could be so cruel as to inform my mother of such a rule, even before she had laid her husband to rest within his tomb. I wasn't aware of this tradition and was surprised that our Nazarite village followed it, since it was clearly the way of the judgmental outer society. I had thought my village was beyond such attitudes. Wasn't that why they had separated themselves, so that poisonous thinking would not taint us?

I had often seen my mother take the hand of a widow and walk her to the well, allowing her to draw up her precious water first. Being gone so much, I hadn't realized just how brave mother was. I thought this was simply her way, not understanding that she was reaching further in the gesture than I imagined. There were other privileges denied as well, I learned. My mother could no longer wait near the doorway of the council chambers with the other women, nor could she directly speak to a council member. Rather, she had to speak with his wife and ask her to give her husband the message; or she could speak to another man, if women were present, and ask him to relay the message to the council. Usually, men preferred not to carry such messages for women, however. Other men took offense at a widow woman's boldness and the man who would promote her cause, didn't fare much better. It was expected that mother would wear a black robe for the rest of her life, and it was forbidden for her to show any outward expressions of joy, smiling included. A widow was supposed to be miserable for the entire days of her life, because without her husband, she had nothing to live for, thus 'was nothing' in the social mindset. My heart ached for my mother, still so young and beautiful.

Hadn't she suffered enough? She seemed more forgiving than me and accepted her role with grace and dignity.

Mother told me to enjoy a regular childhood now. She trusted me to do as I chose, in and around our home and within the community. I helped her with the chores as much as I could; but really, I ran wild having fun with the other children, finally free to be a playful child. I was fascinated with the girls, not having much contact with them until now. I couldn't understand how they could be considered inferior to the boys, since in our games, they beat us regularly, especially in the strategy game we called, 'Mysterious Visitor.' In this game we would place items in and around each other's homes; when they were found (by us of course since we were the game players), we would go about the task of finding out who mysteriously put the item there and why.

One day I found a gourd lying on my doorstep, which had been hollowed out, with a hole carefully carved in it. Upon the gourd was an expertly-carved image of a dove gracefully in flight, with the wings wrapping around the hole-opening. I noticed it was quite a good carving, too, so my first clue was that someone had taken a great amount of time and skill to make this mystery item. That alone eliminated most of the boys in the neighborhood who were part of this game-playing, since they wouldn't have taken the time to carefully execute such a mystery gourd. So I concentrated on the girls as possible 'mystery visitors.' I decided that someone careful and thoughtful, and probably gentle, would have carved the image of a dove. But why the gentle dove, I pondered? I surmised that the dove was often given in sacrifice at the temples, especially in the outside community, and that poor people had to use their last shekels to purchase such a sacrifice when the priests demanded one, which they nearly always did. Clearly, the gourd spoke of an innocent sacrifice. Being carved on the humble gourd, however, it seemed that the poor person's sacrifice was as holy as the bird itself, since gourds and doves were plentiful and obtainable to nearly everyone. The women often made birdhouses out of them, and this looked like one. I loved these games and usually was the first to solve the mystery, but this seemed a bit more difficult than most had been.

I didn't notice at first that there was something inside, until I began to walk around with the mystery item and felt something rolling inside. I gently shook the gourd to see what would emerge and a beautiful blue egg-shaped stone fell out. It was the most intense shade of blue I had ever seen, bluer than the sky and more aqua than the sea. It was the color of both the sky and the water blended perfectly, but much more saturated with pure color. I wondered who would put such a treasure inside one of our mystery items. The stone egg was so realistic, that until I held it, I probably would think it ready to hatch. The egg was the deciding clue for me. I was drawn to a quiet girl, about my age and found her sitting on the ground not too far from my home. I said, "Traleanea, my clues bring me to you, peaceful one." She seldom spoke to us children, but always seemed to be close by, interacting on the fringes of our games. She usually was sitting with a blue egg-shaped stone in her hand, which she rolled over and over, but no one had ever gotten a good look at it. I showed her the gourd.

She looked up at me, smiled sweetly and said, "I can't understand why you would think I planted a mystery upon your doorstep, Esa." That was the first time I had heard her utter a complete sentence. It also didn't escape my attention that she called me by the name only my family used, and she no longer had the blue stone egg in her hand.

"Well," I replied, "for starters, how would you know that the mystery item was found on my doorstep?" I fancied myself quite the solver of mysteries.

"It was just a figure of speech, Esa," she replied, using the family name again, yet still not acknowledging if I was correct or not and coyly teasing me by not confirming or denying my suspicions.

She stood up, but I still had to look down at her; I was now taller since my growth spell than many boys my age, and she was a tiny one. I said, "This mystery item is a gourd." She laughed, because that wasn't exactly a great revelation, since I had it in my hand, and it was quite obvious. I ignored the teasing chuckle she enjoyed and went on, "Anyone might have left such a thing, that's true," and I smiled back at her, "but the hole is so carefully made and the natural contents of the gourd have been expertly and cleanly extracted. That, it seems to me, eliminates the boys, since few have the patience for such delicate, fine work."

I stood, turning the object over and over in my hand and commented further, "The shape of the gourd reminds me of the sacred womb." I guess that was a bit forward of me to say in the presence of a female, for Traleanea blushed and looked away. I ignored her embarrassment, since I didn't yet know that in polite society such things were not discussed. I was inexperienced in delicate female matters, so continued, "But the blue egg that the gourd contained, along with the carefully carved dove on the exterior, are what brought me to you."

"Oh," she said, still not giving anything away.

"I've noticed the mark of the dove on your garments," I remarked, "as well as upon your mother's robes." I became aware of this at the well one day, when I was getting water for my mother, who is not permitted to get water when she pleases now, and Traleanea and her mother were there. I omitted that I had also noticed them on the inner hems of my own mother's clothing. She looked somewhat alarmed and I realized that the embroidered dove shouldn't be a topic of open conversation.

"Don't worry, little girl," I playfully said, "my mother has one as well, inside the hem of her robe, too, and I understand that this is not to be discussed." She seemed a bit relieved at this point, but anxious at the same time, watching me and my response carefully. "Which confuses me," I continued, "why would you replicate the dove, knowing that it might be recognized and revealed?"

She was beginning to show signs of taking responsibility for the mystery and looked like she was ready to confess. She picked up a stick and drew a beautiful rendition of a dove in the sand, as if forming her thoughts first in the artwork, before she spoke them.

I looked at her in bewilderment. She went on to say, "There are among us certain remnants of the priestesses who have prayed and hoped that the dignity of the Sacred Feminine would one day be restored within the communities. I'm but a young one, and my mother told me that there are some lucky enough to be educated at priestess places, hidden away now in the mists. Nevertheless, due to the attitudes within our community, and even greater in the outer communities, I couldn't go to such a learning place. So my mother and a few trusted sisters educated me. Our mission is ever the same–peace and unity. However, that mission, according to my sister-trainers, is against the will of those who are determined to hold control through the power of separation. Unfortunately, even within this community of late, the battle rages. We, of the Order of the Doves,[69] would die for the sake of peace, but we are reluctant to harm or maim anyone to accomplish our greatest desire. Even so, it seems the opposite side of this coin is those who desire to control and separate don't hold the same intentions or guidelines as we do, and they will do anything to keep the power they hold. Thus, according to my sisters, they use fear to intimidate and to gain what they want. Those who don't accept their thinking are eliminated, through rejection, or murder. I was told that the dove is magic, a symbol of the Sacred Feminine, and is visible only to those who are of a peaceful mindset. I also learned that to kill it for sacrifice or food is ultimately the dove's choice. It chooses to help us all learn, that peace is perfect in both its giving and taking form."

I looked at the dove carved on the gourd again, and saw how beautiful it was, there, so clearly incised. Who wouldn't be moved by it? I thought. "I will have to think about why a beautiful bird such as the dove, must die to demonstrate the perfection of peace," I said, "but why give it to me?"

"Because you are gentle, Mary's boy, and I was told to watch you, and if I recognized something special in you, that I was to offer you the 'Egg of Destiny'[70]," she explained, as she smoothed out the drawing she had made in the sand.

---

[69] Secret priestess society that protects and serves the Sacred Feminine and promotes peace

[70] A petrified egg that the priestess cult believed was the symbol of possible divine energetic balance

Just then, the rest of the gang we played our game with found me and asked if I had found a mystery to solve. I nodded my head yes and showed them the gourd.

Interesting, one of the boys said as he plucked it from my grasp. "Looks like a place for birds to make a nest." I still held the blue egg-stone in my hand and had forgotten it, until he mentioned birds. I looked at Traleana and could sense she didn't want me to reveal the stone. She had a pleading look in her eye. I slightly nodded to her to reassure her that I understood her message and continued to listen to the many ideas the other kids offered for solving this riddle, which they decided meant a 'home is like a nest, temporary but necessary.'

What struck me, however, was that the boy holding the gourd made no mention of the delicate engraving of the dove. Several others inspected the gourd as well and made no mention either. Then, one of the girls came forth. She ran her fingers over the dove image and looked at me saying, "Interesting," smiled and put the gourd back in my hands.

Finally, someone asked me if I had any idea of what this mystery was. I said I had some ideas, but nothing firm yet in mind and that this might be a hard one to figure out. "Maybe what you said about homes being temporary is the answer," I replied, "but let's investigate further." The game was no fun, unless everyone was involved in solving the mystery. I sent the others out to look for places the gourds were known to grow, to involve them in the fun and not give away what I already knew.

After they eagerly left to participate in their part of the game, I finally opened my hand holding the blue egg and asked the question that nagged me. "Traleana," I said, "why the blue egg stone?"

Her penetrating eyes locked on mine. Taking her time, she at last replied, "It's a real egg that has petrified, and it has been in my family for as long as anyone can remember." Then she said, "It's sacred and whoever has it is blessed by Mother God."

I inspected it more carefully, and sure enough, I could see a few tiny crack lines, which would be present in such a shell! The color was so vividly unusual in its intensity, that it still mystified me. I opened her hand and attempted to drop the beautiful object into it, but she closed her hand and wouldn't accept it from me. Instead, she held her hands tight to her heart.

That gesture confused me and I said, "It's been in your family so long, surely it must stay therein. I can't accept it, Traleana."

"No", she snapped, "the egg was in our keeping, only until we met someone who would be sent from God to plant the seed of peace. I was honored to hold it for the last time, because it was foretold that I would finally meet the gardener of peace, before I was grown into womanhood." I struggled to understand, and she went on to explain, "This egg symbolizes a peace-seed[71] that will grow and break free one day and change the world. Someday the idea of peace will be ready to 'hatch.'" she said. A flash of vision went through my mind, and I could see how Tara nurtured seeds, which sprouted and matured. Then, I could see a bird eating the seed from a mature plant and finally laying the magic egg, the 'Egg of Destiny'. Mother Earth and Father Sky, united in one purpose, I thought, what a wonderful cycle of creation.

She looked so wise, for such a little girl. Why I didn't notice her before, I can't remember. She then said, "I bid you to keep it with you, until you have recognized that peace seed you carry within your heart and body, dear Esa." She closed my hand over the precious egg with her tiny hands and whispered, "One day, you will give it to someone you love like no other. She will ensure the mission of peace and complete the divine link, to chain forever onward."

The egg felt extremely hot to me, yet it didn't burn in my closed fist. I opened my hand and looked down, wondering why it was so warm. When I looked back up to ask Traleana, she was gone. I never saw her again during our time of playing, nor thereafter; nor did I see her mother either. It was almost as if I had dreamed them.

---

[71] DNA

I asked some of the others about her, but they seemed to know little, just that she showed up shortly after I did, she was always quiet and they seldom gave her much attention. At least, I wasn't dreaming Traleana, I thought, even as it confirmed that the Egg of Destiny was extremely important to my life mission.

I always carried that egg in a little bag attached to a cord around my neck. Its continual warmth reminded me of the mysterious visitor and the mystery that would take a long time to solve, if ever.

I had many days of fun and games with my friends and enjoyed their company as much as I did the lost children in the Far East. I didn't realize that I was finally growing into manhood, until one day, I noticed that when I spoke to mother, I was now looking straight into her eyes, and my voice cracked and went from my normal pitch of sound to a much lower pitch.

"My, my," mother said. "My little son is a grown man now. It was only yesterday it seemed, you were a mere babe." I was strangely embarrassed by that statement. She kissed me on the cheek and said, "Soon you will leave me, and I will miss you."

"I will never leave you, mother," I said. "I love you too much."

"You will," she replied, "and love will be what takes you from me, one day." I assured her that I couldn't envision such a thing. She said, "A greater love than a son's love for his mother you'll find, in many ways, my son. Sadly, you will also find joy and sorrow as companions along the way." I could see tears of dread in her gentle eyes. She gave me a warm hug, held me longer than normal and went back to her daily work.

James was apprenticing with our older brother Joseph, and he was away most days, often staying weeks at a time. My sister, half-sisters and nieces were generally with my mother, helping her or sitting at her feet, listening intently to her words. Mother seemed to be sharing some 'women's secrets' with them. I respected that special relationship among the women of my family, so I occupied myself as I wished.

I drifted away from the playful games and began to take long walks out and about by myself. I liked to spend time with my cousin John, who was what you term now 'a naturalist,' for he was drawn to the wild animals and uninhabited places. He didn't know 'animal speak,' however, and was amazed that I knew it. He was expert at reading animals' body language though. I asked if he wanted to learn their speech. He was eager to expand his world and understand, even more, the beings he loved dearly. He learned the language easily and began to spend more and more time out in the wilderness, not coming home for days. He soon became a 'wild man,' as he preferred the wilderness to the towns and cities. He stopped eating flesh when he learned to talk to the animals, but still would occasionally eat insects for protein, but even that haunted him. He felt anguish for taking their lives for his physical need. He was 'total compassion' and 'one' with the wild places he shared.

I spent more time away from home about then, as well. I found myself drawn to the cities and towns, however, where I would sit near the temples and listen to the discussions of the elders. Once in awhile I would offer an opinion, and I began to gain the respect of many of the council members in the temples, who thought my few comments profound. They would sometimes engage my view, but for the most part, I knew that this was my 'listening' time, and I simply sat and tried to grasp the scope of their arguments. It was quite difficult to hear the warped thinking from many of the elders, and if it hadn't been for the year of silence, I trained myself within, I would not have been able hold my tongue.

One day, I was listening to a discussion of how the kingdom of heaven was only for those whom the priest deemed worthy, and I lost it. I just stood up in the middle of the council debate and yelled, "Rubbish!" They were all startled and looked at me. "I'll go to the dump and sit in better company," I yelled into the faces of the surprised elder priests. "The rats that live there have more sense than you do." I stomped off to the place of discard on the edge of the village and started living with the rats and other scavengers, human and otherwise, who existed on the fringes of society. I stayed a long time lost in my 'madness'. There was more wisdom there then I found in the council chambers.

# MADNESS
## Chapter Nineteen

I can't remember much about my time in the place of discard, or the 'dump,' as commonly termed. I remember the rats and I spoke with them, using the animal-speak technique I learned from my childhood training. They had families and they thought the place a literal palace of treasures; odd how perception can change one's world view. I also remember that the throw-away people,[72] who lived and scavenged in the dump, were afraid of me; for I was literally out of my mind and spoke to rats, no less. Later, when I neglected even my most basic needs, I must have shown something in myself that touched their hearts, as they began to look after me in subtle ways, even though I smelled bad and looked even worse.

I wasn't a pretty sight, I was later told. I didn't notice, much less care, about such things as hygiene. I neglected my health and well-being, had dirty, matted hair and my clothes became stinking rags, as I picked my way through the rotting discarded substances of civilization, accompanied by rats, vultures and cockroaches. Even so, I do remember thinking that the minds of those who dumped all this stuff (maybe some of those council members), were more putrid than anything here.

My rat friends shared everything with me, including fleas; I scratched a lot and tore my skin up with my ever-growing long fingernails. I later carried shame for what I had allowed myself to become for awhile, but eventually realized that this, too, was a lesson, and the castaways were my teachers.

The people who lived on these heaps were those who didn't fit into society, for one reason or another. Often, they had mental problems, as I was exhibiting. Some were thrown out because they didn't make others look good enough, in places they wanted to impress. Some children were there; usually orphans, some just

---

[72] A common term used for those who lived and scavenged in the place of discard or 'dump'

abandoned for not being beautiful enough, or strong, or the right gender, or any of a number of reasons that corrupt compassion and block out love. The ones with mental challenges are often individuals too sensitive to thrive within the aggressive atmosphere of those deeming themselves civilized. They fit better within the place of discard; for there, they established more sensitive rules to survive, be that existence ever so unappealing to most looking on. It might look quite drastic that I ended up at this place, but in looking back, I'm glad I was taken in by the humble beings that survived there.

I didn't know how much time had transpired, when I was finally able to bring my senses back to the vehicle of Esa, the human. I had somehow transformed my self-identity into a rat and was trying to fit into their community. I had periods where I was Esa, and times when I was a simple rat. I struggled within my mind and felt I even failed as a rat, for I was accepted by them, but had a long way to go in understanding the animal group consciousness of the species. They were among many misunderstood creatures.

What I didn't realize was that my beloved guardian Elmira was still on task. He had just taken an invisible stance once again, in that he watched, but I didn't know he was present. He proved to be quite adept at keeping his presence unknown to me. His vow of non-interference, given to the high priest who had sent me off into the high mountain place as a small child, ended after I returned home once again. Jacobite told Elmira that I had to learn to fly with my own wings now; yet, if he chose to do so, he could still guard, but never fly for me. Of course, I didn't know this. It was years later in a dream, that I realized how close he always was. Those times were most difficult for him, he told me. He wanted desperately to keep me from pain and suffering, as he always did. He literally had to shut down the mind communication channel between us that we had perfected, which explained why I didn't sense he was still nearby. It was important that I feel completely on my own, the elder told Elmira, for I had to develop strength of personal guardianship. That type of guardianship meant that one must develop a strong will to live and protect the divine within oneself, so that they can accomplish what they were born to do. Everyone has a divine soul mission, so everyone must experience being self reliant. This often meant experiencing 'aloneness' at some point, so that personal reliance was developed sufficiently.

I went in and out of lucid awareness at the dumping place, and one moment, I was a rat and the next I was a miserable lost soul. I also would pass out from time to time, due to malnutrition. One day as I opened my eyes, I saw a young girl, maybe eleven or twelve years of age, who was looking down upon me with concern and tenderness. She was singing a song, that mothers often sang to little children in my village, to give them courage to face life. Though difficult to translate, it went something like this:

*Don't you worry, little child, for God has sent you from far, far away, so you could have a time to live and play. A time to help others see, how joyful life can be, every single day, you see.*

*And sweet baby true, I see the God in you.*

*Don't you cry, little babe. Your sorrows will be washed away, when those who love you come to see, the truth of your sweet divinity.*

*And sweet baby true, I see the God in you.*

*Don't you give up, little one, on what you must do, for there are angels watching over you. Remember your mission true, a task that only you can do.*

*And sweet baby true, I see the God in you.*

*So be happy, little one, and I will be happy, too, that you came to play, and you came to be part of this family,*

*For sweet baby true, I see God in you.*

I don't give this song justice; in Aramaic, it is much more melodic, and it carries a vibration of gratitude from the singer, for the sake of the one sung to. That's what awoke me, the song of gratitude, within the ancient lullaby. It was an odd feeling, to hear this old song again. It roused me with its gentle message while the child-singer was looking down upon me, laid out on a flat tattered mat. The tiny voice sang with tenderness and innocence. Had I had my wits about me, I would have wondered why this child sang a lullaby to me, and I not to her?

"Who are you," I finally asked.

The little girl's eyes brightened, and she said, "You heard me?"

I simply nodded my head, and my hand went up to where she had been washing. Deep on my scalp was a painful huge gash; my matted hair was caked with sweet-smelling blood. I was clearly confused, so she explained the situation to me.

"Crazy one," she said, "You and your rat friends were rummaging through the discarded stuff, which had just been brought in from the palace of the overseer of the village. Evidently, there was something that was secreted out of the palace, by those who would steal treasures. We believe they followed the discard wagon, intending to retrieve what they had stashed. But you and the rats preceded them, and they reacted out of fear of losing what they stole in the first place."

She laughed in an ironic way, and went on to say, "You squealed at them in a loud shrieking sound. On seeing the company you kept and your condition, they simply took a club out and whacked you unconscious, no doubt thinking you as lowly as the animals you had all around you. When they hurt you, the rats grew furious and swarmed from over the entire region of discards, coming up from the depths. They leaped upon the mean men and bit them and drove them away." She was getting dramatic at this point, indicating how terrible a sight that must have been. "We, the people of this place, were busy at the time in our gleaning of usable items when the wagon arrived; but many of us noticed you being attacked, because your squeals were so haunting. We looked up just as the club came down on your head. The sound still haunts me," she said, as she looked slightly sickened. "Then, so fast, the rats came in droves, like a mighty gray river overtaking the place. We were afraid to go near you, for we felt we would surely be chewed to pieces as well."

"How did I get here then, child?" I asked.

## The Saga-Oracle

"Well," she answered, "it was quite odd. The rats were so many, that the ground was covered like a moving carpet in the area you occupied. Suddenly, the robbers, now covered by biting rats, fled screaming even louder than then you. After that a path opened from you to where I worked. It was strange to witness all that happened. We had never seen the rats behave in such a way, and had no idea of the great numbers that lived in the area. My mother said, she thought they wanted us to go down the opened path and rescue you. Some of us were afraid of you; some had sympathy and compassion and wondered what happened to you to make you crazy, but we agreed there was something that the animals wanted, as they parted a path and didn't seem to be chewing on us. Mother began to move towards you, and the path closed suddenly. Then it opened again, when she retreated. Another adult from our group tried and experienced the same thing. Then I stepped forward and the rats held the way open. I began to move along the opened path and my mother cried for me to stop. She had only me in this world. She couldn't bear to see me harmed and feared for my safety. Even so, I told her I must go to you, and I just turned around and ran to your side. You were bleeding from the head and whimpering like an injured animal. I yelled for help and, very reluctantly, others were allowed to come near you, too. Then as we tended to you and decided to relocate you to this humble shelter, we noticed that the rats were gone, disappearing into the secret places they had emerged from, under the rubble. A few followed us though, maybe making sure you were well-cared for, I think."

"Unbelievable," I exclaimed. "Rats took me in, when I was crazy," I stated, more to myself than anyone else. My memories became clearer, as this sweet young girl brought a cool wet cloth once again to my head, which was aching terribly.

"That's for sure," she said. "Unbelievable to us as well, but the rats liked something about you. Maybe it was the way you talked to them all the time. Kind of, with all due respect," she emphasized.

"How long have I been in the place of discard?" I asked.

"A few moons," she replied.

"That long!" I said, thinking that my family would probably think that I was finally taken by those who hunted down the master children. I felt ashamed of the pain I must have caused my mother and the rest of my family, too. I closed my eyes as I imagined the sorrow I had, no doubt, caused and wept quiet remorseful tears. The release provided a tremendous cleansing process and a river of emotion flooded through me, even as my weeping was silent. I cried, because I had failed. I cried, because the elders who held the positions of authority in the communities, especially the priests, were so disconnected from the truth of Divine Compassion, and I feared they would never 'get it'. I cried, because I had taken a gift as precious as physical life and nearly thrown that gift away. I also cried, because I felt sorry for myself and sorry for my actions. I hurt in so many ways, and right now, very much physically. I released the sorrow, through that great emotional silent weeping, in a river of soul-washing tears.

When I was finally empty of the tears of sorrow and disappointment, after falling in and out of consciousness several times, I noticed another voice, and a slightly different touch of the cloth bathing my wound. The gentle dabbing of the cool cloth on my head brought me back to my senses again, and I felt a wave of peace flow over me, like the energy that rides on the refreshing waves of a warm sea on a hot day. I slowly opened my eyes, and there instead of the sweet little girl-savior of a moment ago, was my dear mother with tears silently streaming down her own lovely face. Her wet smiling face was filled with the joy of finally finding her son alive, even though he was quite a mess. "Welcome back to the land of the living," she whispered.

"Oh mother, forgive me," I pleaded.

"I have no reason to forgive you, my son. I'll have to work on forgiving those who would drive such a gentle soul to such a state as this, however," she said.

"How did you find me?" I whispered.

# The Saga-Oracle

"It took too long, my beloved," she whispered back. "We looked everywhere, but never thought to look in the discard place. Elmira finally had to compromise a promise, he made to Jacobite, and he told me through his mind-talk to visit this place; my presence was sorely needed here. The urgency of his message prompted me to immediately respond. I was desperate to find you and have never doubted Elmira's dedication and loyalty. I knew it must have to do with you, or I wouldn't have heard his inner-voice so clearly. I quickly found my wrap and came forth in all due haste, but by myself, for I wasn't sure what I would find at the end of this quest." She smiled again and brushed something from my face, as a mother often does to a child she loves, and continued on, saying, "I almost turned back, because there were so many rats. They made me quite nervous, but they seemed non-threatening, and gave me enough space to feel safe, even as they walked along ahead of me. Then, I realized that they were leading me somewhere. Being priestess-trained, I knew that animals wouldn't appear in such an odd way, unless there was a divine purpose. They definitely were not aggressive, so I followed them to this little shelter. I just now found you, here being tended by this sweet girl, Alenesha[73] and her mother Bethanisha[74]." Mother looked their way, and I could see tremendous gratitude in her face. They departed, so mother and I could have a private reunion.

Mother looked towards the woman and her daughter as they were leaving and asked if they would be so kind as to help her get me home shortly. Both nodded and came back later with a wheeled cart they used for gleaning—one that probably had been discarded as no longer serviceable, but to the people of this place, a treasure. Others appeared and understood that this beautiful gentle one, who just arrived, was none other than 'Compassionate Mary' from the Nazarite village. My mother was well-known throughout the area. They also realized I must be precious to her, and they kindly helped her carefully lift and place me in the cart. I was soon comfortable on the bed of the cart, or as comfortable as I could be, with a fair sized gash in my head and a headache that pulsed and

---

[73] Means 'noble and kind'
[74] Form of Bethany, which means 'house of figs' the' sha' added to it then means 'kind one from the house of figs'

nearly split my head in two with each throb. However, I felt better, knowing that we were heading home. I drifted in and out of consciousness from time to time, and I would swear that I saw Elmira between the shafts of the cart, as a donkey would be, pulling us along the paths and roadways. I seemed to be surrounded by women, as well, and knew my mother was present, and felt the presence also of my little savior and her mother. Then I slipped out of the physical for a while and watched from a vantage point above my body. It was a peaceful position. I sensed my father's presence. When I tried to look at him, he said, "not yet, son. It's not time for you to look my way, for you still have a mission you know you must do. Hold on, son, and finish what you came to accomplish." Then he dissolved into a misty background. I awoke days later in my family home, feeling cleaner and more mentally clear, and grateful to be with loved ones again.

"Mother," I said upon awakening. "Am I dreaming, or have I come home yet again?"

Since she found me, mother was never far from my side, or I should say, since she was led to me. She simply smiled and said in a tender voice, "It's about time you came back among the living and got on with your work, don't you think, son?"

"It's hopeless, mother," I said. I was feeling despondent at the mere thought of the situation that drove me into the realms of craziness, which really is anger gone into 'madness'. "I spent so much time, waiting for wisdom and compassion in the discussions at the temples. I couldn't make any sense out of the reasoning they applied to the Divine, and how this God, they claimed to know, would exclude those the priests deemed unworthy," I told mother.

She just nodded and replied, "That's because they reason and don't honor their feelings, son." Then she said, "And that's why you are here to bring passion, or feeling, back into the chambers of reason. You are truly my son, the 'compassionate one'," she said as she helped me to a sitting position. My head still ached, but not nearly as bad as it had. "But you shall have to give your compassion more attention than your anger, or surely you will go 'mad' again and again," mother warned me.

# The Saga-Oracle

The place was full of women, all giddy with joy, as I awoke. My sisters[75] moved forward, greeting me with bright smiles, and told me it was about time I woke up. Then I noticed two other familiar faces, and I strained to remember why they were so recognizable. Mother saw me looking towards the elder woman and the younger girl and said, "Behold your saviors, son." She bowed slightly introducing them again, unsure if I had any memory of our first introduction and presented, "Alenesha and her mother Bethanisha."

"They have kindly agreed to stay on and help me with some of my duties as the high priestess within the Order of the Dove, and Alenesha is to be my apprentice as well. I find her a mastra, in need of an opportunity to develop her inborn talents. I'm grateful to have found these two gems." I had no idea that mother was now high priestess in the order, symbolized by the flying dove. Children can be so caught up in their own lives that what their parents are involved in goes unrecognized and thus unappreciated.

Alenesha approached us and sweetly said, "Welcome back to the land of the living, Master," and I recognized her voice and the memory of the place of discard came flooding back.

"The land of the living?"[76] I questioned. "My mother said this and now you. Why is it that you two would welcome me in this way?"

"Forgive me," she said, "we, who live and work, picking through that which has been discarded, refer to those who don't have to live that way as 'of the land of the living,' for we feel like we are within the place of hell, or somewhere near, in the piles of rubbish we survive within."

I thought a moment and then said, "I assure you, beautiful child, that hell is wherever there is doubt that God created you, good, and of God. I found hell in the temples," I told her. She seemed

---

[75] Jeshua had sisters from his father's first wife as well as little Jemima, his full sister
[76] Anywhere outside of the Place of Discard

surprised by that statement. "And I assure you, that hell hides behind closed hearts and inside stubborn minds."

"I understand," she answered.

I regained my strength fairly fast. One day the elder Jacobite, who was once high priest of our sect, sent for me. Now bed-ridden, he no longer served as presiding high priest. I arrived at his doorstep in short order, since his abode was not far from my family's home. I held great respect for the old man, as my father had and my family still did. In great haste, upon my arrival, I was ushered into his room, which was just an area within a large room used for all purposes, with the sleeping area draped off with heavy woven material for the sake of privacy.

It was difficult seeing the old man lying there. It brought back memories of my own dear father on his death bed. The elder could hardly rise from his sleeping pallet and bid me to seat myself close to him.

"I have willed myself to stay in the flesh until I could do one last thing my son," he said, in a weak voice.

I wiped his brow with my hand and asked if he wanted me to bring some fresh energy to him.

He agreed with a nod, but also said, "Just enough so I can talk to you, son. I'm ready to leave this tired old body behind, but before I go, I must have a conference with you."

I nodded, respecting and understanding the request.

"Your mission gets harder now, son," he said in a stronger voice, for my hand was transmitting rejuvenating energy into his forehead, and my other hand was on his solar plexus, keeping that energy spinning within his frail old body. I thought, 'Thank you, Yasma, for your invaluable training.'

"You must go away again, but not so far this time, lad," he told me, as his dark eyes pierced into my soul, imploring me to listen with my heart. He went on to say, "There's great hope that you will break through a wall of resistance to change, which has been forming far too long. This wall is built by the stubbornness of those who feel, to control and overpower is the way to lead others. They believe that they were chosen by God, to be in an elite group that gauges worthiness of life itself. This illusion they feed with their greed. Illusion is an odd thing, lad, do you not agree?" searching deep into my eyes for assurance. I wasn't sure why he brought this up, but he explained a bit more to me, saying, "We are all the illusion of God, envisioning the Divine Self. So if that is true, what illusion would you feed with your attention–the illusion of love, or the anti-illusion of fear?" While I pondered what he said, he sensed confusion and explained further. "Illusion is like 'imagination,' lad. It is creation, plain and simple. Anti-illusion[77] inverts imagination and is like a stagnant cesspool. What it creates is a stoppage of all goodness. It wastes what it holds, and it seeks to hold everything in non-motion, so that it can stop Divine Imagination. In other words, it takes the 'imagination' of God and corrupts, or distorts it, by bringing it to rot within non-motion. God's imagination is pure love; within it, this illusion called 'physical life' is accomplished, so that divine discovery can happen, and that, my dear lad, is why you and all creation came to physicality. It is called 'Evolution of Consciousness' and it is a flowing 'motionated'[78] process. So it matters. It matters how you move through each illusion and how you keep the flow going. Fear is the threat to the motion of evolution. Fear will tell you that you don't matter." I could see by his expression this was what he was most worried about, that I would think my life didn't matter. His strength held, and he continued, "fear supports suffering and judgmental attitudes that separate rather than unite, because that's how you stop evolution. Never allow fear to stop you, lad, for no matter how difficult things get, if you can imagine the success of your mission, then so it shall be. Do you understand?"

I wasn't quite sure how all this would fit into the scheme of things yet to come in my life; but I knew, if this lesson was so important

---

[77] Antiforce
[78] The act of movement as a universal force

that this wise elder would allow me to energize him one last time to utter it, then I should keep it precious in my heart and mind.

He then weakly turned his head towards me and bid me to bring my ear close to his old lips. He feebly said, "In the land of the Samaritans, there is one who keeps a shop here and there. He makes swords for warriors, lad. He goes by the simple name of 'Nod,' Nod the Smithy," he clarified. "He works with anything made of metal, but he is well-known for the strong swords he produces, so he is tolerated in all communities. His talents overcome the bias of his heritage and the judgment of those who see the Samaritans as lacking. Go to him, lad. Tell him you are Yeheshua ben Joseph of the Nazarites. Tell him you have much to learn from him, before you can launch into the mission you were born to do. He will understand. Then obediently follow his instructions. Learn what alchemy is and what it isn't. You will have need of this knowledge. Then, and only then, proceed upon the divine mission, which your heart and soul know it must accomplish. You will be well-equipped to make the difference you were born to make, master." I felt honored to be called a master by this one who surely was a real master. I looked down at him and didn't offer to argue the master matter. I just felt grateful to be addressed as such by one I respected so much.

"I will do as you say," I assured him, "but do I have to go away from my family again, for I fear that I have brought so much heartache already to them, especially my mother, and I dread being separated from them."

"She has close connections with Nod's wife and daughters. Fear not, Esa, for your mother is more linked than you could ever guess, and she will be closer than you realize."

"Now," he said, with a voice that seemed to weaken by the second, "send my family in to bid me farewell and honor me with a firm determination to follow through on my suggestions. You are our last hope, from those we invited into our peace project intention, dear lad." His eyes pleaded for assurance from me.

I nodded and smiled. He knew that was as good as a promise and I departed, sending his family in to see him. Before I got far from his small humble home, I heard weeping, and I knew that Jacobite had quickly departed, after seeing his family one quick last time, before he shed the tired body that had served him long and well.

"Namaste', my friend," I whispered, "and may your journey home be in the arms of angels."

# WHAT YOU SEEK, SEEKS YOU
## Chapter Twenty

I consider this part of my life my true initiation into adulthood, in that I had to seek my last teacher on a journey without the company of my beloved Elmira, whom I had not seen in a long time. It was rather difficult to start out the next morning after speaking with Jacobite, knowing I must leave my mother and family yet again. Mother's eyes were full of sorrow and fear of losing me for a while, or possibly forever. She had taken the responsibility of adulthood far sooner than I had. This last episode of rescuing her 'master child' from the place of discard had taken its toll. I noticed wrinkles had developed like little webs at the edge of her eyes, along with some worry lines in the center of her forehead.

"Today is the day I must depart for my final training," I announced, as we shared our morning meal. Mother was the only one present on this cool pleasant morning, since my little sister, Jemima, was with my aunt for a few days, to help her after she had miscarried a child.

As she prepared our low eating-table for our morning meal, mother informed me, "That little sister of yours has the gift of healing hearts and my sister needs her right now." I always felt peaceful when my sister was present, even when she was pestering me, which she loved to do. She would often tickle me awake in the morning, with a feather dancing on my nose. She couldn't keep from giggling, and it was her joy and sparkling voice that awakened me in a most pleasant mood. I had noticed that she didn't wake me this morning. I would later remember that feather and her joy on many occasions in my life in less happy places.

There was never a mother more gentle and patient, than my own dear mother Mary. It is fitting that she be remembered as the 'perfect mother', because she was flawless in my eyes. My grandmother Anna (her mother) was just as patient and sweet; the legend of my mother having no stain of sin eventually reached out to enfold Anna as well, and it should extend to all women. The idea that women were prone to be sinful was part of the corruption that had drawn me to this plane of experience. That attitude was tilting the balance of peace to the point that cruelty and warring were the norm, rather than the exception. Women softened societies. I always believed that if my mother and grandmother were the queens of the land, then there would be peace therein forever.

On the morning of my journey, which I promised Jacobite I would undertake, my intuitive mother knew before I told her, that this would be the day of my departure. She had prepared my favorite morning meal. I loved flat bread sweetened with honey and nuts, rolled in figs, which was a meal for special occasions. When she laid out the morning food, there was no doubt that she knew of my departure, even though we hadn't discussed it. She proudly seated herself by my side and with a sweet/sad look upon her lovely face, waited to share the bread with me.

"I know," I said to her, "it's hard to constantly be saying goodbye."

Noticing how she struggled to stay composed, I said, "I promise to return soon, but I can't promise to stay, because you brought me into this world to roam and to bring peace."

She nodded and offered me some bread. I received it with both hands cupped like a holy grail, for this was a holy communion to me. I accepted the gift of symbolic love my mother offered. We ate in silence. When I finished, I grabbed a traveling bag I had prepared after I had spoken to Jacobite, and I walked out the door of our humble abode, not knowing exactly where I was going or when I was coming back. I simply surrendered to my promise and headed toward Samaria, remembering Jacobite had told me to seek out the smithy, Nod. I recalled that he assured me, my mother would not be far away and had some connection to Nod and his family. I took comfort in that possibility, but never mentioned to mother that I was looking for the smithy. I'm not sure why I decided to keep the mission private; maybe to spare her anguish. I looked over my shoulder, as I walked away from our home and saw mother standing in the doorway. She nodded her head and smiled the affirmation I needed, to move into yet another unknown time of my life. My heartache then eased and I proceeded in joy and expectation.

Samaria was only a few days to the south of our village. I decided to enjoy the short journey. Compared to some of my other journeys, this wouldn't feel like I was so far from home. As I walked, I wondered why the Hebrews disrespected the Samaritans. I thought I would explore this perplexing attitude, as I walked toward the Samaria homelands. Samaritans were expected to yield the path, or roadway, when anyone not of their own people was encountered. Not long after my departure, I encountered a tradesman who didn't waver one inch, as he came toward a Samaritan family walking together. He forced the Samaritan family to scatter to make way for him. The family held no anger or disgust, they simply split and opened the way, only to reunite once the trader had passed and continued on their journey together.

The trader was coming my way. As he got closer, I said, "Excuse me, sir." He paused for a moment and looked my way. Recognizing that I was not a Samaritan, due to the white robes of Nazarites I wore (since the Samaritans wore brightly-colored garments, unless in sacred rituals), he looked toward me with a rather pleasant smile on his face, waiting for me to explain what I wanted to be excused for.

"I was just wondering," I said. "Why is it that you expect the Samaritans to move off the path, when you walk toward them?"

He looked at me with an expression of utter surprise and befuddlement on his face and said, "Surely you joke with me, lad?"

I said, "No," and he didn't know if he should laugh, or move on and ignore me. After he paused and looked me up and down, he decided that maybe he would answer that absurd question.

"They are ignorant and inferior, lad. Surely, you know that already."

"Why is that so?" I asked. He shook his head drastically back and forth, uttering "No, no, no." Once he got past denying the point of the question, he seemed to ponder it, nonetheless.

"I've never thought of that, lad, but let me think a moment." He finally said, "They don't sacrifice anything worthy to God."

I just stared at him, and he knew he would have to come up with a better reason than that.

Sensing that I needed more convincing, he went on to say, "They see a pig as being as holy as the cow."

That puzzled me and I must have made a funny face at the remark, so he tried to explain further.

"The cow gives us milk to feed our babes and meat to nourish us; the pig just plows up the earth with its snout and will eat nearly anything, thus is considered unclean. One is higher in status than the other. One has a purpose and one doesn't." In his own way, he was trying to enlighten me, for obviously in his mind, someone had failed do so. He continued, saying, "You and I would be like the holy cows, and the Samaritans would be like the swine." I couldn't believe he made such a ridiculous comparison. "They also have been known to eat the swine meat, which we consider unclean and that makes them unclean as well. But worse," he stressed, "many of them see all living things as equal, even their women!" At that statement, he raised his eyebrows as if to convey, 'can you believe that?'

I asked, "But what about their kindness to all beings, especially to strangers? Doesn't that make them blessed in the eyes of God?"

The trader looked at me and answered, "They don't know better, so they don't do better."

I replied, "Isn't helping someone, or something, in need, doing better?" The man became irritated, mumbled something about troublemakers, turned his attention to the road again and just walked off, rigid and angry at my so-called ignorance. I could hear him mumbling to himself about the state of the young people and how they would be the ruin of the world, as he walked away.

It took a couple of days walking to enter the lands of Samaria. I encountered many people expecting the Samaritans to yield way for them, which always happened without question. I spoke with some of those who took over the path, but simply wished them a good day. Mostly, I spoke with the Samaritans and inquired about Nod, the smithy. I never again asked why they accepted that they must yield to others, because I didn't believe they knew themselves.

As I asked for Nod, most Samaritans knew of him, but none knew his location. Samaria was a large land, and they said he moved about, seldom staying put in one place long. His ability to forge steel and work with all sorts of metal was legend, but the Samaritans didn't mention the swords he made, unless I specifically asked. Then they just said, "Oh yes, he makes those, too. They are said to be the best a warrior could find."

It felt odd to be without Elmira. I would often think of him and how much company he was for me on journeys. I tried mind-to-mind communication, but felt a barrier, and knew that I must honor the closed doorway of mind-communication between us and allow him his freedom. After all, I was a grown man now, or at least I preferred to think of myself as such. I had matured nearly to my full height and could look most any man square in the eye, and was a head taller than the normal woman stood. My body had not filled out yet however, for I was late in physical maturity, even as I was early in mental development, which resulted in me being gangly and uncoordinated. That's why I was still called 'lad,' by those who didn't know my name. Mother had washed the mats from my hair, which I acquired in the place of discard. She and little eleven-year-old Alenesha had tried to untangle the matted lice-laden locks, a tiny bit at a time, but finally they had to shear me like a sheep. It was more accepted that men have short trimmed hair than women, so I didn't look unusual. As I remember this shearing I can't help but smile, for Alenesha is such a sweet dedicated child. She snipped away, humming that simple lullaby that she loved so much. Who in their right mind would discard such a child and her sweet mother, I wondered? She had a sweetness about her that reminded me of my own sisters, especially Jemima, who was away now healing a broken heart.

I spent my time, during the first two days on my journey, walking and talking with travelers along the way. Most of the people responded to me as if mesmerized, and I never understood why. One day, I came across a Samaritan man with a donkey cart, stuck in the ditch where it had overturned, when he gave way to a camel caravan. I watched the episode play out. The men upon the backs of camels, which showed higher status, taunted the man and rushed him to clear the path to the point that his cart had toppled into a dirty damp ditch upside down. I immediately went to help him and heard one of the camel riders yell, "Get out of the gutter, lad, for if you roll with swine, you'll smell like one, too." Then he laughed and turned away, riding his huge camel, and continued his conversation with the other camel riders as if this was just another fun moment of the day. Ignoring the plight of the Samarian, they simply went on their merry way.

"Can I be of assistance?" I asked the rather small man, struggling in an effort to unhitch the donkey.

"Go away, lad, before you smell bad," he said, obviously in a foul mood after the insults.

"You don't smell bad at all, but I can't say the same thing for that camel-jockey," I said, pointing to the caravan heading on down the road. That term wasn't meant as a compliment. Those who cared for camels had to pick the camel dung up, too. They dried it to use as fuel for their desert campfires, and they stank strongly from the task. I shouldn't have used the put-down reference, but I was angry. When people are angry, they say angry things. I know that's no excuse, but then I didn't have the patience I developed later in life. I continued to help the Samaritan in the ditch, and the situation hit us both as ridiculously funny at the same time. We sat down, next to the upturned donkey cart. The poor donkey, patiently waited for someone to right him, and it all seemed ridiculous, and we laughed.

"You are a wonder, lad," he said. "I could use a hand unhitching Dankin here. He's in a terrible fix with his cart overturned." As I looked closer, I could see the little donkey quietly waited for someone to do something. He knew he was tethered and couldn't budge an inch. It was rather easy to work with such a docile animal. We simply had to both lift him gently, and unhook some of the harness that bound him helpless at this point. Soon enough, he was safely on his feet. He shook his body like a wet dog and stood quietly waiting for whatever came next.

"I'll take my time and reload the cart, and be on my way soon," the little man said, now in a much more pleasant mood. "I'm grateful for your help, stranger."

"Can I help you right the wagon and reload?" I asked. The Samarian looked me over and said, "Who would want to help the likes of me?"

"Yeheshua ben Joseph would," I replied, as I looked him directly in the eyes. He was a small man, with huge eyes that gleamed with wisdom and strength, and I liked him, even though I didn't know him.

Looking at me in a new light, he said, "Are you the son of Joseph?" Dusting off, making nearly as big a cloud of dust as the donkey did when he shook, he said, "Could you be the son of the Nazarite Joseph, from the village tucked away in the high hills, lad?"

"That would be me, also the son of Mary, the patient one," I titled her thus, as I brought my mother into the picture. Her patience and compassion was legend among many people, and I wanted to convey proper respect to her as well.

A broad smile crossed the face of this weary little man. He looked up at the sky and announced, "He has come and in perfect time." As I stood and wondered about this statement, and who, 'up there in the sky' he was addressing, he said, "Let's get to work, lad, but first let me introduce myself. I'm Nod, the smithy and I have been expecting you."

It's true that what we seek, seeks us as well, and this was one of those defining moments. It didn't surprise me, that I finally found Nod; yet it still pleased me to know that the universal law of attraction was so reliable. Nod and I worked to unload the wagon, which was heavy with the components of metal-making. We talked and he told me that he had been looking for me, ever since a dream in which the Nazarite high priest had come to him and asked if he would take me on as an apprentice in alchemy. He was a bit confused about the dream, he said. Why a peaceful Nazarite boy would need such training, made no sense to him. Then he explained that in the dream the high priest assured him, that this young man needed many skills to be a peacemaker. The fact that it had to do with peace was enough for Nod, since the basis of the Samaritan philosophy was peace and Onement of all creation, even as they struggled, as all groups do, with how to achieve Onement. Since the night of the dream, he had watched and asked those he met, if they knew of a child of peace. He told me he felt the utmost urgency to be about this dream mission. Most he asked just stared at him in disbelief, given that they didn't know what he meant by a 'child of peace'. Certainly, most thought all children were peaceful, until motivated or pushed otherwise.

He put his arm around my shoulders, apologized and said, "I was so angry at the remarks of that stupid 'camel-jockey,' as you called him," chuckling again as he said it, "that I didn't recognize, that indeed a child of peace would be the one, who would come into the ditch to help me. Then you appeared right under my nose, and I didn't recognize you as the one I sought."

The ditch was full of trash from the road; it also held some run-off water from an unusual recent rain, so indeed it was difficult, messy work. Soon enough, we had the cart back on the road, with little Dankin hitched up again, and we were on our way. I didn't have to ask Nod if I could come with him, nor did he ask me if I'd like to join him. We just linked up and moved on, walking alongside the cart, hoping that we didn't have to dive into the ditches again, making way for those feeling more privileged.

"Where's our destination?" I finally asked Nod.

"I have a little place in a cave in the foothills, not far," he said. "I set up shop closer to the source of the material I'll need for a special commission." Then he told Dankin to turn right onto a small trail off the main road, and we began a much more difficult path. However, first Nod took a heavy basket off the cart and handed it to me. I didn't expect the weight of it and nearly dropped the basket when he released it into my keep.

"Careful, lad," he said, "put your muscles into it. Dankin needs some help now. Because of you, I can remove two of the heavy baskets from his burden." He then took a larger basket and hoisted it to his right shoulder, using a rock as a balancing place to get himself into position. The basket looked bigger than he was.

I asked how he would have dealt with this problem on his own. "I didn't think of that," he answered, as he walked the narrow trail behind Dankin, who seemed to know the way. I wondered if I was this heavy to Elmira, the day he carried me across that raging stream, when I learned that he was a Christopher. I prayed that I would be able to carry this weighty pack up the path, for it was getting more difficult as we ascended higher and higher, and I swear it got heavier as we moved on.

Each step seemed to take an eternity. I was sure that my strength would give way at any moment. "How can a little donkey pull such a heavy load?" I groaned to no one in particular, as I struggled along. I appreciated animal helpers, and all those humble ones who carry heavy burdens in our world, even more as I strained under the load I bore.

Nod, ahead of me following Dankin, took the difficult terrain in stride with no signs of extra effort, I thought. It seemed like it took hours to go a short distance, but finally we entered a cave entrance in the side of a cliff. Dankin promptly pulled his cart into the opening and stopped, to wait for us weaker species to bring our load forth. Nod, sweating profusely now, carefully put his basket back on the cart, then turned, took mine off my shoulder and set it beside his. What a relief I felt. Then without a word Dankin moved forward into the tunnel, lit by torches bracketed on the tunnel walls. Both Nod and I were exhausted. We reached out and grasped the support posts on the back of the cart and let the donkey pull us along.

The going was easier now, but not well-lit, since the torches were far apart. However, I could see that the cave was well-tended and kept in good order, for some purpose by someone. Dankin knew the way and pulled us along without hesitation. We went deep into the cavern and passed over an underground stream on a slightly arched bridge. The bridge was so carefully built, that I wondered who might have made it; yet at the same time it looked natural to the setting. It was narrow and had no sides, but Dankin didn't falter and pulled his cart safely across. Nod could sense my weariness and said, "Soon we will rest."

I began to hear sounds, not long after we crossed the bridge. Many voices echoed from the depth of a cavern, which we soon entered. It was huge and looked like an underground city. People of different races, genders and ages were busily going here and there. Brilliant colors in this place brightened up the underground grotto, which was well-lit with many torches and some crystal reflectors, which magnified and multiplied the torch light. The cavern the city occupied was enormous, with layers of open passageways going up and down its stone walls, with small openings, like apartments. Doorways were sometimes just draped with bright-colored cloth; but some had doors of intricately carved wood. Still many were just open to the central grotto. The busy people greeted Nod, after they saw Dankin pulling the cart, dragging us along behind. They immediately helped us. I noticed that overall they were robust, even the younger ones. I watched in amazement, as every last basket was shouldered and transported, even by some very little children, and Dankin pulled an empty cart, prancing along like he owned the world. Nod noticed my astonished look and said, "Yes, they are strong in body, as well as in mind and soul. This place fosters such strength, lad, as you shall see."

We followed Dankin to a lower level chamber, which was bigger than it looked from the entrance off the main path. It was Nod's place now, and he had been busy setting up his workshop, since he arrived a few weeks ago.

"How did you find such a place?" I asked, still amazed. It reminded me of the high mountain sanctuary, but was more open at the central chamber we originally entered.

"I didn't find it; it found me," he said. "After the dream I mentioned to you, a priestess came to get me, told me to gather my things and follow her. She said she had a place for me for the mission ahead. Since I hadn't yet mentioned that dream to anyone, I had no doubt she was part of the plan. I quickly gathered what I could and departed for my unknown destination. I was amazed myself, as you no doubt are, too, lad; for I have encountered those who live beneath the earth before, but never such a bustling place as this. They offered this area for my work, and I quickly accepted. Little by little Dankin and I have been gathering what I require, as we also looked for you. My little donkey loves these kind folk," he added. "They anticipate his needs and help him, just as they do people. He's getting downright spoiled."

"Speaking of which," he said, "let's take our little friend to his quarters." We went deeper, to a place in the far back of Nod's work area, but still connected to his space, where spring water trickling from a rock into a natural bowl-shaped stone, and straw on the floor along with hay, awaited Dankin.

"This is the perfect place for such a loyal servant," I said, as I scratched Dankin behind one of his long ears. Dankin leaned into me and sighed a sound of donkey pleasure.

"Oh no!" Nod corrected. "Dankin's not my servant, but rather my friend. He's free to come and go at will, and he frequently does just that, though where he goes, I'm not so sure. All I know is when I need good company, or help, he shows up, and I appreciate his gift of friendship. The least I can do is honor his comfort, for all he does for me." Then he said, "If you keep scratching his ears like that, I won't have to look far for him."

"Now, how would you like to get a bit of well-deserved rest, too, lad? I have a place ready for you." Exhausted, I followed him back along another narrow path within his chambers, which stepped up into a higher nook. If I had not been shown the way, I wouldn't have found the tunnel that led to a small room. The little space had a comfortable mat, which was laid out and ready for a weary traveler such as I, and a torch was lit, filling the place with a golden light. As I entered the room, it had a familiar smell and feeling about it.

"This feels like home," I said to Nod.

"Does it, lad?" he asked. He often answered my questions with other questions. "Rest now and I'll come for you in awhile. We have to meet the council here, and introduce you to the people of this sacred secret place."

He departed, leaving me to my rest. I lay down upon the mat, which seemed so familiar and welcoming. I instantly fell into a peaceful slumber.

# THE ALCHEMIST'S APPRENTICE
Chapter Twenty-One

The delightful rest I enjoyed in my tiny cave chamber was a pure pleasure and desperately needed. I was allowed to rest as long as I wanted. When I finally felt the urge to arise and move on with my intended purpose, I went to find Nod. I found him working at the forge, in a circular chamber which had an air shaft up to the surface. As I arrived, he nodded indicating his awareness of my presence, and motioned for me to hand him some metal that he was forming on an anvil. However, at this point this piece of metal was languishing in a water basin, fed by an underground stream in one of its 'tempering'[79] stages. He simply pointed and indicated he needed it, when I entered the room. I brought the metal to him, and he laid it in a bed of coals, until it became white hot again. When he was satisfied that it was ready for more forming, he put it back on his anvil and began hitting it, with a heavy hammer made of metal as well. This same process went on and on, hammering, cooling, reheating and hammering again, for hours. He was so focused on his task that he didn't speak to me. The sound echoed around the chamber and seemed musical, because with each impact at different places on the piece, the sound varied. He was so caught up in listening to the ring and ting of the sounds as he worked, that he was oblivious to anyone or anything else.

"Sorry, lad," he eventually said, as he put the hammer down. "One has to form the metal when the fire is receptive, or it won't cooperate. I tell you, if the fire won't work with you, your effort will get you nothing but more burns and bruises. Then he inquired if I rested well, was comfortable and accommodated sufficiently.

"I rested well, Nod," I replied and felt that he would be an easy taskmaster to learn from, due to his concern for my comfort. Maybe this time my lessons will be easier, I thought.

"Good, because from this point on, we rest only if or when there is time. We have much to cover in your training, and I have too many commissions, to be lying about wasting time. When I work, you work." Looking at me with a stern expression, he went on to say, "I fully expect you to do your part and be a decent assistant as a sword maker, since I've taken valuable time from my work to offer you the lessons you need."

I must have looked a bit lackadaisical because his voice became gruffer. He said, almost in a growl, "Do you understand me, lad? Because, if you aren't willing to help me; I'm not going to waste my time with you."

So much for an easy taskmaster, I thought. I assured him I was ready and willing to abide by his terms. I certainly had a new

---

[79] Hardening stage in metal achieved by rapidly cooling red hot metal

respect for this little man, who could growl and bellow with the best and biggest of men.

Forgetting about taking me to meet with the council, he began my training immediately. "Now, the first lesson is the fire. A fire always contains a spirit that uses this form as its body, its opportunity to have 'beingness'.[80] Every priestess knows this and I'm sure your mother has mentioned it."

Feeling a little lacking in that area, since I couldn't remember having that conversation with her, I reluctantly shook my head 'no'. He looked surprised and I felt I needed to offer an explanation. I've been away a lot, Nod, and though I think I've always been aware that there are spirits, or entities within all creation, I hadn't thought of fire that way before, nor has anyone spoken with me of it. The old mountain sages did teach me how to converse with the stone people, however, and since the stones were wisdom keepers, I've enjoyed conversations with them," I said, hoping that this would somehow make up for the lack I had in my fire knowledge.

"Well, you better recognize the spirit within the fire, or you'll get nowhere in alchemy, lad, for the basis of alchemy is a cooperative agreement with the elements; fire is the hardest to work with to get it right, the next being water."

He then said, "There's spirit in the water over there flowing from the underground stream into the bowl. Spirit is in the rocks and earth, which form the walls of these rooms. One day when you have the time, talk to these rocks, since you already know how. They'll tell you a tale or two." I was all 'ears,'–as my mother would say when I'm extremely interested in what someone is saying–and I could see Nod becoming a bit more patient and less dominant, as he noticed my level of attention. He then continued saying, "The very air in here, and out in the open, has spirits, and they show themselves through the dancing and swirling wind. That's how they move about and play, or release any emotion they hold. But for now, let's concentrate on the fire, and before you

---

[80] Consciousness within the form

ask, yes, all creation has emotional responses to its experience. Have you ever heard, or seen, a 'raging fire'? You better hope you don't. Fire isn't nice when it's that mad, I assure you."

He turned to his work, focusing on the fire pit. He said, "I work with a fire elemental I have named 'Ember'. There are many fire elementals, and just as we humans, they are eager to experience being physically manifested. I call this one friend, and I have named him, not because it calls itself by that name, but because it knows that when I speak the sound of the name, I am speaking to it in all due respect. Naming should always be done in respect, lad. So when I make a fire, I'll be talking to my friend Ember, so no need to be looking under tables or around the room when I converse with this helpful friend. Without his cooperation, I wouldn't be successful in my intentional purpose of forging the steel."

He was in his teacher mode now and continued on to say, "As I put the fire components together, I'll do a ritual of sorts taught to me by my dear wife. The women are the true ritual experts, and she is the best I know in that department. I'll talk to the spirit of the wood, or whatever I may be using for fuel, to give fire its moment to be. Sometimes it is camel dung or sheep dung that I might burn, depending on how I need the fire to interplay within my project. I've had to use human dung as well a time or two, but that's a long story, and I'll spare you for now." I must have looked surprised, as Nod found my reaction a bit humorous and chuckled slightly as he continued with the lesson.

"Each component has essence. In the case of the dung, I'm actually conversing with the animal that offered the substance and integrating it into my project. Everything has a purpose and that which we might cast off has many ways to fulfill other missions, even when we think it's just waste." He looked at me with a questioning look upon his face and said, "Do you follow me, lad?"

"I spent some time at the place of discard, and I noticed that," I answered.

Looking perplexed, he said, "I'm surprised that you would go there being a Jew, for don't they consider it a place of the unclean and, heaven forbid, a Jew should get dirtied?

"I was a bit 'mad,' when I was there," I said. "I found the sweetest, most humble people and animals in the place of discard, sorting and sifting the castaway stuff from the city. My little savior, Alenesha, was among those. She and her mother are with my mother now, but Alenesha told me of many treasures they found, including the cart they brought me home on when I lost consciousness. It's odd, the things that people think are no longer of any value, and they discard. Thankfully, Alenesha said, all that unwanted stuff gave the castaway people, and the so-called 'unclean' animals, a place to explore and harvest. Alenesha and the animals helped me see how limiting attitudes are, and how we don't even realize the abundance we already have, so it goes unused or discarded."

"When did you visit this place and why did you have to be carted home?" Nod asked, finding it hard to picture the likes of me in such a place.

"I was there a short while before I came to find you," I replied. "But most of my memories are foggy, due to being out of my head with the madness."

"What were you mad about?" Nod asked.

"I was angry at the pompous priests, who thought they were better, holier, and more deserving, than the people they were supposedly serving. Their lack of compassion and warped logic about being chosen by God to the point that they proposed to be the word of God and deem judgment on others, pushed me over the edge. Arrogance and stupidity made me so angry; I literally went 'mad'."

"And how long did you stay in the place of discard, and why did you leave?" he asked.

"I was told I stayed months, living with the rats and trying to be one of them." Nod looked somewhat amused when I revealed that part. "I left the day I was injured by a robber, who was stashing the items he had pilfered within the waste of a wealthy man's home. He thought that I would get to his ill-gotten treasure before he did, so he split my head open with a club. I don't remember too many actual moments. I have some memory like a dream, or vision relating to the time I left. I vaguely remember that on the trip home in that precious cast-off cart, I thought I saw my guardian friend Elmira, holding the shafts like he was harnessed where the donkey would go, but he was running like a race horse, and the others were having a difficult time keeping up with him. He was like a parent to me from the time I was 5-years-old and sent away to the high mountain sages. He stayed with me, until I was eleven-years-old. Maybe, I was hallucinating within my great pain. He saved my life so many times I can't count," I said with heartfelt memory.

"What became of him, lad?" Nod tenderly asked, as he patiently let me tell my tale with no hurrying.

"He was released from his service of being my guardian, when I came back this last time. He went away to do whatever he wanted to do. He just drifted off and was gone from my life."

Nod seemed to be thinking this over and finally said, "Those that affect our lives this much are never as far away as you think, lad, but now let's get back to the lesson." He turned to the fire and said, "Ember, I'll let you go and dance in other fires if you choose, but we still have much to do yet on this project, and I'll call upon you again, my friend." Nod then asked me to bring water to him, which I did by dipping a clay vessel into the rock basin fed by a little trickle of water coming through the rock above it. I looked into the clear cool liquid, hoping to see the spirit Nod mentioned, but all I saw was sparkling fresh water.

Nod spoke to Ember again and said, "Our friend water will help you sizzle out of here," and he began to poor water over the fire. As he did so, he sang a chant, *"Water, cool and refreshing. Your service is requested to neutralize this fire, thus free my beloved friend Ember therein. I ask that you do your magic to release his spirit for a while, until he comes again to assist me once more."*

As he poured the water over the fire, he continued to chant ritualistic words—*"Please marry together, fire with water, water with fire. Evaporate as you must, and dance with the air elementals as vapor clouds. Fire and water—water and fire—merged and changed,"* he sang, as he poured the last of the water on the fire, *"You are now air-born, and you are free."* After that he bowed his head and whispered, "My gratitude is eternal."

I watched amused and amazed, because I clearly saw what looked like dancing figures in the mist that arose from the sizzling fire. The figures looked male and female. They playfully twirled and entwined in a dance, which I can only describe as 'sensual' in nature. I was just beginning to feel the awakening of sexuality within my own body and mind, and this sight was slightly arousing to me. While I was watching the scene play out, it simply faded and drifted out the portal of the forging chamber. I watched it move into the open courtyard of our complex where it faded away.

Nod saw me watching and remarked, "I know what you're thinking and yes, fire is a masculine element, even as it can take a feminine form. The water is a feminine element, even as it, too, can take the opposite form. As you saw here, lad, they were definitely enjoying the natural modes of their essence. I sometimes wonder if Ember, when his work is done, has more fun than I do. This isn't the first time he has joined with water in such a sensual way."

He could sense that as a young man, I was confused about such things, even as I was fascinated, so he decided further explanation was necessary. "When I told the water to marry the fire, I was, in essence, saying to the feminine, go meet the masculine and then merge and become another form. All creation is both masculine and feminine, in essence, but in the case of humans and many animals and most plants, lad, there is a prioritization at birth or sprouting, as to which modality will dominate, with the other mode being supportive. It's true with elements, as well. Air is masculine in nature, but since it is of the ethers, it's more accommodating to both energies so shape-shifts easier. It has no mass, so solid forms can occupy portions of its being. For the most part, however, remember the air element is 'out there,' thus it is the external energy and being so is most often masculine in nature."

I then said, "But air is both energies, as you said, just prioritizing the masculine. Isn't that right?" I questioned.

"For the most part, that's true," Nod said, "but the emotional wind can be its feminine form, so it's difficult to label the energies that the elements utilize. Remember Tara, the earth, is more feminine, in essence, but she has masculine qualities, too, as seen when she is spouting volcanic eruptions. In addition, the elements are all part of each other. The air feeds the fire, and the water changes the fire to mists. That's followed by the mists raining down on the earth, which sprouts new life or sustains life already upon and within Tara. What is consumed in fire becomes ash, and it goes back to mother earth, too. The waterways reflect the liquid emotional climate of all creation upon the planet and on and on. Just realize that the elements are entities, and that they combine and dance with each other to facilitate creation."

He could see me digesting this information, but he wasn't done yet with my lesson.

"You might then say that fire, Ember today as manifested, is extremely aggressive, very forceful and out there, while the water can be introspective and internal within itself. She absorbs, rather than expands as the fire does. However, water can be turbulent and forceful, just as the fire can be simple warmth. You see, there are ranges of energetic balance, even within the preferred modality." He glanced at me, to see if I was grasping what he was trying to convey. "You must understand this knowledge of energy within elements, to master alchemy," he emphasized, with his brow wrinkled as if he was worried I might not fully appreciate what he was trying to teach me.

I was in deep thought over the revelations he presented and remained silent. He then said, "We'll spend some time getting to know the elementals, especially those that are found in fire, water, air and earth. You'll soon enough grasp the core of this teaching, for in order to understand balance and imbalance, one must understand the energetic dual-modalities and how they work together. Even so, we'll explore those beings that live in metal, wood and stone, as they are families of the original four elements, which are also the building blocks of that body you get around within."

My eyes were glued on Nod's eyes. He said with a chuckle, "You can blink now, lad," and I realized I was locked on his words and intensely staring at him. I did this when I was extremely interested and expanding the parameters of my awareness.

Thus my lessons began and I was pleased to be a student of this learned master. Nod was a smallish man, as I said. He didn't look sturdy enough to handle the heavy loads, he often hoisted to his shoulders, or those he just picked up and carried off in his arms. For that matter, the children who helped unload Dankin's cart didn't appear all that strong either. I was beginning to think I was quite the weakling. Nod, who I discovered regularly seemed to know what I was thinking, assured me that strength comes, when it's needed. When I took on my own share of lifting and carrying, I did become stronger, as the days and weeks progressed. My body also filled out as my muscles developed, but the greater gift was that my mind expanded, due to the teachings of Nod.

Nod made a couple of leather aprons and trousers for me, since when we were within the chamber of fire, Ember's sparks flew all over the place. Leather doesn't smolder and burn like our robes would. I appreciated the lightness and coolness of my robe, after spending many hot hours dressed in leather garments. Yet, Nod wouldn't let me complain. Once I made mention that these animal skins were hot and sticky, and I got an entire lecture on how the poor animal sacrificed its life, for the purpose of keeping my butt from burning up.

It was difficult to gauge time spent in this mysterious place, because we couldn't tell day from night. The only clue I had was there was a certain time they dimmed the torches. Nod kept me occupied, even during that time. When we could take a break, we ate or slept. That wasn't regular, either. If Nod and I were involved in forging a sword (he did several while I was with him), we continued until we were done with the segment, be it the blade or the beautiful, but simple guards, hilts and pommels. He said all his projects were acts of creation. Each had to be correct to the minutest degree and no two were alike. Creation didn't conform to time frames, he assured me.

Ember, the fire elemental, was summoned many times as Nod brought the temperature of the fire to the exact degree of heat needed. In order to do so, he would require the right substance to feed Ember's flames. The earth would supply the substance for the metal to be made, and it had to be 'married' repeatedly to other substances, to get the metal formed correctly. Nod worked with steel, bronze, platinum and even early aluminum of sorts, forming components that would become one with the sword, thus they would be the sword's inner-essence. Nod was ahead of his time in metallurgy. He knew how to make several metals, that were either considered new at the time, or yet to be discovered. He also used gold and silver as well, along with crystallized stones of all sorts, for his work. Sometimes the crystallized stones were ground up and added to the heated molten metal; I noticed that there were ritualistic songs involved, when this was done. One stone Nod prized was raw diamonds. The Nubians often brought him this substance, in trade for some metal items, custom-made for them. These were usually spear tips and ornaments for their body decoration. The diamonds would make a blade hard and extremely sharp, and were an important component of the work, I learned by observation, which was one of the ways Nod taught me. With each step in the process, there had to be a ritual of asking permission from the elemental, to be part of this creation. When the sword was at the finishing state it was etched with symbols of balance and peace, but always slightly different, due to those for whom the tool was intended. That's what set Nod's work apart from other sword-makers; his swords had an intention of ultimate peace, even as they were commonly understood as instruments of destruction and power. Once the sword was forged and etched, it was named by Nod.

"Do you ask the one who commissioned the sword for the name?" I asked.

"Naming awakens the spirit that is attracted to the vehicle of possibility," he answered. Then, he continued, "Sometimes I ask the recipient and sometimes not, but I always name what I create, just as God named all creation. Actually, I usually let the sword tell me its name, for it frequently likes to announce itself as an entity, and claim an identity of its own." Whole new worlds opened up within my mind, as I pondered that remark.

The swords were always beautiful, but not always extremely ornate, unless they were commissioned by someone who wished to display their power, such as royalty or warriors of high rank. Nod wouldn't take commissions from just anyone. It was the priestesses who connected him to those for whom he agreed to create swords.

Thus it was one day, after I had been with him awhile, that I saw the procession of priestesses come forth from the outer world, and recognized the gentle easy glide of my mother leading the group of about thirteen individuals. I was getting Nod some stones he had stored near the entrance of our quarters, when I saw her. My heart jumped and I forgot my mission, dropped the stones, and ran to her, so glad to see her lovely face again.

She didn't hesitate to change her course either and ran my direction. No mother could have been happier to see her son than Patient Mary was when she caught sight of me. When we met, I picked her up and spun her around, and her robes flared out like a beautiful mauve rose. Her robes were a dusty pink color, once red but now worn and subdued from long use, and as they billowed in the wind as we spun with joy, they seemed like rose petals coming to full bloom. Even as we spun, I said, "It's so good to see you out of the black robes of mourning."

"I still miss him every day, son," she reminded me, "but I don't always play the games that restrict women unfairly. I just pick and choose where I'll conform and where I won't."

She laughed and when I put her down, said, "Now you twirl me, son, instead of me twirling you." Standing back she remarked, "You have grown to a man and wouldn't you know it, you do this when I can't watch the wonder of it." She checked me as only mothers are allowed to do with a man and noted that my arms were more muscular; then she ran her small sweet hand slowly down the side of my face, studying it like she was examining a masterpiece of art.

"You are strong like your father and your body has filled out to that of a man in this city of the Brambles[81]. I fear I have lost my little boy, and wonder if the man who replaced him will know that I never had the time I wanted, to spoil my dear child, now a handsome man."

I turned red. I hadn't ever been called a man before, with Nod still calling me, lad. I hadn't noticed my body change, but I was developing an interest in watching the priestesses, especially the ones in the virgin years,[82] as the young maidens moved about the Bramble community. They seemed to be checking me out, as well, and would giggle when they saw me notice them. The leather clothing I wore for the forging process was tight-fitting. I didn't realize that my body was so revealed within the garments of the smithy helper and evidently, for a priestess, I was a sight to behold.

Nod, wondering what had become of me, poked his head out the doorway of our chambers, somewhat irritated. When he saw my mother, he smiled a visual welcome. Before he could speak to her however, one of the priestesses came flying out of the group, grabbed him and twirled him around and around, laughing as she spun. It was a sight to see, since this priestess was a large woman. She didn't look old enough to be Nod's mother, and she was flinging Nod around like a rag doll. He didn't seem to mind, either.

Mother saw my confusion and said, "Claressa[83] doesn't get to see her husband all that often when he's out on one of his missions.

---

[81] Underground network connected to a large cavern where people secretly lived, so named due to the prickly brambles that often hid the various entrances
[82] Simply meaning teenage years
[83] Means 'clear spirit'

Because they don't keep a constant home together, when they do catch up to each other, it's usually gleeful."

I can't tell you how odd their reunion looked to me. He was such a no-nonsense stern taskmaster with me, and here he was, giggling, along with his wife, whom you could tell he loved dearly. She had him off the ground in her gleeful twirl. When she set Nod to his feet, he was dizzy and slightly wavering, as he tried to regain his footing, looking like a happy drunk man.

"Claressa," he said tenderly, "you know you make me dizzy when you do that, my love. I didn't know that you would be paying me a visit in the middle of my project here, or I would be presentable."

"Oh! I assure you that you are presentable to me in that leather garb you wear to make fire, and I shall want you to make some fire for me soon." That was the first and only time I saw Nod blush.

She continued on and said, "There's a lot you men don't know, and we can show up most anywhere at any time."

"I believe that," Nod said as he took his wife's hand.

Claressa looked back towards mother, now joined by Jemima, my little sister and Alenesha, my little savior. It was apparent that they knew exactly what she meant by that statement. They put their arms around me and gave me a tender, sweet and sincere hug. Both said, "Greetings, brother."

I replied, "I'm glad you call me brother, Alenesha."

In her small musical voice she said, "You are my brother, for Mother Mary has made it so and adopted me into the family. I've taken a new name, as well, and I am now Salome Alenesha."

"That's a beautiful name, but why would your mother allow my mother the pleasure of taking you into our family?" I asked. Alenesha subsequently looked sad. She told me that a week after my departure, they had found her mother, Bethanisha, sitting up against the wall of the little adobe house mother had secured for their use, with a smile on her face, looking peaceful but with her spirit finally free.

"She departed, having a real home and people in her life who loved her," Alenesha said. The sad look seemed to ease, as my little savior explained the situation. "Your mother told me, that my mother had asked her just the fortnight, if anything happened to her, would she take me as her daughter. Your mother, of course, was honored to be trusted enough for such a favor. She told my mother, that she already considered me as one of her own. Mother Mary had no idea how soon that promise would be kept."

Giving her a big brother hug, I told her I was pleased to have yet another dear sister to love and adore, and gave her my condolences at the passing of her mother. I could tell she still mourned her. They were very close and had only each other for so long.

Nod and his wife left for his chambers. Mother took my hand and said, "Let them have some alone time. She misses him terribly. She has yet another commission that would be asked of him and this time, it's from a warrior of high rank."

"I don't quite understand how Nod can be a man of peace and make swords," I muttered.

Mother squeezed my hand and said, "Let's go to the well, and sit and chat. I do my best discussion at the well," she explained. "I think the well helps me get my feelings and emotions balanced."

I had a broader understanding of that now. I may have heard such things before, but probably just thought it was simply woman-talk. Like most men, we didn't pay heed to their conversations, unless it was about us. Now I knew better. I also knew the well itself was aware of all the secrets of the community.

The well was located near the center of the grotto courtyard. It was peaceful at this hour; even though I'm not sure what hour it was, but it felt like the mid-day. I didn't go outside of the Bramble City much, but I knew many of the others did, since there were countless tunnels, even some that led into homes–humble and majestic–Nod informed me. I saw processions coming forth from time to time, from many such portals into the city that we seldom left, during my apprenticeship.

"So, you want to know how a man of peace can make a sword, son?" Mother asked.

"That I do," I replied.

She told me, "Change, the only sure thing in our life, is like a double-edged sword. On one side, it's an instrument of right and fairness; on the other side, it's an instrument of power and protection. Nevertheless, most only acknowledge one side of the 'sword of change'," mother said, "And seldom did it have anything to do with fairness or true righteousness. Mostly power and control are the intention because the majority that finds need of a sword lives in fear of someone taking their own power away from them. They are often so fearful, that they frequently pledge their alliance to someone who is even more fearful, thus more aggressive and controlling. They then promise to honor and obey the mighty fearful one, and out of loyalty, die and kill for the sake of someone more afraid than they are." I never expected my mother to be wise in the ways of the warriors. She went on saying, "These types of warriors don't fully understand their relationship to the sword they use. Consequently, they are prone to a path of destruction. If they realized that whatever is created has a purpose and a responsibility, they would be fairer and less likely to be cruel. If the purpose of their sword, when it was fashioned, was to ensure peace, then they would understand that there is a responsibility to peace, instead of to destruction for the sake of fear."

"We aren't just talking about swords, are we, mother? Is the sword than the symbol of protection?" I asked.

"Yes, in a way, that's true, son. The responsibility then is to protect 'the power of peace'. Not 'take the power to control and dominate through fear'. Instead, the accountability is to maintain love and respect, and be secure within that divine intention."

"Amazing!" I said. Women's wisdom has always astonished me. I never could understand why men feared such knowing, and why they sought to deny it even existed.

Mother kept on with her explanation, saying, "There are many warriors who are peacemakers. Nod has accepted a mission of providing them with an instrument of peace, instead of an instrument of destructive ignorance. Those seekers of such swords come to the priestesses, because they are drawn to us through their peace intention. We are open to them, since we know that the peacemakers must integrate into all segments of society, even as soldiers and kings and such. When they finally realize what it is they desire, they find the words to request a sacred manifestation, from those they know still have the power to help them with their quest, the priestesses. At that time, they are evaluated as to intent and sincerity, and I tell you, we take our time in that aspect of the request, as there are those who would do anything to obtain one of the sacred swords. We have nearly let one or two of the unready wiggle through the cracks of our cross-examination, but thank 'Goddess', we have been able to filter out those who are obsessed with power to feed their fears. If the requesters are sincere enough, and finally granted the privilege of a sacred object, then there are a few, such as Nod, who are asked to provide the instrument desired, and they agree to form it. This process is accomplished through the magic of alchemy, and the sword awakens and is ready to serve the cause of peace, even within the guise of war."

"I think I see, mother," I said. "But I couldn't be a warrior, sacred sword or not."

She just laughed that little sweet way she does and replied, "You are a teacher, my son, a true master teacher, and as such, you will open the peace portals in hearts and minds. You'll build doorways, not slay demons. Don't you realize that Nod has the perfect helper in making the sword you are working on right now? It will have your energy within it, as well as his and all the other beings that give of themselves, so the sword could have form."

"I hadn't thought of that yet, mother," I said. And pondered what she had just revealed to me. I was beginning to get a grasp of how the elementals' spirits came together and created another branch of their family within the element of the forged metal. I hadn't factored in that my energy, or especially Nod's, for he was the maker, and I was just the helper, would also be part of the sword.

"He has just named it," I told mother, "Excalibur[84]." She listened with interest, nodding her head in a knowing way. I added, "He says one day it will find its true destiny and pierce evil and overcome suffering. He also told me it would heal the heart with peace and be legendary, always representing the sacred power of a holy mission. He said it could only be activated by a peace-warrior."

I had a feeling that my sword lessons were done, now that Excalibur was finished. However, I still felt that there were a few loose ends yet. I changed the subject a bit and said, "Nod told me that we would work with water, after the sword is finished. But, now that he has another commission, maybe that won't happen. I look forward to beginning my mission, mother, but I don't look forward to leaving you time and again," I whispered, there on the bench by the well as I hugged Mother to my side, so happy in her presence.

"Sons are meant to leave their mothers," she said. "And mothers will always miss them, but if they truly love them, they'll gladly free them to fly to the places they must go, to be the men their souls intended. I'll always miss you. If you'll allow, from time to time, I will follow you. I now must be about my priestess work, as well. With both Jemima and Alenesha at my side, I want to do some traveling and connecting to priestesses from other places, so that we can coordinate our purpose and assist you, as you move about and teach the multitudes. Each group you seek, I intend, will have some of us present to help hold the energy in balance and keep the portals of receptivity ready.

"I'm honored that you're willing to do this for me, mother. However, I fear that I might put you in danger, because I intend to

---

[84] Means 'true king', one who shows the way as opposed to one who holds the power and position

bring about change in attitudes. I'm sure those who consider themselves chosen as more worthy, will surely resist with all their might what I intend to teach, since they don't want to share 'worthiness'. They might try to hurt you to silence me, and it would be the worst pain I could imagine."

She sadly looked at me and reminded me, "That's my responsibility–not yours." Tenderly she explained, "You can't keep that which you love in a sacred box, or you would keep it prisoner. Out of love, I free you in my heart and mind to do what you must. Out of love, you will free me and anyone else for the same reason." Then she looked serene and said, "You'll love so many and will give a great deal of yourself so that they can be free." I knew my mother was a priestess, but I had never realized she was a prophetess, too. Her face didn't show joy, when she envisioned the future that she just alluded to. I didn't ask, for who would want to know?

Mother stayed for a while, maybe a night or two; it's hard to tell, because of the absence of sunlight. Mother and I visited for hours, enjoying each other's company. My sisters were in a priestess quick-teach class, a demonstration of something that they didn't share with me. Mother and I were treated to delightful meals and much pampering from the moment she arrived. Finally, we fell asleep talking to each other, upon my sleeping mat in my room when the torches dimmed. I learned, during one of these conversations, that my own mother had prepared the room for me, and the blanket was from our humble home. No wonder it smelled and felt like home, when I first entered the room. There was no shame in our sleeping arrangements. Within this place, most leaders were women, and they knew that a mother could sleep snuggled with a son, no matter what age and not mar his or her innocence.

A few days later the priestesses left. Nod told me that the new commission would be accomplished at another place and another time, for there were territorial components needed for each commission, with substances from certain places that would better fulfill the need. Nod announced that, now we would move on to the lessons of the water transformation.

Water and fire, according to Nod, were the two most powerful substances that are within the realm of physicality. There are the major building blocks of creational endeavors, which take on biological form, one being masculine and the other feminine. Fire and water absorb each other, even as they change each other into a new form, or a new merged creation. "Once you understand the nature of the substance or essence of the elements, you'll better be able to transform them into other forms," Nod told me.

I was trying to follow along but must have looked a bit dazed, for he then said, "Just like your father merged with your mother and a new form, an 'off-spring' if you will, was begotten–you dear, lad– you have the essence of both your father and mother, yet you are your own person. So too, when changing elements you use this principle. The forms than would have the basic essence of the pure element, but take on characteristics of their own, as 'off spring' of the original element and their purity remains, but in an expanded essence. Metal is such a thing. It is the off-spring of earth and fire, tempered by air and strengthened in water."

My next lesson was turning water into one of its off-springs. Using fire and various other basic elements, I learned to turn water into blood and many other substances; but the one I think most people think of, from the legends of my life, was turning water into wine. It was easier by far than sword making.

In essence, the process goes something like this: the fruit, the 'off-spring' of the vine, which is rooted in the terrain (thus 'off-spring' of the earth) is formed of mostly water that protects the 'seed,' which will sprout and emerge to form another vine in perfect reflection of its parent, if it is allowed maturity. If that 'off-spring' is given freedom from the vine when it's ripe it separates from the parent, and the cycle continues. It's the watery substance that will feed and strengthen the fruit that contains a new seed, until it drops into the feminine earth to renew the cycle. That same watery substance also creates wine. Thus knowing that wine is fermented juice, which is the milk of the fruit, all one had to do is ask the water to take on that form of wine essence, which wasn't difficult and quite pleasurable. I greatly simplify here, because there are ritualistic aspects of this whole process that I'm not free to share in this narrative. It only took a couple of tries to accomplish changing water to wine, but more time to develop the ability to have a good-tasting wine. This was the most pleasant work. It was offset by helping Nod in the final preparation of Excalibur, which included crafting the scabbard for it.

I spent pleasant hours polishing the beautiful metal blade and the stone and wood grips. Nod was usually working on the ornate leather sheath, and he could be talkative when relaxed. With the stress and hardest work done he shared enjoyable conversation with me, often stories about his adventurous life. This stage always put him in a good mood, and I think the visit with his dear Claressa, elevated his normal stoic disposition too.

During this time, I learned much from Nod of the customs of the Samaritan people. I found that they hated being considered unclean, and their communities were a bit more matriarchal than most. They believed that if they ate the flesh of an animal, they then took in its essence and must honor its sacrifice, or it would not nourish them. They had customs of slaughter that hinged on sacred sacraments, but for the sacrificial victim, not for those for whom it was sacrificed. The animal had a choice, and careful attention was paid to them, to ensure the offering was soulfully honored. Thus the rare swine destined for the table of sacrifice, lived a charmed life and was told of the gratitude of those who would benefit from its gift. There were signs they looked for from the animal, which would determine if it was ready to be slaughtered or set free. They also didn't sacrifice for the sake of elitist priests, or to satisfy a blood-thirsty God, but rather for those in need of such nutrients within the community, and they always consumed all the flesh. First the ones in most need were given the meat offering, and then with no pecking order, others who wished could share in the offering of the slaughtered animal.

Nod said, "It's not an ideal society, lad. No, there are many with bad attitudes within the borders of Samaria, I assure you. But my people are more prone to be less judgmental. I'm not sure if we're born with the instinct, or if it's taught to us, but when we see any being in need we react immediately to help them without making a conscious decision. It's simply our nature. If someone is hungry, then to us, they are the most worthy of any available food. That's a concept the priests of the Hebrews forgot, the arrogance of the Romans don't understand, and they fear it so much they call us 'unclean.' That instills harsh judgment of us, so we can't spread our ideas and upset their power and privilege."

"Now, lad," he went on to say, "I must leave on the morrow, for I want to spend some time with my family, before I depart to gather the materials I'll need for my new commission. I may have to go to Rome, to get what I require this time. I want to have some time with my dear wife and children, before I depart, too."

"You don't need me?" I asked.

Nod looked at me, with a knowing smile lightly written across his wise face, and said, "Rather, now, you don't need me, lad."

When I awoke the next morning he was gone, and I knew that I was ready to begin my mission, in earnest.

# THE SAGA OF THE ANCIENTS
Chapter Twenty-Two

As the day of my departure began, I couldn't help but wish I had more time to explore this underground city. Mother told me, when she and I talked all night, that many such places were hidden from those holding power and control of the surface lands and people. They believed that they knew everything, thus were everything, she said. She told me that this city and many others like it, held thousands of people from time to time, and had layers and layers of underground caverns and tunnels going deeper and deeper. The priestess cult, which had gone into hiding to survive, was among those who utilized the forgotten caverns. Those who used the caves were 'secret-keepers,' and for good reason, thus these were secret places. I departed the same morning that Nod left, with a group of priestesses traveling through the tunnels, on a mission to collect rare herbs in the outer realms.

I was the only male, among a group made up of teachers and younger maidens in training. The young girls looked my way and giggled from time to time, which made me blush in embarrassment, which resulted in them giggling even more. The teachers just smiled and shook their heads knowing, no doubt, what feelings and trepidations my presence aroused within the girls. Since I was now full into my physical maturity, the feelings I was experiencing were confusing and pleasant at the same time. I hoped that one day I would have a priestess teacher in sacred sexuality, so I could handle these situations with more grace. I had no clue how to process such things as sexual arousal, and at that point in my life, I wasn't sure what the warm rush was. I felt glad for the loose-fitting robes I was again wearing. Such attire offered a better chance for a shy young man to hide within. If I could have covered my face like a monk, I would have done so, too.

I must say, I loved the ease at which these young maidens moved about within these underground places. Even their usual garb was more colorful than the normal clothing upon the surface. The young women reminded me of butterflies that flitted about in gardens. However, today they wore over-robes such as mine, for on the surface one must not stand out as unusual, especially women who were expected to fade into the background of society. Thus the butterflies had to put on their drab under-wings, as I saw it, to go out into the open air. They reminded me of the brilliant blue butterflies, who folded their wings when they didn't want to be noticed, with the underside an earth brown and a perfect camouflage.

Hours passed, as we moved through passageways. The teachers held torches as they walked, and I noticed some symbols on the walls from time to time. They seemed ancient and quite well-executed, with animals and people depicted. I also saw a pictograph of a dinosaur with people watching it and wasn't sure what the image was intended to relate. There were small niches within the tunnels, which contained earthen jars, some plain and others colorfully painted. I surmised that they were for storage deep here inside Tara, our mother earth. The atmosphere was surprisingly dry and comfortable. At intervals, there were drinking basins supplied by sparkling underground springs, like Nod had in his quarters within the city of Brambles. We stopped often to refresh ourselves, because the dryness, though comfortable, made one thirsty. There was always a spill-way carved within the water basin, so the water could find its natural path upon its journey beyond the cup of refreshment. As one teacher said, "One could always expect a fresh drink of mother earth's wine to satisfy and refresh, especially this deep within Tara." Another teacher reminded us to thank the water for her lovely gift. The air was fresh, I observed. One of the maidens, knowing she was free to chat and ask questions, asked of this. The teacher said there were air shafts within the chambers we traveled in, either natural or put there by the first gods who used the same passageways. That remark sparked the girls' interest and mine, too, but I was trying to be quiet and respectful as a guest on this expedition, and I found myself a bit shy with all the ladies.

"The first gods," a young girl said. "I haven't yet heard of first gods. Who are they, teacher?" she asked.

"That, child," she replied, "is an entire class. One day you'll advance to that class, if you are suited for the knowledge, but for now, be it enough to know that they were not always good just because they were gods. Like all beings, they were on a path of learning, and they had much to learn, even if we remember them as 'gods'."

The girls begged for more information. The teachers decided that to tell some of the tale would help pass the time, and we had a long journey through the underground tunnels, to reach the portal they intended to exit.

The teacher continued, "They were from another place in the heavens. They needed gold for their own planet, because it was losing its breath, or the air that the beings breathed, due to the planet's auric field. The aura belt had developed holes, due to poisons that were coming from the surface. The people of the planet had misused their resources, causing the problem, and depleted the protective barrier that naturally surrounds such places."

The elder teacher, a storyteller, began talking as she walked along in the lead position. The cave walls helped to amplify her words, as the sound was so contained within the tunnels of bedrock that it made her voice crisp and clear, no matter what direction she faced as she spoke.

"They had an ability to make mechanical devices, which would find and change gold, transforming it into an extremely lightweight powdered substance. It would be used as a protective barrier between the void and the planet they occupied," she said as she moved along at a fairly rapid pace. "They did this by spreading the fine essence of gold into the belt of energy, or aura, of their planet. The essence of gold then became integrated with the auric-belt[85] and held a protective seal, as the planet moved through its cyclical journey across the heavens. This insured that their sun's rays wouldn't harm them. They also ingested some of the gold powder to keep their own aura strong," she added.

"Why would they need a barrier between their planet, the sun and the void, teacher?" another girl asked.

The patient elder teacher had long white hair that hung loosely, nearly dragging on the ground behind her when she stood still, which she seldom did. As she moved, it seemed to be weightless as it floated like a white fluffy cloud behind her. She turned to look at the girl who inquired, even as she continued the brisk walking pace forward, and her hair swirled like a white spiral as she looked over her shoulder. I was impressed; she was so gracefully agile at her age. She continued with the tale, saying, "As I said, this is a long story and complicated. However, each planet has a ruler, a mighty hot and bright sun. Those of whom I speak had an atmosphere problem of their own making, and they are one of the rare planets that had two sun-rulers. They share our own beloved sun during their long-cycle[86], but have another sun

---

[85] Same as auric field, but referring to the band of energy that protects the planet, instead of just the field itself
[86] Oblong orbit cycling around two suns

*Jeshua's Song*

planet for their short-orbit[87] cycle. Their planet is much bigger than our Tara (the priestess cult knew that planets were orbs that floated in the void), and it took a lengthy path each year as the planet traveled across the heavens within the void to make its cycles, which looked like an infinity symbol (∞); thus its year was extremely extended beyond ours, as was true for its day as well. Our sun, their 'long-cycle sun,' is the long-timekeeper[88]. The other sun is the major life-giving star of their home planet. It offered an opportunity for physicality upon that plane and served as a balancing factor for the large planet of experience, as it wandered the heavens in the huge double-cycle. When the planet came close to each sun in its elliptical orbit, it had need of protection from the intensity of the light given off from these ruler stars, for there are vibrations and rays of light that they weren't yet physically ready to handle. That being so, the atmosphere, or air, was quickly becoming unable to sustain their civilization. Along with that situation, when a planet floats within the void, there are multitudes of unseen energies that bounce around, helping the heavenly orbs keep their appointed paths. These energies can harm the delicate species that live upon the planets, too. Those energies help the bigger life forms, the planets and stars, even so, smaller life forms just can't handle the intensity of the pure void, unless it is tempered to their vibration."

"How did the barrier deteriorate?" a young maiden asked.

"That was due to not respecting the body of their home planet," the teacher said, with a sound of regret. "The protective barrier, which all planets develop before an agreement to be a physicality plane, was compromised, because the developing physical beings she fostered didn't know about the dangers of depleting resources. When they did understand, they didn't change their habits and ways of co-existing, thinking it didn't matter; little by little they thinned and punctured the aura of their beloved home. All planets hold certain barriers in place, until those beings upon, and within, its realm can accommodate the higher vibrations that the suns and the void emit. It's important to realize that you, or any creation,

---

[87] Smaller orbit cycle around the principle sun
[88] Refers to a longer cycle way of experiencing time

can't move ahead faster than your arena of evolution within the vibration of light and sound. If you do, you destroy your vehicle of physicality. The light vibrations come from the Sun, and the sound comes from the Void. As you evolve, you can expand your ability to interact with higher and higher frequencies. There's a time, however, when the beings of a planet become aware of the energy fields that surround their home. At that time, they have a choice to build a better relationship with their planet host, or to ignore what they know to be true and degrade the delicate balance of their playing field. This step up in awareness also affects their frequency tolerance, but it in no way gives the ruling species a right to ignore the love and respectful responsibility to the planet. Do you understand me?" she questioned, for she knew she was getting into some deep teachings.

Scanning her listeners for a moment and seeing the other teachers nod, as if to confirm the group was following the reasoning of the tale being told, the teacher continued. "So they found what they needed by accident on this planet, Tara, who was just a young girl herself, when they happened to visit due to an unplanned crash landing of their sky vehicle. And before you ask, yes, I know we have taught you that accidents don't just happen; but remember that which is sought, as is always the case, will reach out and seek you. Therefore, a part of Tara pulled them forth, to offer her gifts to fulfill their need."

"Tara accepted them, as they accidentally were marooned upon her surface due to some problem with their flying ships, and lo and behold, the planet was rich in the very minerals that the squadron was sent out to seek." She paused for a moment, then said, "See how it works? Need, or desire, is like a magnet and pulls to itself the fulfillment."

"Tara still had some remnants of beings, from a previous time long before, that were populating her lands. They had their own problems, adjusting to living on an adolescent planet. They were descended from beings that went through similar host-planet imbalance, due to misuse. They were imprinted by their past, even as they were beginning to heal the wounds of the long-ago mistakes upon Tara. The new explorers offered the opportunity to revisit the lesson; however, it ultimately failed once again, since the class was the 'balance of all creation'."

"Some of the surviving populations, that the marooned gods discovered, didn't honor Tara's gifts in cooperative creation, because they still were in a survival-at-any-cost mentality. It takes a long time to mend such deep imprints. Thus, some learned and advanced in evolution, and some were still in the early rediscovery stages. They had formed into small tribal groups, who had to rediscover their relationship with Tara and all creation, all over again. Many of them were like innocent children, in the early stages of learning the lessons of life. Through the years, the survivors forgot. Sometimes, through their shamans, they recalled the wisdom, which was well known but not honored so long ago."

"Tara was familiar with abuse because the early settlers, as I said, had their own struggle between fear and love, and the effects created by the choices they made. Fear being the most aggressive and destructive, took its toll on the planet's lovely body. Finally having had enough abuse, Tara became angry and literally burst with emotion and rage. Mountains blew their tops; hot lava flowed and burned the gardens, leaving the lands charred and barren. The seas rose and created giant waves that the wind blew over the charred land, still raging with fire in many places, and a poisonous sizzling steam resulted when the water met the flames. Most life forms perished. When Tara's anger abated, there wasn't much left. A few survived, among the many species, and they had to revert back to the most basic primal instincts, to save themselves and have any hope to continue on, in this place of physicality."

"Just like all creation, especially planetary ones, Tara learned and grew through the experience. Planets discover through connection to Mother God, how to control their emotional reactions to disrespect and abuse. With that lesson behind her, this time Tara tolerated the piercing of her body (from the squadron that discovered her mineral treasures), and she allowed gold and other minerals to be mined by this new group of gods. Even so, she had a hard time accommodating the gods of the underworld, or those assigned to the mining; for these overseers ultimately had developed slaves from the native remnants of the previous civilization. The slaves were genetically engineered, with their own species, in order to have a stronger larger creature, capable of understanding orders and doing hard manual labor. That was how they obtained the ore they needed. The workers suffered; their pain echoed within Tara, and she grieved."

We were fascinated with this storyteller's tale. Even though we nearly had to run to keep up with her; we craved her every word, knowing that it wasn't common knowledge.

"At the time of gold extraction, it literally hurt Tara to see how the enslaved were treated. It took all her willpower to keep from swallowing up the cruel taskmasters, who treated their own hybrid creation with such poor regard. Mother God had taught Tara that sometimes a mother has to allow her children to suffer pain to learn a lesson. Tara, after all, is a Mother Goddess, a true reflection of Sophia, or Mother God, so she watched, but didn't interfere this time. Tara hoped that soon the gods would learn the lesson of compassion. The poor slaves lived and died in these caverns. Dead ones were dumped into the deep holes where the taskmasters tossed their discarded substances. The gods of the underworld didn't hold these discard places sacred, but Tara did. She received the poor suffering slaves into her arms of love each time they were tossed away, most already dead, and some still suffering.

Since the gods used fire to partially prepare the gold for transport in their sky ships, they carved out great expansive places for their kilns. Those places were none other than the huge caverns we now use as secret cities. In those days, the caverns were full of fire. The suffering within them was so tremendous, that Tara yearned to collapse them and end the torture; but she had matured and knew that she had to restrain her violent temper."

"Now, I'm telling you, maybe, too much," the teacher said. The other teachers were silently listening, but you could tell that they knew the story being told, because they often nodded their heads in agreement as the story unfolded. The girls, thinking that this tale may end, pleaded for more, saying that they were just being prepared for the Ancients Class, and it now seemed more interesting to them. I envied the girls for having such intriguing topics to explore, yet I realized that my teachers had touched on the subject a time or two as well, but from a different perspective. Thankfully, the teacher offering the tale seemed encouraged by that remark and went on with the story of the gods, as we continued our long walking journey.

"The cavern cities were not pleasant places, dear hearts," she continued. "No! They were called 'Hell,' by all who had to be within them. Even the gods revolted more than once, due to the unpleasantness of the work and difficult conditions within the caverns. Originally, the gods thought they were up to the job of extracting the mineral themselves, which proved to be too much for them. That's why the slaves were developed, so that they could use them for the unpleasant tasks. The poor slaves tried to revolt from time to time, but quickly died on the spot, for not wanting to do what the gods themselves refused to do. The way many died was a tragedy; since the supervisors would make sure they suffered in plain sight of others, so that an example of what happened to those who didn't obey the lords was demonstrated. The power of fear was insurmountable to those kept enslaved. The double standard was abundantly clear to all involved, there, within the damnation of Hell, where some were gods and some were slaves. Even within the slaves some were more rewarded, if they spied on the others. Unfortunately, most suffered and died, so that the so-called 'worthy gods' could get what they wanted and needed."

"Why don't the pathways and the caverns hold the sorrow," a very bright young girl asked. "I feel no agony residue as we pass these ways?" Obviously this young novice was already gifted and trained in vibrational echoes[89].

"Tara remembered for a long time," our elder teacher explained. "These tunnels and caverns reverberated with the vibration of suffering," she clarified, "long after the gods had been ordered to withdraw from the planet, by galactic overseers who plainly saw

---

[89] Memory of what happened in a place, by the substances that make up the space

the situation was worsening for all involved. The pain was still so intense that it emitted poison, which made anyone within the spaces very sick." The gods wore masks, while the slaves just suffered. The Galactic Council monitors planets and their interaction with life-forms. There are always those who watch the progress of evolution. Certain lines must never be crossed, or it will affect all the heavens and beyond," she emphasized. "Ultimately, an order came from the Galactic Council demanding the gods withdraw. They simply left, leaving the slaves to their own resources with no explanation and no official release from their drudgery. They abruptly flew away in their sky vehicles and never returned."

She continued on with the tale of the gods, even as we quietly followed. It was a lot to digest. She said, "For awhile, the slaves just continued on with their work, noticing the absence of the gods, but unable to break the habit of extracting the gold, even as they could barely breathe the poisonous air. Then little by little, they realized no one was watching and directing them. They began to break ranks. Even so, a few of their own kind found some of the masks that filtered out the poison and put them on, imitating the guard gods, thinking they became gods due to the magic masks. They began to attempt to force others back to work. They were poor substitutes for the giant gods of the other world, however. Soon the slaves rebelled en masse and stopped the hellish work. They let the fires burn out and wandered away. Some were brave enough to release the imprisoned ones, who waited for their torture and death in black hole prisons. They raided the gods' quarters, looking for food, answers to why they were abandoned, and maybe more masks, because the weakest among them were having difficulty with the air. Finally, wanting to be as far as possible from the hell they lived and worked within, they struck out to find a safe place, breaking up into many small groups and following the maze of tunnels in different directions."

"There were groups who never came out of the earth. They thought they could only escape by going deeper into the depths of Tara; they developed into beings of the inner-world. The fear of going out into the open air was nearly paralyzing to most of the slaves. They thought the gods had just left hell, and would be there upon the surface waiting for them, so they dared not go to the Sun Portals[90]."

"But we live within Tara," a girl commented, "and we sometimes go outside to feel the sun on our face, and it doesn't hurt us. We are afraid of those outside, who have all the light on the outside and none within their hearts, but we still chance it and go out like we do today."

The girl's comment touched the heart of our storyteller, who tenderly continued to explain. "They were living in such fear, that many couldn't conceive of any chance outside in the light of the day. It's true, that fear can thrive in the light, and love can, likewise, thrive within the dark; for the light represents the 'known' and the dark the 'unknown'," she said. "The dark and the light are not places of good and evil, as some believe. The fear of the dark (the unknown) has created the false idea, that the realm of the unknown is an evil place. That's why we teach you to live within love, which is found in both the known and unknown arenas." We weren't sure why she was explaining this in answer to the girl's comments, but patiently waited for her explanation to unfold. "Love unites and, within this vibration, creation emerges, like a babe from the mother's dark womb, finally coming out into the light of the day. Fear can't exist as a power within love," she emphasized. "Fear separates so it can hold power. Beings often fight each other when they are afraid, which enforces separation through wars and slavery. The slaves were all afraid, and had to learn to cooperate in order to survive, when the gods left," she finally said, as she proceeded along the earthen path, once again letting us process the concepts she just shared. The story held our attention and struck us silent at the same time. We quietly followed, waiting for more.

After a short time of silence, the girl relentlessly continued to ask for clarification. As she trotted alongside the teacher trying to keep up with her, she asked, "How did Tara forget her pain and how did the very walls of the caverns and passageways forget all that took

---

[90] Entrances to the caves. From inside the sun was seen as a brilliant light

## The Saga-Oracle

place within them, for surely Tara no longer remembers the sadness, or we would feel it, wouldn't we?"

"You have learned the lesson of consciousness-echoes,[91] too," the white-haired teacher replied, still briskly walking along, amazing me with her strength and endurance. Her patience with the questions didn't falter either, as she continued with the tale, even as she knew she could only give a brief synopsis of this aspect of what the priestess called 'past-story[92]'.

"The answer to that question is, Tara never forgot. The sorrow of the experience will always be there, but through love Tara forgave and in so doing, the poisonous air cleared, too. That's how echo-cleansing[93] resolves things to peace. We priestesses found this refuge, at a time of extreme persecution, when we were being murdered and enslaved ourselves. Many women ran away, if they were lucky enough to have the opportunity of escape. Maybe Tara, understanding our sorrow, opened her portals to us, and invited us to take refuge within her chambers, because the runaway women found a cave that had not been previously noticed before. It was like the arms of mother earth took them into her safety. At first, they stayed near the cave entrance, and then eventually worked up the courage to go deeper into the subterranean labyrinth, discovering the underground city and its tunnel byways."

The other teachers were still content to let the white-haired elder tell this long complicated story, for she was the 'saga.'[94] Sagas had a talent for storytelling. She seemed to enjoy her role and continued on, saying, "Some of the priestesses developed the ability to speak to the ancestors in the spirit realms. The ancestors had mentioned the inner places, but none of us had actually seen them." She must have been one of the priestesses who spoke to the ancestors, I thought, due to her deep understanding of the past. She

---

[91] The memory of what has happened, along with the feeling that was experienced
[92] History de-genderized neither "his" or "her" story
[93] Dissolving the bad effects that a previous time imprinted
[94] The old wise-woman who passed down wisdom and events that happened, through stories or poetry

continued, saying, "I believe they led us to these safe havens below the ground and helped us understand the pictographs we found, as we explored the many inner-chambers. We learned about the previous use of the caves, because of the picture writing the former slaves drew on the walls of their keeping rooms. With the help of our spirit guides, we could understand messages more fully. That's when we learned, that they referred to the mines as 'Hell'.[95] They called the surface gardens 'Paradise,'[96] and overall, they considered the outside world, the land of the gods, or 'Eden'.[97] Through the pictographs, we were warned that Eden was not always a happy place, either."

The saga said, "The ancestors, whom the priestesses called 'Spirit Talkers',[98] spoke of beautiful fruitful places, where the gods grew their food and flowers within spectacular well-maintained gardens."

A young priestess asked, "Wasn't that supposed to be a place to serve the gods as a reward?"

"The Spirit Talkers said that was true, but one had to meet the standards of the reward being: those obedient enough, or pretty enough, or in some other way graced by the gods–the best being both pretty and obedient. The gods loved to be surrounded by beauty," she said. "Even so, paradise was not a happy place for the slaves, who knew that their survival depended on their outer appearance and obedience to anything asked of them. Slaves are never happy," she remarked, as she walked and talked. "Their spirit is denied freedom, and happiness can't be achieved in such a suppressed unnatural state."

"But what happened in the gardens when the gods left so suddenly?" another girl asked.

---

[95] Mines and smelting caverns
[96] Beautiful vegetable and flower gardens where the gods liked to wander and enjoy leisure time
[97] The gods' place
[98] Ancestral guides who can converse with some sensitive's such as those serving as priestesses

"The Spirit Talkers said that those, who found the courage to come out of the inner places within Tara, were in awe of the lushness of the gardens. For a long time, they stayed in the gardens; but there came conflict between the gardeners and the miners, due to their worlds being separated. A value system had formed based on levels of worth connected to beauty, strength and where the people worked, which echoed the way the gods had run things. The gardeners felt invaded, because they had been led to believe miners were less worthy. The miners didn't understand the aesthetic principles involved in gardening, nor how to grow and tend plants, so they defiled the place due to their ignorance and need, ripping out what they desired and trampling the beautiful flowers. It wasn't because they were bad; they just didn't understand gardens and had come from an extremely hostile environment."

"I'm getting ahead of the story here, so let me get back to the memories of lovely Tara and what unfolded within her body-divine, as the lords disappeared and left the slaves wondering why. After the withdrawal of the gods, even the slaves who had the courage to free themselves within their own minds still held some fearful caution and conditioning, as they came close to the sun portals. They had been so imprinted by the mining gods; to believe that they were unworthy of light, they had to develop a sense of worth, before they could muster up the courage to come forth into sunlight, much less feel any form of gratitude for the places and spaces under the sun. They thought they would be struck dead, if they let the warm sun fall upon their faces, because they had been told that they couldn't ascend into the god's realm. Nevertheless, after the exodus of the gods, little by little, as small streams of sunlight found their way down through the air shafts and sprinkled light on the slaves, and no one died instantly, they emerged and found that Eden accepted them and offered new challenges and lessons.

The gods were not there to strike them down for being disobedient; however, many missed them because that was all they knew. That's why they often pleaded to the sky (where the gardeners told them the gods flew off in their great ships), hoping the missing gods could hear their prayerful need, and come back and protect them. They were like caged birds and couldn't imagine a life outside of the barriers of the prison that held them. Some of the gods heard the pleas, because they left monitors in certain places expecting to return. They liked the role of lord and masters, and didn't honor the Galactic Councils demand of non-interference with the native indigenous people, so they would revisit on the sly from time to time, to keep fear in place. The Galactic Council wanted the Tara species to have a chance to evolve. Enslavement made that unlikely. Some of the summoned gods, who visited those whose prayers caught their attention, basked in the glorification for a while, until they were forced to honor the decree of the council. Most of the freed slaves, with good reason, were still afraid. They didn't know how to protect themselves from the only thing they knew, which was, 'fear itself,' and all the ugliness it uses to hold power. They were like abused children, who still loved their abusive parents."

"But let me finally answer your original question," the saga teacher resolutely restated. "How did Tara transform the grief of what she was used for and witnessed in those days of old? To answer this, I must regress yet again and explain the situation a bit more."

"The gods, of which we speak, had two brothers at the forefront, and one sister. They were sent by their father, who was the chief overseer of the other world. They were assigned to run the operation of mining for gold, which was discovered during that so-called 'accidental' landing upon the surface of Tara, so long ago. One brother (the younger one, whom the father favored), was in command of everything as overlord, and the other two (half-sister and brother) were operations chiefs, in that they had to find a way to get things done. The two operations chiefs were lovers, as well as half-brother and half-sister. These kinds of relationships were common among ruling families. They developed the slaves (from the indigenous species crossed with their own genetics) as directed by the overseeing brother, who was also a half-brother to them. It was this ruling brother who realized, that what was needed to extract this precious gold, his people couldn't, or wouldn't do. Afraid of his powerful and desperate father who demanded that they produce the gold that was required to save their home planet, the ruling brother became a force to reckon with, and ordered his half-brother and half-sister to create workers. He feared he would lose his standing as favorite son, should he not measure up to his task. He was ambitious and coveted power. He was not involved in the design and eventual making of the prototype slaves, who his older half-brother and half-sister had created in a vast laboratory. He was given the task to rule overall, and he just wanted to get his job done and return to the planet he called home. Thus, he didn't love hybrid slaves, as those who created them did, nor did he care if they were treated well or not. He was tortured by his own feelings of insecurity. He envied his older brother's sister-lover and wanted her for himself, for she was extremely beautiful. Envy and jealousy breed hate and aggression, and he became an even harder taskmaster. As was the custom of their homeland and time, leaders kept love and marriage in the family, usually taking half-sisters as wives. He decided to claim this beautiful sister as his wife. As appointed ruler he held first right to her and was so angered and jealous of her love for his brother, that he silenced his heart-voice and allowed his head to rule. Thus, he literally forced her into captivity, subject to him, since logically, he thought, his word and wishes were law."

The girls were silent with sadness, no doubt knowing of beautiful women, who were held captive for many such reasons. The teacher continued on with the tale. "Fear uses anything it can, to stay in control. The overseer was the component, within this trio of sibling-leaders, who didn't honor the responsibility of creation. He wasn't making or co-creating, as the operations chiefs were, and control was more important to him than anything else. He was in the position of insuring that the gold mining would be a success, and in his mind, that meant, at any cost. His logical mind could only focus on that. He didn't love the hybrid slaves, even as he told them that he did, so that they would work harder and endure suffering for the sake of the cause. He hadn't bonded through the stages of creation, yet he took credit for both these things–success and the adoration of the slaves–to make himself look good in his father's eyes. He thought his father would elevate his status, bring him away from this planet he considered a prison, and allow him to live in the place he knew and loved, if he accomplished the task assigned to him. His ambition for power was tremendous, and he aspired to step into his father's position, one day."

"He was a poor choice for a leader, but his father knew that he would get the job done, no matter the consequences. So his father appointed this favored son, most like himself, supreme ruler, taking a chance that he wouldn't be too cruel in the process. I don't mention the names here, because there is a vibration within the names, which requires that you be in the right place and within the right moment, to hear them." The girls and I wondered if the names were too terrible to hear. Our storytelling saga continued, "When you take your naming classes–and you all will–you will be ready to hear names of the gods; for when you hear their name, you gain their attention, and if you are not properly prepared, it can be disastrous," the teacher explained.

Returning to her story, she picked up where she left off, saying, "It was the ruler brother, who decided that the women were less worthy and incomplete creational beings. He didn't know how to deal with their passionate intuitive natures, which he found hard to control. He was jealous of his wife's love for his elder half-brother. His own mother wouldn't have approved of his attitude, and he kept his bias quiet around her. She was a woman of power and position in his homeland, and he feared her wrath. In this world however, he ruled, and he proclaimed that the men were more perfect, thus more deserving of divinity, to justify his treatment of his new wife, which echoed into treating all women with scorn. He was also jealous of the feminine role in creation; of her taking a seed and bringing it to full fruit. Secretly, he knew that he couldn't accomplish what his brother and sister had done within the labs, in making beings so much like the gods, yet able to be enslaved. Consequently, due to his jealousy, he constantly questioned the worth of women and all things feminine. He claimed the power of creation as his own. This attitude even alienated the women of his own people there with him, who for a time served as surrogate mothers and birthed the first prototypes of the slave race. There came a time when they revolted at the treatment of their off-spring, and fertility had to be developed into the hybrids to achieve separation from the first surrogate mothers. He was convinced that he didn't need women. That was a great lie.

## The Saga-Oracle

Even within him there was the feminine force. Whenever she emerged, he beat her back down within the depths of himself, not wanting to hear that voice or feel her 'knowing,' especially within himself. Hating part of himself, his actions and reactions imprinted on all that he was responsible to. The attitude spread and corrupted the energetic balance of the planet, which in turn, affected other solar systems and the entire universe, due to the ripple effect which reaches far and wide. That was when the Galactic Council decided to step in."

"The more he carried on with this feminine hatred, the meaner and more heartless he and his sergeants became. It devastated his brother, when his lover was claimed as his younger brother's sister-wife and held captive. They had always planned to be united in the sacred union ceremony. The ruling brother removed his half-brother from the scene, by assigning him to a faraway place on the other side of Tara. He couldn't tolerate their compassion for the beings they created, thus sent one away and imprisoned the other as his wife. These lovers, whose divine union was broken by the authority of the overseeing brother, were heart-broken; for they couldn't disconnect their hearts from each other or from that which they had developed. Because the hybrid beings were like children to them, they couldn't bear to see them suffer." The saga's tale held everyone's attention. This secret story was not well-known; to know it was to be in dire danger, she warned us. She said the ancient Sumerians (who wrote in wedge shapes) had recorded all this. Many other nations incorporated the tale into their own legends, but with adjustments to suit their purposes. They forced their followers to believe their version, or die as heretics.

The saga continued, "The gods had wars among themselves and among others, who would also exploit the opportunity of this developing planet. The arena was miserable, because fear and aggression held rule. There were also advanced beings involved, whose purpose was to watch the portals of entrance to this plane. They could see what was happening and were appalled by the cruel and heartless behavior. Components, at the most basic physical level within the new slave species, mirrored the maker's attitudes, both good and bad, as the new species evolved. Monitors worried, as to the repercussions of the aggressive code, which used fear as its excuse to rage forth. The Watchers[99], as these monitors were known, proposed that if they were granted permission from the chief operations managers to take some wives among the new species, they might be able to implant less aggressive traits. Taking wives wasn't unusual, since the ruler's sergeants had often taken spouses from the slave race. The Watchers intended to implant their own genes, which contained the peace code[100] which would counter-balance the aggressive tendencies. Since they already found the women desirable, they believed this would benefit all concerned. Above all, they wanted to do some genetic engineering, as you would term it today. They hoped to plant a seed, which would sprout in the future of the poor creatures they found so beguiling, through the genetic peace code. They knew this code would pass from them to their offspring, becoming more prominent with each generation."

We were still spellbound, as we followed along in the teacher's footsteps at a brisk pace, paying no mind to the time or progress of our journey, yet each silently processing the information the teacher presented. She continued with the story, realizing that we were not sufficiently informed with the revelations of this tale, to fully understand why the caverns and passageways had forgiven the cruelty they witnessed and her proposed 'brief' tale expanded even further.

"These monitors we have always called 'guardians, or watchers,' for it was their task to keep watch over the entrance portals to this planet. They monitored from great sky-ships that circled Tara; they also had bases on the Moon and Mars. They realized that the building blocks of the bodies of the slave race needed a component that would reflect and respect peace–the principles of love–instead of hatred and fear. The guardians could foresee the future in its many possibilities. They could see there was a missing factor within the structure of the physical body codes of these created ones, and having the foresight, they felt great concern. It

---

[99] Different beings, assigned by Galactic Council to monitor entrance to and from Tara by those from outside
[100] DNA or gene originally transmitted by those of the blue race

was the blue-code that came closest to the essence of love, the first Divine Principle of creation. Because the guardians physical bodies had this code, they had been placed by the Galactic Council as the gate-keepers of Tara at this time of vulnerability, for she was still a young planet and instability was a possibility."

"After much deliberation the guardians were granted the right to intermarry among the women, for the sake of bringing a balance therein. They knew that the balance resided in a true, complete reflection of the Prime Creator, and all that was good (God) had this energy pattern. This Great Mysterious Creator, who is both Father and Mother, had to be reflected in all creation for it to be a success; without balance evolution couldn't be achieved, only destruction, which was often slow and painful. The chiefs of the laboratories–brother and sister, and constant companions, before they were separated by their brother's jealousy–agreed they wanted their creational beings to have success and evolve, as all creation must, or it ultimately destroys itself only to reform again in another way, in another time. The operations chiefs believed this was their choice, since they were responsible for this part of the operation, providing viable workers. Thus, they granted the request of marriage for the purpose of implantation of the 'blue gene'[101]."

"This plan required that the gene had to be implanted within the energy of love, full of passion and physical interaction– not in a lab setting–in order to be successfully ingrained into the chain of physicality. The marriages had to be agreeable unions, and the wives had to love their new spouses with great passion, or the sensitive peace gene couldn't be transmitted. Consequently a wave of interaction began among the two groups, which resulted in some of the male slaves being glad for their sisters and some jealous of the attention they received from the Watchers, as they courted mates. Ultimately, about three hundred wives were joined in divine union, due to this privilege. Sad to say, however, the story has since been twisted to demonize these watchful guardians,

---

[101] Originally this gene was part of a peaceful blue race who had visited the earth plane, but found it too harsh for their gentle natures

whose only intention was peace. That's the way fear hides the truth of love."

"The ruling brother was on the other side of Tara at the time, looking at new places to mine. When the ruler heard about the marriages, he was livid with anger. He held his will and his word to be the only authority of the land. It was upon this discovery, that he devised the banishment of his brother and the capture of his favored sister, forcing her to be his bride. He had been away only a few days, but since he was still within the time frame of his home planet, aided by the gold powder he ingested, it was many years to those upon Tara. By the time the ruler brother heard of the situation, children had already been born and families established. Full of fury, he brought the two operations chiefs to his judgment chambers and demanded they explain why they would grant such a request, knowing he would never agree to it. It was well known that he hated the Watchers, because they were not under his rule. They tried to help him understand, that they, being scientists and he a warrior, viewed the earth project from totally different perspectives. However, he couldn't, or wouldn't, comprehend why there was a difference, and how it affected the decision to grant the wish of the Watchers. His sergeants had taken wives; but for the most part, it had been a forceful claim rather than a loving union, and usually a reward for loyal service. The Watchers were outsiders to the ruler brother, because ultimately they weren't under his authority, being sent by the Galactic Council. At the same time, the slaves were under his authority, and he felt justified in his rage."

"Still, the operations chiefs tried to explain their reasoning further, by saying that the electrical energetic makeup of the slaves, triggered by genetic codes, had to be in accordance with all creation in order to survive and be useful. They thought that might satisfy the angry ruler-brother. The genetic codes were flawed, they said, and the species would ultimately turn on each other and kill their own kind, as well as become a threat to the slave-masters. They also said that if evolution wasn't allowed, a die-off would happen, since evolution is movement and without movement, stagnation and rot occur. The ruler-brother said he didn't care about that, because he would simply breed more slaves. He threatened to wipe out the entire lot and start all over again, if he had to."

"This, my little sisters and brother," the teacher said, looking my way, "is the most misunderstood time of past-story. It has to do with the feminine 'knowing' and the masculine 'idea,' which are how the dual energies interact within all creation. It has been twisted and corrupted within the memories of the descendants, because fear was the greatest tool of control then, and still is, and because those who knew the truth were eliminated."

It seemed these girls could read my mind; for every question, I would have posed to the teacher, one of them asked. Another asked, "What's the difference in 'knowing' and 'idea'?"

"You do jump start your class," the teacher said, "but I'll try to give a simple explanation. In essence, 'knowing' comes from within and has no form; the 'idea' is an active thought form that takes root in the external. Think of Father/Mother God as a huge Onement; within this Onement are endless possibilities. Within the possibilities are seeds or ways that the possibility can manifest. A seed is the full possibility, all compacted into a tiny point. This seed is the idea then, the seed of a possibility, if you will. That is the masculine essence, and it has form. However, the seed, or idea, can't manifest or grow, unless there is a knowing, or believing in its possibility, which feeds it and keeps it safely protected in a formless inner space, so that it can sprout and develop finally to emerge into its fullness. It's the Divine Dance of all creation and how creation extends and expands itself."

We weren't sure what to think of the Divine Dance, and how the creator gods did, or didn't, get in step with it. "All creation is a reflection of these two essences (idea and knowing). All that manifests, and all reaction and action within that manifestation, must follow this divine principle in order to create anything. This being said," she continued on, "I tell you that, in reality, men have the feminine inside them, and women have the masculine inside them, as well; so girls, deep inside you is a boy place (idea), and deep inside boys there is a girl place (knowing)," she said, with a slight chuckle. "If that were not so," she emphasized, "nothing could be co-created and that's the reason for all life in the first place."

"Huh!" someone simply uttered.

Still chuckling a bit, our teacher tried to clarify that last statement, by saying, "To co-create is the great experiment of the Source, who wants to discover via many outlets through this process. So you live to discover (co-create) and manifest, as you discover your relationship to this Divine Source, first within yourself, then within all your communions or relationships. Every time you discover how to manifest something—be it a lovely meal or go so far as to create a new species, or produce off-spring of your own—you are co-creating, and the Divine Source is thrilled and blessed beyond measure. Nevertheless, remember, no matter what you create you are responsible for, even as it must be set free. 'It' will always be filled by the Source, who puts soul into all creation. Nothing is soul-less, remember that," she said. "And the greatest challenge of responsibility is to free what was co- created, to be all that it soulfully can be."

This was deep. I could see some confusion and realized why this was an advanced teaching. I was trying to follow this line of thought and again, one of my walking companions asked what I was wondering.

"I am a boy, too?" a girl asked, giggling as she pondered the idea. "I might be accepting that, but I doubt that many boys would like to think they have a girl within them, especially the Roman boys," she emphasized. The other girls voiced agreement with her statement. Remembering my presence, since the tale we were listening to had diverted our physical attraction, the girls nervously glanced at me. It was their turn to blush, as they wondered how I would react to that concept. Their experience was that boys were insulted to be compared to a girl, much less think they might have one hiding inside of them.

I finally broke my silence and said, "I never thought of that, teacher, because I haven't considered being a girl before. I can see there could be a problem, since biased attitudes prevail in so many minds in fear-based societies. They would see a female aspect as weaker, thus more vulnerable, while one who lives in the essence of love might (since they filter things through their heart) more likely find such a thing reassuring, with a different kind of strength therein and a balancing factor of brilliant design."

The teacher stopped us, turned and looked at me, not saying anything for a moment. I thought I had said something inappropriate. I felt the hot blush crawl up my neck again, to find my face revealing my uncertainty, especially since I was the lone male in this group of females. Everyone was looking at me by this time, and I wished I could find a hole in the cave wall to crawl into.

Finally, the teacher said, "Young man, you are a delight to behold. You have the 'knowing' well within you, and you accept the feminine within your being without question, thus the ideas find clarity in your heart first, then within your lovely head." She kissed me lightly upon my cheek, and I felt a warm blush from the unexpected attention. She continued and said, "I am honored that you are with us on this journey of discovery, in which an unplanned lesson of creation has found us wanting to explore it. You are truly a son of Patient Mary and wise Joseph, and I'm glad you accompanied us." Then she simply turned around, proceeded down the path once again, her white hair flowing and floating in waves as she proudly walked, with us parading behind her like baby ducks.

"So," she said, as she moved in a glide that appeared to float above the path she walked effortlessly upon, "we ladies (those who honor the knowing, because our prioritized gender is feminine) eventually recognized all of this, and we developed the priestess-hood. We had help from the gods as well, because there were among them goddesses, who held great wisdom within their own beings. They shared it to help the slaves in evolution, even to the point of interacting at a close physical level with the female slaves, against the orders of the brother ruler. For a time, we could touch them and feel their presence in untold wondrous ways," she proclaimed, anticipating our question. "Some of the goddesses were mothers of the first prototype slaves, and didn't agree with the treatment their offspring received. They inspired, and loved all, male and female."

"The hybrids needed the gods to love them, as all creation wants its maker's love. Many, especially the women, developed a loving relationship with the goddesses, who taught them about the balance of the polarities of energy. They were the first priestesses and our ancestors. They were instructed that within creation is co-creation, and all were co-created, thus tied to that which made them, even as all creation ever is." This was a huge concept for us to grasp, so our teacher went further saying, "They taught the early priestesses, all creation is part of the Source of 'All That Is', thus they were aspects, or children, of this great mysterious creator, as their co-creators were, as well. Do you follow me?" she questioned, and thinking that we probably did, she didn't miss a beat and went on to say, "The greater gods of the galaxy had a knowing that there was a possibility for the species of Tara to evolve, even as all creation must, into full-blossomed aspects of the Source. These goddesses, for the most part, with only a few lost in the fear-based modes, were our first teachers of the energies we call masculine and feminine. They began helping the women know their true essence, which was equally important to that of the men, you see. They also worked with the men, as well, but were more successful with women, due to our gender-energy priority and its intuitive abilities. Men wanted to use reason and logic to grasp the truth, and they also feared change (natural tendency since the masculine is the protector), and that extended to changing their minds. In some places, the knowing took hold. In others, it became skewed and was reinterpreted by those who held the reins of power. This unbalanced situation always happens, when there is logic first and heart feelings second. Sad but true, learning is often a lesson of 'what is not,' to discover 'what is.' Over-compensation happened from time to time in both directions. Unfortunately, the developing societies couldn't forget the original overseer's biases, which were used to enslave them, and they fell into the old pattern. They only felt secure under this type of rule; thus, fear and power became the basis of their security systems."

"I tell you," she said, "women are a power to behold within themselves and being women, they have their own line of communication, which for eons of time has been ignored as unimportant by men. Women talked and shared their intuitions, mother to daughter, and elder woman to younger woman, friend to friend, down through the ages. They communicated with each other in countless ways. They shared the ways of the feminine as taught by the goddesses, and kept the knowledge sacred and secret. They integrated the 'knowing' whenever and wherever they could, within their lives and their societies. Unfortunately, this was often seen as a threat to fear-mongering leaders, who feared most losing their version of power, and they made it a sin to 'know'. Since the essence of the feminine 'knows,' you can see the problem, can you not?" she asked. Not waiting again for the answer, she proceeded on, "So these priestesses found the underground places. Upon entering them, they felt the vibrations of sorrow, for priestesses are naturally super-sensitive. Within the sorrowful chambers, they decided to help Tara in her grief and depression, by bringing love into the deep sad scars imprinted upon her divine body. They performed rituals–those intentional rites that sealed the deepest most sacred intentions–within these caverns and passageways, filling up the pain and sorrow imprints with pure love. The priestesses accomplished this, never once sacrificing anything or anyone, and created a love-wave that sought out all passage tunnels and the rooms connected to them– rediscovered or otherwise–and washed away the stain of sadness therein. They cleansed and healed the wound—another gift of the feminine–leaving only the scars to tell the story, along with the pictures the past residents left. The priestesses became the midwives, who helped heal beloved Tara, thus today, when you walk inside Tara's tunnels and within her caverns, you feel peace instead of sadness."

With that statement, the passageway became brighter, and we could see sunlight, not in dapples of light from the air shafts as we sometimes did, but this time glowing in front of us. When we could see the entire Sun Portal, our torches were extinguished one at a time in another pool of water. With these extinguishments, a prayer for the transformation of the fire and water into vapor was said, much as I had learned from Nod. We gave thanks for the light and warmth the flame had given us, along with thanking the water for the thirst it had quenched along the way. Then we exited into Eden.

# WANDERING WITH MY COUSIN JOHN
Chapter Twenty-Three

After spending time in the underworld, coming out in the sunlight was quite a shock. It required that we gradually acclimate to the brilliant light. It seemed like Eden, as the young priestesses now lovingly called the outer world, since our walking story of the ancients. The beautiful light, that fosters natural growth like trees, flowers, animals and humanity, is drastically different in comparison to the secret caverns. As you already know, the controllers of the world of light are often biased and cruel, in the tradition of the gods of old. The rulers lived in fear of losing their control, because they feared that if they didn't have power, they would become victims of the same warped world they created. No one has ever felt totally secure in such a system, much less happy. Sadly, that controlling attitude was still the norm.

The first thing I wanted to do was pay a brief visit to my dear mother, who I always missed, even though I just saw her in the city of Brambles. After that visit, I decided I would be on my way, spreading the word and doing what I knew to be my mission. I wanted to change a thinking pattern that was long-ingrained and causing suffering. I hoped to do this by gently bringing the balance of the energies back to their divine equal essence, so that unity would be the pattern and love the principle mode of being. I was idealistic and young enough to believe that change was possible. I still believe so, but know that the old modes of control and power will go to the most drastic of measures, to keep their power in place. My teachers were pointing me in the direction of peace, but no one actually spelled it out for me–it was something I was born knowing. Thus, I emerged into a world of fear, where security was the first and foremost thought of most beings. Yet, in my mind, the only true security–which I hoped to emphasize–is found in love of all creation, including oneself. I visualized a system where there was no hierarchy of worth and people helped one another, because they loved and respected each other. I knew that the only way to honor God, our maker, was within love, a far more appropriate attitude than 'the fear of God' stance so long accepted. It was, and still is, an ambitious mission and I forever believe that love and unity are not only possible, but the only true way. Fear is an antiforce that doesn't give up easily; it dramatically demonstrates its fury and power, when its control is threatened. The system of bullying must come to an end. I knew it then, as I know it now.

After a few hours walk from the sun portal where we emerged, I arrived home, and my family rejoiced, as did I. On my short visit, as always, my mother and sisters spoiled me with attention. My brothers happened to be in the area as well, so I enjoyed reuniting with them, too. Joseph, my half-brother, and I were especially close. James, who looked so much like me, held himself slightly aloof, still not quite sure what to make of his so-called 'master brother'.

My sisters, often with mother, were very much involved in the underground priestess activities and training. To be trained as a priestess is as honorable and intense as being trained as a priest. Even so, it was different, in that their talents and abilities were honed to complement that of the masculine counterpart, the priest, not to submit to it; as a complement, they would fulfill the other. This presented a problem in many minds, and that dilemma has shaped past-story into "his-story" (history). The past records have reflected the controlling attitude that the feminine's purpose was to submit, rather than fulfill, the wholeness of the masculine. The mindset of the day was that, generally, priestesses didn't know their proper place and were a threat to male authority. The sisterhood dwindled, due to persecution, and in most places, was outlawed. The priests often had more power than the monarchs. They saw God as a male father figure and disregarded the mother aspect of God. They also felt that they were chosen to speak for this God they defined, due to a gender-specific hereditary right. That's the climate that I began my mission within.

One of the first things I wanted to do, as I left my family once again, was go on a walking tour of the lands I was born into and reconnect with the people. I also hoped to, eventually, revisit the high mountains and some of the other places I knew as a child, and see my friends and teachers again. I knew that these learning sojourns were intended to prepare me to serve my people and those connected to them. After all, I was called forth to focus on this arena of imbalance. The bias was so tilted, that it threatened future generations, which caused the Galactic Council to intervene. I knew this at a soul level, but when I started my mission it was a strong intuitive urging that guided me, along with the support of family and teachers. Being trained in other cultures as a young child, I learned to appreciate people from other traditions. They weren't heathens, as our religious leaders said; rather they just had the same objective, but a different path to that goal. Imbalance was in those places, too, but others were sent into those arenas. I was born to work in the land where I was born. The nearly-global problem was partially due to the blockage of the evolution of consciousness, which the creator gods established all over the planet. It was time for the pendulum to swing toward its poise, so that true relationship to the Source could be discovered. The age of identity, where individuals had the opportunity to develop a sense of self, so that later they could see themselves within the context of the co-creational purpose, was in full swing. However, the powers-that-be still blocked the natural step-up of awareness. The challenge that faced people of the time was to get past the imprints of times gone by, and sort out what united, and what separated people, within their collective paradigms. I hoped to get people to question the structures that enslaved them. I sought to begin the process of going from fear-based thinking to the unity of love. I knew this was a dangerous mission, since to stimulate change is always a threatening situation to those comfortable within old ways. Examining the status quo provoked the ruling priests who considered it heresy and punishable by death. Those who would dare to think for themselves, or discover any of the secrets that had been buried for the sake of control, were said to be possessed by demons. Fear of the repercussions of thinking, became the fear of evil. It created a fear of the messenger; always an effective way of keeping the masses under control. Fear and ignorance are the main tools of control. I knew I would have to educate in subtle ways. I began using the parable or 'story-form,' of teaching, so that people could simply listen and gently allow the divine truths to dawn on them.

Actually, the gods of old were just more technically-advanced beings, learning to be gods; some in early stages of training, some more accomplished. This may be a difficult concept for many, who might wonder, "What happened to the idea of One God?" To that, I remind you of what you already know. Indeed the One Source–One Being–magnificent and expansive beyond description and ever the great mystery, comprised of total love, and all creation is 'Itself Manifested,' or the God, often referred to as, 'The One'. In ancient times the word 'god' or 'lord' meant positions of authority. God is hard to define and nearly impossible to name, but nevertheless, the Primal Source of all that is calls to creation to be recognized. Generations have argued as to what to call this grand Creator. The closest anyone has ever come is found in your holy bible translation–I AM THAT I AM. The essence of my mission was to explain the truth of this lovely Divine Onement, as best I could, and reveal the lie of fear. Those who play gods are within a stage of evolution, where they are learning the responsibility for that which they co-create and foster. That's why references to the nature of god differ from culture to culture, because different personalities were involved in varying locations. Nevertheless, they were all responsible to the One God of Love, or what some call 'The First Cause.' Those that adored the gods in training loved them and feared them, at the same time for good reasons; they were benevolent; they were jealous; and they were cruel at times, depending on the situation, time and place. They made mistakes, and also made great divine evolutionary progress. They were learning to be gods and have now advanced beyond what your memories recorded.

The use of fear to control others was so ingrained, that the populace expected it. Any power figure, they believed, could only protect them through the fear they knew; thus they were like moths drawn into the flame. They didn't feel worthy to be loved, because they didn't see their own divinity. Believing that any aspect of creation is more glorious than another separates and denies divine discovery the chance to play out, and that has been a major problem in Tara's arena of experience. The microcosm is a true complete reflection of the macrocosm. I wanted people to see themselves as the microcosm that they truly are, and God as the macrocosm. That's true for all creation and key to understanding divine relationship to God.

Humans are not more divine than the doves, or the deer of the forest, or the lizards of the desert, or the rocks, or trees or any created thing. They are different only in purpose and hold more responsibility, due to their ability to live in the past-present-future. All beings have a purpose. In this grand divine plan, all the components fit together like an endless divine puzzle too big to imagine, but nevertheless, known collectively as 'God'. Each being is a puzzle piece in this splendid picture.

I knew that teaching this concept would be a great challenge even then in my early naïve days. The ideas of separation were so ingrained from the days of the ancient creator gods that it caused confusion; change seemed a total impossibility for many who heard my message. The old gods were themselves confused and fearful, as I understood, from the walking-teaching, as I emerged from the city of Brambles. They became experts at control, and their descendents and creations remembered them as frightening gods. The evolution of consciousness, or the learning stages of all creation, must unfold a step at a time. Thousands of years ago the stages of awareness were in earlier learning classes of enlightenment. The creator gods were becoming aware of creation and the responsibility it required. Now, you are moving along in consciousness in some ways, but in others you attempt to conform to the ideas of times past. Most don't even realize that those remembered as gods have evolved as well, and the lessons of long ago are different than the present challenges. The gods of old have incarnated repeatedly, to try to atone for some of the awful mistakes they made in their stages of learning. Some returnees you have recognized and some you haven't. For the most part, you don't understand that you are all gods and those you oversee, be they pets, livestock, orchards, cities or such, look to you as divine, or divinely chosen. How you behave is how those in your keep will judge themselves.

I tell you, the flower you planted and grew in your garden that is not loved doesn't know how to love itself. That is especially true in family units, where the children see their parents as gods of a sort, and like the flowers in the garden, they need to be loved, so when the day comes for them to bloom, they can do so, fully brilliant and perfect.

## The Saga-Oracle

When I left my humble home, mother warned me that it would take a while to gain enough confidence, to hold the attention of the masses, required for my work. People have been brain-washed to the point, that their very bodies hold the concepts, she told me. She said the more confident I was, the better able I would be to reach those I wished to enlighten. This proved to be true. In my early attempts to speak to the people, I was often disregarded as just another crazy man, ranting about his frustrations. Some of those they labeled crazy were genuine message bearers, but few were taken seriously. Individuals who were serious threats to the fear-based thinking modalities were often stoned to death or otherwise dispensed. I soon realized I needed more time to prepare myself for this arduous task, or I wouldn't last long enough to be successful in my mission.

My cousin John was one of those thought crazed. He became obsessed with the falsity of the social thinking to the point that he couldn't live within it. But, then again, he never could live within the human social system. He went to live with the animals early as a young child and relished in surviving like an animal, as well. His mother, my dear mother's cousin, was quite concerned for her son, yet knew there wasn't much she could do, having no power, at least, at the social level, which echoed into her family authority. She was married to a powerful councilman and widowed, shortly before John chose to live permanently in the wilderness. As a widow, her social status was so low, that John, with no father to guide him, had a right to his freedom to think and do as he pleased. As an undercover priestess, she knew why he behaved as he did; even though it hurt her to do so, she honored his choice.

As I wandered around, I found John in the desert one day, looking quite like the wild man he was famed to be. We were close in age, he and I, and I always felt drawn to him. I wanted to know him better–to know why he lived as an animal. When I found him, I became a persistent pest, even though I understood that he wanted to be left alone. Talking to a human, I thought, might be good for him, since he usually only conversed with nature and her creatures.

One day close to a village built near a small oasis, I happened upon him. There was a creek nearby, and he was down on his hands and knees lapping the water (as a deer would), slurping noisily as he sucked up the cool refreshing liquid. He looked odd, animal-like, with his head down and his butt held higher. He didn't wear much in the way of clothing, and this wasn't the most modest position, I assure you. Walking up behind him thinking I would startle him (cousins could be crude in their fun finding), I planned to scare him. About the time, I was preparing to surprise him, he stopped drinking and, without being startled as I had hoped, he simply said, "Don't just stand there, stupid. Get yourself a drink, and while you are at it, take a bath. You smell so bad; I caught your scent long ago."

I laughed, got down on my own hands and knees and tried his method of drinking, and made equal slurping noise. It was actually quite an interesting and effective way of quenching ones' thirst. Even so, before I was done, my dear cousin pushed me off balance and we both tumbled into the water, laughing and wrestling like a couple of rambunctious boys. It was good to see John again. One never knew where he would be, because he held no place he called home. Reunion with him was a rare blessing. For a long time, we played and splashed like children in the water, forgetting that we were supposed to be grown men by this time in our lives. We had always liked each other and had missed being playmates as we grew up. It seemed like no time had passed, as we naturally resumed our close friendship and playfully splashed each other in the stream like a couple of kids. When finally tired, we sat dripping wet on the edge of the creek and laughed and hugged each other.

"Now you smell better," John said to me.

"I smell better?" I questioned. "Have you no sense that, not only do you look like an animal, dear cousin, but you smell worse than one, because animals have the sense to clean themselves once in awhile and keep their tails down. Indeed, I could smell you way down the road long, before I ever laid eyes on you," I lied.

# The Saga-Oracle

John just smiled at me and said, "Your big problem, cousin, is that you think you have to walk on the roads to get anywhere. You miss most of the world by taking those silly confining paths. Those narrow alleyways of repression go nowhere. If you want to know about the world," he emphasized, "follow me around. I'll show you the rest of the world and you'll be truly amazed, my beloved kin."

Since getting people's attention lately wasn't proving all that successful, and sensing that the time wasn't yet ripe for my work after all, I gave John's proposal some serious consideration. I thought I might tag along for awhile and get off the roads and paths, so considered changing my plan. "Watch what you ask for," I answered John, teasing but still not sure yet what I might do, "because you just might get it."

John just chuckled, shook himself off like a wet dog and started walking off into the landscape. I watched him proceed for a while, not sure if I would accept his invitation, but feeling the pull to follow him.

He stopped, turned and said, "You had better get stepping or you'll be lost trying to keep up with me. It's a jungle out here," he said, then made some jungle noises, that children make when they want to be really scary.

I took that as my cue, quickly rose from the stream and trotted off in his direction. He was already striding great steps, going where he goes on his journeys off the paths and into the wilderness. I found it hard to keep up with him, having to trot to his long-striding walk. He didn't say much as we moved along. He stopped and smelled the breezes, from time to time and seemed to be getting information, I was not privy to. I might claim I could catch a scent, as well as he could, but in truth I was exaggerating a bit, and my sense of smell was nothing compared to his.

As mid-day approached and the sun got very hot, sweat poured down my face and arms, and my robes felt most uncomfortable. The scant animal skins that John wore, however, seemed to afford him a cooler comfort. I wasn't sure how long I could tolerate the sunrays, scorching my exposed skin and steaming my body, due to my now-soaked robes. The cool creek water had been replaced by sticky salty wetness.

John stopped and began to dig near a rotted plant. What it had been I couldn't determine, but its remains were hosting other life forms, I learned, as John dug into the thing, extracted some grubs that he bid me to come closer and inspect. I came forth. He took my hand and deposited about ten of the elongated larva into it. He then took my fingers and made me grip them, and nodding his head in affirmation–still not in the talking mood–turned and filled his own hand, likewise. Motioning for me to follow him, we found shade by a stone boulder nearby and sat within the coolness of its shadow. John proceeded to eat the bugs he found, one at a time, with a look of sheer pleasure upon his wild hairy face. I noticed he said a little prayer, breaking his silence, before he partook of his meal. Looking at me watching him in awe, but noting that I wasn't yet partaking of the insect food, he finally said, "Eat. If you are going to learn about the rest of creation, you will have to learn to survive like the rest of creation."

I said my own prayer of thanksgiving, and reluctantly popped the first bug into my mouth. Slowly, I chewed, fully expecting it to make my stomach convulse. At first, I thought I would sicken, for my conception of a bug as unfit food held sway. After gagging a time or two, with a disgusted John watching me, I realized that what I was chewing and gagging on didn't taste all that bad after all. The gagging reflex stopped and I began to appreciate the meal, which tasted like wild mushrooms and nuts combined. As I consumed the larva, I wondered why I had thought them unfit to eat. I realized that I would have to revisit many attitudes about the natural world, to understand my own nature, and that of my fellow beings. It looked like I still had a way to go, before I could be the teacher I desired to be, and my cousin John was yet another divine teacher.

John, sensing my unspoken concern, said, "They don't mind that we consume them, you know." He then continued, saying, "They know before they move into their bodies, that some will be consumed early on and some later. They agree to this and see it as the purpose of that life experience. All they ask is that we appreciate what they live and die for," he emphasized.

"How is it, my cousin, that I have to be taken from my family, travel far and wide, to know such a thing, and you just know it, never forced to leave your loved ones?" I questioned. I felt that he had a better youth than I had, due to the fact he didn't have to leave home. Everyone has regrets–some justified and some not. He had a way of chuckling, low and sweet, which he now did. I must say I found such a sound pleasing, this low amazed laughter that I remembered of him.

"Do you think I spent my early years at my mother's side in bliss, cousin?" he asked. still laughing as he talked.

"I don't know what you did, since I wasn't around," I replied.

"Surely, you've been told of the crazy John, who from three or four years of age would go out into the wilderness and live with the animals," he said.

"Wasn't that your choice?" I answered. "Surely, your mother didn't toss you out"

"Life is a choice," he replied.

I persisted, "You didn't answer my question. I had to go far and wide to understand, that all life gives itself up to other lives and calls such 'its purpose'. If you could know without separation from your family, why did they send me away to learn this truth?" I wasn't above feeling sorry for myself from time to time.

He thought for a moment, then said, "Well, to answer you, I had to go away from my family, as you did, too; but I wasn't given over to a guardian and sent to live with sages and pampered." Little did he know my experience never involved pampering, as he imagined. He continued on, saying, "I wasn't a master child, but still I knew things. I could sense the animals, the trees, the rocks and all sorts of things converse with me. They told me that they would be my teachers, and they bid me from early on to come to them, so that they could foster me."

Thinking for a moment, I said, "I bet that went over well with your mother, no less your father."

Closing his eyes, as if remembering something painful, he finally said, "I think my father didn't notice. He had other things on his mind, much too important to consider the likes of me. Having such an odd child was my mother's concern, and ultimately, she would shoulder the blame for my madness, as they called it. In my father's eyes, I was her failure. For that I'm sorry. I never wanted anyone to suffer, yet I am so compelled to live in the wilderness–which is the only place I feel at home–I can't help myself."

"You didn't know you were one of the master children?" I asked.

At that remark, he looked a bit surprised. "If that were so, wouldn't my parents have told me? Wouldn't they have tried to protect me and train me for the work of such a chosen one?"

Thinking this over, as we both lay down on the shaded ground offered by the huge rock, I answered, "That would depend on if they knew it to be so, wouldn't it?"

"Mary and Joseph knew you were a master child," he said, "from the moment of your first breath and before. I can't conceive that my parents had such a thought pertaining to me, much less that it might be true," he remarked.

I knew that this conversation was long overdue. John had been so separated from people, that he rarely had a chance to have an in-depth conversation with anyone, especially those of his family. Clearly, he had not entertained such thinking as this before now.

"I think your mother must have known, John," I said, "otherwise she wouldn't have allowed you the freedom she did at such a young age, to live under the sun and stars out here in the wilderness." He seemed to be thinking this over, when I continued further along this line and said, "Think about it. Your mother is my mother's cousin. Most of the women are priestesses, secretly holding that part of their lives private, but all closely connected. I know my mother is one, for sure, and she was fortunate to have my father's blessing, but your father was more tied to the social system, isn't that so? Maybe your sweet mother knew, but he never knew. Have you ever thought about that?"

"Thought about being a master?" He questioned, "You ask a question that makes no sense. I've never given it one moment of thought, because I've been too busy trying to learn the lessons that nature provides me. I do, however, give attention to wondering why I can't live like others and accept what they do. I just never thought to give myself the status of 'master,' and then ponder the whys and wherefores of it."

"Hmmm!" I uttered. "What makes you think that being a master is a status? It seems to me, it's more of a burden for most of us. My parents said the majority of the known masters were kidnapped and never heard from again, or blinded, so they couldn't look anyone in the eye. You call that status? I call that a curse, but a chosen one, if my understanding is correct; for if we choose life, we also choose death."

"Maybe so," he answered, "but your parents and village made sure you were safe, with all due concern and cover-up, I might add. The stories of you are as confusing as the sight of you this morning," he said. "I never thought much about being a master or otherwise. I just thought I didn't fit in."

Minutes passed in silence. We both pondered this rare conversation we were having. John was more comfortable conversing with nature than with humans, yet I think he was glad for the discussion with me.

A rabbit hopped into the shade of the space we lay within, to share the coolness with us. I wondered if John would grab it and pop it into his mouth raw, and give me another lesson in surviving in the wild. But instead, he began making an odd noise, much like the very low tone a rabbit might make. He was talking to the rabbit and asking of its welfare. Since I knew animal-speak myself, I could follow the conversation. I remembered that long ago I had taught him animal-speak, and he had easily mastered the language of the wild ones. The rabbit told John that it had a close call with a hawk, but other than that, it was fine on this wonderful day. It asked if we minded if it sat a while with us, before it ventured out there in the land of the hunter. It said, it had to find its nest soon and kept forgetting where it was, and had young ones to tend.

Eventually, the little she-rabbit braved the bright sun and danger a clear day presented, due to her desire to feed her children, and she left us as quickly as she came.

"Delightful lady rabbit," I said. "I hope she finds her children and is able to raise them, before she feeds the hawk," I remarked.

John looked at me in surprise and said, "You understand animal-speak?"

"Of course," I replied.

"How did you learn it?" he questioned.

"For the most part, the same way you did—from the animals," I said. I knew he had forgotten the time when we were children, when on one of my rare visits home, I had taught him the basics of the language. One could pick up the rest by using those basics, and it was evident that he was a natural in communicating with the natural realm.

To test me, he said a few things in various animal dialects, and also did some mind-to-mind techniques. I followed him easily enough and answered appropriately. That caused him to stare at me for a long time, looking deeply into my eyes. Finally, he broke his silence saying, "You are a master, aren't you?"

"Sorry to say, that's true and being so, there's difficult work for me to do. Nevertheless, what is true of me is also true of you, John," I said. I think this was the first time I didn't resist being called 'master'.

He looked confused and unconvinced by my statement. I felt a need to qualify it a bit more, so I sat up—to better communicate eye to eye with him—and said, "Don't you see, that by allowing you to live in the wilderness, which caused people to think you were crazy, your mother was protecting you? I bet she watched you constantly as a young child, and she had to hide it. I don't think your father would've been amused at having a master child in the family, being part of the status quo, as he was. In fact, if I'm not mistaken, according to my mother, before your father passed on, he was among those who persecuted the master children. The Nazerites suspected that he was a traitor and possibly, responsible for some of the lost masters and mastras." That prospect made us both sad, and I hoped I didn't hurt my dear cousin by being so blunt. I chanced to continue, however, and said, "Right under the old man's nose was one of those feared master children and of his very own blood. You are blessed John," I reminded him. "You found safety in the wilderness, as well as education and sanity. You aren't a crazy man, just a sensitive one." John simply listened and seemed to be mulling the idea over in his mind.

Glad that John was finally considering the idea that he was one of the prayed-for children, I said, "Are you seeing that you are also a master child then, John?

He did his delightful chuckle again. "So," he said, "my father's disregard for me and ignorance was a blessing, rather than a judgment?"

"I would say it was both," I replied, "but at any rate, since we are near agreement that we are masters sent in order to change things, shall we agree that 'masters are slaves and slaves are masters,' and someday you will forgive your father? Maybe we were sent to crack open minds of stone and let some light in."

"You confuse me, Jeshua." John said, looking at me, as if I was the one who should be considered crazy. "Are you sure your head isn't cracked just a bit?" he teased.

Answering I said, "Along that line of thinking, I would guess that cracking open closed minds would be a nasty job, since in doing so there are certain physical uncertainties involved like suffering and probably dying as well, wouldn't you agree, John?"

"That would be a certainty, rather than an uncertainty," he emphasized. "Those idiots who think they know everything will hurt or kill you, if you dare to try to open their minds," he answered. "That's why I stay away from them," he continued, "and why I stayed away from my departed father as well. I'm not all that crazy that I desire to suffer at their brainless hands, and though I feel a little guilty, I don't miss my father's disappointed face when he laid eyes on me."

"Then," I continued with my reasoning, "would you say that our agreement to come into this world to shakeup the status quo, or to be cracking open closed minds that don't want to be opened, would either be totally crazy reasoning, or a sacrificial offering of the greatest magnitude, which I might add, is the offering that all servants provide, like it or not?"

"Well, so much for thinking I might be special to be a master," John said, with a hint of sarcasm. "What you're saying then is, I'm a servant," he finally surmised, "But how can I be of service, if I don't even like people?"

"Yes, maybe that's true, but you love them. I know you and you love all creation. We just were born to play different roles. You serve through your so-called craziness; I came to teach in my own special crazy way. We could reason that your father came to demonstrate how ignorance lives within fear and can't see a blessing right under its stupid nose?"

John, now sitting with his back propped against the rock, was resting his head with his eyes closed. He had some long grass in his mouth, and was making the two protruding ends of the grass crisscross back and forth as he was thinking, puckering his lips in the process. Finally, his thought formed and he replied, "You know," he said, "I think a lot out here, due to the peace of this existence, which provides much time for such activity. What I don't do too much of, however, is converse like this. I think I rather like mulling things over with you, discussing some of my thoughts, and accepting and examining some of your thinking. So bear with me, as I ask a possible stupid question."

"Bring it on, cousin," I said, rather enjoying the conversation we were having, too, and the way the time was our own to use as we would.

John said, "If we all have a role to play as you said, and my father's role was to show how an idiot thinks he is so smart–

qualified to judge others 'mad' or 'crazy,' as was the situation in my case–then why would I be sent in order to crack open a mind such as his? Why not let the hard-headed man be totally insane within his illusion, for is that not his role?"

I replied, "Surely you see that others suffer, when they are degraded. Such attitudes dishonor God, who then suffers as well? And if our purpose is compassion, and to be a bridge between ignorance and innocence, we must try to open minds and touch hearts. Maybe it's not our task to change everyone, but rather to help those willing to change, step away from the suffering and humiliation that fear causes? "

"Is that so," John questioned, with a look of disbelief written all over his face, "We have come to keep God from suffering?" After he said that, a tiny bird flew toward us in the shade and misjudged the landing surface on the rock, knocked itself senseless and tumbled down between John and me. John picked it up and began chirping to it, saying, "So it is, little one, you again rush around and forget to prepare for a landing place in enough time to land on your own two feet!"

The little bird, a bit dazed, but regaining its balance chirped back, "I hate to be such a clown, but since I lost my two toes on my favorite foot, I just can't seem to navigate as well as I should."

John gently turned it over in his hands inspecting the toes, and remarked, "The toes have healed well, my little friend, but the mind lags behind. Give yourself time and practice, and soon enough your mind will be healed, too, and you'll land even better than you did before you lost those toes to the weasel." Then John gently put the more-revived bird down and continued with our conversation.

"Then," he surmised, "Since my little bird friend here suffered, lost his toes and lost some of his self-esteem, is it true that God lost a sense of Self, as well? Is that what you're saying?" Before I could answer he asked, "How can God know all and see all and still lose a sense of Divine Self?"

"A great question, cousin," I answered. "Let's think about it. Doesn't God, through this little bird that has lost his toes and thus lost his sense of self-worth, experience what it feels like to be in such a situation? After all, the bird is an aspect of God, created like everything else, of the essence of God, as all creation is." I continued, "If that's so, then wouldn't you admit that even this little bird has a divine purpose, in that God discovers how it feels to have a setback, or a change in form. Thus, God experiences, or discovers through the little bird, how to regain one's perfect concept of self? Certainly, the only way that God could ever experience the wonder of discovery is through creational aspects that are on a mission of divine discovery."

Our little bird friend was now joyfully singing a cheerful song. It could sense that we were enjoying ourselves within our own chatter, and as all animals do, he could see the images within our minds and knew we were talking about it. That made this little feathered fellow very proud. Pride is not a bad thing, when it is illustrative of self-esteem, or appreciation of one's relationship with all creation, which was how the tiny creature felt. He was responding with a blissful song within the moment, realizing that the conversation was respectful. Animals are better at a spontaneous response than humans, not prone to running the experience through their heads first, just feeling the essence of it.

Sensing that John was waiting for me to expound upon his comment, I jumped back into the conversation, saying, "What would be the sense of creation, if it wasn't to experience all things through unlimited possibilities. Don't you think that God, the One Divine Source of all that is, would be lonely with nothing going on? Haven't some of your most treasured moments in this life been, when you discovered something?" I continued on, in that mindset, saying, "If discovery feels good to us, it must, likewise, feel good to God, who experiences everything we say or do, don't you agree?"

"Okay," John said, "I can accept that, but does it also feel good to experience murder and mayhem? Does it feel good to God, to experience meanness and greed and selfishness, or along the same line of thinking, does it feel good to God to feel the deep sorrow of

## The Saga-Oracle

losing a loved one, due to any of these aforementioned deeds? What does it feel like to God, when someone betrays you, or is so jealous that they undermine your successes and cause you to fail? How does it feel to God, when after your best effort, when you have given all you can, you still fail? Answer these questions for me, and then maybe I'll understand better, Jeshua. I want to believe you."

I could see in John's eyes, an extreme need to make sense of the suffering that people inflicted on each other. Those who ruled the land had long held that suffering was punishment from God, thus justifiable, to those less worthy. In their minds, everyone was born in sin and deserved to suffer, because God made them inferior, and the suffering was calculated on a sliding scale called 'worth'. This would be a rather difficult question to tackle, but I tried, nonetheless.

"Certainly, God would be willing to feel anything that we, or any aspect of creation, might experience," I said. "After all, one must often discover the dead-end roads to find the correct path to the destination (John rolled his eyes as I brought up roads, because he avoided them in any shape or form), or how would one know that the journey was fully explored?"

He had to respond, as I knew he would, and said in exasperation, "If they would get off the damn roads once in awhile, they would know!"

"Okay" I interjected, "but back to why we make mistakes, and if we should be interfering in the present mindset. I think those like us, volunteers for the task of compassionate balance, are sent from time to time, so that there might be an opportunity for less suffering." I continued on with this developing thought, as my mind followed its trail, "We come to change the tides of thinking, whether we walk down paths already made, or we get off the path as you have, and find our own way. Maybe your footsteps create new paths, John."

John nodded and agreed to this point, and I continued. "Perhaps we came to crack open closed minds, where the weed-seed of all suffering and degradation takes root. Thus, we are the servants of

God and to all creation, and that could be our divine purpose, and maybe the grand plan, my friend."

"Maybe so," John said, "but the most evil thinking; the most closed minds; the most fearful behavior–which manifests as cruelty–is in human minds. Our little bird friends," he said, pointing to the little bird sitting on the rock–who decided that John's pointing finger was an invitation to perch there, and landing quite nicely upon it–"certainly aren't prone to evil deeds. Birds seldom cook up judgmental attitudes. If they do, it's a reflection of some human they've been hanging around so closely, that they absorbed their attitudes." Then his questioning mind seemed to shift, and he spoke to the bird, saying, "That was a rather nice landing you just did, little friend." He then bobbed his finger up and down, with the little bird hanging on and flapping its wings. John said in a tone of voice one would speak to a baby with, "Balance looks good, landing was good, I think you are pretty much back to great birdie form, my friend." The bird chirped happy thanks and flew off.

"Yes," I said in response, still continuing with the question he posed, ignoring the moment's baby-talk episode; not because it wasn't important, but because it was totally respectful and required no further confirmation. I continued, "That's probably why God sent the likes of you and me, in a human form, rather than as little birds. The gift, and challenge, of thinking in the past, present and future, creates a great responsibility, and I'm afraid that our kind is messing up the job."

John just nodded a knowing affirmation. We both noticed that the sun was going down, and it was cooling off. John got up and began walking away, not inviting me to follow, but not indicating I shouldn't either. I followed. I wanted to have more conversations like this with John. I needed to talk to someone who understood me, and who helped me think deeper and sort my thoughts. I'm sure John felt likewise. I desired to know my, so-called, crazy cousin better, and I found him an open-minded man with a big heart.

# The Saga-Oracle

John and I wandered the wilderness a long time. I also ventured into the villages and cities, when we came close. I kept a more civilized look about me at those times, because I wanted to monitor the situations within the societies, as well as learn from John and experience the peace and solitude of the wilderness. Sometimes I would wake up in the morning, and John would be gone. I might not see him for days, and then he would show up again. I'd run into him wandering out there in his territory. People seldom knew who I was, when I was in their presence, unless I was in my home village. For the most part, I liked being anonymous, because I learned a great deal just listening to conversations and observing behavior. I had once before done the same type of observation. Now I was more patient and much more perceptive–less prone to giving in to 'madness'.

So it was one day, I heard some women speaking of John, the wild man. They were arguing about whether he was to be feared or revered. One said he was smarter than many thought, because he would not settle to live where cruelty was tolerated. His kindness to animals was often the topic of conversation. Most men, if they mentioned him at all, were more likely to simply say he was crazy, and that one day someone would have to do something about the situation. On one occasion a group of men went out to try to find John, so that they could capture him and put him in a cage where he wouldn't be so miserable. Safe, they said, from himself. I feared for my cousin, but little did I know that he knew how to deal with such closed minds and had done so on numerous occasions. As I listened to the ladies, I learned that when the men set out to capture the wild man, they suffered all kinds of unfortunate situations, like falling into traps set by my cousin, traps naturally concealed in holes or crevices; these included snake pits, dung piles, and brambles grabbing and tearing their robes, among other such accidents. More than once the men had their wits scared out of them by some of the more feared wild animals. Once it was the desert panther, stalking them and giving them a cat-hissing comment on their intent, showing lots of menacing teeth and long sharp claws. In the end, as always was the case, John was left to survive in the wilderness, out there where danger lurked for others but where he was accepted.

I encouraged John to visit with his family more often. I couldn't bear totally separating myself from my mother, sisters and brothers. Often his mother would be working with my dear mother on a project that I strongly suspected was priestess connected, and she would mention how much she missed John. The priestess projects or priestess business in general, were seldom discussed with men. The women, due to male dominance and persecution, had to hide their sisterhood in favor of the men's brotherhood. But I knew something was going on. Even as a child I had noted the dove embroidered upon my mother's robes, and realized it was significant and priestess related. It was so tiny and carefully placed that it didn't draw attention. Most, if they saw it at all, would think it discrete decoration. At any rate, John's mother and mine both had the dove on their robes, and they were glad we were together. They had no idea we were hanging out, far more than they could have guessed. We, likewise, had no idea how much time our mothers spent together, either.

I count those wandering years as productive, since within them, I realized that I couldn't just march into community and change attitudes or mind-sets, within one or two short visits, and a few well-chosen speeches. I had to establish myself as someone who listens, someone to be respected and trusted, first. So in my early years, I built that trust. I made friends among those within the human community, and slowly allowed the people to know me, Jeshua ben Joseph. I enjoyed friends within nature as well, thanks to John sharing his life for a while. I prepared myself further, and waited for the time of my greatest challenge to tap me on the shoulder and say, "Hey! Get on with it now."

I was lonesome in many ways, during this time. John didn't seem to care about taking a wife and raising children. He was comfortable in his solitude. He was such a non-conformist, that he felt no connection to the social norms that required marriage, instead he felt totally complete within himself, out there in the natural wilderness. I, on the other hand, had a longing to have a family and children, and wanted to be an accepted Rabbi.[102] That meant that I was expected to fulfill my destiny and take a wife,

---

[102] Teacher

who would bring forth my children. I met many lovely young maidens, when I went into the villages and towns. Some, I was tempted to have a closer relationship with, but I couldn't shake the feeling that there was someone–my own counterpart–who would soon join me. I knew we would be working together on this soul mission, which never stopped nagging me, deep down inside. For the most part, I didn't allow myself to become too committed or involved with the lovely young maidens I met. When questioned on when I would settle down with a wife, I would say, "Soon, when I'm done wandering."

One day John and I woke in early morning as usual, and took our ritual bath in one of our favorite steams, that fed the various oasis communities that dotted the arid countryside we traversed. We looked at each other and simply said, "Good bye." We both knew it was time for us to go our separate ways. We embraced and walked different directions that day, he towards the desert and I toward the sunrise.

# THE GIFT OF THE RED ROBE
Chapter Twenty-Four

My mission awaited my full attention, and I knew it. My early training was complete; even so, at the same time, I felt that with each breath I took, a lesson would be offered every day of my life. I was ready to move forward with my soul's task and fulfill my destiny.

I felt a deep longing for a life-mate, even as I began my teaching. At first, I was by myself, and then gradually I seemed to have followers, who were dedicated to helping me get the word out. Most of my companions had life-mates, because it was the custom and an expectation that some saw as a duty. My followers left their homes, work and, sometimes, family to follow me. Some found wandering with me tolerable; some found wandering not so easy. Early on, I sent those needed by spouses and families back to their homes. I helped them realize that to honor their families was to respect the mission and a divine duty, above all else. "Some will wander," I said, "and some will bloom where they are planted, ready to share their beautiful wisdom in their own garden." They understood this–at least when they were sent back to their homes, they did. Many remembered what drew them to me and the teachings I offered; sadly, some forgot, depending on the circumstances of their lives and the challenges they met. Their minds were confused, during this time of great resistance to change. Fear and hope for a better way battled inwardly and outwardly.

I wandered the lands of my birth, and many seemed drawn to me. I went back to my village occasionally, but each time I felt empty. I was not so charismatic and few ears were open to my message there. Those that remembered the master child project were few now, and the recollections of that intention weren't welcome anymore. The vision and hope were near-totally suppressed. However, one elder woman, who my mother said was a great aunt to me, visited one day and asked me to join her under the shade of an olive tree near my mother's home. There, she told me how the village had devised the idea to invite master souls in through the children and how they intended to fulfill a prophesy-promise, that God would send such beings, in time of the greatest need. She mentioned how the suspected master children had to be hidden, resulting in the project becoming lost. "They've forgotten, because their vision couldn't hold the test of time," she said. Chuckling a little, as elders often do when remembering something ironic, she continued and whispered, "They held a series of tests to determine which newborns, or infants might be those they asked to receive. There were at least twelve sent to our village, two of which they didn't recognize until they were grown. However, time had dulled the vision of the original intention, because the results were subtle, and not dramatic, and they lost faith in their own convictions. They simply quit looking at the glory of the gifts they already received, which I'm sure resulted in the gifts being taken back by the giver. You, Yeheshua,[103] might be the last apparent gift. It appears that your presence, your gift, shall have the best opportunity to be opened and rejoiced someplace other than your home village. This place that invited you to help shift attitudes, I

---

[103] My birth name

fear, has blinders on, and can't see the answered prayer," she sadly said. "Those that asked for the gift won't be those that accept it most graciously. Don't expect to be a prophet in your own land, nephew," she warned me, patting my hand tenderly. "The leaders look elsewhere for fulfillment to their prayers, overlooking the obvious answer right there, politely awaiting recognition. The gift arrived on prayerful intentions put forth by their own fathers, even so, they all lost hope, to the point that they no longer believe in their answered prayer, and are confused as to what they actually prayed for in the first place."

She continued, "The special children were so hidden, that the other children didn't know the scope of the experiment either, and as often happens, they have their own visions, and seek in their own way. Don't feel diminished," she emphasized, looking deeply into my eyes with her own ancient wise eyes, which were deep pools of wisdom. "Realize rather, that you have been freed from expectations, by those who might limit you with their demands. Feel free, master, to teach as only you know is appropriate." She started to cry, and I felt compelled to embrace her. She sobbed into my robes silently, with slight tremors shaking her frail old body. "Master," she said, "I am glad you came." Then she dismissed me as only an elder can, waving me to leave now and let her be alone. I think she wanted to spare me her sorrow.

I noticed that the social atmosphere, wherever I roamed, was one of exclusion, rather than inclusion. Even within the various religious sects in villages, the councils accepted the attitude that others were not welcome, or not 'chosen,' to be part of the tight-knit group they supposedly represented. Then the groups–usually the priests, depending on the power they possessed and the positions they held within the social arena–would set themselves up to be the conscience of others, judging who was worthwhile and who wasn't. Of course, they saw themselves as extremely deserving. This somehow uplifted those who deemed themselves divinely chosen, because they felt better than someone else. They walked around, dressed in fine silken robes adorned with gold and precious jewels, and looked down on the poor who had nothing, expecting them to give their last shekel to God, or be considered sinners and excommunicated from the synagogue, or temple. That warped thinking drove me mad once, but now I was determined to face it head-on and somehow shift this exclusive way of sorting people. In such situations, it doesn't take long for the privileged to offer an opportunity for others to buy worthiness, if they could afford it. Thus, their corrupted power increased in measure with their wealth, and the business of religion became more important that the spirit of it. True power is found within love and connectedness. These I speak of used fear to build walls of exclusion in the religions they supposedly served, with themselves on the inside and their moneychangers posted at the portals of the temples, doing their business of selling sacrificial animals.

This attitude called for divine balance. My early lessons and experience had convinced me that the goal of all creation is to unite, not to separate. The separateness, especially within marriages where women were forced into a lesser role, was the true fall of man. Women, thus diminished and denied their feminine talents, caused a major blockage to divine balance. Addressing this attitude within a community, that had been long programmed in such separation traditions, was my greatest challenge. Change is the biggest enemy of fear, and fear holds tight its horrible grip on humanity through attitudes, ingrained and purposefully imprinted upon the masses to keep them in line. As much as I wanted to bring forth the simple, but complex, core of the matter, I couldn't be so obvious, or I would lose my connection to those I wished to unite. Antiforce used imprinted fear, to shut the door to the truth of love, in any way it could. Thus, I taught mostly in parable, for fear doesn't consider the tales people tell a threat to its control. The assumption that the stories were just entertainment helped me go unnoticed for awhile.

I always loved telling stories. Most often my tales were true observations or narratives of actual life experiences, I heard or witnessed. In some cases, I would take some aspect from one tale and unite it with another to get the point across. I had a talent for storytelling. When I began my parables I would usually have few listeners present, and as the narrative unfolded, I often felt energized and even entranced, as I moved along in the story. Soon the crowd would grow in numbers. I didn't notice, because I was so lost in the trance-like mode as the chronicle unfolded. I was

## The Saga-Oracle

aware of the presence of the others listening, but I felt like I was out of my body, watching the episode, not separate from it, but more an observer of the situation. I would get caught up in observation, noticing reactions and attention of the listeners, but still amazed that I could see through them, into their inner-thoughts. It seemed as though there were two of me–the storyteller and the observer–who would evaluate the success of the talk. As the story ended, I reunited the two aspects of myself back into my physical body, which left me feeling quite dazed. I often had no idea of how much ground I had covered within the parable, or how many listened, much less how many had joined after I had begun the tale. I was always astonished to see how the crowd had grown, upon my full return to my physicality, even as I was drained and spent from the episode.

I began to call those, who chose to follow me from place to place, my apostles; for they were eager to support and understand the work, I was compelled to do. For the most part, they were men who were free to choose their own path. Even so, many women in the villages and towns managed to take time from their busy burdensome days to listen to me, as well. They often seemed to understand the truth hidden in the story more readily than did the men. My apostles, the men devotees, focused on the literal topic, before they could possibly grasp the underlying wisdom of the metaphoric tales I used in order to teach the divine truth. Thankfully, the women understood the greater message of the tales straight away. They used stories as a teaching method for little children. To them, my format of teaching was natural and appropriate.

Later, after the day was done, drained and tired, we would find a place to rest. If we were blessed–and often we were–one of the listeners would take us home, feed us a fine meal in gratitude for the teaching, and we would rest and prepare for the next day. At those times, relaxed and spent, we discussed the parable of the day, lying about outside where we usually slept or in an animal shelter, if we were lucky enough to share one with the donkey or other creatures. I loved those times of discussion, since I often didn't remember the full scope of the teaching until a later discussion. It was like something divine took me over when I taught, and I simply became the observer, thus I remembered little when the teaching ended. As we revisited it in discussion, the day's teaching came back to me as a dream would, and I could then fill out the teaching for my inner group, because while I may not remember it, I understood the concepts at a very deep soul level. The men were amazed; the women were confirmed (intuitively they already knew what I taught) as we enjoyed our follow-up sessions, which fulfilled us even more than the evening meal. The women strengthened me, while the men sometimes drained me, because the men had to be convinced and the women only needed confirmation. This isn't a complaint, just a simple observation of how the men and women interacted and grappled with the teachings. Actually, it was quite a natural way the two genders sorted information, with the intuitive women trusting their feelings, and the logical men wanting to debate.

We passed many peaceful evenings in such discussion. Most of us were in our late twenty's or early thirty's in age, and ready to solve all the world problems, or so we thought. As idealistic as we were, we still knew that what we were beginning to form was a threat to those old ideas that sprang from fear, which had developed a cruel power. We knew we were mavericks, walking a dangerous path. However, we believed that it was our birth mission to be here, in this time and place, and to do all we could to help the suffering people.

Group dynamics are interesting, in that when two or more of like mind are gathered, there is great empowerment, and the energy magnifies and expands. That is true whether the group is focused on love or fear. The power of love is 'God Power,' while the power of fear is a corrupted illusion and consequently 'antiforce' thus anti-God, and destructive in nature. Power intimidates through attitudes and love is a mighty uniting force. Antiforce uses fear to gain power which, through desperation and separation, prevents unification. That has been the real war, which has raged for eons of time–aggressive-fear verses passive-love. I wanted to enlighten people so they would know love is the essence of God in all creation, and fear was the essence of evil. Love is not the enemy of fear. Love is the truth that will dissolve fear. Simple truth is hardest to grasp, and it was rejected time and again, because people were afraid to take the responsibility of living outside of their mental cages of enslavement.

After a long teaching day at another home, due to a kind invitation of both the elder householder and his wife, I noticed that a couple, who had followed us around from village to village for over a week, were sitting close holding hands, with a pleasant look upon their faces. "Zachariah[104] and Judith,[105]" I said, "what is it that makes you so beautiful together, as you listen to the debate on today's teaching?"

They looked at each other, as I addressed them and Judith happily said, "It's the truth of it, master." Then she looked downward, realizing that she had jumped ahead of Zachariah and spoken before he had given his permission, as would have been the custom of the time and place.

He looked lovingly at her and squeezed her shoulders, nodded his head and encouraged her to continue. She was reluctant, having sensed she crossed a barrier that society had created, and she didn't want to offend the group with her enthusiastic answer to my question.

"Please, Judith," her husband said, "answer, Jesus,[106] for you have the ability to phrase our feelings of contentment and connection, better than I ever could."

Judith lifted her head and looked around, as if to gain permission from the other men in attendance, but for the most part, they closed their minds and thought she had stepped out of her place. It was clear that she may have had her husband's permission to speak, but not theirs. Judith looked at each apostle, and at the householders who took us in that fine evening, and finally she looked into my eyes. She saw my gracious acceptance of her

---

[104] Name means 'pure', also means "the Lord remembers'
[105] Name means, 'woman from Judea,' Judea being an ancient region in Israel
[106] 'Jesus' is a translation of 'Yeshua,' a Hebrew way to say 'Yeheshua'. In this narrative Jeshuah, shortened to Jeshua, which are most likely the same name, just now spelled and pronounced slightly different

within my expression. She took a deep breath, and with feminine courage that always pleased me, she tried to finish the answer she was so excited to share in the first place, even as she knew full well that most of the men thought her bold to do so.

"I know that some of you believe that your wives should be home and keeping the hearth warm, out of sight and out of such discussions. I see it in your eyes, gentlemen," she said with her sweet voice. "But," she went on to say, "our master (they were now calling me by this title as most teachers were addressed) has asked a question and my beloved husband has consented to allow me the opportunity to answer it. For that confidence, I am truly honored, and my devotion to him expands," she said.

One of the apostles interrupted saying to Zachariah, "Can't you speak for the family man? Is your tongue so tied that you must let your woman speak for you?"

Zachariah quickly spoke up, saying, "I can speak anytime I choose, and that's true for my wife, Judith, too. We both have a mind to think and a voice to tell those thoughts, and a heart to receive even more to think about and discuss. We are paired perfectly, for our thoughts join us, they don't separate us. When I speak, Judith feels completed; when she speaks, I feel completed. We become as 'One' and for this, I am blessed." This puzzled the others and spurred a further conversation, exploring relationships between the men and the women in their lives, and who should be supportive and silent, and who should be vocally present.

Finally, I said, "Judith has not been allowed to finish her thought, and I would like to hear what she has to say about why she and Zachariah beam when we see them together. Someday, I hope I'll reflect such a glow with a beloved mate, as well."

Judith smiled and explained, "Zachariah and I, from the first moment we met, felt connected. We felt the Onement, as we term it. Our souls joined immediately and we have tried to share as much as we can of our lives, to honor this divine connection. My family didn't want me to wed Zachariah, when we first desired to become husband and wife, believing that he was not of sufficient wealth and power to keep me comfortable. I had to convince them that the comfort of my soul was much more important to me, than the comfort of physical life. They loved me enough to listen, even my father!" she emphasized, as she looked back at the doubting apostles glaring at her. "So we completed our pre-marriage and then the final marriage ceremonies, with the blessings of our families. We have one child now, and since we have met Master Jesus and the group, we have asked family members to keep our son safe, until we are filled with the blessings of 'The Way'.[107]" Looking at me, she said, "When we heard you speak in our village, we were so taken with your story and the truth it offered, we wanted to be fulfilled enough to share the warmth and wisdom of your teachings with those near and dear to us. Thus we agreed that we must follow you for a short time, eventually to finally return to our home and child, to live our lives the way we know is divinely intended."

One of the apostles, ignoring Judith, said, "How can you leave your work, Zachariah, and your child, now without his mother, just to follow us?"

"Didn't you do the same, Bartholomew?"[108] Zachariah answered. Bartholomew didn't respond, just looked down, as it was true he had left his family to follow the master, too, and in asking Zachariah the question, he was also asking himself.

I spoke then, saying, "I'm honored that you both are here, and I'm equally honored that Judith speaks her truth, whenever and wherever she chooses. My mother would love such a woman; for my clear-spoken mother doesn't compromise her sweetness one bit, when she speaks first." Judith blushed at my statement and snuggled back into Zachariah's arms. She had stiffened a bit when she spoke, ready to defend her voice. Now, however, she felt validated and more comfortable again.

So it was; discussions expanded beyond the daily parable and sprang forth from internal situations within our ever-expanding group. After a long evening of discussion, thanks to our

---

[107] How the followers referred to the teachings
[108] 'Son of Talmai'

benefactors who shared a meal and provided a stable for night lodging, we retired and slept well with the humble animals.

I dreamed of a beautiful woman that night. I had seen her before in my dreams, from the time of my early youthful days, but then she was a little girl. It seemed that as I grew, so did she. Her complexion was dark, with long deep reddish wavy hair and eyes that seemed dark one moment and deep ocean-blue the next. She always appeared strong and vibrant. Her aura[109] had a beautiful blue glow, when she visited me in my dreams. I knew that I was waiting for her. None of the beautiful maidens I had met in my life, ever approached the love I felt for the woman of my dreams. I was years past the expected age that men would marry, but I was already in love with my dream-mate and could think of none other as my life-mate.

That night within my dream, she reached out again, as she usually did, but this time her long slender fingers actually touched mine. Always before, there was a distance between our hands as we both reached toward the other. Lately, that space was getting closer and closer. In this dream, we finally touched. That touch caused a flush of excitement, expectation and energy to flood through me. I felt a rush of pure pleasure within the dream, and maybe physically, as well. "Finally, beloved, you have come. Let us begin," I said, and immediately awoke. It was early pre-dawn with just a hint of warm light on the horizon. My body was vibrating and reacting to the passionate charge of the dream vision. I remember thinking, "What a way to awaken and begin the day." I felt that something wonderful for me was on the horizon. I watched the morning sunrise with joy and expectation.

When Andrew, one of my closest friends and devoted apostle, found me sitting quietly watching the sun disc ascend, he said, "Master, you look so happy and refreshed this morning. You must have dreamed well."

---

[109] Energy field around all creation that vibrates with color according to the being it emanates from

## The Saga-Oracle

I answered in a calm quiet voice, "Andrew, why do you call me, master, when first and foremost I'm your friend?"

Andrew said, "Because, dear friend, you're my teacher, and I respect you as my Raboni.[110] This morning, you glow like never before."

I responded, "I have dreamed of a divine connection of some sort, and this dream revisits me throughout my life. That which I seek seems ever closer, but just out of reach. This time it was different. I could touch the vision, I have dreamed for so long. I don't know how it will affect my work, but I know it completes me and enhances my mission, and I have long waited for this moment to arrive."

Andrew sat down next to me, put his arm around my shoulder and said, "You are worthy to partake of all that is good, master, and if your dream announces such a gift, I rejoice in your happy expectation."

To have a friend share such sentiment is a blessing, no matter what form joy takes as it enters into one's life. I felt grateful to share my dream and the new dawning day with my friend Andrew. I appreciated that I didn't have to explain further. Acceptance is sweet, especially coming from those you call 'friend'.

At full sunrise our group arose and went about the new day's morning chores. We cleaned and prepared ourselves with our usual morning rituals, and just as we were about to leave, I went to the householders to thank them again for their hospitality. Our hostess gave us three gift bags. As she handed them to us (handing me the third bag) she said, "These are for your journey. I believe you will find a need of these basic things, and I'll feel great joy, if you would accept them." She bowed down and took my hand, lightly kissed it on the back across my knuckles, then raised my hand to her cheek and held it there a split second. This was a rare show of love and gratitude, and I appreciated the sincerity of the moment. "Go in peace, and may peace always be with you," she

---

[110] In Jesus' day it was a term of dignity given by the Jews to their distinguished teachers, a form of Rabbi

said, looking into my eyes with compassion, as her husband stood beside her smiling agreement. Women often said this to me, and I had come to know that they were the true essence of peace, when they were supported and respected, and they didn't say these words lightly. Men would frequently say, "May you be successful," while women most often would say, "May you be in peace." Each was given in love, and I accepted them equally with my heartfelt thanks, knowing that the sentiments were complements to each other, and meant to bless me fully.

We accepted the three gifts—which I assumed was food, because I could smell fresh baked bread—from the householder's wife who handed the bundles to us. The one she gave me, however, didn't hold such smells, and I felt it probably was something else that we might need along our way.

Around noon, we decided to rest, as the sun offered the greatest heat of the day. We came to a creek, which fed a well downstream where there was a small community. The well was a hub of activity, until the sun drove the water seekers back into the shade, but a few women and girls lingered to fill their buckets or goatskins with the refreshing spring water. We could hear them talking, in the distance.

We found a shady spot a short distance away and expectantly opened our bundles. First, Bartholomew opened the one he carried. It contained twelve loaves of flatbread and one jar of olive oil, sealed with bees wax. "More than enough to satisfy our hunger," he rightly commented.

Then another apostle, a young boy, John, so sweet in his early years, who felt honored just to carry the second bundle, opened it and found sun-dried fish and vegetables therein. He looked at me and said, "Master, the gift is far beyond what we could have hoped for."

"I know, John," I replied. "True gifts of the heart, no matter what form they take, far exceed what one might expect and such gifts are endless blessings." John was like a son to me. He usually positioned himself as close to me as he could, due to his admiration. I knew that this gentle young man loved me, as none of the others did; not more, just differently, with child-like wonder. I felt responsible to him for this adoration, yet I gently steered that love into a wider, more expansive and appropriate manner, that would benefit him as he grew and matured, so that he could, in like manner, know how to love unconditionally and totally, those he would meet and greet in his adulthood. Many teachers had blessed me, and I adored them much the same way. I knew that I was an important teacher for this young lad, as well. I hoped I would be up for the task of his intense adoration.

It was my turn to open my bundle, as the other two were now revealed and all eyes were on me, and I untied the linen covering that held a basket within it. Inside the circular basket, I found a cloth, soft and a most brilliant red. I pulled the cloth from the bundle basket and looked at it in wonder, for the red was so intense that it had a warming and comforting effect on me and anyone who touched it. It excited me, and puzzled me all at once, and I had no idea why it did so. It was an exquisite red robe, soft, velvety to the touch, and I noticed it had a small dove embroidered on its inner lining.

"Is that for you, master," John said, "for if you wear that robe, you will surely stand out, and there will be no doubt as to your passionate intentions."

"Well, John," I answered, "passion certainly describes my intentions, but I have no plan of wearing such a robe. I can only wonder at what the purpose that such a fine garment might have." I then noticed Judith looking at me, with a sweet knowing gleam in her eyes.

We turned our attention to the midday meal and enjoyed it, and at the same time, all wondered how the robe of passion would be used. Many touched it, but no one could think of how to use it, and I noticed, they couldn't hold it for long. Finally, it came back to my lap, where it comforted me. I carefully folded it again and put it into my satchel, where I carried my items of ritual and physical needs. I handed the basket to John and told him to give it away, or use it as he would like. He announced that he would put shoulder straps on it and use it as a carrying device, so that he could be more helpful to our group. We all laughed at his enthusiasm, but appreciated that he wanted to pull his weight and be of more help. We often wondered how his family could part with him at such a young age, for we guessed he was about 10-years-old, and he never explained why he was free to wander with us. I wondered if maybe they didn't appreciate his unique feminine manner, so delicate yet so strong. Sometimes, families thought all sons should be mighty warrior types. John's strength was not in physical strength, but rather in deep commitment and joyful passion.

After our meal of bread dipped in olive oil, dried fish and vegetables, I became quite thirsty. A stream was nearby, but I was drawn to the community well. I didn't consciously choose to go in that direction. It just seemed my feet and thirst pointed me towards the well, where I knew my intense thirst would be quenched.

The closer I came to the well, which now had a few additional people present since the day was cooling slightly, the more I noticed a blue halo around it. I wondered why the well glowed, when suddenly, I realized it wasn't the well that was glowing, but rather the glow surrounded a woman getting water. When I first saw her, she was quietly bringing up a bucket of fresh well water. I can't describe the way my heart fluttered upon setting eyes on her, or the way my knees seemed to weaken, along with an overall faint feeling, I was experiencing. I had never felt such pleasant sensations, and they confused and befuddled me.

It seemed as though I floated to her. The blue halo emitted from none other than the woman of my dreams. As I approached her, I spoke, since it appeared that she hadn't noticed me, but that wasn't so. I can't remember what I said. She gently looked up at me smiling sweetly and said, "At last we meet." She reached her hand out to me exactly as in my dream. Without hesitation, I took her tiny hand into mine, and the same feeling that awoke me from my dream this lovely morning, again shocked me with a wave of pleasure. I helped her to her feet and just looked at her for a long moment.

"Again, you awaken me as none other could," I finally said, as I twined my fingers around her glowing sweet hand. "Come with me, now," I beckoned, knowing full well that she would. She simply put down her water jug on the rim of the well and walked away with me. It was exactly what Judith was trying to convey about the Onement she felt with Zachariah, and I knew what the intention was for the passionate red robe.

# SONG OF THE SEA
## Chapter Twenty-Five

There aren't words to adequately describe, how it felt to walk beside the woman of my dreams. I have loved her from the moment my soul was sparked into the realms of discovery from the Divine Source of all creation. It's true that everyone longs to be reunited to that other part of them, that some call soul mates, twin flames, soul twins and such. The deep yearning is for the one so closely entwined with your own soul, that they are part of you, as you are part of them. Long ago, when your soul was first sparked from the Divine Source, you were actually one. Then there came a time that you split, so that the discovery of both aspects of the spark of you could be fully explored, and one could be as an anchor for the other throughout your many sojourns into discovery through incarnation. It's rare that both aspects of the one soul would incarnate at the same time. It's always true that one ever longs for the other, however. That's by divine design since the yearning is a motivating factor, and also the way that you discover that your beloved is within your very soul, inside of you and, forever and endlessly, loving you totally.

I was fortunate, and unfortunate, to meet the one I naturally yearned for. That's because, what one experiences, so too does the other; the plan of one incarnated and the other in the heavenly realm affords a more easily accomplished soul-goal. This insures a greater opportunity for the soul to stay connected to its pure essence, the true reflection of the Source. The counterpart, the one who never rejects, always loves without conditions, encourages and stands true with you, usually as a spiritual anchor, keeps you on track in the mission you incarnated to accomplish.

Nevertheless, in this lifetime, within this mission of balance, the project required that both, I and my soul mate, be incarnated at the same time. The joy of this arrangement is beyond description. Unfortunately, the pain of it is equally indescribable. This union would present the greatest challenge to both my beloved and me as we doubled the joy and the sorrow. To explain that a bit further, I would not only feel my own physical, emotional and spiritual pain, but my sweet soul mate's as well, and she would, likewise, feel mine. That was our greatest challenge in this agreed-upon undertaking, that I can only tell you now from the other side of experiencing it.

We walked a long way hand-in-hand, just basking in the pleasure of the other, saying nothing. My group of followers walked a few steps behind us. At first, they thought I was just being nice to a woman I found by the well. I could be that way. I often connected to people, alone and in need of a friend, but this time they sensed there was something different. I was in a daze, and I'm sure my body language was that of pure joy. We were lost in our own world and hardly noticed anyone, much less my close followers. My group consisted of mainly men who didn't have family responsibilities, or if they did, they were in a position to turn that responsibility over to someone else for a while. Women were usually day-followers, since to join me for longer would mean they might spend the evening with the group of men, and society frowned upon such things. I had a few women who came with husbands, and I found them gentle and comforting. Now that I found my beloved by the well, even though I could sense the confusion of my followers, I was too caught up in my own joy to care what anyone thought.

"Aren't you going to tell me your name?" I finally asked.

"Aren't you going to announce yours, as well?" my sweet love said.

"I won't announce, but share my name," I said. "I'm not important enough to proclaim myself by announcement," I clarified. "I am Yeheshua ben Joseph of the Essene Nazerite people. Even so, my family calls me 'Esa'."

Smiling, my beautiful beloved replied, "I am Mary of Magdala, daughter to the world and servant to all. My family calls me Miryam.[111]"

"This union won't be easy," I said, as we walked together, assuming that we would be betrothed, even without formal permission from her family, much less asking if she approved or desired such a union.

"I know," she responded, "but we knew before we were born as we entered into our soul agreement, that what was asked would be difficult." She confirmed what I knew to be true. I always sensed that an agreement for partnership had been established, before my emergence into the physical.

I answered, "Of course, and even those who walk with us, probably won't understand the true purpose of the mission and union between you and me. Can you sense the confusion already, as my followers walk behind us, wondering why the one they call Raboni, is so light of foot since taking your hand?"

"I can sense it, and I would have expected nothing else from them, since first they must question, then they might see how it can be, and finally they may shift their attitudes. Isn't that why we came into this mission we shall share, to help people shift attitudes a step at a time by being living examples of balance?"

I simply nodded agreement and we proceeded to a village I planned to visit. As usual, a crowd already awaited us. "It always amazes me that crowds know of our arrival, before we step foot

---

[111] Her family did not, yet call her MiryAmah. Mary, or Miryam, means 'sea of bitterness', 'rebelliousness', or 'wished-for child' from the Hebrew, or to be derived from the Ancient Egyptian word *mry* ('beloved'), *mr* ('love'), Also, secretly, 'beloved if Isis'.

into the villages," I remarked, because I didn't plan my visits that far in advance. Often it was a spontaneous decision.

"It doesn't surprise me," Mary said. "I knew of your visit. The priestess network is reliable. There was word that a teacher would arrive this morning and have need of the sisters within the crowd to keep a feminine presence therein. I had planned to be in the very village we now approach, since our messenger mentioned the location. I was about to head towards the meeting to be a balancing factor as requested, after my well duty. I had no idea that you were the one called 'teacher'.

"I suspect my mother Mary has something to do with that," I said. "She once told me that no matter where I was, she could sense my location. She said she had this ability, so she could keep me safe, and help me in her own special maternal way. She's a priestess, too." I said. "She is known as Patient Mary."

"Oh my!" Mary nearly shouted. "Patient Mary indeed, the one who so many love and respect is your mother?" she asked. Mary was a common name, but it was more a title than a name. Those called 'Mary' were expected to be the wise-women of the family. They also secretly were designated to be the connecting link to the ancient Isis Priestess Cult[112], which had been actively practicing the feminine wisdom secretly for ages. Isis was one of the creator god women I learned of in the tunnels as I left the city of Brambles. Mary meant 'Star of the Sea.' I thought how appropriate that my mother and this sweet lady, now walking by my side and filling my soul, should be called such. The calmness and peace I felt, was very much like what I felt when I walked by the sea.

"I'm grateful that my mother is appreciated," I replied. "Patience is her greatest strength and has no doubt been the only thing that helped her through the difficult times in her life. I regret that I've been the cause of many of those hard times."

---

[112] One of the feminine creator gods, who befriended women and trained priestesses, the tradition secretly continued

Mary seemed to be thinking this over and finally said, "She is well-known for her patience and her endless compassion. There's no one gentler with the new initiates than she. How she is so patient with the priests, yet manages to get her point across, is famed among the priestesses. Little do the priests know, that she holds a high rank among the underground Isis following and that under their very noses, the humble little Patient Mary is actually one of the most important and strong leaders of the feminine priesthood. And now, here I am walking beside her beloved son. I feel honored and blessed."

"No, I'm the one honored and blessed, or maybe we both are. I still can't believe that the woman who has visited me in my dreams all my life is finally here, walking and talking with me. I couldn't be happier."

We chatted on and on about anything and everything, with the conversation bouncing around like a child's toss toy, but never becoming boring or repetitive. We finally arrived at our appointed destination and were greeted by a smiling woman, who ushered us to a sloping terrain for the purpose of our visit. Hillside locations were favored, due to the way I could see everyone, and they could see me. Today's location fit perfectly, and had ample date palms and olive trees scattered here and there for shade, as well as some well-appointed boulders to sit upon, for the listeners' comfort.

We rested for about a half hour, as people silently began arriving. They seemed to keep a distance giving us time to prepare, but I suspect that the priestesses were out there orchestrating that, as well. At some point I just stood up, held my arms up and began. It was as if something inside of me triggered at that instant, and I said, "It is time." I always began my teaching that way.

When I raised my arms, all became silent, turning their attention toward me. "Welcome, beloved ones," I began. "I'm pleased that you have come to hear my humble stories and consider my teachings. I'm but a servant, and you are all my masters. I thank you for the opportunity to be of service."

As I have mentioned before, I found that the people understood my message better if I told them a story. The story may be based on a true happening or may be totally metaphoric, but the message was always a truth. I felt that it wasn't my head thinking up these tales; rather it was the truth flowing through me. I had but to offer myself as a channel of such.

I quickly moved into the teaching that I hadn't prepared, or rather allowed to flow through me, coming down through the top of my head and ultimately forming the teaching of the day via words. "Today, dear ones, I want to tell you a tale about the song of the sea. You all know of the water places, which soothe and help calm your worries, when you walk along its shores. It doesn't matter if it is the Sea of Galilee or the inland Dead Sea, the Red Sea or the Gulf of Arabah or whatever large body of water you may visit–it's ever the same–the shores magically calm the soul, ease the mind and heal the body. The sound of the waves washing in–be they gently rolling or crashing–soothes and comforts, because it is the Song of the Sea–God's Song, if you will."

"I want you to picture the land and the sea, as important aspects of a single entity you may refer to as Mother Earth. She is a Supreme Goddess and known as Tara to the ancients of long ago. She has soul and personality, just as you do. Her body has solid surface, watery depths, and she mothers all creation that calls her home. She has secrets, regrets, talents, but most of all, she has a great love for all that live upon, within, and around her because she is a good mother."

One of the men listeners, interrupting me, said, "Surely, you're not saying that there is a Goddess within this ground we call holy, are you? How would God permit such a thing and why would the sea sing His song?"

I kept quiet a moment, as was my developing habit, so the questioner could think about his question, especially the words that just came forth and the implications they afforded. Finally, I said, "What bothers you, friend? Is it that there is a possibility of such a being as Goddess? For surely, if there is God, there is

## The Saga-Oracle

Goddess, as well. How would it be otherwise, for all creation depends on this Divine Principle?"

The man remarked in a rather offhand way, "We are past that nonsense about the Goddess. We have a Father God in command of all creation, with no need for a Goddess to share His glory."

"How do you know that within this Father God, there is not the Mother God, as well? Isn't all creation consummated by the love of the father and the mother?"

The questioner just shook his head, to signify his bewilderment at my stupidity, and he walked away. Many walked away at first. Later they stayed longer for various reasons.

"This is a story," I said. "Let me return to it. When I'm finished, you can judge it as a good story or one that does not enlighten. It's your choice and even having a choice is a blessing, is it not?"

"For now, I will call our dear mother earth, Tara[113] and I hope you will be able to connect to her as a being worthy of the name, meaning 'Mother of All Goddesses'.

"Tara has a large family of those who depend on her for life itself, and she has a counterpart, too, the solar Sun, bright and warm, which brings the day to her night, so that the two can unite and offer a chance for all creation in this realm to flourish and expand awareness, thus evolve. Tara is aware of all those beings she supports, or mothers. She knows what they think and do, for constantly, they are near and dear to her, as their lives play out. She offers her gifts aplenty, and we call her our home. She has times of joy and times of sorrow, as she perceives those she mothers, in all their relationships. As all mothers do, she wants her children to love and honor each other, and appreciate the love and service she offers, too."

---

[113] Tara is a Tibetan name for 'Mother of All' and the name means "Star", the Druids also called their Goddess Tara, many indigenous cultures called their major Goddess 'Tara' and believed that all life sprung from her.

The people were quietly following me, and only a few had left with the disgruntled man. I continued, "Upon and within her body are watery wonders that carry her emotions. Upon the edges of such divine places, where water meets the land, there is a zone, a place where the balance of her emotions and her intentions are most at peace. Those edges are the shorelines, where water kisses the land. She has rocks that form her memory banks, too. She keeps these memory stones in her water places, and upon and within the earth of which she is composed. The soil is the substance of her womb, which along with water, births creation into her realm. Without the womb of Tara, no life would manifest upon this plane. All that happens on Tara is recorded within the stones, for they are the divine record of all actions and reactions within this arena. There are some who can read these records, but most often, they must keep silent or be murdered by those who don't want you to know. Tara has seeds aplenty, as well, planted within her by the light of the day, to nurture inside her sacred dark earthy womb. Those seeds of possibility will only grow through the emotional assistance of Tara's waters, poured forth through passion, as the powerful sun pulls the water into its realm making clouds, to rain the water down upon the fertile fields. That passion must couple with the father energy of the sun to warm and bring forth the seeds of possibility, so that they can reach for the light. Without the dark earthy womb and the bright sunny light, nothing would grow and know the joy of discovery in the physical plane known as Mother Earth. The dark and the light are not enemies; they are the God and the Goddess and, unless they dance and find joyful passion, no life springs forth."

I knew I was taking this story to a depth, which not many of the listeners had heard before. In the olden days when the Isis Priestesses could practice their wisdom, this would be their tale to tell. Knowing that the priestesses couldn't speak openly now, and for the moment, I could, I continued on. "Mother Earth then is of the dark, but not its totality. She is the sister to the Divine Void, which you see between the stars of the night, where the light dances within her dark womb. Both are the feminine aspect of God, or the Sophia, who nurtures other suns and stars of light beyond imagination. The Mother is always represented by the darkness from which she emanates, because she is the space and place of creation, even as the Divine Light is the spark and manifestation of creation."

"Tara offers physicality upon the earth plane, a place to experience and discover its divinity. She experiences evolution, too. How she experiences her task is important to all who share the space she affords. Sometimes, she is glad, and the days and nights are blessed. Other times, she is sad, and the very soil seems to be in sorrow and will not sprout as much as a tiny blade of grass. Sadly, other times, Tara gets angry and, in her emotional anguish, will stir up the ocean and the land will be lashed with her watery tears. Or she may spew out her frustration through her volcano portals, sending the fire of her rage to the surface. That violent response is due, in large part, to how her children behave. Yet, even within her rage she doesn't punish; she simply reacts to the heart-wrenching events that play out among those she loves and nurtures. The human children disagree so much it seems; who is more worthy, who is less; and who is right, and who is wrong; which family is divine and, which is not and so forth. She sees all as her children, God's children, also. Her love of her children is the same as yours. You see your own children as yours, yet God's, too. Like you, she knows her family is divine and when they behave badly, she is angry and disappointed. When they demonstrate love, she is at peace."

"But Raboni," someone said, "I don't see how she could be a mother to me, since I have my own earthly mother who gave birth to me. I didn't sprout and grow like a plant from the earth, either."

"A good point," I replied, "it's known that our bodies are made of water and earth, according to our legends? Remember, we are taught 'from dust you came and to dust you shall return.' That being so; isn't your mother made of earth, thus an aspect of Tara? And if your mother is made from earth, then she is earth. How can you separate the two mothers, or are they in some way One?"

The crowd seemed to struggle with the story, so I reminded them. "This is a story, a tale, that's all. It is simply intended to get you thinking about how you see yourselves and your lives, so allow me to continue, so you can see how attitudes affect all that you encounter and how all relationships are one divine bond."

"I want you to think about how God, the creative Source of all we know, would stay active and interactive within all creation; if you were a loving father, what better place to lay your babe than in its mother's arms? Who could love the newborn more? My brothers, where does your baby emerge from? Whose arms does it need?" I gave the crowd a moment to ponder this point, and I watched their faces to see if I could sense a breakthrough of any measure. "All creation is 'birthed' from the Divine Source. You were all created male and female within yourself, even as you prioritize one modality over the other at birth, as gender. You have been taught down through the ages, that you are a true reflection of God. So where has the Goddess gone? Just think about it."

Returning to my story, I went on and said, "Tara realized that she wasn't honored as mother, as a feminine being, or as Goddess with a purpose, for that matter. She saw that her children used her and didn't hold gratitude for the many gifts she offered. That was sorrowful enough, but she also realized that the lack of gratitude for her mothering role, reflected in all mothering roles throughout creation. She saw women used and abused, reflecting the attitude that had developed within her realm, to the point that they are seen as less deserving, and mere possessions. It was the human children, who developed this attitude of ingratitude. The other creative beings accepted Tara's gifts, her life-giving essences, and held great respect for all she gave of herself for their sake. The humans, however, the ones entrusted to keep the relationship with Tara sacred, simply ignored her role and the importance of it and only glorified the light, the Father essence. They began to use the dark void as a symbol of evil. It was as if they spit upon the earth and, at the same time, looked to the sky asking for blessings. They couldn't see inside Tara's womb, or in the voids of the heavens, so they deemed them bad places, or nothing places. In fact, anything they couldn't see, they suspected as wicked. They didn't honor the marriage within themselves, because their own inner sacred space was denied, since it couldn't be seen, either. That echoed out into all relationships. Chaos held rule upon the land, and corruption resulted from the imbalance of the dark and the light, the father and the mother, the external and the internal."

I realized that I was perhaps taking my teachings too deep for the general masses, and even as I told this tale, I had doubts that it would be totally understood. I hoped, however, that somewhere inside the listeners, due to the attentive state, with which they patiently listened, that something would take seed and grow from my tale. So I continued on with this story of balance. "Thus the Divine Parents, the One Source of all that is, was sad and wondered how to teach the children to respect both aspects of the Source. Until they could balance their awareness of the Divine Creator, they couldn't see how each aspect of creation echoed and reflected the original Maker of all creation."

"There are heavenly helpers to the One Source I mention. They set some guidelines, some hard and fast rules for each plane that is evolving. As they looked to Tara, it was decided that the full process of choice, right or wrong, would play out within free will, so that what is 'not' would help define 'what is'. This results in some grief, unfortunately, for the Divine Source who experiences through all creation. The pain of error is experienced, even by that which is total love, through creational freewill of the eternal sparks of you and me. The Divine Source is two distinct energies, married into One. Hence in agreement, the Divine Parents decided to offer opportunities, for the children to learn how actions create reactions in this arena. Thus, there were floods, draughts, wars, and all kinds of effects, from the chaos that disrespectful children had created. In addition, there were times of plenty, when the lands and the sky danced in unison, and the balance was evident and bountiful. The dance is always the same; unite, come together as One. Even so, as often is the case with children, it takes many opportunities to learn to walk, much less dance. The Divine Parents allowed the effects of the children's ungracious thinking to manifest unbalanced effects such as depression, which felt like the dark night of the soul,[114] or times when the light was so bright that it felt like the fires of hell. The intensity of the light caused destruction upon the lands and stopped the growth of their crops. All extremes were caused by one factor, without the balancing other factor. This wasn't done to punish, rather to show the children that the parents loved them and wanted them to learn, that the misuse of all that is good, could cause suffering and stagnation. God never intended the flood to be viewed as punishment, even as there were those who would use the occasion to their advantage,

---

[114] A period when the unknown is so deep that one feels lost within it

proclaiming it so. Rather, God wanted the children to see, that when the emotion of sorrow, springing from disrespect and heartless actions regarding their home, happened, Tara's pain was their grief, and they could drown in her tears."

I could see the crowd was struggling to follow this story, and I was definitely taking them too far, but I was past the point of stopping now. I would have to simplify my parables next time, I thought. So, I decided to bring this story to a close.

I continued, saying, "Then one day, one of the elder leaders of the children, a high priest, was walking down the shore of the sea. He was old now and depressed, thinking that he had done everything right in his life, so why did he feel miserable? As he walked along the seashore, waves washed in and out, with a soft whoosh that seemed to speak to him. He clearly heard a voice say, 'Why do you hate me elder, for I have loved you so much?' He stopped and looked out to the water, thinking he was losing his mind, since he distinctly heard a voice singing the words. He decided he should just move on and get some rest, before the evening services and meal. Surely, he must be hallucinating from his weariness, he surmised. Even so, before he stepped back from the shoreline, a powerful wave rushed in and surrounded his feet with water and mud, holding him in place. He was a bit irritated that his holy feet should be soaked in this muddy manner. His beautiful sandals and the bottom of his priest robes were awash. As he tried to move out of the offending pool of water, he found he couldn't budge. Again he heard the same feminine voice say, 'I have given you life, yet you don't know me.' "

"Feeling even more confused, he struggled to be free of this offensive wetness. The voice continued, 'Inside your very body, I reside, and you don't know me. I surrounded you within the belly of your dear mother, and you forgot that I protected you and fed you until you came forth. When will you honor that which loves you so dearly?' Then the water receded, and he went home, thinking he experienced a bad dream, and was ashamed that he had soaked his feet and the bottom of his priest robe. How undignified, he thought. He rejected the Song of the Sea, and he remained depressed."

# PETER, OH PETER, MY ROCK
## Chapter Twenty-Six

My story enters a time that history attempts to focus upon when remembering my mission. Sad to say, the records have forgotten the importance of my beloved, having excluded her due to the tradition of suppressing women. I won't try to correct the book you call holy, so confused now, for it would be difficult for even me. There were situations remembered but not understood, and situations understood but not remembered. Thus there is truth within the pages and propaganda, as well as outright lies. Memory can be a molded commodity, and the bible is a book of memory–be it historical, spiritual, or in many cases, political in purpose.

People have been taught for ages that this book was God's book. Of course it is, but not in the sense that many believe. Once a lesson is experienced, it is internalized where it merges with the consciousness of the student. It is attached to many different scenarios, depending on who remembered it, and what perspective they saw or heard it within, which could be a logical, 'this is how it happened' to an internal 'this is how it felt'. Depending on the storyteller, there were countless ways the events of the biblical record were remembered and retold, and still be truth, revealed or hidden. At the same time, propaganda, or assumptions based on outright distortions connected to the powers-that-be at the time and place and many other influences of that period from which the story sprang, are within the pages, too.

Memories of your own life are shaped by perspective, agenda and sometimes, by plain confusion as well. Should someone write your life story from their perspective, it would be quite a different tale than from your own memory. Thus, many varied versions of my mission were recorded, depending on memory, perspective and political persuasion. It can be confusing at best, and it's not my intention for you to lose your faith, just broaden the possibilities of what happened and what might yet be revealed. As for the prophesy of the bible, remember that prophesy is only a 'likely' result, and the main reason for foretelling such outcomes are so that different choices can be made, and different results achieved.

While oral history has been quite accurate in some places and within some cultures, your bible became a more political book. Literally, 'his-story' and very little of 'her-story,' was allowed to be remembered, thus my beloved's contribution to our common mission was lost and there are few references of her importance in my life within the book many call 'holy'.

I must rephrase and translate as best I can, into the language of your time and place, as I share my life story, so that you can visualize and integrate this account of my time as Yeheshua son of Joseph, eventually to be known as Jesus or Jeshua, and my companion MiryAmah, remembered as Mary of Magdala[115], or Mary Magdalene. The difficulty with languages is that the verbiage and rhythm are different, due to the time and location, and not easily translated.

In the days when my beloved and I walked, what you now term the 'holy land,' there was a much different consciousness that colored and formed the events that took place. The perception of what played out was different depending, again on perspective, while the truth was ever the same within the moment of that life opportunity. I can only offer my story from my own perspective—how it felt to walk and talk and become the man I was. My beloved MiryAmah has already told her own story and how it felt for her.[116] For instance, there was the idea that disease was punishment; that a demon would find residence within one who had sinned and cause havoc within their physical bodies and minds, because they deserved it. In modern times, you know that isn't true, yet you are aware of such ideas as the eastern concept of karma, in which attitudes and thoughts are connected to these conditions of dis-ease[117], not as punishment, but as cause and effect. There's still much to learn about disease and you expand your awareness every day. Truth is diverse and difficult to define,

---

[115] Triple Goddess Mari-Anna-Ishtar who was popularly worshiped at the time of Christ. 'Marys' corresponded to worship of this Goddess

[116] For her story read *"Magdalene's Well"* by Saga-Rhose which preceded this narrative, Infinity Publishing, 2004

[117] Being out of the perfect physical pattern thus not healthy, or not at ease

and a constant unfolding understanding, depending on perspective, readiness for expansion of consciousness, and a multitude of other considerations.

Onement refers to the balance of the energies–positive and negative–within all creation. Not separate from each other, but integrated, different, equally representative of the One Source. The energies are comprised of the same stuff as all creation, the original essence of the one popularly known as 'God'. This is true within all creation and true, as well, within all spaces and places that manifest creation, which is everywhere, infinite. Remember, all creation has consciousness. I remind you of this, so that you will know where my beloved MiryAmah, as I came to call her, and I, wanted to take our teachings. We had to tread softly, because there wasn't a common understanding of the negative energy and how it balanced the positive energy, completing the Onement. That knowledge was suppressed and held secret, for the sake of controlling the masses. The Egyptians knew about the energy balance and even had electric lights in the tombs, operated by power cells they made in earthen jars[118] that utilized the positive and negative energy to create light in their tombs. They had an entire priest division responsible for keeping this secret hidden, because knowledge was power. Think about that, as you ponder the tale of the Garden of Eden and the Tree of Knowledge that supposedly led to the downfall of humans.

Other cultures, especially in the Far East, openly spoke of this dual energy that produces Onement. They called it yin (feminine) and yang (masculine) and the symbol of this principle shows a divided circle that has a winding division, but equal and a little of one in the other[119]. Even though the symbol indicates that this culture was informed in the dual nature of the balance, they too, ultimately struggled with the dance of the positive and negative energies. This is due partly to the positive being naturally more forceful and, left unbalanced by the gentler feminine, it tended to take over. There was also an echo of the influence of the creator gods, who

---

[118] An ancient battery, or electrical cell
[119] ☯

had insured that their male offspring, the Demigods,[120] would rule. They had outposts all around the globe, thus influenced many cultures at a deep core level. One of the greatest lessons of this plane is the understanding of the yin/yang energetic dance of balance within all creation, and especially within relationships, the most important one, your relationships with yourself.

Change of mind is perhaps the most difficult challenge of all within human physicality. Changing a mind means that one must rethink what they may believe is safe and secure, and move into a new realm beyond the old parameters. Due to the human ability to conceive past/present/future all at once, change can be most daunting. Humans grieve for the past and fret about the possibilities of the future within the 'now' moment. Living in past/present/future at the same time is fertile ground for fear, which becomes a wall that prevents any change. Fear will constrict mentality, if it gains control. In reality, all mental walls fall sooner or later. It's far better to make the choice to dismantle these mental blocks a little at a time, than to have them blasted apart, because you have outgrown the constrictions. Evolution is by definition change, and all creation must move along within physicality, or it stagnates and dies. Death isn't the end however, because the energy just tries again in another form, often living the same lesson all over again in order to finally 'get it right'. Nothing can remain the same. It must grow and evolve, or it will be forced along the path of change. Force is always painful, especially when it meets resistance. However, the normal movement of evolution, just like a growing child who changes every day, is a natural flow and the pain of change is minuscule compared to the wonder of it. Can you imagine forcing a child to stay in one stage of its development, never letting it grow or change its form? That's the essence of what my beloved and I hoped to nudge along, so that humanities' growth would not have to be forced.

We came to bust dams that blocked the flow of consciousness, and make portals in walls within minds. MiryAmah and I knew that the time was ripe for the blockages to be broken, so the people

---

[120] Not the children of the Watchers, but of the ruler in command and his sergeants

could begin to be free. We had no doubt that we were born to work side-by-side in this mission, be it ever so complicated, even within its simplicity. That balancing part of our work has never been fully understood, and there are many who haven't yet fully comprehended the essence of Onement.

Perhaps the hardest part of our mission was getting the apostles to open their minds and change long-ingrained attitudes. Those blockages had been imprinted for eons of time, and our followers wanted change, even as they resisted it. Imprints developed into genetic blueprints, or pathways, and passed down generation after generation in the family lineage, and the urge to fall into the old patterns was unconsciously followed. Some traditions were indeed taught, but the inclination to follow certain mindsets was often deeply ingrained in genetic family imprints. That doesn't mean they couldn't be changed, just that it was difficult.

Some people think everything is possible, and some people think nothing is possible. That's due to a genetic imprint influencing their choices. The 'optimist' has an easier time making changes. The 'pessimists' are afraid of change. Knowing the diverse situations within each individual, as well as how those mind-paths affected the greater masses, my beloved and I knew we had a difficult task ahead of us, but also knew that we came to meet and greet this situation and would follow through on our commitment.

People, over the span of time, came to think that men were chosen to serve God, and that women were made to serve men. They couldn't see the Divine Mother within the God they called Father. This, of course, is the war between the positive and the negative energies. The true fall of man was when this separation concept took hold and became reflected within the genders.

The old slave mentality never really went away. The story of the ancient creator gods, told to the young priestesses and me in the tunnels from the underground city, helped us understand that the gods of old served as models for how to judge self-worth and people naturally adopted that system. Sadly, it is often true that when one evaluates their self-worth, they too frequently go outside themselves and look back through the eyes of others, instead of seeing through their own divine vision. Lack of self-confidence is the greatest tool of slave masters. When people view themselves through the clouded eyes of others, they accept that foggy judgmental attitude and reflect it. Even though the slaves of the ancients hated the cruelty and judgment of the gods of old, after the exit the slaves ultimately emulated it, since they knew no other way. They also noticed that the beautiful women were treated differently than those deemed not so lovely, and they copied that ideology, as well. Thus, many didn't discover the true depth of beauty in them, nor in others. Some moved beyond the limiting attitudes, but the group consciousness echoed standards that were not divinely balanced in the first place, because their gods were in a learning stage of balance. True, the old gods were more aware than the slave race they co-created, but they had a long way to go in terms of understanding their own energetic balance. The lesson of fear and love played out for them ages ago, too. They weren't 'whole' and 'complete' in their minds and hearts; therefore, they weren't as 'holy' as they claimed to be. Even within the situation after the withdrawal, the freed slaves had a great opportunity to learn valuable lessons, for nothing is wasted and all situations can be 'resolved to peace.' Consequently, cause and effect were allowed to offer their lesson of balance and wisdom, in order to teach the evolving race upon this divine playing field the responsibility of co-creation.

Souls, such as MiryAmah and I, were sent in from time to time to stimulate a different response to old corrupted attitudes, so that the evolution of consciousness could progress and equalize the scales of justice. When there is no movement, awareness cannot expand. Stagnation then occurs, and things begin to rot and force a change in form. We were sent, as others were, and still are being sent, to unplug a stuck place within the group consciousness so all can grow towards Onement. It's not something you move away from, but rather something you are drawn back into. That's why the negative force is so important in this Divine Dance of discovery; it absorbs and pulls into itself, even as the positive reflects and explores the external places and spaces. It's the combination of the two that builds balance, and affords the opportunity to recognize your own divinity. Religions struggle with this concept; some move towards it, while others move away. What is important is that, at least, they have a core intention of building the bridge back to Oneness, even if they don't call it such.

To get things moving is a complicated and huge task. We felt honored to be asked to assist and willingly volunteered to come through the portal of forgetting (birth). Our forgetting was not as drastic as usually needed in the new life experience, for the sake of the mission. We simply came in order to change the mind-set within individuals, thus affect the collective consciousness. A mind can never be forced into change. Consequently, we souls who came for the purpose of bringing the balance had a difficult and extremely delicate job to do. We trained ourselves for the task, on many a plane and planet, through eons of time and within multitudes of incarnations. We were never better than anyone else, just experienced and trained to assist evolution in places needing our expertise. We didn't want adoration, only cooperation and consideration.

Even within the group of apostles, I learned to offer lessons through parables, before I eventually took the stories to the crowds. The early followers were training me, you might say, as I attempted to prepare them to be co-teachers in the quest. Their preparation convinced me to maintain the parable plan, while my beloved MiryAmah was more successful teaching through ritual. I knew that if I couldn't reach those closest to me, then I couldn't share much with the masses. Hence my followers were also my teachers. I will forever appreciate each and every one of them for the lessons they offered, that helped me be the leader I was born to be.

Even though I found that stories were effective as a teaching method, it was the follow-up discussions that proved to integrate the deeper wisdom, for those who would be entrusted to carry on the work. Information (inner-teachings) that I couldn't discuss with the crowds, but shared with my apostles and disciples,[121] was usually discussed later. After our evening meal, or at the time of our rest, we enjoyed expanding on the daily lesson. We had become quite bold now with MiryAmah at my side, and had a

---

[121] MiryAmah's women followers

group of women followers, who began to travel with us. Our followers were so dedicated that they left their former lives, knowing something was terribly amiss within the culture of the time. It was that determination, which opened the door of further discussion of the parables and allowed our inner-circle a clearer vision of the message we were born to bring.

The women followers, disciples, weren't called such to separate them from the apostles. Originally, both words actually meant 'devotee,' with an apostle meaning male devotee, and disciple meaning female devotee. MiryAmah had women committed to her, who looked to her to teach them. Often they were of the secret Isis Cult, known as the Order of the Doves, that both my mother and my beloved were involved deeply within. I had men committed to me, too, and our groups merged, when MiryAmah and I found each other. Now with MiryAmah at my side, women dared to stay longer and walk further than ever before. Their reputations wouldn't be damaged, since they followed a woman leader.

MiryAmah had good connections in most communities–as my mother Mary did as well–and the disciples were invited into safe places to spend the night close by us, but not so close that it caused public concern. This pleased me tremendously. I often found the most fulfilling company among the women, who didn't require everything logically proven to them. They seemed to know the truth when they heard it, while the men held a 'prove it to me' attitude and were more difficult to reach. It was simply the natural masculine and feminine talents of logic and intuition, yet logic can often be harder to resolve.

The apostles more easily joined the movement, because men enjoyed more freedom, thus we had greater numbers of men followers. We often ended our evenings out in the moonlight, under the starry canopy of the night sky, still discussing the daily parable lesson, usually in small groups. MiryAmah and her disciples would normally be guests within a home by this time, for their own safety. To find a woman unprotected was to assume she was a harlot or cast away. It was permissible for men of narrow minds to do as they would with the poor woman. Within compound walls, MiryAmah and her devotees would have their evening discussions, too. Later she and I would chat about our talks with the followers, thus integrate the sessions through our conversation. Sometimes we began debate and discussion at our evening meal, if we ate together. Sadly, there were places even dining together wasn't allowed, depending on locality and social customs. Conforming to the law of the land, while we tried to expand the restrictive attitude, proved most challenging; we were not law breakers, rather simply wisdom promoters. Nevertheless, we had to pierce dams in society's attitudes, in order to start the flow of consciousness and dissolve blockages that separated for far too long. We hoped to begin the unification process based on the principle that 'love unites' and 'fear separates'. Those that opposed us tried to make that an unlawful offense.

On one beautiful starry evening my apostle Simon, who I lovingly called Petro or Peter (my rock), and I were reclining upon the ground on our sleeping mats, looking up to the star-filled heavens and reflecting upon the daily message. Peter was a huge burly man, strong in body and mind, and I loved him dearly.

Peter said, "Master, why do you tell stories to the people? Why don't you just give them the truth?"

"Why, Peter," I said, "being such a big strong man, what would you have me do; go out into the crowd and beat the truth into the seekers?" I watched a look of surprise on his face, since he saw me as gentle, never one to resort to violence, and he was openly confused. I continued on saying, "First, you have to gain their attention. We each have our gifts, mine being the storyteller and yours is your might. So do you suggest that I not use my gift within my message-bringing?"

"Why would you say such a thing, Jesus?" he responded, looking over at me, as if I was going mad. "I wouldn't ever use my strength in such a way as you suggest. But, I would use it other ways should need be. Surely, I wouldn't force the issue."

In equal consternation, I said, "Why do you suggest that I take a truth, that is a power just as your mighty body is a power, and force it upon the seekers then? Don't you train your muscles little by little to be strong? I've seen you lift rocks–first smaller ones, and then bigger ones–to train your muscles so that they could do something very different than lift rocks. Why don't you just tell the muscles to be strong and demand that they pick up the fishing boat and move it off the entangled net that restricts it? Isn't that what I found you doing when I met you, untangling fish nets from the keel of your boat? Surely, your strength goes far beyond this one thing you ask of it. In all cases brute strength isn't appropriate or even able to move mountains, as they say. Even so, I assure you that to change a mind is easier than moving a mountain." Peter looked at me, shaking his head, thinking, 'there he goes again' with the stories.

I just couldn't help myself. I spoke in parables. "If you had to move a mountain, strong man, wouldn't you use your strength and remove it little-by-little? And since minds can be as daunting as a mountain, can you not see that I must also complete my task, little by little? I use stories to do that. You would use a shovel."

I could see he was thinking this over, but not responding, not quite ready to see how these two things were related. So I decided to expand the analogy. "You conditioned yourself to be physically strong, by using rocks that have nothing to do with the tasks that you would ask of your body one day. Within the parables, I condition the minds of the listeners, so that one day they can use their expanded thinking power in the way it was meant to be used, as a device to understand the intent of God. Just like your muscles are strapped upon your bones, dear friend, so you can lift heavy loads, so too, is your mind housed in your consciousness, so that you will know that all creation is really One House with many mansions (rooms) therein. How would you know where your room is located within the mansion of God, if your doorway is shut and locked tight? You would only know your own cell-room, a limited space of illusion. While you might feel more secure, your creative life would be restricted from interaction with other rooms, which merge into larger arenas of divine awareness. Remember, Peter, cell-prisons, restricted by keys and locks, are seldom a growing place. Your heavenly divine room within the One House of God was not intended to be a cell, only a place where you can begin from, and return to. Humanity has all the keys to unlock cells, but antiforce, made up of the collective power of fear, doesn't want them to realize this. Even when the cell door opens, too often the caged birds are afraid to fly free and escape that which enslaves them, which is their own mind. My intention is to reveal the key to unlock minds and open hearts, so the caged birds can be free."

He listened without comment. He just seemed to ponder what I was saying, no doubt trying to understand what I was getting at, for as strong and loyal as he was, he had problems turning the key to his own mind. So, I continued on, "Fear hides the key and love reveals it. Don't you see, Peter?" I asked.

Still withholding comment, he struggled to grasp the essence of this chat we were having. That's why I loved him so, because he never gave up trying to grasp my teachings. He always supported me, even though his personality made it difficult for him to expand his assumptions and beliefs.

"Peter," I said, "consider this. We have spoken of the universal law that stipulates 'like-attacks-like'. We have even experimented with it, noticing how the muscular strong men gravitate toward you, and those more physically like the other followers seem to move towards them as well. We have also experimented with the sorting stones, when we played the game of organizing the pebbles, did we not? And the sizes and colors of the stones were naturally put in order, even though the only guidelines in the game were grouping stones."

Peter at least nodded his head to the affirmative, remembering the experiment, realizing, yes, the big guys gravitated toward him.

"So it is," I continued, "if like attracts like, as we have concluded, those who are controlled by fear, due to what attracts them to it, will naturally fear the unknown. That's all they know–fear. The unknown is just an undiscovered void, or a dark place like a womb, but fear would make it an evil place, because what it doesn't know it can't control. What it can't control, it fears. Those of such a mind-set, which has been cultivated by controllers for eons of time, can only find comfort with others that are also afraid–thus, 'like attracts like'. They don't want to go outside their cell. Likewise, as I have said, 'love reveals the key to freedom and knows that there is just more love outside that door'. Love leaves the door open and fear keeps it tightly shut."

Peter asked, "What does this have to do with the stories you tell? Why can't you just tell the truth of it, without the complicated tale and shorten the whole process?"

Peter was indeed my rock and sometimes, I thought, his head was the hardest part of that rock. "You are persistent, Peter. That's what I like about you. Also that's what pushes me to my wits limit, as well," I said as I playfully slapped his shoulder, making us both laugh. "I'll try to make this as simple as I can, dear friend, but simple is not always 'short'. Because people have lived within the room of fear so long, which I have referred to as rooms in the Divine Mansion, and because those they know and interact with are of like mind-set, they would then occupy an entire wing of the temple, or mansion of God. That entire wing in the mansion of God might be a religion that is locked from the rest of the glory of God. That could be considered the collective consciousness within this closed-off arena, which is in agreement. It's not a bad place, just a restricted place that isn't growing in awareness, thus it is 'locked' into its own ideology. Do you follow me, Peter?" I asked, hoping that his stubborn mind would give way to his courageous and loving heart, because if I could reach Peter, I was sure I could reach anyone with my teachings.

He didn't answer, so I continued on, saying, "Within this corridor, they're all afraid. Even when they interact, it's within an agreement that fear rules and doorways are kept closed to keep danger out when all the time they are keeping God out. They put their faith in wall-builders because they find security therein, or think they do. By telling a non-threatening story, I knock gently on such doors, so as not to startle those who know nothing but fear. This is basically what I do in each village I visit. I must knock gently, or they'll be too afraid to crack the door open and let me into their frame of mind, or room. Gentleness and persistence can't be blunt, or it triggers the fear all over again. The House of God does indeed include many mansions, some beautiful, some neglected, some under construction. I'm determined to gain access to those prison cells that fear created, to begin freeing the enslaved

Peter," I explained. "When I tell stories, I'm hoping that the people look out windows of their mind to situations that they may not have considered possible, and perceive the lesson of the story, even as they absorb it unconsciously at a personal level. It may be a simple narrative, such as the one about the blind man who grabbed the cloak of another blind man, because he couldn't see. He wanted to be led, because he had no confidence in himself. Another blind man might grab onto him and so forth, all eventually towed along and ending up in a ditch, because none of them could see where they were going. They were alike in their condition of blindness, thus were attracted to each other (like attracts like). Because they all were trying to find someone to lead them, they kept following each other into ditches, into perilous situations, always ending up worse than they were on their own. Then one day, one finds his courage and breaks away from the others to pierce the unknown, where he finds his path easier and his vision returned." Peter nodded his head in the affirmative, indicating that he had known of many situations where the blind led the blind metaphorically. "If the underlying meaning of the story seeps in later within their dreams, as they converse with their own inner-voices seeking truth, then love's expansion of consciousness can free them, a little at a time. The parable slips through the slightly-opened door, Peter, and that's why I use this type of format in my teaching. If I can unlock just one of the many locks in the seekers' minds, then I'm delighted and fulfilled. However, better yet, if I can help someone find the key that lies there waiting to be discovered, my 'cup runneth over'–that overflowing cup, my friend, is the grail, the cup of my soul."

"Well, I have to admit your stories are entertaining, and I do love to listen to them. Sometimes, it takes me too long to digest the tale myself, and I wish I just knew the truth, straight out," Peter replied.

"If I'm that direct, I'll be talking to myself with no listeners, in a short time, dear friend. Even so, sometimes I am direct, especially with you, my close friends and followers. Didn't I tell Bartholomew to stop calling himself a weakling? He thinks that if he can't lift as much as you, my powerful friend, then he must be less a man than you. Didn't I tell him that his true strength was in his devotion to me, and that I loved his loyalty? That aspect of him is the gift that keeps me going on this difficult mission, as much as your physical strength. Wasn't that a direct statement? After all I didn't make him suffer a long story. Surely, sometimes you are hard on me, Peter," I said, with a bit of exasperation in my voice. Peter's hard-headedness often drained me.

"I'm sorry, Raboni," Peter said in a humble voice, looking down at his huge hands and wringing them like an apologetic boy. "I just wondered, that's all."

"Why must you call me teacher within the personal time of the evening, when we are such close friends?" I asked, (I always preferred my close apostles to call me friend, but they seldom did), "You are indeed my rock, Peter. Without your strength, I doubt if we could stay together as a group and survive. I always want to hear your concerns, and I want you to know that I respect your opinions as well. I'm not in perfection–I'm learning to be a Raboni, or teacher, and you are my teacher and my friend. But Peter, if I can't convince you, how can I convince anyone else? You worry me and you define me at the same time. Obviously, there are those who lose patience with my long narratives, and you speak for them, dear friend. I thank you for being you."

"But you are a master, Jesus," Peter said, "and that makes you specially chosen, doesn't it? And how could I ever 'define' you, master?

"Dear Peter," I answered, "to be a master just means that one has a greater responsibility. It's not a jewel to wear, or a crown upon my head. It simply means that I have agreed to a huge task within my soul mission, as I walk through this physical life experience, because I am aware of my relationship to All that Is. It doesn't make me better or different than anyone else. A master, or mastra, is simply one who knows that they are the essence of God, sent out to discover that divine relationship through countless situations, and to help others on their path of discovery, so that they can merge back into the Oneness of God. You 'define' me, because you make me speak clearly, more concisely, and more heartfelt. That's surely the only way I can penetrate into fearful minds, my friend. I don't mean to say you have a fearful mind, Peter, rather that you require a complete mental image, so that you can begin the process of understanding deep within your heart."

Not seeming to be offended by my statement about fearful minds, but more fixated on something I had alluded to as a master who knew that they were the essence of God, Peter asked, "Are you saying that you are God, because you know you are."

"Yes! And so are you–you just don't know it yet. All I'm saying is that to be a master or mastra, one understands that what comes from God is God's essence, thus God. What I am, you are, too, but so much greater, because you're unsure of that principle, and still in the difficult stages of going through opportunities to learn the divine truth, walking a path of faith, which is extremely difficult and courageous to do."

Peter gazed into the star-filled sky and finally said, "Are those stars, then, God?" Then he looked at me with piercing eyes, which even in the moonlight sparkled with intensity and interest, and continued, saying "Surely God made them, and since God made us as well, how do you know that which is God and that which is not?"

"You do ask enormous questions, friend," I said. "Yet, your great mind is thinking out of the closed fear-room, so I am delighted with your inquiry. Let me try to clarify. Whatever is created is formed of God stuff—all made by the One Source. If God made all things then God is all things. It's what we do with creation that is our responsibility." I almost pleaded because he was now sitting down holding his head like he had a terrible headache, rocking back and forth, and my heart went out to the big man who tried so desperately to understand me.

He stopped rocking for a moment and said, "Are you saying that the Jews are God as well, then, and the Romans, too? Our enemies are God? What about the animals and the trees and the very earth we lie upon this puzzling night?"

"I am. However, in the case of the Romans and some of our so-called enemies, since they might not be aware of that truth, then they may not be 'masters' or 'mastras'. Even so, I tell you, that even within their ranks, there are such ones, for God sends the master souls to bring the light of awareness in, where the motion of evolution of consciousness is slowed or stopped. It's not for us to judge who is or isn't 'Godly'. All are 'Godly', but not all reflect the goodness of God, which is the essence of this Being of Love. As for the rocks and trees and all other creation, I sometimes think they were born masters and mastras. They just know and never question."

Ignoring what he couldn't grasp, Peter focused on the Romans and the enemies, as well as our own Jewish people. "I know a priest or two who believes they are closer to God than most, but they don't claim to be God and would condemn to death anyone who uttered such an idea." Peter watched me, to see how that remark affected me.

"I tell you, Peter; they are like undeveloped babes in the dark womb. Not in a bad place, but a place of preparation, and since they can't grasp the true nature of their being, they aren't ready yet to be born into the truth." My beloved apostle still seemed to struggle with our discussion. However, seeing that he was intently listening, I went on to say, "So, masters and mastras are sent to be mid-wives to help birth such babes into the light of awareness, where they can see who and what they are, and rejoice. When one knows this basic truth, they pierce the darkness of their own soul (not a bad place, but in an inner 'knowing' place), when they choose, and plant seeds of awareness into that fertile womb. One day, the fruit of the womb reaches for the light of day and fulfills God's greatest desire, for all creation to be happy, fruitful and loving."

Peter still looked puzzled, and asked, "Who are the mastras?" This part of the conversation just dawned on him, and now ignoring the happy God concept, he demanded that I explain something that troubled him.

"Oh, Peter, you have them around you all the time. They are the feminine aspects of god, who walk and talk within the form of a woman, thus they are mastras who have come for the same purpose as the masters," I emphasized.

"Surely you have fun with me, Jesus!" Peter said. "I would know a holy woman if I saw one, and I haven't seen many in my short life, nor do I think I care to."

"Peter, oh Peter!" I almost cried, for his reluctance to understand this most important part of the mission tore my heart out. "You are like the blind man. I certainly hope you haven't hooked up with me, thinking I am also blind. You make me wonder what you saw in me and why you followed so willingly, when I told you I would make you a 'fisher of men'. I perhaps should have said 'fisher of men and women', Peter. Sometimes I have fear, too, and I fear you have a blind eye to the wonderment of the feminine. If that's true, you can't ever understand the scope and wisdom of creation, or God, who is both He and She." Still a bit frustrated, I said, "There are so many wise-women who you can't see, due to your fearful mind. They are near and dear beyond your wildest imagination, dear friend. We have encountered several mastras and have one within our midst. You, blind man, can't see the blessing that is close enough to kiss your cheek."

"We have one in our midst?" Peter exclaimed, with a slightly crazed look in his eye, which the nighttime couldn't hide. "Who could that be?" He asked with a scowl written all over his face. "For how can we seriously do our work with a mastra present?"

My patience was challenged at this point. I wanted to shake him by the shoulders and yell into his face, but instead I gained my composure and said in a very low, but firm, voice, "How can we do our work without a mastra present, Peter? Didn't we discuss the need for balance of the attitudes within the minds and hearts of the people today, and on every day of this mission we share? How can we have balance, if we believe the mother is less than the father, or the daughter less than the son, or the mastra is less worthy than the master? I see alarm in your eyes, because we are graced with a mastra. I'll not tell you what you already know, if only you would allow your heart to enlighten you. When you are ready to see her divinity, you shall. However, remember, how would God create your very body without both parents, each different, nevertheless, each so vital in the divine plan of creation?" I said, hoping that Peter would finally grasp what I was trying to convey. "If creation of the body needs a man and a woman, don't you think creation of the mind and soul does, as well?" I had high-hopes that one day he would go on to reach the most challenging characters within our society and share the truth, as only he could. "I know you had a bad experience with your mother, Peter. No one is perfect or what would be the purpose to be born into this life, for perfection needs no lessons. Forgive your mother for her insecurity and how that affected her behavior. Her anger wasn't aimed at you, but at the system that denied her divinity."

"You haven't told me who the mastra is," he demanded again, ignoring his relationship with his mother, obviously not ready to deal with that yet. The determined look on his face revealed that he was fixated on the fact, that there was a woman of mastra status nearby. I could read his mind enough to know that he would try to drive her off, for my sake. He still couldn't understand why I loved the presence of women. He was sure they were tempters and distracters. To me, they were peacemakers and understood me without draining my energy. They nourished me with their love and devotion, and I appreciated them far beyond what I could openly admit.

"I won't tell you what is obvious. I only hope that one day you'll open your mind and honor that which honors you. Maybe, if you listen carefully to a few more parables, you'll ultimately see how important the women are within all creation. Maybe you'll recognize God within the form of a woman. Perhaps you'll even come to love your mother and honor your wife, whom you have left to follow me. Possibly, you'll understand what she sacrifices, as she supports you in whatever decision you make."

Peter just looked at me and yawned, turned over, and said "Good night, Raboni," and went to sleep.

Those followers who loved me the most were my greatest challenge and, as I have said before, my teachers. I prayed a thanksgiving for each of them, before I also went to my slumber, but especially I prayed thanksgiving for my own sweet mastra companion MiryAmah, who would have to suffer far more than I ever would, within this drama we came to adjust. "Dear God Almighty," I prayed, "give me the strength and the wisdom to continue as a teacher to these reluctant children of yours, and brothers and sisters of mine. I don't know if I'm up to the task." I had my insecurities, too.

# DIVINE UNION AND THE SPARROWS
Chapter Twenty-Seven

My greatest ally and equal in this mission, of course, was ever my beloved MiryAmah, known as Mary of Magdalene. Her early training prepared her for our work, as my early training years also did for me. Those who called us forth into incarnation knew this difficult, but vitally important, mission would require such early interventional training. MiryAmah and I were aware that we weren't the only masters and mastras sent forth to plant seeds of balance. Others were also sent. If they were lucky enough to have the opportunity, they would have the same intention, but move into it from their own direction and talents. It was the divine marriage and family unity that we would pattern, because within it, we could address the balance of energies that all creation merged–individually and collectively. Other masters followed their own path, as was the case with my cousin John, who became known as, 'The Baptizer'. His need to retreat into wilderness and nature was just as important to his mission, as my need to go far away and explore mysterious environments to learn the truth of integration of spirit, or Onement, and as my beloved's internship on one of the Mysty Isles[122].

I knew that all creation was 'One' from as far back as I could remember, and many before me knew as well. Even so, this

---

[122] Mysty Isles were places that floated between dimensions, Avalon being one of the best known, where the Cult of Isis taught the feminine mysteries

'knowing' was suppressed, hence had to be re-learned. John received the same lesson from nature. Thus, it was that he also held high respect and understanding for all elements, especially water. By recognizing the conductivity power of water, as well as a healthy respect for its ability to cleanse and nourish, he began the practice of baptisms within the streams near villages. There had been baptizers before, but he put his own spin on the ancient practice and improved the old traditions, which had been forgotten and suppressed. He had his favorite places, and people knew, through the discreet social grapevine, where to find him for a divine cleansing and ritualistic blessing. Bear in mind, it was extremely hard for him to interact with people, but he forced himself to endure, because he knew his intentions were pure and his faith out-weighed his anxiety around crowds of people.

One warm special day, I found John, wild-looking as ever dressed in his animal skins, with matted hair and the usual crazed look in his eyes, about his baptismal tasks within a pool of water fed by a tiny stream. As uncivilized as he looked, people were lined up to be immersed and blessed by this wild holy man. My followers were aware that John had developed a following. John had finally taken to heart the revelation that he, too, was a master, which we discussed when we lived together for awhile. He had since confidently stepped forth as 'teacher.' I was genuinely pleased to see him about God's work in his own unique way. I knew that it would take many to accomplish the goal of divine balance. Sadly, many of his followers, and mine, saw us in competition with each other. Thomas, one of my dear companions, could be the greatest one to doubt intentional actions and interactions.

Upon arriving at the place where John was baptizing that day, Thomas said, "What makes that cousin of yours think he can conduct such a sacred ritual as baptism? What good comes of getting people all wet and near drowning them?" It has always been a sorrow to me that when groups encounter one another, they begin to haggle and judge the others' worthiness and an egotistical competitiveness emerges.

My other followers and I, mostly men today because MiryAmah and the disciples were in preparation for our wedding that would seal our intentional purpose, were out and about just walking and talking. I, like any expectant groom so in love, was processing my anxiety by taking this walk with supportive friends. My beloved was attending to her preparations with her women followers, the disciples, and maybe that was her method of relieving the anxiety of our approaching important moment of wedded union.

When Thomas voiced his opinion, the other apostles showed similar thinking, nodding their heads in agreement. I noticed the smug look of superiority on their faces. I knew these men to be good-hearted, but often hard-headed. They didn't hesitate to speak their minds either, since our way was that all could speak freely. I decided a demonstration was in order. I went to my cousin, embraced him fondly, and said, "Isn't it time for my baptism, cousin?" I could feel the surprise of my followers, and John's as well, since I made sure they all heard me. I also had a deep intuitive feeling that my cousin should baptize me on this, my wedding day.

"I have waited for you to come," John said, in his usual raspy whisper, as he embraced me. His followers assumed the same look that mine were demonstrating, because in their minds this was a validation from their perspective that John was the chosen one. Neither he nor I ever claimed that we were the one and only voice of God, but we did tell our followers that God spoke and acted through us, because we had given our lives to that purpose. We never intended our every word become a creed; only that it helped free people from the beliefs, which controlled and abused them.

We knew our devotees were in a learning stage, and all leaders at heart, nonetheless, still learning about ego, they sometimes felt superior to the lesson of the day. As John hugged me, I felt our old bond strongly. Then for a moment, he looked me in the eye and with sincerity asked if I was ready for a divine cleansing. I could see his admirers looking at each other, exchanging that, 'I told you so,' look. I wish sometimes that I couldn't read thoughts and body language, because I knew they found confirmation in the moment, proving John was the long-awaited messiah and me the upstart. The hope of a messiah was powerful in our time, because there was such a deep level of soul pain, due to the judgmental attitudes of those who controlled people within fear. People yearned to be rescued. It was something both John and I gently addressed in our teachings. We spent a lot of time when we once wandered together, exploring the immense questions. We concluded after long discussion that the messiah, or savior, was really the inner-voice of the divine in each of us, and a direct channel back to the Source. I still found listening to the inner voice the best way to describe the 'savior.' However, people were conditioned to disregard the inner-voice and only listen to those who deemed themselves worthy to speak for God. Too often these self-chosen ones controlled the idea of a savior by shaping it as an external event. Baptism was how John opened the channel of the inner-voice, and stories or parables were my method, along with demonstrations of healing. Healing the bodies of the seekers was easier than healing their hearts, and unfortunately, most of the recorded events only speak of physical healing.

I looked at my cousin and nodded, indicating that I was ready. He gently pushed me backwards into the water. I had totally given him control of my body, to allow the backward-falling motion and sank into the fairly deep water, with only his hand in the middle of my back. Falling backwards can be intimidating. John was a genius to baptize this way. It forced the seekers to give up fear and totally trust him. Perhaps I had an advantage, since I wasn't afraid of the water, as the majority of people were. Given that swimming in the sea was only done for medicinal purposes, with people never going into deep water, and other bodies of water were reserved for animal thirst, humans seldom learned to swim, thus, were uneasy in the watery realm. Maybe I didn't fear the deep water because I had conversed with the fish that saved me as a babe, as I fell into the river that day. We had swum together for awhile until my air bubbles ran out. As I fell backward in John's arms, I simply relaxed and asked Holy Divine Spirit to cleanse and bless me. As I came out of the water, a dove surrounded by a bright light evidently hovered over my head—I didn't see it—others did. I noticed that everyone was looking above me. I wondered what made their faces glow and why they smiled. I felt sparkling clean, like never before, and a peace flooded through me. People began to talk about the radiant dove, which I assumed was the Holy Spirit answering my prayer.

I was sure that the Holy Spirit came to me as the 'Holy Dove of Love.'[123] I thought of the embroidered doves on my mother's robes, and a new appreciation for her work filled me with warmth and comfort. The Dove is a symbol of the Divine Feminine, and it all made sense to me now, why the priestesses chose this tiny symbol to recognize each other. The apparition provided a fuller confirmation of my baptism and reassured me. My teaching moment became my sacred moment of blessing, as I approached marriage with my beloved.

John's and my followers stopped leering at each other and actually merged and were smiling. They laughed in joy and accepted my baptism as a sign that we were all blessed. I felt no pre-marital anxiety now and all the emotional insecurities I had as I began this walk eased; instead I was full of love and readiness to meet my bride. I bid my cousin farewell, inviting him to the wedding, knowing that he wouldn't accept my invitation since crowds made him extremely uneasy, but still wanting him to know that he was welcome to this blessed moment in my life. I departed with happy expectancy.

It seemed like the day had flown by. As dusk approached, one of the most beautiful sunsets I had ever seen further blessed me. Love makes everything more vivid, and I felt love like never before, as I anticipated my union with my lovely MiryAmah. Called Mary of Magdalene by most, and recognized as a Mag-Delah[124], my bride was priestess-trained and a feminine leader within the secret Isis cult. It was during the wedding ceremony, that we officially sealed our names to Jeshuah[125] and MiryAmah, emphasizing the 'ah,' so that our union was divinely linked on the wave of sound. Those who meditate using the 'om' sound feel the vibration the sound makes. They would recognize how that pulsation is slightly different than the 'ah' sound. The om brings the vibration to the body and mind, linking the two with the divine through the heart. The 'ah' sound links two beings together and merges them with

---

[123] One of the ways Sophia, or the feminine aspect of God appears
[124] Derived from Magdala which meant 'Tower of Strength' but in this case it means the high priestess who is a tower of strength.
[125] Later the 'h' was omitted from the spelling of my name

the divine in holy union. The sound is closest to the essence of 'beloved'. A subtle difference, but to us, it was important that we affirm our unity within our marriage and be jointly linked to God. I get ahead of myself, as I try to explain my beloved's importance in the work we were born to do. After my baptism, I quickly prepared myself for the ceremony and returned to the garden, now feeling fresh and ready to meet my bride, proud to be the lucky groom to be sacredly united with her.

The garden that served as the sacramental place for the ceremony was located only three abodes from where the apostles and I were staying, making my walk short. The disciples (women followers of my beloved) had the garden interior decorated beautifully. The flowers were in full bloom in this wonderful natural setting. There were also vases of flowers placed along the pathway that we would walk. At the end of the path in the middle of the garden, candles surrounded a circular center lined with flat stones. In the heart of this stone circle, a small fountain stood spilling its water into a ring that had small grooves, directing the overflow in channels that watered the garden. This was an 'artesian well'[126] that flowed constantly and was a rare luxury. There were petals of pink and blue roses strewn upon the path and surrounding the flowing fountain, too. The smell was intoxicating, yet not overpowering. Everything looked stunning, but not as beautiful as the moment my beloved come forth in all her feminine glory. She beamed and indeed looked like the Goddess manifest. She had dark blue eyes that she could shift to black at will; however, for this special day I could see the rare deep blue in them. She wasn't hiding the difference from the norm today, as she usually did. I also had similar-colored eyes that could look brown, or I could lighten them if I so chose, as was the case today. Joy always lit up my eyes and looking upon my bride was the most joyful moment of my life. Our eyes of deep blue didn't make us more divine. It was simply an indication that the peace code (gene as you call it now) was extremely active within us. The reason those in our region, with eyes like ours, were feared was because we tended to disregard the rules of fear. Within peace, love holds reign, thus we were harder to control. In other areas of the world, this might not

---

[126] Tapped into an underground stream and never stops flowing

be true. It would always be the difference that was intimidating to controllers, who promoted separation; consequently, a difference became a reason to pass judgment on beings. Those naturally blue-eyed people would occasionally have a dark eyed child; that child often was subject to fear, as well. Our eyes were obviously dark; just the base color was dark blue, rather than dark brown, so we didn't look that different than those of our area of experience. On this holy day and at this sacred moment, I only had eyes for my beloved. The love I felt was reflected in my eyes, as her love shown in hers. She waited for me in a robe of blue, holding a single blue rose, the color of the divine feminine. I felt a tear of joy roll down my cheek. I wore a magenta robe and carried a rose of deep pink, the color of the divine masculine. As I approached her, I felt as if I was floating.

When MiryAmah saw me, she walked my way on the rose path. When we met, we exchanged roses. The ancient goddess symbolic custom meant that we brought to each other the divine counterpart. I kissed the top of her head, held her face in my hands and asked if she would be my wife.

She said, "Yes, now and forever, as it has always been." Salome, my sister, then gave her an alabaster jar and MiryAmah anointed me, head to toe with spikenard, rubbing it on the chakra locations[127] and on my feet. When she got to my feet, she bowed down and wiped the anointment of nard upon them with her beautiful dark reddish hair, saying, "Would you be my beloved husband?"

I replied, "Forever and ever as it has always been and ever meant to be."

She performed the ritual of the goddess, which signified the same blessing I gave her as I kissed the top of her head. After my acceptance, she kissed each foot, which sent chills up my body like only a beloved mate could. Thus it was, that I had kissed her head and she my feet, and the dual energy of love met dramati-

---

[127] Energy vortexes within the body; crown, brow, throat, heart, solar plexus, abdomen, base of spine

cally within both of us through the channel of the ritual– the crown of the head the masculine sky; the feet standing on mother earth, the feminine ground. We sealed our wedding vows and finalized our betrothal with a light mouth to mouth kiss–the only public kiss that our society usually accepted. I have to admit that we didn't always worry about this public idea, that to see a man and woman kiss was distasteful. We couldn't help our urge, since, in reality, such tender kisses were divinely appropriate and our greatest joy. Our wedding wasn't the normal Jewish wedding and required no permission or presence of a high Jewish priest. The priestess ritual had been denied and deleted from most ceremonies by this time, yet we felt that in order to truly be united, we had to honor the Divine Feminine as well as the Divine Masculine in our vows. We shocked a few of the wedding guests with our ancient ceremony. We were non-conformist; that could be a dangerous path to walk, and we knew it. As we slightly bent the rules of judgment, we gently pierced the attitudes that kept love at bay on this our most sacred day.

After the ceremony, all enjoyed a feast and then, the so-called, miracle of the wine occurred. My mother had forgotten to order wine and came to me in tears. I reassured her, "It isn't important enough for you to bear sorrow, mother."

She replied, "But son, this is a most important day for you, and you have every right to expect, that your wedding guests have wine to drink in honor of your union to your beloved bride. We have some wine donated by our friend who hosts us, but only enough for the wedding couple and family," she explained.

"We'll not drink wine while our guests drink water, mother. Perhaps it's time for the wedding couple to do something about the situation," I said to set her mind at rest. By this time, the home and garden were overflowing with people. We had only expected our immediate followers, but many more showed up at the ceremony, which pleased us. They were full of joy and happy wishes. It was thought a good omen then, to have more guests than one expected at such a sacred occasion.

Both my wife and I knew how to do the alchemy of changing water into wine, by blessing the water and merging the grape essence into it. We had learned slightly different methods, but the same principles were involved. We asked for bottles of artesian well water. MiryAmah performed the ritual of the grape by putting one grape into each bottle so that the water could marry the fruit, and as she did so, she chanted an invitation to the elementals of the grapes.

I also spoke to the spirit of the water and grape, and invited them to merge and dance as one. It might sound quite simple but there were mental and spiritual steps, as well, that merged the physical with the elemental realm. In this way, the essence of the two substances could find common ground and actually accelerate a natural process to become wine instantly. The making of wine this way had been long forgotten, or kept secret, so we quietly accomplished our goal, and only shared the water, now wine, when it had fully transformed.

The symbolism of the water to wine was a complement to our matrimony. Sadly, even during this joyous occasion, many of my followers didn't approve of my marriage. They wanted me to be a maverick through and through, and deny my need as a man for a life-mate. They actually feared that if I married a woman, I might love someone more than I loved them. It's difficult to shed the old patterns of thinking, and women had long been suppressed and considered an unpleasant necessity in a man's life. Thus, later, my apostles didn't talk about what actually happened, but rather what in their minds they believed should have taken place. As it turned out, the wine we made, because it held the essence of joy, which married with the pure artesian water and grapes, was the finest wine many had ever tasted. Mother was pleased, and when mother was pleased everyone was happy. Not because she was unpleasant when not pleased, but because she was so joyful, she could affect one and all with her grace.

My bride left me for a few moments to attend to her followers, as the festivities continued into the night. The disciples weren't merging with the men, but standing to one side. MiryAmah wanted her followers to integrate with the apostles and their wives, who were present but maintaining a distance. We couldn't be messengers of change in attitudes, if our own followers kept men and women separate from each other. The disciples, being priestess-trained, before, or after they came to the group, were especially sensitive to the judgmental mind-set. The aloofness of the apostles and their families troubled them. After urging both the apostles and disciples to mingle and celebrate our love, MiryAmah, so joyfully happy, finally managed to get the groups to let their guards down. They finally blended and enjoyed our sacred celebration, as we hoped they would.

I took a short walk in the garden with Thomas, whom I loved with all my heart, as I did all of my followers. I wanted to show him a little attention, for he doubted his own worth at times, and I could sense he needed some encouragement from me. Unfortunately, he was also of the mind that by taking a wife I was moving away from him and the others, and he worried that I would ultimately forget the mission due to the temptation of a woman.

As we walked in the garden, a bright red sparrow lit in the path in front of us. It was quickly grabbed by a small child sitting nearby and crushed in his hands. The child evidently had been stalking the bird, waiting for his chance. As he held the little dead bird, he offered it to me saying, "Jeshua, I have a gift of red feathers for your wedding day. If I can catch the mate to this little sparrow, I'll get your bride the bright blue feathers of the female." Sparrows, rare then, were brightly-colored song birds, often captured and caged, or killed and plucked for their feathers to be used in decoration.

I took the bird and looked at the child, so eager to please me. I knew his intention was to honor me, but nevertheless, the lifeless body of the bright red male sparrow was now lying in my hand. I stooped down and said to the boy, "I would rather that you give me a live sparrow, lad, for life is a gift that is most divine."

He looked at the dead bird and said, "But the red feathers are so beautiful and these birds are rarely seen. I don't have a nice cage to put him in. How can I present you with the feathers, if I don't kill the bird first?"

Realizing that the child just wanted to do something special for me, I tried to respond in kindness. I said, "The reason you don't see the sparrows very much, and folks think they're so special, is because people only appreciate the exterior of them–the bright plumage–and they kill or capture them to take their beauty. So the pretty birds hide from us, so that they can live and be free. True beauty can never be captured," I told the child. I watched him mull over what I said, as he looked at the brightly-colored bird now lying dead in my hand. He stroked it and said he was sorry, and a tear ran down his tiny cheek.

"I promise I won't kill another living thing, Jeshua," he said in all earnest, and I knew he would keep that promise his entire life. These flashes of 'knowing' happened from time to time and always proved true.

Thomas was watching, while I gently stroked the little bird and talked to the sad child. He was caught up in the moment, and as I stood up, Thomas looked surprised, because the bird began to stir and awaken in my hand. He said in amazement, "Master, is a bird worthy of healing, too?" His statement no doubt echoed the encoded attitudes that sorted those worthy and those not. To Thomas, it was a logical question to ask, but to me it was a terrible thought.

"Why not," I replied, looking deeply into Thomas' huge brown eyes. "Didn't God make this bird as well as you and me?" I wasn't mad at Thomas for asking the question–just sad, because his inquiry echoed the belief that only man was worthy, and women and all other creation were commodities for man's use, which often included abuse.

He seemed to be thinking for a moment, even as the small child rose and stood on his tiptoes to see the bird coming back to life in my hand. Then Thomas said, "But now he'll probably be crushed again, because his beauty is so bright and noticeable, that surely someone will do just what this little child has done, and capture and kill the bird for its beautiful feathers."

By then the little bird was fully revived, but didn't escape from my hand where he felt safe. His mate, the bright blue female sparrow, was chirping from a nearby almond tree, and she was clearly distressed. I began to speak to the red bird, fascinating the small child, and even more Thomas, the doubter. Children naturally think that everything is possible, thus it is until they are taught it isn't, but Thomas always had to see with his eyes to believe. At this moment, he saw me carrying on a conversation with a bird that had clearly been dead, but a moment before.

The little bird asked me in animal-speak, "Why does your kind kill me for my feathers?"

I tried to answer, saying that humans never felt as beautiful as he and his mate were, and people thought if they wore the bright-colored feathers, they could approach such beauty.

The bird looked at me and chirped its talk, saying, "But you're quite beautiful in your robes of color, and you didn't have to kill anything to get them. I've watched the process of weaving and dying the thread, but still that's not enough, and you hunt and murder my family and my kind."

The bird dropped its head and silenced its song. Its mate flew to my hand and fluttered down next to her mate, who she sensed needed her, which overrode her fear. The two sad birds represented to me how the divine marriage could experience extreme sorrow because, as beautiful as it is, ignorance and jealousy could destroy it. I wanted to do something to lift the sorrow these two little creatures felt on this our wedding day—for them, myself and my beloved, and all present. MiryAmah approached us, noticing the two birds in my hand. She looked at them and read their minds instantly. She was also an expert in animal communication.

She looked up toward me and said, "On our special wedding day, or on any day, isn't there something we can do for these gentle little creatures, so that their lives, and the lives of their children and kind are better?"

Her tender request moved me. I thought for a moment and answered, "If only these birds were the color of Tara, mother earth, who has such beautiful tones of browns and russets within her essence; maybe then they would blend, instead of stand out, and their beauty wouldn't be something people desired to possess."

"Why can't we change them?" MiryAmah asked, in the way that only women who know no limits or boundaries could.

Thomas began to scoff. He couldn't help such a reaction, because he was naturally the 'doubter'. We accepted this from him, because we knew that he was honest about his doubts and being so, he spoke what others feared to reveal. Actually, his personality was a gift, keeping us aware of how uncertainty could cloud our teachings.

"Why not, Thomas," I asked. "Why not help these birds assume a new color, one that blends into the land, which they rest upon, but complements the air they fly through?"

"How would you do such a thing?" he asked, as the pair of little birds still sat on the palm of my hand, watched intently, becoming more alert and lively.

MiryAmah said, "I'll call the sparrows forth, one and all, and if we make a portal of our hands and ask Tara, mother earth, maybe she'll share her colors with these humble little beings." We felt the energy from the earth vibrate in answer to her request. We looked at the flowers in the garden, who called our attention with a humming sound. Those that hadn't yet bloomed came to full bloom before our eyes. We knew Tara had heard our request and would do her part. Thomas stared at the unfolding petals of the flowers, his eyes widened and his doubt evaporated.

MiryAmah was already explaining what we proposed to the birds, still perched on my hand, and they thought this would be a good thing, but only if they all could be forever changed to earth colors. My beloved then looked to me and repeated the request. I agreed that indeed, that was the only way to approach the situation.

The little pair of birds began to sing and my beloved bride began to sing, as well. That was the first time I had heard her sing, and I was delighted with yet another talent blessing our union. Her beautiful song brought the wedding guests out into the garden, and they thought it so precious to see such a spectacle, the bride singing to her groom along with brilliant red and bright blue birds–males and females of the rare species–swarming above us in numbers too many to count. They soon filled the garden and air space above it in dazzling colored flocks. The wedding guests exclaimed that they had never before seen so many sparrows. It was rare even to see just one pair, now too many to count flocked above the garden. It was truly the miracle of our wedding day and so soon forgotten.

The singing sound of the multitude of birds was beautiful and in harmony with MiryAmah's song. MiryAmah faced me and took my hands. We made a portal of our arms, for the birds to fly through to be changed. By doing so, we created a gateway of transformation. With our raised arms creating an archway, a portal into to another dimension opened. We became entranced and suspended between the physical and the spiritual realm.

MiryAmah urged the brilliant blue female sparrow, mate to the one that had been healed, to fly through the portal. Her mate was a bit hesitant, not sure if he could muster up the courage, since he had already been through so much, being crushed and then brought back from the dead. The bright blue female, without hesitation, flew through our arms. When she reached the other side, she was changed. Her color was now a rich earthy brown with splashes of white and some black details that emphasized a delightful pattern. The male bird, now sitting on my shoulder, watched in awe, and I urged him to fly through the portal, too. When he found the courage and flew through, he was instantly changed, too. He wasn't so different from his mate, just a bit blacker in places, thus his pattern was more intense than his female counterpart. He knew that would be a good thing. Now, if anyone wanted feathers, they would see him first, and she would be safe to raise their chicks. They flew in joy in their new earth colors and beckoned the swarming others to fly through the portal, too. It was a sight to behold, my beloved and I holding hands fashioning an archway, with birds flying through the space we created. It looked like a red/blue striped ribbon that streamed through our upward arms, emerging a rich earthy-colored ribbon of russet and brown. As all the sparrows finished going through, now changed to the beautiful colors of the earth, we gazed into each other's eyes and couldn't help an intimate kiss to seal our happiness. The sparrows, russet and brown, danced upon the wind in their joy of being forever changed, and sang their delight, then disappeared back into nature. It was an erotic and passionate moment. To MiryAmah and me, the birds always represented the joy of our union.

The guests who witnessed the event held various responses, ranging from, 'now, how will we find the bright feathers?' to 'did you see them kissing there in the garden without shame?' But thankfully, there were also those who understood that beauty could be imprisoned and that the birds were set free.

Our doubting friend Thomas, asked "How can this be?" and we knew that the others wondered the same thing.

I answered, "Tara, our dear earth mother, changed the birds by sharing her spiritual essence of color and hue with them." It wasn't commonly known then that color was a vibration, therefore sound, as well as light. I kept my answer simple and just called it 'spiritual essence'. Tara has much to do with how vibration, the sound of color, meets the light, thus, creates the hue within the visible spectrum to those experiencing the time and space. It takes the planet, (the female aspect), and the sun (the male aspect), to blend vibrations, which are felt, heard and seen as color. As a result, the visible rainbow of colors is created. There are a multitude of colors yet to be seen. One day when the time is ripe, even more colors will be revealed. I didn't explain all of this, however. It was my wedding day, and I kept my teachings simple and to the point, as Peter had suggested not so long ago.

After the bird transformation, Thomas was emotionally moved and apologized again for his doubting ways. "Oh, Thomas," I said, "it's your courage to reveal your doubts, which gives voice to those who feel the same reservations, but can't voice them. You keep us connected to the issues that underlie the attitudes, my beloved and I hope to align. I love you for that." Each follower's fault was also their strength. That was why they were such good teachers for the cause to which my lovely bride and I were committed. I loved their imperfections, as much as I loved their willingness to soulfully grow and change. It took courage and commitment to be devotees to 'The Way'[128].

I hadn't informed my followers of the priestess tradition of the married couple going into seclusion after the wedding. I thought I might as well update Thomas now and said, "I leave soon, for time to be with my bride. I've asked Peter to be in command of the teachings, while I'm away. I'll be gone a month, and this'll give you all time to try your wings as teachers of 'The Way'. I know Peter can be overwhelming, Thomas, but gently try to share this responsibility with him. I need his strength, as much as I need your ability to understand the fears within the minds of the listeners. If you'll do this, I'll be grateful beyond measure. It'll give my bride and me time to know each other better as man and wife.

"Consider it done," Thomas said. He gave me a heartfelt hug, and walked back to the disbursing crowd. I took my beloved's hand, and we walked away. It was considered bad luck to tell the guests good bye at a wedding. We were still full of vibrating energy from the bird portal episode, and needed to be alone together to bring our energy levels back to normal. As we walked along and spoke of the sparrows, we discussed how we, too, must blend into our world as much as possible, or we could be murdered for the beauty of our love.

Just before we departed, however, the little boy from the garden stopped us, blocking the path at the gate. He said, "Now that the sparrows all look the same and no one will notice them, what will happen if God can't see them?"

MiryAmah smiled and allowed me to address this heartfelt question. "I promise you, little one," I said, "that not a sparrow will fall from the sky that God doesn't notice." He smiled, as I went on to say, "And that goes for you, too, little one. You are like the precious sparrow, and are always watched and loved by God."

---

[128] How we referred to our teachings

Satisfied with the answer, the little fellow smiled and stepped aside, waving goodbye to us.

# A SABBATH DAY HEALING
## Chapter Twenty-Eight

With the official wedding ceremony and our second joining feast now behind us, my beloved and I, brimming with hope and love, moved into our mission full force. The first joining was our engagement. Usually it was an arranged union between families, but sometimes, as in our case, it was a personal choice. Accepting MiryAmah as my equal, sad to say, was the apostles' greatest challenge. They still held firm to the concept that the leader was greater than the followers, who should bow down in humility to him. I didn't blame them, since this attitude was long imprinted in the system that shaped their minds. The imprint, or pattern, deeply embedded in the structure of society, was the norm. So, I found that to adopt the priestess tradition of making a circle when in conference with my inner-circle of devotees was best, so that there was no obvious seat of superiority. I, of course, wanted my beloved by my side in this circle. She in turn, wanted her close twelve inner-circle assistants, the disciples, present within the arena of conference and confidence, too. There was a great debate over this. It took long hours of arguing the case to and fro, to convince the male apostles to accept the expanded circle of twenty-six that included my beloved and I, and our close followers.

Some would rather remember the events that have come down through history regarding my lifeworks; however, those recorded times–if they happened at all–were from a different perspective than mine and thus perceived differently than my memory. Considering that history has shaped the story, as well, by manipulating the written accounts, creates a difficult web to untangle. I can only tell you how it felt to be me in the journey of Jesus, or Jeshua, as I came to be known, and how I saw and understood the situations of my life.

The reluctance to heal on the Sabbath, considered a punishable sin, was a custom that made no sense to me. While others might accept it, I could not. The priests and those in seats of power became so legalistic, that they forgot the spirit of the Sabbath law. The rule of no work whatsoever on the Sabbath was intended to give all a chance to honor God, even as it was also used as a way of getting the masses of people together so that they could be trained and observed. Those who might meet with an accident or have any other life-threatening issue on the Sabbath day, the last day of the week, known now as your Saturday, were most unfortunate. The rules, made by those who sought to gain and hold power, were meant to keep control over others. Rules all too often create a place of security and superiority, in life, death and beyond. The priests were bold enough to think that their authority extended even beyond the grave. Fear's power is accomplished by separation. The greatest tool, in the mind of those in control, was to separate the good from the bad, but their labels had more to do with obedience than with actual qualities of character. Hence, some classes of people were deemed more worthy than others. In this mentality, the idea of the hierarchy of creation, with man at the forefront, and animals and women somewhere down the line, created to serve men, flourished and still tilts the axis of balance within your present age.

This context, the audacity of such laws, confused me at first, and then finally angered me, as I held no regard for that nonsense. I could only believe in love–love unites and doesn't separate creation into better or worse categories. I knew this was true from the depths of my soul. My years of learning from the great masters, who took me on as a young student reinforced this truth of all creation. My teachings, parables and outright discussions brought up the imbalances within the social structure. People's repressed anger, frustration and grief came to the surface, as they listened and questioned the rules we discussed. Their minds began to open, and a change was shifting in many minds and hearts. Fear can't risk change. Thus, I became a threat to the established religious leaders, because I dared to challenge their deeply-ingrained fear-system.

## The Saga-Oracle

One Sabbath day, MiryAmah and I were talking to a large group of people. We were addressing the idea of 'master and slave,' and discussing who was most holy. Of course, my beloved and I were trying to lead the crowd into realizing that both were equally holy; but it takes awhile for that simple truth to dawn on minds that have been brain-washed into thinking that wealth and privilege equaled more worth, and that servants were naturally chosen by God to be underlings.

One woman said, "Raboni, are you trying to say that my servant girl is equally divine as myself, who she serves?" I found it interesting that the first person to discuss the idea was indeed a wealthy woman. She was wearing fine silk robes, and it was evident that she was from a well-off family.

I replied, "Why wouldn't she be?" Contrary to what many believe, I urged people to talk and think through questions for themselves, and I simply invited her to think and speak her thoughts, by my short reply. I was, and always will be, the storyteller, since I find that I teach best through that mode, but I am also a leader, and I know that a true leader directs and does not dictate. I wanted to direct those listeners to explore the truth, not give them my version of such and expect them to integrate it into their minds and hearts, just because I deemed it so. Truth is an odd universal commodity, if you pardon my description here, but for the sake of this narrative, please bear with me. Truth must come from within a being, no matter what form of creation that being occupies. Truth, thus, can't be given to anyone; it must dawn on them. All messengers can do is help open inner-doorways to truth, which can never be forced. It must come through the portal of the soul and only the being responsible for the physical vehicle knows when they are ready for this 'knowing'. This is true of all creation, since creation does indeed have awareness of itself and truth is Divine Essence within Its Own creational experiment.[129] If you can understand this one concept, you'll understand how religion can go astray. Religion at its very basic core-concept level has a good (God, if you will) intention. However, as those who run the show seek to make everyone believe that they are more worthy,

---

[129] God experiencing God

thus more deserving of holding the power of position, they reshape the conceptual truth until it no longer resembles its divine intention. Minds may wrap around the convenience of such thinking, but the heart/soul will never be fooled. Sadly, the outcome is the soul-voice recedes and becomes so small, that the entity can't hear it and nearly loses its divine connection. Forgive me, if I preach a bit. MiryAmah has often teased me about that tendency. I just mention these things to prepare you for the conversation I am remembering with the wealthy woman.

"So, Raboni," the woman continued, "if we are equals, why then is she my servant, and I her master?"

"Because you desire someone to serve you, dear lady," I replied and watched her mull the simple explanation over in her mind.

"Did she desire to be a servant, teacher?" the woman asked.

"That's true, and I tell you that she is not lesser than you, because she desired to serve. She could have played the role you hold if her soul had preferred, but she chose to take a role that has no glory–a role that puts all emphasis on helping another being through their life's journey. I assure you, being a servant is a totally unselfish position, which is a lofty choice for a soul to select as they enter this physical world. It takes great courage, but doesn't indicate greater worthiness, or less." I noticed the woman of wealth seemed a bit puzzled, yet behind her stood her loyal servant girl, ever faithfully watching her intently, because in her heart, she knew the truth, and her soul and heart were so connected they were one. The servant girl loved her life in service, as she loved the woman she served.

"I see," the lady murmured and turned to look at her servant girl. She then reached out and put her arm around the girl's shoulders and gently pulled her to her side. You could see the joy spread across the young girl's face. Joy is the greatest emotional expression of all creation and the echo of God pleased. Both the master and the servant became one as they finally embraced tearfully, hugging each other. The crowd looked on with great bewilderment; for what had dawned upon these two had not yet cracked the doorway open in their own hearts. The emotion of joy was, nevertheless, affecting them and spreading as it always does, and some were beginning to feel something change.

The moment was interrupted by commotion coming from within the group. Confusion began to take hold, as resistance to change of attitudes caused fear to erupt in many of the listeners. The energy of the group became chaotic. MiryAmah spoke up, which didn't please my apostles, thinking she was stepping out of her place, given that she didn't ask my permission to speak, as was the custom of the time.[130] We spoke when we knew it was time.

"Peace, dear people," she said. She then sent her disciples out among the people. They laid their hands gently upon the back of the heads of many of those most troubled in the group, and simply said 'peace' and the crowd began to settle down.

Then they noticed that MiryAmah began to build a small fire in front of her, on the side of the hill we were using for our teaching this fine Sabbath day. Building the fire seemed an odd thing to do in the middle of chaos, however MiryAmah was calm in the process; even as confusion was still apparent in the crowd, her calmness settled them. They wondered how MiryAmah could be so detached from the chaos. They didn't realize diverting their attention was her way to bring peace to them, and it worked like a charm.

MiryAmah added some herbs to the flames that were now consuming the dried sticks she had gathered, while I was conversing with the woman of wealth. She used the flint stones, from the bag of supplies she carried, to light the fire, cracking them hard against each other in the process until the desired spark occurred. As the flames quickly took hold, she added pinches of an herb I didn't recognize. My lovely wife surprised me regularly, and it pleased me. I had no idea what she was doing, but I completely trusted her. The smoke mingled with the burning herbs, and the result was a scent that was near intoxicating, but in a most wonderful peaceful way. The astounding effect on the

---

[130] Women customarily had to gain permission to speak from a male, usually the husband or other male family member

crowd astonished me. People were in a daze, as they smelled the fragrance drifting out over them, and they became more serene.

In her sweet, but resounding, voice she said, "Dear Ones. What is most important to this fire's success? Is it the tree that provided its twigs, which had to die and dry to the stage of brittleness to be consumed? Is it the stone that must aggressively hit another stone hard enough to produce a spark of friction? Is it the final addition of the sacred peace herb that held top priority? Tell me," she said, "which is the master and which is the slave here?"

She had a magical way of gaining the attention of a crowd and her voice carried well as she spoke with confidence. By then most were focused on her. Someone said, "Isn't it you, MiryAmah, who used all of these things that is most important, thus in this case 'master'?" And the crowd seemed to agree with the questioner, with many heads nodding in affirmation. I thought, at least they are beginning to see her as a master soul and affording her the respect, she is due.

"No," MiryAmah said, shaking her lovely head back and forth, as she repeated it again, "No, I was simply the servant."

"Servant!" someone questioned, looking confused. "How so, and whom do you then serve–surely not the sticks, stones or herbs."

I was enjoying this assistance from my sweet counterpart and trusting her to take this conversation to its full conclusion, stepped back letting her have full command of the moment. She calmly looked at the crowd with love written all over her face and waited for the truth to dawn on them. At that point, our little friend from the garden (the boy we met at the time of our second wedding) came forth. I hadn't seen him since our wedding day, when he offered me a brightly-colored, but dead, red sparrow for a wedding gift. After the transformation of the sparrows, MiryAmah and I went to our wedding retreat, and he wandered off to places that only little boys go, the same little boy, but still as changed as the sparrows were.

I noticed my mother within the crowd, too, which surprised me, since the place we were visiting was on the opposite side of the inland sea from where I believed she was staying. My mother seemed to show up from time to time without announcement. Some of my apostle friends, especially Thomas, who ever struggled with doubts, thought she was keeping an eye on me, or spying to make sure I did her bidding. I told him more than once, that love doesn't need to keep track. Only fear keeps track, and my mother was fearless! "All any mother wants, is for their child to be fulfilled," I reminded Thomas, my doubting friend.

I saw the little boy look back at my mother, as if for approval. She was motioning to him to move in our direction, and finally, she said, "It's Okay, say what you will, your brother and sister will understand."

Slowly, the child approached and stood before my beloved MiryAmah and me, as we sat upon the slope on the higher ground with the fire burning beside us. He said, "My brother, my sister, I know the answer." He was excited to share, because he was sure he knew the answer to the question posed by MiryAmah. I remember thinking that he was addressing us as brother and sister, because he understood the truth that all creation is related. MiryAmah however, kept looking at the child and then at me, and a bright smile crossed her face as if something that brought great joy, just dawned on her.

I said, "Tell us the answer then, child."

"The master is us," he said, "we who listen, for we had a great need for a servant to help us find peace, because we were confused by what you said. So, the twigs, the stone, the fire and the herbs were offered to us by God's servant, my sister here," he said as he looked at MiryAmah. "Isn't that so?" he questioned, looking right into her eyes. His child voice was heard clearly by everyone, possibly due to our location or by some unseen divine force that wanted this child's wisdom to be heard by all present.

"So it is, and so it shall be," MiryAmah replied, as she softly looked deep into the eyes of the bright child.

He turned again to me and said, "I love you, brother," and returned to where my mother was standing. She put her hands on his shoulders in a tender manner, and pulled him closer into a loving hug. I thought the familiarity between the two something I would ask her about later.

Before we could carry on with the day's message, a woman collapsed within the crowd. Someone, knowing of our healing abilities, called me forth and said, "Jeshua, please come and help this poor woman." I moved quickly through the crowd to the place of the collapsed woman, where I found her being held by another woman, cradling her head in her lap.

"Can you help my sister," the woman cried, with a look of desperation in her eyes.

Someone said in astonishment, "But it's the Sabbath! One cannot do anything that is work-oriented on such a day and isn't healing your work, teacher?"

I looked into the crowd that was closing around me. I could see that the idea of work, in any capacity, would be the gravest of sins, so deeply ingrained that the people couldn't conceive of me helping this poor woman. I looked long and hard at those who would condemn me, for they glared at me, as if daring me to break the sacred law.

Finally, I said, "Would you sacrifice this woman's life, for the sake of labeling healing as work that is not worthy to be done on the Sabbath? How can an act of love, which helps those suffering, be work? Isn't it divine service, to recognize that God's creation should not be in misery, if there is something to be done? I ask you, one and all, what better day for such 'work,' than on the Lord's Day?"

The crowd quietly looked at me, obviously at a loss for words to answer such questions. They had been well-trained to accept rules without exception.

"Is this ban on working on the Sabbath, a rule worth a life?" I asked. I then looked down at the wilting woman and knew that her life force was rapidly leaving her. The ground under her was running red with blood. Some of those nearby made a face of revulsion, clearly repulsed by the realization that this was the blood of the womb, she gushed.

I stooped down and put my finger in the blood. I noticed that MiryAmah was there beside me on her knees, leaning over the reclining woman in need. We looked into each other's eyes for a quick moment, and I took my finger from the blood pool and anointed MiryAmah on the forehead with the blood, saying, "This is the blood that has been shed for me and for anyone who comes through the womb of their mother." Then I continued and said, "Blessed is the blood of a mother."

She, likewise, put her finger in the blood pool and said to me, "This is the blood of my sister. Without her sacrifice, no one would know the glory of life, including myself." She then anointed me as well, but putting the blood to my lips.

The crowd gasped at this demonstration, and wondered how I would react to the blood they considered unclean on my mouth. They were taught, and believed, that the blood of the womb was tainted and vile. I then floated my hand over the pelvic area of the woman, slightly above her robes, to check for the level of energetic balancing needed to help her stop hemorrhaging. Her sister informed us that this had been going on for over a month, since she had delivered a stillborn son. She had heard that many were healed, when people listened to me teach, and she hoped that her sister would be as well, thus she had helped her sister attend our Sabbath teaching.

I didn't notice that MiryAmah slipped her hand under the robes of the bleeding woman. She later told me, she placed her hand directly upon the sacred portal where the blood gushed forth so profusely. The disciples came in close, as did some of the apostles, for they instinctively knew that their assistance would help in this situation. I felt comforted that they were not haggling about who was first and who was last among them. They just reacted to the time of need, with all due concern and compassion, they surrounded us.

The poor woman was barely conscious now. I blew into her face and said, "Let the breath of God come through me and bring you healing, woman, for there is no need to blame yourself for the child you think you lost." She barely opened her eyes, but nonetheless, they emitted a river of tears, flowing in streams down her cheeks and dropping to the same ground that her blood now soaked. I knew that it was the blaming of herself that began this ordeal.

She whispered, "But the child was the son my husband always wanted." She squeezed her eyes tightly shut, to the point that her forehead bore tight wrinkles of tension, due to deep sorrow. "If only I had tried harder to shelter this child within me maybe he would have survived," she cried.

MiryAmah then said to her, in a soft voice that was meant only for her ears, "What better shelter than your own womb, woman." She kissed the poor mother on the forehead, brought her bloody hand from under the woman's robe and pulled back the grieving mother's robe to reveal her bare chest. The disciples flared their robes at this point, so that there was privacy within the moment. Their thoughtfulness surprised and pleased me. I appreciated that our close companions and followers now worked together, sharing this task of making a circle of privacy, something we had never before seen them do, nor had we discussed it. It was totally spontaneous.

MiryAmah placed her bloody hand upon the woman's heart. She said, "You gave all you could and this child was born, due to love." She further explained, "The reason the child didn't stay was because he sensed the love of the father was in confusion. His father had a great struggle within his mind, which pushed his heart away and altered readiness for this sensitive son."

The poor mother sobbed softly, christening the ground with even more tears and said, "He is a good man, and I love him."

MiryAmah, understanding, responded and said, "This doesn't make your husband a killer of babes or guilty, dear heart." She gently wiped the tears from the poor woman's eyes, and continued to explain, "It just means the father was not ready for the son yet, thus the son was not ready for the father, either." The face of the hemorrhaging woman was so wet with tears; it almost seemed that she might drown. MiryAmah took her own robe, soaked the tears from the woman's face, then wiped the bloody handprint from the suffering mother's heart, saying, "I wipe the sorrow from your heart, dear one, in the name of Mother/Father God, who has no need to forgive you, but wishes you to know that you are loved and shall live, so that this son can come again. Your daughters need you as well, as does your beloved husband."

Watching my lovely wife tenderly perform her tasks always pleased me, even though I never knew what she would do, nor when, but I always knew it would be appropriate and compassionate. This part of the healing was privately done, with our circle keeping the crowd from seeing the process, thus keeping the dignity of the afflicted one intact. As I watched my wife wipe the bloody handprint from the heart of the woman, I saw in wonder, upon her breast, there was a smaller hand print that didn't wipe off. It was the size of a tiny baby's hand. I looked at my wife, and she nodded affirmation, for she knew that I understood the source of the baby hand print. It was not red like MiryAmah's bloody hand print had been, but blue and every little mark of the flesh of a newborn hand clear and present. MiryAmah then brought the robe back to its purpose, to cover the flesh, and she kissed the woman, as I did as well and our devotees opened the circle. I knew that it would be her husband who discovered the little hand print, and he would resolve his inner conflict and be ready for his son to come again.

The crowd was eager to know what was happening and pressed in to see how the woman faired. Knowing that the healing was complete, I said to the formerly afflicted one, "Rise and go forth now, woman. You have not sinned and you are not condemned. Your life shall be as a blessing to all those you meet, and you have blessed everyone here."

The woman opened her eyes, looking like the weight of the world had been lifted from her. Her sister helped the new mother rise from the blood-soaked ground. Another woman came forth with a wrap of the finest silk, and wrapped it around the waist of the healed one. In so doing the blood soaked robe she wore was covered, so that she would go home without the stain of sorrow showing. Then other women came forth to assist her, and another, and another. It always gladdened my heart to see how women come together to help in times of great need, without a thought, but within a heartbeat, without judgment. I noticed Thomas take sand into his hands, and like the trickle of an hourglass, he let it stream down through his fingers and cover the blood on the ground. I could see him praying, and not a trace of doubt in his face could I detect.

I heard a man calling, "Selene,[131] Selene!" He finally worked his way through the crowd and approached the women's group that was assisting the newly healed mother. It became apparent that Selene was, none other than, the mother we had just worked with, or I should say 'served,' for surely healing is never work, but rather a service.

Selene's husband found her being assisted by helpful women. He gently picked her up and carried her in his arms, while her sister explained the situation. He could see that the spark of life was burning brighter in her face. When he last saw her, he thought she was near death's door. He walked away with her cradled safely in his arms and hugged to his chest. He stopped, turned and looked back across the crowd. He was a tall man and could see over the heads of those between us, and simply offered a grateful smile to MiryAmah and me. We needed nothing more, and didn't need that gesture, but we were glad for his recognition, so clear by the expression upon his face. We knew that the healing was successful in more ways than one.

Some of the men had tears in their eyes, at the living example of how truth reveals the divine through healing and the example of love at its finest between a man and wife. Other men, especially those of the ruling class, which had been keeping themselves separate in a small group, were not so happy, and they were shouting insults at MiryAmah and me, for defiling the Lord's Day. I sensed that things could become dangerous since the crowd was

---

[131] The woman healed on the Sabbath. Greek origin, it is likely connected to the word selas (σέλας), *meaning* 'brightness' also means 'brightness of the moon'

taking sides and getting agitated. I asked my wife to remove herself and her disciples to safety. She reluctantly did so, not out of wife obedience, but rather out of respect and concern for the women who followed her. In the eyes of my enemies, not only had I broken the law of the Sabbath, but I had involved a woman in the crime. Anger and fear are a dangerous combination.

I faced my accusers and asked, "Would you rather see that woman die, her family lose their mother and a man his much loved wife, so that your rule would be obeyed as you have ordained it? Surely, God didn't make a rule that wouldn't honor love and compassion, and life itself."

One pompous fellow stepped forth and said, "God was punishing her for not being good enough to bear a son, thus you have interfered in God's plan, and that is a grievous crime." Evidently the essence of the situation had traveled fast through the crowd like a mighty tidal wave and everyone understood that there was a healing, while not all agreed with it.

"I tell you this woman holds no sin," I said, "Rather it's you who judge her that commit the sin, because you haven't honored the tragedy or success of love. Your lack of compassion is 'un-Godlike'. You and those who make rules that hurt and deny mothers and others the compassion they deserve are what offends God."

"Blasphemy!" someone yelled. Then someone else said, "Along with working on the Sabbath, now he makes blasphemous statements, speaking for God and not even a priest."

"I am a priest, as my wife is also a priestess," I responded, "but that doesn't matter. Our calling isn't of the same spirit that yours is. We were trained that suffering is never unattended, no matter what day or hour."

The mood of the crowd had shifted. Those in opposition to our teachings became more aggressive and loud. They pushed the others aside, and since many of them held power and position, the people dared not oppose them. One of the men closest to me said,

"You sound like the dirty Samaritans! Are you a Samaritan priest then?"

I just looked at him in silence. Then I quietly took in all the judgmental harsh faces now staring at me, which made them become uncomfortable. It's interesting how a penetrating look and silence can speak louder than words. Since I had learned to read hearts and auras (or the energetic fields), as a young child, I just looked at the lack of brilliance in the auric fields of the aggressive accusers. When the occasion warrants I can see past-actions in individuals; memory of their actions and reactions dances within the aura that surrounds people. These men had murky depressing energy surrounding them. I noticed one man, in particular, the one doing most of the talking, and could read his aura like a book.

"Jacobus,[132]" I said. He looked at me wondering how I knew his name, since he had been anonymously sent by the High Priest of the temple within the community, to observe me, not to get to know me or reveal his identity.

"How is it, you know my name?" he angrily asked.

"I know you more than you would like me to," I responded. "You once ran a Samaritan's cart off the road. His donkey was trapped in the traces of the cart in the ditch, and you laughed at him and told him to get out of the way, when someone of your status moved through. You didn't attempt to help him, and just went on your merry way, leaving him to solve the problem alone. The donkey died and the man lost his only means of supporting his family–all because you felt superior to him." This was a common occurrence, and I thought of Nod, the smithy, and Dankin and was glad that I could help them.

"So what!" he replied, leaning forward with his fists on his hips and a snarl on his face. "How can I remember how many of those scoundrels I have cleared from the road? They need to show more respect."

---

[132] 'Holder of the heel' or 'supplanter'. Takes position by force

## The Saga-Oracle

"Yet, when you were just a babe within the sacred womb of your mother, and you decided to emerge before your time, it was a Samaritan, who found her collapsed in early labor by the well, took her in and eased her pain, so that she could hold you a while longer, and thus ensure your survival," I revealed to him.

Jacobus looked puzzled as I said this, then his expression changed to anger. "How could you know this? Surely, you lie!" he shouted, clearly irritated. His older sister was in the crowd. He looked her way and could read the truth of my revelation on her face. He then raged and screamed, "My father told me my mother died, because of the poison the Samaritans fed her and because of them, I had no mother to hold me as a child!"

"No, Jacobus," I said, feeling compassion for the son who never knew his mother and missed her tenderness in his growing years. "Because of them, you lived. She died, because they couldn't save you both, and she begged them to save you. Out of love she chose you, and out of respect and love, they helped her survive long enough to bring you forth. What they did was help her accomplish the last gift she could give her family–you."

He seemed confused. His face showed the struggle between hate and love, but his long-held attitudes couldn't be penetrated by this tale. He finally said, in a most forceful low voice, "You are a sorcerer and evil." Then he turned and walked away.

I could feel his hate puncture me as he left, and I near buckled under the load of such resentment. That kind of hate squashes whomever it is aimed at. Just as nausea was about to overcome me, a small hand touched mine, and I immediately felt relief. I looked down and there standing beside me was the child again. He said, "Brother. I think this bird needs his feathers changed to a different color. All that brilliance and no heart is dangerous."

327

# MOTHER'S SURPRISE
## Chapter Twenty-Nine

It would take volumes and volumes of dialog, to untangle the web of stories you've heard in the records of my life, and that web is difficult, if not nearly impossible to unravel. I only relate how it felt to be me in this tale I tell. I don't attempt to justify, nor link myself to the records of old. It's my story, I share, not their story, or history, for that matter, since that is always the tale of the victors. Even my beloved wife and I would have slightly different memories of our life experiences within the time we remember, since what impacted us emotionally shaped our memory and remains our truth from our own unique perspective.

However, both MiryAmah and I wanted to shift the scales of balance, so that it would begin to find its grail position[133] at the personal level, and also reflected out into the social arenas. That relationship, we believed, would be the foundation of a better life and less suffering for all creation within the playing fields of Tara. We were trained in the old religion of Mu, along with other ancient spiritual traditions. Due to our wonderful teachers and the knowledge they shared, we knew that always, when there was imbalance of the principles of masculine and feminine, there were losers and winners, so-to-speak, and the losers were many, while the winners were few. Those who perceived themselves as winners (victors) would do anything to hold onto their misguided status. That elitism is the root of all judgments that lead to suffering. My beloved and I wanted to go as deep as we could–to the very foundation of the corrupted concept–and build a solid foundation of balance, so that suffering would stop and people could work together to reach their earthly and spiritual goals. Idealistic, you may think. Indeed it was, and still is, but there is divinity in being idealistic, because one acknowledges that it is possible to achieve what the divine planner envisioned all creation could be—perfect.

---

[133] A symbol of the balance of power in its perfection, not tilted to patriarchy or matriarchy, but as perfectly balanced as the sacred holy grail cup that all seek within themselves

## The Saga-Oracle

Sadly, even among our followers the attitude of superiority could disrupt our teachings. MiryAmah, my beloved high priestess wife, had to keep her contribution hidden, for the most part, with only a few chosen ones realizing her mastra status. This weighed heavily on my heart, and I hoped to live long enough to allow her the glory she deserved and queen-ship[134] she represented. Even so, she didn't seem to mind the suppression and often said she was my most loyal follower. When she voiced her devotion, I frequently told her, "No, I'm your loyal follower and will gladly follow you anywhere, my beloved, in this physical world or within the heavens, for I pledge my love and devotion forever."

Little did we know how far we would have to follow each other and to what ends those journeys would take us. She usually positioned herself at my feet during my teachings. Her presence was a calming influence, as she quietly sat there upon the ground beside me, as I shared the parables. She anchored and honored me, especially when she lovingly looked up keeping silent, but saying so much through those beautiful eyes. Her devotion, and love, was my channel of strength. She knew that whenever she wanted to speak, she could. She just chose to be my strength, and allowed me the space and energy I needed to tell my tales of balance and love.

Mother would often visit us, but seldom followed us. She just showed up here and there, and by some odd coincidence, she would have lodging already arranged for MiryAmah and me and the followers who accompanied us. She was what you might term, 'an underground network specialist,' and was more reliable than the town criers at getting the word out that I would be sharing the teachings of 'The Way'.

We met mother in the little village just outside of Jerusalem months later. We were heading to Jerusalem for the festival of Passover. I noticed that she had the child from the garden with her. She told us to come to a little village nearby later and walked back the way she had come.

---

[134] In a soulful sense, as queen, or leader of the Sacred Feminine

We knew that there would be multitudes of people present for the Passover in Jerusalem, and we also were aware of the legend of the messiah who offered the oppressed hope of a better day. It was an old tale in which a savior would ride through the city gates one day on a young white ass.[135] White animals were always considered gifts of God and sacred messengers. Since we had planned to make a dramatic entry, so that we could gain the ears and eyes of the crowds, we decided to play the role that was spoken of in prophesies from long ago. It was always hoped that someday, someone would come and save the oppressed people from the suffering others inflicted upon them, so we believed this was the best time and place to gain the attention of those wishing to make a positive change. The people were always looking and hoping for the redeemer, and in many ways, I was the one they sought.

We had to bring a few details together, however, like finding a white donkey colt for me to ride through the golden gate of the city. That was purely a dramatic ploy, because we needed to gain support and respect from the crowd to accomplish our goal, so decided to play into the legend. Our goal was to challenge the practice of sacrifice for the Jewish Passover holiday, and to show that God's angels didn't need the literal blood of a lamb to spare the innocent, as they avenged evil. In fact, we wanted to teach the multitudes that avenging anything was never the answer, that only forgiveness would wipe away sin. That was a politically dangerous stance for us to take, and we knew it was pushing the limits and possibly dangerous.

As we prepared for our grand entry, all the followers, men and women alike, were nervous. There had been talk that Caiaphas,[136] the high priest, would cause some trouble for us, should we show up. He not only stood to lose control of the crowds should they listen to our message, but he also feared the business of Passover might be affected, too. He made a lot of money from selling sacrificial animals, which were mainly lambs, goats and white

---

[135] Donkey

[136] Caiaphas was the high priest of Jerusalem who, according to Biblical accounts, sent Jesus to Pilate for his execution

doves. Caiaphas also held a personal vendetta against me, since I had rescued and taken into our fold, his daughter, Sarah. MiryAmah and I had found her at a community well, beaten nearly to death–first by her father for not accepting an elder Roman statesman as her arranged husband; then by the townspeople who thought she was too beautiful and independent to appreciate her blessings, and thus she deserved to lose them. They beat her even worse than her angry father had. Hate and jealousy are a terribly destructive force. Poor Sarah was as close as anyone can come to being totally destroyed–body, mind and spirit–when we found her. Her beautiful face was torn, her spirit crushed, and her body broken. When we came upon her, she looked like a heap of discarded laundry lying by the well. We noticed that the pile of dirty laundry covered a body, and we originally thought her dead. MiryAmah discovered a slight pulse, however and asked me to carry this poor discarded human to our present sanctuary, where the priestesses could try to save her. Beauty, in any form, was victimized in many ways.

Caiaphas, the high priest, was an extremely jealous man. The elder Roman, to whom he betrothed his daughter, would have been an exceptionally powerful ally for him, and afforded him even more power and control over the people. Caiaphas lusted for power. He loved authority more than he loved God, who he professed to be serving. He knew the Roman elder was cruel, but that didn't cause him concern. Sarah, in his mind, was too headstrong. He felt such a match would be good for him and good for her, in that she would finally be put in her place. She reminded him of her mother, who he had rid himself of long ago, replacing her with a more manageable wife–not quite as beautiful, however. What good was beauty if you couldn't control it, he reasoned?

Thus, while I dreaded the vengeance of Caiaphas, I knew that our mission had reached a critical moment, and I had to push my fears aside and follow my heart. At this point, we either made a bold statement or faded away. To fade away would be un-thinkable, since so many had prayed for the change we came to initiate, and countless others had suffered for the sake of the divine mission already. Down deep inside our minds and hearts, we all knew we couldn't turn back now, just because things might be more difficult. We would play messiah if that would get the attention of the people. In reality, weren't we already messiahs, one and all? Certainly, anyone who understood their true relationship with the Prime Creator we call God, was a messiah, since all creation is 'of God,' thus God incarnate, which we often discussed. That was the hardest concept for most to accept, especially our closest followers, hence it kept coming up repeatedly in our inner-circle, as our followers wrestled with the idea. All their lives they had been taught that they were unworthy, and that to love and affirm the self was blasphemy. Blasphemy, the man-made crime, usually resulted in a death sentence and the fear of the accusation was more powerful than the realization of divine truth. All this death, and suffering, was rationalized, because the leaders of religion convinced the multitudes that God was a vengeful deity, and that they were one-and-all, sinners. The imprints of lies were deeply ingrained.

The dangerous message that 'all were chosen', was what Caiaphas didn't want the people to know. If they knew, why would they come to him and his priest followers to purchase sacrificial animals, or to buy forgiveness, or to trade their riches for blessings? He was also determined to make sure that Sarah found no happiness, since she challenged his authority by not being obedient. To allow her to live would diminish him, he believed, thus his bruised pride plotted revenge.

Some of the followers were sent into the city, previous to the day of the grand entry, to prepare the crowds. We often sent people in, to judge the energy of the place and the mood of the crowds. Our people this time, however, dropped hints that the messiah was coming and as a result began a great anticipation, especially among those excluded from the blessings of the Passover celebration, because they weren't important enough, or rich enough, thus not the 'chosen ones'. They were the lost sheep I mentioned in parables from time to time, lambs all, sacrificial offerings lost by the very shepherds who were supposed to watch over them. When I spoke of the 'good shepherd', and later was called such, I was talking about the good religious leaders who would leave the larger flock and seek out the lost lamb and save it, not sacrifice it! There were so many lost lambs among the people, and the shepherd-priests seldom cared about them, unless they enriched them personally. What could a mere poor lamb do, when a priest, or shepherd, was fleecing an entire flock! During this time such concepts as ours were indeed radical. More and more, those who held the reins of command were seeing me as a troublemaker, dangerous to their sense of security.

The nearby town where mother had arranged for us to stay was a peaceful quiet little village and the perfect place for us to rest. When we arrived, she greeted us as usual, giving MiryAmah a warm hug and then a mother's kiss on the cheek for me. This time she introduced me to little Simon, the child I met on our wedding day. He greeted me as a brother again. I thought he had just adopted me, and I asked mother where she found this delightful child, thinking she may have adopted another child as she did little Salome,[137] who had saved me at the place of discard long ago.

She looked at me and said, "I found him the same place I found you, dear heart." And then she looked down to her own belly and rubbed it.

I must have looked quite astonished, for clearly she gave an indication that she had birthed the child with this gesture, and I knew nothing of such an occurrence until this moment. I just stared at her with my mouth agape, and she laughed at me.

"This child, Jeshua, I assure you, is born of love and has lived within the priestess sanctuaries. I thought it was time that he came out and met the world, especially you, his true brother," she explained.

I looked down at him astonished, and he just shrugged his little shoulders. I said, "We've met before a time or two, here and there, and never did I sense our brotherhood." He nodded his head, confirming that he had indeed been on the fringes of my presence, and I think he was delighted that he had kept the secret so expertly from an adult no less.

---

[137] Alenesha's adopted name as she became Jeshua's sister

I imagine he was about six or seven years of age, maybe younger. His hair was snow white with a tinge of reddish highlights, quite unusual for a child of this region. I wondered how mother could have kept this secret from me for so long. She must have read my mind, because she answered my question before I had a chance to ask it.

"Son," she said, "just as in your case, there are children who are in danger from those who would judge them not worthy to live, because of how they look, when or where they were born, or who their parents might be. The children can't hide their natural wisdom and compassion, which speaks volumes with each glance they make. I had to send you away to keep you safe, and so you would be prepared for your mission, did I not?" she questioned. Then she said, "It broke my heart to have to say goodbye to you so often. Joseph was older and a stepson grown before I met him, and I never got to be a part of his childhood. James came along so I could spoil a son as I wished I could you and for a time I enjoyed this brother of yours. Then too, James grew up, as you did, my dear one, especially after your father, Joseph, passed on. I thought I would never love again, nor see the manifestation of love through the eyes of another sweet child. Nevertheless, I did find love, Jeshua," she said, with the sweetest voice of remembrance, "and I was blessed with a child of that love."

I was still dumbfounded and bid my mother to come sit with me in the shade of a nearby grape arbor. We settled in the shadow of the vineyard. MiryAmah was close by as usual. She looked towards me and nodded, and moved away, giving us our privacy for a talk long overdue.

"Why have you waited so long to tell me of this brother, mother?" I asked, as I watched Simon take MiryAmah's hand and go off with her.

"Because you were otherwise occupied with your work and because the man I loved was not exactly a logical or understandable pairing for me," she answered. Then she looked away and gazed into the now-setting sun that lit up the sky in beautiful blues and pinks, delicate like mother. She turned back, looked at me and said, "Jeshua, Simon's father is Roman, a soldier, and he kills people. He is bigoted and thinks that the Romans are so superior, they should prosper and others should not. He is the most unlikely man for me to fall in love with. I didn't know what had got into my heart, much less my head, when I became involved with him, but I couldn't help myself. I could see past his insecurities and his bigotry, and I knew that I had loved him before and would most likely love him again, beyond my choosing. I simply couldn't help it, son," she said, searching my face for understanding. "I reasoned that I'm a priestess, and as such, I can take lovers as I choose, so I gave in to my passion, which I know would have won the battle, no matter what I might have intended. Yet, I didn't think I would conceive another child at my age. When I found myself blessed again, the entire relationship took a different turn, becoming more complicated, for now there was another soul involved in this affair of the heart. At that point, I ended up having to make a choice between my priestess ways and the way of the Romans. I chose the priestess-hood. Even though I loved this man dearly, and we certainly must have been lovers in other lifetimes, I couldn't leave the sisterhood. Your father, Joseph, never asked me to do so, and he was such a gentle and wise man. I was fortunate to have the years with him, I had. I never believed I would love another, but it happened," she said in a very low voice, not a voice of shame but a voice of gentle truth.

I hugged her to my chest, and she knew that I wouldn't judge her, but still she cried tears of relief. When she stopped her sobbing, she continued on with the story. I knew finally, she had to tell me this tale of her life, how love had visited her again, because to keep it secret any longer would be to somehow separate us from each other, and we had been separated too much in my lifetime.

She continued, saying, "I'll not discuss who Simon's father is, for I don't think it's important to reveal him. I also want to keep his present life from being complicated by the love we shared and the result of that love, our dear Simon. When Simon was born, my Roman lover didn't know that I was with child. I finally told him when Simon was about three months of age. He wanted me to be his wife and to claim we adopted the child, saying his true mother had died at the time of emergence, or childbirth. Making this request meant that he loved me, for Romans often had lovers and seldom wed them, just because a child resulted from their unions. However, he wanted me to give up all contact with the sisters, and to run his household and to birth more children as a dutiful wife should. In short, he wanted a Roman marriage."

"I couldn't serve such bondage, and I told him I didn't know why I loved him as I do, but that I couldn't give up my sisterhood, nor probably would I ever be lucky enough to conceive another child. Simon, this late in my years, was a miracle beyond measure, I told him, and anymore children would be asking too much of my body. I told him that I couldn't be a proper mother in my elder years. He knew this was true, but he loved me and wanted to believe what suited him. I said that one day he would realize that what he needed was a wife, much younger and stronger, especially one not so independently oriented. That statement must have awakened him, for in a flash, after I mentioned the younger wife, he had a surge of anger, even as I felt the instant loss of his love. He screamed at me, saying that this child was no son of his; stormed out of my humble home and I never saw him again. He sent spies to watch for a while, so I moved to the underground sanctuary nearby my little house, taking my newborn with me of course, fearing he would do something drastic to this babe I loved so dearly. Even in the sanctuary I felt threatened by his fear and anger over my rejection, so I gave my house away and began moving from sanctuary to sanctuary, enjoying the love and companionship of the sisterhood.

"Simon, I have to say, at times is quite the wild-child. He has much passion for life, and his imagination seems endless. He is even more independent than you were, Esa. Since the sisters all shared in his watching, I think some of them allowed him explorations I might not have approved." She looked over at Simon playing with the children of our followers and love for the child was written all over her face.

"I'm blessed by my mother, as my brother is, too," I said. "A child born of passionate love is doubly blessed. So many children are born of duty and conceived in imposed shame, with their true divinity unrecognized according to the old priests."

"Once, mother," I said, "we did a teaching upon a hillside, and the children showed us how to perform the greatest of miracles, which was to open hearts to love and close the doors of fear. These children, because they believed in themselves and in idealistic dreams, were able to make the very trees tremble. I know that Simon is a child who believes in miracles, because he is a miracle. Maybe someday, somehow, he'll open the heart of his own father. Regardless, I love him with all my heart. I don't care who his natural father is, for his Divine Father is the same Father of us all. I just wish I could have helped you with this little brother of mine during your time of heartache. I pity the man who didn't understand the gift of your love, and I pity him the loss of a beautiful son and his glorious priestess mother."

Mother shed a large crystalline tear; it slid down her cheek at hearing what I said. Then quickly she changed the subject and said, "Son, now what are you planning to do in the great city?"

I only told her of the essence of our goal, not the details. She could tell I was keeping a lot from her, due to love and consideration, and she looked at me with a wrinkled worried brow.

"Don't worry, mother," I said. "I know what I am doing."

"I hope so, son." she said. "I hope so." I could tell she was trying to convince herself that I would be safe.

# THE CROWN I DID NOT WANT
Chapter Thirty

As the celebration of Passover was about to begin, great crowds gathered in Jerusalem. It was an opportunity to reach the masses of people, who would be on pilgrimage to celebrate the occasion. Our message was beginning to worry the powers that be, especially Caiaphas, the high priest. Sarah, his daughter, now our devoted friend and follower, worried about the revenge her father could wage. She warned me not to underestimate his wrath. I had no idea of the scope of his hate.

Philip, one of the apostles came into our Bethany camp (which Mother had arranged) with a tiny white ass colt on the morning previous to my famous entry through the gates of Jerusalem. By playing into the legend of the Messiah, we felt we could reach more people who yearned for a savior. Nevertheless, we knew it would be a massive threat to the priesthood and to the Roman overseer of the region, Pontius Pilate. We even discussed the possibility of death resulting from our boldness, but we hoped that the people would protect me, believing that I was a divine savior. With all due trust and faith we proceeded with the plan. We intended to skirt the law, rather than to outright break it.

Shaking my head, I looked at the tiny white yearling donkey, saying to Philip, "Surely my friend, you wouldn't subject this poor little creature to carry such as me through the gates of the city?" I feared the poor thing would drop on the spot, or become swaybacked for life, or at least become bow-legged, all of which would diminish its ability to work as a pack animal ever again. It was barely a year old after all and so small.

Philip looked at me with a pleading look and replied, as he beckoned me to look closer with his hands, and said, "Master, I have looked long and hard to find the perfect animal for your service—one that would match the requirement for the legend." He then said with a look of remorse, "The only other alternative I can think of is to white-wash a bigger animal, and surely you wouldn't ask that. Pure white donkeys are rare. I had no choice."

Using the language of animal-speak, I looked at the tiny little white colt, and I could hear him tell me, as his big brown eyes pierced my own, that he was very strong, and that he would bear me proudly upon his back, if only I would trust him. I conveyed my concern that I would damage his young back. He assured me he was strong enough, and he added that he was born for this task, and pleaded that I would not deny him his soul mission. He reminded me of 'Little One,' the donkey that my mother rode to Bethlehem just before I was born. She had served our family for years and was also young at the time of her service; She, too, convinced father, that she was born for the task. I must say, I instantly loved this little white fellow and consequently, accepted him as my proud steed for the grand entrance into the city. Both he and Philip were relieved. I, however, wondered how ridiculous the sight would be–a big man on the little white donkey. I'm not above vanity and never was as perfect as some would have you believe, and the thought of such a ridiculous sight crossed my mind. Then I spoke to God, saying inside my head, "You do test my determination, don't you?"

My beloved MiryAmah and I seldom had personal time together outside our inner-circle, because few knew of our relationship as man and wife. We had been man and wife a mere seven months, but didn't publicize our union. We had enemies, and I didn't want to endanger MiryAmah. There was also the custom of men and women remaining separate while in public, which was enforced in some places and not in others. We had to comply with the regional customs, in order to have a chance to teach. Jerusalem was one of those places that had a strict code of separation of men and women in public, married or not.

I was up especially early the day after Philip located the perfect steed for my grand entry into the holy city. I think I was probably a bit anxious. I hoped this early morning, that I might have a little time for myself and my wife just before sunrise. I walked to the place the women stayed and gently called her name. She was already there waiting for me, dressed and sitting on a rock outside the compound where the women slept. She read my intentions before I could announce them, so this wasn't surprising, even as it was unexpected and appreciated.

"It's about time you arrived," she said. We chanced a private greeting kiss and walked together to a garden on the outskirts of the village. It was a place where they grew grapes and where olive trees shaded flowers that were too sensitive for the sun's direct rays. The owner of the garden was a friend and had told us to come for some quiet time, whenever we wanted. The garden had paths winding through the olive groves and the keeper of this orchard loved the delicate flowers that grew in the shade. There were beds of these flowers, in shades of pink, white and blue, on either side of the path as we walked. It was enchanting, to say the least, and I was glad that we had the opportunity to accept the kind invitation of this master gardener who we loved and trusted. We discovered a bench, uniquely situated in a semi-circle of olive trees, deep in the grove. The tree limbs had been trained and molded to form an arch over the seating accommodation, giving it shade and privacy. We settled into the grotto to watch the morning sun find its fullness over the horizon.

MiryAmah was in her $7^{th}$ month of pregnancy now. Her belly bulged under her robes ever so slightly, unnoticed by those not knowing her condition. Among the women, the $7^{th}$ month was a time of confirmation. It was assurance of the likely emergence of the gift of the mother, and the blessing to the father.

"I feel the impatience of your child," MiryAmah said to me, as she touched her belly gently. "She wants to come forth and be proof of our marriage, and especially of our great love."

I put my hand upon her rounded stomach beside her hand, feeling the active babe within. I took my hand away for a moment, put my ear upon the raised abdomen and said, "Speak to me, daughter, for your father can't wait to hear your sweet voice."

I heard her speak to me, as clearly as I hear the inner-voice of the animals. She sweetly said, "Father, I fear that you will not be able to be with me in my baby years. Please be careful in what you say and do, because I have great need of you and mother, even as I love you more than any need could require. Please take care." A child not yet born doesn't baby-talk and my child's voice was the ageless voice of her soul.

MiryAmah asked, "What does our sweet babe say to you, dear heart?" I didn't want to alarm my wife, since this part of pregnancy is so critical to the survival of the child, so I simply said, "She wants me to assure her that I will be a dutiful father."

"She!" MiryAmah remarked, "I was right then. We'll have our wish for a firstborn to be a daughter?" We could have determined this information in many ways, including some old priestess predictive processes, but we wanted to be surprised, so hearing me refer to the babe in the womb, as 'she' was a slight slip-up. MiryAmah had called her 'she' as well.

## The Saga-Oracle

Trying to assure my wife, who was still uncertain if she would bear a son or daughter, and knowing she would love both equally, I said, "I have a strong feeling the voice I heard was that of a daughter, my love, but should I be wrong I would love the son who holds such a gentle vibration as well."

Full sunrise arrived too soon for us, and we knew that we had to regroup our followers for the mission of the day. There was sadness and worry in MiryAmah's eyes, as she looked long and hard at me, just before we headed back to the others. After one very long passionate kiss, we reluctantly parted to be about our individual tasks.

My apostles were already preparing the little white donkey when I arrived back at the men's sleeping compound. They had the animal all decked out in bright colors, which its pure white coat complemented perfectly. I noticed red tassels protruding from behind its large ears, which made them look even longer and more prominent. I had to laugh to myself, and thought I was glad it wasn't my ears that they put those crazy decorations on. They were also busy going over the plans of the day that would culminate in a Passover dinner upon the rooftop of one of the follower's relatives. It was the only place we could find that was large enough for our group, including myself, MiryAmah, our followers, plus some children, the householders and a few trusted assistants who would serve the traditional meal. My main concern for the celebratory meal was that usually a lamb would be sacrificed for this occasion. I had instead asked that eggs of the dove be served. I argued that the dove could lay more eggs, which had not yet taken their first breath of life. The lamb had already experienced its first breath and should not be taken from its mother, since the sorrow of the separation would be against our message, that all creation be allowed its chance to reach its full potential. To consume an egg was much different than to kill a lamb, I reasoned. It was not a sacrifice, but more an offering of the bird, as it is also ever a symbol of the feminine gift of creation.

This threw the plans off somewhat and Thaddeus[138] asked, "What else shall we ask to be served then?" He had already made arrangements for our food and prided himself in accommodating everyone to the best of this ability. Evidently, he believed that the meat of the lamb was the cornerstone of the meal, since it was the lamb's blood traditionally, that was thought to alert the angels to pass by (Passover) a household in the days of the exodus in Egypt. He thought the occasion warranted the flesh and blood of a sacrificial lamb. I wondered–had he really been listening all the times we spoke of the waste of sacrifice and how the God of gods, the Divine Creator, would never create something to be wasted in the mistaken idea that God wanted innocent blood to be shed? This concept was a huge part of our mission intention during the celebration of Passover, and I insisted that we hold true to our convictions.

"As far as I'm concerned, only unleavened bread and wine is necessary," I said, "but I'm sure the householder has some contributions to that rather limited menu." I then told him to send Peter and John to assist and prepare the Seder (Passover) meal with the eggs of doves instead of the sacrificed lamb." I could see that Thaddeus was not thrilled with the change in the menu, but obediently he complied and my attention went to other preparatory tasks. Thaddeus was the apostle who could accomplish what others thought impossible. I had no doubt; he could shift his plans for our meal without sacrificing the sanctity of it.

The women were organizing the laying of the palm boughs, which would be part of my entry into Jerusalem, and were bundling and loading them onto their backs. Some were already at the city by the gates awaiting my arrival, which was planned for mid-morning. I may have had stage fright, because I was beginning to feel a bit weak in the knees, but when the time came, I took my seat upon the tiny little white donkey, and we proceeded toward the gateway with my caravan of followers behind me. The last of the women arrived at the gate just moments before me. There were crowds already gathering in anticipation of my arrival, and waving

---

[138] A term of endearment meaning 'dear one' or 'courageous one' given to St. Jude

the palm boughs in glee, that the women had distributed. The oppression, and depression, of the people ran far and deep and the possibility of a messiah compelled them forth in great droves.

This massing of the crowd brought the attention of the officials; both from the Priest, as well as the ruling Roman segment. I knew my enemies, there among the welcoming crowd of people, were watching me, and it made my skin crawl, because I felt their intense hate.

I prayed that the little white donkey would bear my weight long enough to move through the gate. To have him collapse would be the opposite message, my group and I wanted to convey, but he bore me proudly and firmly. He managed to prance at the apex of our entry as the shouts of joy from the multitude energized him. The women began laying the palms to carpet my path and quickly others in the crowd followed suit. I must say I felt elated and blessed by the reception. I chanced to see Caiaphas on the edge of the crowd. The look on his face was pure evil, as his stare pierced me and then shifted to his daughter Sarah, now our faithful follower, too. She was among those laying palms down directly in front of me, and I saw her shiver for a moment, as she noticed her father. She glowed with the joy of her service to the point that the ugly scars upon the right side of her face (that her father had inflicted) nearly faded from sight. In his anger, he intended to take away her beauty, because she wouldn't do his evil bidding. Another chill ran through me at that point because his expression of utter hate shook me, as I couldn't fathom how a father could ever hate his own child with such intensity. I had to refocus my attention on the joy of the crowd, or I would sacrifice this moment of elation and triumph. I was determined that our mission would not be diminished by the high priest's hatred.

As soon as I passed through the gates, I dismounted from the little donkey and proceeded to the temple, where I planned to protest the slaughter of the Passover lambs and free the doves. The crowd followed me into the temple grounds. As it became apparent what my intentions were, the venders were not pleased. They had anticipated an impressive day of profits from the sacrificial lambs and doves. Due to my message, their sales suffered as never

## Jeshua's Song

before, and they watched their potential earnings fly away, as cage after cage of doves were tumbled. The lambs were freed as well and ran for their lives, out of the temple gate, back to their mothers.

The issues at hand consumed the rest of the day, and we made our point repeatedly. As the sun was finally setting, we found our way to the home of our host for the Passover celebration meal. We had a code for our invited guests, since we wanted to feel safe and secure within this blessed moment. We devised a system in which those who would attend this sacred banquet would go to the well and follow a guide who had a bright red water jug, to the appointed place. Jugs were usually terracotta or goat skins so this, we thought, was a safe way to get all of us to one place and still keep it secret. There were three wells in the vicinity, and we had guides posted at each place. It wasn't a time to feed the multitudes, which we had done many times–once by multiplying fishes and loaves of bread. That moment was for a different purpose, to show how the law of abundance worked. To accomplish our task that day we had to pull some advanced training into the teaching moment. This evening, however, wasn't the time for the miracles that caught the attention of the masses. It was a private celebration for families who, during the original Passover, and on the anniversary of that day since, come together to pray and ask for the forgiveness and protection of God. We were a family now–perfect and imperfect as all families are.

Upon arrival at the place of our meal, I noticed that there were already several red water jugs at the doorstep, indicating that most of the others had arrived. My beloved wife approached me waiting outside the doorway, not wanting to enter the portal until she could do so with me. I wanted to kiss her again, passionately, as we did when we parted from the olive garden this morning, but I couldn't do so in this more public place. I took her hand and kissed her with my eyes, and she responded with a like kiss that only two in love such as we, would have understood.

"The others are within awaiting your arrival, my beloved," she said as she hugged me, and then she chanced a little kiss upon my cheek, and we entered the humble abode.

## The Saga-Oracle

There wasn't a long table, as depicted in some of the popular artwork, which has come down through the centuries, rather many lounges and pillows were used and we ate like the Romans did, in leisurely positions, placing our food and utensils upon the floor nearby. Before the meal, we spoke of the day's events and of each task we had accomplished, then we pretty much followed the traditions of the Passover rituals, doing the cleansing of hands, (our hosts had already cleansed the house) and remembering the events of the exodus. After the purification, those who went to the temple with us spoke of how angry the venders were, yet how relieved the pilgrims seemed, when I made my point about moneychangers in the temple. The others who were assigned to other tasks, like preparation of this meal, or keeping watch of priests and soldiers, spoke of their day as well.

Judas was especially elated by the success of the day, and he asked me, "Master, now do you see that the people surely would have you as King?"

I looked at my dear friend, who I had known since youthful days, and I felt sorrow for him. He clung to a vision of me being a King, a ruler of the land. I had discussed this issue with him many times, saying, "Surely you know, Judas, that should I take a crown, I would also have to take up a sword and kill with it." Remembering that conversation, which we discussed numerous times, I gave him a sympathetic look, shook my head and said, "Oh Judas, what am I to do with you and your King vision?" Little did I know, that he had met with a Roman soldier whom he believed was supportive of our cause and the two of them had decided I would be crowned this very night.

My greatest challenge was that, while everyone wanted me to be an instrument of change, even among my closest followers, the role I would play within that change differed in their own minds and hearts, depending on what they idealized. Some wanted a messiah. Since I had decided to play into that role, they felt like their vision was correct. Some wanted a master teacher. Maybe that idea was more accurate; except that I wanted them to become master teachers, as well, not establish them below my status, but alongside me and my beloved wife. We wanted to be living examples of how men and women should work together, equally important and divine, for the good (God) of all creation. Others had their agendas, as well. I had one apostle who actually loved me to the point he wished to be my physical lover, in the same way that the Romans often took male lovers instead of loving their own wives. The practice was not uncommon, since the Romans occupied our land and their ideas began to be more and more integrated. They felt that to love someone at a deep core level meant that they had power over them, because love was hard to deny. Romans loved power and didn't want to give any of it up, especially to wives and women in general, thus they feared to love their own wives, mothers and daughters. That influence caused many arguments among our followers.

MiryAmah and I had spent considerable time and energy, educating our followers, especially our inner-circle. Attitudes ingrained by the occupying Romans were like demons that ate people up from the inside out, particularly women. The general population had been convinced that suffering was caused by evil spirits. They believed that anyone who suffered deserved the condition, because they housed it within their body. It was a terribly flawed philosophy. The casting out of the seven demons remembered and recorded was MiryAmah and I, demonstrating how the body energy vortexes housed the pain of the corrupted attitudes. Together we purged her body of the residue of the pain in each chakra center[139]. We intended that by doing this, we could symbolically free all women, who would understand the teaching and release the concepts that caused them deep sorrow and shame.

Even though we weren't all yet in the same accord, we still felt closely united to the cause of peace and looked forward to our Passover meal. Finally, the time arrived for us to share the meal, and we enjoyed the offerings, including the eggs of the doves, which had been boiled hard and brined in wine. I didn't have a

---

[139] Chakras are our energy centers. They are the portals for life energy to flow into and out of our body. Their function is to vitalize the physical body and to bring about the development of our self-consciousness. They are associated with our physical, mental and emotional interactions

## The Saga-Oracle

beautiful golden goblet to drink from as some may think, but rather I had a bowl made from olive wood just as the others had. It was the householder who came forth with an alabaster goblet, old and chipped, and asked, "Master, if you would drink from this cup, I and my family would be eternally blessed? It is our treasure and has come down through our family from ages of old, and we hold it most sacred." It reminded me of the alabaster jar in which my wife, MiryAmah, often used to mix her sacred herbs, but was more broad and flat, and the color was deep translucent pink.

To be accommodating, I agreed, poured the wine left in my wooden vessel into the chipped alabaster cup and raised it, saying, "This is the wine that has blessed us with its essence. Blessed is the wine, for it is like our blood that, likewise, blesses us and therefore gives us life."

I raised the cup and all there said, "And so it is," which is much like the 'amen' that developed from the old Egyptian tradition, that some would say to affirm a statement.

I then said, "Before I partake of this blood of the vine, the wine, I want you to remember that the womb is a cup, a sacred vessel and the blood of the womb is like the blood of the vine. Without it, you would not know the blessing of life." I drank the goblet dry. Those few who knew of MiryAmah's expectancy knew full well what I meant. The others thought it was a reference to my divine birth. I had often spoken to them regarding the divine birth of all creation, especially their own birth, but the imprints–the demons if you will–of generations of attitudes that would separate all creation into worthy and unworthy were difficult at best to overcome. Therefore, some understood more than others. I was planting seeds again, in their hearts and minds, and hoping that the essence of my beloved's and my own work would ultimately be understood and shared, through this inner circle of followers who we loved so deeply. We also traditionally broke pieces of the unleavened bread and shared it with each other, symbolically sealing our shared vision and mission. The entire meal was sacredly observed and enjoyed until finally we rested and silently gave thanks for God's blessings.

I noticed Judas leave about that time. Quietly, he slipped out, thinking I didn't observe, but my sensitivity was high, and I was very connected to the mood and presence of everyone present, including the animals that had found their way to the table, which included a stray dog that had leaped from the rooftop next to us. Several of my special friends, the sparrows, now feeling safe in their earth-colored feathers, helped clean up the crumbs and offerings of the diners, too. As Judas took leave, I had a flash of intuition and saw a golden crown form above him as he exited. I knew I saw this mental image, because he intended to push his agenda. I dreaded his return and what I would do, if he tried to crown me King of the Jews, as he often said he would do one day. It wasn't long before he slipped back into our fold. His face wore an expression of extreme disappointment, while he held a small coin bag. He looked at me with such a look of sadness, that it was all I could do to keep my joyful mood intact and not run to comfort him. I quickly looked away and continued with the joy of the Passover celebration, but part of my heart was broken, because I knew something terrible had happened, and it was connected to Judas, who I had loved and trusted for so long.

We finally finished our meal and were very tired. The day had been long and full. We didn't have a place to stay within the walled city of Jerusalem and were too tired to return to Bethany. At this time of the night, the Roman guards at the gates would be a problem, as well. At the suggestion of our host, we decided to go to the garden of Gethsemane where there would be ample room to rest and return to Bethany tomorrow, to prepare for further teachings that we would offer within the area where the returning pilgrims would pass. It was the custom that all Jewish men would take at least three pilgrimages a year to the holy city of Jerusalem and Passover was one of those times most men choose. It was the men whom we had to reach first, to cast out the demons of inequality that would label all things feminine as weak and unclean. That's why we came, at least in MiryAmah's and my mind, it was. We also hoped that the women who bought into this flawed way of thinking would finally cast out the demeaning demons in their hearts and minds, too.

The Gethsemane garden was beautiful even by starlight, which was the only light we enjoyed this late evening after our Passover meal. We entered and found places to rest. I had a terrible feeling within me and asked for some time to pray and reflect on the events just past. I found a rock that supported me and kneeled down to pray. I was suddenly physically weak and nearly overcome with a feeling of dread. Kneeling in front of the rock, I put my forehead upon it for support. As was my custom, I put my hands over my heart and bowed in quiet reflection. I knew that God was the Father to all, even as I knew God was the Mother, too. However, now, with my earthly father long gone to his heavenly home, I prayed to the Holy Father, "Oh God, why do I feel such anxiety and dread? What has transpired, that would bring such a sad feeling over me?" My answer came at that exact moment as Judas, anxious himself, broke into my prayer and asked to speak with me. Peter and Andrew tried to hold him back, since they knew I deserved a moment of privacy after such a long dramatic day. He managed to break through the barrier that the brothers, Peter and Andrew, were creating between us. He looked like he was about to break into tears. He still held tight the moneybag. I though he probably received it as a donation from a follower and wanted to give to me. I wondered why it couldn't wait until morning and why he was so close to tears. Seeing his state of mind, I arose and went towards him, indicating to Peter and Andrew that I was okay with the interruption. Judas embraced and kissed me on my cheek and whispered, "I'm afraid I may have betrayed you."

When I heard his whispered words, I saw instantly what had transpired, like a slow-motion replay of the events. I saw a Roman soldier who had been the actual betrayer. He was sent to befriend someone from my close inner-circle, to find out our intentions. He found that someone in Judas, who shared his vision that I desired to be crowned a king one day. Only, to Judas it was a blessing and to the Roman it was a threat. The Roman agreed to have a crown made, to endear himself to Judas. He would bear the expense, he assured Judas. It was to be ready for the Passover meal, where Judas would crown me as the king he believed I was intended to be.

The soldier had no intention of having a crown cast, however. He just wanted to affirm that I had political intentions, which was not the case, so that he could alert the officers of the Prefect,[140] Pontius Pilate, who sent him. It was planned that he would give Judas thirty pieces of silver instead of a crown, telling him the item was not yet ready, and that he would receive delivery in the morning. The silver, the Roman said, was a donation to our cause for the inconvenience. My enemies knew well that by morning they would have me in custody and also recover the money from Judas. They had the evidence they needed to charge me with crimes against the Jewish nation, in that they believed that I had planned to overthrow the government. Since the venders of sacrifice at the temple had to pay taxes on their sales to the Romans, they would claim that I was against paying Caesar his due, as well. High priest, Caiaphas was pushing Pilate to arrest me. He saw me as a troublemaker, who he hated more than he feared. In his mind, I had rescued his unworthy daughter, who he had condemned to suffering and death, and to go against his wishes was treason in itself, as far as he was concerned. There's no force more evil than hate and power united, and this high priest, in many ways, was more powerful than Pilate, who the Romans had placed in command of the area. The Priest controlled peoples' minds, and the Romans could only threaten them physically, or take their money, or kill them. It was with the threat of the loss of their soul that the priests terrorized people. The priests had convinced them, that, unless they did as the priests dictated God would strike them soul-less and condemn them to everlasting suffering. That became fear's most powerful weapon—the loss of one's soul.

This all flashed through my inner-vision in a second, as my friend Judas kissed me. I could sense his tremendous sorrow, so deep, it was as if an endless black pit had opened up to swallow him. I simply said, "I already forgive you." I hoped it would be enough so that Judas could forgive himself. He loved me with all his heart and soul, and I instantly feared what he might do to himself. It was he who was betrayed, but under the circumstances who would understand?

---

[140] Position of authority, overseer of a region

Just as I whispered to Judas, I heard yelling and Roman soldiers burst into the garden, with the betraying soldier at their forefront. He saw Judas and headed straight for us, knocking Judas away. He grabbed me and threw me to the ground. My head hit the stone path so hard I was nearly knocked senseless, but still I was beaten and carried away. All I was really aware of was screaming. I hoped that my beloved wife didn't see me in this state, or surely she would go into early labor and possibly lose our child. As it turned out, she was so exhausted, that she had fallen asleep with her head on the little white donkey, and was spared the scene that I feared she might see. I'm sure angels kept her asleep through all the commotion. I hoped I would have the wisdom and strength to endure my fate.

# DEATH OF A MESSIAH
Chapter Thirty-One

This is the saddest segment of my life. I knew that our mission had come to a critical point, and as I drifted in and out of consciousness along the pathways of Jerusalem to the office of Pilate, I had no idea that things would deteriorate even further. I had forewarning flashes all day, which cautioned that the situation would shift to the point that men would be in more danger than women. Always, we had to protect our disciple women; now even the apostle men followers had to hide, to guard their own lives from those who would silence their voices. We had often had discussions about such times, when the danger of all of us being killed at once might occur. We reluctantly agreed that the followers must hide so that the message could survive, thus the voices never silenced.

The Romans were complex people. They could be generous and calm one minute, and within an instant, be most violently brutal. That was their culture. While there were gentle-natured people among them, it was the bullies that ruled and conquered the world as we knew it. They seemed to nearly worship meanness, and I noticed that they often became drunk upon cruel actions. Taking me away from the garden became the fuel for the soldiers' malice.

I was smashed repeatedly with fists to sensitive parts of my body, including kicks to the groin and spittle in my face. I saw the look of utter wickedness as it took over these same soldiers who, at the time of my entry into the city, were quite docile even as they remained watchful, no doubt as they were sent to do.

Mercifully, I fell unconscious. When I awoke, a man in rags within a dark chamber of horrors, the prison in the house of judgment near the residence of Pontius Pilate, was gently holding me. The man, a prisoner himself, was wiping my face with a water-soaked rag he had torn from his own tattered garment. Water was precious in such places. He offered more than just compassion, since most likely this may well have been the only water he would have for days. As my eyes opened, he must have sensed my confusion, for he said, "Master, you are within the dungeon of judgment, but you are in the arms of gratitude."

I was confused and too injured to know what he meant by that statement, but I felt comforted being held so gently, even as my body screamed for attention, with its aches and pains. I hurt so badly that I literally sweat blood, which now soaked the cool rag that Dismas[141], the thief, offered to comfort me as best he could.

The atmosphere in the space was extremely quiet, not normal for a room full of shackled and chained prisoners, who typically cried and moaned their sorrow constantly. There were some that could move about freely within the near-total darkness. Overcrowding from the Passover celebration had brought this sad place more prisoners than it was intended to hold.

I could hear questions and answers from those I couldn't see, but sensed present. "Is that the master who so boldly entered the city yesterday?" someone asked.

"Yes, what a brave soul to enter this haven of hell in such a dramatic manner," someone answered.

---

[141] Prisoner with Jeshua in Pontius Pilate's prison, now considered a saint

Then Dismas said, in a voice that echoed off the unseen walls, "Blessed are we to be in this man's company, for God has sent him to free the oppressed and to bring love to everyone, even these Roman bastards who have beat him senseless."

Dismas, who I could feel was muscular and strong, went limp and cried, after his pronouncement. His face drooped over mine, and his tears washed me. Those tears somehow soothed and transferred his great strength to me. I truly believe that if it were not for his tears, I wouldn't have survived this hellhole they called a prison. My injuries were already such that my physical body could easily have given up the spirit then and there.

As strength flowed into me through the sweet/sad tears of this man they called a 'robber and criminal,' I noticed shadows beginning to form on the walls. The shadows indicated that many were close to me, including those chained to the wall in shackles. Soon the shadows began to be more defined, and I realized that another light was coming closer. I saw torches outside the bars, heard the clanking of keys and again saw Roman soldiers, but this time I saw the robes of the priests, too. I felt some relief for surely the priests would not allow such unjust treatment of one of their own people. Little did I know that they were the true enemy, due to their fear of losing status and power, they felt God-given to them. The Romans could become drunk on cruelty, but the priests certainly also became intoxicated on the so-called 'Power of God' they believed they represented. The priests, believing they were the chosen ones, didn't intend to let anyone alter their status.

The captain of the guards had no intention of going into the pits of hell and demanded that the prisoners deliver me to him. He yelled, "Bring Jesus to the gate. I'll not step in your putrid space without being angered." He continued his instructions and threatened further. "If I have to send in my sentry, I'll order him to kill anyone he can reach."

"Dismas," I said, and how I knew his name, I can't remember, "Give me up to them, so I can give you back to God." What I meant, of course, was that I wanted him to survive so that he could live fully the life he was created to explore and experience, thus in my mind, given back to God. He kissed me upon the forehead and arose, picking me up and yelled out, "I bring the one you request." He lifted me quickly, yet gently, and further said, "Tell your guards to put their fists and swords back at their side. There's no need for killing today."

Dismas had given me so much through his watery tears, yet he seemed to still have enough strength to lift and carry me. He walked proudly in the semi-darkened room to the gate. Upon arrival, Caiaphas stepped forth, torchlight reflecting off his gold trimmed robes. He held a posture of importance as he stepped from behind the captain of the guard, now moving to the forefront of the group. Hate is ugly. No matter how beautiful the robes he wore, the look on his face made him grotesque. At that point, I knew that the priesthood would not be my savior, nor would I be theirs. Evidently, Caiaphas wanted to be sure that they retrieved the right person. Upon inspection, he nodded his head to the affirmative, and the guard opened the gate, so that Dismas could bring me forthwith.

"Let the wannabe king walk on his own," Caiaphas said, and Dismas gently set me down upon my feet. The strength he gave me was now taking effect. I felt strong enough to stand on my own and stepped forth. Wisely, Dismas quickly stepped back into the cell, realizing that the soldiers wanted an excuse to beat someone.

I had long hair, which in itself was seen as somewhat obscene to the priests and the Romans, who kept a shorter clip of their locks. Long hair was too feminine in their minds. Women, they believed, used their tresses to tempt men into sin. Caiaphas, grabbing me by my long hair, bending my head back, hissed into my face like a viper about to attack, "You will rue the day that you befriended the likes of Sarah." I could see in his eyes, that this was more about his hatred of his daughter and her mother, than about political or religious issues.

I was pushed and directed to walk ahead of the priests along an inner underground tunnel system, to the chambers of Caiaphas. Even within the pain, I found it strange that the temple was connected to the prison. Emerging into his quarters, I was interrogated, as you would term it now, with all sorts of questions thrown at me, including, 'do I think I'm the son of God, and the king of the Jews?'

Caiaphas wanted to trap me into blasphemy, so that I would break, the so-called sacred law enough to be given the ultimate punishment.

"You know me not, even as I look into your eyes," I replied to his question. I then said, "What I am, so too are you and would you, as the Son of God, condemn your brother?" The historical records have been spin-doctored and Caiaphas himself altered my reply, so that his agenda could be achieved. I'm sad that the confusion of my true intention and response has been reworded and misunderstood.

Again, I was dragged by the hair of my head, only this time blindfolded, to the Court of Judgment where Pontius Pilate,[142] the Prefect of Judea, overseer of the City and nearby territory, would have the final say in the matter. His wife Claudia was a friend of my dear MiryAmah. I hoped that my wife had not put herself in danger and tried to influence the situation through contacting her friend. As I moved along blindfolded, but using skills that I learned as a small boy in the dark tunnels of the high snow mountains to navigate blindly, I was aware of my passage and of those who spat upon me, as I walked past them. Some of the very people I knew were present at the gates of the city during the grand entry, participated in the degradation, and I could feel a shift in their energy. They were caught up in the hope and joy of the crowd at my entry, but now they were equally snagged into the hate and loathing of my captors.

As we passed one man in the courtyard of the temple, he spat upon me. I said, "Jacob Jabiah, I forgive you." Even in my blinded condition, I could sense that his knees gave way, and he collapsed. He didn't expect me to know his name. The full scope of his

---

[142] Overseer, or fifth Prefect of Judea, appointed by Julius Caesar, the Roman Emperor

fickleness immediately depleted his strength, when he realized his betrayal.

Caiaphas shouted, "Don't let Jesus threaten anyone, guards, shut his mouth now!" A rock hard fist found my face once again. Hot blood poured from my mouth, and I could feel some broken teeth. I spit them out and said blindly, to the one who just hit me, "I forgive you, too." Expecting a less than gracious response, I had the presence of mind to duck. His fist went past me and somehow hit one of the priests, who went sprawling to the ground. The priest had been positioned on my right side and the words that came forth from him were not temple words, I assure you. At that time, however, we arrived at the doorway of the Judgment Chamber and there was no time for repercussions, since Pilate was expecting us forthwith.

I could hear the echo from the floor as my sandals slapped the surface with each step. It was as if all my senses were compensating for the blindfold I wore and everything was magnified tenfold. I could smell the sweat of the soldiers, as it merged with their leather garments and weapon sleeves. The clinking of their weapons sounded like a symphony out of harmony. That, along with the swishing of the silky priest vestments, sounded cold and impersonal. The smell of incense on the priests' robes was sickening. The entire parade was like a terrible nightmare, where everything had been inverted to wickedness.

Finally, we arrived in a space that echoed more than the others, and I felt the openness of a large circular room. They told me to stand still, removed the blindfold and then withdrew, leaving me alone in the exact middle of this great space. I stood in the midst of a mosaic circle upon a grand floor. I'm sure many an accused man and woman noticed the beauty of the spot, where judgment had cast its, often, evil shadow. Within the circle, were little mosaic fishes swimming, each with the tail of the other in its mouth. There was an outer-circle of them going one direction, and an inner-circle of them going the opposite direction. All this was in brilliant greens and blues. The spot on which I stood clearly showed the goddess activation grid[143] with blood red at its center. This symbol meant that all things radiate outward and then reverse back inward, to recycle and radiate back to the origin. This, I surmised, must be how they see judgment passed on those who stood upon this very spot. I wondered if they realized it was true for them, as well as for the accused. It's odd, what can run through one's mind in crisis. It seemed my mind processed everything, to divert me from my physical pain.

"Who condemns this man, and for what?" Pilate finally asked, as he sat upon an ornate thrown elevated on a platform, which could only be approached from circular steps that cascaded down onto the tiled judgment floor.

Caiaphas said, "The people condemn him, for he says he is the Son of God, and he claims to be King of the Jews."

"King of the Jews?" Pilate questioned, "Why would he be King of the Jews? Don't we have our Emperor Caesar? Who cares for another king?" Then Pilate, looking at Caiaphas with a slight frown on his face, further said, "Sometimes, I think you believe yourself King of the Jews, Caiaphas. Would you have me condemn you as well, high priest?" The two had been feuding a long time, over who was in command of Jerusalem and the surrounding areas.

The anger written upon the face of the high priest was all the answer given. The continuous battle between the two for power constantly shifted and changed. For the moment, Pilate was slightly more in command as the Prefect of Judea than the pompous high priest. However, Caiaphas held control over the people and Pilate was not fool enough to think that he could do his job without some cooperation from the priesthood.

Caiaphas finally spoke, "We, the Sanhedrin, bring you this blasphemer for judgment and ask that you perform your duty, as governor and Prefect of Judea, and hear our argument against him."

---

[143] Spiraling circle which symbolizes that everything evolves from the 'center', or from God

Pilate responded, "I see a man that is no threat to the Romans, nor our Emperor, or any of our citizens. What I do see is a man who threatens the priesthood, especially you, Caiaphas." Before a response could be offered, Pilate's wife, whom he loved dearly, interrupted the proceedings in tears. Pilate was concerned for her, even if the interruption was considered an infringement upon the office of the Prefect, especially during the time of judgment.

Caiaphas was a hater of women. His anger ran deep, from what he considered betrayal from his beautiful Leiona[144] and her brat daughter, Sarah. He shouted out at the interruption, "Surely Pilate, you would not let this woman interrupt such an important judgment time!"

Pilate knew that indeed this did look bad, and realized that he should have responded in the expected way and driven her off with chastisement. Instead, he had a flash of an idea. He thought of a solution to the problem. He said, "Every prisoner has a right to have someone speak for them and Claudia has come to speak for this man." Caiaphas couldn't deny this right since it was Jewish law, not Roman law. It was the only thing Pilate could think of, to save her dignity and side-track the accusation of Caiaphas.

Claudia rushed from the doorway where the guard had been holding her back, ran to the feet of her husband and collapsed, kissing his feet. He took her face in his hand, pulled her from the embarrassing position, and brought her face level to his. She whispered, "Save him. He's not guilty of anything, but keeping Caiaphas from collecting more taxes and profiting from the sacrificial slaughter."

Pilate whispered back, "I'm trying, my love, but you have now taken the place of anyone who might have helped me free him. I fear the opportunity is lost, because you are a woman, they probably won't hear you." At this revelation, she fell back to a kneeling position at her husband's feet once again, weeping.

---

[144] Caiaphas first wife and mother of Sara

Gathering herself, she finally arose and looked at the Sanhedrin council, which by now was filling the place of the accusers, with Caiaphas at the forefront. She could tell that they wouldn't listen to her, but she had to try. The moment, like it or not, was hers. It would likely be more difficult for her husband to fulfill her request, now that she had come forth without considering the consequences.

She rose to her feet and stood by her husband. Tall for a woman, directing her eyes to Caiaphas, she said, "The only so-called sin of this man Jesus is that he loved women, as you never could or would." She tried to continue her defense, but the shouts and angry words of the Sanhedrin, who believed that women were the source of all evil, drowned out her words. Pilate had to have her physically removed from the proceedings for her own safety. It was difficult for him to order her out, because he never denied her anything, and he wished he could, yet again, fulfill her every desire. She didn't leave gracefully. A soldier finally carried her out, as she shouted at Caiaphas, words that he didn't want to heed, thus he didn't hear.

Pilate could see he was in a difficult situation, yet he thought he could devise a plan that would save Jesus at the last minute. Because of Passover (and its tradition of remembering those exiled people who had been spared slaughter by the angels of God, who passed them by, as they avenged the anger of God in Egypt), there was a Jewish custom he recalled. According to the Jewish faith, a special opportunity during the celebration was allowed. Pilate remembered pardon was possible, at this particular time, for one prisoner. He was sure that more people loved me, then hated me, and he believed if he could give the crowd a chance to ask for my life to be spared, they would do so and ease Claudia's grief, as well. I could tell he felt compassion for me. He liked the tales his wife had told him about the teachings, during their most private times. He knew it would be a risk, but he had to chance it, because I wasn't backing down from my claim of being the Son of God. Even as I made that claim, Pilate didn't realize that what I had claimed all along included him, and every man and woman, too. Knowing one's true relationship to God the Creator was dangerous to those who wanted to shape and mold attitudes and opinions.

They put themselves in charge of God relationships. For a price, they might allow someone to rise up a step or two. My arrest was more a matter of revenge and economics than religion.

Reluctantly, Pilate thumped his silence staff, due to the chaos in the chamber of judgment, while people argued my fate. It took the gonging of the bell on top of his staff to bring silence. When that sound was given, an official statement would follow.

"I shall pass judgment," he announced. Looking at me with regret, he said, "I condemn thee, Jesus, as a troublemaker and someone who deprived Caesar of taxes, by interfering with the business of the temple, by influencing people to forgo the purchase of a slaughter lamb at Passover. I realize that the priesthood collects the taxes and takes a share," he explained "but the greater sum belongs to Caesar, and you have taken his due."

"I further condemn you for claiming that you are the Son of God, for only the Emperor can claim that status." At that statement Caiaphas rolled his eyes. It was clear that he didn't agree with the declaration, but if Pilate needed it to justify the result he desired, so be it.

Pilate continued, "But what I condemn you to die for, Jesus, is that you claim to be the King of the Jews, not by word but by action. When you rode into the city so blatantly, upon the back of a white animal of burden, you violated the rules of the land thus set forth by the Roman Emperor, which rules that only a king shall pass through a city portal on a white steed." I hadn't been aware of such a law and think it probably was not often enforced. Pilate proceeded, saying, "That is an offense punishable by death. By your deed, you have condemned yourself. I order you immediately to be prepared and crucified until death, before the sun sets today." As Pilate said these words, I looked directly into his eyes and could see that Pilate's heart was not behind the words he spoke, and that there was something, some sort of hope, still lingering within the mind of the Prefect of Judea.

The Sanhedrin yelled and congratulated each other, slapping one another on the back and showing great joy at the verdict. Pilate then pulled his last hope-card, saying, "I'll take Jesus to the people and ask if they want the angel of death to pass over him, as is the custom during Passover." And he motioned to the guards to bring me forth.

Caiaphas, clearly agitated, spun around with his golden robes flapping and flaring out as he twirled and yelled, "No!" He didn't expect this turn of events, and he had to think fast. He remembered another custom and said, "We have the right of ritual preparation of this condemned man and to take him to the people after the preparation."

"Do as you must," Pilate reluctantly said, knowing that during such a rite my safety would be in the hands of the Sanhedrin. "But within two hours," Pilate said, "I'll expect Jesus alive on the steps of the Hall of Judgment, or I'll have you in the circle of judgment before the day is done," he threatened Caiaphas.

The two, still battling for power, stared at each other. Finally, Pilate turned and left his chair of authority, before Caiaphas turned. In this action Caiaphas had won, because he had held his ground longer and wasn't dismissed before the Prefect left his throne. Pilate couldn't stay a moment longer, even as he understood the implications of his exit. He was beginning to falter himself, and he knew that the old priest would see the opportunity of weakness and show no mercy. As Pilate left the Hall of Judgment, he hoped that the people would free me. He wanted this outcome, not just for the sake of his dear wife whom he knew loved me as a master teacher, but also for him, because he saw divinity within my eyes, and he didn't want to kill me. Part of him knew that if I died at his command, he would be killing himself as well.

Now I was in the hands of the Sanhedrin, without the benefit of Roman protection. They planned to use the two hours as efficiently as they could, to prepare the lamb for sacrifice. They had come to view me as a representative of all the lambs who weren't sold for sacrifice at the Passover meals, which impacted their authority and security, as it was perceived through the eyes of wealth. Finally, they would have my blood, to avenge their pocket books that didn't jingle with the money they had hoped to enjoy as profit on the recently-past celebration day. Greed and anger, thus paired, again created evil actions, and I knew that the rite of passage to my death would be a living hell.

As with all cruel people, there seems to be no limit to how they will torture the object of their hate and unfortunately, so it was with me. After some grueling torment, it was reported that the women were approaching, boldly walking to the temple with my own beloved wife at the forefront.

"One leads them in the red robes of the priestess," I heard being reported to Caiaphas, who inflicted much of the abuse upon me, in the so-called 'rite of purification'. He decided that, if he couldn't make my body hurt enough, he would hurt my heart and said, "Bring Jesus to meet the women who he loves so much. See what company he keeps? If we didn't need these women for mothers and servants, we would put them all to the cross and be done with the likes of them, who don't know their true place."

As can happen during dire pain and agony, thoughts flashed through my head and whole scenarios formed in mega-seconds, as I thought about what my destiny would be, and worried about those I loved. Remembering the Romans' favorite form of execution, I thought, "Oh yes, the cross!" the very symbol of balance would be used to kill me. The symbol of the masculine, reaching upward toward the heavens, and still downward toward the earth, and the arms of the cross being the feminine leveler, keeping him balanced so that he can stand tall. This divine symbol would now be used to end my life and mission." To crucify usually meant to be put to the cross and hung out for vultures. While it was a convenient shape for the task, my mind dwelled on the symbolic aspect of it. Odd, I thought, in my suspended moment of reflection, that the very symbol of the balance of life would be the chosen instrument of death.

I was dragged to the temple steps, where the women demanded to talk to the priests and see me. My heart dropped when I saw my sweet beloved wife, my MiryAmah, there in her red priestess robe, which she never wore, unless the moment was sacred–the very robe I gave her, having received it just before I met her. She looked beautiful, yet so miserable. She was extremely vulnerable in her late pregnancy and this worried me. I wanted her to stay hidden and safe. If Caiaphas knew of her pregnancy, he would kill her and our baby, for sure. I pleaded with her with my eyes as she sobbed and fell upon the steps, pleading mercy for me. My mother was there also and Sarah, the daughter of Caiaphas, which didn't go unnoticed by him. She actually cried at the feet of her father, saying, "Father, take me. Take my life, for that's what is in your heart. This man isn't a threat to you father–spare him!" and she too collapsed into a pile of robes at his feet, reminding me of when we found her at the well, beat senseless, and left to die by the same man who looked down on her now, her father.

All this emotion seemed to feed something in the high priest. He smiled wickedly, showing no pity for his daughter or anyone. He seemed to get a sexual kind of elation from the drama that was unfolding. He actually moaned an orgasmic sound, as he kicked Sarah aside. I wondered how the real judgment that comes at the end of one's physical life would be for him, for surely he would have to see his own motives and reasons for the pain and suffering he had inflected on so many innocents. He, who should have known better as a spokesman for God, took all the goodness (thus 'Godness') he encountered and killed or spoiled it. What, I wondered, would ever correct that madness?

He looked at my wife–my dear sweet MiryAmah–there clad in her red priestess robes and said, "See harlot, what happens when you go against the word and will of God."

MiryAmah raised her head and said, "Your word is not God's word, Caiaphas." I worried that she may go too far and be crucified alongside me, should she stand up to him further. She then said, "You may kill Jeshua's body, but you'll never kill his soul. I know that you will be dammed for all eternity, for what you do."

It became evident that the scene was getting worse by the minute. Some of the Sanhedrin had already been sent out, offering payment to those who would sell their soul for mere coins. They had been hired into service to shout down and deny my followers should they try to defend me. They were already earning their little bags of coins, shouting insults at the women. Possibly, they felt if their voices were loud enough, what their heart pleaded wouldn't be heard. The power of their screaming overcame the gentleness of the disciples, and the women's voices were lost in angry words from people who didn't even care, one way or the other.

I noticed that my mother and my mother-in-law had a quick conversation, and then spoke with my suffering wife. MiryAmah and I were so close that we always felt each other's pain in all ways–in the physical sense, emotionally and especially spiritually– and it was difficult to gain her attention, because she was miserable at seeing me in this condition. I felt her pain and we both remembered again why twin souls–those two souls that are really one, in essence–don't usually incarnate together. It leaves no anchor in the spirit realms, for difficult times like this in the arena of the physical. They finally got her to listen to reason. It must have been decided to have quick words with me without further confrontation with the priests, so the women directed their comments towards me and promised not to desert me, believing that my apostles had done so in weakness. The high emotions of the moment didn't bring any peace, only more pain and that was the point of allowing the women to see me—to extend the pain as far and deep as possible. I could see the toll the grief was taking on all of them. What good would more sacrifice be? Surely, the apostles would die if they were present, and I feared the women would go that far, if I didn't send them away.

I never took my eyes from my wife's, once the women directed their attention to me. In our unspoken language of love, I pleaded for her to keep herself and our child safe. She knew. She always knew what I was thinking. I begged, "Leave me now, all of you. What I must do is not for your eyes to see." Then I was taken away, back to the Hall of Judgment, for the last judgment of the crowd in a short while.

To go over the details of my suffering would be pointless, but I'll try to address a few things. There are no words to describe how I felt. I had so many mixed emotions swimming around in my head, along with the severe physical pain from the torture I received from the Sanhedrin, on top of what the Romans inflicted. Disappointment, feelings of betrayal followed by the greater emotion of forgiveness, complicated by fear (yes, I was very afraid, more for my loved ones than myself and fearful of what other forms of torture Caiaphas might think of for all of us, before I passed from this world) all flashed through my mind.

The women followed me to the Judgment Steps, determined not to abandon me, ignoring my request that they leave me to my fate. The steps were located at the approach to the Hall of Judgment that Pilate used when he was in town to pass sentence upon the accused or to declare new rules. The women were scattered within a greater crowd now, a crowd formed because they had heard of the situation and knew the opportunity of Passover pardon would be offered. There were three of us to be executed shortly. Dismas was among the condemned. He was a compassionate man, and I remembered that he had cried me strong with his tears, which helped me through the last agonizing hours. I wished with all my heart that he wouldn't share my fate. The other man I also felt compassion for, but didn't get a chance to interact with him. We all stood side-by-side and Pilate demanded the attention of the crowd by thumping his staff of office, which had the bell at its apex, as he did before. It was the official sound of attention, and all were required to honor it with silence. The gong rang and the crowd quickly silenced, looking at the three of us pitifully displayed before them. I was the most battered of the three. Many of the on-lookers looked at me and quickly looked away, as if they might sicken.

"Silence," Pilate began. "As is the tradition of Passover, I offer you a chance to free one sacrificial lamb among the accused here, for mercy was the request of your people from the angels at Passover, and now you shall bestow mercy, as well. Which condemned man shall be freed?" he asked, fully expecting that they loved me enough to free me.

He didn't know that Caiaphas had spent many silver coins, and even some gold ones, to pad the crowd with naysayers. His instructions were for them to choose Dismas. Caiaphas chose him because his crime was against a Roman, and not against a Jew. He had killed a soldier of Rome, who had raped and murdered his wife; but until he found this particular soldier, he had raged havoc on many Roman people of authority, thinking that they didn't protect or respect his wife, nor care about her fate. As was the practice and attitude of the day, it was she who was blamed for the situation and was labeled a tempter and harlot, thus according to those in authority, she deserved what she got. To choose Dismas then was to give Pilate one last slap in the face. It was a brilliant strategy, Caiaphas thought.

Immediately, my name was offered, but as quickly as it was spoken, someone yelled louder, "Free Dismas!" My followers were by nature softer personalities and their voices reflected a peaceful nature not loud enough to rise above the shouting of the hired thugs Caiaphas had arranged to have present. Thus, the forceful voices of the conspirators overcame my followers' pleadings, and Pilate had to grant freedom to Dismas instead of me. It was difficult for him to concede, and he nearly buckled under the weight of the verdict. It was not the outcome he had hoped for.

There was a moment of near silence, before he made the official declaration, which gave me a chance to say to this compassionate criminal, "You are free to be all that you can be. Be love. Don't hate anymore. Bring strength to the power of love. Starve fear of sapping your strength, which it would feed upon if it could."

He cried like a little child, sobbing uncontrollably. As he was cut free of his bonds, he said, "I'm not worthy to be loved this much." He looked at me and said, "I would gladly take your place on the cross, Jesus, if only they would allow me."

I whispered, "Yes, you are worthy and don't disappoint our father in heaven who has freed you. Our Divine Father wants you to live and do more good works."

"How is it that our Divine Father would choose me over you?" he asked.

I answered, "Because you have something to offer which I cannot give, dear friend." I knew that there was divine guidance within this moment. I'm sure that the mercy this strong man showed me in the dark of the dungeon cell was the moment that Father/Mother God decided to offer him compassion and total forgiveness. I finally said, "I will meet you again one fine day in heaven, dear one."

I was immediately taken to the street where the symbol of balance, the cross, already formed from two rough-hewn cedar trees,[145] waited for me. I knew the tree didn't want to be part of this ritual of evil. I could sense the tree's spirit as easily as I could each person present that day. I had learned so much in my short life about the consciousness of all creation and I could feel the agony of the very wood that had the power to pre-vision its destiny. As quickly as the thought formed within my mind, it seemed that I was given the burden of carrying the very symbol that I loved. The weight of the cross, as it was lowered upon my shoulder, was massive, and I realized that I would have to carry it myself to the place of the skulls, Golgotha.

Someone had crowned me with a crown of thorns, which had been forcefully pushed into the crown of my head. Warm blood was streaming down my face, stinging my eyes and blurring my vision; again, I had to use techniques learned from the sages of the mountains to find my way, because I couldn't see much through the veil of blood that covered my face. I did see my loved ones, from time to time within the crowd, as I struggled along the path. I wished I could spare them the experience of this horrible event playing out before them, in the streets of the same city that had welcomed us a short time previous. As I began my long journey, I faltered and fell every few steps. Someone stepped up next to me, and I could sense a gentle soul there. My face was wiped of the blood that was blinding me. A woman whispered, "Love is here to give you strength," then she stepped back. Not long after her act of kindness, with a crowd still peppered with hecklers screaming obscenities at me, I felt the weight of the cross lift from my aching shoulders. It was such a relief. As reluctant as the tree was to be an instrument of pain and suffering, it couldn't help its weight and

---

[145] Sometimes called 'timber of the gods' also is symbolic of birth or death of someone you love

mass. I'm sure I could never have carried that cross to the place of skulls, where I was destined to die. The hate that condemned me wanted me to experience the maximum degree of pain. Even so, what force lifted this burden, I thought? I wiped more blood from my eyes, with painful hands already ripped from trying to carry my cross, now free of that burden. As the blood was cleared for a brief moment, I beheld a Roman soldier, not too tall but strong as an ox, who had taken my load. He wasn't ordered to take it. He simply had followed the path of mercy, rather than give in to the drunkenness of the torture, like most of the other soldiers and many in the crowd were. He looked at me and I nearly fell in my tracks; for he was no ordinary soldier, but Elmira, my Elmira, whom I thought had long ago found another life and a different purpose other than protecting me. I was so glad to see him, I almost gave him away. He quickly diverted his gaze from me, adjusted the heavy cross upon his great shoulders, and we went forth, with me trailing along behind him near dumbfounded.

We had learned mind-speak when I was but a child, so I could talk to him as we trudged along the endless path to Golgotha[146]. It was the longest journey of my life and here was my protector again, taking the journey with me. I said within my mind, "Where have you been, dear man?"

He answered, "Not far."

Then I said, "This time you can't protect me."

He answered, "If I could I would. I carried you across that raging stream, when the old wise-woman called me a Christopher. Now I complete the task I was born to do. I gladly carry the burden of the 'Christed one' and if I could take your place on the cross, I would."

Another one willing to take my place, I thought. I couldn't keep track of those who had said they wanted to suffer for me. People were so compassionate, I thought. Maybe our work found fertile ground after all. I hoped that love, radiating peace, would come to

---

[146] Place of the skulls, one of the many places used by Romans when they crucified people

full harvest. I knew that I suffered for everyone who was oppressed and enslaved, in a system that denied their divinity.

"Oh Elmira," I said within my mind-speak, "please don't die for me. Live for me." I feared that he might do something to try to protect me, maybe even offer himself as a proxy in this execution.

Soon we reached the place of the skulls. I was thrown to the ground, stripped of my robes and nailed upon the wooden cross as it lay flat on the earth. I could hear it scream its reluctance within my mind, for it didn't want to accept the nails. I could feel it all, but I could feel the tears of my beloved wife more profoundly than the reluctant nails. Her tears were my greatest pain. She was, and still is, so much a part of me, as I am, too, of her, that we shared all things, including this moment of pain and sorrow. Her tears stabbed my heart, and I never knew such agony. Even the nails entering my wrists and ankles didn't compare to the anguish of seeing my beloved's sorrow. It was with a sad and terrible dread that I was finally lifted up to the sky. I could see my loved ones, pushed aside by the paid shouters, who were throwing stones and mud at me. Finally, they allowed my mother, my wife (they thought she was just a persistent woman follower) and my dear little friend, the youngest apostle John, to come nearer to me. Again, I think they wanted to torture me and pierce my heart, not satisfied that my body was mutilated. They had broken my legs before hoisting me up and there wasn't much left to do to this poor body; I knew they wanted to kill my spirit, too, and would use my loved ones to accomplish that dire deed.

I looked at John and said to him, "Please, little John, promise me that you will take care of my beloveds." He nodded that he would. However, I didn't realize then that he didn't consider MiryAmah as one of my beloveds, only my mother would he acknowledge as such. He loved me with all his heart, but being the son of a Roman soldier and a Hebrew mother, he was conflicted between the Roman way to love and the Hebrew way. Sadly, he was jealous of my dear wife. I understood his love, but didn't see his jealousy. I never condemned him for his love. Love finds many ways to express itself. I knew that some women loved women this way and that many men found this the only place they felt they could really trust love. I didn't see it as wrong; just as a situation they lived and suffered within. I had often spoken to the followers about the essence of love, and to John directly, and how unconditional abiding love, no matter how it manifested, was always divine. Insecurities within such loving opportunities were usually the cause of their downfall, since insecurities are fear-based and antiforce will pierce the bubble of unconditional love if it gets a chance. Even so, at that moment I believed John intended to keep his promise as he understood it, and I loved him dearly, and still do, for his divine intention.

My words were getting harder to speak now. From some place deep within me, I felt the terrible force of disappointment and screamed, "Why have they forsaken me, father?"–meaning why had those I came to reach with the truth of Oneness come so far, only to return to the very demons, the attitudes that denied them their own divinity?

The pain was beyond horrifying as it affected every aspect of my being, and I saw a soldier come forth. He had a sponge on a long stick and offered me a drink from it, knowing that I must be thirsty. He seemed bigger than the others I had previously seen, but I was now losing consciousness and thought I might have been hallucinating. The substance on the sponge seemed bitter. I almost didn't partake of it, until I looked at my mother, and she showed me the small bag from my childhood that I had always carried. It was a gift from one of the magi long ago, and it contained myrrh, along with some other herbs. How she obtained it, I didn't know, since I kept it with my personal items, which had been taken from me at my imprisonment. Maybe she got the bag from Claudia, who was secretly one of mother Mary's priestesses. Mother nodded her head affirmatively, and I sucked in the substance, sensing that it was meant for this moment. It immediately began to numb me. I felt more peaceful and in less pain, but I was having great difficulty breathing, with the full weight of my body pulling me down due to my broken legs.

Another soldier came forth. He, too, seemed larger than life and said, "It's time to help this king of the Jews die." He pulled a grand sword from its sheath at his side. Instantly, I recognized it as the sword with which Nod taught me sacred metallurgy. It was 'Excalibur,' the same sword we had infused with the intention that it only be used as an instrument of God, and that it could never serve evil, solely peace. As with all such moments, time seemed to be suspended in slow motion as I watched the sword I helped form pierce my left lung, which was filling up with body fluids and drowning me. I felt the water in my lungs burst out the hole Excalibur made; I realized that I had seen the face of that soldier many times in my dreams. He was Michael the archangel and messenger of God–the same angel whom our people believed ran through the neighborhoods, killing and avenging for God and passing over the houses that had the blood of the lamb over the doorway. In my dreams a few nights previous, Michael said it wasn't quite like that. He said those who died were blessed and released, and those that had sacrificed a lamb lived to suffer more. The fluids that were drowning me flowed like a stream from my side, relieving me. Glancing at my precious wife and mother, I mouthed, "I love you," and lost consciousness. The myrrh made me go into a deep sleep, and I wasn't physically aware of anything until later in the tomb.

A brief second before the deep sleep took me from the pain, I noticed that the skies revolted and brought great turbulent clouds forth, and mother earth shook. I remembered how she also trembled, but in a much different way, when MiryAmah had asked permission to change the colors of the sparrows. Tara's emotional responses are dramatic, and she grieved for me. Somehow, this lifted some of the sorrow that overwhelmed me.

I wasn't thrown in the ditch of the dammed, which was the place they usually put crucified criminals. My half-brother Joseph had managed to take possession of my body and offered his tomb for the pre-burial. He had gained a seat on the high council by keeping our true relationship private. Being the son of my father's first wife, who had died when he was but a teenage youth, helped him keep a low profile as he watched over me, honoring a promise to father. Even within the extended families, our relationship wasn't common knowledge because of much separation of years and the locations of our homes. My half-brother, known as Joseph of Arimathea, after the town where he lived, felt that he could best be of service to me, who he had come to love and honor, by placing himself in positions and places of authority. He had, through his travels, already managed to build foundations of change in many lands. Lazarus, the brother of my dear wife, helped carry me, believing I was dead, to my place of rest when they finally lowered the reluctant cross.

I remember bits and pieces of the procession, and especially Lazarus speaking of the time I had raised him from the dead and how he wished he could do the same for me now. Actually, he wasn't dead, but in the deep coma, then. I learned to recognize this condition, from my time with Yasma the healer in India. It was a simple healing and meant much to my beloved, who was my betrothed at the time, to have her brother healed and awakened.

Even though I was physically unconscious, I was quite aware of what was happening as I followed the procession, and my body like a ghost. I was delivered to the tomb and a great stone rolled in place. Anointing usually took place in the morning. Since the sun had gone down on this Sabbath evening already, and tomorrow being full Sabbath, it would be another day before anointment could happen. Even so, my beloved didn't wait for the first day of the week to seek her rightful task. She came the next morning, the Sabbath, and found the tomb already empty.

It was a great shock to her, and she was despondent, finding an empty tomb. She wanted desperately to do her wifely duty and prepare my body for my death journey. She didn't know that during the night, I became aware of the smell of incense and awakened in great pain within the tomb. Some candles were left burning, as my ghost merged back into my physical vehicle. All was utterly quiet. Had it not been for the pain, I would've thought I had passed on to the land of spirit, but the pain was everywhere and relentless. I could see the shadow of the candle dancing on the wall and realized that I was alive in a tomb, when I expected that I would be discarded in the ditch like other criminals. Noticing the chiseled names upon the openings where the bone boxes were stored, I recognized family names, and realized I was in the tomb of my brother. I heard a great grinding sound and looked up from the stone slab I lay upon, toward the portal of the tomb. The shroud had fallen from my face, so I had clear vision of the huge stone moving aside and a blast of light entering the chamber. I remember thinking this must be God coming to get me. Then in the midst of the light I saw Michael again, and the other soldier. They didn't have Roman uniforms on now, but seemed to be wearing garments of light. The glow around their heads and shoulders looked like wings made of brilliant rays of radiance. They came to me and Michael laid his hand on my forehead. I felt instant relief and white light filled me with peace. I must have been taken from the tomb, for my next memory was of being out of body and seeing my beloved coming to the tomb at dawn, with sacred oils for anointment, and seeing her finding the doorway open.

She ran into the tomb as I watched from outside, my body floating pain-free. Her grief at finding my body missing was overwhelming. I knew that somehow I had to tell her I wasn't suffering any longer. I saw a nearby gardener and jumped into his body, or I should say the essence of me entered him. Without even asking permission, I took him over and spoke to my beloved. At first she didn't recognize me. After I spoke an endearment that only she and I knew, she was convinced and relieved. I warned her not to touch me. I knew that the touch would bring the gardener, the rightful soul of this physical vehicle, back in, and I would lose my chance to speak with her.

I said, "Fear not, MiryAmah, for you have not lost me, rather you have found me. Go and tell the apostles and the disciples that I am raised, and I will come to them soon, in dreams and otherwise if I can." I didn't really understand yet, if I was dead or alive myself.

She seemed a bit confused, due to the grief of all that had transpired, so I said, "Go to safety and don't mourn me. I am only dead as Jesus, never as Jeshua." Then before the energy depleted from this abducted host, I said, "Our mission will never be dead. Remember, and keep that ever in your mind and heart. It will be you who will carry on the truth of our divinely sacred intentions." Then I lost the ability to hold the energy within a host who had never agreed to such a situation. As the gardener desired to come back, I was pushed back into the light.

The light was peaceful and I felt no pain, I floated within it. I felt the strong connection to my beloved wife and family, and also my child's presence as well. I prayed there in the light, that they would be kept safe from the evil that would extinguish the essence of love I was now engulfed within. I knew my prayer was heard.

# THE HEALING SKULL OF MU
## Chapter Thirty-Two

I can't begin to describe the pain of being crucified, nor do I think you want to hear such agony. It affects more than the physical body and all sorts of torture rips ugly gashes, caused by fear-based thinking into your very soul. Just know that it is terrible and never deserved, no matter what the priests would have you think. Archangel Michael's touch in the tomb was the end of the unbearable pain and proof of God's mercy.

I remember my body being taken from the tomb as I watched from above it. I slipped in and out of body for a short while, as I lost consciousness and finally, just left my body and floated near it, yet still connected. It felt like one second I was emerging from the tomb and the next I was in the high mountains again. I recognized the underground passages and could hear the chants of the monks. I was laid on a soft bed and finally, physically opened my eyes. I saw the same master teacher who had greeted Elmira and me, when we fell into one of the tunnels so long ago when I was but a wee boy. This teacher again filled the room with radiant light and love, just like he did in the tunnel so long ago, and I welcomed his wise old face.

He gently wiped the bloody sweat from my face, the result of extreme suffering and said, "You've returned to us, dear one, but you come back all worn out and used up."

I tried to answer him, but he indicated for me not to try to find the strength to respond. In fact, he said, "It's time for you to leave your body for a while and attend to the affairs you just left." He gently smiled and added, "Don't worry. We'll keep your body safe until you return, but you must return before sun sets on these mountains tomorrow, or I fear we can't hold the physical body suspended without the soul any longer, dear one."

I must have looked a bit confused, since the elder one said, "You have done this before in your early training here. Go now and ease the hearts of those who love you. Ride the wings of the eagle to the place you desire to be."

Oh, how I had loved that lesson of flight, when I had become the bird and looked through its eyes, as a young boy. But, I wondered where I might find an eagle now. The elder sensing the question said, "Just visualize wings. You don't need the actual bird this time. You have several ways opened to you to communicate; the more heart-tied you are with the individuals, the easier it will be for you to speak to them."

I remembered the lessons of long ago, and closed my eyes and through my imagination could release the soul from my body, much as one does during a deep sleep, and fly away. As I lifted out of my body, I saw the thin silver and gold cords, the same twining cords that connect to the Divine Grid, or Holy Cloak of God, that surrounds all creation. It was attached from the crown of my physical body, even as I was free of this vehicle. Flying in space this way can only be described as heavenly. I could perceive the area around me and felt freedom beyond description. Watching my body below, I observed many monks arrive in the chamber, and they began to tend to me. I saw them bring in a pregnant woman who was huge with her yet unborn babe. I heard the master teacher say that no harm would come to the child, but likely it would be born forthwith after the procedure was accomplished. They put a tube directly into her navel and attached it to my body through the incision in my lung–the one Excalibur had so cleanly made, relieving me of the fluids that were drowning me as I was nailed on the cross.

While I was watching all of this, I heard a voice I knew, but never actually experienced hearing physically. This pleasant strong voice was most welcome, because it was Elmira.

"Master," he said, and I saw him floating there with me above the scene playing out below. "Don't fear, for the waters within the womb will not drown you, even as they enter the collapsed lung. They will instead expand the lung, seep into the other tissues and help rejuvenate your battered body." He then said, "The gift of the Mother is endless; is it not?"

I looked at him. He looked young and strong, and his tongue was there and no longer missing as I had known before. Since I was so recently in the physical I had some confusion at seeing the perfection within the image I now perceived of him. For a moment, I was engrossed in the beautiful sight of a tongue, now part of Elmira's face, apparent as he spoke. The last I had seen of him, he was in Roman uniform and lifting the cross from my tired battered body, as I was forced to march to the place of skulls, through the streets of Jerusalem, to the killing fields.

"Master," Elmira said, "we must go now. I shall, as ever, be your guardian on this journey back to the place of your pain and suffering, but this time, there'll be no pain, and I will not have to yoke your cross on my back."

I understood the urging and knew that the proceedings below didn't need my presence. My thoughts naturally went to my beloved MiryAmah.

I immediately could feel her emotional pain and tears. Her pain became mine again. Elmira told me to let the pain move through me and not find a home within me, so that I could be a source of relief for her. It took a moment for me to understand the process, since the pain was all encompassing again, but finally I achieved what Elmira suggested. I could still process the pain and not hold it within my being this way. I released it to dissipate into the ethers that surrounded me and all creation, and in so doing, I could relieve my wife's sorrow, too. I wondered why I hadn't remembered this fundamental law of release, when mired within the terror of the crucifixion.

Time and distance mean nothing outside of the physical plane. Now that I was beyond those limitations, just thinking of my beloved drew me instantly to her. I saw her enter the tomb. It was the day of the Sabbath. Ordinarily, one would not enter a tomb on that day, so she was alone, yet there were those close friends following her from a distance to keep an eye on my grieving widow. According to the Jewish law, no physical labor, not even for the sake of the dead, was allowed on the Sabbath. People even had to prepare the meals before sundown Friday, for all day Saturday, known as the Sabbath. Evidently, my dear wife couldn't keep herself from coming to me, having been awake all night crying and in terrible grief. The laws of man couldn't stop the law of love. As she entered the tomb, she quickly wondered who had rolled the great stone back; instantly fearing our enemies had taken my body. Her thoughts were mine, too, and so being, I felt the dread that coursed through her, even though I knew the truth. Not seeing my body, she fell to her knees sobbing and crying, "No, no, no." My heart ached to see her so.

Salome, her friend who followed her as she ran out of the sanctuary where she was staying that early morning, entered the tomb now, as well. She knew that my beloved could bring herself to premature labor, should she become too physically affected by her grieving. She and many others in MiryAmah's inner-circle were trying to protect her and our unborn child. As Salome entered, MiryAmah just looked at her with great wet tears streaming down her face and cried, "What have they done with my dear Jeshua? What more can they do to us, now that they have murdered him?"

Salome helped my grieving wife to her feet. As she was raised, MiryAmah took the shroud from the stone slab, all that was left behind, and brought it close to her heart. She buried her face within the fluid-stained material, trying to breathe my scent into her body. Salome gently urged her toward the doorway. When she emerged, I knew I had to communicate with her, and that was when I possessed the gardener.

Once convinced it was me, I could give my message to my beloved, and then gave up the body I had taken without permission. After I departed from the gardener's body, I asked his guides' forgiveness and was granted such. As it turned out, they were actually aware of what could play out and had positioned him in the proper place, should the need arise.

I floated around the area for a while observing the situation, after the cruel punishment for crimes I didn't commit. My only crime was to threaten the power of fear, which is the security that binds the twisted control system. That, along with loving and honoring my wife and all women, as well as all creation, was why I was executed. I had questioned and resisted religious authority in many ways. While not a crime, just knowing certain truths was a sin in the minds of those who held positions of power, especially the Sanhedrin Priests.

With my apostles now scattered, I remembered the 'Whisper of Inspiration'[147] technique I learned from my time with the great master, Yasma in India. Finding Philip, I whispered into his ear, gently but still with enough force to vibrate his eardrum, "Find the others and regroup, Phillip, for I will come speak with all of you."

I loved Phillip's confidence in the inner-voice. He didn't question everything, as dear Thomas would. He just immediately paid heed to the voice within. This was his talent, and as always the case, was his weakness as well, for there were other forces that would slip in to confuse him while he perfected the fine art of 'divine listening'. Demons are not only false attitudes that deny or demean God's creation, but also voices of those who die in fear and can't find peace thus they seek to feed on other's terror. They band together and support fear-based power structures and will often serve those against good (God), because they think if they align themselves with wickedness, fear will not target them. Therefore, they are anti-gods, evil in nature. This was a teaching of the inner-circle. I finally got Phillip to stop listening to demons in his misery, to have confidence in the whispers of his guides, and hear my spirit voice.

In Philip's case, we had practiced the Whisper of Inspiration many times, when we walked together from place to place. I have

---

[147] Communication (Audiovoyance) between those in spirit and those in the physical through hearing

actually whispered messages to him, thinking I was just illustrating how intention of quiet communication would sound, when it was brought forth for the purpose of 'good,' thus 'God'. In so doing, however, not only did he become better at listening to the voice of good, but he became accustomed to my own vibrating whispering sound, and he immediately knew I was with him on this day of miracles. He jumped up and began looking for the others, to give them the message. Oh Philip, I thought, my precious believer, thank God for the likes of you!

I didn't prioritize my visits in terms of importance, and after Philip, I sought my mother, and just moved through the window of opportunity. While I was visiting Philip, my beloved wife was telling my mother of her vision in the garden near the tomb. MiryAmah shared this information with other followers, too. Some didn't believe her, sympathetically thinking that her grief was deceiving her, but my mother knew–as only a mother can–that somehow I had survived the terrible ordeal, and she eagerly listened to all the details. Mother took MiryAmah to her chambers to rest, and then went to her own allocated place to await my visit. She knew I would come.

I found her there, quietly sitting and waiting for me. I was beginning to be able to materialize into a misty form by then. She could see me as clearly as if I was fully physically present, because her love and open mind opened a channel between us.

"Can I touch you?" she asked, remembering what MiryAmah had said about my warning to her not to touch me.

"I wish it could be so, mother," I replied, "but not yet. I hold no touchable form at this point, but let me kiss your heart as a greeting of love." Just the mere desire created the deed. My mother swooned in maternal pleasure that only mothers could feel, and I was glad that I could give her at least that form of affectionate response.

"I see another form with you, son," she said. "Is this your guardian angel?" she inquired.

"Oh yes," I replied. "This angel is none other than Elmira, who is still watching over me."

She nodded her head, because it made perfect sense to her. Then she asked, "Has Elmira passed on as well?" Not waiting for an answer, being so full of questions, she went on to ask, "What would you ask of me, dear son, for any request you put forth is my desire?"

"We are not yet ghosts, only able to leave our bodies. I've been granted permission to come home again and bring assurance that I'm not gone, just changed." She was trying to follow the conversation, but as is always the case, time and place can cloud meaning. During this time, sorrow and fear that I might be dead confused the message I wanted to impart. So I changed the subject and said, "I have asked little John to care for my beloveds, mother. That includes you, MiryAmah and my child. Nevertheless, I fear he may be conflicted in this task I know he wants to do, but may not be able to bring himself to honor. Can you help him understand that MiryAmah is as much me, as I am, and that to love her, is to love me as well?"

Mother understood that this young half-Roman child/man was one of those who passionately loved men and in his heart that passion was aimed at me, whom he loved beyond measure in all ways. She also knew that this confusing situation caused little John, so immature and inexperienced, to want to deny MiryAmah. She witnessed it at the foot of the cross the night of the crucifixion, when he turned his back on MiryAmah and gave all his attention to her. He didn't know of the child. Only a trusted few knew of this situation. I knew he couldn't handle the knowledge yet. Even so, I still felt that he, above any of the others, would want to please me, since he stayed with the women at my execution, unlike the others who had to hide. I trusted him with my last request. I had hoped he would understand the scope of my appeal and honor it in all ways. After all, I was upon the cross suffering, and he was there for me to ask. I know now, that it was out of the foggy vision of pain, that I asked too much of this boy who loved me. I thought that if anyone could help John see through more mature eyes, it

## The Saga-Oracle

would be the one who helped bring myself to maturity, my sweet mother.

The truth was I did love John without end, but my love for my wife was first, and foremost, because she and I are one soul. We had often spoken of the teaching, "love your neighbor as you love yourself." What it really meant was that you had to realize that you were a divine creation, thus a child of God, and respect and love yourself as such, before you could ever know real love with anyone, or anything else. This teaching was so simple yet complex and the hardest for my followers to understand, especially little John. He tried to understand out of love and devotion to me. I have to admit that I hadn't yet openly addressed the truth of MiryAmah as my twin flame[148] and one spirit, split for the cause we served. It was on the agenda, yet we couldn't seem to prepare the men enough for this simple truth, so how could I expect little sweet John, young brother of James of Alphaeus,[149] to understand what far more mature men couldn't grasp? I didn't love John less because of his shortcomings; we all had them. I wanted my mother to watch over him as much as he over her, thus he became John the Beloved.

Mother's maternal instincts were the best I had ever known. I have always counted myself the most fortunate soul to have her as a mother in more than one incarnation, but especially in this time I now remember.

She fully understood my request and said, "Don't worry, son. I'll take John under my wing and bring him to maturity, but this understanding that you want me to help him achieve will take a while," she emphasized. "Be patient with him. He'll arrive at the truth one day and when he does, I only hope that he can forgive himself for denying the greatest gift of all to the one he loved so totally."

---

[148] Two parts of one soul, one primarily feminine and one primarily masculine but both essences in each
[149] One of the Apostles

## Jeshua's Song

Then mother asked the question she had to ask, "Son, what does it feel like to die, and are you in heaven now?" Clearly, she didn't understand my condition and how I could come to her, as I did, and still be in the physical.

"I'll tell you when I die," I replied. "I'm not dead, mother. From this perspective, I can tell you, sometimes it's harder to live."

"How can that be!" she exclaimed with confusion. "You come to me as a ghost, and you say you haven't passed from the physical. Are you trying to affirm that death isn't permanent? Help me understand," she cried, upset for not getting the story straight in her mind.

"I'm not dead," I reassured her. "My body was taken by angels to a safe place in the far mountains. The same place you and father sent me as a child for a safe haven. The people there are attending to me, even as they sent me back to reassure my beloveds here, in this place and time, that all was not lost."

The wrinkles of worry and dread began to ease a bit on her beautiful forehead, so I continued. "I'm not sure, what is in store for me, once they mend my physical body. However, the situation is that, for some reason, I will not be permitted to pass from the physical plane yet. I'm pleased, because I can't bear physically leaving you, or MiryAmah and my child yet to come forth."

"You've laid eyes on angels, son?" she questioned, remembering what I said about them a moment ago.

"Yes, mother," I replied," and I tell you they are a sight to behold. One day, I'll tell you how close you were to the very same angels that saved me, during your deepest grief."

That seemed a bit puzzling, but she had other things on her mind far more important than if she was near angels and simply said, "What would you have me do for you then, son, until your soul and body are one again and can return to us somehow."

"That will probably not be possible in the way we might prefer," I explained, realizing that politically my entire family would be in danger of murder, should I reappear on the scene, and having no idea yet how we would ever be safe again.

Mother looked sad and the worry lines reappeared between her eyes. She had no idea how we would manage such a complicated situation. Then she said, "So it seems, as Jesus, you are dead." Her face showed the deep sorrow of a mother who has to admit that her child is gone. Then she said, "It was Jesus, they wanted to kill, son, but as Jeshua you still live, and it has always been Jeshua, or Esa, that I knew as my beloved son." She seemed to brighten and the lines of grief lifted. "I look forward to the new life you will create from the ashes of the sacrifice you endured."

"As I said, mother, it's easier to die than to live." She nodded her head in agreement. "That was the message that brought all this down upon my head, isn't it? That, the true sacrifice God wants, is for us to live, not to kill innocent lambs!"

At that moment, I couldn't hold form any longer, and faded away into the ethers from which I came. I found myself back within my physical body again, Elmira kneeling at my side. I felt heaviness and pain returning. The pregnant woman was sitting near me, smiling down at a newborn baby in her arms, still wet from the water and blood of its mother's womb. Its face was scrunched from its journey through the portal of forgetting, from the womb to the physical world again. My wounds were now being packed in pieces of the placenta, which the new mother shared with me for my healing. Even the thorn wounds on my head and face received the ointment of the placenta. I knew this meant that less of this sacred substance would be preserved and dried for the child's safekeeping, for later in its life, as was the priestess custom. Evidently, she felt there was more than enough for both of us, as she happily just looked down and smiled at me, content in new motherhood. She was a young mother and had the look of the Mongolian people of this land that I find so beautiful. As I smiled back, my master teacher came forth and laid his hand upon the crown of my head.

"Back so soon," he said. "Too soon, I believe, but evidently your soul had to be re-energized. You, no doubt, have more to do yet, so I will bring the sacred crystallized skull forth and charge you up, so you can depart again and prepare your loved ones for your transition into a new life." I must have looked confused, because the elder chuckled and said, "Don't worry. I'm not talking about you being reborn as this babe here has just done. We must prepare you to live in a new way, in new lands, that's all, and this body will have to serve you for a while yet, dear one, so we have much work to do and energy is needed for healing purposes."

I tried to speak and ask of the crystallized skull. I had seen it before in my youthful days, but didn't know its many uses. I did remember that the day I saw it was a special occasion and its beauty was enough to raise the vibrations of all present.

"He wonders how the skull will be utilized, master," Elmira, so adept at reading my mind, said in this thought language.

"Oh!" the elder replied, "is that all? Well, Jeshua, as you know, the skull is an actual skull crystallized and once was the head-bone of a great master. We spoke of this before when you apprenticed with us. This master was from the land of Mu, and he was both, he and she—one of those who had not yet split their beings into two distinct gender components. He/She was one of the principal leaders within the arena, being the spiritual advisor to the one who held rule over the land. Everything this one touched was infused with energy. After awhile, that became a problem, because as the energy-keeper achieved a great age the infusion of energy upon contact with his divine battery was increased, too. As such, eventually no one wanted to come near enough to be touched by him, since the jolt near killed them. It became a great burden for the energy-keeper, not being able to enjoy the touch of others, so the soul decided after long service that departure time had come. Those who depended on the wise spiritual council of this being were devastated at the decision. They wanted this wise one to leave them something they could feel connected to and still enjoy wise guidance. Being a kindhearted being, the energy-keeper thought this wasn't too much to ask. The people were assured that indeed, a relic would remain. Instructions were made that at the time of cremation, which was the custom of the land upon physical departure of the body, to have the head taken from the body. The head was to be placed in a specially-made box and not opened for a period of eleven days, at the eleventh hour. At that time, eleven priests and eleven priestesses, having already read instructions, would know how to utilize the relic."

"At the appointed time the box was opened, with all due ceremony, in front of the people, so that they would know that this was reality and not trickery. They had their challenges in the land of Mu, too, and there were those who would play games to gain power and those who doubted anything they didn't understand. When the box was opened, all the flesh had vanished from the skull and the bone itself had crystallized into a clear substance, the color of the summer sky. There was no flesh or decay present, only the cool crystallized skull. From that time to now there have been successions of the keepers of the skull of Mu, which is one of many skulls that were either handmade or transformed from actual bone. Each keeper has been able to unlock yet another service the skull can perform, considering that all services are energetic in nature and blended with that of the keeper."

"My own discovery through my time with the skull was in healing the seven bodies[150] of physical form. Once the information and lesson is learned, one doesn't need the skull to accomplish the task. That which I learned consisted of being able to bring this restorative energy through each body of the entity, such as: (1) the soul body, or body that holds the Christ Consciousness and knows it's true relationship to God, also known as the God Body; (2) the spiritual body, or body that knows the relationship to all creation and is One with such; (3) the emotional body, or body that feels the experience and offers that feeling back to all creation and fuels the force of passion, the creative force of God; (4) the mental body, or body that seeks to understand how this all works within the experience and the body that makes ultimate choices for the entity; (5) the etheric body, the body that has no boundaries and can find its way through ethers to any desired place in time or space, while holding the blueprint, or pattern of the physical intact;

---

[150] Soul, spiritual, emotional, mental, etheric, astral, physical bodies all echoed in one being, all having their own properties and purpose in the physicality of the person

(6) the astral body, which helps the physical form stay within the desired pattern and marries the subtle and the soul as one; and finally, (7) the physical body, which is the pattern manifest within the realms of limitation and is the container of all bodies in one. The order of the bodies is not important and some might line them up differently, but you get the idea how they all unite as One being."

"What I plan to do," the ancient elder said, "is bring the energy from this Skull of Mu through each of your bodies, finally culminating within the physical vehicle here, so that healing can happen and perfection be achieved once again. Since you have just been traveling using some of the other six bodies you have a disconnected unit to deal with. Since the physical vehicle is still viable and connected through the silver/gold cord,[151] it requires all available energy to survive. Thus, this cord has called you back, so that you can live. Since you have unfinished business with your loved ones, it will be difficult for you to keep from reuniting with them upon the mere memory of your great love and this won't help the situation. I have to keep your bodies all together here, for this part of the charging."

"Do you understand?" he asked. "Blink at me if you do." Having little available life-force left, I blinked my affirmative answer to him.

Just to be sure, he said, "I will trust Elmira here to keep your seven bodies safe and present until the energetic charge has vibrated them into a balanced rhythm. When that point is reached, you may go back to your loved ones. At such time, he will take you out of your body once again, and you can feel confident that you'll have the energy to finish the task you must do."

And so it was that I simply fell into a peaceful sleep, catching a glimpse of the glowing sky-blue skull, which sat beside my head, as I drifted off into darkness.

---

[151] Double twining cord, silver the sound vibration, gold the light vibration, is connected to each being in the physical and its trail of actions and reactions are part of the Cloak of God, or Divine Web. At physical death it unlinks with the physical body but stays with the soul

My next recollection was being above my body again with Elmira beside me, looking down and seeing the monks with their bald heads bobbing to and fro as they seemed to be rubbing light into my body. Elmira explained that they had now transfused enough energy, so that I could come back to consciousness within spirit to see the end of the process, or be about my unfinished business with my loved ones. What I looked down upon was the sight of blue light from the skull being directed to areas of my body that didn't reflect brilliance. The monks seemed to be able to make a cup shape of their hands, scoop up the light and apply it to the darkened areas, rubbing it in like a healing balm. The master was working on my heart. No area was unattended and I was quite fascinated. Elmira had to remind me that I had work to do elsewhere.

I left the monks to their divine task and felt tremendous appreciation that such people lived upon Tara, the earth place of this sojourn. I intended to go to the apostles and hoped that they were re-formed by now as a group as I had asked Philip to do through the Whisper of Inspiration. Even as the thought and intention formed within my being, I was there with them.

They were grouped, but not united, I noticed. Some were still scared—actually most were terrified. Some were angry; some sad; some couldn't feel anything but fear and confusion, especially my rock, Peter, whom I loved dearly for his willingness to use his great strength for the service of our cause. Now he seemed weakened and lost, and sat separate from the others. I sat down beside him as he held his face in his hands, suffering despair, nearly to the point of breaking his great heart. I said, "Why the misery, strong one? Didn't you believe what I taught you?"

He nearly jumped out of his skin, at seeing me well-formed there speaking to him. His mouth fell open and he clearly couldn't believe his eyes.

"I'm as real as you are, dear friend," I said sensing his thought that he might be going crazy. "Now shall we join the others?" I asked. He simply nodded his head yes, as if in a trance and arose. We both walked toward the others. He didn't utter a word and kept looking at me, to make sure I wasn't an imaginative configuration that sorrow and grief had formed. The energy I had received from the Skull of Mu was enough, so that I could now form a more solid physical body. As I walked, dust was disturbed, even as it also was from the feet of Peter, too. But, his dust always was more prevalent, being the big man he was. How strange that I noticed the dust so profoundly today, I thought, when surely many times we had raised the dust walking together. So much of the physical experience goes unnoticed, I reflected, in the short moment it took to reach the group.

We stood awhile, at the edge of the circle the apostles had formed, unobserved. I sent Elmira to get MiryAmah and her group. I knew they would be together, and I wanted them here as well. The group was quieter than I had ever seen them, wanting to believe Philip's message and wondering what would happen now. Philip was beginning to doubt the voice he heard, due to the mood of the group and his proximity to Thomas, who sat next to him. Emotions and thinking modes hang in the air around people, and the attitude of Thomas could be catchy, as the group often commented upon. Philip finally looked up into the rising sun and saw, through the glare, Peter and me, on the fringes of the group. He couldn't quite make out who was who, until Peter said, "Arise and greet our master." Everyone looked toward us, standing there awaiting discovery, and they all came to life instantly. It was good that I had formed a semblance of a physical body, because the need to touch was overwhelming and my reception was emotional. It seemed that everyone desired to touch me, with Thomas wanting to put his finger into my nail wounds. Mathew was appalled at this request, and voiced disgust at Thomas.

"Don't reprimand Thomas," I said to Mathew and everyone present. "His doubt is his strength." I offered both my hands to Thomas, who at first touched gently and then more forcefully, to see if I could feel pain. He needed this confirmation and so did the others, but they weren't bold enough to demand it, as he was. That's why his doubting was his strength, because he posed questions others couldn't bring themselves to ask.

## The Saga-Oracle

"You're not all here," I said, seeing only eleven apostles and sensing a missing element. Then I realized who was missing. "Where's Judas?" I asked. I didn't know that he had hung himself after the crucifixion, suffering from deep sorrow and self-hatred for failing me, as he saw it.

"That traitor has done us the favor of killing himself," Thaddeus[152] said. I could see that everyone believed Judas had betrayed me, by the look of disgust on their faces.

I spoke softly but firmly to the group, just as the women arrived. However, I first smiled a welcome to my wife as she joined us. I kissed her lightly on the cheek, but firmly enough so she could feel my sentiment. Again, this was a private moment only spouses partook of–and nearly never in public–so I knew that there would be tensions among those who saw my tender gesture. Then I turned to them and said. "Know this! Judas was the one betrayed. His only lack was in not understanding my teachings. All of you have such a lack, in one way or another. Would you then, also, be betrayers? I have tried to give you eyes to see, but I can't take the blind spots from your inner-vision. I don't feel betrayed by your blindness so why would I feel betrayed by Judas. I just hope that one day you'll have your true vision restored. I pray now that wherever Judas is, he can see that I love him dearly and forgive him, as I must forgive all of you and myself, for not being perfect. We strive towards that goal, but we aren't there yet, my friends, my brothers and sisters, not yet. I also pray that you have the ears to hear me today, for too often what I say you don't hear."

They didn't want to be thought of as betrayers, so they dropped the accusation against Judas. I could tell they wanted to blame someone other than themselves; the sliver they saw in others eyes was nothing, compared to the plank they had protruding from their own. They knew this parable well, since we had discussed it often enough.

I then said, "I have come today to make sure that you carry on with the mission. I come from the house of my master (most

---

[152] Also remembered as St. Jude

thought they heard me say, 'My father') and I'll stay there with him, until I'm sent to do more of God's work. I want to review some things with you, and I would like you to listen with your hearts, not your heads this time. It's vital, if our mission is to be saved."

"But master," Andrew said, looking uneasy, "why do we need the women here? Surely, it is we, the inner-circle of twelve now eleven, which you must instruct in such important matters." As he said this, he looked over at Sarah, the daughter of Caiaphas the high priest, whom we had rescued so long ago by the city well, beaten to a pulp. He loved her, I could tell, and wanted her approval but not enough to change the imprint of keeping women from important spiritual business, as was the custom of the time. She looked at him with a pleading look. It was apparent that she found him appealing, too. She beseeched his heart, as she looked back at him, hoping he would release this concept that women would somehow disrupt or corrupt God's work. After all, it was that attitude that nearly killed her. I knew then that this love wouldn't materialize as a divine union. Poor Sarah, I thought. She certainly deserved love after all the suffering she had endured.

I answered him and the others saying, "Without the women, we aren't One. God the Father is God the Mother, too. Haven't you learned that important teaching yet? Would God the Father deny God the Mother His presence or would She deny him Hers? What you fear, my friend, is that the women may understand more easily than you do, and may have to teach you how to receive the grace of God, and you think that diminishes you."

I could see that the truth made the men uncomfortable. Even so, I continued on, saying, "I came to make sure that the teachings continue. Do I have to re-teach you the lessons? Why can't you understand that to deny women respect is to deny your very essence? Until you learn to love yourself, and your own feminine essence within your being, you'll never be able to reflect that understanding into all your life relationships. That's the imbalance and that's what fear uses to control and enslave you. Can't you see that the hatred and distrust of women is the source of all corruption?" As I looked out over their collective faces, I could

## The Saga-Oracle

see that some still had no concept of that which I spoke. They could more easily understand that I came back from the dead as some sort of Holy Ghost, rather than see the divinity of their own wives, mothers and daughters.

MiryAmah looked at me with an expression of sympathy and sorrow. We had spoken in private on many occasions of the frustration of not being able to teach this simple, but important divine relationship. Finally, I asked all to sit down on the ground in a circle. It was a bright hot day. Without thinking, I summoned a cloud to make shade for us, and we commenced reviewing the teachings in a rare shady spot, with a cloud not moving but hanging above us offering protection from the hot sun. The group was so entranced at seeing me, that they didn't notice the gift of Mother Nature and simply sat and waited for me to speak further.

I could see that many minds in this group were confused as to the core of our beliefs, the energies of positive and negative, or masculine and feminine. We had discussed, time and again, in countless ways, how this was an equally-balanced divine plan, how it couldn't be enforced yet when it fell into place naturally, it became a 'force of good,' or God. Elmira was there with me, but they couldn't see him, because he didn't physically manifest as I had. He asked me if I would like him to create a channel to their minds, so that I could pour wisdom therein. I looked at him and wondered of what he spoke. He told me of a custom his people had, of creating a channel for wisdom within their most sacred ceremonies.

"How can this be?" I questioned, since I hadn't heard of the technique.

He said, "It's not always successful, but if there is sufficient heart intention, a bright flame-like light will appear at the crown of the head, which indicates the channel is open."

"Give it a try," I replied, not realizing that the group was watching me speak to thin air and were just getting one side of the conversation. It wasn't stubbornness that closed their minds; it was imprints from years of slavery to those who held power, and always feared losing control. Thus, they needed to control others (love cooperates–fear enslaves). In a way my apostles were still slaves to the system, through deep imprints of attitude that were encoded into their very bodies from father to son, and from mother to daughter. The persistent demons of fear were relentless.

Elmira began his task and went to each person, even though they didn't know of his presence. I simply watched the progress. The followers couldn't understand why I silently looked above their heads, one by one. They eventually noticed the light where I looked; flame-like illumination appeared where I stared. They thought I was creating some blessing, when all the time my dear guardian Elmira was blessing them by opening a channel of wisdom. The more close-minded the individual, the brighter the flame burned above the crown of their head, due to the channel being opened more widely. Thus it happened that gentle lights appeared before the intuitive inner-circle of women, but above the men some very bright flames appeared. They could see the lights themselves and as easily happens, the brighter lights captured the greatest attention. Unfortunately, the light above the women's heads, and the women's presence, was forgotten in time. When Elmira had opened channels for all, I continued with my intention of refreshing their minds and thus touching their hearts.

I reviewed the essence of the teachings of 'The Way.' I knew the information found its way to the hearts of everyone, since I saw a light appear within their eyes–the windows of the soul. I knew that at least during this moment, they understood. What I didn't realize is that a few of the most headstrong would close the heart portals and reshape their memories of our day of wonders later. I worried that some would choose that course, yet I knew I must at least try to get them back on course. So it was, that alongside my beloved MiryAmah, we planted seeds of knowing again; her by being supportive, as I reminded our followers again of what they had already had been taught on many occasions as we wandered and shared the teachings of 'The Way'. All we could hope for was the seeds of wisdom would somehow find fertile ground within them– for their soul growth–so they could help lead others out of slavery.

By nightfall, I could feel my energy slipping and my form began to dissipate here and there. It looked like I had holes in my body,

# The Saga-Oracle

and the followers were beginning to tire, too. The sight of me breaking up was upsetting them. Elmira reminded me, it was time to go. I asked for a quiet moment with my beloved wife; we took our leave and walked away from the group. She clung to me for a short moment, but by this time, there wasn't much to cling to. I said, "I'll not desert you, my beloved."

"I know," she said, "but I wish we could have had a life together and more children, I sense that this child of yours wants, and needs, her father in her life, as well." She rubbed her belly and said, "We love you, Sarah." We had already named Sarah after our dear faithful friend, the daughter of Caiaphas, now our devoted follower.

"I don't know how I'll fulfill that wish, but I'll find a way," I replied. "I'm not dead. Remember that. I'm just in a safe place." Then I lost the energy to remain and vanished from her very embrace. As I drifted off, I could see her sitting and hugging her knees, rocking back and forth quietly sobbing. I looked at Elmira, who was guiding me along and asked, "How is it, Elmira, that those I love the most, I cause the most pain and sorrow?"

Before he could answer, I re-entered my body and was awakened by the monks, who were trying to see if the energy transference was successful and the re-mergence[153] of the bodies had happened. Now, the physical body needed the major force of the energy from the Skull of Mu. I could not appropriate it anymore for other purposes, the master told me. The healing had begun and the tissues needed all my soul's energy to re-knit, as the broken bones did as well. I would have to go into a coma-like state for a while, my master teacher told me, but one that would not allow my other bodies to freely wander. Thus a peaceful darkness descended upon me, and I slept.

---

[153] All seven bodies as mentioned, back together in perfect sync

# THE GREAT GIFT
## Chapter Thirty-Three

Being within the mountain community and with the old master was like being in heaven, even as the pain told me otherwise. One minute, it seemed I was in the grip of hate that would destroy and torment me, and the next I was being gently healed and attended to by those who I totally trusted. I found myself within the most profound relief imaginable, in the presence of love and wisdom. As I awoke from my deep sleep one day, the events past and present all flooded through my mind and body, resulting in great healing tears gushing forth from eyes, which saw too much suffering for everyone.

The visits I had made to my beloveds, which included the followers of course, were like a dream. I wasn't all that sure I hadn't imagined it, due to the pain I was enduring. The master assured me I, indeed, had visited my loved ones, and that he had a hard time getting my spirit back into my body, because I wanted to stay longer with those I loved. They were in terrible emotional pain from the events which took place, too. The memory of what happened overwhelmed me with sadness. Feeling that my mission had failed, I felt that I had let my followers and loved ones down, along with those who had entrusted me to this sacred task in the first place. I sometimes could remember the great Galactic Council and how determined I was to take on the mission they proposed. Emotions took over completely. The sadness drained me; I felt my life force quiver, and I began to shiver. It's quite true that one can die of a broken heart, and I believe I was heading that direction at that moment.

The old one put his hand upon my heart center, and gently whispered in my ear at the same time, "Don't waste the strength you still have on remorse, lad, for you didn't fail. Rather it was those you were sent to serve who failed, for they refused to take the servant's gift. You have planted good seeds, lad, and I tell you that they'll sprout and reap a good harvest, when the time is right. Now, let the sadness go. I ask you to let it go; so that your heart can help you thrive and not die for what you didn't do and live for what you did, and will continue to do."

His voice touched me. I released the overwhelming sadness and merged into peace. Letting the feeling of regret and disappointment go wasn't easy, but with the old wise one helping me, I arrived at one last great heaving sob, and it was done. My heart stopped feeling the effects of extreme sorrow and regret, which would stop it from beating its life-giving rhythm of sending life-force coursing through my body. I felt immediate relief and strength coming back into my chest area, where the hole in my aura had developed due to the grief I was feeling. That strength, spread from my chest and throughout my entire body. The aura, or energy field, around a physical body is the protection zone; extreme sadness can rip a hole from which the spirit may leak out, and become disconnected from the body, before the intended time of departure. That wouldn't happen today, and I was thankful that I had the wise elder there to help me through the situation.

The healing room was quiet, but not silent. There was a calm peace therein. Still I sensed a harmonic sound, beyond what I could normally hear, within the healing chamber, echoing off the walls and surrounding me with a symphony of greatest loveliness. A strange light was also present, that changed from marbleized green/blue to another mixture of red/pink. The color floated in the air around me. The master used his gentle old hands to direct the colored substance here and there, swirling it around my body like a magician doing a magic demonstration of controlling the mists. I remember the shift between the cool colors of the spectrum, the soothing blues and greens, to the warmer red and orange hues. At times the full visual spectrum was present, creating a vibrating rainbow. Then I noticed colors that the eye usually is unable to see and became mesmerized by them. I saw the color beyond violet,[154]

---

[154] Ultraviolet, consists of electromagnetic waves with frequencies higher than those that humans identify as the color violet.

which was present but carefully controlled by the master. He pulled this light into his ancient hands and applied it to various places upon my ripped and torn body like it was a lotion. That was followed by a white light, the purest I had ever seen, and beyond imagination, thus hard to describe. It was the Divine Light manifest. I had seen such a light in my own healing ministry before, but never in this intensity. The effects of the ultraviolet light, followed by the light of the Divine were pure bliss, and I could literally feel my tissues find their perfect pattern. It felt like an electrical frequency coursed through my body, with the pulsation causing a vibrating sensation, which somehow brought the tissue and bone back to its ultimate state of connectivity. I had a flash of regret, because I wished I could have helped people in this way. So many came to me suffering pain; to help them in this manner would have been the relief they longed for, just as I now longed to have my physical vehicle soothed and healed.

The vibrational frequency combined with the light healing, sounded like angels singing. Sound waves, along with light, were used in my healing. The result was like divine voices with no words, just notes of pitch, followed by echoes that reverberated around the healing chamber, encompassing myself and the master, who I believe was the only other soul present at the time. I became so lost in the wonder of it all, that I didn't dwell on the terrible events that had recently taken place and wondered again if I was entering heaven. If I had my wits about me, I would have remembered the heaven that so many, in times of crisis long for, was actually a higher purpose, not a place. It is a state of peace within the soul, not a place achieved by a system of judgment ushering you through a golden gate into an inner sanctum that only the chosen could access. I knew heaven as a peaceful sense of self, due to forgiveness of self-judgment, and acceptance of relationship to the Divine Essence. Yet, here I was reverting to the idea of a lofty place as I wondered where I might be. My beloved MiryAmah and I had spoken of the heavenly state of mind to our followers and tried to help them understand, but it seems that often the most difficult concepts to understand are those that begin and end with self-realization, and even I, in my agony, could be forgetful within my misery.

## The Saga-Oracle

The result of this serene condition I now moved into, due to the healing of the light and sound, was that I drifted off into a dreamless peaceful serenity again and awoke later in a personal chamber that had been prepared for me. When I awoke, I noticed I lay on a bed, and a lone candle burned nearby. The room, although carved out of bedrock, was polished to the point that the one tiny candle gently illuminated the entire space. I noticed I wasn't alone. There was a little mountain woman, a nun by the look of her, within the room. At least I assumed she was a nun, for in my day those of the quiet-sisterhood[155] were called such, and she reflected the confidence and wisdom that the sisters were well known for.

She looked at me and exclaimed, "Little master, you're awake."

She looked vaguely familiar. My foggy mind then recalled her, and I realized that she had looked exactly the same the last time I had seen her as a boy, when I was in residence in this holy underground mountain city. She was the playful one. I was seldom given names of individuals, since they wanted me to integrate the people into Onement, seeing them all as part of the same vibrational group, there to mentor and share with me. Each had a distinct personality and hers shone no less bright now, then it did before. As a little boy with a huge imagination back in those days, I would notice the personality traits of those in this secret city. She was indeed, 'the playful one.' Here she was again, in my presence, bringing the joy that forever rode in upon the tail of her flying robe tails, as she went about jumping and dancing her glee. She always moved in a wonderful dancing motion, skipping as she went through her daily tasks. At first it looked a bit ridiculous, causing one to laugh; maybe that was the idea all along. Today she was hopping around the room, dusting the few objects within the space, with the end of a sponge-like object she held. It was actually mountain moss that was used for this purpose; the dust it absorbed would feed the mushrooms. These people, I remembered, didn't waste anything.

---

[155] Women who devoted their life to service, and while they used ritual, their main dedication was to serve others

As she danced and sang in her own language, which I had come to understand in my early years, and now remembered with ease, her robe, as always, was fluttering like the wings of a butterfly. Since they were rainbow striped, indeed she was a beautiful sight to see. When she noticed my eyes open, she fluttered her robe-wings over to my sleeping shelf, which was comfortably padded with the wool of mountain sheep and covered with finely spun orange linen sheets, and practically lit by my side, like the giant butterfly, she reminded me of.

She continued her song and gently kneeled beside me looking intently into my eyes, still seeing me as the little master, as I ever saw her as the 'happy one.' Time between our last meeting and now, seemed to dissipate. We picked up where we last saw each other, she still ever the pretty one, full figured and happy, and I felt like the little boy again who loved her presence and her joyful attitude.

She often sang her communication with me, never falling out of harmony, and again she sang *"You will always be the 'wee one' to me, dear heart, and I am glad that you've finally come back in the world, such as it is, to be with us once more. I've missed your sweet curiosity."* Her singing statement was the natural way this butterfly-like person communicated. I would have sung back a reply, but I had no strength yet for words linked in song, and barely for any other mode of linking words in reply. I struggled to respond to her, then finally found strength enough to propel my voice, and asked her, "How long have I been suspended in this dreamless place I return from?"

This time not within a song, she answered, "Many moons, dear heart, a long time."

"Months!" I exclaimed. "How can that be?" It certainly didn't seem like that long, since I had fallen into this healing slumber.

Noting my astonishment she sang, *"Anything you can imagine can be, and some things you can't imagine happen, too,"* as she gently kissed me on the cheek. Excusing herself, she fluttered out the door, but not before throwing something that looked like a ball of fur in my direction. *"Here,"* she sang, as she tossed the object to me, *"this will make you laugh and bring some joy to energize you."*

I instinctively reacted and reached out to catch the object flying my direction, which seemed to please my playful attendant. She nodded her head, affirming something that she wanted to know, which I surmised, was that I still could move my body in sync with my automatic reactions. My hands had flown from under my covering to catch the soft ball that came hurtling toward me. Immediately, I felt the pulse of life within the object. As I inspected the fur ball, I found it, mainly white with stripes of gray encircling it, and velvety to the touch. My attention was diverted from my departing nurse, to the soft ball that throbbed with warmth and life. She had taken it from a basket by the doorway.

Being naturally curious, I didn't notice I was no longer in pain, and that my wounds had healed. All I wanted to know now was, what sort of a living being was this warm fuzzy thing I held. Even as I wondered, a head emerged from the ball and a cat-like face, with a very flat nose and whiskers looked at me with piercing dark eyes. Then legs appeared and I had in my hand a small animal that I couldn't remember ever encountering before. It purred like a cat, but it looked more like a stripped ferret and acted like one as well, for it had a playful nature.

It soon tired of staring into my eyes. It was naturally curious, too, and wanted to explore me as much as I wanted to see and understand it. After unfurling itself from the ball shape, which I now understand is how it slept, it ran about my body on its four short legs, sniffing and checking me out, head to toe. It even found its way under the warm light-weight feathered quilt that covered me. The antics of this inquisitive ball of fur made me laugh and that was how the master found me, laughing and playing like a boy with a new toy, when he entered the room a short time later.

"Finally, you are sufficiently strong to awaken, lad," he said. Since there was no need to answer him, as just seeing me was answer enough, he reached down and took the little animal gently from my coverings, where it was sliding up and down the hills and valleys of my body on its little sleek back. "Rema,[156]" he said, as he stood by me, elevating the little animal in his hands to eye level, "have you checked out the little master and do you find his energy in balance?"

I could hear a very high-pitched sound uttered from the tiny animal, but it wasn't an animal language I understood. I asked what Rema was saying.

"Oh!" the master said, "I'm sorry to be so rude. Rema here is a guest from another place. He came to us just after you left as a boy, so, of course, you didn't learn his language. He's a healer of energy. He has been sleeping and living with you, since we brought you in from the emergency chamber, where we had to do some major adjusting of your energetic fields. His expertise, if you will, is to keep the energy fields balanced. He does that by rubbing his sensitive fur over the surface of your body, which is quite pleasurable to him, as well as to you. I think you may have already noticed. When he finds a place within the pattern of your being that isn't in balance, he's able to move the energy, ever so slightly and gently, to the place that needs attention, by rubbing the area blending it to perfection. He's giving me an update now on your energetic fields, and he finds that it's time for you to arise from your bed, young master, and get back to the realm of physical living."

Amazed and amused by this cute little being, Rema, I threw back my comforter of feathers and stood up. I felt no stiffness upon arising. Without a stitch of clothing upon my body, I remarked, "The playful one who just left, said I have been sleeping for many moons, but I feel as if I just lay down for a few moments. I'm not stiff, nor do I feel fogged from long sleep." As I said this, I suddenly noticed my nudity and very, frail thin, skeletal body. "Oh!" I exclaimed, "I'm sorry, I'm not clothed. This body has wasted so; I must be a sorry sight, dear master." I meant no disrespect and felt I needed to apologize for my lack of garb.

---

[156] Small animal that had the ability to check the energetic field and find places that needed to be balanced, or needed an infusion of energy to heal them. He came from another plane, or place.

He just laughed, handed me a bright blue robe to cover myself and said, "I've seen your nude body many a time, lad. From the days when you first came as a wee child, and we swam in the pool of reflection, and now as a grown man, and I find it not much different, but I must admit you have shrunk to the bone." Then he helped me belt in the waist of my robe, as I found that I was a bit uncoordinated. Helping me tie the sash at my waist, he further said, "A diet of only energy doesn't hold much physical weight on the body, but is sufficient to sustain physical life upon this plane of being." Then he went on to say, "But I think we should give you your first meal, so that you can gain the mass you'll need for the work that awaits you." Thus, he ushered me out the doorway of my small room, with Rema now perched on his shoulder. How the little fellow managed to get there, I hadn't noticed. We went to the place of communion; the master strolling along at a slow pace–no doubt to accommodate me–with the fascinating animal Rema riding his shoulder.

In this underground mountain city, the place of communion was where food was prepared and served. It was considered the holy center of the city and the act of eating was Holy Communion to these people. It was customary for groups to sit together to share the meal, but also to feed each other from time to time. Therefore, it was quite natural when the master joined others at a small low-built table upon a floor carpeted with soft mountain moss. He kneeled down upon his knees and invited me to do so as well. Rema scurried down his arm, onto the table, and the master explained to me, "Rema likes the hall of communion, and he can't wait to feed you a tidbit or two." Then the master said to Rema, "Remember, it's hard to digest some food stuffs after being on a diet of pure energy for so long. Be wise in your choice of what you share with our little master, or surely he will suffer, and the result might not be pleasant." Rema, taking no offense at the caution, just nodded agreement. I looked at Rema and thought of how I was still referred to as 'little master' here in this sanctuary. I was a grown man now and to me, Rema was the little master.

The hall of communion was occupied by several other groups of people. Mixed in here and there, were a few individuals clearly not of the tribe of the mountain folk; many other species were present, such as birds and animals of all sorts, too. The people all looked at us as we entered. They put their hands together in a prayerful manner, touching their lips with the tips of their fingers in the welcome gesture, smiling then went back to their communion and quiet conversations. Soon food arrived at our table, and I was offered a bowl of vegetable broth, but not solid food. Bowls were provided for all three of us, and I noticed that the master and Rema were served delicious broth, as well. I found it comforting that they shared the same version of sustenance that I must consume. Conversation in this place was never of the chitchat variety, and it was common to see individuals just enjoying each other's company and eating in silence. So, too, it was with us. The taste of the soup was incredible. Each vegetable, fully blended in the broth, offered its essence in full measure, including the mushrooms of the mountains that I loved so much as a child. I didn't miss solid food due to the intense flavor. As I tipped my bowl and drank directly from it each slurp I pulled from the rim of the bowl was satisfying and fulfilling. I noticed, as we sat and dined, that Rema's front paws were like hands. He also picked up his tiny bowl and partook of its essence much as the master and I did. He noticed me watching him and smiled. That's when I knew that he was of a highly aware species, for the smile denotes humor, and humor results from a heightened emotional ability. Picking up his small bowl in his little hands, he walked upright across the table to my position and held his tiny vessel up for me to sip from. Knowing the custom and sentiments of this sharing ritual, I gladly took a sip of his offering. His soup was different from my own, nuttier in flavor but still as satisfying.

"Easy now!" the master cautioned as I took a small sip, careful not to drain Rema's bowl of food; "our little master can't have too much of a good thing yet, or his body will not perceive it as nourishing, and he will spend the rest of the day in the cleansing chambers." I wondered how could there be enough within that tiny dish to cause such havoc within my digestive system. Evidently, the amount of food was not equal to the effect of it; I heeded the warning and partook lightly.

The fact that I had tasted his offering pleased Rema, who after waiting to be offered a taste of my soup, which I presented, went back to his former position. He said something to the old master as he passed by and the master told me that Rema thought my soup was a bit bland for his taste, but otherwise acceptable.

"Tell him I'm glad that he thinks my food is good, but I'll be happy when we can speak directly," I said.

"When you are strong enough, lad," the master said, "Rema will give you the gift of understanding his language."

I don't remember much after that. The food was so comforting to my body, that I immediately fell asleep. I awoke again in my sleeping place wondering how I got there, with Rema doing his fun-loving gyrations all over my body. He was acting very otter-like as before, sliding down the crevices of my comforter on his back and twisting around so that his body spun like a cork screw. I was sleeping on my side, so there were many hills and valleys for such fun and service. When he noticed my eyes open he came up to my face and literally examined each eye intently, getting as close as his flat little nose would allow and peering into each one individually. It was all I could do not to laugh at the tiny one, for he was quite comical in manner and action, and even this eye contact was amusing. As he looked into my eyes, I could sense energy going directly into my middle eye, or pituitary gland, and my face began to heat up between my eyes. I then felt quite awake and wanted to arise, but I had to wait for Rema to finish his work. Then it happened–his essence merged with mine within the arena of the pituitary. He spoke to me through mind-speak, and I heard, and saw, his essence quite clearly. His physical body may have been in an animal form, but his spirit was much more expansive. I saw a being without form, within my inner-vision, beautiful beyond description. There, light and sound united, married and merged to the point that it was pure energy. Even as I call the little fuzzy version of this being a 'he,' I knew that its essence was both male and female. Rema said to me, "Fear not, young master. You have much work yet to do, and I bring energy and balance into your physical being, so that you can be back on track with your mission."

Watching the light shimmer and change hue, I answered, "Who are you, little one, who doesn't seem so little to me now?"

"I am that I am, just as you are that you are," it answered, vibrating in its non-form essence.

It must have sensed a bit of frustration on my part as I struggled to understand this being, so it expanded its answer a bit, saying, "I take whatever form I need, that fits within the place and space where I find myself for energetic work. In the case of the high mountain city, it's quite cool here for my physical comfort, so I keep a small body covered with warm fur as my preferred form. I must have a physical form to work with, when I am in a physical place." I understood, because being in the physical realms, I had to work from that perspective as well. Rema went on to say, "I devised a way to curl into a ball, to conserve the heartbeat and energy, I need to sustain a physical presence. I come from a far place where days are much longer than in this plane. So, in my experience of time passing, which is not linear but cyclical in nature, I have been here but a short time, while those I visit, feel as if I have been here nearly a lifetime for some, or about twenty-seven years in your cycle of understanding."

"When will I understand your language outside of my head?" I asked, because I wanted to know what he was saying while communicating from the little body, he just described to me, when I encountered him outside these inner-chambers of my mind.

"I'm planting the codes now within your third eye and also putting a trigger inside your ear drums, so that when beings such as I, want to talk to you, we can on any level and in any manner. Your days of learning languages are over, little master," he said. "Now, you will instantly understand any spoken word, as well as any thought a being transmits. This will be a necessity since, as you slept so soundly, your soul was in communication with the Council of Elders, and it was decided that you would travel in all manner of ways to far places and plant the seeds of peace wherever you go. That intention requires that you must have a way of totally understanding those you seek and speak with. That's why I'm working with you and a few others of the same intention.

## The Saga-Oracle

Do you accept the responsibility of having these codes I have just placed, activated?" Rema asked in a voice of authority.

"I do," I responded without hesitation. Even if I couldn't remember being with the council, I knew this was the desire of my soul, to continue with the work of peace and balance, and I was ready for the responsibility it required.

I felt, heard and saw the brilliant bright light again, the one that followed the ultraviolet light in my intensive healing sessions with the old master, but this time it was not exactly just healing in nature. It was an activation vibration. Again it came with the choir of angels sound. The combination of the sound and the light filled my being. I felt a huge release within, not unlike the sexual release I felt during the most intimate times with my beloved MiryAmah, when our lovemaking matched our love feeling. A flood of pleasure and soothing energy coursed through my body, and I realized that my entire body was releasing. It couldn't have been more than a moment or two, but when I came out of the reverie, I was covered in tears, sweat, mucus, blood, urine and feces, and the smell of my release was not what I would term pleasant, but strangely, it didn't bother me.

"Well, the release was total," Rema said. He then pointed to a copper tub filled with steaming water in a small grotto off my chamber. I hadn't noticed it before. It was an overflowing tub with volcanically heated water, channeled into it from a source within the rock wall. It held a constant temperature and overflowed the rim of the copper tub draining away, back into the rock. I didn't need any urging to cleanse and headed right for the tub of inviting bath water. I carefully put my big toe into the water as it looked very hot, steaming to the point that the fog was nearly engulfing everything in the tiny room, and found that it didn't burn me. Cautiously, I slipped into the soothing tub of water and enjoyed the feeling it afforded, as it bubbled around me like a boiling soup. The bubbles, as it turned out, consisted of sulfur and other substances that the volcano offered within its sacred waters from deep within the body of Tara (mother earth). Those bubbles were full of healing properties, and the magic of the bath, I now enjoyed. Interestingly, however, the sulfur didn't have a strong odor, as usually was the case; rather it had a fresh essence that pleased my sense of smell. The smells of the fluids that I had just released quickly dissipated, due to the agitation of the bubbles, along with the constant flow from the volcanic channel that naturally cleansed me and recycled the water through the overflow back to mother earth. In mere moments, I was simply relaxing in the clear sparkling hot water, feeling re-energized and relaxed.

While I was in the tub, the playful one–the little nun–came into the room, cleaned the linens from my bed and had them sent to be laundered. She came to me with a clean robe of blue, and motioned that I should get out of the tub, and be wrapped to dry. She noticed that I was a bit embarrassed as I climbed out of the tub naked, before a woman not my wife. She laughed at me and told me that she had seen me in the nude on many occasions as a small lad, when she had helped with the sacred baths. It didn't bother her then, so it shouldn't be bothering me now, she reminded me. I had conveniently forgotten that part of my stay here, and wondered how many times I had paraded around without clothing, since the master had mentioned pretty much the same thing. Her request, however, was easier said than done, since she had not aged a bit in all the years I had been away and still looked young as ever. To a little boy, she may have seemed motherly, but now that we were both adults the situation felt different to me. She muttered something about being old enough to have given my great grandfather baths and just shook the robe, indicating I was to get my bare butt into it as she suggested. Her constant movement and laughter was not about the situation, just her natural way of being. Her mood uplifted me as she helped me into the warm dry robe.

There were candles burning within my space, as I left the bathing nook, which gave a delightful odor to the room–quite different from the odors I had just recently created due to my great release. I was grateful for the transformation. The old master came in and my attendant nurse just fluttered out the doorway, giving us our privacy, leaving behind a neater and cleaner space than she had found.

"Now, that must feel better," the old one said to me, as he headed toward a jutting rock that held a cushion upon it. He carefully settled his ancient-looking body upon the cushion and just looked at me with such love, awaiting my response.

"You know, master," I said, "I certainly do feel wonderful. If you had described the process to me, I wouldn't have thought it to be a pleasant affair at all, this releasing of body fluids and toxins." Then, sensing that Rema wasn't present, I asked of him.

"Rema is preparing to work on another project," The master answered. "Rema will speak with you from time to time, if circumstance and opportunity allow," he explained. I already missed the wonderful little being, who had energized me to the point that I could release so many toxins from my physical vehicle, and feel the lightness and cleanliness I now enjoyed.

I must have shown disappointment at Rema's quiet departure, because the master said, "Don't worry, lad. That Rema shows up in the most unlikely places and chooses the best times to materialize. Now that you have been encoded to communicate, you'll be surprised at how Rema will bless your days to come."

"Now," the old one said, "It's time to leave this sleeping place, where you have spent so much time and be about other business."

## BI-LOCATING TO MY BELOVEDS
Chapter Thirty-Four

My strength came back enough so that I could move about, and I visited many old friends within the mountain place who I knew from the days of my childhood. This was a homecoming for me in many ways, but still I missed my own family intensely and wanted to know of their well-being. One of my teachers from my childhood, Eocha,[157] watched me intently; as we reminisced about the playful pranks I pulled in my early days in this place. She seemed to be looking through me even as I remembered those

---

[157] This name means 'watcher' and in this case a 'nun watcher.' It is old Gaelic and often a boy's name

days of carefree fun. I wondered if she heard me at all, since she wasn't one to show emotions.

When she could get a word in edgewise, Eocha finally said to me, "You miss your beloveds, dear one." I didn't expect the comment. I had been laughing and enjoying remembering a special prank I used to play on her, where I would put a noise maker under her seat, and as she sat upon it the noise would be like a mighty passage of body gas. She just ignored it, as I recalled the situation, and went on as if nothing happened, while I rolled around on the floor in laughter. I was never reprimanded, as joy was encouraged. Even the joy of a boyhood prank was considered sacred, as long as it didn't hurt anyone. Eocha was always able to hold a calm presence no matter what the emotion might be, but she did slightly smile at times such as that, and it was my sweet success. Her calm didn't mean she missed the delight of the occasion. Depending on what she experienced, it didn't mean she couldn't feel the pain or cry the tears, either. I saw her tears flow once, and it was a sad moment that moved us all to sorrow. However, this time, her comment brought me to full emotion, and I broke down before her, when she mentioned my beloved family and friends, all dear to me. I missed them beyond measure. I sobbed and shook as all the raw emotions (my frail body nearly couldn't accommodate the inner pain) coursed through me, which always hurt more than physical wounds did. The cleansing, evidently, had not washed away the sorrow of separation.

Eocha calmly moved toward me, took me in her old arms and gently rocked me. She made a soothing sound, almost a sing-song melody, and I finally found my way through the ordeal. She said nothing—just sang and gently rocked me.

I finally regained my strength again, and apologized for my lapse into self-pity. Eocha said, "You have nothing to apologize for, Jeshua, for love is like that mighty sword you helped forge, with two sides, quite opposite but necessary in its work."

I looked at her and tried to understand the full meaning of what she said by peering into her deep blue eyes. That was when I first noticed that, while she had the dark skin of the mountain people,

# The Saga-Oracle

her eyes were deep pools of blue, like my own. They were so dark, they at first seemed dark brown as was the common look of these people of the high places. I suddenly realized that because I expected them to be like everyone else's eyes, I never looked closer.

"Oh! Now you are trying to look deep into my eyes, and you see something you haven't noticed before," she said, as she returned the stare in her own piercing way. I could feel the connection of spirits between us and wondered how I had missed this as a boy in her presence.

"Why didn't I notice that your eyes are blue like mine, mastra?" I whispered, for my blue eyes were always something I hid, so that I didn't gain too much attention within my travels and teaching time.

"Probably because it doesn't matter, since having a difference in one place is not a difference in another," she answered. I must have looked a bit puzzled, as she went on to say. "There are places where the deep brown eyes are unusual, and they scare the blue-eyed majority, because they can't see their own reflection in the earthy pools of color therein."

I forgot my sorrow, as I pondered what she had said, and drifted off in thought. Even so, Eocha brought me back to the moment, asking if I would like to learn how to be in two places at once. I wondered what that had to do with missing my family and the color of eyes.

Eocha could change the topic so fast, one forgot what was being discussed and why. When she mentioned bi-location my attention was instantly diverted. I knew bi-location was a possibility, since I had heard of it before. I thought it would take many years to accomplish and said, "If only I had the time to accomplish such a feat, for I would surely disguise myself and take one part of me back to my family, just to check on their safety and well being."

She said, "It's possible and we'll begin the conditioning you'll need, to hold a double presence in the physical. I believe that you desire quite strongly to touch and hold those that you love. That

409

isn't an option right now in your present condition. It takes too much from the one body and depletes the other to the point of demise in the physical state, should you push your energy vibrational frequency too far."

"You see, dear one, even when you went back in the etheric state to visit your followers and beloveds after your ordeal on the cross, the energy was nearly used up and there wasn't much to hold life within your body. You may think that you were unconscious for only a short while, but the truth of the matter is, that you were nearly three years suspended from daily physicality, while your body repaired itself sufficiently enough to hold a balanced energy grid again," She informed me. "Rema had his hands full, getting your energy grid back in sufficient balance to hold life-force."

I remembered the little furry master, and was thankful for all that was done for me by the tiny one, especially giving me the ability to understand the spoken word, no matter what language it was voiced within.

"Yes," Eocha said, sensing my gratitude to the little Rema, "as has often been said, good things do come in small packages, and your little energizer worked a long time to bring you back fully present and physically perfect again."

The statement about the years passing astonished me. I thought I might have been unconscious for days, or at the most weeks, but she said I was asleep in a coma for years. "How can this be?" I insisted to know, thinking that my family would surely think me dead by now and wondering what could have transpired in all that time in an unconscious state.

"It can be and it is," Eocha said. "And now there is work to do, so that you can carry on with your mission in a new modality." She looked at me and could see that my eyes were glazed and my thoughts were again with my family. I was still carrying raw emotion from my ordeal. She walked across the tiny chamber within the mountain city that we occupied and found a shallow bowl made of quartz, sitting upon a shelf. She brought it back to a flat rock that jutted up from the floor of the chamber; I noticed how she cradled it into a natural depression within the rock, which

## The Saga-Oracle

held it perfectly level. She then found a pitcher made of the same quartz, white and nearly clear, and she took it to a spring water spout in the wall, which drained into a stone-hollowed basin below the tiny trickle. Filling the pitcher, she poured the water into the bowl. She blew upon the water. It began to swirl like a whirlpool. Mist came upward and engulfed her face in a purple fog. She stopped the gentle blowing and summoned me to come forward. As I stepped towards the bowl, she simply said, "Look."

What I saw was my beloved MiryAmah with a delightful child at her side, golden-haired with the suntanned skin of a child that played in the sun. I noticed that her eyes were the same deep blue of my own and her hair had the reddish glow that my own had, as well. She looked so familiar to me; I became lost in the vision of her. She was with my beloved wife, and I could clearly see she loved this little one beyond measure. Then it dawned on me that I was seeing little Sarah. Again the emotions overtook me. My tears mixed with the waters I was scrying[158] and I nearly lost the vision.

"Stay calm within the moment," Eocha gently said. "Your calmness will hold the vision that takes you to Egypt, where your loved ones are now in exile. Remember that sweet love is stronger than sorrow, and recall the dreams of your coma, Jeshua. You often journeyed there, while you slept to the world." I then realized why this child seemed so familiar, apart from the knowing a parent has for their own children. I remembered the dream visits, I experienced quite often, how my beloved wife always embraced and encircled me with her immense love, and ever this little one was there as well, giving me love in her own childlike manner. I'm sure that their love was responsible for a great deal of my healing.

Just as I was thinking about the dreams of my coma, my child looked as if she sensed my presence and looked directly at me through the gentle swirling scrying water. I saw her mother's look of concern and she said, "What do you see, child?"

---

[158] A way to look into other dimensions, times and places, much like crystal ball gazing

Little Sarah cocked her head one way, and then the other in deepest concentration, and said, "My papa." Evidently that was the way she referred to me. MiryAmah tried to look the direction of Sarah's intent gaze but I could see that she wasn't able to find my face as I had found hers. However, she knew that I was there and said, "Jeshua, we miss you. We are doing well, but are still in hiding under the protection of your brothers and the priestesses. I wish you could come back to the land of the living, but even as I wish for your presence, sweet husband, I also know that where you are you are safe and that's more important for my peace of mind. You'll always be the love of my soul, dear heart. Be at peace," she finally said, and the vision disappeared.

I looked up at Eocha, questioning why I had lost the vision.

"You've done well, Jeshua," she said in answer to my unspoken question. "You've held the scry longer than I thought you could, taking into consideration the state of your physical body. Maybe next time we'll scry your sweet mother, for I know you miss her, too. Now, however, we must not push too far. Go back to your chamber and get some rest. Tomorrow we'll begin your lessons in bi-location."

And so it was–I would go daily and learn how to take the energy of my body and double the grid that it used to envelop the mass of physical form that I held, as does all creation, so that I could activate two identical grids for the one body I used. It is a very complicated process, but Eocha was persistently patient, and she taught me the power of the calm. This power of the calm was evident all around in the physical world. I was surprised that I had overlooked it, while I walked as Jesus. It was the calm just before the storm, the moment of repose just before action. Calm is the scrying pool of the mind. Who would have known what wonders could be accomplished within the calm, I thought. I knew that meditation brought answers and communication from the divine, but I didn't know that physical alterations could be made within calm surrender.

Two more years passed and it seemed more like merely two weeks. I, eventually, was offered the bowl of reflection to see my mother; I could see that she was also in a safe place, at least, for the moment. When I came to her presence, I saw that James, my brother was with her. He was encouraging her to be careful, because there were those who would harm her, if she became too visible in the social areas. She was assuring him that she was taking every precaution, but that she had to go to see her granddaughter, Sarah.

"I just have to see that child!" she said and I could see James accepting that our mother wouldn't be denied her grandmother's right. She added, "You know, James, she claims she has seen her father, and I must know how that happened. Little Sarah doesn't know what a lie is and surely this child has seen what I would desire with all my heart–to lay eyes on my own child again."

"We may have to move them soon," James announced, watching her to see her reaction to this statement.

"Where?" mother replied, looking at James, almost as if she dared him to take her loved ones further from her than they already were. Even so, she still encircled him in her arms and kissed him on his forehead because he was her child, too. He looked so much like me, which had caused him some moments of danger and insecurity.

"To a safe place," he replied to mother. "Joseph has been preparing a safe haven in a faraway land, mother," he said. "His trade routes take him many places, and he knows where our family can disappear."

She asked, "Safe from the Romans or safe from the very people who claim to be our friends?"

"The Romans have taken control of lands far and wide, mother," he replied. "The place Joseph has located, Romans aren't so concerned, due to the population being mostly forest people and tribes not of interest to the mighty Roman Empire." He went on to say, "But how long that will last is beyond my ability to perceive, for they keep spies in all areas of their lands of conquest. Also, we have those among our followers, who are people who would shape things to fit their vision. I fear that they may accept you, but never the family of my brother."

Then the vision dissolved. Eocha didn't offer the bowl again, instead concentrated on teaching me the calm and the re-weaving of a duplicate energetic grid for my physical body. Over and over we traced the pattern–at first with a stick in the sand floor of the chamber, then in the air, and finally we brought light to the drawing and made the light patterns merge with sounds, that I can't describe, but can say were like symphonies.

I learned that energy is a truer form, than the actual physical manifestation. If the energy grid is well constructed, the physical body then naturally forms to its natural perfection. I remembered Yasma healing the man's misshapen arm long ago, as he talked about finding the perfect pattern. Of course, that was for healing; now I was working on bi-location, but I could sense a connection in concept, nonetheless. To make a duplicate grid is tricky; for when two identical bodies are formed, one has to sustain the other and vice versa. This duality can only be sustained for so long, and then must merge back into the body's Onement. Within bi-location what one does the other body also feels. If one is in a position of peril and harmed, both bodies are injured and could suffer physical death. It reminded me of my twin soul MiryAmah, but in this case it was the double of my own part of that twin-age I worked with. That alone was a major problem. Few undertake the doubling grid, due to its extreme difficulty to manage and how carefully the first physical vehicle must be monitored.

Finally, the day came, when I was given the chance to duplicate my body. Time, day, or week, didn't seem to matter to me anymore, so I can't tell you how long it took to get to this point. I spent most of my time adjusting, and becoming accustomed to, the energetic grid of my physical vehicle. When I viewed, and listened to myself, I became well acquainted with every nuance, and how the sound and light cords entwined, until they were totally familiar. I had to learn to step out of body to do this monitoring, since the grid could only be matched from that vantage point. Eocha said that by stepping out of my body, viewing it and inspecting the grid, I was actually accomplishing the first step of bi-location. I carefully placed the new grid over the original grid and adjusted each intersection to correspond with the original pattern. I could hear my soul-sound, and became expert at hearing the finer frequencies, which I had previously overlooked. I adjusted them to match as well. Fine-tuning was a difficult process but had to do with entering the calm and carefully using intention, to move the components to and fro, up and down, in frequency and so forth, until they were the exact echo of each other. It took concentration, pure will and determination, and, possibly the hardest part, the total acceptance and love for oneself, to accomplish this feat. Love is a creational vibration. Fear is anti-creational, or a destructive de-vibration[159]. By that I mean vibration is movement and life. To stop the movement, or de-vibrate then, is to destroy the natural growth life affords. Not honoring yourself is fear that you are not worthy; you can't work within such a destructive atmosphere, much less improve or activate anything. I had to stop beating myself up for my so-called failure to bring balance and love into the priesthood, and the social context of the time and space I had just left. I also had to get over feeling like the father who had abandoned his family. It took great leaps of faith to forgive myself. I tell you that forgiveness of self is the greatest challenge in the evolution of consciousness.

I eventually arrived at the day of my first body-doubling. I was allowed to mentally choose a place within the area I now resided to bi-locate. I chose the cave of the snow leopard, since I have always loved the memory of my time therein. Eocha nodded her head and instructed me to prepare for my first journey. As I entered the calm, I noticed she, too, entered the calm state. I wondered if she was taking me on this expedition, or if I was on my own in the process. I envisioned the cave, as I had learned to do, and became calm enough to step out of my body and see my two grids separate. The two identical forms of me stood side by side in grid pattern and could move separately. I then visualized the cave and intentionally relocated one of the bodies to the place I intended to materialize. I could see the snow leopard there with kits. She was washing them from head to toe with her huge

---

[159] Stopping the natural movement of a life-form, through thought and action

tongue. They were playfully resisting, but still loving the attention. All the purring declared the sanctity of their cave dwelling.

I came into full physical form with a loud pop. The mother leopard reacted by immediately jumping to her feet, kittens tumbling down around her. With her fangs bared, she nearly attacked me. A light enveloped her and she calmed within it, and I saw Eocha there with me, also fully physical.

"You don't think I would allow you to go and get yourself eaten by a snow leopard, do you?" she said. Then she continued, saying, "This is a good lesson for you, in planning your destination. There are definitely places you may not want to visit unannounced. This den of the snow leopard is indeed such a place. It was her mother that you knew so long ago, who has since moved on. Before you materialize, you'll have to consider all possible scenarios, for fear will react faster than love can recognize you. Love is of the calm; being such, it comes through on a slower wave, even as it is a higher vibration. Fear, which is reactionary to its framework, lashes out to protect against the monster that would change its world. In some cases that reaction is justified, so that physical life can continue. In other cases the reaction harms that which would not have threatened its security, but may have enhanced it." At this pronouncement, she allowed the mighty feline mother a chance to come to full presence again. It calmly purred and watched us converse. Now it was curious of me and my mastra, there in her safe haven.

Remembering my animal-speak days, I told this mother cat that I was a friend of her mother, and I was just learning to go to sacred spaces. She stopped her purring for a moment and a low growl emerged from her great speckled white body. She was telling me that she was not willing to share her sacred space, which I should immediately depart and leave her in peace, or I would be her dinner. I saw Eocha smile slightly, which in itself was remarkable, for she seldom showed emotion; though I know she felt it. She nodded to me and I knew it was time to depart, before dinner was served, and I was the on the menu.

# The Saga-Oracle

As we came back, our other bodies united and merged, as Eocha had taught me to do, I was concerned, because I felt I had failed my first try at bi-location. Eocha assured me that I hadn't failed, but had learned a good lesson. "Any time you learn something, you never consider it a failure," she assured me.

After a period of time, and much more practice, I felt ready to do a most serious visit–one that had been on my mind since the first day of my scrying vision of my beloved MiryAmah and little Sarah. It had been a couple of years since that comforting vision, and much had changed, including their location. I was now able to follow them outside of my dream state. I knew they had sailed across the Mediterranean Sea to the land of the Gaul, guided and guarded by my brother, the merchant traveler, Joseph of Arimathea. Joseph had created a safe haven for my family there. I knew from dream conversations with my wife, that she was carrying on with our work as best she could in the new land, one of the places of the Druids. Finally, the day came and I prepared to go to her first, before going anywhere else.

Eocha assured me that there were those who would anchor me here, and watch the body left behind. She also said, "We'll make sure that part of you remains calm and rested, so that the other part of your being can fully experience all levels of interaction at your homecoming."

Thus, I departed in anxious anticipation, but still able to keep within the calm surrender. I fully manifested in a castle-like complex, but within the chamber that my beloved now occupied. I saw her by herself, sitting on a shelf used for sleeping. She was so sad and lonely. She sat with her eyes closed and tears leaking, as she rubbed them with her sleeve. I walked up to her and could see a slight smile appear upon her lovely face, as she stopped the soft sobbing. Still keeping her eyes closed, she raised her face and looked upward. I believe she thought she was having a good dream of me again.

"I miss you so much," she whispered.

"I have missed you, too," I said and her smile broadened, still with tightly closed eyes not wanting to lose the dream vision. I gently kissed her on the cheek. Her eyebrows wrinkled slightly, for the feeling of touch had never before accompanied such sweet visions. She was still somewhat reluctant to open her eyes and chance losing the sweet moment, so I kissed her again, this time gently, but fully upon her mouth. Her eyes flew open at this gesture; she shrieked with joy and surrounded me with her hugging arms. Such strength, she had. I couldn't have escaped that hug, if I had wanted to, and I certainly didn't.

Finally coming to her full senses, she asked, "Am I dreaming out loud, now?"

"And what would that statement mean?" I replied. "If you are wondering if I am really here, wonder no longer, wife, for the husband has returned, alive and out loud!"

Our emotional response wasn't what I would describe as calm. We joyfully voiced our joy and twirled each other around and around. The thought crossed my mind that those watchers of my other body might perceive all this and, since every part of me wanted every part of my wife all at once, for a split second, I blushed. We couldn't stop our physical reaction to our reunion, nor could we label it unholy. My blush gave way to the lust of love, too long denied. We simply had to merge and be one, thus we gave in to our physical needs with full passion.

After our frantic reunion, we held each other tightly, there upon the sleeping shelf we occupied, now disrobed and entwined together wrapped in a blanket. I explained how I came to her chamber this happy reunion day.

"I don't care how you got here, only that you're here," MiryAmah said, laying her sweet head back on my shoulder. The feel of her silky dark hair touching my skin excited me again. Then she asked the question I didn't know how to answer, saying, "How long can you split your physical body and stay, my love?"

I answered, "I'm not sure, but I can't stay with you always as I would love to. Even if I could, I'd be putting you and our child in dire danger, as well as, all who love and protect you." Then I remembered, "Speaking of our child. When do I get to meet her?"

## The Saga-Oracle

"After you tell me how you survived the crucifixion, or are you but a lovely dream, husband of mine?" MiryAmah replied.

It took a while to fill her in on the events as they played out. She was not surprised when I told her of the day I scryed her and little Sarah, and how pleased I was that she had chosen the name we discussed before my leaving.

"I knew it!" she remarked. "I knew she saw something. When she said it was her Papa, I had no doubt that somehow she had tuned into you. I thought at first, it might be just a child's imagination vision, but still I knew it was important. Children see much clearer than we do."

We weren't disturbed during this time, which didn't surprise me, knowing that the intuitive people who gave my family safe haven would have sensed a need for privacy. But I was anxious to meet my little daughter, so we dressed and went to the great hall, where there was a celebration awaiting us. It was like a surprise party. Standing in the midst as we entered the hall was none other than our sweet little daughter, beaming in pride, since it was her intuitive knowing that had instigated the preparations and materialized this gala event. Cheers greeted us. My little girl came running to me. I swept her up in my arms, as I had done so many times in my dreams. I remembered whispering to her, "This time it's not a dream, dear heart." Oh how good this little one felt in my arms. Sweetness could never be better, I thought.

The overseers, Rainald and his lovely wife Bridgett, came to me as I set my little one down. They bowed like I was royalty, even as they both wore the crowns of authority in this principality.

I felt a bit embarrassed, and said, "Don't bow down to me, because I'm not worthy of such an honor." Even as I made the statement, I felt a physical pain in my body. I realized that I almost pierced the calm that held my bi-located body in place, by feeling less than worthy. So I quickly rephrased by saying, "Let me bow down to you, for you are just as worthy as I am, and I'm honored to be in your presence." Then we all bowed again, nearly bumping heads, and my wife and little girl laughed in glee at the situation, as it released the tension of the moment. I knew without a doubt that these people were true friends. I was, and will ever be, grateful for the honor they offered us, with their devoted compassionate love.

I must admit the homecoming was beyond delightful, well into complete bliss. Surely, the only word that could suffice is 'heavenly' as that term has come to mean. I felt fully in a divine place here with my family and newfound friends. My little Sarah seemed so grown up, as I watched her reluctantly share my presence as the others met me. She had a presence that a child as young as she would rarely exhibit. Most present didn't fully understand exactly who I was, however. It was understood that I was Sarah's father and MiryAmah's husband, but the full measure of our union and previous experience, as master and mastra in the holy land, was kept private. We couldn't chance that my survival became known, or the safety of my wife and child would be compromised.

I noticed that there was a little white donkey following Sarah around. She was talking to the wee white one like it was a brother, saying, "Beeba, this is my father. I told you he would come home some day, and here he is." She was saying this as she walked. He followed her, all decked out in a colorful back pad, with tufts of bright-colored yarn tassels attached to his mane and tail. Then she stopped, turned around and said, "Do you believe me now?" This interaction fascinated me. I interrupted my conversation with some people, went to her and said, "Do I know this little fellow?"

"Oh father," she said, "don't you remember Beeba, who bore you so majestically through the gate of the great city before I was born?"

"And how do you know about something, before you came through the channel of forgetting? Surely, you would have forgotten such a thing, once you emerged into this world, child?" I asked.

"I don't forget like other children, father," she said. "I have talked to Beeba, since I can remember. He has told me many times, you thought he couldn't carry you through the golden gate of the city, and he knew that he could. He sometimes wishes he didn't carry you into the city," she continued, "because some of the people were bad and killed you. So, sometimes he's sad, father," she explained. As she said so, Beeba flattened his long white ears to the side of his head, and I didn't doubt that these two conversed and understood each other perfectly.

I remembered the day she spoke of, the gate of Jerusalem that the little ass colt had carried me so proudly through. I also remembered how the little fellow communicated to me that he was born to carry me, and how I had feared I would be too much of a burden for him. I stroked his pure white coat and said, "You aren't much bigger now than when I nearly flattened you in a bed of palms at the gate, little one." I could read his mind, and he said that his growth was fulfilled the day his destiny was.

"Well!" I replied to his mind talk, "it seems that your destiny has expanded. Here you are, keeping good company with my little girl."

The proud little donkey stood as tall as he could and pronounced in a donkey heehaw, much to the glee of the crowd, but addressed to me, that he was given a new task and was the guardian of this holy child. Sarah and I understood what the verbal statement was, others though Beeba just being cute.

I'm not sure what the others thought as I conversed with this donkey, however Sarah did all the time. Maybe they figured it was a family trait. I said, "I'm grateful that you find my child holy, and I'm sure that you know all children are holy, no matter what form they take."

The little one went back to mind-speak and said, "But master, your mastra child is my charge, so to me, she is the holiest of all. I'll serve her all the days of my life. If I'm lucky enough I'll live long and stay strong for the task I've accepted."

Animals give so much to us, I thought. They give their flesh for our nourishment, their fur to keep us warm, their backs to bear our burdens and now this little fellow gives his heart to my child as her personal guardian. They are all masters, these animals some would think inferior, I thought. We are the undeveloped species, not them, and I thought of how much this little humble animal had given to my family and me.

We retired to the private chambers reserved for my beloved family. Beeba, MiryAmah, Sarah and I sat by a fire, and we caught up on years of separation. Time didn't pass as it normally would, but rather slowed down, for it seemed we talked for hours when it was merely moments. Being graced by being outside of time, we caught up on the news of the followers, which was not good. Many of our closest friends, the apostles and the disciples, were persecuted, my wife told me. Even my brothers and sisters were in danger. Joseph had instructed my sisters to keep our relationship private to insure their safety and the safety of their families. That was troubling. I felt the pain again, as well as the drain of the calm leaving me, as anger and disappointment began to take its toll on my dual body. I had to bring myself back to the calm. I found that joy energized me, but sorrow depleted me. In order to stay present with my beloveds, I had to stay within the joy and put disappointment in its proper perspective. I needed to turn the sorrow of my sisters having to deny our relationship over to the joy of their survival. After all, MiryAmah said, they all had good marriages, and their husbands treated them with all due respect. I suspected my mother was seeing to that. She, being a priestess, could be most persuasive.

We spent the remaining time, discussing how I must continue with my part of the divine mission and how my beloveds might continue with theirs. There was discussion of a religion emerging from our teachings. I said, "I hope they don't try to make me into another God. We have enough versions of God. If people would just look into their own hearts and souls, they'd see the true reflection of God, right there waiting to be discovered."

"Well," MiryAmah said, "I think they will deify you and make me a fallen woman; for what they can't reconcile, they'll make into a god or a demon."

"Don't say that, dear wife," I pleaded, "I can't bear to have you defamed or denied. You are as pure as my beloved mother. How could they not know that?"

## The Saga-Oracle

Looking at me for a moment as if weighing the thought, MiryAmah said, "If your beloved follower little John didn't know it, how could you expect others who didn't see our union and walk with us daily to know?" Then looking pensive, she said, "Remember, John loves you with all his heart, but he can't share your heart with me. How do you expect those who, likewise, love you ever to consider sharing that love with a wife, much less a child?"

I didn't like hearing what I already knew. I knew the boy John was in love with me in all ways. I thought that by accepting and loving him, I could show that God created many versions of divinity, and that love was always good, no matter how it was manifested. What I didn't take into account was that poor little John was but a child when he joined us, and that his Roman background had not prepared him to share his love, rather it became as a passionate possession. It was a complicated situation at best, and I didn't have the time to bring John to full realization that I loved him without end, much less convince him my wife was the other part of my very soul, and if he loved me, he would love her as well.

"I fear there'll be a version of remembrance of the teachings from each follower," I said. "I can only hope that somehow the truth will hide therein and come out one day, when there is great need accompanied by open minds and hearts. Hopefully, that day all the pieces of the puzzle can be assembled, and the simple truth will unite all creation."

"What I need to do now," I told my dear wife, "is to take the message of peace far and wide, and plant it like a mighty gardener on fertile soil all over Tara, our mother earth, so that it will grow and link all creation, nations and people. Even as I plant the seeds, I don't want to change their religions. Rather, I want them to see the divine balance of all things within their perception of the Creator. I'm not sure if I can bi-locate to do this, or if I must keep just one physical body to accomplish this work I must do. I know I have got to travel far and wide for this mission and keep my true identity private." I could see that MiryAmah knew that would mean we couldn't be together as much as we wanted, and it saddened her.

"I love you with all my heart," my wife proclaimed. "And whatever calls to you, I know you must do. I only hope that the life I already feel within me will be proof that you are still my husband in all ways, and that I once more will see you and hold you tight against my yearning physical body, even as I will always, and in all ways, keep you ever present in my heart."

In my reluctance to leave, I missed the comment about 'the life within her,' instead focusing on the fact that loving enough to free, that which you desire to keep close, is the greatest test of divinity. Her divine love was all I could see at this parting moment. Thus I had to leave my family behind and go back to the high mountain place, to prepare for the journeys I must travel and the work that was yet to do. With reluctance, I walked away from those I loved most, secure in the knowledge that my brothers and my mother were closely connected to my family and would fulfill the duty of protecting my little clan, in many ways.

I remember walking away and not wanting MiryAmah or Sarah to see me dissipate, as my bodies re-merged someplace else. I looked over my shoulder and nearly lost my calm surrender to the process. I could hear Eocha remind me, "Stay calm. Stay in the calm and let the gratitude of love fill your being, for your family is safe and healthy in this moment. Live in the moment. Stay calm."

And I awoke within one body, with Eocha standing behind me and holding her hands upon the crown of my head, grounding me to the place and space where I returned.

I cried a long cleansing cry. No one spoke. They understood.

# THE FARAWAY LAND
## Chapter Thirty-Five

My beloved wife, MiryAmah and I were as One Soul, which you might understand as Twin Flames.[160] As such the reincarnation of

---

[160] The masculine form and feminine form of the same soul

both of us was already a difficult proposition, for it meant all experience would be doubly felt, including joy and sorrow. Due to the dangers for my family, we had to endure the pain of separation, which to me was worse than the crucifixion.

When I merged with my primary body in the inner-chambers of the high mountain place, after my visit to my family upon my first bi-locational journey, I found that Eocha awaited and guarded the 'other me.' I was nearly inconsolable upon leaving my beloveds and wept and retreated into myself for days. I was brought food, which I didn't eat; given warm blankets to warm my body, which I didn't use; and a fire was set in the fireplace, which I didn't approach for warmth. Depression set into me, body and soul, yet even within the sadness was the memory of the faces of my beloved MiryAmah and our dear little Sarah, so brave and adult-like in her demeanor, and that kept me holding on. My poor child had grown up before her time, and I regretted the loss of her childhood. She was but a little girl in body, and yet her mind and heart were caught up in responsibility to her mother and my memory, and what she believed to be 'my expectations of her'.

I don't know how long I drowned in self-pity, but one day Eocha came by and stood looking down at me in the coldest corner of my chamber, where I lay shivering and curled in a pitiful fetal position, nearly nude. She stood there with her hands on her hips, looking down at me and finally spoke saying, "Master, how long will you beat yourself up for that which you didn't cause?"

I just looked up at her; not bothering to answer, for the will to speak had long left me.

"Well," she said, "I guess you might as well die and abandon your family once again, and fulfill the true disappointment you believe yourself to be."

I looked up at her, wondering what madness she was uttering.

"Shall I get you a sharp knife, master?" she asked sarcastically, "so that you can cut out your heart? Then I can send it to your family, and you can finally be with them."

I began to emerge from my stupor and said in a rather irritated tone, "What utter nonsense are you saying, Eocha?"

"What utter nonsense are you doing?" Eocha answered. Then she went on to say, "If you want to be tortured, I might be able to take you to a place where they enjoy such horrible pursuits. I'm sure they would love to mangle and mutilate you and might even do as good a job of it, as you've been doing lately."

That really made me mad! I arose from my pathetic fetal position in the cold corner I occupied. It wasn't easy but anger empowered me. Heat coursed through my body, due to my fury more than the fire that was trying to keep the room comfortable. I found my full height and stood very close to Eocha, nearly chest to chest. I was much taller than this little powerful woman, and I leaned down, looking her right in the eye and said, "What are you saying, Eocha? Would you then waste all the effort that has been done to keep me alive and turn me over to those who would enjoy killing me?"

She looked back at me, with a look that pierced right through me and said, "What does it matter, master? You've already turned yourself over to a killer, haven't you? You have fallen into self-pity so deeply, that the only hand that reaches out to you is the killer called 'regret and remorse.' You can't even see they are fear-based illusions, which antiforce sends to pull you from your mission and dissipate the power of good. Such destruction would best be turned over to the experts of torture, don't you think?"

That impacted me hard, and I answered with my voice now more soothing. "Eocha! My dear Eocha," I said, as I put my arms around her little body. "Forgive me, for I am such a fool. The pain of separation from my family caused me to go insane again," I told her. "I have visited that place of madness a time or two and maybe that was by divine design. How can I possibly understand the depths of despair, if I haven't been there?"

Eocha pulled my face down once again to her level and looked into my eyes without speaking for a moment. I noticed her eyes were dark pools of wisdom, which locked me to their gaze. Such eyes could see the very soul within you. She ultimately said,

## The Saga-Oracle

"Then let's launch into the new phase of your work, master. It awaits your attention and now surely, you have sufficient understanding of how deep depression takes those oppressed into the hell that consumes them."

I simply laid my weary head on her tiny shoulder, having to bend even lower to do so, and nodded 'yes.' She kissed my cheek, found a robe for my body, wrapped me up and led me from the chamber to the dining hall. I could hardly keep up with her, as I feebly walked beside her. When we arrived, it was filling up with those about to partake of the evening meal. I was famished and eager to share the bounty.

The hall was mostly silent as usual. The people of this place didn't chatter or talk a great deal during the evening meal. It was mostly a silent ritual of thankful prayers as the sustenance was consumed. Eocha and I sat down on one of the floor cushions at one of the low tables and awaited a bowl of food as the others were doing. The servers rotated. Those, whose day it was to serve, silently provided bowls full of rice and vegetables, and sometimes a bit of meat, if there was a natural offering from an animal that accidentally died. Nothing was wasted with these people. The protein from the meat would help them through the cold months outside the inner city compound, where many had to come and go. As we waited, we prayed our silent prayers. I asked forgiveness for denying the food left in my chamber its mission to nourish me. After our meal, we sipped butter tea, a Tibetan drink that also helped the body stay warm in the unpredictable mountains I was exiled within. I came back to my peace, the balance within.

If you are in total agreement on all levels, (physical, mental and spiritual) the food that you consume works its magic to the tenth degree. By that I mean the energy that they bring to your body will multiply ten-fold, when you fully understand how the cooperative effort is played out. I gained my strength and health within a short period of time and, with gratitude, immensely enjoyed every bite of food during our meal times.

Having come to my senses again and regained my strength, I began preparation for my continued mission. A council of wise elders was assigned to assist me. Never did they direct me. They were there to help me think things through, and to remind me to bring the intention through my heart first, then use my head to move into the mission. To pull intentions through the heart first, when in planning stages, is easily forgotten. One can over-think challenges and lose the vision very easily. The council expertly guided but never shaped my mission, which was mine alone to accomplish in whatever way I was steered to do so.

My intention has always been to bring a balance within the attitudes of the human realm, which would reflect in all other domains of physicality, and beyond, for nothing is isolated and all is 'One'. I planned to interact with people, and help them with the process of understanding themselves and how their very bodies and minds react to their self-concepts. First, people had to identify the available energies that shaped and molded attitudes within and around them. Once they could see how they envisioned themselves, which literally shaped them, too, they could work on attitudes of self-worth and fine tune themselves into a better balance. Then they became pillars of peace, because the energies they reflected outward affected their families and social settings.

Energy at the time was understood as 'life-force'. However, people had been conditioned only to see half of that force. The conditioning was deeply ingrained within them. I wanted to help individuals honor the balance of life-force energies, both aspects, complements of each other. I had studied with the masters of the Far East, and the symbol of yin/yang[161] is an ideal visual of this concept. When people understood the balance within themselves, they would also understand the balance of all creation, especially that which is known as God. All creation echoes, or reflects, the Original Intender. Some might call this a duality, but in actuality it is Onement,[162] as the ancient symbol of yin/yang illustrates with its circle containing two distinct but different, complementing sections, representing the masculine and feminine energies equally divided in a graceful arc. It represented the completeness of all

---

[161] Ancient far eastern symbol of energetic balance ☯
[162] Wholeness achieved by two equal, complementary components that make a complete unit also known as "at-one-ment"

creation, each part totally balanced and perfectly reflective of that which made it in the first place.

The so-called fall of humanity was due to the misunderstanding of when the separation of the souls into genders was prioritized[163]. Not long after that, there was a huge forgetting of one's totality, or Onement. This genderization offered a choice to test the awareness of spirit beings, as they discovered the other complementary energy within themselves, and also outside of themselves. It's difficult to explain how, for instance, MiryAmah was within me and another being as well. The miracle of creation is that it has mysteries to solve and that's perhaps the greatest divine unknown of all. Nonetheless, there is always a part of the other within, as illustrated by the yin/yang circle where you see a little of the opposite energy in each section. The divine intention instills the deep desire of the soul to reunite with its counterpart, within itself and also with its twin-flame, usually anchoring it within the non-dimensional home. People would always sense that there was a component so perfectly matched, that it was the other part of them. For animals and other beings of nature, the design was a bit different due to their unique responsibility to Tara, the free-will planet. However, for humanity, desire is a great motivating factor, thus always yearning for your counterpart activated a longing to move through physicality. This echoed the even more intense desire to 'go home' and reunite with the Source. Desire launches this journey, but it is love that keeps it moving forward, or I should say moving 'back,' to the Divine Source. Desire and love motivate divine action. On the other hand, it can be interrupted or corrupted by fear, which interferes and attempts to stop that forward motion, creating chaos, which drives one in the opposite direction from God. The sole agenda of fear, or 'antiforce,' is to stop the journey home to the Divine Creator, because without fear in place the illusion dissipates.

I revisit the same concepts constantly because every phase of my life is connected to the points that I make, and I remind myself, during my remembered tale, time and again, why life affects me and my loved ones as it did. My joy and my sorrow were all

---

[163] Previous to this all beings were androgynous, both male and female

affected by the balance of attitudes within the social arenas I lived and interacted within.

Being twin-flames and incarnating at the same time, MiryAmah and I faced our greatest challenge, but we were determined to finish what we had begun. We willingly met the resistance of antiforce in all its angry power. We knew that stagnation would sooner or later rot itself out. We were certain that we had started a trickle of good (God) that would gain energy and become a mighty river of flowing consciousness one day, and the pools of stagnation would finally clear and life would reflect its divinity as originally intended. An idealistic cause, but that was what we were born to do, nudge all creation towards the ideal.

We didn't want to create a religion, just shift those already in place. As it turned out, however, through our teachings three streams of Christianity emerged: the Roman stream which my rock, Peter would anchor; the Greek Orthodox stream which his dear brother Andrew would anchor; and the Celtic stream which my beloved MiryAmah would anchor. Of course these all developed a bit later as time went on and memories and intentions gained momentum. My beloved's followers suffered the greatest resistance and persecution, due to their connection to the only feminine stream of Christianity. From its beginning, shortly after my wife was exiled in the land of the Gaul, that stream was in constant danger. It was the only stream that honored the essence of our teachings–the balance. The Grail Keepers[164] did everything in their power to protect my family and the message of balance we tried to establish. They were aware of the various peace-code projects. These guardians existed long before we entered this time and place and still exist even as you read my narrative. The secret guardians of balance had to remain under the radar of those in power, so were always feared by the rulers who abused their seats of power. The various groups that sprang from the guardians of the

---

[164] Those who monitored power and attempted to bring balance into the places most affected by imbalance. The Grail is the symbol of balance, thus they were secretly known as "Grail Keepers". Knights Templar were Grail Keepers who came out of secrecy to be known as 'Poor Fellow-Soldiers of Christ and of the Temple of Solomon'

grail were slandered, so that people would hate and fear even the idea of a secret society. The Magi were among those who were secret monitors of power and had indeed come to me early on in my life. They were descendants of the Watchers, who the Galactic Council had assigned to watch over the progress of this planet, way back when the gods of old mined the gold. They've been demonized, too, by those who bought into the patriarchal system. The Grail Keepers, among which were the Druids and Magi, and countless other groups, still watch over my family and all powers that be, but now they must adjust power from a different perspective.

My true agony at the time, however, was that I had to be separated from my family. I had to accept that for this incarnation I wouldn't have the opportunity to walk side-by-side with my soul mate, but I would always walk with part of her heart within me as she would mine, no matter where we found ourselves. We would ever be one, like the yin/yang symbol, with a little of each other in our hearts.

Knowing this, my council and I decided that it was time for me to walk the paths of people in other localities, so I could see how much of Tara was affected by the imbalance. We also decided that I would go physically instead of bi-locating, saving that for more intense situations that might arise. When bi-located, Eocha had to be present and protective of my dual physical vehicle. I felt to bi-locate often, would be too much to ask of Eocha, even as she protested that this was her pleasure and her work to do.

I wanted to go to a land far away I had heard of, across the vast sea of the lost continent of Atlantis. It was rumored there were those there who lived a nature-oriented life. I wanted to meet them and see how they organized their societies. I would have to find passage on many ships, to travel across the great water, which in itself was nearly impossible, for few chanced such a voyage. If I gained passage, I knew it would take months to arrive using this method, but still, I thought it best to be fully physical in this journey of discovery and learning. My council was concerned for my physical safety, and we debated hours over the matter. Few ships dared to go near the edge of the world as they knew it, and it would take a long time to reach my destination. Of course, my counselors and guides knew that the planet did not have drop off edges, as most ship captains believed. The only regret I had was that I would be away from my family. I still hoped to secretly visit them from time to time, even though the area of Gaul they exiled within was still Roman dominated.

I suffered great agony over how to move into my mission. Finally, I was wisely asked to consider that I could bi-locate while aboard ship, since I would be able to hold place within its protection, but that I should therefore, not be traveling alone over sea or land. It was agreed that bi-location would be seldom used as I walked the paths faraway; since I needed to fully submerse myself within the cultures I visited, to gain the knowing I was seeking. Even so, I knew I could have time with my loved ones while the ship found its destination, so I looked forward to the opportunity.

It was decided that Eocha would take the trip with me, to help accomplish the shipboard bi-location. The council insisted that I also accept a guardian for the entire journey. Eocha would return once I reached my final landfall destination, they told me. The Council agreed that I needed a protector who would stay by my side. They said, none other than my dear Elmira would do. At that pronouncement, he was immediately ushered in.

What a lovely sight he was. I hadn't seen him, since he took the cross from my weary shoulders, and later went with me to visit my followers and had opened the wisdom channels. I sprang to my feet to embrace him, like a child finding his long-lost favorite uncle. Elmira just chuckled in his silent way and said in mind-speak, that we had perfected while I was a child, "Master, I have never been far from you. I've always honored the request to give you space to accomplish your sacred tasks. Even so, I couldn't stop the horrible drama of the crucifixion." His face was sad when he remembered the terrible event. "Will you ever forgive me for not saving you?" he asked.

I responded, "I wasn't meant to be saved. It had to play out as it would, even as it tormented me most in denying my greatest desire, which was to be with my beloved family. It wasn't my destiny. But it was the choice of those of the place and time," I explained. "There was nothing you could do to change their closed minds on the matter. Hatred was, and still is, firmly ingrained within them, and it has shut down their heart centers, Elmira. It wasn't your fault, or the fault of any of those that supported MiryAmah and me," I reassured him.

Elmira, looking a bit older but still strong as ever, nodded his head in agreement, but I could see he wished he could have spared my loved ones and me the agony of the entire episode of that terrible time. I offered him my hand to shake in agreement, saying, "Shall we again be on another great adventure, my friend?" His smile was all the answer I needed, even as the grip of his strong hand infused me with his love and devotion.

We began preparing that very night. It wasn't difficult to prepare our travel gear, since we always traveled light. Not much in the way of supplies was needed, and the three of us set out, to go to the coastline of the Mediterranean Sea and gain passage on a ship. That involved crossing through the land called 'Holy,' where I had been crucified and thought dead, and where many of my followers still suffer as well. It confuses me when I think of our message of love being seen as evil and a threat to God and the Emperor. The only threat was to those who would use their positions of power for self-gain and the enslavement of the people.

Again we joined caravans going in the general direction we wanted to travel, as we had done when I was a child. Elmira kept close watch for our safety, as always. Little Eocha was often thought to be his wife, due to their common Mongolian look and coloring, and people thought I was their son, even as I was lighter in complexion due to some of the drastic healing techniques used at the mountain sanctuary. I kept my hood over my head most of the time and seldom did anyone pay us much heed. We wore the robes of poor people and blended in with the invisible lower class. We didn't confirm or deny their assumptions, finding it safer to keep a low profile and to say as little as possible.

We found our way to a shipyard on the Eastern Mediterranean Sea and paid our fare for accommodations, along with the cargo of olive oil, far eastern silks, and other such trading commodities, some animals, including donkeys. We would cross the Western Mediterranean, stopping at a few ports of call, proceed through the Hercules Gate[165] and around the coast of what is now Spain to the great island of the Celts. The final departing port on our journey would be at the far north on the great island in the place that the Egyptian and Scythian people had jointly founded and later became the Scottish nation. Our accommodations were with the donkeys, and we were very happy to accompany the sweet animals on this journey. Their soft bodies comforted us; however, they became sea-sick, and we, in turn, comforted them. Eocha had several ways of putting pressure on points of their bodies, which instantly relieved their discomfort. It was amazing to watch them take turns being near her, so that she could help them. Finally, she had to teach Elmira and me the technique, so we could help out as well. Donkeys were not meant for sea travel, and many suffered.

Once we reached the top of the great isles as arranged by our mountain sages, we would be kept in safe chambers until a ship departed for the lost continent. For the most part, such ships still embarked in secret, since it was feared that the warring and conflict of the lands that we inhabited might spread and contaminate the faraway place. The attitude of war and the act of overpowering people to control them was the norm in our known world, with the Romans setting the pace in taking over lands and people. Those that knew of the faraway place didn't want to see the indigenous people dominated or destroyed, as happened in the lands we knew. I wondered what the great crossing would be like. I was told the ships looked very much like Viking or Egyptian barges, with both sails, and oarsmen to move them, and were often shaped and carved to look like dragons. I eagerly looked forward to the journey over the vast Atlantic seas.

The first leg of our trip took about four weeks; during that time, with Eocha there to anchor me, and Elmira protecting me, I bi-located again to be with my family in residence in Gaul. However, this time they were at a place within the forest, at the home of the midwife. It felt odd to me to be on the sea and also with my beloved wife and child Sarah, and I had to work hard to

---

[165] Now known as the Straits of Gibraltar

concentrate on one location at a time, or I would force full-impact mergence of the two bodies, which could be deadly. Previously, the monks who sat in meditative silence during my dual body experiences, reinforced this anchoring in the high mountain place, and were deeply involved in helping me when I split myself. My mission was considered important enough for an entire team to give me support. When I thought of the great effort, they had given to me from the time of my childhood, I understood why they didn't want anything to go wrong now. I had heard that one could even expand to three or four places or more, but I knew that it would be far too dangerous for me to attempt such a feat, and would probably drive my team of helpers over the edge should I attempt such a division.

As it was, with the preparations and my traveling time, it had been about nine months, since I last saw my beloved. My arrival at her sanctuary coincided with the birth of our son, James. At first arrival I couldn't find anyone about; and then I saw a young priestess running down a hall carrying white linens in great haste. I followed her to the birthing chamber and wondered who was bringing a babe into the world. When I saw my beloved wife there in full labor, sweating and heaving great birth spasms, I was at first shocked. Then it dawned on me that our passion at our first reunion had proven fruitful, and that I was about to be a father once again. It was with great pleasure and shock, I took my place at the portal of emergence,[166] gently tapping on the shoulder of the one who was a stand-in for me, not even noticing who that blessed one was. I just wanted to be the first to physically hold my tiny child. I no sooner took my position as a great contraction had ended, and MiryAmah was catching her breath, when a new contraction was already building to bring forth another entity into this land of the 'living.' She looked down through her knees and noticed me, but she couldn't interrupt the force that wouldn't be denied its power, which quickly took her over once again. The look upon my beloved's face, however, was a sight to behold. She thought she would have to go through another birth without me there to catch the newborn, as was the priestess custom. I could

---

[166] Between the legs of a woman giving birth, the portal being the birth canal

tell at first that she thought she was having a great dream, even as the contraction had its way and the babe burst forth into my waiting hands, slippery and wet with the blood and water of life. My joy and emotion was as intense as my dear wife's, and that's when she knew I was really there, where a child's father should be, at this sacred moment. If all men could experience the emergence in this way, they would never again trivialize the wonder of birth. Truly, women are much stronger, and certainly braver than any man, I thought, as I cuddled my newborn son. I nearly fainted from the drama and the joy of his arrival.

Eocha, in the meantime, held my energy within my quiet body back upon the cargo ship, and Elmira made sure that no one disturbed our threesome in the donkey stables. Thus, my time with my family was a great blessing, and I was safe in both of my bodies. I stayed about a month. During that time, the ship had docked at its destination and unloaded its last cargo, including us, and took on yet more trade items for its return journey.

Eocha, according to Elmira, was quite concerned, for I hadn't merged my bodies as we disembarked from ship, and I was in a bit of a daze as we took to the land. She told the captain and others nearby, that I might be coming down with an illness. That was enough to keep them at bay, as we departed from the ship and made our connections with those expecting us, since the last thing a ship needed was illness raging through the crew.

A group of women took us to safe quarters within a seaside cliff dwelling, where the entrance required the lowering of a platform made of planks of wood to bring goods and passengers down to a cave entrance. Again, we entered the safety of caves. Eocha and Elmira carried me into the underground sanctuary, where I was offered a place of safety and rest.

I was happily involved in my other body, the one in Gaul with my family. Eocha and Elmira monitored my anchor body keeping it very quiet, though functional, and I didn't need as much food and activity since the other provided more than enough. Bi-location means that you are literally in two places at once, but you still have to navigate in both bodies. One becomes dominant, and one more quiet at such times. All Eocha and Elmira had to do was offer me an occasional sip of water and some broth.

The interesting thing about bi-location is that what one body experiences the other does as well, so while my bi-located body was feasting and enjoying all sorts of physical pleasures in Gaul, my other body just required safety and quiet. Had I been suffering it would have affected my other body, too, and the process would be reversed. Elmira and Eocha had a great responsibility in keeping watch, so that I would be safely protected and monitored.

All too soon, it was time to merge myself back to one, and I had to take my leave from my family once again. The short time we had together with our children was a high point in my life. I am blessed to have known what few have ever experienced in terms of true love and devotion, thus, the quality of time outweighed the quantity of time.

With Eocha's help, I merged with my body. This time it was less traumatic. Her funny little face met mine as I opened my eyes, and she knew that I was no longer two, but one again with myself.

"Well, master," she said, "that must have been a sweet visit. Even in your quiet meditative state here in the sanctuary of this cave chamber, your face glowed with love and pleasure, and I think I saw a smile or two written gracefully across your lovely mug."

"Wouldn't you like to know?" I said and just chuckled, and then I told her and Elmira of my new baby boy, and remarked on the beauty of my dear wife and little girl. "I worry though," I said, "that Sarah grows up too fast. She has already taken over the care of her baby brother, and no one can seem to stop her from being his guardian."

Elmira in his mind-speak said, "You grew fast, too, master, and it hasn't harmed you. It sounds like your little girl is right out of her father's mold."

"Yes, I know," I replied out loud, "but I would love for my child to have more of the sweetness of childhood."

I noticed that Eocha also could mind-speak, because she said to me, "And how many children are allowed that sweet privilege, dear Jeshua?"

I must have looked at her in surprise, because she laughed that funny way she does and said, "What's so surprising about my ability to understand the unspoken language? Didn't you learn the language within our care as a child yourself?" Then she went on with the conversation, saying, "I bet that little girl of yours is already talking to the animals. That's the first form of mind-speak, so don't be amazed at what naturally develops if given a chance."

"I also began with the animal realm," I told Eocha, "but I got into mind-speak full-swing when Elmira and I wandered a year, and I kept my chattering mouth silent." I noticed him smiling agreement as he remembered, too. "It was the only way we could communicate, and I was glad to gain a two-way connection to my loyal guardian. I realized that I had gotten into the habit of chatting away at him but never really listened to what he might have to communicate. So, I decided to remain silent awhile."

Elmira was finding that a bit humorous, since as he followed the conversation, he remembered that I used to sound like a chattering monkey. We all started to mimic the monkey family, all talking at once. What a sight we were, three adults jumping around in monkey fashion and making the sounds of the monkey tribe.

Eocha finally stopped her playful antics and said, "That chattering may be good for the monkeys but for us humans all talking at once, means no one is listening. The monkeys have a better ability to unite the chatter and to harmonize it into one voice, even if it sounds chaotic to our ears," she explained. "The temple monkeys in India and the high mountain tribes of monkeys might make a lot of noise," she went on to say, "But they are all talking about the same thing and all understanding even as they chatter." Then she added, "Remember the monkeys who went to the hot springs and soaked in silence? Chattering is not their only way," she reminded me.

I remembered seeing the monkey tribe, soaking in the steamy spring in a high mountain plateau volcanic pool, their heads

## The Saga-Oracle

silently sitting on top of the water among the clouds of steam and heat. Their eyes were shut as if in a deep meditative state. Upon their heads were sprinkles of white snow. The entire group was completely silent and peaceful. I was but a wee boy when I saw them, and I asked my teacher why they were so quiet. I remember him simply saying, "So they can listen, boy! So they can listen."

I remembered thinking about his answer for a moment, and then asked, "Why is it that humans can't do the same thing?"

My teacher said, "Some do, but unfortunately most can't be quiet enough to listen in the way the monkey tribe does. Maybe one day you'll know the truth of silence," he said. We often had very deep conversations about what might seem like trivial matters, but within the discussions came great understandings.

"Humans don't even listen to each other, when no one is talking," Elmira mind-spoke, as he was following my memory trail. I had forgotten I was within the mind-speak mode to him, so the channel of communication was still wide open. He then went on to say, "I can't speak, so I have learned to listen and observe conversations. I notice that there is usually a lot of talking, but not much listening going on, when the human tribes communicate. Even within a conversation", he said, "the one who pretends to listen is just formulating what he or she will say, when they get a chance to take over the talking part of the conversation, instead of really listening to what is being said."

"I hope I didn't fall into such a situation during my teachings," I replied, remembering how I would tell the stories called parables to those who came to hear me. I worried that I might have been doing just what Elmira was referring to. Everyone harbors insecurities and I'm no exception.

Elmira, reading my own inner-dialog, said, "For the most part, you didn't play the game of all-talk-and-no-listening, Jeshua. I was always in the crowd watching and ever listening." Then he continued saying in our silent language, "That year of not talking taught you to listen, and I only know a few instances, when you didn't hear the full extent of our inner-conversation."

"A few times!" I exclaimed. "That's too many." Then my mind skipped to the second question in my mind, and I asked, "You were always in the crowd when I taught?" I thought he was sent away to live his own life apart from mine when I released him from his guardian post. As I thought of this assumption, I remembered the times I thought he was gone, and he really wasn't. I wondered how I could doubt that he was ever my 'Christopher,'[167] and always nearby, even if invisible to me.

"Usually I was there," he said, "I always tried to stay close. As for the few times you might not have been listening," he went on to explain "it was when those closest to your heart did not understand the full extent of your intentions. Judas revealed his expectations of your kingship to you one day and his dedication to that cause. All you heard was love and devotion, which was there, that's true, but you didn't hear that he would go to any ends to make you his king."

That remark saddened me. "Oh my God!" I said in a low whisper, "I betrayed him more than he ever betrayed me."

Eocha quickly moved closer to me now seated upon the ground, and took my chin into her tiny hands. Tilting my head back so she could look directly into my face, she said, "You can't blame yourself for focusing on your friend's strength rather than his weakness, any more than he should blame himself for the same thing. You forgave him. Now, forgive yourself." Not convinced I was accepting her suggestion, she said, "It was a difficult concept to implant into a society that hates the feminine to the point, it hates a part of itself. Kingship was the only way Judas knew to honor you. Someday, your message will be understood. The crown represents power in many people's minds, because they have been conditioned to think that way by those who hold authority over them. What's important is that you tried your best and Judas did as well. He was courted and betrayed by the Roman, who was a spy who wanted to please his overseer with the news your enemies desired to condemn you with. You got caught up in a game of

---

[167] He who protects and carries the burden of a 'Christ' who is a totally enlightened being

hate; you and Judas were victims, not demons. Forgive yourself for being human as you have forgiven so many others who you love, no matter how many mistakes they made. And so, too," she added, "love yourself for being human, as you have always loved him and all others, as well. It's not easy being in this human state," she reminded me. "Judas is at peace, if you let him be. The only way you can do that is to forgive yourself, and understand that perfection is not normal to humanity. It's an achievement and a potential, but seldom is it achieved in every moment of every lifetime," she emphasized. What a wise woman she was. Our second leg of the journey was full of such discussions, where we traded wisdom and supported each other.

One day, we boarded another vessel and headed Southwestward across the great sea, finally landing on a peninsula of land surrounded by swamps, but with shores of white cool sand. This place was sunny and bright, with no real seaports, so the ship anchored off shore. Those conducting this voyage knew where they were going, no doubt, having been there a few times before, and after being taken ashore in small boats with cargo, we followed a path into the depths of the jungle-like place, led by people who were on the beach waiting for us.

A well-worn path led us through the land, which was beautiful, with huge lush green trees towering over us, as we pierced into its dominion. I had never before seen such giants of trees in my travels. In the lands I knew, the trees seldom reached great height and such fullness. Before we left the land of the Scythians,[168] I had noticed large forest tracks in some locations, but nothing approached the height of those that now surrounded us, here in the place of the sun. There were palm-like trees, as well as other lush greenery, full of birds of many colors. The shapes and the sounds of the animals and birds were like music within a temple. We also saw alligators and other reptiles in the swampy areas, sunning themselves where the sun peeked through the trees and warmed the waters that dotted the forest. I remembered the crocodiles of the Nile River, and how they also laid still in the sun, like logs floating on the water. A time or two, I saw what looked like a

---

[168] Later it became known as Scotland

large dark brown panther, that seemed like a mere shadow gliding alongside our pathway, unseen but watching. I did my animal mind-speak to ask of its intentions. It was just curious as cats can be. I asked for safe passage and was granted my request, with all due respect, since it was pleased that I knew of its presence, as the others seemed not aware of it. Cats are clever animals and appreciate awareness in all species. From that point on it followed us; somehow its mate understood its intention and the mate preceded us, keeping watch at the point, with its counterpart keeping watch at our backs, always unnoticed by our guides. Eocha and Elmira looked my way, and I knew they understood the situation and were feeling safe within the protection of the great swamp cats, too. We hoped that the armed guard around us didn't see our protectors, for they probably wouldn't understand and might attack those that were honoring us with a safe passage.

It took about a half day of hard walking to arrive at a village, made of huts of bent saplings covered by the giant green leaves of the ferns of the forest. Our group leader called out, announcing our arrival in their native language. I understood every word and gesture, since I now had the gift of language from little fuzzy Rema, my mountain sanctuary energy healer. When the people rushed to meet our group with joyful hearts, I realized that not only did I understand the language fully, but could easily speak it as well. I could see how this gift was essential to the expansion of my soul mission and sent a prayer of gratitude to little Rema. I heard him clearly acknowledge my thanks.

An elder woman, dressed in colorful feathered garments, came forth. She was quite tall and stood her full height with pride. She seemed like the queen of the group, I surmised, only they didn't have a king or queen system. She greeted us, told the others to prepare a welcome banquet and to move her things into another hut, as her home would be our home. I noticed many of the people were busy moving their belongings out into the open, so they also could accommodate the other members of our traveling party within their humble homes. Obviously, our beach welcoming group was not of this tribe. The village people were as gracious as the Samaritans, and felt honored to offer us their modest dwellings. The people were dark-reddish in complexion and both men and women had long straight shiny black hair. They were mostly tall people and carried themselves proudly. I found myself wishing I could walk the way they did. The bright feathers they wove into their dark tresses just made them look more impressive and the black hair accented the color of the decorations. Their garments were mainly leather breeches, or dresses upon the women. The children, both boys and girls, were mostly nude and seemed to pay no mind to their nakedness. I only saw one frail person in the encampment, and that person was among a group of mostly healthy elders. The frail one arose to greet us, and the young adolescent children dressed in skimpy garments, helped him. He had the finest crutches I'd ever seen. The supports, which this frail one used to walk were carved jewel-studded works of art. Overall I saw a happy group of people with no obvious hierarchy.

They immediately presented us with a banquet of fish and fruit. I wondered how they knew to prepare this meal to coincide with our arrival. No doubt, watchers had been posted on the trails. As I walked into their village, I noticed bright feathers adorning the living spaces, along with animal skins hanging on the interior and exterior walls of their huts. I learned later that animals were ritually harvested for their meat and fur, which was used for their sleeping pallets, too; but never was a life wasted, just for sport or to prove a point. The floors of the dwellings were covered in woven palm leaves. Firewood that gave the richest aromatic smells was neatly stacked by the fire pits. The village, obviously, was prepared for us, and soon the fires were lit. Our few belongings were placed in baskets inside the huts they had allocated as guest quarters, so we would feel at home when it was time to rest after our meal. The hospitality couldn't have been better, had we been of the royal families of our homelands.

After the wonderful feast and rest the tribe, seemed drawn to me. They surrounded me. Some touched my, now long, hair which had been sun-bleached making it a bright auburn color, due to the time I spent on the deck of the ship on our ocean voyage. I imagine that with their deep black hair, my reddish locks caught their attention. They touched my face and began to talk among themselves about the light coloring of my skin and my beard. They had no facial hair. My skin was indeed much lighter in complexion than even my father and mother. I didn't seem to tan very well, since my healing in the high mountains making me quite pale in comparison with everyone else. This sometimes happened with those born with blue eyes, due to the pigment of the skin being unable to hold the protective tan. Along with that, the restorative herbs used in my healing after my ordeal on the cross, were known to cause paleness of skin tone.

I understood every word the native people said, and one child reminded me of my own dear little brother Simon, probably now grown. As the people were commenting on my appearance while I sat on a boulder in the village, I lifted this child up to my knee and in their language, said to him, "I must look funny to you and your people, little one, being so pale of skin, and you are like the sunset, beautiful, reddish and warm."

The little one said, "We find you beautiful, too." Then some of the adults asked if I was taught their language, since my speech evidently was perfect. They explained they had a hard time teaching their simple language to the Scythians who came to visit them from time to time, seeking trade for the blue stones, the turquoise, that their Egyptian wives so long ago loved, and now their descendants loved, as well.

I said, "I had the gift of language given to me not so long ago. With you, I have greeted my first understanding of the importance and blessings of this endowment."

Then the lady chief arrived, hearing me and asked, "And what does that wonder of wonders gift represent?"

I liked the directness of this woman, who quickly came to the point, and I could see that she took an instant liking to Eocha, who could also be quite direct. Wise-women always seemed to recognize each other. Eocha, as always, looked slightly amused, waiting for my reply. She is ever the teacher who wants her student to get the answer right, so that proof of success is evident. As she patiently waited she beamed her pride in me, even though she knew Rema was responsible for the gift. The high mountain people all shared in the successes and failures of their intentions.

That was obvious as her bright, satisfied smile and nodding head, affirmed her pleasure, as I answered the high chief.

"It represents that I have had the honor to 'hear' what you are saying and 'know' your true intention. It also means that I can respond and speak to you with the same knowing that you will hear my true intention, thus we can enter a divine conversation."

"If that's so," she said, "then you are the promise kept from our ancient of ancients long ago, who said that one such as you would find us one day, and remind us that we are blessed and loved for who we are, not for what someone else believes us to be. We are honored that you've come. Whatever you desire, if within our ability to provide it, shall be yours," she said, as she bowed down to me.

I waited for her to come back to her tall commanding position and said, "I just desire to walk the land and meet the people of this place. I would like to walk among the people of the land and see how they are alike, and how they are different, from the people of my homelands. I want to learn their ways and see how they love the territory that keeps them fed and protected. I want to learn from all tribes of this beautiful place, that most of my people can't even imagine existing, much less understand their natural ways. I desire to see your relationship with all creation, especially as it unfolds around you. I yearn to know if the world can live at peace."

"And what will you teach us?" she asked.

"I didn't come to teach. I came to learn," I replied.

"Then you will teach us to be good teachers, even as you show us how the grateful student soaks up the lessons through the fine art of listening," she said.

"Yes!" I confirmed. "I've come to listen. I've also come to see. I wish to know the spirit of your communities and how each soul within them links to the Great Spirit. I hope that you and those like you will help me understand my own people better."

"And hopefully we shall help you understand yourself better, as well," she proclaimed to me. She went on to say, "I am White Eagle, leader of my people, and I welcome you to the land of the ancients."

# THE GIFTS OF THE SEA-GODDESS
## Chapter Thirty-Six

Since Eocha would be going back to the high mountain place soon, I wondered how I would bi-locate if I needed, without her assistance. At least, she would stay within the village until the word arrived that a ship was again near the place of the white sands.

She and White Eagle became instant friends. I felt a bit abandoned as she spent most of her time with the chief. Even though I aspired to be an example of the highest good in human nature, that didn't mean I didn't have moments of insecurity, too. After all, it was in the pitfalls where the greatest life lessons were learned, I reasoned, as I yearned for Eocha by my side. I could feel sorry for myself better than anyone I knew, and I felt comforted in the presence of this lady of the high mountains on my journey of discovery. I had Elmira with me, too, yet Eocha's mothering presence could only be likened to my own mother, who I missed, along with my little brother Simon, who had found a special place in my heart.

It interested me that White Eagle had mentioned a legend that one, such as I, would one day come to the Fisher People, as they called themselves. I remembered I was taught that time wasn't a straight line, but a rippling tide, washing in and washing out. No doubt, somehow the Fisher People prophetically saw this time washing up on their shore of experience, and me riding the waves into their lives. These old stories have a way of shifting and changing, to the point that the expectations could be so removed from the truth of the prophecy, that no one would fit the pre-imprint of the tale, but they were sure I was the promised prophet.

## The Saga-Oracle

Wandering among the tribe, I noticed that they were indeed a 'fisher tribe', or those that survived from the bounty of the sea. Their leaders were women, yet I found the men to be commanding in their own right. Their stature was interesting in that the men and women were nearly the same height and quite tall, with six foot being the norm. I wondered if that explained their society of equality, at least it seemed that way, as I watched the interaction of the tribe within the camp, and noticed how the men and women treated each other. I found them especially patient with the children; the men were as gentle as women with the little ones. I noticed women were as likely to show the children how to make fire, or how to construct stone slings for hunting, as the men, who were often traditionally teachers of such things.

One peaceful evening around the central fire where most of the people congregated in the twilight hours, one of the men asked if I would like to go to the sea for a hunt with them the next day. My intention was to understand the people of this faraway land, so I eagerly accepted. I asked if my dear friend, Elmira, could come as well, and it was agreed that he, too, should learn the ways of the Fisher People. We arranged to meet again here at the central council fire at the break of dawn.

I slept lightly that night. I wasn't sure what to expect of these quiet, yet strong guardian type men. They laughed and joked with each other a lot. Maybe Elmira and I would end up having some grand hoax played on us, so they could laugh some more.

When Emira and I approached the fire pit at the breaking dawn, our fisher friends were already waiting for us. Proud Foot (the man who asked me to come on this expedition) introduced me to another man, Little Turtle. I loved the animal and nature names the people took, not yet realizing how the names were developed from visions, and one had to earn the use of the sacred name.

Proud Foot told me that he earned his name after being bitten by a snake. The bite caused his foot to swell. "The shaman of healing couldn't seem to get the angry demon within my foot to stop its path of destruction," he explained. "She feared that my foot would have to be cut from my leg to save the rest of me. I was but a young boy and all my dreams of being a mighty warrior-guardian of my people seemed to dissolve, like paint on a talking-skin[169] that told the story of my life, but now it had all changed. I could envision my life as it should play out painted in pictures. Suddenly, it dripped off the surface of my imagination, leaving an empty shell of a person with only one foot, hopping around on the other. My destiny was murky and sad." Then he looked down at his two perfectly normal-looking feet and continued on saying, "I decided that I needed to talk to the Great Spirit."

I asked, "How do you talk to this great one?"

"One can only talk to the Great Spirit in isolation from all others," he answered. "No one can do this for you, and no one can tell you exactly how to approach the Great One, who made all that is. I knew that only Great Spirit could help me understand and accept, or alter, the situation with my poisoned foot. So, I just hobbled away from the care of the healer, asking first for her blessings, telling her I had to talk to Great Spirit and would she please tell my family."

I said, "In the land of my people, there are those who believe that only they can talk to God, our name for Great Spirit. If someone such as you wanted to converse with this Great Creator, you would have to petition them first, and if they deemed you worthy, they would be the go-between. Often, they would think you deserved the pain and would shun you."

Proud Foot looked at me in astonishment. "Do your people believe this nonsense?" he asked. 'How can it be they don't know only they can talk to the Great Spirit on their own behalf and the Great One never desires suffering?"

"Understanding God, as we call the Great Spirit, is ever the challenge for all people, don't you think, Proud Foot?" I asked.

"Surely, you know that the Great Spirit can only walk through the portal of the seeker's heart," he replied. "This is so respected by us

---

[169] Hide of an animal that pictographs were painted on, telling the history of the tribe and its people

Fisher People, that when I asked the healer to tell my parents I had gone to talk to Great Spirit, I knew they wouldn't interfere and would respect and allow me my quest, even if it meant I might ultimately choose to give up my life, rather than be a one-footed man."

"I agree with you and I believe that your people have made remarkable progress in understanding their true relationship with Great Spirit. But how did you save your foot, or is that wonderful appendage I see in your moccasin but a carved replica?"

"Oh!" He exclaimed, "That's how I got my spirit name." As we walked down a well-worn path in the tropical forest full of the sounds of nature, he told me of his naming.

"I went to the swamp forest when I left the healer," he said, "trying to walk with a huge purple throbbing foot, which might have to be separated from my body, if I chose to survive. I eventually found an enormous tree on a small dry island in the midst of the deep misty swamp. I was burning up with the heat that consumes a body in distress and began to see distorted visions. Some were terrible and scared me. Then a peace seemed to overcome me, and I saw a white panther. We have swamp cats but they're usually a golden bronze color, not this pure white. It came quite close to me; to the point, I noticed it had blue eyes. I sensed that I could read its mind, and it could read mine. It told me to follow it, so I did. The forest became a blur. I was in so much pain I couldn't even see well. I began to weaken and fell into the swamp water. I wondered if I would end up being a meal for the alligators that lived in such places. Then I felt the huge cat pick me up, like a mother cat picks up a kitten, by the back of my neck. Its teeth were so sharp that I thought death was near. The teeth didn't pierce my flesh; instead, they gently held my weakened dangling body, and I was dragged to that huge tree I had seen, just before I saw the white panther."

"The large cat pulled me ashore, upon that tiny oasis where the giant tree stood, and took me to the base of it, where I could lean against the huge trunk and wonder if this would be my departure portal into the Great Spirit world. The panther licked my face, and what a rough tongue it had, immediately bringing me fully awake. It looked into my eyes (I was in too much pain to be afraid) and communicated with me; it told me to talk to Great Spirit about my situation, that this was a sacred tree, and it would give me the strength I needed."

"Then it left me there. My mind just wanted to process the pain, watch the red line come up my leg toward my heart and contemplate the relief I would feel when I died. I knew this experience was holy, and it was time to have a talk with my maker–the purpose of this journey into the wilds of the land–no matter what my destiny was. So, I determined to go on with my intention."

"'Great One', I said, looking out through the dense swamp that had steam rising from it like a magic mist. 'Do you want to waste this life of mine and take me back to the land of the ancients?' I asked, as I watched the mist swirl, creating shapes and forms in the air."

"I saw nothing that I thought might be an answer, and I didn't hear anything either. I wondered what to do now. I looked at my foot growing bigger and blacker, as I sat there with the pain near intolerable. I knew I had to make a cut someplace soon in this poor foot, or it would surely burst and that wouldn't feel so good either. I took my knife from its sheath on my belt and held it towards the sky, saying, 'Bless this knife so that it can do its work and release the pressure that threatens to explode my foot. Help it cut a portal, for the poison of the snake to find a way out and release me from pain.' I took the very sharp knife and tenderly, but painfully put the knife tip into the very top of my blackened foot. As the sharp blade pierced my skin, the blood burst from this tiny hole, splattering me on the face with some streaming down my leg, and I felt immediate relief. I then looked at the bloody scene and said, 'I am proud of you, foot, for you didn't falter or move, when I had to pierce you to relieve the pain and pressure. You are a good foot, and I do so desire to keep you attached and safely part of my body'. In my child mind, it was perfectly natural to be conversing with my foot."

"About that time, I noticed the white panther again. It came close enough for me to see the twinkle in its deep blue eyes. It's odd how a twinkle in the eye is the effect of a high spirit. Then I realized the blood might have attracted it and hoped it was not hungry for a tasty boy such as me. It did the most extraordinary thing; it transformed into a person dressed in long white robes. It was a shape shifter and the first I had ever seen. This person, I believe, was a man of great age. He was light of skin and seemed to be one of the sacred albino ones, which happen from time to time in all creation. He still had the eyes of blue, and the sparkle that told me he was, indeed, a spirit helper. I had even seen an albino tree once, and I knew the legends of the spirit helpers, appearing as pure white ones. He walked to me on top of the water, floating above the mucky liquid. I must have been in total awe, for I just sat there, watching him come to me, lost in the spectacle of the moment."

"He finally broke my trance and said, 'Let me look at that foot.' And he proceeded to examine my foot. 'Now that you are proud of it,' he said 'it has decided that it will stay with the mission it has agreed to and be the lead-stepper it has been created to be.' "

"I must have been dumbfounded, as I was still just sitting there with my mouth open, watching the shape shifter move about examining my foot of which I was so proud. I was totally engrossed in the scene, and didn't realize that my foot was no longer throbbing. It was shrinking to its normal size, even as the white one spoke with me."

" 'Proud Foot', the white one said to me, holding his arms up high in the air with his robed arms looking like huge wings, 'your prayers have been answered. The Great Spirit sent me to remind you that the body is one with the foot, just as you are one with Great Spirit, and as the body and soul are one as well.' Then the shape shifter said, 'It's time for you to commit your intentional mind to the service of your spirit. You are 'Proud Foot' and, as long as you appreciate your entire being through holy appreciation, nothing will stop you from accomplishing your soul mission'. Then he transformed back into the great white panther and slipped into the forest, leaving me awestruck."

"When my wits returned, I looked down at my leg and watched the red line return upon itself to the now perfect foot. It reduced to a tiny red spot upon the place of the snake bite, and then totally disappeared." Even as he remembered this moment, Proud Foot had an expression of amazement. "Interestingly, as I watched this happen," he continued, "another swamp snake came slithering up onto my small dry island. When I saw it, green like the swamp with the tell-tale yellow spot on the back of its head, I recoiled since they are dangerous snakes and we, fisher people, avoid them. Then I found some courage, thinking of the shape-shifter Great Spirit had sent and his message. I found my voice and said, 'Snake, I respect your right to the swampy place, your home, and I apologize for any discomfort I have caused you in your sacred space. I have come to this place to speak with the Great Spirit, and I thank you for the safe passage you have given me so far. I ask that we part in peace'."

"And what happened then?" I asked Proud Foot, very caught up in his story. "Did the snake understand and leave you, or did you have to do some walking on water, too, as you ran for safety."

He thought a moment, like he was not sure how much I would believe and then said, "You know that ancient tree lifted up one of its root legs, and made a hole, neat as you please, that must have looked quite enticing to the snake. It immediately slithered down into the ground, and the hole just swallowed it up. Another root started moving, working its way out of the ground. It was long and spanned a great distance within the underground. Before I knew it, there was a long root bridge to dry land, where before was only dark stagnant water. I got up, tried my leader foot and found it strong, and carefully tried the new root bridge. It held me with the strength only a tree can offer. I carefully found my way to the higher ground."

"Incredible," I said, totally amazed by this story.

"You don't have to believe me, Jeshua," Proud Foot said, "yet this is the truth of my life, and my good lead-foot is evidence of the blessing I received."

"Oh, I believe you," I said. "What a powerful way to honor your soul and body, and take a new name. I never realized how important my foot that steps out first into my day, and on my pathways, really is. I don't know what I would do, if I lost that vital part of my physical body. Do all of you have such incredible experiences, so that you can find your name?"

Proud Foot stopped a minute along the path to the fishing place. "Not the same way," he replied. "White Eagle, our chief, as a young girl, had a white eagle come and sit on her head when she was quite small. It sat there for all to see. No matter where she went all that day, it stayed there. It wasn't easy for a small girl to be carrying a giant white eagle around on her head, either. It took tremendous bravery to do such a thing, for the bird could have pecked her eyes out at any minute, or even taken its great eagle talons, grabbed her and flew away with her. Even so, she, wisely, didn't try to dislodge the bird and walked bravely for an entire day, not complaining, nor bragging, just accepting the situation. That's how she became the chosen one, to be trained as chieftress,[170] since it was known then that she could carry the burden of such a position with great calm courage."

"Again, the animal was white," I remarked. "Does Spirit always send white animals to you for naming?"

"Not always, yet it is understood that a totally white animal is always Spirit visiting us."

Proud Foot explained further, "Little Turtle here went on a vision quest as a young boy. He was taunted by other children for being so gentle and quiet, and he felt confused about the situation." He looked at Little Turtle, as if to ask permission to go on with the tale. Evidently, the look that passed between them was sufficient to finish the account. Proud Foot continued and said, "He stayed in the swamps for an entire moon cycle, a long time for one so young and small. He proved that courage knows many shapes and forms. It was hard for his parents to honor his vision quest, because they

---

[170] A female form of the word chief or chieftain, meaning the leader of a tribe or clan

wanted to protect him from the dangers in the wild. Yet, the dangers the other children presented in their teasing games, diminished his self-confidence, and was far more destructive, and they had to allow their son his chance to prove himself."

"He doesn't like to talk much, being a shy one," Proud Foot explained, as he nodded toward Little Turtle who was leading us down the trail. "So, I'll tell you his story. When he slept out in the wild unprotected by his family dwelling, he was at first quite afraid. He couldn't even find sleep and enter the dreamland. The night animals might have easily carried him off to their dens and fed their families with such a small boy, and he knew he had to face that fear of being small and shy. Eventually, sleep came. In his dreams, a little turtle said to him, 'Do not to fear, just go into your safety shell at times such as these and come out when you feel like you can face the world again.' Finally, when he could sleep, and move about without fear when he was awake, he knew his vision quest was done, and he came home to his family a more confident son. His mother had a little turtle on her lap, when he arrived at their dwelling place. She had painted a bright symbol of the sun on its back, the day she found it near her weaving basket, the same day her son had left for his quest. The little turtle, she said, was her proof that her son would come back safe and sound. She had painted a sun symbol on its back to remind her that her son (sun) would accomplish his quest, and he would ultimately find his way home to his family. Thus, she took this as evidence of his true divine spirit name, 'Little Turtle,' and never has anyone doubted his courage since, even when he has chosen to go into his shell for awhile for a bit of peace. Turtles are sacred to the Fisher People, and we respect those who know how to live within themselves. We even call our homeland, 'Turtle Island', because we know that great seas surround the land, since our ancestors left legends and pictures on the rocks nearby."

"I think your naming conventions are much more interesting than ours across the great sea," I said, as I reached ahead to Little Turtle and gave him a friendly pat on the shoulder.

About that time, we began to smell the freshness of the sea and hear the gentle waves washing in. The sea smell is very difficult to describe, but there is freshness about the air in such locations that carries a healing feeling. I felt like I was walking closer to something grand and sacred.

Proud Foot said, "Soon we will be at the departure place where we keep our boats, and you'll be in the Sea Goddess realms."

As we broke through the forest, the sea was so beautiful it left me speechless. I had seen it many times, but there was certainly something here that made one observe the shoreline, through all the senses. The turquoise water enchanted me, and I could feel waves of something peaceful wash through my soul.

Elmira, who had been so quiet that I nearly forgot he was with us, immediately began turning over a huge boat that was laying bottom up, high on the shore. Proud Foot looked pleased that Elmira had anticipated the need of righting the boat. We found places to hold one's hands, to drag the heavy vessel to the water's edge. Under it, we found the nets that the village people made, from vines that naturally grew in the woods. The nets were as finely-woven as any I had seen in the Mediterranean. There were also great hooks, made from tree branches, used to position the nets. I found some small nets, as well, with long handles on them, and wondered how they would be used.

Proud Foot, seeing my wonderment, explained them to me, "These are for diving into the sea. They are light and one can swim into small places and find the most wonderful offerings of the Sea Goddess," he said.

It was full morning now. After getting the boat afloat, we all jumped in. Little Turtle pushed the boat out further, and then hopped into it alongside the rest of us. Paddles were snugly tucked under the rim of the boat, which had been carved in such a way, that there were also sitting and bracing places for those who would paddle the huge vessel into the deep water. It felt good to be bobbing along through the rolling waves in such a sturdy vessel, with all of us paddling to propel it.

The craft was sea-worthy and broke the incoming waves easily. Once past them, we enjoyed a more peaceful motion. I noticed a smaller boat coming our way, first as a little dot, and then as it closed the distance, I noticed it was a small canoe. One man navigated it. He had some of the smaller nets with him, full of fish and crustaceans. Proud Foot was familiar with this lone fisherman, and they exchanged blessings. The fisherman went on his way, after telling us where the good fishing was today.

"He gets out early and goes alone," Proud Foot said. "He's called 'Lone Fisher' and lives up to his name," he explained. "We usually don't fish alone, but everyone must do what they must do and his life is a lonely life by choice."

Proud Foot went on to explain, "He is a loner. He likes to live alone and desires no village to surround him. He lives in a high tree and provides for himself. He doesn't desire, nor need a wife, or child, or anything or anyone. He's the lone fisherman. Sometimes though, he leaves fish for families who are in need. For that, he is loved and respected even more. There's no one way to be in this life, is there?" he asked me.

"That's true," I said, "so true, but extremely hard for some to understand."

We paddled in silence for a while towards the rising sun, along the coastline of white sandy beaches. Breaking the silence, Proud Foot said, "Now, you shall see the domain of the Sea Goddess." He handed me a small netted bag as we stopped rowing. It seemed that we had found our fishing place. Elmira and Little Turtle quickly became busy, dropping the large nets. Elmira, I noticed, was at ease with the task, and mind-spoke to me that he had been a fisherman long ago and loved this work. Proud Foot had other plans for himself and me. After stripping nude, we slipped over the side of the boat, the handle of a small net bag crossed over our shoulders, as we dived into the aqua seascape of the Sea Goddess. Indicating that I should follow him, Proud Foot first taught me to hold my breath underwater, then to allow it to escape in carefully spaced tiny bubbles. He also said I should always keep three bubbles for surfacing, since one should never surface without air left to expel. We practiced as we bobbed along the beautiful surface of the water. When satisfied that I could hold my breath sufficiently, he turned his body toward the ocean water, swimming deeper and deeper, with me following.

Once my eyes adjusted, I couldn't believe the beauty of the undersea world. Fish of every color swam by; coral in the most graceful shapes and colors formed magic places for sea creatures to hide and live within. Truly, this realm of the water goddess is a sight to behold.

Proud Foot pointed towards a huge lobster, scurrying around on the sea bottom. He very quickly grabbed it by its back, being careful to stay away from its giant claws, and put it in his bag. He indicated that I should do the same thing. I managed to get one, but felt close to having just three bubbles of air left, so I rose to the surface. I took a great gulp of air, dove down again and rejoined Proud Foot, who had many more of the sea creatures secured in his bag by then. I grabbed two this time, and then again, had to head for the surface. As before, I gulped air and went back down. Proud Foot, not having surfaced yet, must have lungs like a whale, since he was still filling his bag. I began to notice the release of bubbles from his mouth, and quickly captured a few more lobsters before surfacing. This time Proud Foot followed. We both had full bags by now, and he didn't seem winded at all as we floated along the gentle waves. His smiling face just looked my way and he told me I had made him proud.

"Proud?" I questioned. "I had to come up three times to your one. I would say I'm not the fisher you are, dear friend."

"Most first-time divers don't go back down as you did, my friend," Proud Foot said. "They get one of the creatures and feel that getting more is not worth their breath. You filled your bag. I'm proud of you and you should be happy yourself," he said. "It took me years to stay down as long as I do. Certainly, on my first attempts, I didn't do as well as you did, Jeshua. You are a true fisherman," he said. "May I call you 'Fisher?' " he asked, then took my bag from me and reached into it and pulled out a blue lobster, releasing it.

"I would be honored to be called 'Fisher,' Proud Foot," I answered. "I hope I don't have to go on a vision quest and suffer, to get the name to stick." Then I remembered the lobster he just released and asked, "Why did you release the blue one?"

He laughed at me and said, "Not all spirit names come from the same type of vision quests; Spirit talks to us in many ways, my friend, isn't that true? By the way, the blue one belongs to the Goddess. She only gives them to us as a sign that she approves of us; we give them back to her, because we love her generosity and honor her message."

By the time we got back to the boat, Elmira and Little Turtle had filled it with fish from the sea. Little Turtle finally spoke up and said, "The Goddess is pleased with us today, my friends, and she provides plentiful gifts."

Proud Foot explained that many times they came in from the day's fishing, nearly empty-handed. When fishing was good, their people and those of the neighboring tribes always shared information as to where to find the best catch, as the Lone Fisher had done. According to Proud Foot, the lobsters that we had been hand-harvesting were a rare treat and difficult to find. This day we were doubly blessed, he assured me. Then he looked serious and said, "The Sea Goddess offered you a rare blue lobster. That, my friend, is important, for there are many among our people who have never even seen one, and this is a sign that you are specially chosen."

When we reached the shore, instead of taking the catch out of the boat, a fire was built on the beach in a place I could see was used many times before. I wasn't quite sure what to do, to be of help. Realizing that the fire was the main concern of our two fisher friends, Elmira and I helped gather the dried wood. The fish and lobster were ignored in the boat, and many still wiggled and gasped for their last breath.

When the fire was flaming good (since this was a hot day already, I wasn't quite sure what the purpose might be), Proud Foot and Little Turtle took an old oar, from a pile of old broken, used oars near a tree on the beach path, and put it in the fire until it ignited, due to the natural tree sap still in its wood. The smoking oar was taken to the boat. The two native men began to sing a song of thanks-giving, passing the smoking oar between them and smudging the boat with the smoke it offered. I can't remember the exact words of the song, but they said something about how the fish and the people were one, how the oar had found new life within the fire, and how the fish and sea creatures would find new life within those who consumed them. After the smudging, a fish and a lobster were selected from the boat and examined closely, to see if they had taken their last breath. When that was determined, they were brought to the fire, placed on some hot rocks that rimmed the burning pit and cooked. When they were sufficiently cooked as determined by our native guides, they were put in a broad leaf, used to keep one's hands from being burned. The lobster was pried open to reveal the succulent meat it had to offer; the fish was broken into bite-sized pieces, as well. The leaf then became the serving dish. Proud Foot explained that the fisherman, who had caught the fish or sea-gift, had to be the first to partake of it, so that Great Spirit would know our gratitude. Thus, Elmira and Little Turtle shared the fish; Proud Foot and I enjoyed the lobster. When we had finished, the fire was allowed to consume the old oar and burn out naturally. Then we bundled the remaining catch in netting and devised a sling for it. Our catch swung between two long shafts that we carried on our shoulders. Elmira and Little Turtle had the heaviest burden to carry, with many fish, but both were strong and determined. Proud Foot and I had a lighter load, but it still took both of us, to carry the gifts of the Goddess, found at the bottom of her ocean.

"The village will rejoice. There will be a celebration feast," Proud Foot said, as we walked along. Thus we returned to share that which the Great Spirit, through the Sea Goddess provided.

## 'FISHER ONE'
### Chapter Thirty-Seven

Eocha had left, by the time we returned from our day of fishing. I felt a bit uneasy, since I was comforted by her presence, knowing I could bi-locate from time to time and be with my loved ones. I was with them often within my dream time and could feel the emotional and physical situations my beloved soul-mate, MiryAmah, experienced as she could mine. For the most part, it was the pain of longing that I felt–my wife's longing and my own longing for each other. Now that our work had been diverted, with the same goal calling us but now to be accomplished differently, I was somewhat at a loss as to how to carry on, yet still following my intuition.

The Fisher People were gracious and loving to me, but this type of community, I could sense, even in this faraway land, wasn't the norm. According to White Eagle, there were many warrior tribes. They often violently targeted tribes of peace, because they knew they didn't naturally desire to fight. I planned to visit more communities in this land. I still wanted to keep an eye on what was developing in the Middle Eastern place of my birth and early work, along with keeping an eye on the land above the Mediterranean where my family ultimately settled. To do all of that meant, that I might have to be in at least two places at once from time to time and my anchor had just left! I wondered if I had marooned myself.

After the feast of the gifts of the sea, White Eagle, who often watched but seldom spoke with me, bid me to walk with her. I had moved out of her little hut before my fishing expedition, thinking I would find it more comforting to sleep under the stars.

She asked me, "Isn't my abode a comfort to you, Jeshua?"

"Oh yes!" I replied. "It's a great comfort, but I need to talk to the stars right now. Under their canopy, I can better understand my next step in this long journey."

I also shared something that I didn't think I would share with anyone, which was, "I used to lie under the stars and make love to my wife."

White Eagle smiled at that remark, not because it was funny, but because she knew how much I missed MiryAmah. She probably had intimate moments of her own under the blanket of a starry sky. Then she asked, "And what do the stars tell you about the next step, Fisher One?" Her voice was a bit playful, since the name had come up in conversation and merriment, as we ate our bounty, during the feast we had just shared with the village people.

"You call me 'Fisher'. How can it be, I should be so honored, when I only delivered a few lobsters to their doom?" I replied. "Anyone from your village is a much better fisherman than I am."

Laughing loudly, she said, "Maybe you brought those lobsters to their destiny, thus helped them fulfill their soul-mission. They waited for you a long time and grew to perfection, so you would choose them." Then she just walked away quietly, not waiting for an answer. She stopped, looked back at me, and I knew she expected me to follow her, so I quickly caught up with her on the path.

"We call you Fisher One, because you are like the fisher of men." Then looking to see if I was listening, she went on to say, "A fisher of men is one who brings spiritual food to those who hunger. You can give the hungry a wide variety of food, but only when you give them something that satisfies their soul are you a true 'Fisher'," she explained.

I was trying to follow her reasoning. I hadn't done anything, since I arrived but accept their hospitality and didn't feel worthy of this honor. Surely, Elmira was the fisher, and I was but a bad diver who couldn't hold his breath very long, but who had the luck to happen upon a good catch. I hadn't yet processed what she said about 'fisher of men'. I called Peter that once, so I should have understood her meaning easily enough, but I had a problem with seeing my own worth, as everyone does.

"I see you struggle with self-worth, Fisher One," White Eagle said. "Is that due to being so closely soul-tied to that other part of you,[171] the part that usually holds the life-line from the Great Spirit Realm, yet, this time came down into the depths of this learning place with you? She can give you her support and love, but cannot fulfill your sense of self-worth. Only you can do that."

---

[171] Referring to my soul-mate (twin flame)

She clearly understood how the soul was split into two parts and how they usually worked toward the success of experiential incarnations. I answered, "I suppose. I, like everyone else, sometimes wonder if I'm accomplishing any good in this learning plane." I couldn't talk about how much I missed my beloved wife and children, because it was too painful for me to voice.

She continued on, "You are a little insecure, with Eocha now journeying back to the high mountains. Isn't that so?"

"You read me well, White Eagle. Are there no secrets you can't pierce?" I questioned.

"One of my talents, and also my burden, is that I can read what others have in their hearts and minds," she explained. "The day the eagle came and sat upon my head, it opened channels that resulted in my hearing and seeing what others are thinking and feeling. At first it near drove me crazy," she said. "But I remembered how I felt so peaceful and calm, when that big bird came down and landed upon me. I reminded myself to have patience with all the new chatter going through my head, since the visit of the spirit bird."

"How could you hold such a huge bird on your child head?" I asked.

She rolled her eyes, perhaps because everyone had probably asked her that question many times, but patiently explained yet again, "It was nearly as big as I was, but I wanted it to stay there on top of my little head. As for how I could do that, it seemed near weightless to me. I saw the amazement upon the faces of the people of my tribe and family, and I thought this would be fun—to see how long this great weightless bird would stay there upon my head. It was like a child game, you see."

"And how long did it stay, White Eagle?" I asked, visualizing the spectacle.

"Well, it stayed all day," she announced, as if I should have known; "from the dawning of the sun until the end of the day, when the sun goes to sleep and awakes in another place. All day long everyone was following me and the great bird. I was having fun, doing my chores and acting like I didn't even notice I had a huge bird on my head, much less an audience in awe. Then it simply lifted off and flew into the setting sun, with me and my entire tribe watching."

"I was more entertained at that point by the whole thing," she continued. "I had no idea of the blessing that had just taken place. The elders knew and they were very attentive to my every action and reaction, during and after the eagle visit. They were following me all day, nodding and whispering to each other. They believed the Eagle had chosen a future leader of our tribe. Following this episode I spent months in council with the leaders, being groomed to one day take the chief position. Eventually, they sent me to observe the eagles and report back to them after one full moon cycle. I was young for a vision quest, but my mother agreed and allowed me to go to the home of the eagles at the lake of tall trees. I learned that the eagles were fishers. I also learned that they could see into the underwater world of the Goddess–her seas and lakes, or whatever water she provided. I heard the eagles ask for her fish, before they partook of her bounty. As they dove, grabbed the fish and took flight again–taking the food back to their nests–I heard them thank the fish for its gift." Then White Eagle said, "Don't you agree that the need and the fulfillment are one? The blessing is to honor this Onement in both its giving and taking."

"I would agree with that," I replied "I realize that I was blessed when I was given the ability to understand and speak languages without learning them. Nevertheless, even with this ability, I often feel helpless in the face of such overwhelming imbalances in the way people think and behave. I can't find the right fish to feed their souls, White Eagle. So I'm not a good 'Fisher,' I fear."

"What hungers within those you desire to feed?" she asked.

I thought for a moment and then said, "They hunger for truth and connection. However, there's a false ideology of what the Great Spirit is and wants; the multitudes have accepted the lies as truth, while at the same time they still feel empty. In most places I go, there's a split attitude of creational essence, with half being evil and half being divine. Those who consider themselves divine are usually the men. They feel justified in enslaving that which they believe less worthy, which includes women and other beings. Within this illusion, they are drunk with power and judgment. If I'm a fisher of men, I'm also a fisher of women. I wonder why I can't find the fish that will offer truth to the people and nourish their souls. I see starvation in the spirit of my people."

As I talked with the chief, I thought of how this tribe of tall men and women held an attitude of equality as I had never seen before, even in the high mountains where the monks and nuns usually lived apart. I said to White Eagle, "I don't see women leaders demand power as figureheads in your society. Rather they seem to be in positions of encouragement and direction, of the design and purpose of this arrangement and I want to learn more. Eocha has been a force that has sustained me, and she has much to offer as a leader, yet even in the high mountain place which sent me, I noticed the one in command was a man. I wonder, why not she?"

"Oh, my dear friend," White Eagle said, easily putting her arm around my shoulders as we walked, due to her being taller than me. "Just because women leaders are not visibly powerful, doesn't mean they aren't at the forefront in full command." Then she stopped, turned me to face her and said, "Your sweet wife is as much a leader as you yourself, but she could never step out in the manner that you once did, to lead effectively. Isn't that so?" Then she said, "Eocha is a leader of the highest degree, you just don't know how expansive her role is, do you?"

"I guess you're right. In my interactions with her, she's usually always concerned with my bi-location endeavors. As for my dear wife, she has her band of followers with her inner-core of twelve disciples, as I had the twelve apostles, but the overall attitudes in place kept her from being openly the leader she truly is."

"Yes, but she still commands respect without even asking. She doesn't demand respect, as has become the way of the imbalanced tribes." White Eagle gave me a lot to think about, and she continued, "She and her followers had to adjust to the atmosphere and the need of the moment and time, so they could more effectively do their work. I would guess that even in their quiet leadership, they were more courageous and loyal to you, than those who paraded around after you in your footsteps, feeling specially chosen by their son-ships."

"You're right about that," I agreed. "When I was put on the cross, all the women were there agonizing over my suffering, while most of the men went into hiding. However, I don't judge the men for their actions. They had to save themselves, so the work would carry on." White Eagle and I had briefly spoken of the crucifixion previously, when she had seen the scars on my wrists and ankles.

"Hmmm!" White Eagle pondered for a moment. "And I suppose that with everyone you encountered, you would have a slightly different way of sharing your divine message. Isn't that true, Raboni?"

I was surprised that she called me 'teacher' in my own language. "I see you also understand and speak other languages well, chief," I said.

"I know that a Fisher of Men is also a Fisher of Women, for the two are one," she said. "That's why I call you 'Fisher One' for you bring the two aspects together and unite that which should never be separated." Watching me to see if I understood, and being satisfied, she said, "I know as well that what you catch is people's attention, then you give them the tools to enter the portal of 'knowing,' which leads to compassion."

I could see a huge doorway open in my mind's eye, as she spoke. I had never thought of my work as a doorway before.

She continued again, saying, "But that portal can be intimidating, for once opened, if the truth revealed is opposite to what was thought to be true, it shatters the walls that were perceived as security. The awesome light, as it comes through the opened door, threatens their past, present and future. That can be so dramatic, that many can't survive the vision. Your mission is most difficult, Fisher One."

## Jeshua's Song

What a wise woman, I thought, as I listened to her. I was used to doing all the talking as a master teacher, but since I had come to this land, I was doing a lot of listening, and even more learning.

She wasn't finished yet and continued on. "Thus Fisher One," she said, "you bring in the catch, you share the specialized food in terms of your teaching, then once again you release it all back into the big blue ocean called humanity, to prosper and spread good seed."

That philosophy, I realized, was the deepest spiritual truth of these Fisher People. They may be fishers of the sea, but they were also fishers of spirit. I felt a great honor that she would see their qualities in me.

White Eagle confirmed my observation and said, "If you can understand that concept, then you understand who we are."

"I'm glad to be considered your friend, White Eagle," I said. Then I admitted, "I'm still a bit confused as to what my next step will be. I'm not getting much rest these days. I have nightmares of my homeland, where I see my followers at odds with each other over what I really meant, when I shared the teachings. Certainly, some of the fish I offered to them were not appreciated. In addition, my supporters are persecuted by the Romans and, especially, by the priesthood. I tried to feed their souls, but I fear I have been unsuccessful and just caused them more misery."

"Misery is often the companion of change," White Eagle said.

Her wise words hadn't sunk in yet, when I shifted the topic, saying, "I sense my wife is expecting again. I dream of a sensitive son, wanting to come through us. I worry that he will find this world too crass for his beautiful soul. I know my mother is worried. She has suffered so much. I fear for my brother James, because when he appears in my dreams, a black cloud consumes him. I wish I could be just a fisher for my family and nourish and protect them. Their suffering haunts me."

White Eagle stopped, turned to me and said, "I, of course, know of your dilemma, and I wish to send you to see the one called 'Clear

# The Saga-Oracle

Water'. She is what you would know as an oracle. She will help you see through your misery and assist you to find a path to begin this part of your journey. Can you leave tonight?" she asked.

It was already late after a day of fishing, a huge meal, and now this rather long walk. I wasn't sure if I had any energy left, yet White Eagle seemed determined, so I agreed to leave immediately. After all, I wasn't sleeping all that much anyway, and my meager traveling items were already bundled. So, I just nodded my head in agreement.

"Good!" White Eagle said, "Because an escort is in place for you and Elmira. They await you, even as we speak."

Then I realized that all the time we had been speaking, we were going down a trail I had not noticed before, which led deep into the dense forest full of night creature sounds, as we walked along. Ahead of us, I could see a small fire burning and hear voices around the parameters of it. Confidently, White Eagle walked to the clearing where the fire was lit and nodded at three young men, sitting with Elmira. They rose up, took some bundles upon their backs, and Elmira kicked some sand onto the small fire, putting it out. As the smoke rose, White Eagle took a white feather from her hair, and used it to direct the smoke around each of us, as she sang a song I couldn't translate. It was a song of sacred sounds only, but I knew it was a blessing. Once she had smudged us all to her satisfaction, she simply turned and walked back the way she had just come, and we went in the opposite direction.

Lucky for us, it was a moonlit night, and we could easily make out the path. I could sense the night creatures around us, some watching, some choosing to keep their distance. I felt the presence of the panthers again, but I never communicated with them. I just sensed that they were there once more, one at our forefront and one in the rear, keeping watch.

We traveled through the night and rested during the day. After three nights of traveling this way, we came to a village. This place had a different feel from the village of the Fisher People. The people immediately surrounded us and took us to the chief, who seemed familiar with our guides, yet not all that friendly to them.

The people felt more aggressive and had spears, bows and arrows, and clubs dangling from their waist belts. I sensed they were willing to use the weapons in a heart-beat, if necessary. The chief was a strong man in his mid-life. He sat on a pile of animal pelts and didn't arise when we approached. Standing, looking down on him didn't seem to bother him; it felt like he was looking down on me instead. He was a plump little man, not appearing physically fit. Women nearby apparently served his every need, thus, there was no necessity for him to move around much, I surmised. He didn't look pleased to see me or Elmira, and already our guides had hastily left without much fanfare or even a goodbye. The language they spoke in this location was different than the Fisher People, not as harmonious and musical. I understood it, however, and answered a remark from the chief as to "What are the Fisher People discarding now?"

"They discard nothing, chief," I said. "I was sent here to see Clear Water the oracle, for I have need of her great wisdom."

"And if I allow this, what in return, will you offer me?" the chief asked.

Sometimes I react within total intuition and, to my own surprise. I said, "I'll cut off my hair and give it to you, so that you know my gratitude is sincere."

At that answer, he arose, with some effort, from his sitting position with the help of a couple of his hand-maidens and walked up to me, looking closely in my eyes. Then he shifted his attention to my hair, which was very curly due to the humidity of the area. My hair had grown long, as I hadn't thought to trim it on my sea journey. The bountiful forest made it grow at an accelerated rate, as well. He picked up a lock in his soft chubby hand and felt the texture. My hair is fine and silky to the touch. He kept running his fingers through it, with an odd look on his face like a man holding gold.

"You have fire in your hair," he finally said. Due to the intense sun in this land, my normally dark auburn hair had become nearly reddish blond. "And your eyes shift color," he commented, looking back into my eyes again. "One moment they are the color of my own, then when I look once more, they are the color of the forest, and another time they change to the color of the sea."

I wasn't trying to shift the color of my eyes, which I knew how to do, and was confused as to how he could see a shift, where none was orchestrated. I almost felt I should apologize, but decided not to ask forgiveness for being myself. I was sure that gesture would be wasted on this chief.

"You can't hide from me, stranger," he said. "I can see more in your eyes than you want me to see, and I see no harm intended. I see sorrow and a past of great suffering. I see a need for you to keep yourself as the chameleon does, blended in with the surrounding space. I grant your wish. You shall see Clear Water and your guardian friend will accompany you," he said, pointing towards Elmira.

Then he said, "After you leave this village and go to the place of the oracle, I'll forget I saw you. I just saw a chameleon and its follower move through and go beyond our village." He nodded to a small boy and indicated for us to follow him. We left the village, after only being there a short time. I was glad to be on my way. As we followed our boy guide, we foraged through the dense forest, not following a path, but taking routes that only little animals could comfortably manage. I was thankful for the clothing that White Eagle had provided for both Elmira and me. She said robes wouldn't do so well, while moving about in the tree world. Our robes had been bundled, and our guides had carried them, but now we had them strapped to our own backs. Following this young lad through rough terrain, required agility that leggings and leather shoes offered, I couldn't imagine sandals on my feet, as I could barely keep up with the forest child.

I saw doubt on Elmira's face, and thankfully, I could mind-talk to him as we struggled to keep up with the sprinting boy. He wasn't sure this was such a good idea, especially when we had to wade up to our chests in swamp water, which was full of unseen slithery things, while above water insects were keeping us miserable. He was a man of the desert; all this water without a boat worried him. The boy was swinging through the trees using vines, which was easy for him being so slight of build. For us full-grown men that wasn't an option, and we had to trust that where we waded, we wouldn't sink too far.

Elmira found a small high dry spot and climbed up, grabbing an old stump and clinging to it, he looked like he might go no further. The boy looked back at us and said, "If you don't have the courage to go through the swamp, then how will you have the courage to look into the clear water?"

Elmira doesn't give up easily, and he waded back into the water again, following the precocious child, pushing past his fears of what might be under that dark murky surface.

"How is it the chief has seen fit to torture us with this child?" I asked Elmira, out loud in our own language so the boy wouldn't understand my complaining. He just shrugged his shoulders and kept moving through the water, which was beginning to get shallower now. I felt all sorts of things touch my body underwater and decided to mind-to-mind speak with the water goddess, asking her to keep us safe in her domain. As we walked, or I should say, waded, it seemed like hours and miles. I thought of the life forms that depend on this watery place for life. I decided that to hold gratitude would be the best protection available to us, and the only way to keep from climbing a tree, never to come down to the muck and the biting bugs again. The more I could foster this feeling of gratefulness, the clearer the water became. I also noticed that the colors of the places we were moving through became brighter and more colorful, too. The air smelled better as well. The boy looked back smiling and seemed to beam with some secret knowledge, as we kept following him.

Finally, we came near the domain of the Sea Goddess again. I could hear the crashing of the waves on the shoreline. The fresh energy washing in over the water was rejuvenating to me, even before I could see the water. As we came through the density of the forest, the same beautiful aqua color greeted us as on the day we fished, but this time the sky seemed to be purple and deep blue, with a beautiful sunset sitting upon the horizon. I realized that we had traveled all night, the next day and into the next evening. It

## The Saga-Oracle

was about the same time of day that we departed from the village of this jungle boy. Upon that realization, exhaustion overtook us. The boy, as fresh as the moment we departed from his village, walked to the shore, held his hands up to the setting sun and sang a song of rejoicing. His mostly bare bronze body glowed like gold, as he performed his ritual of thanks-giving. I noticed he was not all bitten up with bug bites, as my guardian and I were. With his arms raised in praise, his youthful body looked beautiful against the setting sun. Following his lead, I joined him and sang my own song, and Elmira just sang a song within his heart.

I wondered if Clear Water was the sea, the great Goddess to these people, and the oracle after all. Why the chief would have to be so guarded of such a vast resource I couldn't guess. Surely, there was enough of Mother Sea for all to enjoy. Why the big deal over something so abundant? I thought.

The lad turned and stared down the shoreline, with a smile of recognition spreading across his face. Following the direction of his gaze, I saw a woman approaching along the beach. She walked barefoot in the washing waves. She was so graceful that for a moment I was mesmerized, just watching her approach. She had long black hair that floated in the breeze. I couldn't guess her age, because she seemed young and old at the same time. Her garments were a weaving that I hadn't ever seen before, a material, wispy and soft, that was tinted the colors of the sea. She had a water lily in her hair. When she reached us, she gave the boy a loving hug and introduced herself to us.

"I'm Lily", she said, "Lily of the Lake. I've been expecting you, since I envisioned you coming, now for nearly a full moon."

That was puzzling, since it had only been a few days, since I had departed from the Fisher People. "I'm Jeshua," I said, extending my hand to her.

She gently touched the back of my hand, and said, "No!" You are the Fisher One." Then looking quite satisfied that she had my attention, she went on to say, "You used to be Jeshua and before that you were Jesus ben Joseph, and Esa. Now you are all of these, but in essence, you are the Fisher King."

"I'm not a king," I assured her, but she was not easily dissuaded.

"Yes, you are. This must be your beloved guardian, who has kept you safe for nearly your entire lifetime on many journeys," she said, looking at Elmira, who seemed as surprised as myself as to how much this beautiful lady knew about us.

"We have come to see Clear Water," I said. "Do you know this one?"

She seemed to ignore us, looked at the boy and asked, "Did you bring them the easy way or the hard way, Little bird?"

He looked very pleased with himself and answered, "The hard way, of course, my lady. What fun would it be to choose the easy path?"

She ruffled his short-cropped black hair, then looked at my hair and took a handful of it. The chief hadn't yet taken me up on the offer of my hair for this favor. "It's a shame to part with such hair of sunshine," she said. Before I could comment, she whisked out a knife from under her dress and whacked off most of my hair. I must have looked totally shocked, because I didn't see that coming. Then she took another handful of straggling hairs and did so again. I stood still, stunned, as I felt no ill intent from her. She continued chopping off most of my hair, as Elmira just looked on, amused. He did nothing to save me from this lady with a knife, intent on separating me from my hair of sunshine.

"There," she said, finally satisfied with most of my long curly reddish hair now in her hand. She then walked out into the sea up to her knees, with her dress floating around her, making her look like a beautiful water lily. She reached under the water and grabbed some seaweed. Returning to where I still stood watching her, as if dumbstruck, she wrapped the cut ends of my hair in the seaweed. Finding a few little shells with natural holes in them along the shore, she laced them with the sea weed, too, making a most beautiful bundle.

Then she said, "Here, Little Bird–a promise is kept. Give this to your father and tell him that as long as he honors this gift, the sun will shine upon him and his village."

The boy, taking my hair, ran off in a totally different direction from where we had emerged on the beach. No doubt, he took the easy way back.

Lily turned to us and said, "I'll take you to Clear Water. She comes when she chooses. If you are lucky, she may choose to honor you. If your luck is not with you, she will ignore you."

She turned and walked along the beach in the direction she came, I assumed expecting us to follow. That wasn't difficult. She was nearly as beautiful as my dear MiryAmah. Her confidence and the flow of her walk brought my wife's memory to my heart, and as usual, I felt pain due to our separation. I wished that she could be here beside me, walking upon this beach following lovely Lily of the Lake, going to find Clear Water the oracle.

## LILY OF THE LAKE
### Chapter Thirty-Eight

We followed Lily for a short distance along the shoreline, where she abruptly turned and proceeded into the swampy forests. Elmira and I were not pleased to see her select that direction, but our fears were unfounded. Unlike Little Bird, the chief's son, she didn't take us into the forest 'the hard way.'

She followed a nearly invisible trail, but quite easy to traverse. The path seemed more like a deer-trail, used only by the animals– for it was barely discernable under the ground cover. She walked at an easy pace through the forest with her dress floating like a ghost of the sea. After we had followed her for several hours, she came to a large tree and asked if we would like some rest. Since we hadn't had any in a couple of days, we were eager to accept her invitation.

## Jeshua's Song

Inviting us to climb the great tree she had chosen for a rest stop, she ascended first with the nimbleness of a tree monkey, moving swiftly upward through the tangled branches, and we followed. I guessed that we might be resting out on a limb, somehow clinging to a branch. Any rest would be greatly appreciated. Higher and higher she climbed in this enormous tall tree. Finally, she did venture onto a limb, and I saw what looked like a vine hammock swinging from it. "This will do for Elmira," she said and indicated that I should go still higher with her. A few more branches above, she assigned me to another hammock. Above that, where the tree narrowed down and danced on the breezes overlooking the forest she settled into a strange-sitting-up type sling and told us to get some rest.

We were still carrying our back packs. At this moment, the softness of the robe seemed like it would be a good choice to line the vine hammock assigned to us, so Elmira and I unwrapped our bundles. Inside them, since we hadn't had a chance to check them out, we were delighted to find dried fish, fruit and nuts. I offered some of my food to Lily, but she refused, saying she had earlier enjoyed her meal of the day. She just closed her eyes and began to immediately snore, already in a deep sleep, rocking in the soft breeze like a baby in a cradle.

Elmira looked at me in wonder and thought, "Don't you wish it was that easy for us to nod off?" I returned the look and finished my most wonderful meal, saving some food for another day. As I settled back into my high bed in the tree, the cool breeze swung the hammock ever so slightly, and I was as comfortable as a rocked baby. On the ground, the mosquitoes had been annoying us as we walked, but up here the breeze blew just enough to keep them away. This is a perfect resting place, I thought.

I already liked sleeping under the starry sky, but had been having nightmares of late and not sleeping so well; thankfully, that wasn't the case this evening. I was so exhausted from my journey that I soon fell into sound sleep.

In what felt like a mere moment, I heard the song of a bird and awoke to the little fellow sitting very close to my hammock and singing his morning song, full throttle. The sun was up and the day was new. I felt rested and cozy, there curled in my robes from home, feeling like a bird in a nest. I looked up to see if Lily was awake yet and noticed she wasn't in her sleeping sling. She was already on the ground and bathing in a pool of swamp water, which looked much less murky in the light of the day. She was humming and washing her beautiful black hair. I saw her garment hanging from a nearby bush, and I made a throat noise, so she would know I was awake. I quickly looked away, not wanting to embarrass her, since she was totally nude.

"Hello, Sunshine!" she yelled to me. "You might want to climb down out of that tree now and get yourself ready for the rest of this journey." She didn't make any effort to cover her nakedness; just kept washing herself using some herbs she found growing near the pool of water.

"I'm not sure I want to take a chance on getting submersed again in the swamp." I replied. "The water Goddess might be tired of me by now."

"That's ridiculous!" she exclaimed. "Get down here and get yourself clean, if you want to be seeing Clear Water. Otherwise, if you approach her without cleansing, she'll smell you a mile away and might decide to be someplace else."

'Oh well,' I thought. I gathered my things and descended the tree, tapping Elmira on the foot when I passed him, indicating it was time to pack up. When I reached the bottom of the great tree I looked for a private pool of water and found there were many, with the trail winding through the pools on higher ground. I laid my robes down by one such pool. Looking over my shoulder to see if I was too exposed to the others, I took off my leather breaches, vest and shoes and slipped into the water bare and shivering, since the morning hadn't yet warmed the water. The cold water felt refreshing though. All that wading up to my chest yesterday didn't feel this good. Yesterday, the water felt mucky and heavy. I rinsed my body, closing my eyes as I rinsed off my short-cropped hair, and washed under my arms.

"How do you expect to get clean bathing like that?" I heard louder than I liked and Lily was standing there, now dressed, be the dress ever so skimpy, staring down at me with her hands on her hips.

She startled me and I nearly jumped out of the pool, but remembering I was naked, I decided to stay in the water for now. I just looked back at her with the thought of 'are you crazy woman?'

She stooped down and began to pick some yellow forest flowers that were growing around the pond. "Here," she said, "the pool always provides for those who would enjoy her waters."

I took the flowers and she looked at me, realizing I didn't know what to do with them; she shrugged and said, "Oh, you aren't a forest person, that's for sure. You take the flowers, thank them and smash them in your hands until they feel sticky. Then you wash your hair with them. After you're done with your hair, you take these large leaves (she was now picking) and smash them into a paste as well, and you rinse your hair. But," she added, "This is not for the body. At the bottom of the pond, there are some plants that grow on long stems with fine leaves–use them as a body cleanser. They repel the bugs that love to suck your blood. They also help heal the scratches, where you've been making trails for the bugs to find more blood."

I followed her directions, hoping that would cause her to leave. I was quite pleased with the resulting feeling of cleanliness as I followed her directions, but she stayed to make sure I did the process to her expectation. I looked up at her like a boy wanting approval, but I really wanted some privacy.

She must've sensed my embarrassment, because she spun around and went to look for poor Elmira. He was trying to work up the courage to bath as well, but water was not his favorite substance. I thought of the bravery it took, for him to help me across the stream that turned into a raging river when I was a small boy. That was when I learned that he was a 'Christopher,' or one who protects a 'Christed One'. I had been so caught up in him being a Christopher it hadn't dawned on me that day that I might be a Christed One. Maybe that is what a Fisher One really was, I thought. I didn't feel especially chosen, or more deserving, or closer to God. Even so, I did know from early on that I was part of God, and that I had a divine mission.

I used my robe to dry off, and then dressed back in my forest clothes and moccasins, as I now understood my soft shoes were called. My short hair was much easier to manage. I soon walked back to the tree and began to bundle my robes and supplies. Elmira joined me and his eyes danced in amusement, so I assumed he had been given the lesson of the bath as well. It didn't seem to bother him as much as it did me. I could swear that someone once told me, that he was a harem caretaker. Maybe he knew how women can be about bathing and cleansing.

We quickly moved back to the trail and traveled on throughout the day, stopping from time to time, once about midday partaking of the food we had with us. Lily brought us several beautiful flowers. I thought she was presenting us with a lovely bouquet to gaze upon. 'How sweet,' I thought. I took the flowers, smelled them, showed them to Elmira, and he did the same. Lily didn't look pleased. She selected one of the flowers, popped it into her mouth and ate it. Then she pulled another one for me and unceremoniously shoved it into my mouth. Elmira quickly took one and ate it, not needing a repeat demonstration. The flowers were very tasty and gave us a feeling of fullness that I hadn't expected. After a short rest, we moved on again following the same trail, still nearly invisible.

About sunset, we came to an inland lake. Its waters, reflecting the setting sun, mirrored the purple/pink hue of the sky, and lay peacefully still in all its colorful glory. Beauty in nature is always a pleasure for me. I walked up to the lake and just stood there drinking in its grandeur. Lily was busy getting some dried wood and building a fire. Eventually, I took my eyes and heart away from the colorful scene and helped her. She made a small fire and told us to warm ourselves, she would be back soon. She then slipped into the dense forest and was gone.

I looked at Elmira, who was somewhat chilled from the cool evening air coming across the water, and he looked back at me; our unspoken question was, "What now?"

I began to feel my mood slip, as I thought of my family again. I could sense that all was not well with them. I put my face in my hands, as I sat by the fire and wept. Elmira watched. He knew that I needed to release my emotions, even though he hadn't expected that the glory of the moment would dissolve into the tears and sorrow he now witnessed. Here I was in a faraway land, body and soul, however, I knew those I loved were suffering, because I could feel it, even as I was cut off from them. 'Oh Eocha', I thought, 'where are you when I need you?'

The night had completely fallen by the time I stopped sobbing and lifted my head. Elmira had left and I couldn't see him, still I felt that he was close by. He must have given me my privacy in my moment of self-pity, I thought. I needed that time to weep, and now I felt drained but cleansed from it.

I heard someone clear their throat as if to gain my attention. The fire was still blazing. I thought I saw a figure step out of it and take a squatting position on the opposite side. 'Great,' I thought. 'Now you have yourself in such a state that you are hallucinating.' I berated myself in my head voice.

"I'm not a hallucination, I assure you," a familiar voice said.

I stood up to better see, and there was none other than my master teacher from the high mountain place. It was he who found Elmira and me after we tumbled down into that dark cave shaft. He was always orchestrating my lessons at the school of masters and mastras.

"Teacher," I cried, for I knew him by no other name, and I quickly went around to the other side of the fire. "It's been so long and I've slipped much since I last saw you. How is it that I'm worthy enough for you to come to me?"

"You have always been worthy, and you are not a failure, Jeshua," he said, and walked toward me and embraced me in a long strong hug of true love and friendship.

"I'm afraid that you found me with a heavy heart," I said.

"Your heavy heart is why I came," he replied. "We are heart-tied as teacher and student, you see," he went on to explain. "That means that what you feel, I can feel as well, if I choose to keep that channel open. Since you left to continue with your mission, I have chosen to keep the channel between us open, so that if you need me, I'll know."

"They suffer!" I said, meaning my followers and especially my loved ones.

"I know," he replied in a whisper.

"I feel helpless and cut off from them. I feel like I've abandoned those who depend on me. I know that the doorways into their minds and hearts, I opened, cause them to suffer. Those who don't want such doors open, try to slam them shut. I'm a complete failure and I don't know why I'm allowed to stay in the flesh any longer. I fear I've let the great God of love down in this sojourn."

The teacher didn't reply, just let those statements hang in the air and dissipate, as all feelings must. Finally, he sat down upon the ground and indicated to me to sit also, by patting the spot next to him.

In a tender quiet voice, he said, "You are not helpless–far from it. You didn't abandon those you love, even though you must live separately from them. Within their hearts, you are still present and leading them through the trouble they encounter."

After making sure I was following his conversation, he continued, "As for the suffering–yes you came to bring change. To do so often means that those in resistance will inflict suffering on those that insist on evolving and moving into a better way."

Still he watched me and paused, before he went on to say, "As for God, who you and I know is present in all creation within love–

holding creation in form unifying it all at the same time–you are not a disappointment. No experience is wasted. I tell you, the One who sent you out as a spark of a soul so long ago recognizes your loving courage, which you have shown throughout your life, as proof that creation will succeed in the Master Plan. You have no idea how much you have changed the entire realm of the physical on this plane, and how many eons of time your memory and legend will be pondered. I wish I could say the change is complete and perfect, but that's never the case. Change must come to its perfection gradually. You have started a mighty wheel rolling. Your legacy will be that you gave your life for the cause of Oneness and unity, instead of accepting the elitism and division that have brought so much suffering down through the ages. It's not God's will for anyone or anything to suffer. It's God's will that all aspects of creation, one day realize that together, united, they all are good and all God!"

"I am not telling you anything you don't already know," he concluded, rustling my frazzled hair. Then he pulled his hand back, inspected my new hairstyle and said, "What's this? Are you trying to shave your head like a monk? If so, you had better get some help, because you've made a mess of it."

"Oh that," I said, "it's a long story. Right now, all I know is I need to see my sweet wife again. I miss her. I miss little Sarah and baby James. What a beauty Sarah is, master. She takes after her mother." Then the sobbing took me over again. I was inconsolable. I had been through so much and now here I was in the dense forest of a land faraway sitting with my master teacher crying like a baby. "I'm sorry," I said. "My heart has its way with me."

"I heard your heart pleading," the teacher said, "and so it is; your desire is not unheeded."

Again I washed my eyes and face with my tears. I knew that I must appear as a pathetic fool. Many families had suffered worse separations than I had, but my grief caught up with me and couldn't be held back a moment longer. On the other hand, maybe I felt safe in this serene private place in the wilderness–safe enough to indulge in self-pity. When I finally looked up, Elmira and Lily were there, quietly watching me. I quickly dried my face on the robe I was sitting on and didn't offer an explanation. They didn't ask for one, either.

Finally, Lily said, "Tomorrow, you'll meet Clear Water. I go now to prepare. I have given Elmira instructions on how to find her. I'll see you when your thirst is quenched." Then she arose and left.

I didn't sleep well that night. I had nearly forgotten why I desired to see Clear Water at all, much less why I was in this forest land so far from my family. I had no answers in my head and nearly forgot what the questions were, to begin with. Elmira awoke early, began to clean up camp and bundled our robes. I was but a helpless lump, and sat stooped down, by the lake looking out across the water. There was a mist upon the water that was rising, due to the warmth of the morning sun. As it rose, I saw an island out in the lake. Funny, I hadn't noticed it before, but there it was, getting clearer by the moment.

I felt a tug at my shoulder. Elmira helped me get my robe pack secured on my shoulder, with straps that crisscrossed my chest. He led me to a hidden boat, and I walked like a zombie, just moving along. The boat was nestled in the reeds, not far from our camp. He indicated I should get in. He found a paddle and pushed the boat out into the lake with it. I thought he would jump in and join me, but he didn't. Nor did he offer the paddle. Great I thought. Here I am in a boat with no paddle. That pretty much summed up how I felt about myself right now.

Then I realized the boat was moving along, with the prow headed towards the island, on its own. I saw no wake in the lake, or waves, which could account for this forward motion. I have witnessed many wondrous things in my life. Each time I find myself in the same awe, and this moment was no different. The boat made steady progress to the island, then went down a winding stream, overhung with vines and arched trees, which pierced the interior of the isle. Still, it moved of its own power, with no direction from me. The mists of the island hadn't completely lifted. It seemed quite enchanting, as I floated along through a tunnel of trees and plants, in an otherworldly mist. Birds of colors

I had never seen before chirped and hopped from branch to branch or swooped in flight past me. One dipped down and pulled a hair from my head, and I thought it quite interesting that a bird would gather a hair for its nest, right off my head. I saw other animals and had a feeling of being watched by many eyes, as I silently floated along. Then I saw her.

Standing on the shore of the channel was a woman, all dressed in white, and she seemed to glow. She reached out and acted like she was pulling my boat with an invisible cord, reeling me to her. Finally, my boat was at her feet. She offered me a hand and bid me come out of the vessel and into her domain. I would go anywhere with this woman, I thought.

I asked if she was the Goddess of the Water. She said, "No, I'm Clear Water, the oracle."

I followed her, like a puppy dog, to a clearing ringed by the same type of giant trees we had used for refuge in the swamp. Inside that ring of trees grew another low ring of delicate blue flowers. In the midst of that ring was a flat rock and on it, a bowl made of an iridescent seashell. The bowl contained crystal clear water and upon it floated the most perfect water lily one could imagine.

We stopped at the edge of the flower ring. "Are you ready to step into the sacred oracle realm?" she asked. "I must warn you that what you wish might be granted, and such a request is always a two-sided gift." Watching me to see if I would take that opportunity to retreat, then finally deciding I was up to the challenge, she said, "One side of every gift is perfectly fulfilling; the other side is extremely draining and sorrowful, yet at the same time both sides lead to the same goal."

"Does that mean if I step into the oracle circle, I will cause suffering?" I asked, "If that's so, I can't trade fulfillment for suffering, thus I can't accept the gift."

"What is fulfilling will fill its cup, one way or another," she answered. Then she said, "What is sorrowful must run its course as well." She watched me, knowing my dilemma and said, "You can make both situations better by participation. To do so means you will need to have my assistance within the circle. I see the gift that would fulfill you, and you are deserving of your desire." Then she said, "Suffering is often the wrapping upon a greater gift."

"Then I'll take my chances with you," I answered. Feeling somehow reassured with her oracle-like explanation, I stepped over the blue flowers and entered the sacred space.

I had heard my wife speak of the Mysty Isles[172] before and of some of the power places upon them. I loved hearing her memory tales of such magical realms and wondered why I had to be an apprentice to hardship, more often than a witness to enchantment. I knew, since MiryAmah, my soul mate, had been there, and we experienced all that the other does, I wasn't lacking in my training. After all, we can't be everywhere and do everything together, though I think it would've been delightful to be a boy trying to keep up with a girl from the School of the Mysty Isle. Now, however, the magic here lifted my mood, and I hoped that something good would come of this. There were two sturdy but small trees next to the stone with the bowl upon it. The trees began to move, as I entered the circle. Twisting and twining until they reduced and reshaped themselves into two comfortable-looking chairs by the water bowl. Clear Water indicated I should choose one and be seated. It didn't matter which I chose, she told me. So I sat in the one closest to me, and she took the other.

"First," she said, "let's look in on your family and see how they fare in the land of the Druids."

The water in the bowl immediately began to swirl and shift, bubbles formed and lifted from the top of the water, drifting off skyward. Then the water settled and I could see my beloved. She was in trouble. Something was terribly wrong, and as I suspected, she was again expecting a child. Little Mary[173] was running and pleading for help. My daughter Sarah looked frightened and was holding baby James.

---

[172] Islands that appear in the mists, mysteriously, called 'Mysty Isles' for the 'mystery' of their appearance

[173] Caiaphas's daughter Sarah[173] changed her name to Little Mary, in honor of MiryAmah and Mother Mary

Then I noticed MiryAmah, large with child, being escorted to the place of birthing. Joseph, my older brother, was following closely and assuring MiryAmah that all would be well.

I had dreamed that I sent Joseph to take my place at the birth of this child–sensitive and fragile–agreeing to enter this harsh world. In a split second, I saw the next vision, and MiryAmah was in the labor chair. I saw the crown of the babe's head coming forth. My brother was sweating and stressing at the situation, and I felt remorse for having sent him in my stead. As the child slipped into Joseph's hands, all noticed how dark blue he was, choking on the life-cord, which was wrapped around his neck. Quickly, the handmaidens, with Little Mary's help, unwound the cord, but the babe still didn't breathe. Joseph, feeling terrible anguish, brought the babe to his face and gently breathed the breath of life into its tiny body. He kept giving small puffs of life's breath, until finally the baby's hands opened and gripped again, like they were grasping at this chance to enter the world of the physical. Then the tiny boy cried and so, too, did everyone else in the room, including myself as I looked into the scrying bowl.

"I wish I could have been there," I said.

Clear Water simply said, "There is a place you are more needed right now. The gift has two sides. One fulfills and one is more sorrowful, but both will indeed fulfill. Shall we leave your family for now and go where you are most needed?"

I reluctantly nodded 'yes,' as I noticed the bowl again, sitting there with a lily floating peacefully.

The oracle simply said, "And so it shall be."

# THEY KNOW NOT WHAT THEY DO
Chapter Thirty-Nine

I sat looking at the lily floating in the sacred bowl and thought about the vision I had just seen within the watery depths of this chalice. I felt like an entire dream had unfolded in a split second. Surely, it was just a moment I glimpsed in the scrying water, but I could remember the pain my MiryAmah felt before, during and after that instant. I knew my own body had processed the terror in the form of physical suffering as well, for what MiryAmah felt, I did, too. It was as if I had also given birth. Again, I thought that every man should experience the entirety of birthing, to fully appreciate the strength and courage a woman must muster to bring a child forth through the portal of physicality.

I remembered the fear and disappointment that my beloved felt, when she saw a limp blue babe in the hands of Joseph, my brother, who immediately began the kiss of life. At that point, the drama became too much for my dear one to endure, and she lost consciousness.

As I sat by the scrying bowl with the lily gently floating on the water, it became a fixation point, and all the memory flooded back to me. Through the small instant moment, I knew how it all played out. I wasn't even aware of Clear Water's presence, I was so entranced. I remember my concern was for MiryAmah, and somehow I met her in the spirit realm, out there floating and in agony. I caught her and merged with her to offer my strength by wrapping my soul around hers. I told her not to give up, that the children needed her, and that I couldn't stay in the physical without her. Our love, thus merged, began to glow brighter and brighter, and I could feel her strength grow. Then as she understood, she dissolved the stupor of sorrow, stepped out of our joint soul vessel, and told me she loved me more than life itself.

I said, "Love me and live, and make that life a sacred altar to our love, dear heart."

Her soul, so beautiful, floated before me. She kissed me lightly, bid me farewell and slipped back into her body.

When one goes back into their body, they also go back into the mind-set of that moment of experience. She became concerned for her baby, who she thought might not have made the journey from the spirit realms to the physical, and our meeting was forgotten.

She immediately remembered Joseph giving the kiss of life to our child. Being a fully-trained priestess, she knew that to do so, with great intention and devotion, might deplete him to the point of taking all of his life-force, and he might perish from the physical realm.

As all of this came to my mind, I looked up, feeling Clear Water's piercing gaze. She simply looked at me and told me to continue with my memory, so I could go on to another matter that needed my attention.

I said, "How can this be, Clear Water? I haven't been gone from my marriage bed long enough for a child to emerge. Wasn't it just weeks ago that I arrived in this land? How can it be that a child comes forth now?"

"You are on a Mysty Isle," she said, "a place of mists and mysteries. Time isn't a sequence, but rather a constant cycle, happening all at once." Watching me to see if I comprehended, she went on to say, "Also, dear one, when you take yourself out of the illusion of sequence and begin dancing around in the time realm, which is a cycle, or circle, like the one you just stepped into here, you can easily skip over to alternate cycles of time, that play out a bit differently."

"Does that mean that there are many versions of our life experience?" I asked, "And can I ease MiryAmah's pain?"

"Not exactly," she answered. "What it means is that you can review possibilities outside of the actual time cycle. Being able to do so, there are places where the time cycle can be adjusted, for nothing takes shape in stone, rather it's first molded, and an opportunity to choose a different outcome is possible. It can only be done at a very subtle level, however, for the growth of consciousness as a whole, has to have its chance to interact and learn from all interactions." She said, "You shifted the sequence between dimensions, when you merged with your soul-mate and the decision was made for her to stay and see this episode of time through." Sensing my concern, "She's not in pain any longer; she's blessed, and so is your family. All will be well."

I certainly felt blessed myself, in this faraway land, where wise women shared such insight with me. Then I asked, "Must my brother die for helping my son find his life?" I remembered, while my wife and I were merged, when her soul wanted to leave her body behind, that I had promised her that I would do all I could to prevent such a thing. Joseph had given our son nearly all of his life-force, as he drained himself and filled our delicate son with his precious energy.

She reminded me, "All will be well. Your brother has saved himself, isn't that true?" Clear Water watched me, to see if this sank in, as she could watch my mind process the memory. "His intention, combined with yours and your dear wife's gratitude, as you agreed during your out-of-body meeting to name this child in honor of him, restored the depleted energy."

Looking at me like a teacher reviewing a lesson for the tenth time, she said, "You know this already. Energy feeds on gratitude and depletes within fear. Joseph was so happy the kiss of life was successful, that he didn't care if he survived, only that this baby would have the opportunity of life. He wasn't afraid of dying. He was grateful for life. He was thankful to offer his life-force through the kiss he offered. Thus, he saved himself." Then she said, "That, coupled with yours and MiryAmah's gratitude and magnified by the gratitude of all present, was sufficient to cause the energy to grow, and fill the physical vessel Joseph uses, once again."

"And all of this has not happened yet?" I asked.

"Everything has already happened. Due to your time traveling, you changed the outcome ever so slightly, but quite dramatically."

I relaxed a bit and wished my beloveds didn't have to go through such drama. Then my mind returned to the 'other matters' to which Clear Water had alluded.

"You must rest now, Fisher One," she said. "Lily will take you to a place where you can find some peace." Right before my eyes, Clear Water transformed into Lily; the flower on the water was gone and was instead in Lily's hair again, where I saw it before.

She was dressed slightly differently, not in the white robes that Clear Water had worn, which seemed like a garment of light. She reached to me across the bowl, took my hand and led me out of the ring. We didn't have to step over the flowers now, due to an opening I hadn't seen before that offered us exit.

I don't remember much after exiting the ring. I awoke in the boat, floating upon the water of the lake. I was comfortable, lying on a bed of moss with my robe unpacked and covering me. As my eyes opened, I saw a beautiful sky with soft white clouds floating above. The fresh air filled my lungs as I made a great sigh. I could feel a gentle rocking motion, and then realized I was in the boat, just floating. What awoke me was an inner-voice, one that I recognized as Elmira's.

"Wake up!" It demanded repeatedly. I reluctantly sat up in the boat, where I was quite comfortable; I could see that the boat was just off shore, near the place of the reeds. Elmira was standing on the shoreline, looking very worried. My wooden vessel didn't move on its own as it did before. I tried to use my hands to propel it, but couldn't make much headway because it was too heavy. Elmira picked up the paddle (he had previously used to push me off shore), and threw it out as far as he could. It splashed near the boat, floating just short of the target. I could barely reach it, but finally my fingers coaxed it close enough to grab, and I used it to propel the boat to the shoreline.

Elmira helped me out of the wooden vessel, since I seemed stiff and disoriented. His mind talk told me I had been gone many days, before he saw the boat again. He watched it constantly, but didn't see anyone in it. He feared I had drowned. An entire moon time had cycled, he said, as he paced the shoreline, before the boat got close enough for him to climb a tree and look down in it. He then discovered that I was lying inside the boat, like it was a floating tomb and this distressed him greatly. He couldn't swim and he thought he had failed to protect me, as was his role as a Christopher. 'So much grief and worry we go through in this life sojourn due to not knowing,' I thought, 'Poor Elmira.'

## The Saga-Oracle

Then he said, Lily showed up on the beach and yelled to him, "Don't worry, Elmira. He just sleeps. He needs the rest," Then she left.

He climbed the tree for three days straight. He could see the boat drifting closer and closer. It finally got near enough that he could see my hands move and my face twitch, from time to time, when the dragon flies landed on my nose. Then, evidently, he waited for me to get close enough that he might be able to wade out to get me. He decided to try to wake me up using our inner-voice technique, since he still feared the water. His inner-voice worked, as his smiling face confirmed.

It was then that I realized that he was getting on in years. The poor man had been with me over thirty years. I wasn't an easy project for him. He assured me, however, I was an interesting assignment and not to worry, because he would be my Christopher until I moved on. I still had a hard time, thinking I could be a 'Christ Master,' but Elmira was convinced of it, so I left it at that.

Once I could walk without wobbling again, we decided to make camp on the lake. It was a clear day and there was no sign of an island. Elmira couldn't remember seeing an island, but if I said there was one there, he believed that to be true. His faith in me was unshakeable.

Our food supply was dwindling, so we decided to go to the forest to forage. We found some newly-laid eggs and asked the bird for a donation. The water bird, an egret, at first wasn't all that happy to participate in filling our bellies, but her mate convinced her she could lay more eggs. We found some berry bushes. When I remembered the bounty of the water Goddess, we took to the lake, wading along the shore and found some clams. We made a fire, hard-roasted our eggs, steamed our clams and feasted, making a berry juice out of the freshwater from the lake with our fruit. After a long fast, due to my peaceful sleep in the boat, the food had to be consumed slowly, and each bit tasted extremely delicious.

"Now, what do we do?"Elmira mentally asked, with a look and a gesture with his hands, and shoulders shrugging.

"We wait," I replied. "Something I must do is still not done."

For some time we lived on the shores of the lake in solitude. Now that I had seen and experienced the cycle, or circle, of time, I find it hard to gauge it and give an accurate remembrance of how long we resided there. My strength returned, as the lake and land provided nutritious substance for us during this waiting time.

The rainy season came and water fell from the sky in great torrents. We had to take to the trees again to find a high dry place. Even with a canopy of huge wide leaves, we were soaked through most of the time. Lily showed up again one rainy day, climbing up to see us. She was a welcome sight, even though she was drenched, too, looking like she had just emerged from the lake. I must say her smiling face was a delight to both my companion and me with her ever-present water lily in her hair, looking as fresh as the day it found full bloom.

"Hello, Sunshine," she said to me.

"Hello, Lily," I replied, "I could use some sunshine soon. Can you accommodate that request?"

"Now, why would I do that?" she said, with a slight look of disdain, for in her mind that was a very stupid question. "The land needs the water, and the water needs the land," she stated. "How could anything grow without both?"

Then she said, "I come to tell you that Clear Water has a visitor who wants to see you. You must come now and take to the boat again."

I could see Elmira thinking that he would be abandoned, for who knows how long, and I felt sorry for him.

Lily said to him, "This time we need you, too, Elmira." Then she said, "Follow me."

The rain was coming down so hard I could hardly see my hands as we descended the tree. Luckily, the water lily entwined in lovely Lily of the Lake's hair had a particular glow, so we just followed the glow. It led us safely down to the water-soaked ground, then towards the lakeshore and the anchored boat. We nearly stumbled into the boat, because we couldn't see it, even as Lily was already inside and making room for Elmira and me. She was dipping water out with a seashell bowl, and indicated that we needed to do the same with some other seashell bowls, found under the seats. As I was dipping, I wondered how my body could have been so comfortable, lying suspended on these three seats we were now sitting on. As the boat became emptier of the rainwater, it began to move again as it had the first time I rode in it.

We moved out into the lake, now full of splash rings and bubbles from the ongoing hard-driving rain. The level of the water had risen significantly, I noticed, because I could see that some of the shore trees were now submerged. There were plenty of old logs and debris floating in the water, due to the area being quite flooded. The boat didn't bump into them or anything else. What a smart magical vessel, I thought.

I didn't see the island in the mists, until we were at its shore and moving through the inner channel. It was very quiet on this trip, unlike before when sounds of the forest animals filled the air. It was a peaceful, silent passageway today, and as we entered, the rain gave way to the magical mists.

Lily said, "Do you love our Mysty Isle?" to Elmira. He nodded his head mesmerized at the transformation once we reached the island, that not so long ago he wasn't sure existed.

"Do you call it a Misty Island because of the mist, Lily?" I asked.

"No," she answered. "It is not always in the mists. The mist comes when the inner-dimension, where it resides, moves into the outer-dimension, where it visits. Thus," she said, "it is what one calls 'of the mystical realms'. It's but one of many such places, called 'Mysty Isles'–'Mysty' meaning, 'mystical' " she emphasized.

"It seems different today," I said.

"It's a different day," she replied.

I saw the same landing where Clear Water had stood before, and wondered where she could be, as no one was there. As we approached, I remembered the transformation that overtakes Lily, and she was in the boat with us, after all.

Then I saw a small figure, walking along the path down to the landing. The figure had a familiar rhythm in movement. The boat moved to the stepping off place and the small robed one, reaching the shore at the same time we docked, swept back the robe hood and there stood Eocha. Her wrinkled old face had a rare smile from ear to ear. I was so glad to see her; I literally flew out of the boat and practically jumped into her arms.

"I thought you had left me!" I said.

"I did," she replied. "I have a life, too, you know, and I had things to do."

I just laughed at her honesty, hugged her and spun her tiny body around in place. She was like a messenger from home, to this long-lost wanderer.

Lily and Elmira were already walking down the path, so Eocha and I followed. The going was not as rough as before on the shore land, because the rain didn't pound this island as it did our camp. We walked in silence. I think this place invited such a quiet demeanor; hence it seemed natural to be wordlessly following each other.

We took a different trail this time, and I was surprised to arrive at a small village. The dwellings consisted of domelike shapes. They blended in with the vegetation and, at first, weren't visible to me. Then as we got closer, I could see the village, laid out in a circular pattern with a large dome building in the middle. We entered that building, which was open to the outside all around, with just a thatched roof and structural posts holding the entire thing together. There was a hole in the center of the roof and an inviting fire was already burning under it. Several women were present, some weaving and others busy with other tasks, like cooking and sewing clothing.

# The Saga-Oracle

"Is this a place of women?" I asked.

Lily answered, saying, "Women are most at home here. Men pass through from time to time, depending on the cycle and where the circle of time needs adjustment."

"Are they, then, the keepers of time?" I asked.

"They are more than that. They are the 'influencers' of time," she said. "They come to be trained, so they can integrate back into segments of time. We have some of them training to merge into time-past, time-present and time-future. In order to influence time, all three phases must be adjusted simultaneously. Others are here for many reasons, such as teaching, learning, or just in exile," she explained.

"Are we going to be working on time, then?" I asked further.

Eocha answered, "You are such an inquisitive one. Everyone influences time," she said, like I should have known that. "We are always working on time, in or out of the physical!"

Now that I had been reminded, and that issue was answered as far as Eocha was concerned, we sat down by the fire, and Lily bid us farewell. She said she had another important matter to attend to.

I asked about the welfare of those back at the high mountain place and Eocha, as best she could, filled me in. I told her about my master teacher coming through the fire, and she said she had heard. She said he had sent her to me, that was why she was here now, sitting beside me in this Mysty Isle place.

We were brought food, which was welcome to Elmira and me, since we had been tree-bound for quite a while and had been reduced to eating the bark and some of the tree's foliage. A delightful berry soup and a drink were offered to us and a wine of some sort, potent and delicious. In no time the party seemed to blossom; or it might have been that Elmira and I had too much wine and joy was leaking out.

Just when things were getting wound up, a quiet descended upon the group. All the women who had been dancing and enjoying

493

entertaining us quietly sat down, and bowed their heads. We did as well, but we didn't bow our heads as deeply as they did, nor close our eyes, since we wanted to see what was transpiring.

I saw the glow and recognized it moving into our presence. I looked at Eocha. She smiled and nodded, as if affirming what I already knew. She, too, closed her eyes and bowed her head. Elmira just sat there, with his mouth hanging open in amazement.

Clear Water materialized, or just floated, within the light and entered into the circle under the dome. There was something about her, that made noticing the dynamics of the moment important, and we became peaceful in her presence.

She walked right over to me and touched my head. I swear I saw sparks. Then she walked to Elmira and did the same. I was certain I saw sparks. She visited everyone in the circle, and the same effect happened. Then she came back to me, took my hand and pulled me to my feet. I floated weightless to a standing position. As I said before, I would follow her anywhere. I believe the same effect would happen to anyone she beckoned. She also did the same with Eocha. Then she turned to Elmira and winked at him! Even in my day that familiar signal has a playful meaning.

"You enjoy yourself with the ladies," she told him. "And ladies," she said, looking at the group who all raised their heads and opened their eyes in full attention, "you give Elmira a good time here among us. He deserves it."

Then we walked away, with beautiful Clear Water leading us through the forests of the mists. After a short walk, I recognized the sacred scrying circle again; still the beautiful blue flowers ringed it. This time I noticed, they were little blue bells dangling from delicate shafts. We stepped over them into the circle. I held out my hand to steady Eocha, more out of respect for my elder than for need of balance. She managed to get around high mountain places like a mountain goat. Stepping over a few flowers would be nothing for this agile woman.

The bowl was in place, but this time, there were three seats made of reshaped sapling trees. The lily was floating quietly on the water, as before. We each silently took a seat.

"It's time to attend to the matter of which I spoke before," Clear Water declared. "This won't be easy and there are many dangers. For that reason, I have called in your council, and they have agreed to assist. I also requested that your bi-locational anchor Eocha be here as well."

I could feel the presence of love all around me. Even as I looked at Eocha and Clear Water, I could see behind them the forming shapes of monks, both male and female, in the natural setting. In the high mountain place, they both often dressed in the same saffron robes; I could see that they were again in their sacred robes. I swiveled my head, scanning the entire circle, finding familiar faces, including my master teacher who nodded at me and smiled slightly. I saw a serious demeanor, however. I wondered what could assemble this council, and I feared to guess.

Eocha said, "The situation in the land some call holy is dire. Where you have laid a foundation of love and balance, there are now those who distort it," she explained. "The reshaping is neither in line with your divine intentions, nor your soul mission of a balanced way of being."

"First, you must remember, you have not failed, because they have misconstrued what you taught them. Teaching and learning are two different things," she said, with all due inflection and conviction. "You have offered the teaching, now they must learn. Nevertheless, we are hopeful that you can bring some ripple of sanity back to the mission, and we have decided that this is the time and place to bi-locate you. Always, you have done this technique to visit loved ones. The pleasure of reuniting has kept you whole and sustained, within the multiple bodies involved and as well, given you the opportunity to train in the technique without danger. This time, you will also be visiting a loved one, but pleasure will not visit you. There is no one thing that you should or shouldn't do in this situation. Remember that!" she said. "It's our hope that your pure intention will affect this time-space place;

that somehow there will be a redirection back to the truth of the foundation of your teaching, for the good of all creation is the motivation of this mission, you have undertaken."

I was very worried now and all my loved ones passed through my confused mind. When my brother James appeared to me, I knew it was he I would visit this time. "It is James, whom I must see, isn't it?" I asked.

Eocha nodded affirmatively.

Clear Water said, "Now, we shall get started."

At that announcement one by one the monks came forth and, one at a time, stood behind me, put their hands on my shoulders and offered me strength. As they returned to the circle, they put their right hands on the shoulders of the monk next to them, so all were connected, encircling me. The energy each one shared was different, and I realized that each gave me a special type of life-force. Finally, my master teacher approached, for he was not in this circle now and simply kissed me on top of my head and left. Even so, before he left, maybe so that I could be sure that this was all happening, he ruffled my hair, still somewhat stubby but now much longer than the last time he did the same thing.

Then Eocha prepared me for bi-location, which meant that I changed back into my robes. She instructed me to look in the bowl. The lily was gone so I knew it was ready. Eocha said, "Remember to find the grid of light and sound. Find where you are right now and then look for the energetic imprint of your brother James."

It was easy to follow the directions, since I had done this a time or two already. I slipped into the time and space I sought so naturally, that I thought I must now be near expert at achieving; not realizing that all the strength I had just been given was propelling me.

Very quickly I found my beloved brother, who looked so much like me that I was momentarily taken aback, for it was like looking into a mirror of who I once was. This time, not only did I bi-locate, but I also had to take on another body, so I wouldn't be recognized. The only time I had ever done this type of appropriation of a body was at the tomb after the crucifixion. I found a man in a stupor from drinking, due to lack of lust for life, lying along an alleyway. I borrowed his body for the mission that I wasn't sure how to accomplish. Now I was not only in two places at once, but I had a body within a body and the physical condition of this body was a bit tipsy from too much wine. I didn't have time to ponder this, since a crowd of people listening to Peter was nearby, and I felt pulled in that direction.

I yearned to go to Peter, hug him and say, "I am here, old friend." But this body I had borrowed was pretty ragged and abused, and I wasn't sure Peter would see me in it, especially since it was reeking of the drink.

He was telling people in the crowd, that I had appointed him as leader of the cause. I actually told all my apostles and disciples that they were leaders of the cause, which we referred to as 'The Way,' so he was not in error on that point. However, he was telling the women to go back to their chores, and leave this work of spirit to the men, as it should be. That was totally different from what I had taught him. I was disappointed that he didn't remember how we had argued that point time and time again, and I thought he understood the basis of my teachings sprang from the important issue of both women and men, equally working towards one goal of unity. I pushed through the crowd, saw my brother James on the fringes just listening, and I approached Peter.

"Do you not know me?" I asked Peter.

Peter looked at me and softened for a moment, then put a mental wall between us and ignored my question, thinking I was just a disoriented drunk. That was partially true, since I was confused and trying my best to get this body to cooperate. Other listeners, men, for the most part, pushed me aside, to listen to Peter. He was getting it all wrong, my rock, my friend Peter. He had slipped back into the old attitudes of exclusion of women. I wanted to scream my frustration, but no one would pay heed to a drunk, much less would Peter hear me.

*Jeshua's Song*

Then my brother stepped forth and began correcting Peter, reminding him of what I had really said. Peter seemed afraid of James, what he represented being my brother and possibly closer to me than Peter was. There was a heated argument, in which the role of women was discussed with James, emphasizing that no man would be there to ponder the question, if it hadn't been for their own mothers, and how their very sisters would be the wives of others, so they could have children and continue the evolution of all consciousness through their descendants.

Peter said, "Yes, I agree and that's where they should stay, raising the children or warming our beds, not confusing the teachings of Jesus."

James, I realized, had changed since I last saw him before the crucifixion. Before that time, he had removed himself as much as he could from my teaching and didn't seem all that interested. Maybe he was just giving me space to do my work. Now I realized, in his own way he had naturally absorbed that which I worked so hard to get the other apostles to understand, which was, of course, that the balance of masculine and feminine was Onement with God, and knowing this was 'The Way.'[174] The woman followers of MiryAmah, the disciples, were better able to grasp the concept, but then again, they were the oppressed, and they longed to have their wings unbound. The women in the crowd now were accepting what James said, except for a few privileged wives who feared losing their, so-called, positions of status connected to their husbands, should they take up the cause. It is sad to say, that too often those who oppressed the women the most, were other women themselves who had found a way to survive in the corrupted situation of patriarchy.

As I was listening, an old man approached me. I tripped and fell to the ground, due to the drunkenness of this body I had taken over, and the old man offered me his hand and asked my name. I have to admit, I didn't know my name at that point. Was I the discarded crumpled man I found in the alley, or was I myself, bi-located to this place and time? I stammered and couldn't find my voice. So

---

[174] How Jeshua's and MiryAmah's teachings were referred to

he introduced himself, saying, "I'm Stephen, and I'm glad you have come to this gathering. I fear the atmosphere is different from days when Jesus walked and talked among the people." Then he said, "That's James, brother of Jesus. He remembers the master's teachings well. Peter," he said, "forgets what is convenient."

The women in the group began to ask their husbands to listen to James and consider what he was saying. However, the men were more inclined to agree with Peter. They were becoming more and more agitated and forceful with their wives, because the women were begging them to listen to James, not Peter. It was like madness had overtaken the multitude. One man began to beat his wife, and the other men cheered him on. The scene made me sick. Other men began to beat their wives as well, and the women ran screaming from the gathering. James yelled at the men to stop the madness. Peter looked confused. Since he would rather have the women someplace else, he didn't try to stop the crowd that was turning violent, with men pounding their wives.

"You aren't remembering what my brother taught you," James yelled above the crowd.

Peter looked at me again, and I pleaded with him with my eyes to remember. I even said, "Remember Peter, you are my rock." But he just walked away, ignoring the crowd in a state of chaos, and did nothing to attempt to stop the madness.

Things got worse at that point and James said, "Stop hurting the women. If it weren't for them, you wouldn't have a life to live." The old man, Stephen, began to cry. A wall or building was being constructed nearby and a pile of small stones lay there. Someone picked up a stone and hurled it at my brother. I was frozen, unable to physically move, as I viewed the horrible scene. I couldn't believe what I was seeing, as a stone hit James in the temple, and he stood there, with blood running down his stunned face. Before I could react, others picked up stones, and they flew forth with a vengeance. The old man ran towards James to protect him. Doing so, he became a target. Since he was elderly and frail, he collapsed, and then arose again. By this time James was on his knees, with a look of utter sorrow written on his face. I started moving towards him, but was held back by a hand that reached out to me, Stephen again. Thoughts race at times such as this, and I realized that both my brother and I could lose our lives, along with the old man and the unknown man whose body I borrowed. Should that happen it would cause a great wave of grief for all connected to us. That moment of hesitation was just enough, so that more stones found their intended goal, and James collapsed totally, a bloody mess.

The old man yelled at the crowd, saying, "How can you say you loved Jesus and then kill his brother?" Someone uttered nonsense about cleansing the memory of me, by killing the taint of sin. They were already denying my siblings any connection to me, I realized.

How awful, I thought. Again the remorse, that I hadn't made things better, but worse, washed through me. Then Stephen became the target of the stoners. They didn't want to hear the truth he uttered. He quickly fell. I crawled upon the ground below the stoners, found Stephen and held him in my arms. His last words were, "Forgive them; they know not what they do." I had said the same words myself once.

I crawled over to my brother. He was a bloody mess, but I didn't care. I wept upon his limp body. I can't remember exactly what I said, but he recognized me. I asked his forgiveness and he said there was nothing to forgive.

"Someday," he barely whispered, "they'll understand." Then he smiled and looked over my shoulder. I looked in the same direction, because his expression was so different now, relieved and loving. I saw my father there, and I thought, how can this be, can he bi-locate, too? I clearly was disoriented, forgetting that father had already passed. I noticed yet another rock thrown, this time from behind my father. Still confused, I thought, now they will kill my father, too. In panic moments, logic doesn't click in. I couldn't reason as I reacted, seeing my loved ones attacked. I saw the rock pass right through father and land near James. I knew, then, that my father had come for James, at the same time I remembered he had long passed on.

Father looked at me and said, "Forgive yourself son. You have not failed." I turned back to James and lost myself in my sorrow, lying there upon his bloody chest. I couldn't feel the beat of his heart now and was grateful that father had come to get him. Knowing this gave me relief. Who better to escort James back to the heavens, I thought–who better?

# HOME TO HEAL
## Chapter Forty

After father took James from his body, I looked up and saw ugliness in its worst form. Contorted faces full of hate had replaced the once-beautiful beings that now hid behind the masks of ignorance in its most destructive action. It was obvious that both James and Stephen were helpless, and probably dead, lying in pools of deep red blood. Nevertheless, the rage of the aggressive madness continued at a fevered pitch. I couldn't control myself now and threw back my head screaming at the crowd, and echoing Stephens's words, yelling, "How could you kill the brother of one you say you love?" A man, holding a stone, just glared at me and said that Jesus wouldn't want the taint of these two near him. He didn't even know he was looking into the eyes of the one he proclaimed to serve. Then he let the stone he was holding fly towards me. I felt sharp pain and saw sparks and lost consciousness.

When I awoke, Stephen was there with me, or at least his body was, for his soul had departed. I wondered where my brother's body had gone, since the place was now empty, except for Stephen and me. We weren't considered worthy to be carried off, it seemed.

I remembered feeling some responsibility for the body I borrowed. I dragged myself to the well, and somehow brought the water bucket up and poured it over my head. Then the body I occupied collapsed, and I could do no more for it, or myself.

## Jeshua's Song

A woman approached and bent over me, as if to inspect this pitiful pile of human flesh. Small yet strong, she lifted me to a sitting position and leaned me against the well. "Eocha!" I said, as I recognized her. "How did you find me?"

"The same way you found your brother," she answered. "Now you have me in three places at once, master," she informed me. "I think it's time to leave this poor body you've borrowed. He'll be taken care of, since we have priestesses already coming for him. Now step out and merge with me, so that I can carry you back."

I don't remember much after that. I don't recall the process of rejoining my body, nor do I remember seeing my council afterwards. Eocha took me to the priestesses of the Mysty Isle and left me in the care of Clear Water, or was it Lily of the Lake. I couldn't separate those two and realized that they were one body with two personalities, one the oracle and the other the priestess.

Evidently, Elmira was very happy with the priestesses. Whenever I saw him, he was always smiling and looking younger by the day. But I only got glimpses of him now and then, when I was conscious. Obviously, he enjoyed being tended by the sisters. I can only imagine the pleasures, they afforded him in every manner. I knew that whatever was given was a divine blessing, so I released worry for him.

It took me a while longer to become physically well, for what happened to the body I borrowed also happened to my body. Clear Water only visited me a few times, in the many weeks I healed. One visit, she asked if I would like to go home to my family, and I, of course, said, "Yes, more than life itself."

"You put things into a strange perspective," she told me. "How about you want life, so that you can be with them?"

"That's my intent and I do want life, Clear Water," I answered, understanding how my words were paving paths of possibility.

"Then you must cooperate with Lily better," she said.

Lily had been bringing me herbs to drink and rubbing them on my wounds. I was very reluctant to allow her to tend me. I think I felt that I needed to suffer more, so that I could make amends for the misery I had caused. I realized I was in the village on the Mysty Isle, hearing the familiar sounds of the women and the forest birds and animals. One bird's song would go, "Woop woop," again and again, and it soothed me.

I looked up at Clear Water and said, "I'm sorry, Clear Water. I just can't stop feeling responsible for all of this misery."

"You didn't cause it. You came to stimulate change, to sway that which was playing out as a path of error, and to influence the Akasha[175] flow in a better direction. Pain and suffering were already in place and having their way," she explained.

She continued on, saying "All players, including you, dear Jeshua, in this drama of time and space, have agreed to come into the flesh and try to be an agent for change, for good, or God. Some are more successful than others in their intended mission. It's an expansive endeavor. That's why so many are sent. Don't take the responsibility for all messengers. Remember, you can carry the message, but you can't enforce it."

I lay on my mat and stared at her. Beautiful and wise, yet the truth of what she said would take time to sink in. I wondered if she ever felt like she caused suffering, and did she know times of failure. I was sinking into self-pity again.

"Yes! I've felt suffering and I've thought I have failed, many times," she answered my thought. She had been reading my mind! I should have known that, in places such as the Mysty Isle, the veil was thin enough to read thoughts. MiryAmah told me many times. I would have to be careful what I'm thinking.

"No, you won't," she replied to my thought, "Soon I send you home and your thoughts will only be pleasant ones."

---

[175] The record of all actions and reactions recorded in light and sound, which are sometimes called 'the Cloak of God'

She walked away and Lily came with herb tea nearly immediately. I gratefully drank the tea, even though my heart wasn't in it. I felt a warming sensation run through my body, then I peacefully nodded off into a deep sleep. In this peaceful sleep, I saw my teacher. He beckoned me to enter a cave with him. I followed him willingly, for I trusted him completely. I remembered being so small and scared in the dark cave long ago, when he came to Elmira and me, and how the cave lit up when he indicated to us to follow him. In my dream, I followed him again, and he took me to a sanctuary. It consisted of a room that glistened with walls of crystallized stone. An underground stream filled an overflowing basin within it, and the overflow found another way to reunite with the stream. I remember that there were soft woven blankets and jars, lining a shelf. I saw a small fire in the room, as well. I was lying down on blankets and being covered, and I heard my master tell me, "You have to rescue yourself this time." I sighed and went back to a peaceful nothingness.

I think there was a part of me that didn't come back to consciousness. My reluctance to the herbal tea was part of my denial of healing due to my self-judgment. When I finally woke up, I could recall a firm decision, within this dream, to stay and finish my sojourn, accomplishing my soul mission. Once I removed the barrier of self-judgment, I came fully awake.

Clear Water came again, shortly after my awakening. I was still within the Mysty Isle compound. All she said was, "It's time." She sent for Elmira, and then asked another attendant to bring the lily bowl. Soon Elmira was at my side, helping me to stand on wobbly feet. He put me in a chair beside the lily bowl. Clear Water sat opposite me. I didn't know the scrying bowl could be relocated and was grateful it could, since I didn't feel strong enough to go to the circle in the woods.

"This is the plan," she said. "We are sending you to your family. You will stay for an extended visit this time. Elmira will stay with us and tend to the physical body here, which, as always, will be identical to the one that we send home. In this secure place, you'll be suspended in a peaceful sleep in the temple of dreaming." Looking at me to see if I was agreeable to the proposal, she said,

## The Saga-Oracle

"If you like I'll take you to that temple first through the scrying bowl."

Of course, I agreed and we continued with the process. The lily was not floating on the surface of the water, I noticed, so I knew all was in readiness. Clear Water waved her hand over the bowl, and I saw a small interior space. It reflected the colors purple and pink, and there were windows that looked out on a fern-filled scene. I could see dragonflies zipping around. I swear I saw the tiny elemental folk riding them. I must need more rest, I thought, again forgetting my thoughts were as loud as my words for Clear Water.

"You can certainly use more rest, Fisher One," she said, "but you will rest better in the arms of your lovely wife. What you are seeing is a place we keep here in this inner-dimensional island, which is guarded and kept by the elementals, who serve Isis. They take many forms and are quite adept at keeping someone in a peaceful sleep, which we need to anchor your body for the bi-location we have in mind. We will send Elmira to this location, not far from here, to monitor your sleep. He will not have to sit by your side day and night, only check once a day on your dreaming. The elementals are trustworthy and will keep you well."

"What of Eocha?" I inquired, remembering she had shown up at the well, helped me out of the borrowed body, and I assumed, brought me back.

"She monitors and keeps her watch from her home in the high mountains. She and your master teacher have been here several times, while you dreamed of escaping this life. They have been healing your physical body. Now, it is your soul that is wounded; the body is just weakened, at this point. Only you can heal that. You have taken the first step by accepting the help of the healers and waking up.

"Are you ready, then?" she asked; reading my thoughts, she knew I was.

## Jeshua's Song

I looked at the water and found my Akasha grid[176]. The silver sound cord, wrapped around the golden light cord, was not hard for me to locate, since it was my own. Then I found the grid of my beloved wife, the other part of myself. Since we were as 'One in spirit,' her Akasha was easily located.

Clear Water anchored me as I matched the two grids, then closed my eyes and willed myself to be in two places at once. I must be getting better at this process, as I was more aware of a shift through space and time, and I could see and hear a humming light tunnel coming closer to me. It changed colors as the distance shortened. When it became the same color as my major auric shade–a vibrant violet that I could clearly see in this suspended state–I stepped into it. I lost control of willful progression at that point. A force picked me up, and I was spiraling through this channel, seeing a blur of different colors flashing past me as I rushed forth at unknown speed. Then I heard and felt a large zapping sound, or a crack, and found myself in the garden of my dear wife. I looked at my body, making sure I had come through this tunnel with all parts still connected. I noticed I had my robes on, but I must say they looked very tattered and worn. My body seemed a bit frail, as well, and I touched my hair, still quite ragged but grown out somewhat, from when Lily hacked it off to keep the promise made to the chief.

MiryAmah's followers had prepared a small remote cottage for her. I had been here before in my dreams and loved the place. Anyplace my beloved resided, I considered home, but this was a most pleasant compound she occupied now.

I could hear people's voices, and I recognized several of those sounds, especially my dear mate's voice. I realized they were dining, and I worked up the courage to enter their lives again. I knew I looked terrible, and that my second son had emerged while I was gone. There would be explanations to make after the sweet reunion, I thought, about a lot of things. That would be the hard part, for I could hear my mother's gentle laughter, and I didn't know if she realized yet, what had happened to James. The women

---

[176] Place on the Akashic Record grid, connected to an individual soul

in my family had more courage than we men, I thought. I wished I had an ounce of that courage now, for I couldn't make my feet move forward. I stooped down and just sat there rocking on my heels, listening to the beautiful music of my loved ones in conversation.

As I kneeled there rocking in silence, a beautiful young man came forth and gently made himself known. I looked up at him, and he looked familiar, and I smiled spontaneously.

Smiling back, he said, "We always seem to meet in a garden, don't we?" I tried to remember what garden he spoke of. He sensed my need for a reminder, cupped his hands and opened them, and a little red bird flew forth. Then he did the same thing again, only this time a little blue bird flew out."

"Are you a magician?" I asked "or are you my little brother Simon, all grown up?"

"I'm not even here," he said. "I'm dreaming you. I dreamed that you needed a little shove right now." He pushed me over, and I fell flat on some flowers. Then, looking a bit amused, he offered me his hand to rise, so I could gain my footing.

"Well, if you aren't here, your hand seems solid enough," I said, as I took the outstretched hand and found my feet.

"You're not the only one who knows how to be in two places at one time," he said. "Don't tell our mother that I'm here. She doesn't feel I'm ready yet for this part of my training. I have a habit of jumping into things, before I have officially graduated from the course, you see."

He gently nudged me towards the garden gate to the house and said he had to get back into his dream, before it was discovered he took a side journey.

Thus, with a little help from my brother, I walked into the doorway to the room my family occupied. Silence fell like a mighty cloud upon all therein, at the sight of me. I found my mother and my wife with my newborn son, who was already chubby and active, about two months old, wiggling in her lap. I couldn't make an announcement of 'hello', nor speak in any manner, so I just stood there. Finally, I found the strength and courage to cross the silent room, locked in the gaze of my wife. I took her in my arms and enfolded her with my love. I can be so emotional and, sometimes, I think I should learn more control; but I couldn't stop the tears nor could she. When we finally let our sobs run their course and remembered we weren't alone, there wasn't a dry eye in the room. Even my newborn son had silent tears dripping off his tiny cheeks.

"I'm home," is all I could say. Then I reached for my mother and drew her into my arms, and somehow my sweet daughter fit between my mother and me and little James as well, and we had a wonderful group hug and many more tears of joy.

When things settled down a bit, I kissed Sarah on the cheek and little James, too, and looked at this new perfect baby. Sensitive, so sensitive, I thought, as I drank in his perfection. "Is his name Josephus," I asked, as I let his little fingers grasp one of my own.

"You know it is so," MiryAmah said, "as you requested."

The entire episode of my son's birth–especially the fact that I was not present–came flooding back to me. The remembrance of the event and what my beloveds had endured, along with the relief and joy of our reunion, proved to be too much for me. I wasn't yet strong enough to keep my composure. I collapsed, I'm sad to say, into a pitiful pile of human flesh and tears.

My brother, Joseph, who was still staying with my family, helped me regain my footing. Little Mary was by his side, too. My brother, along with mother, my wife and children, managed to get me to our private chambers. Joseph actually picked me up at one point and carried me, realizing I didn't even have the strength to walk the short distance.

I must have looked a sight to them. Clear Water did say I would heal better in the arms of my beloved wife, so I relaxed in expectation of such bliss, but knowing I had to talk with my mother first.

"Joseph," I said, as he carried me.

"What, brother?" he answered.

"I bring news that might break our mother's heart. I can't hold it any longer. I must tell her and hope that she can find the strength to hear the words I have to say. She'll need you more than I do. Promise me you'll stay close to her," I begged.

"You know I will," he answered.

We had reached the chamber, and he gently set me on a soft seat near a blazing fireplace. MiryAmah heard my words to Joseph and looked worried. Mother Mary soon came into the room, and MiryAmah knew that the news concerned family, since she could feel it dreadfully. She asked the family to sit by the fire and most just sat on the floor, surrounding the chair where I was resting. MiryAmah sat on the floor at my feet, rubbing them lovingly; my mother sat on the other side, just looking up at me. Little Sarah was holding one-year-old James, who was very quiet for such a tiny child, and Little Mary held my newborn son.

She asked if she should put him in the cradle and give us privacy.

"You are my family, Little Mary," I said. "I need you here as well. Please stay."

Reluctantly, I told them about being in the faraway land and how I could see in the lily bowl events before they happened, and knew before Josephus was born, how it would go. I told them I wanted to make it better and more than anything I wanted to be there, especially catching the babe as he emerged, as a father should. Then I told them about Clear Water, how she told me another matter needed attention. I tried to explain that time could be influenced, but events not drastically changed, only slightly shifted. Then, I finally found the courage to tell them about James.

My mother wailed, as only a woman in total sorrow can. It echoed throughout the dwelling. I'm sure all within the compound heard the howling of terrible sorrow. The sound pierced my heart, and I wished there would have been some way to keep this information from one as tender and loving as my mother. I had only heard such a sound once before, when I was nailed to the cross, and she thought I had died.

We all cried again. So many tears flowed it seemed we would drown in them. I apologized to my mother for what I still believed was my fault.

She stopped her sobs long enough to tell me again, "Forgive yourself. It wasn't your fault. It's the fault of those who live within hate and fear, and block truth. You don't live there and you never have." Then she smiled through her tears and said, "You always blame yourself, son. You can't carry the blame for others' sins, even if you try to save them. Ultimately, everyone has to face their own choices and correct their imbalances. What you give them when you bring your teachings through is a choice, son. That's all you can do."

I brushed the hair back from her wet face and kissed her forehead. She looked up at me and said, "My baby James is with his father now. I'm pleased that Joseph came for him, at his hour of need. I'm also grateful that you were there as well, because I believe you helped him move through the terror he endured."

Then she looked down a moment and said, "Bless the old man Stephen, who tried to help both my sons."

Joseph gently picked up my mother and carried her away to a private place, to grieve and rest. Dear, strong Joseph, I thought, his strength sees us through, and he literally carries us all. Little Mary followed him, but laid my new baby son in his cradle before she left. Sarah, who already looked like a tiny grown priestess, took little James and went to the cradle, gently rocking it until both babies were asleep. Then, she curled up next to her brothers and slept herself. It was as if the grief had drained us all.

MiryAmah gently helped me to our sleeping-shelf bed, where I laid my head down and closed my eyes. I felt her come into the bed beside me and we all fell into a deep exhausted rest.

# The Saga-Oracle

We must have slept all night. I remember awakening to the sound of bird song, as morning broke the stillness of the dawn. I was the first to awaken. I watched my sleeping wife in my arms and drank in her loveliness. She smelled like fresh air and the flowers of spring, all mixed together. I watched her peaceful face and noticed how long her lush eyelashes were. I could see some lines of strain around her eyes, but that just made her more beautiful to me. Such perfect loveliness, I thought.

She moaned with the sound of sleep slipping away, opened her eyes and said, "I must be having a very good dream."

I hugged her closer to my body and responded saying, "I think I am having the same beautiful dream. Do we have three precious children over there across the room dreaming, too, dear heart?" I whispered.

"That would seem to be the case," she whispered back, giving me a gentle intimate kiss.

Our children must have heard our quiet conversation, as they came fully awake as well, stretching and yawning. Sarah picked up the tiny babe, and with little James toddling along, they came across the room to MiryAmah and me. They crawled into bed with us and snuggled. Sarah changed the baby's diapers at one point, while James just sat watching, sucking his thumb, content in the moment.

"She's like a little mother," MiryAmah said, as she picked up the now cleanly-diapered babe and offered her breast milk. James wanted some milk, too. As I watched her nurse both babies, I realized how close in age my sons were, and I wondered how my wife could produce enough milk for both babies.

We lay back again, with the boys nursing and just enjoyed being wrapped up all together. Sarah lay on my chest, listening to my heart. She said if she could hear it beat, then she was sure she wasn't dreaming.

James soon got his fill of milk and just lay sucking his thumb, snuggled under my arm, looking into my face and wondering who this nice soft stranger was.

My other arm was around MiryAmah, with Josephus still lying across her soft bosom taking the milk of life at his leisure.

It's moments like this that are highlights of an entire lifetime. I will always remember that moment through eons of time. One couldn't ask for more bliss. This quiet time together was healing for all of us.

Too soon we realized that we had to rejoin the rest of the family. I wanted to be sure my mother was being tended to, so we dressed and emerged from our chambers.

Sarah had somehow found her best friend, the little white donkey she called Beeba, and carefully placed James on his back. She already had the new baby wrapped in a swaddling bundle and was trying to secure him on her back as well.

"Sarah," I said, "you don't have to do everything. We can carry the boys. You work too hard for a little girl."

"I'm not a little girl," she announced. "I'm a big girl now, in case you haven't noticed, and I help my mother take care of my brothers, all the time."

MiryAmah just smiled as if to say, "That's the way it is with her."

"Can I at least carry little Josephus, Sarah?" I asked. "Then, when we come back, can I carry James, too?" I asked further.

"Okay, but be careful," she cautioned me. "They are precious, you know."

I could sense there was a bit of anger, as well as self-chosen authority, in her voice, possibly due to my absence from her life. She was, in her own way, telling me that life had gone on without me, and I couldn't just march in and take over. My little Sarah was a very commanding child and always had been. I loved that about

## The Saga-Oracle

her, yet realized that I had to respect her strength and not in any way squelch it.

She handed me Josephus and we joined the family now, gathering in the dining area again for the morning meal.

Mother looked better, but still hollow-eyed from the sorrow she processed. Joseph was at her side. I walked to them and handed little Josephus to my mother. I knew that babies had a healing effect. She willingly took the baby from me and cooed baby noises to him. He knew her well and smiled and wiggled his joy at her baby talk.

Little Mary came up to Joseph, my brother, taking his hand in a familiar manner. I nearly missed this gesture, because I was asking him if he dreamed of me requesting him to come to my wife in her time of need.

"Yes, Jeshua," he said. "It was such a strong dream, I couldn't deny it." Then he squeezed Little Mary's hand. He looked at her in such an intimate loving way. He looked back at me and said, "Little Mary has taken her old name back. She loves the name Mary, which she took so that she could honor MiryAmah, but her soul keeps telling her that she is still 'a Sara' thus we now call her Asara.[177]"

"Beautiful," I said. I've always loved the name Sara, and Asara is even better. I kissed Asara on the cheek.

"Is there something else I should know?" I asked Asara, noticing she was rubbing her slightly-rounded belly and looking at Joseph.

"We are married now," Joseph said. "I have found another life and a new wife, and can't believe that I would be blessed twice in my lifetime with such treasures. I have turned my business over to my grown sons. Since I've traveled many years after my wife departed, I find that I would like to settle in one place for longer periods of time now. Asara and I want to bring up our child in this new land. I ask your permission to stay with MiryAmah and the

---

[177] In Thailand this name means 'magical grace and happiness'

children, or at least somewhere close-by, so that our children can know each other and also, so that I can help her when you aren't here."

"You don't need my permission to offer such a blessing," I told him. Then I said to Asara, "I thought your father abused you to the point that you couldn't bear children? I'm glad for this miracle and pleased that you are not only my friend, but my sister as well."

It's true, that what hurts us, can destroy us, or make us stronger. Asara's glow affirmed that good does overcome evil intent and action.

Mother, looking up from her attention to my newborn son, said, "That's true, but one can only regain the preciousness of life, if they can forgive. That's the key to everything," she emphasized, "to forgive!" My mother was reading my thoughts; she always did know what I was thinking.

# LOVE HAS TO LET GO
Chapter Forty-One

I felt my strength return near immediately, now that I was home with my beloved wife, MiryAmah. She was looking lighter and brighter, too. Our entire household knew of my presence. Asara, who I learned was a trained oracle now, warned that we should take all due caution, for there were enemy spies for the Romans getting nearer to us. The priesthood, having also heard rumors, was presently doing follow up investigations; if they should discover me or my family, they would destroy us, one and all, Asara warned.

A few weeks after I returned, Asara gave birth to a son. She and my brother named him Bran, honoring a Celtic god, who journeyed to the Isle of Women, the place of joy, according to the singers of tales.[178] Joseph said my account of Clear Water reminded him of this legendary god's realm. Thus, he wanted his son to be connected to the Mysty Isles, so if he ever needed refuge, or exile, his name would open the portals therein.

MiryAmah didn't have quite enough milk, for both James and little Josephus, and was struggling to keep them both satisfied. One day when she and her dear friend Asara were nursing the babies together by the fireplace in our private chamber, Asara said, "Josephus and Bran are like twins, with Bran being a large newborn. He's already the same size as your little one, MiryAmah."

I was watching the two women enjoy each other's company chattering as women often do. I could see some struggle and concern from MiryAmah, as James was older and more aggressively taking her life's milk, and Josephus was slow to nurse. They were like two opposites, each attached to their mother's breasts, one draining her and one like a puppy pushed out of the process. Little wrinkles of stress were showing their paths on my wife's face.

Asara was full of milk, still glowing as she had when she was expecting, and she had more than enough mother's milk for her babe. She looked over at MiryAmah and said, "Let me try to nurse Josephus, my friend. Maybe I can help, since I am full of milk, and I see that James nurses so robustly that he drains both your breasts."

MiryAmah looked down at her baby boys, considering the offer. Men are seldom allowed to hear such conversations between women. Women have the ability to have close intimate relationships with certain friends, and they'll share all sorts of private issues with each other. Men, as a rule, didn't worry about milk for babies. If that became a problem, they expected the women to solve it with a stand-in. This was a matter of commerce for those affluent enough to afford a wet nurse. The ability among

---

[178] The bards who went from village to village and sang the news and songs of legend

the poor to be a fully-blessed mother was rare however, since their diets were lacking. That was one of the reasons for a high child mortality rate. Men usually just concerned themselves with providing security, housing and if the child was a son, bragging rights. However, here I was, with nothing hidden from me. I loved watching and participating in things other men would normally not witness. I loved women pure and simple. They were much more interesting than society would admit, and certainly a lot stronger than men understood.

MiryAmah looked over at me and said, "What do you think, Jeshua? Should I take my friend's offer and maybe fatten up this little guy a bit?"

"Give little Josephus the decision; if he likes the arrangement, then why not?"

Sarah, never far away from her brothers, was sitting by Beeba, her donkey companion, who was more a house pet than a beast of burden. It was hard to believe Beeba was the same little white donkey I had ridden through the Jerusalem gate, now part of my family. He was but a young colt then. He had matured, but not grown a great deal and was totally devoted to little Sarah. She was listening to the conversation and, I believe, was contemplating it as well, for Sarah didn't miss much.

MiryAmah, knowing how responsible Sara felt for her brothers, said, "What would you say to this proposition, my little queen?" It was a playful name she used often of late, because of Sarah's ability to take command of situations and evaluate them in a split second. She was usually right on the mark with her opinion, too, which she didn't hesitate to offer.

Looking much older than her years, she said, "The Goddess provides, does she not? I would agree, why not give it a try." At that statement, she jumped up and went to her tiny brother still trying to nurse at MiryAmah's breast, easily detached him in a gentle way, and taking him to Asara, laid him at her free bosom.

"You wouldn't get James to give up the nipple that easily," Sarah remarked. Then petting the forehead of Josephus with the tips of her fingers, she told him, "You must learn to take your milk more vigorously, little one, so you can keep up with Bran and grow up big and strong."

Asara was sitting in a rocking chair made of old tree limbs and twigs. It had comfortable arms giving her a place of rest as she cradled both babies, now nursing. She just closed her eyes and seemed to be in a trance, as she rocked back and forth, with both babies taking nourishment from her body.

I looked at MiryAmah and she looked back at me; we both nodded in agreement. We had spoken to Asara and Josephus, before the birth of Bran, about being godparents. We didn't exactly make fully plain what we wanted, which was more than just stepping in, should we be taken from our children's lives. We had been devising a plan for the safety of our family. Neither of us wanted to follow this route of protection, but it was the best idea we could think of.

"Asara, can you summon Josephus, my brother," I asked, as she was nursing the babies.

Without opening her eyes or stopping her rocking motion, she said, "I've already done so, and he comes forth any moment."

She reminded me of Clear Water now, and I wondered how much of my thoughts she was reading. I contemplated that, if she was an oracle, maybe I should guard my thoughts.

"I only tune in on your thoughts, when there is need of me," she answered, so much like Clear Water had. "That's how I knew I should share my milk. I knew, if this tiny babe of yours would take my milk, I could fulfill your request, whatever that request might be."

"She's very aware, Jeshua," MiryAmah said, "but she never intrudes, so don't worry. We still have our secrets," she said, winking at me, and then looking back down at James, who was full to brimming with nourishing milk, and had fallen asleep in her lap.

I blushed, because we had some very private intimate secrets between us. One secret, especially fresh and foremost in our minds, was when my wife told me she was tired of moving about in the village, making sure she didn't cross the line that held women in their proper place.

"It's so degrading," she would declare. Wanting to bring some joy into the moment, I decided to be playful and divert her mind from the limitations unfairly placed on her for being a woman. I picked up one of her dress robes and began to dance around the room in it. She laughed and started walking like a man, pretending she was full of pride and importance. One thing led to another. Because we felt securely isolated even as we playfully danced around, we decided to trade genders; I dressed in the robes and garb of a woman, she dressed as a man. She chose the robes I had worn home, since they were tattered and faded. She had a robe I found that she would wear when she wanted to be invisible. It was a very old robe, too, that her mother had given her years ago, before she passed on. She said the robe may be humble, but it held a certain power of invisibility, so I wrapped the layers of material around me.

"Can you still see me?" I asked.

"Yes, my love," she said, "but if I was a street merchant, I wouldn't give you an ounce of my attention. Anyone with robes such as those you wear, surely wouldn't be spending much in my shop."

Then she cut some of her beautiful waist-length hair and made a beard. I gasped as the tresses were cut. She told me not to worry, that her hair grew extremely fast and never stopped growing. We had such a good time, dressing each other up. We decided to take our game a step further and go out in the village. We discussed that if we appeared as very poor humble people, no one would scrutinize us. Our playfulness became serious and we ventured out, walking along the side of the road away from our safe sanctuary. If it were not for us giggling, we would have been totally ignored. As it happened, we were nearly run out of town, as being 'crazies' and just more riff-raff. Episodes such as this are definitely private. I wouldn't want to think Asara could perceive, or share that drama, nor anyone else, even as I share it now thousands of years later. They were our sacred secrets, tucked away in our own hearts.

"Don't worry, Jeshua," Asara said.

Joseph entered the room. Seeing his wife nursing both babies, he came to her side saying, "Oh! We have twins." Then playfully, he said, "Why have you kept this hidden from me, woman?" He kissed Asara on the cheek, lightly touched little Josephus's pretty head and whispered; "You have my name, now you have my wife."

Asara looked lovingly at her husband, and then back at me, since the question in my mind was still hanging there. "Your private thoughts are your own." She explained further, "A thought will not be shared, unless there is divine reason for it to cross the path of one such as me, or anyone, for that matter." Then she said, "I sensed that you desired to speak with your brother and myself, and expand on our conversation not so long ago, when you asked if we would godparent your children. I knew there was more to it. I also knew that if this baby took my milk, it was confirmation to you, and to us, to have a deeper agreement."

"Please, Jeshua," MiryAmah said. "Let's at least discuss our idea with Asara and Joseph." She and I were reluctant to accept the only solution we could think of.

I nodded my head in agreement. "Joseph, I have a favor to ask of you and your dear wife. You don't have to grant this favor, and I'll not think the less of you, if you should decline. You can say 'no' and I will not in any way be angry or feel hurt."

He said, "Ask what you will, my brother, and we'll see what might or might not be granted. Even so, I can't imagine ever saying 'no' to a request from you. You are my brother, after all."

"First," I said, "the easy part. I want to ask again, if you and Asara will be godparents to all my children. It is customary for godparents to be chosen, as you know, so in case something happens and the children are orphaned, they'll have another set of parents to raise and protect them. I have given you time to reconsider this responsibility, since what this asks, could result in a great accountability to children not of your making."

Looking at Asara, who was still rocking and nursing the content babies, but now staring at her husband and nodding her head, Joseph said, "Yes! Of course, we still want to be godparents. God forbid that anything should happen to you two. There has been too much suffering in this family already. We need you two in this world and your children need you more," he emphasized. "We choose to keep our word, and our intentions haven't weakened," he reminded us, looking down on Asara and the babies, as he spoke for both of them. She nodded agreement, as he knew she would.

"There's more," I said. "It's getting dangerous for it to be revealed that I survived the crucifixion. We have spoken of this before. There's a cult following of 'The Way,' which has developed several leaders in my absence. Each apostle, and disciple, was trained as a leader, and as you know, the disciple women must lead quietly, undercover. The apostles, however, are trying to follow the teachings and take the reins, as I attempted to teach them, and go directly to the people. But they suffer, I hear, in their dedication; they themselves can't totally agree on what I meant, or didn't mean, when I shared the teachings of 'The Way'.

Joseph reminded me that we had spoken of this before, and in his travels, through his line of connections, he had heard some sad stories. The episode with James had been a terrible wake-up call for all of us.

I went on to explain, "The followers are a great threat to the corrupted priesthood and the authority of Rome. Rumors of my presence are reaching those in high positions of power. They keep their power through the fear of the people. Our message has nothing to do with fear and that alone makes us their enemy, as you know. They are determined to follow the trail of tales and exterminate anyone connected to me. The temple priests also want my memory cleansed, or rewritten to their satisfaction. Added to those situations, many of the followers are basing their strength on my death, not my life. Should they find that I survived in a physical natural way, I fear they would turn their devotion into hate and attack my family, as already happened with James."

My brother and Asara listened quietly. I could tell by the look on their faces, they had surmised the same possibilities.

"MiryAmah and I want to give you our children," I stated flatly.

Little Sarah came to full attention, shocked, and said, "What! You can't just give us away." She ran to her mother and cried on her shoulder, to the point that we had to stop our conversation and deal with her reaction.

"We aren't really giving you away," I said, stroking her pretty long golden hair. "We are just giving the world the impression, that you sweet children are from another family, so those angry enough to harm you, because they hate us, can't find and hurt you."

"How would that work?" Joseph inquired, as Mother Mary entered the room and quietly found a seat. In her priestess way, she knew this was a critical moment.

"For the outside world, or those not in this room at this moment," I said, looking around the room at everyone– Asara, Joseph, my mother, my wife and the children–"MiryAmah is still Mary of Magdala and is a beloved disciple of mine, the one I loved first and foremost, for those who have enough sense to understand at least that much. Nevertheless, to the world, we must spread a fog of protection." I emphasized. "That fog is this; we did not wed, nor did we have children, because I died on the Roman cross on that fateful day." I looked at my mother, and I could see pain, but resignation in her eyes.

"Furthermore," I continued, "Sarah is a servant girl, who came from Egypt to this land, to assist Mary of Magdala, who exiled there." The look on Sarah's face told what she thought of that idea. Then I went on and said, "Little James and Josephus were born of you, Asara and are brothers to Bran. Josephus is Bran's twin and James your first born."

"But none of that's true," Sarah cried.

"It's fog around the truth," I told her. Then, even though I knew she was hurt, I had to go on, saying, "They are your godparents because they adopted you, the little slave girl, into their family. Your brothers, within this protective fog, since you have been formally adopted, are still to all appearances your siblings. However, as I said, they have to be Joseph and Asara's sons. That's the story we must foster, for the sake of survival. I wish it didn't have to be so. Even as it breaks my heart to devise this plan, it gladdens it as well, for whom would I trust more than my own half-brother, Joseph of Arimathea, and his beautiful wife, our dear friend Asara?"

No one was happy with this lie we were developing. My mother looked devastated, but I could tell she was, nonetheless, relieved, for she knew a threat was closing in on us.

"The truth has to be hidden, so that we as a family can survive," I said. "We need to live. The lineage of your mother, Sarah, and me, carry the peace code. Since we have joined two peace code components in our marriage, combined now in you, our children; your survival is the success of our mission. We have to keep our family relationship private and our public relationship as I have just proposed."

Sarah looked like she was finally accepting the proposal. "Someday, I promise you, little queen," I said, "the truth will pierce the fog."

Asara arose from her chair, carefully laid Bran in Joseph's arms, walked over to me and laid Josephus in my arms. She then, without even covering her bare breasts, went to Sarah and took her in her arms and let her have a good cry.

"I love you, child, with all my heart," she said. "I know I can never replace your mother, and your uncle Joseph knows the same is true with your father. I assure you, that our love for you is just as deep and full as what we feel for our baby Bran." She wiped Sarah's tears with her robe and closed it. Taking Sarah's face in her hands and looking intently into her beautiful eyes, Asara said, "You and I have play-acted many a time, haven't we?" Evidently she and Sarah used to play dress-up all the time. "Now, we will just keep the game going strong, for people who are not of this secret family. We will show the world a loving family, even while the real family, just as loving, will ever sacredly be honored. When people are ready to live in love instead of fear, the fog will lift. We'll do this, because your mother and father love you so much they have to give you up in the eyes of others, so that you can live to your full potential. Even so, in their eyes and hearts, you are forever their baby girl, their little queen, and they'll never abandon you."

Sarah stopped sobbing. Regaining her composure, she announced, "But I am still the guardian of my brothers, because they need me to help them."

"Yes, little queen," Asara said, "you'll hold reign as guardian of your siblings. That may prove to be more difficult than you bargained for."

"Then, is it agreed upon?" MiryAmah asked, looking at me, my mother, Joseph and back to Asara, still holding Sarah.

"We are honored," Joseph said. "Your children are my children, and mine shall be yours, as well."

Even that statement from Joseph didn't make it easier to give up my family and children in any manner. We trusted Asara and Joseph completely. Even so, to have the pleasure to walk within the village without disguise and in full pride, as a family, is a blessing that few realize until they lose the opportunity. Saying, 'hello' to a neighbor without worry of judgment and fear, which might hurt you, is seldom appreciated until lost. Helping someone while not having to wear a mask to conceal oneself is true freedom. Constant attention, to prevent our identity from being revealed, was like continuing to carry the cross of the crucifixion upon our backs. We decided to live in the moment and enjoy every second we shared, no matter what games we had to play for the sake of survival. That's how we kept going day by day, because we knew that on some tomorrow I would go away again.

This time I stayed about six months. The village people and followers of MiryAmah knew me to be a close friend of Mary of Magdala. We made sure that we weren't seen as ourselves, by anyone except our close inner-circle. We often disguised ourselves, when we needed to be seen together in other places and spaces. I spent my time working around the compound. I even made a few secret passages, so I could disappear, or could hide the children if need be. Only Sarah, Asara and MiryAmah knew of the passages. Sarah helped me plan them. She had an excellent mind and could strategize better than many of the leaders of the time.

Asara began working with me. She allowed me to use her scrying bowl, a lovely alabaster one given to her by MiryAmah at her final initiation as oracle. Asara had a cave sanctuary, where she preferred to work. She told me that my beloved wife was planning to spend more time in the cave herself, when the children didn't need so much attention. I made an underground passage to the site, which was not so far from our dwelling. When I visited the cave and looked at the scrying bowl, I thought of an alabaster jar MiryAmah had kept for her sacred ceremonies. She mixed holy substances within this jar. My dear wife was an expert in healing using the essences of nature, mixing things like flowers and roots with oils. Asara told me that MiryAmah had told her alabaster could hold an essence in its purest form; thus, when she gave Asara the scrying bowl, she had given her a hallowed tool for her Oracle work.

I remembered, once MiryAmah had used the oils in that alabaster jar to anoint my feet. She dipped her long hair into it and washed my feet in our ceremony of marriage. It's odd how just the sight of something like the alabaster bowl can bring back a flood of memories. Images and objects can be triggers in many ways. Even the Peace Code that we carried within our bodies–double now due to our union–was programmed to be triggered by various sounds and sights.

Working with Asara, I could keep in contact with Elmira, through Clear Water, in the faraway land across the ocean. He said my anchor body was looking well. His mind easily spoke through the bowl, saying I must be having much pleasure, for there is usually a slight smile on my face. I told him he, too, seems to have a little smile. He also looked younger and refreshed. I asked if the ladies were taking good care of him, as well. However, as the scrying bowl is not for idle chitchat, I had to bid him farewell and go to Eocha, who I knew awaited me.

She had the master with her, when I found her. She was at that very moment, peeking in on me, so the connection was especially bright and light.

"You have work to do elsewhere," she reminded me.

I knew she was right, but I didn't want to go just then.

"You can visit your family again, but your path calls you. If you don't willingly step forth, it will grab you and force you to fulfill your mission," she reminded me.

I said, "I regret that I have to visit with my family like an outsider. I want to be with them as a father should." I didn't want an issue forced either, so I took her quite seriously, since a forced matter usually meant pain for all involved.

The master teacher then came into my view and said, "In this lifetime, to be a good father, one must make hard decisions. Have you put your plan for the security of your family in place yet?" It didn't surprise me that he knew I would have to do such a thing. He was expert at seeing the larger scope of things and would know of the dilemma we faced.

"Yes, the plan is in place. I've watched it work now for a few months, and I believe it to be a good plan," I answered. "Asara and Joseph are proud parents, when out and about in the village, of three sons and an adopted daughter. The children enjoy getting out of the compound from time to time, too," I added.

"Then, it's time for you to reunite your bodies," he announced as he faded away.

I looked at Asara. She suggested that I spend the evening with my family and come to see her at high midnight the next evening. She and Clear Water would have the preparations in place. When Asara was in her Oracle mode, she had such a faraway expression in her eyes. I wanted to hug her in gratitude at this moment to thank her for all she did for me, and my loved ones, but I knew that I could only lightly touch her outstretched hand, lying beside the alabaster bowl. I carefully touched the back of her left hand and sparks of light danced in a swirling pattern around the spot. She quietly looked down, took her own opposite hand and did the same quiet touch upon my right hand, which produced similar effect. The feeling of this event is hard to describe; it was like being pleasantly shocked. Then she nodded and I knew I was dismissed.

# THE LITTLE QUEEN
## Chapter Forty-Two

When I opened my eyes Elmira was looking down at me. I was in a small round dwelling made of stones, which were carefully fitted into a perfect circle about thirteen feet across. I lay prone on a comfortable swiveling platform in the middle of the circle that turned, with my head to the east and my feet to the west. Elmira later explained to me, that I was slightly rotated each day, to keep the energy balanced and flowing into my quiet anchor body. He told me that the small airborne elementals who rode the dragonflies showed him how far to move the pivoting platform by hovering in their sparkling-lit flight at the point to which my head must be moved. Thus, when I came back, I had come full circle, according to Elmira, much like a sundial clock.

I had no need of rest, once my bodies had been re-merged, so I just got up off the swivel base, stretched and announced to Elmira that I was back. Elmira and I met with Clear Water. She helped us speak with my master teacher in the high mountains, so we could evaluate how to carry on from this point.

I must have looked rested, because my teacher greeted me with, "You look well, lad." He still saw me as a mere boy, I thought. If he could reach out to me, I'm sure he would mess up my hair again. Instead, we got down to business. We talked of how my mission (which originally was regional as Jesus, teacher of 'The Way') was now becoming global. "Fisher One," he said, "you will have many names in the lands that you wander, because each place would describe you slightly differently, depending on their unique perspective." Then he offered advice, saying, "Fisher One, cast your nets wide and true, that's all you need to do. Then set your catch free, as was meant to be." His words were often poetic and sing-song in nature.

My teachers and guides often spoke in riddles. The sing-song words of wisdom open sacred channels in the mind and heart. The metaphors, especially if they have a rhyme, allow a personal-oracle channel from your soul to your consciousness at all levels. Nursery Rhymes are a prime example of how children are programmed to a higher truth, through meter and metaphor. The rhyme connects the words in rhythm form and just like all song, it will play over and over within the mind. That is how bards worked their magic, too. Many a song of current events was metered to open a channel of love and cooperation. The bards were known to be the most romantic of all message carriers, since they often sang of love and union. This message from my master teacher was intended to attach itself to me, and sing over and over, as I moved through this more expanded stage of my work.

I wished with all my heart that my family could have been with me, wherever I was sent to wander. I never wanted to be separated from them. They were part of my heart and soul, and I was only truly happy in their presence. That would not have been possible, of course. Even my children had volunteered at a soul level to be secret peace code planters and activators. We couldn't chance that all of us might have perished at once, should something go wrong.

Elmira and I set out to explore the lands in which we now found ourselves. We went down some animal trails, some well-worn paths of people, and sometimes we blazed our own trail. The scenery was amazing to Elmira and me. We had to learn how to accept the changes in climate and the rain that might turn violent within a moment. All this water gave me an opportunity to perceive a different type of world. One day, when storms were upon us, we saw the clouds come down from the sky in a great funnel. The end of the funnel whipped around and everything in its path was twisted and torn. I had new respect for the power of nature after that. We learned to watch the skies carefully, when we felt the change in weather approaching. I thought of the cycles that all creation uses to cause movement, some easier and some violent, but nevertheless, all natural and intended to foster growth and evolution of creational awareness. Elmira and I frequently spoke about the wisdom of going with the flow, rather than against it, especially after we saw what happened when the great funnels whipped across the land. That which wasn't flexible was ripped and spun, and left somewhere else.

Being in a place of water, however, meant lots of streams and ponds and lakes to enjoy. In the land of my birth, occasionally an oasis offered such wonder, but never to this magnitude. As a result, I could scry from time to time in still ponds and clear lake waters, and see visions of what was happening within the movement. I no longer needed an oracle to help me find my visions. I also taught Elmira how to scry, which wasn't difficult because he had spent so much time with the 'ladies' on the Mysty Isle. As I looked into the clear water, I could see that my followers were determined to carry on, in spite of the suppression back in my homeland where this project had begun. I saw continued confusion over my intentional teachings. I grieved that I hadn't been able to merge their hearts and heads, as I had intended to do. I wished that I could somehow go back, interject myself through bi-location, and correct some of the corruption of my teachings. My advisors, both in the physical and otherwise, cautioned me against such a drastic measure. The seed had been planted, they assured me, and the greater consciousness had to process and change gradually, or there would be a terrible conflict between those who wanted change and those who didn't. I couldn't expect the seedling of change to sprout, if I went back and dug it up, I was reminded. I often checked in on my family, too. They were the garden of my soul.

I was assured the seedling would sprout, because change is necessary for evolution of consciousness, on a personal level first, then echoing to the group level, which affects the universal level. That is simply the way of it, like it or not, I was reminded. Change has to be waded into, like a swimmer going into a lake from the shore. To dive into change causes such shock and upheaval, that it affects everything far too fast, my guides reminded me time and again. "You just can't dive into change," Eocha and Clear Water told me, when they spoke with me through the water. They were always glad to have a chance to communicate in their favored way, and it was comforting to know I had their advice to guide me. "Forcing change never works," Eocha said. "Give it time."

Thus, I continued on through this land, wandering and walking among many people. I listened to their traditions and asked some questions to enlighten myself. Hopefully, I begin weaving the thread of balance into their lives, if they were off center. In most cases, it was I who received the enlightenment, and I was brought to balance.

The swamps and dense forests teemed with life, which shared itself back and forth for the sake of survival. There was a harmony within that system, even as it could seem brutal when an animal died to sustain another being. That was the way of the physical; that all creation would have to give and take, in order to sustain the physicality. The people I met all honored that balance, and the natural world demonstrated it perfectly. It was the cooperation and gratitude of the offerings of nature–the give and take–which was the truth of divinity manifested in the physical. Elmira and I lived and survived in a natural setting that had little interference from the hands of man. It was easier to see the balance in such a beautiful unspoiled place.

We eventually came to vast plains of tall grass, blowing in the breezes. It looked like an ocean. Often we saw the near-endless flow of sacred bison, or buffalo, which sustained the tribes of the area, offering food and skins for shelter and clothing. The people, in their high reverence for this noble animal that lived in great herds, never wasted one hair of the sacrifice the buffalo offered. However, I did find that many of these tribes waged war with other tribes. I often asked, "Why not cooperate and unite? Why do you fight?"

That was usually the first question out of my mouth in their language. Upon coming in contact with me, they assumed that I would be ignorant of their language. They were quite shocked when I asked such a question in their native tongue in perfect dialect. It caught their attention and commanded some immediate respect. I bless the day I was given the gift of tongues.

I found that their reasons for not getting along were not so different from the people of my homeland. They said they fought because they didn't understand each other, or they were slightly varied in some way, or because one tribe was abundantly blessed and another may not have enjoyed such blessings. Instead of asking for help, they gave in to envy. Or, if they did ask for help, the other tribe may have harbored greed and didn't care to share. In many cases, however, there was cooperation, even as they kept the separation of the tribes in place. We found many separate nations, some more sociable, some more reclusive and suspicious, than others. All the tribes, however, had an extremely soulful attitude about how all creation is related. I loved that aspect of the people.

I also discovered that the more patriarchal tribes, holding their women and daughters in low status, were more aggressive and war-like. I found some matriarchal tribes, but they were few. They were more peaceful and willing to negotiate and trade, but unfortunately they were also more vulnerable to aggressive tribes.

We located some well-balanced groups, that didn't hold the genders unequal in worth. White Eagle's group was one such tribe. Since they were the first I encountered, I had high hopes that all the people of this great expansive land would be the same. I should have guessed that my high mountain protectors and guides would naturally have an alliance with those most like them, which was the case with White Eagle's tribe. I also should have expected that tribes would be different, depending on their unique circumstances and influences.

I found that the tribes we encountered had many origins and traditions that caused differences. One thing they held in common though was the way they kept their true origins and principles alive in a metaphorical manner through their stories. They had great respect for the spirit world and kept the doorway of their dreams open to guidance from that realm. Thus, they had an opportunity to experience life beyond the basic rules of physicality. They were aware of how matter and space surrounded them. Yet, their reality also included the unseen natural kingdom. Their life was rich, because they could see more connections to all creation. One old chief told me, "What one does not believe, one doesn't see." He then wisely advised me, "Believe in life, and it will believe in you."

Many of the mystical tales I've been telling you in my story will seem like science fiction. To those whose awareness has expanded beyond their physical vision, these tales are within their understanding of possibility, because they believe anything is possible. The native people saw visions and accepted the guidance offered. They chose their names based on these visions and other supernatural events in their lives, like White Eagle's childhood experience when the mighty eagle sat on her head all day long. I learned much from them and was better able to visualize myself and the success of my soul mission thanks to walking the paths of this faraway place.

Clear Water had asked the ladies of the Isle to fashion a new robe for me, while I was visiting my family. When I returned, I was gifted with the garment.

When one bi-locates, their clothing also bi-locates. I would have to make sure that I had changed from the skin garments the natives made for me, when I bi-located back to my home. My old robes were not holding up as well as the clothing of animal hides in this less arid climate. Thus, were so tattered, they literally fell off my anchor-body, when I was in the circle chamber.

Clear Water had the fairy folk weave magic into the new robes. They were the softest white material I had ever felt. Clear Water said they were woven from a puffy white flower that grew upon the island. They resisted stain and dirt. She had the robes made without seams; cross-woven, so I could bundle them as I had before, and strap them to my back with no points of strain upon the precious material, so it would always hold its shape. I have never had a finer robe.

I changed back into my leather clothing, upon arrival at the Mysty Isle in Lily's lake. We immediately departed to continue our journey of discovery. As Elmira and I wandered into the plains, however, I was more chilled than Elmira, who loved the leather leggings and breach cloth of the native peoples' style. So, I switched my garb and put on the new robe, as I walked. Elmira, more and more, resembled one of the natives, due to his skin tone and his ability to tan. No one found him a standout. I, on the other hand, couldn't tan, and seldom did my skin burn either since my healing after the crucifixion. The only discomfort I felt was I chilled easier. As we entered the grasslands, I changed my native garb to the white robes, and found them extremely comfortable and comforting. The native people began calling me, 'White Robe,' and sometimes, 'White Beard' due to my beard, now pure white and grown long. My hair was getting more streaked with white as well with, and the reddish hair losing prominence, as my crowning glory faded.

One day I saw a white buffalo standing upon a small hill. It caught my attention, because it nearly glowed there, among the blanket of brown and black buffalo. The other animals were grazing quietly around the white one. I spoke to Elmira saying, "Spirit sends a message," and I pointed to the white buffalo upon the rise. "Wait here, Elmira," I said, because I wanted to go forth and see if I could communicate with this spirit animal messenger. Elmira, had no desire to be in the middle of a stampede of thousands upon thousands of these huge animals–on more than one occasion having seen them on the run in fright–had no trouble agreeing to wait. I could see in his eyes he was fearful for me, too.

"I'll be fine," I reassured him. "I'll speak to the animals, as I move through them, and let them know I mean no harm."

A few of the cows looked up as I approached, but quickly went back to grazing as I explained that I wished them no harm. A bull came forth, put his head down and kicked up some dirt to warn me. I had to have a word with him as well, but he finally realized I wouldn't harm his charges and left me be. Buffalo, like many animals, can smell harmful intent or fear, but even more, they sense love. They sniffed the air, picked up a love smell and just parted, giving me passage to my intended destination. It took me but a few minutes to reach the white one. I slowly approached her and she looked at me. In our mind-talk, she complimented my robe of white.

"I like your robe of white, as well," I said. "Do you bear a message from the Great Spirit?" I asked. The white buffalo, transformed into an elderly native woman; even before I finished my question and she sat down cross-legged there, upon the summit of the small hill, like it was the most natural thing to do. I did, likewise.

"I am White Buffalo Woman,[179]" the elder woman announced, "and yes, I do have a message for you."

"I'm blessed," I simply said, as I bowed my head in reverence.

"Don't judge my people by their weakness," she said. "They are in different stages of learning and come from different perspectives." Then she continued, "They are aware enough that they knew you were coming. You are indeed a message bearer yourself, bringing change and hope to the people."

Her eyes were piercing black; her long white hair was straight and loose. It drifted ever so slightly on the breeze that rippled over the plains' grass. Her words drifted like wind chimes, gently tinkling on a gentle breeze.

---

[179] Also known as 'White Buffalo Calf Woman'

"How is it, the people of this land knew I would come, when I didn't know myself?" I asked her.

"Because they called you forth," she answered.

"Why would they summon me?" I questioned. "I haven't changed them, nor have I tried. Surely, I have learned more from them than they have learned from me. So, it is I who am changed, not them," I said.

"White Robe," she said, "you know that change is the way of life. Sometimes, it comes more easily than other times, but the nature of life is to ever change. You are transformed, that is true, but you bring the seeds of a greater change," she said. Then sensing my next question, she added, "You bring the message from Great Spirit, that all creation is sacred, that the male and the female spirit of 'All That Is' can only be fulfilled, when both those spirits dance as One."

"Oh, but I wish I could demonstrate that, by bringing my own beloved mate to this moment and dancing with her, so I could show the wonder of that divine dance," I said wistfully, remembering our dream of teaching by example.

"She is here!" she announced. "Don't you recognize her?" she asked.

I looked around myself full circle, seeing Elmira now perched high up in a small tree to better keep an eye on me or to feel safer. Besides that, all I could see was a sea of beautiful buffalo in colors of reddish browns and black. I looked back at Buffalo Woman and there sat my beloved MiryAmah. I think my mouth just opened in surprise, and I sat stunned, not quite sure what to do or say, still not yet believing what I was seeing.

"Well," MiryAmah said. "Is this all the greeting I get, this look of bewilderment?"

I jumped up and went to her. I lifted her up into my arms, then swirled and danced around the hilltop. "How can this be?" I asked. "Have you learned to bi-locate? If so, how can you do this and still be nursing our children?" We had been delaying using this technique, because the energy needed to nurse a child was not compatible with bi-location. We had two little sons needing MiryAmah's life energy through her nourishing mother's milk.

"It's the dreamtime portal, my love," she said. "Where your children and I reside, it is nighttime and the freedom of the dreaming comes forth. I saw you speaking with White Buffalo Woman. She asked if I wanted to dance with you, and here I am, for I always want to dance with you, my dear," she said. She twirled and spun me around, repeatedly, accompanied by the sounds of nature, on the top of that knoll, surrounded by a sea of buffalo calmly grazing and some watching contentedly.

Dancing to the tune of Mother Nature hours passed, with us lost in the moment. Then MiryAmah said she must go, since it was time to awake and tend to her motherly duties.

I gave her a great passionate kiss. Before the kiss was done, I noticed I was kissing the elder, White Buffalo Woman. It surprised me and I said, "Oh! I am sorry!"

"Well, I'm not sorry," she exclaimed. "I haven't enjoyed a kiss like that in a long time. It seems I jumped back into my body quick enough to share just a bit of your passion. I hope you don't mind, White Robe." She looked almost embarrassed, as she told me this.

"Was it you all the time, and I just thought I was seeing my wife? Have you played a great trick on me, White Buffalo Woman?"

"No," she answered. "I completely gave up my body. You received the message, thus you received a gift as well." Then she turned back into a white buffalo and wandered away, going down into the vast herd of other buffalo, eventually completely disappearing.

I looked back at Elmira, still clinging to the tree and looking a bit frazzled and worried. I asked the buffalo between us to give me a safe passage to reach him and access to the outside of their group. Animals that live within herds are expert at group consciousness

## Jeshua's Song

communication. They parted, making a clear path for me, all hearing my request at once. When I finally coaxed Elmira to come down out of the poor little over-burdened tree, he kept a nervous eye on the large animals.

Once out of the path of the herd we followed a little creek to the higher country and made camp in a rocky alcove. Elmira had found some vegetation along the way that he knew was edible. His great passion, as we moved through this place, was learning how to live off the land and discovering how to prepare and eat what nature offered. At the creek, he managed to catch a spawning fish, which was destined to die after she fulfilled her destiny of depositing her eggs in the land of her own birth. Carefully, helping her release her eggs by squeezing her rounded belly, he quickly released her soul and prepared a fish dinner for us, by wrapping the herbs he had collected and the fish within leaves from one of those same small trees that dotted the plains. I wondered if all the time I was busy dancing with my beloved, or was it White Buffalo Woman, was he collecting those large leaves for later. He was a hard one to figure sometimes. Just when I thought he was paralyzed in fear, he was still functioning, anticipating my needs and welfare.

Since the mind-to-mind speak doesn't always satisfy my need to hear my own voice, I decided to pose a few questions out loud to Elmira. When one perceives on a level of awareness beyond the basic physical, it's easy to think that you have imagined the events. That's probably because all creation is Divine Imagination. Without this imagination, you couldn't experience anything. In short, I needed reassurance that I wasn't going crazy again.

"Did you see that white buffalo?" I asked Elmira.

He nodded 'Yes.'

"Did you see it transform into something else?" I asked.

He nodded affirmative again.

Just to test him to see if he was only agreeing to humor me, I said, "Did it turn into another animal?"

He looked at me with a look of slight contempt and mind-spoke, complete with exasperated hand gestures and said, 'You know it didn't, so why do you test me, master?'

"I'm testing myself," I spoke out loud to Elmira. "I'm trying to see if I'm going crazy, or if I've been blessed," I further explained.

He pointed to me and made a hand gesture of finger to head, twirling it in circles and pointed back to me, which indicated that I was crazy. Then he smiled and laughed in his own silent way.

"What did you see, Elmira?" I asked.

He arose from sitting by the fire and imitated an old woman, bending slightly but looking wise. Then he straightened up, pointed to me and using his hands, drew a smile on his face.

"Okay," I said. "Yes, I was happy to see an old woman, but did you see anything else?"

He mimed the elder woman again. Then smiling mischievously, hugged himself, and danced around the fire.

"You saw me dance!" I gratefully exclaimed. "So you did see something else!"

He vigorously nodded his head 'yes'. Then, showing his mastery of mime, he took his hand and making a flat plane of it pulled it down across his face and gave his impression of someone much younger by simply raising his bushy eyebrows. He touched his heart with both hands, crossed them and making his hands move like a great pounding heart, pointed to me, laughing in his quiet way again.

I found his mime quite funny. "Then you saw her, too?" I asked, "My MiryAmah," wanting to confirm my suspicions.

Elmira put his arm around me and gave me a slight kiss upon the cheek in a teasing manner. He fell into silent laughter and gleefully slapped his legs as he found the conversation quite amusing. Then more serious, he finally nodded 'Yes.'

"I have to go back again," I told him. "We don't have Clear Water or Eocha nearby, but I know I have to go back for awhile," I informed him, now extremely serious and determined.

He nodded 'yes' again. He understood the seriousness of the proclamation and was resigned that I would do what I must do. He would be supportive as always.

"We'll look for a place, where I can look into the scrying water," I said, "and where you can hold my anchor body safe for a while."

He didn't look all that enthused, but he was resigned to the task. He opened his arms and bowed to me, as if to say, "Your wish is my command."

We went upstream the next day and found a waterfall. We explored the space, like a couple of inquisitive boys. Then we decided to take a bath in the cool waters of the pool, partly because the water was so clear; and also we were beginning to smell each other. Behind the falling water, we discovered a small cave, about twenty feet deep with ancient drawings on the walls. The images were of bison and larger animals that looked like giant lizards, etched and painted upon the stone. We discovered these pictographs, when we had made torches for the purpose of examining the cave. It reminded me of the Bramble city tunnels, where I apprenticed with Nod. I knew this was a sacred space, too, and it would fulfill our needs perfectly.

The cave was dry and comfortable. It didn't look as if it was in use right now, by anything or anyone else. We both agreed that it would do fine and spent the next few days in preparation, building a swiveling bed, lining it with leaves and moss we pulled from the pond and dried on rocks, and stocking fuel for a fire for Elmira. I was concerned, because I didn't know how long my journey would keep me. I asked Elmira if we should try to find food to stock up for him. This land had moon-seasons, we learned from the people we met. It slept, in what they called 'the winter moon,' when a blanket of white cold snow covered the plains and mountains. They pointed out to us snow on the mountain peaks. I was once taken high enough to see and taste the cold snow and ask it to favor us on our journey. I worried about Elmira with the winter moon approaching soon. He assured me that he could keep himself safe and fed, and that I should worry about other aspects of my bi-locational journey.

A bright day presented itself to us, the evening after our preparations were finished. This scrying technique required a still clear reflection in water to gaze within, so that one could have a safe path. The sky was a vivid blue, without a hint of clouds. Later in the day, the pink and purples of the setting sun were low on the horizon, and I knew the time was perfect. I found a comfortable flat rock just offshore in the small pond, far enough away from the falls so that the water didn't swirl, but stood crystal clear. I never knew how my anchor body was relocated to the location of keeping, and this time I asked Elmira.

He told me I shouldn't worry, that he had taken care of me before and would do so without a problem, and indicated I should get back on track. I began to wonder what the hurry was, and if he had a harem someplace he wanted to join. I had forgotten that he could read my mind if I forgot to close it, so he seemed shocked that I would have such a thought, and remarked in mind-speak, "Don't I wish!"

First, I found Eocha in the crystal clear water, looking back at me. She told me that I should find Clear Water as well. Even as I agreed, Clear Water appeared next to Eocha and greeted me.

"Fisher One," she said, "shall I assist you once again on your secret journey?"

"I would be doubly blessed, if you would," I answered, saying, "Eocha always keeps me safe, but you seem to help me have a clear vision as well."

When all was ready, I found the grid again. Using the technique I knew well by now, I merged my energy path on the ley-line of my beloved's, and quickly found the tunnel once again. I waited for the violet color and jumped into it, when the color matched my own aura. I spun and fell, then ascended upward, only to feel like I was falling again, over and over, until finally zapping through into a different location this time.

I expected to emerge in the courtyard of the compound within which I was familiar. Instead, I was in a different place and saw a huge building being constructed upon the crown of a hill, with a little community around it fanning out like rose pedals. The place was quite orderly and beautiful. As a matter of fact, I landed in a prickly, but beautiful rose garden. A woman working nearby heard the sound and noticed me lying there in her flowerbeds. She seemed shocked and I had to explain my sudden presence, so I said, "Oh! I'm sorry. I threw a rock and when I saw it enter your garden and crack against another rock, I tried to retrieve it before you noticed."

She reluctantly seemed to accept that explanation, since I found a big rock at my feet and picked it up and walked out of the garden, a bit scratched. She yelled at me and said, "Don't be throwing rocks in my garden, stranger, or I'll be scratching you worse than my roses have."

I walked down the streets of the little community, which was growing bigger by the moment, with workmen on several projects. It was very early morning here, with the sun just peeking over the adjoining mountains. The streets were paved with flat stones. It was laid out in levels like a rose pattern, with petal terraces that unfolded as one went up or down the hill. The long shadows defined the rose-like layout of the village, making it appear more like a flower, than the lay of the land.

"What is this place I've happened upon?" I asked a workman I found, working on the paved path.

"This is the city of the Rose," he answered, looking at me like I should know this.

"And who is the overseer of this developing beautiful city?" I asked.

"The Little Queen," he answered, then dismissed me, going back to something that needed his attention.

I had no idea why my bi-location had brought me to this place. Since I was sure my grid and MiryAmah's was properly crossed, I knew she had to be close by. I decided to walk along the pathways and feel my way to her side.

I definitely felt something pull me in a certain direction and followed that urge to a beautiful building located near the last terrace of this little town. It looked like a public meeting hall that had apartments within it. I could see living spaces at a second story level. Overhanging the balconies were the familiar feather coverlets used for sleeping times, being freshened in the morning air. I had chosen to bi-locate at the latest moment in the land faraway, when the sun was about to give way to the moon, remembering that our time of day was different, so I wasn't surprised that this place was just waking up. No doubt the gardener was an early riser.

I sensed that my beloved was within the walls of this building. I entered the building without notice and followed my intuition around to a central meeting hall. Walking through an arched hallway, I heard some voices, one of which sounded like music to my ears. Guards appeared and halted me, saying, "Stop! Who goes there?"

"I'm a friend of the family," I announced.

"Be more specific," one of them demanded, stepping in front of me.

Things had changed since my last visit, I thought. It had been over five years since I last saw my family. I had been wandering and visiting the tribes of the faraway place, longer than I realized. I had changed more than I knew during those years, too, with a long white beard and nearly totally-white hair as well, now grown long again. My white robe made me look like a Magi Sky-gazer. If I had worn the checkered turban upon my head, I would certainly have been able to pass myself off as one of those mysterious astronomers.

All I could think to say was, "I'm a close friend of Joseph of Arimathea." Evidently, that was the right thing to say, because they stepped aside and allowed me to pass into the room where I heard the voices.

I saw MiryAmah speaking with several men and women. She was talking about the city, which she insisted have a 'petal-like' layout. "The symbol of the rose must be followed," she explained. "If you get lost, go to Martha's garden and get a rose," she told the leader of the group. "Look at it and you'll have your plans," she suggested.

I thought, 'Martha's garden.' No wonder that woman seemed familiar. She hadn't recognized me, nor I her. How much we've all changed, I thought to myself.

MiryAmah looked up to see who was entering the room. She froze in mid-sentence, as she was further explaining her plan for the city. She just looked at me and said to those present, "Leave me now!" A bit confused by her abrupt change, from pleasant manner to the demand of their departure, they looked at one another, shrugged their shoulders and left. I heard one say as they walked past me, "When she gives an order, there's a good reason."

"It's you," she simply stated, never taking her eyes from me.

"It is I. Ever late, but still, nonetheless, I've come," I announced. Then we ran to each other and embraced, and pretty much did the same dance we did when the buffalo woman allowed MiryAmah to come from her dream time.

"The last time I danced with you like that," MiryAmah said, "I was dreaming a wonderful dream."

"It wasn't a dream, dear heart," I said.

Before I could explain further, a beautiful little woman came into the room, preceded by someone saying, "Ecknoreial[180] wishes to see the Madeline.[181]" Then the announcer backed out of the room.

What I saw was a little Queen, complete with a beautiful delicate gold tiara. For a moment, I wondered if my wife was taking up acquaintance with the royalty of the land.

---

[180] A High Priestess placed in a position of power and leadership
[181] Way the people of Gaul referred to Mary Magdalene

The little queen said, "Oh! My goodness–look who's back!" She stood in place, looking astonished at her parents embracing tenderly. "How is it that two people can be so old and still be so taken by passion?" she asked. Then she began to move in our direction and was transformed into my little girl, and cried, "Father" as she came into my arms.

As I hugged her, I looked at my wife and asked, "Ecknoreial? The Little Queen? What's this all about?"

"Who better, my love?" MiryAmah said. "The Priestess becomes the Queen. Isn't that a good combination? We have long needed to honor Queen Nor[182] again with the Eck.[183]" She was referring to a legend in which the Nordic Queen Nor of ancient times kept the energies attracted to each other, the masculine and the feminine, so that Oneness could be achieved. Thus, secretly, Queen Nor's influence spread far and wide to all those who honored her message. Countless stories illustrated this law of divine attraction. Down through the ages, Ecknoreials were secretly placed here and there where needed, according to the priestess legends.

Sensing my confusion, especially knowing how I never desired to sit as King to accomplish our work, she explained Sarah's regency and how the Roman overseer of this territory was married to one of MiryAmah's own inner-circle of followers. The plan to bring in a leader the people could follow, who would influence unity, instead of separation and elitism, was accomplished through our own little girl, still little in stature, but all grown up in mind and spirit, she explained.

"But she's so young," I reminded my wife.

"I am nearly fifteen years old and women get married younger than that!" Sarah proclaimed. There was never a doubt that this child of ours was up for any leadership challenge. I had to admit what my heart didn't want to acknowledge, that my little girl had matured so quickly.

---

[182] Nordic Queen who monitored balance of energies called "Eck"
[183] Masculine and feminine energies as they interplay and influence the greater masses

"You are married," I replied, "to the people. But if you are happy with taking a husband, I wish you the same happiness, your mother and I enjoy in our union." I further explained, "However, I wish you none of the separations we've endured and please don't rush into anything you aren't ready for yet."

"I know, father," she said. "I'm dedicated and trained in my role as way-shower and leader. I won't disappoint you," she assured me.

"You could never disappoint me," I said, "but I fear that you are too vulnerable in such a visible position."

MiryAmah reminded me, "She is the daughter of the oracle, Asara, who came from a very high-ranking family from Jerusalem. She is betrothed to a man who has a Roman father of high rank and a Gaul mother of equal status. His mother is a priestess from the old Druid people, and this union is planned to bring strength to the movement, as we hope to expand it through the Order of the Rose," MiryAmah explained.

"If it makes my daughter happy" I said, "then so shall it be." I needed to emphasize that she was my daughter, even if I had to admit that we had a plan in place and must live as if she was Asara's and Joseph's child.

Then I continued saying, "I've heard my mother speak of the Rose Orders. I can only hope that this means our work is in the hands of those, who can secretly hold the energy constant even as it gradually unfolds."

"And so it is," MiryAmah confirmed. "Our daughter has come to her work early, even as we can't claim her publicly, yet we can feel pride of her conviction and ability to lead within our hearts my love," she reassured me as she stroked my face.

"It sounds like you have things under control," I said, as I put my hand over her hand. Sarah, our little Queen, just rolled her eyes and said she had things to do, giving us the privacy she knew we needed. As she left, she remarked that her new husband better be half as passionate with her, or she was going to be greatly disappointed.

Our private reunion I shall keep private. Your imagination will fill in all the possibilities of such a meeting. I will share that there was an explanation of my long absence, but that came after the closeness we needed. I also needed to be updated on the relocation of my family. I learned that the Romans were now suspicious, due to hearsay about Mary of Magdala, or the Madeline, being in the area. They didn't find my body after the crucifixion and that, along with the high priests of the temple being nervous because an official had never confirmed my death, caused alarm for my family. They were actively seeking my lovely wife and intending to watch her closely.

"We moved to this location for several reasons," MiryAmah said. "One being, we wanted to make a place for followers to meet and hold the memory of you. There are other such places as well, being constructed underground in the burial catacombs in the land of our birth and in some remote villages," she explained. "The people can't meet out in the open anymore, because the Romans and the priests persecute them. In this place, we hope to be able to be more open about our teachings, but we aren't yet sure if we can pull it off, even here so far away. The hilltop location offers some security, too," she told me "because we can monitor who comes and goes. Unless," she qualified, "they are able to pop in and out of time and space as you do."

Thinking I needed more convincing, she explained further, "We have master builders, who have carefully chosen every rock for our complex and placed them in the precise location needed to keep this site safe. We have used a priestess power place, already energized with protective forces, for our church."

"A church?" I questioned.

"Yes, my love," she answered. "A temple is a place of ritual, and a church is a place of memory." Then she went on to say, "It's my hope that the memory of what was really meant by your teachings can live on through such a place as this church I have envisioned.

Although what you actually meant in the teachings of 'The Way' is a topic of much debate," she added.

"So, beloved," I said. "You may well have created the first church of my true teachings, since you know what our intentions actually were."

"Yes," she answered, "but how long I can keep those teachings from being conveniently reshaped, will be the challenge. I plan to incorporate ritual within the meetings, as well, because the rituals marry the intentions. I hope this will keep the teachings of "The Way' purer."

"Have you been interrogated by the Romans?" I asked, worrying that she may have been mistreated.

"Oh yes," she replied, "but don't worry. When they come to visit me, all they see is a mad woman who lives in a cave." Sensing my confusion, she explained. "I have a cave nearby, accessed by an underground tunnel, from the days of the ancients when the miners were in this area, looking for the sacred gold for their alchemy."

She said, "The gold-hungry conquerors missed what was right under their noses, because there is much gold still veined through the passageways, but it takes on a greenish color. The veins of gold were quite different than what they thought was the color of the mineral, so they gave up and tunneled elsewhere and left secret places for those who know how to find them, and only took the obvious yellow nuggets they found."

She continued, "The priestesses have used such passageways for years. The location for the City of the Rose was chosen because it was on a hill, and an excellent overlook for miles. It also had a passageway, right in the midst of the site, to the mountains a few miles away full of caves, which the priestesses knew well and continue to use in secret."

"It's the priestesses who support us now," she explained to me. "They warn me when I'm to be interviewed, as the Romans call it. I go to the cave and keep them waiting as long as I can, then emerge in an outrageous condition, so they think I've lost my mind. I heard that one persistent interrogator intended to take me captive and haul me back to Rome to be imprisoned. I decided to change his mind by giving him a lesson."

I already felt sorry for the man as I listened to my wife, since a priestess giving a lesson might not be something a man wants to encounter too often.

"I hesitate to ask what you did, but I shall," I inquired, nonetheless.

MiryAmah laughed a little and said, "I had the priestesses strip me down to my naked body. I had them smear me with the dung of pigs, birds, and any other source that had a strong-smelling release of fecal matter. I had to have them put herb oils in my nose and ears and all openings to my body, so I could stand the smell myself and not bring any problems into my physical vehicle. Then they wove all sorts of things one might see as nasty into my hair, like dead birds and lizards, topped off with a dead snake. When the fellow came to one of the caves, directed to that particular one by one of the priestesses in disguise as an old woman, he was not pleased to see me and certainly not willing to take me with him in the state, he found me. It was a very difficult path on which the old woman led him to the cave occupied by a multitude of bats. He was already exhausted and the will to make a grand capture was mostly gone by the time he saw me."

"You amaze me, woman," I said, "and I thought I was the only one who ever saw you unclothed," I playfully exclaimed, not out of disgust as anything that kept her safe was quite welcome news.

"Well, there wasn't much to see since the sisters had me mostly covered with hair. It has started quite a legend already in the village, in the year or so since we changed the mind of the one who would capture and transport me," she said. "Let it be said," she added, "I was not a treasure, he wanted to take home with him."

"You'll always be my treasure, no matter what condition your body is in, because what I see is part of my own soul," I said, even as I noticed how much the last five years had aged both of us.

MiryAmah was starting to have strands of gray hair running through her lovely reddish black locks. Her hair had grown so much that it, indeed, did reach nearly to her ankles. She allowed it to flow freely, not covering it with a robe as she had to in our teaching days. She explained to me that she used to keep it cropped shorter, to her waist, but now she figured she might need it again as her 'robe of madness'. Mental illness has always been misunderstood and feared. In that time, it was thought to be demons possessing the individual. Others thought if they got in close proximity, they, too, could be possessed. Thus, it was an efficient way to be left alone, my wife assured me. There was always the danger of being killed, however. MiryAmah said the priestess disguised as an old woman told the Roman, as she led him through the difficult trail to the cave, that the demon had spoken to her and told her, that anyone who harmed so much as a hair on the Madeline's[184] head would take her demons into themselves–and forever take her place. That was a daunting possibility to most anyone.

My wife looked at me head to toe, saying, as she ran her fingers through my hair, "You are ever beautiful to me, dear heart, but you have turned white as snow. I hope you haven't had to witness suffering and sorrow in your absence."

"Time marches on, my love," I said, "and being apart from you makes me feel like a widowed old man sometimes. I haven't revisited sorrow as terrible as when I last saw my brother James. Mainly, I've been walking and talking to the native people of the faraway land. I've been learning their ways, for the most part," I explained "and watching my dreams and visions, to keep track of our followers and how they fare."

"You haven't found a native woman attractive?" she asked, knowing the answer, but having to be reassured anyway.

"I find many women attractive," I answered "but I'm attracted only to you." Then I said, "I could ask the same of you, pretty one."

---

[184] The way the Gaul, later France, referred to Mary of Magdela, also known as Mary Magdalene

"Oh, are we not the ones?" MiryAmah said. "Do we not play the game of life as all others do? Are we so insecure after too long a parting?"

"You're full of questions, dear wife," I said. "Let's find the answers through closeness." Then we disappeared for a few days into the underground tunnels, where there was a private cave comfortably kept for her, with whatever one would need to have some time alone. Only, this time we weren't alone, we were together at last.

## HOLY COMMUNION
Chapter Forty-Three

Mary Magdalene, or 'The Madeline,' as she was known in the region, disappeared again into the mists of the mountains. Those who missed her knew that, from time to time, she faded away from the City of the Rose. They thought she secluded herself to mourn for me and that was partly true.

As for myself, I was just a traveler, a friend to Joseph of Arimathea, and a frequent visitor to the city complex, who the people believed to be a devoted follower of the Christian movement originally called 'The Way.' I also disappeared, unnoticed. This way of living and survival wouldn't be possible in our old homeland. There was far too much confusion and social fear there, to allow untied ends to dangle before the eyes of those holding power and place of authority, so we avoided the Middle East and wandered other places.

My wife and I needed some private time together to catch up on each other's lives, so we could feel our divine union linked, as it should be. We did some scrying in the secluded caverns and sanctuaries of the nearby mountains. There were places, not easily found, that had little private valleys totally enclosed by rock formations, with streams and ponds that offered the peace and tranquility needed to use the ancient technique of water gazing. As we scryed, we watched in dismay, as some of the situations unfolding in the old homeland played out very differently than we had intended. We finally had to agree that change was always difficult, but in the end it was necessary for the sake of evolution, or that steady process of learning our relationship with God. Those who would gain power and control through enslavement of mind, body and soul are always against change. MiryAmah and I talked about the state of 'slavery' and agreed it was a state of mind. That was why we always taught that the heart should be the director of the physical life sojourn, and the mind should be its servant, not its slave, but helper. The only one who can totally free a slave is the one enslaved. Even when a master finally frees the oppressed, until the mind changes, there is never liberty. We gave the followers of 'The Way' the key. We accepted that part of our soul work, and took responsibility for all aspects of the movement we came to begin, but we couldn't turn the key for them.

Out in the far reaches of the Roman controlled lands, we found breathing room, which was just enough to cause a less drastic ripple of change. MiryAmah had begun that ripple in the lands of Gaul. I had planted the seeds of change in the far-off land you call the Americas, among the tribes I visited. I didn't preach to them, however, I listened to them. Sometimes, that's the best way to make a difference in this world of experience—to listen.

It's true that the voice one must heed first is your own voice. I had taught through parables, based on actual situations from several perspectives, in the old homeland as Jesus and people had listened to me. They were so disconnected from their own voice that they would never understand the tales of my native friends. They were mind-tied to a system that forbade them to think for themselves, much less speak for themselves. 'Obey blindly' was the unspoken rule, thus, those in obedience didn't speak what was in their heart, and I spoke for them. That was the threat. Someone was speaking for the people and showing them how to access their inner soul-voice. Ultimately, that is why I died as Jesus on the cross, and why many of my followers suffered, too.

MiryAmah and I decided to go on a journey together. There were peoples of the far north that we wanted to listen to and understand. They were descendants from the long-ago lineage of the original creation project of this age. Some descended from the Watchers, some of the first peace code implanters. There were other such projects, but that long story is another tale to tell one day. Look to your legends with an open mind and the pieces of the past will slowly connect like a mighty puzzle.

The people I speak of now were those of a lineage that could be both aggressive and receptive, as they protected themselves with a fierce determination to survive. Their intuition was greatly developed, and they could still experience amazing insight even at the basest level of physicality. This ability resulted in a richly expanded awareness of nature and how it affected and interacted with all creational experience. Many of them knew of the Mysty Isles, since they were aware of that place between physicality and the spirit realms. Respected shamans within their social groups were the bridge to such places. We wanted to meet these people and see if they had achieved a better balance of the opposite, but complementary, energies of the masculine and feminine within their societies. If so, we wanted to learn how they preserved that knowing, or was it a constant unfolding state of discovery?

It was time for my wife and me to take a journey together, and share our mission once again. Thus, we packed a few things and left, telling our family, we would see them in a few months. We traveled alone, we thought. Elmira, bless his heart, was never far from me, even if he didn't reveal his presence. He was my 'Christopher' through and through, and intended to remain so, as long as I needed him. I knew he was protecting my anchor body and that this would be a long bi-location; however I didn't know that he had learned to bi-locate himself, if need be.

We went to what you now would term Scotland. At the time it was known as the land of Alba or Caledonia. There we met with the painted people,[185] who tattooed pictures on their skins. We stayed with them for a time, inquiring why they adorned their bodies this way. They told us it was not adornment to them; rather it was wrapping themselves in grace and protection. It also was to help

---

[185] The Picts, or Picti known to Romans as Pictis, also referred to as 'the Pictish People' or 'Painted People'

the gods identify them. Each person had very specific designs and images, which were closely tied to how they perceived themselves as a soul. Their names were usually taken from nature and subject to change as life changed. I saw a similarity to the natives of the Americas, who usually adopted names from nature, too. However, if they painted themselves, it was with paint that was used in the moment and washed away later. The Pictis, as the Romans called these people, permanently tattooed themselves, covering nearly every inch of their bodies, by the time they were full grown. The tattooing started at birth, with the mother telling the shaman what her vision was, just before the child emerged. That image was put over the small one's heart, and it expanded as the child grew.

They passed their leadership down from mother to daughter, or if she only had sons, the rule reverted back to her sister or niece. The men were usually the guardians, but some were shamans and healers, too. We wanted to watch them and see how such a matriarchal society interacted. Still having to protect themselves, warriors were important in this society. Even so, those powerful men and women who took that role didn't make the decisions for the tribe. Talents were felt to be gifts of the gods. All roles were important, including hunters, those who prepared food, and those who acted as servants to others in any way, and so forth. We saw the occasional beggar type, which was not the norm. They, too, were respected and seen as an example of learning for the tribe, through the role they played.

Through generations, the elder woman chief called the council of other elders together, who made the major decisions, both women and men. This had worked best for them, they told us, and they asked if I took the wise council of my wife, MiryAmah, allowing her to lead me through difficult times.

"Actually," I told them, "we both lead from time to time and we both follow as well, depending on the situation and who is best equipped to handle the dynamics of it."

"Then, you are free," the chieftress said, "and we thought we were the last of the free people."

Freedom is a state of mind. These people demonstrated the principles of that mind-set, which could be in place through generation after generation. You could see the freedom in thinking, just by watching them move about their villages and doing their daily tasks. No one seemed to be more highly esteemed. They didn't consider nudity a shame. Usually, in warmer weather, their children didn't wear garments, rather, were allowed to run about completely nude without the problem of restrictive clothing. Since body pictures on the babies began early, the colorful designs gave the impression that the children were dressed, due to the ornamentation in bright colors. Often entire families might appear nude during the few sweltering hot days of summer, and walked about with no fear of shame, quite comfortable. Since we arrived in the last of the warm season we had a chance to see how the body pictures developed from mere babe to full grown adult, both father and mother. This time we were learning by 'seeing'. We realized that we had progressed from speaking, to listening, and now to 'seeing,' in our soul mission sojourn.

What we saw in the Picti People were peaceful beings, but people who could be fiercely protective of their lifestyle, if need be. They were a constant thorn in the side of the Romans, who wanted to bring them under their control and civilize them to their standards. That was never successful, however. They considered the Pictis quite barbaric, as they didn't permanently build villages and would relocate on a whim. Also, they only recognized the authority of their own leaders and not the Romans, whose disgust was partly due to the maternal order of things, which was the opposite of the Roman fiercely-patriarchal way, where women held a low status in their world.

The Picti People were prime examples of the concept of nonresistance. They didn't resist the Romans; they simply refused to join into their agenda, resulting in times of violence, but never initiated by the Picti People. While we were with them such a moment happened, and we saw that which we would rather not have seen.

Erudia[186], the chieftress, gave full authority of protection for the people to her faithful husband, Normic[187]. The names are hard to pronounce, since they are of a language which is not part of the root language that unites most tongues. These tribes have an elemental origin going way back in time. Erudia, translated would mean 'Queen of the Forest', and Normic, 'King of the Hills'. The Picts often named themselves after places, like rivers, the ocean, the hills, and mountains and such. The native people from the America's often took their names from the animal kingdom, like White Eagle, Gray Wolf, Raven, or the effects of nature, like Gentle Rain or Rolling Thunder, etc. In the land of the Pictis, the name would be followed by their role, as 'Manocha,[188] Shaman of the People,' or 'Lillithath,[189] Song Healer,' and such. The origins of the names were sometimes connected to other cultures, since the people were nomadic by nature and interacted, bringing new words to the tribes with which they integrated. The names in this culture were an ever-unfolding thing. For example, when the Queen gave up her leadership, she passed along her name 'Erudia, Old Queen of the Forests,' and she was then renamed. They called me 'The White Wanderer,' and they called MiryAmah, 'The Lady of the Well'. We thought that was ironic, since we met in this lifetime at the well. They tagged her with that name because they also had shallow wells they used as they set up temporary villages, and she had a habit of singing down into the echoing well as she brought up water. Odd, I thought, how I hadn't noticed that until someone else mentioned it, however it was true. She did sing into wells and the echo sounded like an entire choir of women singing.

So, as was their custom, Normic didn't have to ask his wife's permission to act in defense of the tribe. While we were there, a group of Roman soldiers were found to be too close to the encampment of the Picti People's village. Their demeanor indicated their purpose, as they were closely watched by the

---

[186] Queen of the Forest, she called Jeshua the 'White Wanderer'

[187] Similar to name Norman, means 'Thor mind, Thor courage,' also meant 'King of the Hills'

[188] (male) Sanskrit: 'air, wind', one of the commonest names of the wind god Vaui. Charioteer of Indra

[189] This name also connected with the 'tree of life'

tribe's sentries. Normic was expert in defense strategies, and put one of his many plans into action in short order, causing the enemies to lose many men and to suffer to the point that they had to turn back. The leader, however, was wounded and abandoned by his men, because they believed him dead, no doubt. He was brought back to the Picti village, which was already in the process of packing up to move to a safer location. Erudia had as good an inner-communication system with her husband, as my own wife and I enjoyed. She knew a danger was closing in, so had already given the order to prepare to move on.

When Normic arrived with the leader of the Roman brigade on a drag cart, even though the hate and distain could clearly be seen in this enemy's eyes, and it was evident he was ready to suffer for his cause, he was treated with the utmost of gentle care. The healers, many of which were women, attended to him to ease his pain. He couldn't bear to look upon them, tattooed and bare breasted, working on him, so looked away with disgust. Due to his ingrained judgment, he nearly sickened from their sight and flinched from their gentle healing touch. The Romans held little regard for women, thinking them vile and dirty. The so-called 'great society,' the Romans believed they enjoyed, seldom depicted a nude woman in their artworks, but often their sculptural art consisted of nude men whom they found perfect and beautiful. The semi-nude Picti women repulsed the Roman captive. It took the easing of his pain for him to begin to get past his bias, ingrained since birth. It didn't go unnoticed by him, that he was being helped and not out of duty either, but genuine concern. The women healers had the look of determination on their faces, not the look of revulsion. As a severed shoulder was gently packed to control the bleeding and carefully stitched, a song healer sang a tune of relaxation. The fallen warrior finally understood that no matter how they appeared to him, they were willingly helping an enemy. This was something that he had to mull over within his mind, since he usually dispatched his wounded enemies quickly and cruelly, to satisfy his lust for blood. The implications and impact confused him.

Erudia came forth and leaned down over him. He didn't have much strength left, but he quietly spoke saying, "Why do you make an enemy comfortable?"

She said in perfect Latin, "We comfort the body and soul, which are not our enemies, soldier. Only your mind is our enemy, due to your corrupted attitudes."

He seemed to accept this explanation. Sometimes pain opens portals of understanding. Then he asked, "Are you going to kill me?"

Erudia said, "Yes, you know we must."

I think he thought about how the Romans killed, instilling as much suffering as possible. He must have been wondering if he was being prepared to suffer.

MiryAmah and I were impressed that they would comfort the man, before they took his life. We didn't feel they would inflict more pain on him. We watched Erudia put a finger to a place on his neck where the main highway of life's blood went from the head to the heart. She gently pushed until he lost consciousness, and then pulled a tiny knife, she kept strapped to her thigh. It was decorated in bright-colored red and green jewel stones, and was made of the jawbone of a boar, I think. At moments such as this, time always went into slow motion, and I would notice every detail. Erudia quickly pierced the man's heart, while he lay unconscious and gently took his life.

His lifeless body was put on a pedestal prepared from branches of trees, raised off the ground well over six feet high. He was laid on the skin of a wolf, symbolic, I think, of the predatory nature of the animal. His hair was cleansed and his helmet was put on a pole at the end of the platform closest to his head. A single circle was drawn upon his face, and then tattooed by the shaman of pictures. It was a red circle with a blue spot in the middle. It represented God.

He was covered with his own blue robes and breastplate. The people brought wild flowers as well and laid them by his side. He was treated, with all due respect, we observed, as we watched the event unfold. The Picture People were nearly ready to relocate and knew that soon other soldiers would come for their comrade. The ritual of sending off the dead had to be done without pre-ceremony, so Erudia came quickly and said a prayer for the journey of his soul.

"Oh, great Mother/Father of All Creation," she prayed. "Take this soldier back into your fold and forgive him his ignorance. Remember the good in him and help him forgive himself for that which he has done in the name of the power he thinks is God. Forgive us for taking him prematurely out of this existence. Our only choice was to prolong his suffering and to sacrifice our people, should we have tried to sustain his life. We send him back to you, in all due respect and honor." Then she left him to be found by his people.

We all left at that point. No one really knew where the next encampment or temporary village might be. It was the leader's intuition that would plot the course and within that highly-developed intuition, she would know where to settle once again and how to get there.

We left the group, as they intuitively moved forth through the hills and forests. We wanted to see more people of this land. We knew that, since I was still in bi-location, it could be difficult for MiryAmah, should there be a problem with either body. The decision not to have her bi-locate, but to rather be fully in one physical vehicle was to ensure that one of us would survive, if we encountered problems. A bi-located body had its limitations as to endurance.

As we wandered, we encountered a tribe of light-skinned tall people. They had blue or green eyes and hair the color of fire or light wheat. They are referred to now as the Vikings, but to us, they were the Far North People, or the Norsemen. Their social system was different from tribe to tribe. Most were aggressive, due to somewhere down through the ages, they had developed a love of conquest—brutal conquest.

When they encountered us, they wanted to capture MiryAmah and enslave me, or better yet, kill me by doing battle. We were walking up a rocky trail heading for high ground. We knew that there were tribes that wandered this region, but it was our intent to make contact, so we didn't try to hide our presence. We didn't resist when a small raiding party overtook us and that didn't please these rude vagabonds. They liked the thrill of the fight and wandered far and wide, for just that pleasure. We surrendered too easily. They thought they could make me fight, if they abused MiryAmah. Certainly, they were correct, since I was ready to battle to the death to protect her from being raped. At that critical moment, a flaming arrow pierced the heart of their leader, and he fell dead at our feet. The others took cover, leaving us exposed to the danger. One at a time they came out, looking for the archer. Each time, more flaming arrows flew. One by one, each burly man went down with an arrow in his heart. The Viking warriors were notorious for their insane ability to face an enemy. The men kept charging the unseen assailant and dying on the spot. Finally, with one left, I pleaded in a language I had never heard before. "Whoever you are spare this man, I ask in all due urgency." I couldn't stand to see anymore death.

Then Elmira stepped forth. Evidently, I had spoken his native tongue, which he had never shared with me. He looked like a Picti warrior, being about the same size as they were, but without pictures on his body. His face was painted half blue, however. I could tell the lone Viking warrior was prepared to die. Using my gift of language, I said, "Maybe this is not your day to die. Maybe this is your day to bring a peaceful man and his wife to your people, so we can better understand each other."

The warrior looked at me thinking this over and wondering why I would have need to understand his people or, for that matter, him. He speculated maybe I didn't have the courage to fight, let alone have a healthy lust for blood. MiryAmah reached over and touched his shoulder and just looked at him, eye to eye and nodded 'yes', answering a question not yet asked, which was 'Do you really want to die now before you understand what you die for?'

## The Saga-Oracle

He did something, which I later learned was a great honor. He gave his long knife, his main weapon, to my wife and bowed to her and headed down the trail. She followed him with the knife, and I followed her. Elmira disappeared back into the landscape, ever close but like a ghost unseen. A thought passed through my head. I wondered who was anchoring my body back in the faraway land, in the safe place behind the waterfalls.

We arrived at the nomadic encampment of the Vikings. We began to wonder if anyone set up permanent villages in this far land. The group consisted of mostly men and a couple of women who were warrior-like. We passed a sentry who kept watch. Evidently there were several such sentries on guard, allowing others to take turns being by the fire and bragging about their conquests. We were allowed to pass, as it was immediately noticed that MiryAmah carried the warrior's long knife with point down, as we followed the lone survivor back into the camp. This, evidently, was a signal of safe passage and also indicated that there was some kind of respectful truce in place. When we entered the camp everyone stopped talking and looked toward us. Their faces were rugged, and if I allowed the surface to define the person, quite scary, being full of scars along with ornaments pierced into their noses, eyebrows and ears. They all wore helmets with animal fur and horns, resulting in a pretty intimidating-looking lot.

It always surprised the people we met, when I could speak their language instantly and with the same rhythm as they themselves spoke. The first assumption was that I had been closely connected to their people at some point, since I spoke so fluently. This ability opened doorways to their minds, as the question formed and the possibilities paraded through their thoughts, clearing a line of communication. At least there wasn't a misunderstanding of the spoken words.

Sensing conflicting thoughts, I said, "I have come in peace." That didn't impress them much, but at least they knew right away that I didn't intend to fight them. Then I introduced them to my wife and said I was seeking them out, so I could understand their people better. I explained to them, we wished to understand all people, by discovering how different tribes were alike, rather than how they might differ.

One of the men, who had an ugly scar that nearly covered his right eye, said, "Well, I must say you have the guts to be a warrior, even if you don't have the will, walking in here with only this little woman for protection with one of our own warrior's knives." Then he said, "How is it you can speak our language as if you were born to it, but you are as unlike us as a bird is to a cat?"

"It's my gift," I said.

I could see he was in command, for the others watched him to see what he would or wouldn't do. Then he asked about the other men from the raiding party and was told by the one spared warrior, of their demise due to the flaming arrows. The leader seemed to be pondering this turn of events and looked into the fire, as if seeking to sort something out. Finally, after a few moments he turned back to me and asked, "Who is the ghost with the fire arrows?"

"He's my protector," I replied. "He has always been devoted to my safety. Just when I think he's not with me, there he is," I further explained.

Contemplating this answer, he looked back into the fire again. Finally, he turned to me and said, "Why did he suddenly appear from nowhere to protect you from my warriors? Why doesn't he walk at your side?"

I answered, "I didn't know he was with me. He doesn't always do what I expect, and I thought I had left him behind, when I came on this journey. He appeared, because I would die before I would see my wife harmed, and he knew it. My protector is determined that I shall not die before my time."

He asked his warrior where this protector was now and the answer was, "Who knows? Probably back in realms of the ghosts, watching."

"And why did you give your sword to the woman?" the leader inquired, as this was seen as an unusual decision.

"Because she touched my heart with unsaid words and her courage impressed me," was the answer.

Then looking back at me, the leader motioned that MiryAmah and I should sit by the fire. The circle quickly expanded to make room for us.

"Anyone who can convince such a warrior as this one," he said, pointing to the spared man, "to give up his sword due to unsaid words is worthy to join us for a time." Then he said, "As for my other men, they died in honor, since a flaming arrow is the sign of a noble death, even if the cause was far from dignified." To him a noble death was to fight in battle. According to the story he just heard, there was no such battle, only a ghost-archer protecting this unusual man and woman.

The leader never offered to introduce himself, or the others, and was careful to mask any reference to such. I believe he thought that if we knew their names, we would be able to capture their soul.

He spoke of my protector again, stating, "Anyone who is protected by a ghost surely is sent by the Gods." Maybe that's why these rugged warriors decided to allow us to roam with them for a while. We just watched, for the most part. They knew that was all we wanted, and they respected us. To accommodate our presence, they made sure their actions were in accordance with their intentions. It was like a language of images, without words, (both MiryAmah and I could see mental images) that resulted in actions. It reminded me somewhat of how the Pict's used the images upon their bodies to define them as individuals, as a group, and how the pictures held the secret of their intention, as well. These people had different ways of depicting intention, within pure action which, unfortunately, was often brutal. It was hard to witness their customs.

We had seen enough death and violence, so hoped that we wouldn't witness these Vikings in their most brutal mode. One night MiryAmah and I had the same dream, of this group of violent raiders finding a small Picti encampment, and they brutally raped, pillaged and killed the entire tribe, down to the last baby.

We both awoke in a cold sweat after the dream vision. It was Erudia's people. When we left for our morning bathing ritual by a small inland lake, we quietly slipped into the cold clear water before dawn as usual. Once we stopped shivering, we floated with heads above the water surface. We looked at each other, and shared the dream and our concerns. We had to decide what to do. Should we continue with the non-resistance plan, or should we do something? We decided on the latter, but we had to devise a way to stop the slaughter and still respect the aggressors, who were our hosts at this point.

We knew if there was any conflict, death would be certain for the tribe of Pictis. We didn't want death on either side of this situation. We decided to try and scry a line of communication with Erudia. As it turned out, she was also in water at the same hour, taking her morning cleansing dip. The water is a great conductor of thought energy, thus we could see her and communicate easily. We told her of our dream and asked that she not sacrifice anyone to conflict this time. We asked that she simply take a different path to another location and spare her people and those who would harm them.

She thought long and hard. Then her husband joined her and he, too, became part of the discussion. He said they could make a trap for the invaders. She said, "What good would that do? A few would be killed, but there were many more where they came from and when would it end?" And so it went, until it was decided that they simply would go to another safe-place, and avoid killing and suffering on both sides.

We went our own way that very day. We later ran into the Viking group, going back to the sea to their long boats, thinking that there wasn't much purpose to staying in this land since it didn't offer all that much in conquest and treasure. Thus, they decided to return home and plot a new course, where plunder was worth their effort.

"We thought that we knew of a village of the Pictis," one of the warriors said to another, as we were leaving. "But our scouts tell us, they aren't where we thought they would be. Our leader said they weren't worth trailing, since they usually didn't carry precious things with them and their women aren't to our liking."

We ran into a few other tribes, with some more matriarchal in nature, and some downright mystical people, living in the mists beyond physicality in the realm of elementals, along with more of the aggressive-natured, as the Vikings were. We decided we had seen enough and turned for home.

The City of the Rose was calling us back. We came back from a slightly different direction, but still had to cross the great channel. We found longboats-men[190] willing to take us over this daunting body of water. Our crossing before had been on a small ship heading for the highlands, for trade in wool. Even as we traveled back towards home, we didn't spend long periods with people, but only interacted as traveling wanderers would. We finally arrived early in the morning on a rainy late fall day. The streets of the little city, that entwined the petal-like terraces, were like rivers. We had to walk on the walls of the terraces, which had been made wide and slanting for this purpose. For some reason, we wanted to go to the church being constructed at the apex of the hill first, so bypassed Ecknoreial's palatial home. We would see her soon enough. No need to wake-up the entire household, we felt.

The building was nearly finished now and even had a roof in place, made of thatched reeds, as was the norm in this area. We entered into a small dark room, through double swinging doors with carvings of the sun and the moon on them, and other images of heavenly orbs, like stars and comets. Once our eyes adjusted to the unlit entry room, we entered another set of doors, which had a woman and a man figure carefully carved on the surface, with the man on the left door and the woman on the right. Where the latch was located, the figures' hands were clasped. To enter, one had to turn the clasped hands to release the handle. Entering this room, we found a long narrow isle, made of a path of flat stones of a natural red hue, which led to an altar of stone. The outside walls

---

[190] Men who had long canoe-like boats that ferried people and small amounts of cargo across the English channel, especially to the Scottish shores where ships rarely went

had high windows and were extremely tall, because there were walls outside of them, like wings, that held up the main exterior walls. Jutting out either side of the altar were circular corridors leading to small rooms. MiryAmah had designed the space to represent the inside of a woman's belly, the true sacred alter. In the small rooms were kept the eggs, or ova of the ceremony, she explained. The priestesses would bring these symbolic items to the altar, and a priest would unite them with the masculine intention of Divine Marriage, and the Oneness would be ceremoniously achieved within the ritual. We knew that you could teach people a lesson verbally, but to show someone a ritual and involve them, was a way that the real sacred essence of the truth could merge with the soul, beyond logic and judgment. The corrupted priesthood didn't enter ritual with the same intention. To them, it was a sideshow to appease the ignorant populace and a way to deepen the ingrained attitudes they had fostered. MiryAmah told me she wanted to marry the priestess tradition with the need for public involvement through ritual. I was impressed that she had wisely chosen this path.

My sweet beloved wife told me to wait for a moment. She chose one of the side corridors and disappeared into the inner-chamber. Emerging with a golden chalice, she said to me, "This is the chalice of life. It is the symbol of my womb. Fill it up and all life will be blessed." Then she placed it upon the altar.

There was a flask of wine inside an ornate cabinet on the altar. I instinctively took it out and realized how I should respond to what MiryAmah had just done with the chalice. I poured the wine into the chalice and said, "This is the fruit of the vine. It's full of life and possibility. I fill your chalice, dear wife, to overflowing and together we are 'One.' "

After carefully pouring the wine to the brim, we lowered our lips to the edge of the chalice at the same time. Without tipping the cup, we sipped until it was a bit below the edge. We didn't want to waste a single drop. Then we lifted the cup together close to our faces, and I put the chalice to MiryAmah's lips and said, "Drink of my blood of life, dear wife, so that life itself will be blessed."

She drank a good swallow, licking her lips sensually afterwards. She then lifted the cup to my lips and said, "Drink of my blood, combined with yours, so that life can be fed and grow strong within me and all that I represent as Priestess and woman," and I emptied the cup.

MiryAmah, looking at me, licked inside the cup, and it was such an intensely sexual thing to do and appropriate. I did the same enjoying the moment and feelings of arousal. It was still early morning and no one was out in the rain, which pounded the roof. It was quite natural that we end this ritual with the actual coupling of two lovers, who desired each other beyond their control. Sexuality is not a sin. It is a gift from God. To enjoy and merge due to such love and passion is the gift given back, in full measure, and a sacred sacrament.

Someone had left rose petals in a basket on the steps to the altar. We didn't plan to spill the contents, but our bed of rose petals was appropriate for the occasion. We both knew that we had implanted another child within the blessed womb of my beloved. This kind of passion always was fruitful. We rejoiced in this sacred moment together—One.

# OVER LAND AND SEA
## Chapter Forty-Four

Leaving this time was most difficult for both my wife and me. We didn't know then, that this would be our last physical time together. At some level, we realized the truth of the situation, because there was something about this parting that was more agonizing than any before.

After a proper visit and tearful farewell to my family, I left to rejoin my bi-located anchor body. I had to go to the exact place that I zapped into this duality, thus went back to the garden of Martha. This time, however, my sister-in-marriage recognized me, as she walked among her beautiful thorny roses. MiryAmah didn't reveal my presence, when I came, to anyone except my brothers if they were in residence, since they were her protectors, and they needed to know that I was not someone who was a threat to her safety. Of course, mother knew, too. Other than my immediate family, I was a beloved guest from time to time. My wife's family situation had changed. Her parents had passed on and her brother Lazarus and sister Martha joined her in exile. MiryAmah didn't burden them with the scope of our reality, however. She had never fully explained our unique relationship to her sister even though she loved her greatly, as knowledge was dangerous, and to know could mean to die. So when Martha saw me, she thought I was a ghost visiting from the spirit realms.

"Hale, Jeshua!" she said. "You have come to my garden, and I'm not worthy." People had been so ingrained to believe they were born unworthy and would ever be so, that their first response was, "I am not worthy." I, too, struggled with that feeling from time to time.

"You are ever worthy, my sister," I said. "Haven't my wife and I trained you to know that? You were always one of those who understood the teachings at the highest level," I reminded her.

"Why do you show yourself to me this fine morning?" she asked with a worried look upon her face, for she already thought the worse scenario.

Realizing that this moment would affect her life, I decided that this would be a good time to affirm her worthiness and ask a favor as well. "Don't worry, sister. All is well," I began. "I've come to ask a great favor. I want to ask that you remain at MiryAmah's side throughout her life journey, for I can't be there as you can. I trust only you to know how a woman must feel, to be abandoned in her lifetime in her greatest hours of need. Will you grant me this request?" I asked. "If you will, I will rest more peacefully, and you will forever be among the blessed of God."

"Of course, Jeshua," she replied. "You know it's my honor to serve my sister and that is the reason I'm here now, because I believed she and the children she fosters needed me." Martha was always a hard worker and to serve others was her soul mission in life. I remembered the day long ago in her home, when she was busy serving my followers and me. She was serving a delicious meal after a day of teaching. I had just met MiryAmah at the well, and we were so taken with each other, that we didn't have eyes for anyone except each other. Martha was getting frustrated, because her sister wasn't helping, only sitting at my feet and looking at me. Martha complained and I answered, trying to clarify that the divine gift of love reunited was as worthy as the selfless service to others. Because Martha was so dedicated to her service, she didn't quite understand that remark, and I always wished I could have been wiser in the handling of the situation.

Nodding my head even as I remembered this, I said to her as I dissipated, "You are indeed blessed, Martha, and we are blessed for your dedication and devotion."

Going back, I often don't remember going through the tunnel of transition and this time it was again so. After the zap in Martha's garden, I awoke in the cave where Elmira was monitoring my anchor body. He had pivoted the body as before and thus knew when I would return. It wasn't a matter of time measured by increments that he had to follow as he turned my pedestal bed, but rather he had to sense when to turn the spinning platform since the fairy folk weren't there to light up the adjustments. He knew the position of return and was prepared to attend to my needs, and he had just shifted me into that direction when I awoke merged once again.

It's not easy to reunite the bodies after bi-location. It takes some time to become oriented, and massage of the body is necessary to get one's life's blood flowing again within the merged vehicle. While I was with my family, my life's blood was active within that body and nearly dormant in the body left behind. The overseer of the anchor body must do light massage from time to time, but vigorous massage at the re-joining is necessary. Thus I awoke to a deep vital massage from my friend and guardian, Elmira. His strong hands were working on my chest area when I opened my eyes.

I could see he was glad for my return. He had a tea made of herbs for me, to help get the digestive system awake, and he quickly poured me a cup. The herbal teas one needs in such situations vary depending on location. The herbs had to be gathered from the location of the body merging, so that the body could fully readjust back to the locality from which it emerged. The tea, made from the vegetation that grew under the waterfall in front of the cave, was warm and quite soothing, and I was fully awake within an hour.

"My friend," I said, to Elmira, and he nodded his head, glad that I regarded him more than just a guardian. "It's time for us to go across the vast ocean again. I have a mission to complete and time is becoming short." Then I remembered the ghost and the flaming arrows that had saved my beloved and me from the brutal attack of the Vikings. "How is it, Elmira that you also can be in two places at once while still being an anchor here with my primary body?"

He just looked at me and shrugged his shoulders. Then I heard Eocha chuckle, and I looked around for her. She was sitting upon a stone shaped like a chair, thus looking throne-like, perfectly fitted for her, watching us. "Bi-location can be a community affair," she said, and then she dissipated.

That very day we scryed and asked that transportation be arranged to cross the sea. Eocha and my master teacher told me to go northeast. "I see you are home again," I said to Eocha, and she just laughed that same chuckling way. My master said all was prepared, so we set out in the direction of intuition towards the sea, leaving the sanctuary of the warm and comfortable cave. The weather was cold and there was snow on the ground, outside the cave dwelling. We forged northward, using the sun and stars to navigate, when we could see them through the blowing snow.

Going north in the time of winter is never easy. I was in my white robes and now had totally white hair and beard, so I blended into the landscape. While I was bi-located, Elmira had tanned the skin of a buffalo that had been killed by a wolf pack. He had spent many hours preparing the hide and making it soft and comfortable. He had another huge pack upon his back, when we left, I noticed. I assumed it was extra provisions, he had prepared on those many long hours of sitting by my side in the cave of repose.

# The Saga-Oracle

About the second day, with the wind whipping and drifts hampering us as we moved along, I said to Elmira, "The high mountain people trained me to keep warm in the cold, but I feel my energy for this technique is waning," and I began to shiver violently. The technique required that I mentally send blood to the exterior of my physical vehicle, for usually when one is very cold the body will only send blood to the vital organs. I had to adjust the energy to override the natural security system, but it couldn't be kept indefinitely in that mode. In a meditative state, one could last much longer, but now fully awake, I was extremely cold and numb.

"If I don't make it back, will you leave me and save yourself?" I asked Elmira, worried that he would stay with me until the end for both of us.

Constantly, I learn and relearn the lesson of 'asking' or 'admitting to need.' As I said this, Elmira stopped and took down the mighty bundle, that was clearly a burden to him as we trudged along through the drifting snow, and unfolded it. I was surprised to see it was another buffalo robe, but this one was white. I was flabbergasted, to put it mildly, for he had been wearing his robe of reddish brown, since we began, and I had just my soft white robes and my skill at keeping the body warm through mind control.

Elmira motioned to me, as I stood with my mouth gaping, and asked in body language, "Do you want to wear this robe or not?"

Looking at him with exasperation, I said, "Yes, I want the robe. What took you so long to offer it?"

I clearly heard his mind-speak voice say, "You didn't indicate a need."

I can't tell you how welcome that white buffalo robe was. It helped me keep my body heat constant enough to continue. The struggle to trudge through snow sometimes waist deep kept me from physically talking, however. I had to save my strength for the trek. Elmira and I had spent a year not speaking when I was a child but still communicated through body language and mind-speak, thus we carried on a mind-to-mind conversation as we

569

moved along that was not energy draining. It felt like I was back in my boyhood days during that quiet year. I asked how he got the second robe. He told me White Buffalo Woman showed up at the cave with it one day.

In mind-speak he said, " She told me that I was only to give you the robe when you asked, and that I was not to tell you it was available," he explained.

As we moved steadily along I said in my mind-to-mind speak, "But I didn't even know you had such a wonder as this robe, so how could I request it?"

Evidently, White Buffalo Woman had come often to the cave and, according to Elmira, she had spoken of many interesting and wondrous things with him, in the same manner we now spoke. She told him to make a backpack out of the robe, with the inside skin as the outer layer, and not to tell me about it until I needed it. She also told him I would have to be fully aware and up front about my need, as the robe of the white buffalo is sacred. She said the white buffalo robe is Great Spirit's Divine gift. It is never offered to anyone, unless it is called forth through unselfish need, not called specifically, but called through pure intentional need. She evidently shared great teachings of 'divine need' with my guardian. It was a state of receptiveness, she told him. Thus, according to Elmira, I had to arrive at a state of receptiveness, before he could offer the robe.

The bulky white animal skin was a perfect warm wrapping for me. Elmira said, White Buffalo Woman also told him, it could only be warm and comforting, if the gift of Spirit came at the perfect time of need. Thus, the rest of my journey to the ocean in the far northeast was more pleasant than the first couple of days.

We arrived at the point I recognized through our scrying vision. We met with a group of indigenous people, tending a fire on the frozen ocean beach. Through our long trek, we seldom encountered people, because they were tucked in for the winter or had gone south. These people, though, were comfortable in the cold and evidently expecting us. They were dressed in warm coats of fur. Their feet were protected by fur as well, looking like animal paws as they moved about. Every two or three hours, Elmira and I, having leather shoes, had to stop and warm each other's feet. I wish we had thought of the fur shoes, or had some of the warming gel Elmira had used on me as a tiny boy, when first we went to the high mountain place.

Again I could communicate with the tribe by my gift of language. They told me they were waiting for us. Their shaman came forth and said he had a vision of the approach of a white spirit-man and his native helper, who needed help from him and his people. Elmira's physical appearance was always a good blend with the native people, and he looked like one of the tribes. I, because of the whiteness now of my skin since my healing, complemented by my white long hair and beard, was always seen as a spirit walker. Remembering that albinos were associated with Great Spirit, I found that my appearance usually worked for me, rather than against me.

It was comforting to be by the fire. We often built a fire at our resting places, but to be with this group now was delightful. We hungered to interact with others, since it had been somewhat of a lonely journey thus far. This tribe was refreshing as the people were near childlike in their happiness to see us and make us comfortable. They soon prepared fish and some type of dried flat bread their women made, from a finely grown powder they carried in their backpacks, baked in the fire. We hadn't eaten well on this passage and were losing our body insulation of fat. According to the people we spoke with, we had been at least two moons on our trek. As we had traveled, we had mostly eaten bark. If we crossed a stream, we might ask for the gift of a fish. Elmira had made a rack from twigs that fit on his back. Sometimes we would cut a few fish into strips and hang the strips from this frame, where they quickly froze. He wouldn't let me carry the rack. He appointed himself chief cook and keeper of the food. The frozen fish were a great help in fueling the energy we needed, to carry on at the physical level.

The fish we now enjoyed were prepared by digging a hole and putting the entire fish into it, then making a fire on top. When the coals of the fire had become red hot, the women sang their song of thanks-giving. At the end of the song the red-hot coals were pushed aside, the fish was dug up and removed. Then more wood was added, to bring the fire back to a full blaze. Brushing the sand off the now-baked fish, it was served on platters of bark that were passed around. Everyone pulled some of the cooked flesh from the bones and partook of the feast, all seated around the warm blazing fire. Fish this fresh and taken within a respectful manner has a taste that is nearly indescribable. Children say it best, when they say "Yummy!"

As I was enjoying the meal, I began to think of how the little things in life were the foundation of the bigger things. By that I mean the simple sharing of this meal, the happy faces of our hosts, showed that these people had an attitude of gratitude. No matter what corruption of attitudes manifested, under it all was a divine truth I realized. That truth was that all creation knew it was One, and that Onement attitude was the essence of God. On this journey of understanding, in which my work became global in scope, I needed to see how all creation kept its goodness, or 'God-ness'.

My mission hadn't changed but my perception of it broadened, right there in that moment of sharing, as I realized that the essence of God's true intention was always present, no matter how many shaky structures of fear masked it. God's intention was for all creation to love itself, not fear itself. Fear was responsible for corruption of self-worth. These people didn't struggle with issues of feeling worthy of sharing their abundance. Nor did they think Elmira, and I unworthy strangers.

Fear is a great liar, but still a huge force when those who live their lives within that false concept feed it. Fear eventually devours itself. Even so, it is not always a destructive thing, as it could be life-preserving in situations of danger; that's true. My mind was racing a mile a minute and those around me were respecting my pondering and quietness.

I realized that it was the misuse of the fear instinct that stopped the flow of evolution. It was this very thing that brought me and my dear wife to this planet to plant seeds of change, along with others on the same soul mission. There are rules to incarnational[191] experience and one is that you emerge into this physicality through the channel of forgetting at the time of birth, so that you rediscover the reason you came. That discovery is your journey of experience. Some have a talent to remember easier and those of us who were sent into this time of need had that ability. God's Divine plan is always discovery. On this day, upon this frozen beach, it clearly dawned upon me. I discovered that I didn't have to change attitudes at the most basic core level, because that is ever a place of Onement–a place where sharing is natural and judgment is not allowed to separate creation in action.

These people knew the fish died so we could live on in the physical, and they honored the sacrifice. They also respected the grain their bread was made from, and water from the streams for drinking and cooking and so forth. Thus, they were at this moment in time, in complete balance and within Onement. They were the 'grail manifest',[192] the symbolic union of the masculine blade and the feminine womb, the receptacle of the soul, filled with gratitude and shared with us in Holy Communion.

On this journey I wanted to see how the tribes compared with each other. I had found many attitudes among them, some more fearful and violent than others. Now I realized that under it all, in some way, Elmira and I had managed to arrive at a point with each group we visited, in which there was a non-judgmental sharing of something divine. We had pierced the fear. I now knew that to pierce the fear was the first step in dissipating it.

A couple of children came and performed some dances for us. In spite of all the food and entertainment, Elmira and I both quickly fell asleep there by the fire, and I don't remember the children finishing their gift of dance. We awoke in early morning, and no one was present. The fire was still warming us, but now back to red embers again. We lay upon pine boughs, covered by our robes. Next to us, carefully laid on tree bark, were more cooked fish and bread. Each dish held a lone feather, not to eat, of course, but as an

---

[191] Being incarnated or in the flesh at the physical level
[192] The receptacle that symbolizes perfect balance and fulfillment

## Jeshua's Song

offering of love. My feather was that of an eagle, Elmira's feather was an owl's; the power birds of day and night. They understood the balance needed between us. We arose and performed our morning ritual of bathing and cleansing, then enjoyed the meal left for us. This private maintenance of the body we accomplished alone in the forest that hemmed the beach. We both found a private place to prepare for the day and used the cool white snow to scrub our bodies clean. Then we shared the hope for the day over the morning feast, blessed by our gift feathers, which we used as we had seen so often done, to smudge the smoke over ourselves.

As we finished our morning rituals and wondered what next, we noticed two men standing on the beach near our fire. They looked more like the Vikings of the land of Caledonia[193] than the people of this land. They stood next to a long boat, with a high carved serpent head at the front and an equally high carved serpent tail at the rear. They just stood there and stared at us. As we walked toward them, they gestured that we should get into the boat. Going back to retrieve our robes and meager supplies, we soon climbed into the serpent boat. The strong men who had fetched us rowed this strange vessel out to sea. No one spoke.

The boat had to dodge floating ice as we moved ever outward. Elmira was never comfortable with large bodies of water, and I could see he was a bit nervous. Putting my hand on his trembling hand, I indicated that we had trusted our intuition to this point, and that I was sure all would be well. His hand stopped shaking. We began piercing a fog that arose from the sea, colder than the air. One of our boatmen took a bell and rang it three times. He did this at three intervals, and we heard three rings come back, nearly like an echo. This continued; the three rings, then the returning echoing rings that got louder and louder, until the rings were right upon us. Visibility in such a fog is difficult at best, but I didn't expect to nearly collide with a huge version of the same boat in which we were afloat. I simply saw a wall of wood and heard the bell right over me. We had arrived at an enormous longboat ship. Our boatmen maneuvered our boat into a sling that floated just under

---

[193] Another name for Scotland, along with Alba

the water. Then I heard the cranking of a wench. We were lifted from the water and swung to the deck of the bigger ship and surrounded by other rugged looking sailors.

Elmira and I were glad to step out on the deck of the much larger boat. The waves were getting quite high and choppy, and I was getting as nervous as my guardian about the endless rolling sea and what our fate would be. Once, long ago, I had managed to walk upon the sea, but that had been a calm warm day and my concentration sufficient to levitate. The cold water and ice were too daunting for me to consider this technique here. I was grateful for the sailors, who knew how to manage a small boat in rolling waves.

Helped out of the smaller boat, we were taken to a cabin at the front of the ship. An ornate door, with carvings depicting dragons painted in bright colors, was opened. We were ushered into a small space, to the man in command, the captain, no doubt. He said, "I've been asked to pick you up, on this god-forsaken frozen beach; for what I don't know, but the request was urgent according to my spirit talker." He looked toward a man standing to the side of us, who I hadn't noticed when we entered the room. I had the feeling this was none other than his 'spirit talker.'

I immediately recognized the garb of the Magi. He stood tall and lean, and was much darker in complexion than the burly others of this group, who were light of skin with red or gold hair. He didn't wear the horned helmet either; instead the distinctive checkered turban of the Magi covered his head. He had a long red robe wrapped around his body, with one corner thrown over his shoulder. He looked at me, bowed his head and said, "I'm honored to be of assistance."

"I'm honored that you have recognized our need," I said.

"It's you who have recognized your need," he replied, as he quietly left the cabin. Elmira and I remained with the captain.

I introduced myself to the captain. He didn't tell me his name, however. It wasn't his custom to utter his name, unless in a conquest or in sacred ceremony, I sensed. To do so would be to give away his power. He needed as much power as he could muster, just to keep this ship afloat. He was a Viking, through and through. These men, as I saw no women, were a rugged lot and reminded us of our previous experience in the land of Alba, where the Vikings had come to pillage and plunder. They were a strange lot, I thought, so prone to violence. There was something about them, they didn't reveal often to strangers, that could be just as giving as the Picti People tribes I met, and also as the beach people had demonstrated last evening.

"I ask that you don't talk to my men," the captain announced with a firm commanding voice, breaking the silence between us. "If you need fresh air, stay at the forefront of the ship, get your breath of fresh air, then immediately go back to your assigned quarters, which are directly under the deck and accessible by a trap door behind the head of the dragon," he ordered. "If we have food to spare, we'll bring it to you and leave it in a basket by the trap door. If we don't have any food to spare, the basket will be empty. When we reach a place to drop you off, we will immediately unburden ourselves of your presence. We have a small boat; we will donate to your cause. It seems my good friend, and spirit talker advisor, believes that giving you safe passage and a boat, when we come close to landfall, will bring us good luck. We always accept good luck." With that, he dismissed us.

We were shown to the tiny compartment, at the front of the ship under the deck. It was cramped and the ride was rough in that ever-bobbing location. The great prow of the ship, looking like a fierce dragon, coursed through the water, going up and then down over the waves it pierced. Before we were unceremoniously deposited in the compartment, I noticed we were under sail and still oarsman rowed the huge vessel, as they sought to redirect it. I could hear whips snapping and someone yelling at those who rowed the ship, to reorient her to the direction we would take. I felt sorry for the oarsmen already, even if it was partially by their power that we were underway.

Elmira and I huddled together in that small dark place, but comfortable in our buffalo robes with some dry frozen fish and a little bread, thanks to our friends on the beach. We could hear the head oarsman singing his song of rhythm, so the slaves, chained at the oars, would row in the same unified moment. I felt sad for those men, feeling the sting of the whip if they got out of sync.

Our little compartment seemed as a haven compared to their lot. I prayed for them. After my prayer, Elmira and I fell asleep, wrapped in our warm skin robes. I awoke hours later and didn't hear the song of the rowers. The wind had taken the dragon vessel out into the open sea, and it was nearly flying across the top of the water at a good speed. I felt nauseated, not being used to the motion of the ship still slightly bobbing along with us in the position of the greatest motion. I opened the portal from our chamber, climbed to the deck, hung my head over the side and purged my stomach. The men on deck laughed at me and made fun of my wrenching. I stood there, letting the cool air clear my senses. Feeling eyes watching me, I turned and saw the captain, standing just behind me with his arms crossed looking, as usual, displeased. I thought I had better disappear into my chamber again. Before I managed to descend, he nodded toward the basket he promised. It held two lemons. I hadn't seen lemons, since I had left my family at the City of the Rose. They were a precious fruit, no matter where one found them. I looked again to make sure I wasn't hallucinating and yes, there were two beautiful large yellow lemons in the basket.

The captain said, "Make a small hole at the nipple end of the fruit and nurse it like you would your mother. Only take a sip at a time, and you'll not feel the ache in your belly so bad." Then he turned and left.

Elmira had the same reaction upon awakening, as I had. The lemons made all the difference in our comfort. They cut through the nausea and eased the spasms of the stomach. I realized another divine gift came forth in our time of need. I knew that lemons were precious to these men, and I was grateful the captain saw fit to share them with us. The next time I saw him, I thanked him.

"I hate the smell of vomit!" was all he said, and then dropped two more lemons into our basket.

After that we didn't seem to be bothered by the motion anymore. From time to time, we would find coarse bread or raw fish in the basket, too. We pretty much slept most of the time, not having any light in our compartment. The logistics of such a tight space kept our minds busy. It was difficult to do the elimination process of physicality, but we managed to find a bucket with a rope on it and realized our waste went into it. Then we dumped it overboard and cleaned out the bucket with the water of the sea. We used the same bucket in which to wash our clothes as well. We learned why cleaning was a constant activity on such a ship. We didn't eat much so having a toilet was not a huge problem. I finally had to ask for fresh water, remembering that outside of the agreed upon food, drinking water hadn't been discussed. It was the Magi who brought us water from time to time. He had a certain musical knock, he would make on our portal door on the deck. Since he was the only one who ever summoned us like that, it was a welcome sound to hear from time to time.

I believe we had traveled a few weeks, before we heard a different knock and the captain announced we would depart from the ship. We were put in a small dugout boat and lowered to the rough sea surface. The Magi, who seldom spoke, said, "I wish you well, master," he put his hands together and bowed his head, as he had when we first met. This was comforting, since we weren't sure what was happening, and we couldn't see land. Yet, I have to admit I wondered–was this a version of walking the plank, as I heard some ships did to rid themselves of undesirables, as I saw no landfall?

We asked which direction to take and the captain just ignored us. The Magi pointed in the direction we should go, and then pointed to his heart. I knew this meant 'follow your heart.' As our little vessel was lowered, we found two very old oars on the floor. Rowing our rugged dugout boat away from the huge vessel, we began our separation from the dragon ship.

This little boat had no fancy carving. It was just a dug out tree made in the shape of a canoe, yet it was a precious gift. Had we not had some practice in navigating such a vessel, from our time with the native tribes in the land we left behind, we would've been in great trouble. When you coordinate the rowing, with one person at the forefront, one at the aft, and with the oars paddling on alternate sides, it's possible to course through the huge waves and still hold a direction. We soon saw landfall. It was dawn, the sun just coming up over the sea we were gliding upon. The morning light revealed a rugged shoreline. We could see big splashes of water, as the waves broke through a stony path to the sandy shore. We wondered how we would make it to the beach unscathed. Then I heard the Magi's voice again, like the mind-speak Elmira and I do.

"Lay flat inside the boat," he said, "you and your guardian face-to-face, and hug each other like never before. Your weight will keep the boat right side up and with no resistance; you'll allow it to find its path to shore."

We did just that, and felt no embarrassment as to our closeness; hanging on for our dear lives. The boat dipped and dove. We feared that it would smash on the boulders that protected the shoreline. But it found a path, as the Magi said it would, between the daunting boulders, following the flow of water. As our boat didn't resist the natural path of the incoming water, we ultimately ended up gently arriving on the beach. We climbed out of the boat, wondering where we had arrived. Pulling the craft ashore we followed our intuition again and proceeded north on the beach, walking along the well-smoothed sand for hours. Finally we decided to make camp for the night. The sandy beach skirted a jungle. We sensed we were being watched by all kinds of birds and animals, as we walked along. I assured them in animal-speak that we meant no harm and wished for safe passage.

We found some firewood. Using some flint rocks and dried moss, we soon had a blazing fire. This would be helpful just in case the animals didn't want to grant that safe passage I requested. We had taken off our buffalo robes earlier and strapped them to our backs, as it was a hot and humid. Now we would use them as sleeping mats, making ourselves comfortable for the night. We found some fruit in nearby trees and bushes, bananas and berries, and enjoyed them immensely. We hadn't had any fruit since our lemons on the ship. Exhausted, we laid back and fell asleep again asking the animals for safety and asylum, as we drifted off into a deep slumber.

I awoke in the night feeling like someone was watching me. Looking up into the dark night, since the fire had burnt itself out, I could see two sets of eyes shining even without the benefit of moonlight, since this was the time of the new moon. One set of eyes was higher, one lower. I could also hear what sounded like the loud purr of a cat. I startled and sat up. I could barely make out the outline of a person and a large cat.

"Greetings," the person said in a clicking language.

To my surprise, my language ability even included this difficult tongue, and I clicked back a response, saying, "Greetings as well, to you and your friend."

"You know us then, since you speak our tongue so easily," the female voice responded. There is something about the voice that can reveal gender, even in a dark night with no light from the moon.

"I don't know you. I just have a gift for languages," I replied.

"What a blessing, this gift you have," she replied. "I've been called to give you safe passage through this land. And I never travel anywhere without my own guardian," she said, as she stoked the cat. I could hear its pleasure in the slight shift of rhythm of its purr.

My guide began to play with the now dark coals of the fire. She must have added some fuel, for soon a small flame appeared, and I could see her face more clearly. She had short-cropped hair, bright-colored beads around her neck and also woven into a band around her head. Her breasts were bare and dangled freely, as she leaned over the fire. She wore some sort of skirt, wrapped around her middle, which hung to her knees. As she stooped there by the fire, her skirt covered her knees and just barely touched the ground. The huge cat, I found out later, was a cheetah, and it had a multi-colored beaded collar around its neck, as well. It was totally relaxed by her side and looked at her like she was the most beautiful sight to perceive. To us that was true, too.

Elmira, awake, just lay there, quietly watching as he often did, evaluating the situation. Then our new friend greeted him, calling him 'guardian,' which pleased him.

She stayed there in the same position, coaxing and tending the fire, until the sun rose, not saying much. Elmira and I went about our morning cleansing ritual, respecting her silence. Since the seawater was so warm we took our bath in the salty tide pools. Given that our visitor was nearly nude, we didn't think our striping down for our bath was a problem. We did strategically position ourselves on the other side of a beach boulder, however, as we enjoyed the dawning of a new day and the refreshing dip.

We found some more fruit and picked enough for our visitor, as she still sat there with a pleasant smile on her face. "Welcome to the land of your people," she finally said, as we prepared to leave. I looked at my whiter than white skin, then to her nearly blue-black skin and said, "Yes, all people are my people," thinking that was her meaning.

"That's true," she said, "but we are also the blood of your blood through your marriage, thus your children are our children, and that makes you one with us." It was then that I knew where we were. We were in the land of the Nubians, of course. MiryAmah's people had come from these regions. How did this wonder woman who talked so wisely know that, I thought?

Sensing my question, she said, "I am the shaman of the cat. I am from the priestesses who, for eons of time, have kept the line of communication open between our sisters. I have been asked to meet you and give you safe passage." She reminded me rather playfully, "You have, in addition, asked for this service, knowing that you need help to keep from being a food offering, for those that would see you as delicious." She sat quiet for a moment, as if considering if she should reveal more to me and finally said, "I know, because I read the water, as well. Your wife worries about your safety and sensed that you were in the land of her ancestors. She asked during her dreamtime, that you be kept protected on

581

your journey and her wish is granted. What then, is your intentional desire, master? For the new moon is the time to ask for fulfillment," she explained. MiryAmah had never let a new moon pass that she didn't do a ritual of intention.

"I wish to meet your people, to wander for awhile and meet some other tribes who live in this land of my wife's ancestors and probably mine as well," I answered. "I intend to learn from them," I explained. Her guardian, who was giving me the eye that cats do so well, caused me a little nervousness, and I said, "And I also wish that your great beautiful cat friend would not look at me, and then lick its lips that way."

The beautiful black priestess laughed in glee, throwing her head back and said, "She just wants to clean you up as she would a kitten."

I wasn't totally convinced. I knew that cats, such as this one, in the land of Egypt were kept at the royal residences for a purpose other than beauty. They were long legged and built for speed, and used to chase down and kill enemies. Once they saw their prey, nothing could out-run or out-smart them. I may know animal-speak, but this cat was keeping its mind closed to me, and I couldn't read its thoughts. It reminded me of the snow leopards in the high mountains; I had great respect for them, too and knew they wouldn't communicate either until they were good and ready.

"I'm known as Cheetah Woman," the shaman priestess finally said. I introduced Elmira and myself. "Shall we begin with the tribe of my birth?" she asked.

"Do you have another tribe?" I asked, because she had made reference to her birth people.

"All people are my tribe," she replied, echoing what I, myself, had said earlier, as she arose with her cat guardian by her side and moved into the jungle.

# THE PATH OF PEACE
## Chapter Forty-Five

Elmira and I followed the beautiful priestess and her majestic cheetah guardian, along narrow paths through the dense jungle. We would never have been able to pierce the landscape we now entered, nor move through such entanglement on our own and still hold a direction. We had total faith that we were headed in the right direction, since our travels had long been journeys of trust.

Life itself was a miracle to me. Everyone performs miracles on a daily basis. If someone wanted to 'deify' or 'demonize' you, they would do so by remembering those occasions and magnifying them, molding them into the shape they desired. My entire life was a miracle; so, too is yours. I was born a 'sensitive' as many of you are, as well. As such, you are finely tuned to the full scope of physicality and how it connects to spirit, through a divine web that encompasses 'All That Is'. They call this awareness, 'spirituality.' In truth, all creation is spirituality and physicality exists within this realm of divine relationship. It's important that this be understood, since I soon will be telling you of the shifting of my work yet again. Just remember, 'spirituality is the umbrella of the Divine, and all creation is under its protection.'

The global shape of the earth was well known by the ancients, especially the Magi, the expert stargazers. They understood that everything physical and experiential, including time, was a circle (cycle) in the $3^{rd}$ dimension sense, thus the circle was a globe. Later this truth was suppressed for the sake of control of the populace and because there were those people positioned in high places that enjoyed an ignorant arrogance. They didn't want to expand their awareness. They wanted a flat earth, where the threat of falling off would keep explorers within parameters. The seats of power, for the most part, had one agenda, to maintain their control and power. To do so meant to stop awareness, thus no exploration beyond what they foresaw was allowed.

Remember, 'Truth will set you free.' Thus, stories and legends that came down through time were often blocked by walls, or barriers, to 'knowing'. These barriers are the false structure upon which societies built their mental faith. Mental faith is not accurate; it is brain-training. Within such a state, you can convince people that they are unworthy. You can stop their inner exploration, as well as their exterior exploring. That's how you keep beings enslaved. The mental part of your being is intended to help you sort and shift your experiences. The faith part of your being is your intuitive confirmation that you are a divine entity discovering God.

The faith I was speaking of, when Elmira and I followed the people we encountered on our global journey, is the 'faith of the heart.' The heart will not lie to you, but the mind will. The mind can't handle a superior role, for it needs the heart to lead it, or it falls prey to fear. That doesn't mean one is better than the other, for the toe is no better than the thumb. It's just that the mind was created to serve as a supporter, not leader. It's not much different than trying to get a hand to do the job of a foot. It can be done, but it is best to let the feet do the walking and the hands do the grasping. When the mind is put in the leadership role, it becomes overwhelmed and begins to follow fear, disconnecting itself from the heart which would put it back on course. Thus, to preserve its 'fear of losing control,' the mind will manipulate what you think you are feeling within your heart. This very thing confuses many who don't know what they really feel, because feeling can't be rationalized even though the Greeks tried to do so. If the mind allowed the heart access, indeed it would push the intellect back into the position it was intended to hold, that of sorting and keeping guard. When the heart and the head are not in proper relationship, the heart will somehow find a way to correct the corruption. As a result, a nagging unsettled feeling haunts those, who live within the framework of fear. They know, at a most core level, that the structure of fear is shaky at best. Inside them, as always, there is love, a heart-oriented essence. Fear has its place but it must not be the ruler, it is intended to be the servant. The heart is the love portal and never afraid. The mind is the only place that fear can live. I'm not talking about physical organs here; rather I'm talking about the way the soul interacts as the body experiences physicality. I tell you this, so you will understand what my soul intention was, in this complex life I remember and share.

I want you to know that I wasn't only educating myself on my journeys, but I was spinning a heart-line that connected one person to another. When I met the Pictish tribes, then the more aggressive Vikings, even though they were as different as night and day in their attitudinal expressions and actions–one being more peaceful but would fight if necessary and the other more aggressive but could be peaceful from time to time–a fine filament of peace, which is the intention of God our Creator, was strung from one to the other. That filament of peace is what my global work was about.

I looked forward to meeting more of the people from the land of my wife's ancestors and faithfully followed Cheetah Woman through the jungle. By sunset, we entered the village of her people. They lived along a great plain on the edge of the jungle. They had herds of cattle that grazed upon the sparse grasses of this land. As we approached, I noticed several village children tending the cattle. The cattle watched the Cheetah who accompanied the priestess, but showed no fear. They could tell that this time Cheetah was not interested in their calves or the mothers, full of life-giving milk. So they just watched and eventually went back to grazing.

There was great excitement when we arrived at the community. They didn't often see a couple of people as odd as Elmira and me. They helped us set our bundles down, and then proceeded to inspect our backpacks. We didn't carry much; a few flint stones; some dried fish and fruit; a small knife and some herbs; as well as a gourd cup to hold liquids and our bison robes. I had given the sacred begging bowl away long ago. Those inspecting our bundles were most interested in the animal robes, not recognizing the species from which the skins had come.

The chief came forth, looking at Cheetah Woman, and in the clicking language said, "And who are these men you bring into our village?"

Cheetah Woman looked at me, and nodded for me to answer the question, as she wanted the chief to be as amazed as she had been, at the grasp I had of the clicking language.

I answered, "I am the Fisher One. This is my companion and friend. Elmira." I didn't use the name Jeshua, or Jesus, because we were too close to the land of my birth and persecution. I didn't want to reveal my survival of the crucifixion for the sake of my family, and because, at least in the illusion of my death, our followers had found strength.

"Fisher-One" the chief said the name, as if he was trying to understand it. "Does that mean you are a fisherman of the sea?" he asked, showing no sign of amazement at my grasp of his native tongue.

"No, I'm more a fisher of men and women," I answered. Seeing the confusion on the face of the chief, I went on to explain, "I don't catch men and women; rather I connect them together through a divine web, like a fish net made of love and respect." Then I drew an image of a web on the ground with my finger, showed him how I was in one location, and he was in another. Due to my visit, there was now a path from me to him, thus from my people to his people, making them united. I wanted to demonstrate in my drawing, that a new link in the web was then formed.

"This looks like the web of the poisonous black spider," he said. "How do I know that you aren't a demon, much like the spider, and what you want is to get me stuck in your web, or fish net, so that you can feast upon me and bring sorrow to my people?"

"The web is not sticky, and I'm not a demon spider, nor do I want to take your people in a net that would remove them from their comfortable home," I assured him, or tried to. "I come out of respect and ask for nothing. I have nothing to give, except connecting you and myself in a united peaceful alliance, I explained. "My net doesn't constrict; it unites and expands."

"Alliance?" he questioned. "Why should I ally myself with you? What is the benefit for me or my people?"

"People who don't feel connected don't respect each other. They feel separate. Thus, they justify the enslavement and killing of those to whom they feel no connection, due to that faulty-oriented mind judgment." I wanted him to realize, I wasn't from a certain tribe or group, so I explained, "My people are all people. I don't represent a tribe, even if my parents were of the tribe of Israel and my wife's ancestry is of your lineage near Egypt."

"Your wife is linked to us?" the chief asked, now looking more interested.

"Yes," I answered. "Her grandfather was Nubian."

"Go on then," he said, "convince me further."

"As I have lived and traveled, I have discovered that all people are more alike than different," I emphasized. "I have found that most aggression and suffering are caused from the separation within one's self, and within families and tribes."

"How is that so?" the chief asked.

"First, and foremost, I've found often, it is those who beat down their wives and daughters, who are the unhappiest. They know beyond their mind-logic that their heart-faith can't support this lie, thus there is always uneasiness inside of them."

The chief nodded agreement. "Is that what killed your wife?" he asked.

"She's not dead, chief," I answered, "but we are forced to keep her in a safe place. She continues our work from where she is. With the two of us working together, but from different locations we can do more good. There are those who don't want to be united. They would kill my wife and family, if I didn't keep them separate from me. It's my greatest sorrow to leave them."

He looked genuinely sad at this news. He told me that among the tribes were those who attributed bad luck, to their wives inviting it to them. He could understand why I would keep my family in a safe secret place.

It troubled me to hear this, yet I had seen it many times, women being blamed for bad luck in any shape or form. I replied to the chief, "I think when there is this confusion within oneself, always an underlying feeling that something is not right, haunts you. Most think the uneasiness is due to vulnerability of security. They attribute that to the women first, then to the enemy, or those they feel separate from." Carefully making sure the chief heard me right, I continued, "They separate themselves, because inside of us, we are all equally male and female, in essence. The genders are but a physical manifestation of the essence of our beings for this life sojourn and that which is the reflection of our maker. At birth, we choose which gender to wear on the outside while the other stays inside to balance us." I think the chief understood my line of reasoning, so I went on. "And when we reject our tender feelings, our intuitions, and favor the logical mind, it makes us lose track of our hearts." I knew this was a pretty philosophical concept, but as a chief, he would have pondered such ideas in many ways.

"The mind separates, as it should; for it's a place to sort and keep track," I explained. "The heart unites, as it was divinely designed, so we would know the divinity of all creation, thus respect and unite it. We are made so we have a balance inside us–masculine or active factors, and feminine, which are reactive aspects–so that we can meet the challenge of physicality and find the divinity within. Wisdom is our ability to use both aspects of ourselves. Strength is our ability to act upon the wisdom appropriately," I explained, "and you know this already, or you wouldn't be the chief here." Realizing I was teaching again, I hoped I hadn't overstepped my dedication to listening. I didn't want to confuse the situation and cause a change that would be too drastic, thus could be destabilizing, since I wasn't sure what the customs were for this chief's tribe.

"I am Vulcan," the chief said, finally introducing himself to me. "My totem is the vulture. I know how to utilize that which others may think is beyond use. I'm now looking at a stranger, who comes bearing a robe of white from an animal I dreamed of many times. Each time the animal, bigger than the water buffalo, came closer and closer to me. Last night, I dreamed the animal walked into my village. But what walks in? You arrive, a man, as white as the snow in the high mountain places, carrying the skin of the noble animal that dream-talked to me. I have to ask myself, why is this so? Did this man, who understands my language and speaks it as well as one born to it, take the soul of my spirit animal, the buffalo of another place? Is this man, who might be a demon hiding his true identity, about to bring suffering and pain to my people? I must circle around you like a vulture, see if you are putrid and dead inside, or alive, and not ready for me to tear you to pieces and reuse your essence yet," he warned.

The chief was tall, as was everyone in this tribe of blue-black people. He also had colored beads in his hair and around his neck. In addition he had a necklace with talons and black feathers from the vulture, dangling from it. Arising from the stooped position he had been holding while speaking with me–I hadn't realized how tall he was–he looked down at me with a most piercing look. He walked in circles around me again and again; his long legs seemed bird-like. I noticed Elmira was watching the entire situation very closely. I flashed him a glance that said, "Be patient." This was a critical moment of evaluation, and I didn't want violence to flare. I wanted to defuse it and infuse peace, instead with this man and his people.

"You don't fear me, Fisher One?" he asked.

"Yes, I do," I answered.

"Good answer," he said. "Why do you fear me, Fisher One?"

I replied, "Because I'm not sure if you understand that I have come in peace, and that I speak your language, not because I'm a demon, but because I'm divinely blessed."

"Oh! You claim the Gods sent you then, as one of their own?" the chief asked.

"The Gods sent us all. What I'm telling you is I was given a bequest when I was on the brink of death. I entered the spirit realm, ready to give up on this physical life, and was sent back to walk this land, near and far, and pave a path of peace. To do so, spirit gave me the gift of understanding and speaking every language I encountered without learning it, just instantly knowing it, so there would be no barrier of confusion. This gift has been a great tool to understand all creation. It also has been perplexing to many, who believe that to speak as well as I do in their own tongue means, either I was adopted into their tribes as a babe and was forsaken, or, they fear I'm some demon who took their language, so I could pierce their confidence. None of these are true. The truth is that by dying and coming back again, I have a message to bear. That's the divine part. That message is peace—first within oneself, then within one's family and finally, within one's tribe. When that happens, tribe-to-tribe peace is possible. I'm a weaver of peace. My visit is an important thread in this Cloak of God, some call the web. If you choose to kill me, my weaving ends here. I hope you allow me and my companion safe passage however, for we have more peace paths to make before I have accomplished my mission."

Vulcan looked over at Elmira and asked, "He is not of your tribe. Why do you travel together?"

I answered, "Because he accepted the call to be my guardian from the time of my childhood."

Still looking at Elmira, he asked, "Is this true, man?"

Elmira nodded 'yes.'

"Speak up," the chief commanded.

Elmira pointed to his mouth, opened it, showing no tongue to form words.

"Who did this to this, man?" the chief demanded, looking back at me clearly agitated, with his eyes blazing. "You, who claim to speak for peace, would have your guardian silenced?"

"Elmira came to me without a tongue," I answered, "but he speaks eloquently in our mind-to-mind silent speaking. His silence has made me listen to myself better. He's one of my greatest teachers and his devotion to my safety has been my blessing. He keeps a promise better than anyone I have ever known. He's a great man and I hope one day to be worthy of his unending devotion," I said, as I looked toward Elmira, who was now closing his eyes and trying to disappear, as he didn't want praise, and felt uncomfortable receiving it.

"I can see, by the way you look at your servant," the chief said, "that you love him."

"He is not my servant," I clarified, "he's my friend. He's a free man, and always has been, since I met him when I was but a small boy."

"Hmmm," the chief murmured and I could see he was in deep thought. "I don't think you are dead enough yet in spirit, so I think I won't have to tear you to bits. So, I shall receive you as an honored guest, instead of an enemy, and leave your bones to pick another day."

The entire village had been standing quietly, watching and listening to the proceedings. They let out joyful clicking yells and danced, jumping high into the air like excited children, eager to enjoy a great party. When the chief made up his mind, the fear and rejection were immediately replaced by joy.

We were given a hut to rest within. Our backpacks were carefully laid out for us, with nothing missing. Water was brought to refresh and cleanse. Some fruit was left as well. We were told that we would feast further at sundown. We could hear the village people hustling about, preparing for celebration. As guests of honor we wanted to give something back to the people. Elmira and I decided, we would wrap up our buffalo robes and give them to Cheetah Woman and Vulcan. We didn't need them anymore. Vulcan had dreamed of the white buffalo, shaggier than the native wild water buffalo of his land, so there must be a connection between him and the robe. Dreams are often pathways for spirit. I heeded the message that this robe should be his now and was glad that someone who understood the importance of it would receive it.

At sundown, we were ushered into the center of the village, to the place of festivity around the central fire. The fire was huge this evening and the heat of it kept the people back in a wide circle around it. Elmira and I were taken to the chief and Cheetah Woman, who was seated next to him, with her ever-protecting guardian cat by her side. Before being seated, we stood facing these two on the ground, sitting cross-legged comfortably. We stooped down, so our heads were lower than theirs and at the same time offered our gifts. Elmira handed his reddish robe to Cheetah Woman; I offered my white buffalo robe to Vulcan.

"We offer these gifts in gratitude for your hospitality," I said. "These robes come from a noble animal across the ocean, and they are vital to the natives of that land. These buffalo roam along great seas of grass, like a mighty ocean with no water. There are so many buffalo; one can sometimes see a herd pass by on the run from sunup to sundown." The chief looked pleased and said they had plains herds too, the wildebeests that migrated once a year. He said they often took hours to pass by as well.

I continued, "These buffalo give a sacrifice of their meat, so the native people can live. They give their skins, so the people can make homes that they carry across the land and move where the huge herds of buffalo roam. This mighty animal also provides hides to make clothing from, and bones to make tools, which made the peoples' life easier. They are sacred to the plains tribes," I emphasized, "and once in awhile, a white one appears as a messenger of the Great Spirit. It's never sacrificed for the sake of the people; but when it dies, nothing is wasted. A woman, who reminds me of Cheetah Woman, shape-shifts so that one minute she is a white buffalo, the next she is a wise elder. She gave me this robe, which I now offer to you, Vulcan. Consider this a gift of spirit, left behind as the soul of the white buffalo departed and shape-shifted finally into one being. You, Vulcan, know what to

## The Saga-Oracle

do with such things, and the extent of the gifts of transition, which most can't comprehend."

He nodded his head, as he was named for his ability to process that with which others couldn't bear to deal.

"May this white buffalo robe unite your people with those across the great ocean," I said. "And, the people of the jungle and the savannahs, now unite with the people of the grasslands and the forests, and become brothers and sisters, so there is always a path of peace between you."

Vulcan gracefully reached out and took his gift. As he did, so the lovely priestess who brought us to these people took her gift as well.

"The spirit gods work in mysterious ways," he said. "I can't think of a gift more welcome to me than this robe of white. I didn't realize the white spirit animal of my dreams was sending such a gift to me in this form. Now I know it was trying to tell me it had died or transformed, and still had gifts to offer. I am Vulcan, the vulture chief," he said to everyone, holding up the robe so all could see. "Death has brought me a Divine gift. Death is just a change in form. I accept this gift for myself, but more for all of you, who shall be blessed by the path of peace that connects our tribes."

Cheetah Woman simply wrapped herself in her robe, hair side out, and petted it in appreciation.

We only stayed about a week. We found a peaceful tribe after all, somewhat of a surprise, after the interrogation from the chief. Nevertheless, since the people shared the land with other tribes, many of which were aggressive, he had to be strong and careful when dealing with strangers.

Cheetah Woman was their guardian priestess, yet she didn't live with them. She was more solitary like the cats she loved. I learned that it was a rare occasion she visited, nonetheless, she always watched out for them. Those, such as she, were born with the ability to see more, were super sensitive, and mysteriously in tune with nature. They were nurtured and trained to be intuitive guardians of the tribe from which they emerged. One day she might take a child under her wing and train another guardian priestess. Upon the age of maturity, these priestesses married the tribe, instead of a man, and went to live in isolation. There were few in number–as we understood, as rare as White Buffalo Woman–and were held in high esteem. They showed up now and then, only to disappear as quickly and quietly as they had come, which was the case with Cheetah Woman. She arose from the fire, after receiving her robe, and just walked into the jungle. She was not spoken of, nor did she appear again to us, before we left. Elmira was delighted that she walked out of camp wearing the buffalo robe he had given her. Obviously, she had accepted the gift full measure.

We wandered the land of the black people for many months. Again we met tribes of a peaceful nature and those more violent. As in the land beyond the ocean, I asked the people to explain to me, why they harbored hate and aggression. I listened to their answers and didn't attempt to balance their thinking; rather, I just let them listen to their own reasoning. I hoped that seeds of peace would be planted. In every case, there was eventual acceptance of Elmira and myself. When I explained the Path of Peace, some understood and some didn't. In a way I believe Elmira and I were healing the invisible web, the 'Akasha records' some call the web of light and sound, that we all weave upon our journeys of experience, even as we forged new connection paths. My beloved MiryAmah loved to call this web, 'The Cloak of God.' Elmira and I, in our global wanderings, could begin the healing process at certain points upon this Divine Cloak, just by connecting the pathway of peace, as we wandered from tribe to tribe. I was grateful for his constant company. It would have been a lonely walk unaccompanied. Sometimes, it appeared that I was alone. For at times we decided he would stay quietly behind the scenes. This was done as the need arose, however, most of the time we walked together, as we did when I was but a wandering boy.

We moved from the nation of the black people, to the areas I had visited as a child, near the high mountain place. There were vast lands peopled by Mongolian tribes and people of Asian descent. Elmira came from the Mongolian people, and it was a sweet/sour homecoming for him to enter the region again. I could see the strain on his now-elderly face. The wrinkles and deep, sad, eyes of the elders is not so much due to age, but due to what they've seen and the challenges they've met in their long lifetimes. His face was full of opposing memories. He didn't mind-speak of his childhood, nor did he tell me about his days as a slave and the torture to keep him silent, as we walked his homelands. Even so, we did make a pathway of peace.

One day upon the open land of the nomadic Mongols, we encountered a lone walker. This one walked slowly, stooped over, every step obviously an exhausting effort. I worried that the wanderer would fall and not be able to arise, for fragility was apparent. I walked over to the lone walker, put my arm around the person and quietly asked if I could help.

"You have learned well," the lone walker said to me, and I realized my master teacher was this frail elder one. He seemed to have shrunk in size and was no bigger than a child.

"How can this be?" I asked. "You can't have aged so much, since I last saw you in the water," I remarked, remembering the most recent time I scryed and he appeared.

"You look different to me, Jeshua, as well," he answered, as he just realized I was now an elder myself, with long white hair and beard. "I've been looking for you, lad," again reverting to seeing me as a young boy.

"How long have you looked?" I asked out of concern.

"A long time now," was his answer.

"Why didn't you urge me somehow to come to you? Why is it that you and I look different in the scrying water?" I asked.

"Because we see each other as a soul essence, not as a physical presence," he explained, to answer one question. To the other question, he said, "I wanted to encounter you this way before I left this old body of mine. I wanted to just run into you, without the use of bi-location, which I have never been all that good at," he emphasized. "I wanted to touch you and know that you have found your path, and that finally you have arrived at peace within your time in the physical. You have had such a difficult mission, lad," he said, with such gentleness and conviction. "How you managed to keep your soul from retreating, I have no clue."

"Without you, I would never have stayed the course," I reminded him.

"And without you, there would not be a path of peace either, for your gift is in being a master of peacemaking," he told me.

We found a nearby rock that offered some protection from the wind, picking up across the vast open lands. We made a fire to comfort my teacher. We were all silent while trying to make a temporary sanctuary. Finally, I put my thoughts into words.

"I think I have accomplished making a path of peace," I said to my teacher. "But I fear I have failed to accomplish a good path in my own first homeland. I tried to open pathways within the minds of those my beloved and I visited. I tried to open the minds of men, so they could see into their own hearts, but I fear I failed. I suspect that for a long time war and violence will have its way in that region of my beginning." I began to weep, for I knew all was not well in the Middle Eastern place of my birth. "I don't think I pierced the hatred the people hold as walls around their hearts," I said, through my sobs. "I haven't stopped the suffering of the women and fear I have made it worse for them to bear. I wanted to be an example of love in balance, and I became a threat."

My teacher put his arm around my shoulder, pulled me to his chest and let me cry it out. Finally, he said, "You have given all any soul can give to that situation. People will say you died to cleanse their sins, and they will deny the great love of your life, but that's not the truth. You died as Jesus, because of their sins of ignorance. Not to know is not a sin; but to refuse to know, when the opportunity offers enlightenment, is a sin," he said, in a rasping

## The Saga-Oracle

whisper. "You showed them divinity within themselves and within their relationships with their wives and daughters."

Stopping to gain some strength, he continued on and said, "They defiled the divine gift. For that, their nation will hold karmic debt, for what is sown will be reaped. You have sown good (God) seeds. I promise you, someday what you planted will be reaped," he assured me. "Those who live in fear of change have sown corrupted thorny weeds. Those thorns will eventually tear them apart. When all misconceptions are cleared away, the Divine harvest will be celebrated and shared," he whispered.

He held me and rocked me like a baby, using his waning strength to comfort me. Elmira had wet eyes as well. As usual, Elmira silently suffered his own regrets, here in his homeland.

At the dawning of the day, my teacher was so weak, he could hardly speak. "Son," he called me. "You are like a son to me, even as I know you had a father of greatest gentleness and wisdom. I am grateful Joseph shared such as you with us, trusting we would be able to keep you safe and help you develop your level of mastery as a peacemaker. I have to leave the physical body now. I ask a favor of you. Will you burn my body and take my ashes back to our mountain sanctuary?"

"I will do anything for you, master teacher. You know that. But must you leave now?"

"I must and you know I must." Then coughing and mustering up enough strength, he said. "You will follow me soon. You have taken the path of peace around the globe and reached nearly every land. The places you have not reached, other masters, possibly from the places you already touched, will make pathways. Soon, I will meet you in the land of spirit, and we will work at a universal level. I will look forward to our reunion," he said and passed out of his body, which sagged lifeless in my arms.

I held him all day long and well into the next night. I rocked his body, which also rocked mine, in its love. As the morning dawned, I saw Elmira had been up most of the day and night, preparing a great platform for the proper send-off for my master. To find wood in this open land was not easy. It had to be wood already down, not still connected in physicality to mother earth, our Tara. I hadn't even noticed Elmira's absence. He had found enough sacred downed wood to make a great fire. He had also dug a security channel around the fire bed, so the grassland didn't become part of the cremation ritual. He had lots of dried pine boughs, dropped from the trees dotting the open land surrounding us. They were lying on the platform he had made. He ripped strips from his own clothes to tie the structure together. He waited until I looked ready to release my master, who I loved dearly. Elmira knew me well, he could tell just by the look on my face, when the time was right.

I looked at him and nodded my head. He carefully lifted my beloved teacher from my lap and holding him easily, walked over to the platform, which was about knee high, and laid him gently down. We both arranged the teacher's tattered robes and smoothed his face, making sure his eyes were closed. I kissed him on the forehead. He had no hair to smooth, but I ran my hand over his baldhead anyway. I wished he did have some hair, because I would have cut a piece to carry with me until the end of my days in this physical realm. Getting my flints out of my small bundle of supplies, I ignited the pine branches. Elmira knew I must light the fire. Even though I knew my master was not in his body, I still felt much sorrow as the fire consumed the physical vehicle of one so near and dear to me. I sat upon the ground with my head in my hands, waiting for the spark of the last ash to fade. Then I sat some more. I don't know how much longer, but evidently it was long enough for the ashes to cool. Elmira gently took his wide knife and began making a pile of the ashes. I had found a brass vessel among the master teacher's things, brought it to the fire pit, and we put his ashes inside it. I had seen such containers before. That was their purpose. My master teacher knew he was not going home the way he left.

I'm not sure if we were there one or two days, or maybe more. But when we left, we headed toward the mountains to take my master home. His spirit was free, however, and I felt his love and gratitude, which was what I needed to give me strength to fulfill his last request.

## PRECIOUS INNOCENCE; LOST, THEN FOUND
Chapter Forty-Six

Moving in the direction of the mountain sanctuary, we encountered fewer and fewer people. The terrain wasn't easy to navigate, as it went from grassy plains, to low mountains, and then the higher peaks of the Himalayas.

I reflected upon this life sojourn as I walked along and entertained myself with 'what if's,' as in, 'what if I could live openly with my family?' and so forth. I thought about the different languages I could speak and even write if I wished. A walking meditation can take one anywhere. Even as I relate this story, I think of how languages hold keys of discovery. For instance, the word 'live,' in this language I have used to share my life story, is just one letter different from the word 'love'. The 'i' is like a symbol of the individual, who refers to themself as 'I'. The 'o' in love is mindful of the circle of unity, which is how love unites all that is. I thought about how fear holds things back by reversing energy, and pondered the word 'live' again, how if you inverted it, the word 'evil' came forth. Yet, as I remembered these walking meditations, other words in other languages had the same keys. My gift of languages seemed to race through my head, showing me many codes to understanding how attitudes and paradigms work within different cultures. I realized the underlying key, to understand the people who spoke the tongue, was to look carefully at the words they used for good and bad. It was all there in the speech they spoke, that echoed out into their actions and reactions to the situations they encountered. I knew your English language even then, for there was not a language I didn't know backwards and forwards in time. I thought about the way antiforce was viewed, personified as the 'devil,' which is 'lived' in reverse. Walking quietly invites much pondering; walking with my best friend who can't speak and the ashes of my master teacher in my backpack invited much reflection.

All this walking and thinking finally brought me to the realization that I was getting weak and feeling old. I couldn't hold a scry session, even if I could find an appropriate reflective place to try it. I knew in my heart that I was a father again, for passion, combined with the deep devoted love my wife and I felt at our few intimate times, always proved fruitful. Lately, I often had night and day dreams of a sweet little girl. She would always just look at me and say, "Tomorrow. Tomorrow." I thought that meant that one day I would see her, but not today. Actually, as it turns out, she was referring to her chosen name, Tamara[194] and I was not hearing her correctly, as I was beginning to lose my ability to mind-talk clearly.

Names carry the vibration of sound, just as bodies carry the vibration of light. The two together are the components that create the web of God, or Akasha, I have spoken of before, as experience through discovery is accomplished in the realm of the physical. Children pick their own names. If the chosen name is overridden by their parents or anyone else, they will ultimately get themselves oriented to the point where they will adopt the name they were born to carry, sooner or later. In cultures where names are chosen at different points in one's life, this custom helps the soul achieve the name it prefers as well, as progression along that sojourn unfolds. When wives adopt husband's names upon marriage, there is a shifting in vibration to accommodate the connection. The intent can be one of power or honor, depending on the situation. Life experience will bring a need to change names as well. By this time, I had been known by many names: Yeheshua, Jesus, Esa, Jeshua, Fisher One, White Robe, The White Wanderer, and on and on. Perhaps my favorite one was just being called 'Lad' by my master teacher, even though I was now an elder myself. Pet names are full of love. Petty names, however, are the opposite. Those who tag others with false names are trying to defuse their divine energy and bully them out of the sacredness of their life's journey.

---

[194] Derived from the name Tamar in the biblical times which meant 'Palm Tree', in India it means 'Lotus Blossom'

# The Saga-Oracle

Quiet walking is one of the best forms of meditation one can do. Even the animals meditate upon such rhythmic movement, because the act of walking is similar to the evolution of consciousness, it just keeps going forward, slow but sure.

Even with the rhythm of movement as I walked, I was still feeling weaker and weaker as time progressed. Maybe I was giving my aches and pains too much attention, I thought, and then I heard something unusual. It sounded like weeping, but in a soft form of the sadness. I could feel someone close by. When you walk in the wilderness, you get a sense of who is present within your path, be it human or not. I was definitely feeling something other than the nature creatures usually nearby. Even Elmira was looking all around, trying to identify the sound and from whence it came.

I saw some birds sitting on a large rock. They would flit up; fly around, then return, clearly interested in something. They were little birds, not birds of prey, thus I found this behavior odd. What had their attention was a small woman curled into a ball, holding her protruding stomach.

I bent down and pulled her robe from her face. I knew she was from the land of India at first glance, for the indigo spot upon her forehead was my first vision of her very young face. "Why do you weep, lady?" I asked.

She just looked at me and said in her tiny voice, "Why do you care?"

"Because I do," I said, as I tried to sit her up, noticing she was full of child and about to burst, it seemed. She was very weak and probably had not had food or water in too long a time. I offered her a sip of water from my flask.

She refused the water, saying, "No, I am not worthy."

"I doubt that's true, child," I said, and really, that was all she was, a child someone had brought to womanhood too soon. Then I said, "Drink for the babe you are about to bring into the world then."

"My baby is not worthy, either," she answered, refusing the water.

"Someone has convinced you of lies, child," I told her. "Now are you going to drink this water, gain some strength and tell me about it, or do I have to have my friend here, Elmira, force-open your mouth, so we can fulfill the need of the worthy body of yours and your child?"

Reluctantly, she accepted the water. She also nibbled on some dried fish. We made our camp that night, right there in the place we found this poor woman-child. After the sun had set and our camp fire was at its most welcoming warmth, I again tried to hold a conversation with this pitiful vagabond we had found who, through shame, couldn't look us in the eyes.

I asked, "Why are you and your babe not worthy?"

She finally looked at me astounded, for she thought it was obvious in her condition why she wasn't worthy, and said, "I'm not a married woman." If she was married, the Bindi[195] spot on her forehead would most likely have been red. I had forgotten the custom. A child often preferred indigo.

"Of course," I said, "you are too young to carry the burden of marriage, yet you seem to be carrying one of woman's heaviest loads, with this child about to emerge, nonetheless."

"Precisely," she said. "I have shamed my family and my village. I am an outcast."

"So," I asked her, "you gave yourself a death sentence?"

"It was either that choice, or become a woman of the night. Surely that's no way to raise a child. Since no one would take my child and raise it, due to the taint of my sin, the best I could do for my baby and me, was leave this world and come again another day." She then looked ashamed, her eyes downcast, as she turned her head away from me.

Talking to the side of her head, since I wasn't about to end this conversation just yet, I said "True, you could come again, but what

---

[195] A form of decoration found in the far eastern countries

is left unfinished this lifetime will still have to be revisited and resolved."

"You mean I will have to be raped again and have the same decision once more," she cried.

That was the way I found out this woman-child had been violated. Her innocence had been taken from her, and then she was punished for a crime someone else had committed. I had to remind her that should she willingly kill herself, she was also killing her soon-to-be-born babe.

"This baby in your belly," I said, "has come past the time of decision to turn back its incarnation. To go this far into the physical body means the soul is tied to the physical vehicle now and wants to have its chance at life. Because the child is so body-merged at this point, you are not just dealing with one life, but two," I reminded her.

That set off great loud sobs and a river of tears. "I asked my mother to help me rid my body of this pregnancy, but when I knew of my condition, the baby was already moving within me, and she wouldn't hear of it. She didn't know what to do to help me, as every day I grew larger and larger, and my sin couldn't be hidden. When it became obvious, my father threw me into the streets, calling me a harlot. My mother has other children who need her. She could do nothing for me."

"Is this your father's child?" I asked.

She vomited the small amount of water she had just sipped, at that question. She couldn't stomach the thought of it, yet she had to live with the consequence. Remembering my healing ways I laid her down and put my hand on her stomach. At first she resisted, maybe thinking I was another man not to be trusted. I began to sing a song in the same rhythm a lullaby would be sung, and gently rubbed her stomach through her robes, careful not to make her feel uncomfortable. As I sang the words of my song, I told the stomach to relax and hold its life-giving contents. Then I sang to the baby, telling it that no matter how it was conceived, it was divine, that the world of the physical needed its blessings. Just singing these words over and over helped the little mother relax and the nausea subsided.

"Your father is a fool," I told her, as she finally lay still there, on the ground by the warming fire. "An angel was sent to him, and he didn't recognize her. He dishonored the gift of God." That made her smile slightly, for she knew I meant her. Then I said, "I want to take you and your babe to a place that is safe and loving. You are without sin, child, and so is your baby. Bear this child into the world, sweet one, because one day this babe will bring great blessings to your people. You, dear heart, will have brought the greatest blessing of all, by bearing the burden of motherhood before your time."

She slept then. The next morning Elmira and I helped her to her feet. Taking turns we got her to walk, until she could stand no longer. Then we carried her. The going wasn't easy, yet it didn't dampen our determination.

I prayed, as I walked along with this child-mother in my arms, that my strength would hold until I got her to safety. In truth, I was myself almost to the state of not being able to walk, much less carry anything. Elmira, much older than me, but always a strong man, would take longer and longer turns with the young mother in his arms. Finally, we saw the snow capped ridges of the Himalayas. We also saw a caravan, in the distance, going away from the direction we needed to take. We watched it move out of our sight. We couldn't afford to lose time, going the opposite way.

As we began our assent to the higher cliffs, the air was colder and snow began to cover the path. I sensed an animal watching us. It showed itself upon a high rocky ledge. It was a snow leopard on the hunt. Remembering my old days, not so far from here, and my animal-speak teacher, I spoke with the beautiful cat, as best I could with my waning skills. It circled us, I thought, closing out my words and not responding at first, as if evaluating the others and me. Then it stopped in front of me, too close for comfort, and began to purr. I sat right down in the path, face to face with the purring cat, posing no threat and honoring the peace offering the purr afforded.

# The Saga-Oracle

To my utter surprise, it knew of me. I didn't realize animals kept legends. The purring, I learned, was a language of its own. When a mother cat purrs to her kittens, she is passing along the past stories of her clan. This cat was of the same clan as my first animal-speak teacher. After posing a few critical questions to me, as I was beginning to hear clearer and clearer, she became satisfied that I was, indeed, the Jeshua of legend in her clan. Wanting to know what brought me back to the mountains, I showed her the urn of ashes of the master teacher. She stood up and bowed down to the urn. She knew this teacher, as all the animal clans did in the area. I told her of Elmira, and she knew of him as well, from her family legends. Looking at the little mother, the great she-cat told me this people-kitten was too young to be a mother.

"I know," I said, "I found her trying to die. I have convinced her she should accompany me to the high mountain sanctuary and live a little longer. I just pray I get her there in time, as I'm not sure I have the strength, nor am I sure this child will wait."

"It will not!" the leopard announced. "It's time is very close. Follow me," the cat said, in the mental language we shared, and she got up and moved off the trail towards higher ground. Elmira and I were both worried about going off the meager path we were following, especially in this high elevation where blizzards could manifest in a moment's time. The leopard looked back at me, saying, "My den isn't far."

Sure enough, after a mere stone's throw distance, she slipped into an opening not easily seen. A perfect place for a den, I thought. Inside, it was snug and cozy, lined in her own fur, which she had pulled during her grooming. She would have kittens in the spring and was clearly preparing a warm place for them to be born.

We carefully crawled into the opening, first me, then Elmira, who handed me the shoulders of our little mother, now in full labor and scared beyond reason. It was difficult to get her swollen belly around the portal path of the cave den, but we managed, even though she was fighting us, maybe thinking we intended to sacrifice her to the leopard.

## Jeshua's Song

We just got her situated in a comfortable position, and she raised her knees and in fear she began the screams of birthing. Her spasms were taking her breath away. I forgot about our leopard host, who had left the den anyway. My experience, as father and catcher of the babe at least once, helped me know what to expect and do. I had Elmira get behind and hold the little mother in his arms, making a vise around her chest and helping each spasm by pushing on her stomach. Gently, but firmly he pushed, but to no avail. I had to look inside the poor child, who was so far past embarrassment at two strange men attending her instead of the usual mid-wife, that she ignored what I was doing. She just wanted help. I tried to transfer strength and energy to her by healing hand transference, but that didn't work, because my strength and her receptivity didn't match. I could see the child pushing against her stomach, trying to emerge. She screamed with each spasm. Then I knew I had to help the child and its mother, the way MiryAmah had told me was done sometimes. I had to reach into the mother and help the head of this child come through. Because she was so young, I had to use my knife to widen the channel. I hated making those cuts, first at the exterior of the birth channel, then inside at the portal to the womb. I had to gently insert my entire hand into her tiny womb, now stretched far more than a child's womb should ever be. I could barely get my fingers in place, but I found the soft head, which I gently guided into the channel of emergence. At that point the child burst forth so fast it scared me. I wondered how it could go through the forgetting process that all babies go through, emerging so fast. The dim light was sufficient to see blood, fluids, afterbirth and baby, coming all at once. My moment of wonder was soon side-tracked, by the drama playing out in this den of the leopard.

The leopard was back with a dead bird she had caught. She had watched the entire situation. When the baby had arrived, she commented that was how the kittens came, too, very fast. Then she began licking the baby. I was at first not sure if she intended to eat the baby or what. As she licked the baby, she told me she was, not only cleaning this people-kitten, but was stimulating him so that he could scream and suck in its first breath. That is exactly what happened. The baby boy screamed his head off, not liking the

## The Saga-Oracle

roughness of the tongue of this one giving him his first bath. It was quite a sight—a leopard cleaning a newborn human.

Elmira, our little mother, and I were so exhausted. We just watched in astonishment, as the cat, purring a lullaby to the newborn people-kitten, took care of things for us. It did shock us though, when the leopard gently picked up the babe, by his entire head in her mouth, and deposited him on the chest of his mother. The child stopped crying then, sensing his mother, and instinctively looked for his mother's milk-giving nipple. I hoped she would be able to produce the milk needed for her child. After all, she was still a child herself.

The leopard devoured the placenta and the umbilical cord, it had chewed off from the babe. I didn't know what to think and must have looked confused, for the cat stopped and looked at me. She communicated that she had to ingest this life-giving substance; that by doing so she was pledged to be the guardian of this child throughout his life. I finished the cleanup of the little mother, using some moss I found on the side of the cave to stop the bleeding, where I had to cut the poor woman-child. She and her babe finally slept peacefully.

"Why is it, Elmira?" I asked, "That we find ourselves in the strangest situations?"

He just smiled and chuckled silently, as he always did.

It was dusk when the child came forth. Not wanting to venture out into the night, we all rested. The snow leopard eventually left again, being a nocturnal animal. At the first dawning light, we wrapped up our little mother and child, and began to take leave of this warm den. As we carefully exited the den, we saw the large tracks of our host in the fresh fallen snow. Since we were not sure how to get back to the narrow pathway, we followed her path. The going was rough and I began to worry we would all perish for lack of strength and warmth. About that time the leopard showed up, upon a rock overlooking us. Snow leopards are mostly silent creatures, but she roared with a wail that echoed off the mountain peaks. Then I heard them; people were talking. A rescue party was searching for us. As they approached, I recognized Eocha leading the others. She looked at the leopard and nodded acknowledgement of her role in this rescue.

Eocha found me, sitting on a rock, holding my bundle of mother and child, wrapped like a huge backpack. "Jeshua!" she said, "Is that you under all of that white hair and beard, or are you the yeti man?"

I saw others were tending to Elmira. Glancing at him, I saw how frail he was, as well. We must have been a sight.

Eocha looked at the leopard, now leaving. "She brought you, didn't she?" I asked.

"Yes," Eocha said. "She told me she was the guardian of a great man to be, that I had a friend who needed me, and that the two were as one."

Then Eocha noticed my bundle was not supplies for a long trip, but a young girl curled around me, clinging for life. "Rescued a little girl?" she asked.

"More than just a little girl, for look at what she holds to her breast," I said.

Eocha carefully folded away the robes and saw the tiny newborn face, suckling at his mother's breast. "What wonder is this?" she asked. "Surely, this is not this little one's child."

"It is a long story, Eocha, and not mine to tell. Yes, this is her child and this is the beginning of the life of the great man, who now has a leopard as his guardian."

Someone gently lifted the mother and child from my arms. I was so tired, I didn't notice who took her from my grasp. Then I was lifted myself and wrapped in a warm woven yak blanket. It felt good to be carried, so I just relaxed and fell asleep, as the procession moved along towards safety. When I awoke, I was in the high mountain sanctuary, in the same chamber I had used in my youth. There was a warm fire in the hearth and Eocha sat watching me.

"You still look like a Yeti to me," she said. "I have never seen anyone sleep so soundly," she remarked, with a sweet smile on her old wrinkled beautiful face.

"Like a baby as always, within this sanctuary," I replied. "And what of my friend Elmira, and the little mother and child, are they rested, too?"

"The child is spoiled already," Eocha said. "We haven't had one so young in our midst for a long time, and we argue over who gets to hold him. His mother is doing better, but it will take time for her to forgive herself for guilt that is not hers to bear."

"I know," I said. "The victim is always accused by those who harm them. It's the abuser's way of shifting the blame. Sad but true, most victims blame themselves, because those that abuse them, are often those they love and trust, and they believe them when they shift the fault."

Eocha agreed, nodding and thinking, then she said, "We will help her find her divinity, and we'll offer her a place to raise her beloved son, who–because he is the son of her father, the one who betrayed her–will also be the path to forgiveness.

I knew then that Eocha had spoken to the girl and knew what had happened to her.

"Now," she said, "what do you know of the master teacher, for he went in search of you months ago?"

Suddenly remembering, I looked around the room for the bronze urn. I saw it, sitting with my other things, untouched and unopened. I had sealed it with bee's wax, just after Elmira and I had put my teacher's ashes within it.

I nodded to it. When Eocha looked in the direction, her face dropped. She looked back at me and said, "Tell me it's not true." She and he were very close. Once as a boy I wondered if they were lovers.

"He found me and I've brought him home, as he asked me to do."

"How can it be, we didn't know of his passing?" she asked, looking confused.

"He was so weak when I found him, that maybe he had no strength to communicate his situation," I explained. "He wanted his ashes brought back to this place he called home. That was his last request."

"May I take them with me now?" she inquired, looking sadder than I had ever seen her look.

"Of course," I replied.

Very carefully, with tearful eyes, Eocha lovingly took the urn into her old hands. Holding it to her heart, she asked to be excused for a while and left me to rest.

I don't know what happened to the master teacher's ashes from that point on. I knew that whatever was done, it was proper and appropriate to his wishes.

Under the wonderful care of my second family, as I considered them—even though many faces were different each time I came back, but always the essence of them as a whole was constant—I soon found renewed strength.

I was aware that within my dreamtime, I was interacting with my family, MiryAmah and the children and my brothers and sisters, as well. I frequently saw Jemima, my little sister, in those dreams. She was talking about preparation for my second daughter. "The priestesses prepare for one of their own," she kept telling me. "The Little Rose will have a sister rose," Jemima said. "Tomorrow, tomorrow," I thought I heard her say. Those words haunted me. With all the training and experience, I've had, I was still confused by soul communication from time to time. My emotions got in the way, when I thought of yet another child of mine born without its father. Somehow, it felt better knowing that I could attend the little mother who birthed her son in the leopard's den. I couldn't read the signs as normally I could. As dream-visions do, I couldn't tell if the birth of my child was now past or yet to come.

I never did hear the name of the little mother, nor did I see much of her outside of a glimpse, when she passed near me with her baby firmly cradled in her arms. Eocha saw me watching her one day and said, "Little Jeshua grows stronger day by day."

"Jeshua?" I questioned.

"Correct," she said. "We hope you don't mind, as the child's mother wanted to be reminded time and again of your kindness. In fact, the child's name is actually Jeshua Elmira."

"I'm blessed," I said. "And where is my faithful friend Elmira?"

"When he's not sitting next to the doorway to your chambers he's lurking somewhere nearby watching as only he can, like a ghost unseen," she said.

"I must go to my family. My wife needs me, for we are about to have another child. Tomorrow," I said.

"Tomorrow," Eocha repeated, "tomorrow, tomorrow." She repeated again. "Maybe tomorrow has come and gone."

"What does this mean, 'tomorrow, tomorrow,' I keep hearing it?" I asked in concern.

"It is the hope of today, is it not?" she asked. "But if it's true your child comes tomorrow, then without bi-location, you'll not be able to attend the occasion," she reminded me.

"Are you sure I can't bi-locate, Eocha?" I asked. "I would gladly take my last breath, helping to bring one of my children through the channel of life."

"I wish it could be so, master," she said. She didn't often call me master and that impressed me. "But it's impossible, and we might lose you between dimensions. Then how could you carry on with your work?"

"What work?" I asked in frustration. "What is more important than my life with my family, who I love so much it hurts?"

Eocha just looked at me, saying, "Love doesn't hurt, Jeshua. You know that. What hurts is that which tries to stop love or separate it. Your love for your family has never faltered, nor has theirs for you. What hurts is the battle against fear, dear one. Fear is an awful enemy."

I knew she was right. I also knew no matter what the case may be, I needed to head west in the direction of my loved ones, who kept sending me the mysterious message, 'tomorrow, tomorrow.'

That day while I sat resting and meditating, I saw my master teacher materialize. I squinted my eyes a few times, to make sure I wasn't dreaming, but after a misty moment, he looked as solid as my own body was.

"Greetings, lad," he said.

"Greetings, master," I answered. "You look much better than last, I laid eyes on you."

"It's refreshing to shed an old body," he told me. "I thank you for bringing my ashes back to this place I love so much. I see you returned something else precious as well."

"And what might that be, master?" I asked, not knowing to what he referred.

"Innocence," he said. "You brought back the innocence of the feminine and the masculine, when you brought the little mother and her baby boy to us. They belong here," he said.

"How is it that so?" I asked.

"Just as you belonged here," he answered. "Sensitive souls are lucky, when they're born to parents who understand the gift they offer. Lucky for you, and appropriate for you, such was true when your parents realized you needed safety and training to fulfill your soul mission. In the case of this child-woman, her mother was not priestess-trained and had no network of support to sustain her in times of trouble. Her father tried to kill the innocence of the gift he sensed, but didn't accept. If he had recognized the daughter as a gift, he would never have hurt her. His rape was evil and lust

## The Saga-Oracle

combined, as it defiled the sacredness of true union. He hurt his own soul more than he did her body. He tried to hide his guilt, by making her the sinful one and throwing her away. You and I know, you can never throw away guilt, nor transfer it. The situation must be resolved to peace, by both the guilty party and the forgiveness of the victim. The gift of the divine will not be stopped," my master said. "Little Jeshua will fulfill his divine purpose."

"I was honored to be able to help him into the world. Now, I only wish to do the same for my own baby."

"You will be there," he told me, "but not as you are now, nor will you be bi-located."

I tried to understand what he was saying. Then it dawned on me, I might die soon.

I felt old and weak, true, but I wasn't ready to leave just yet. Eocha had said my crucifixion experience had aged my body before its time. "I'm not ready to die yet, master!" I said. "I have work yet to do."

"Your work constantly evolves, as you know, lad," he explained to me. "The next cycle awaits you and so do I." Then he became a mist again and was gone.

I stood in my room. I could neither speak nor think. Elmira entered my chambers for the first time, since we arrived. He bowed to me and began packing my few belongings.

"Are we leaving?" I asked him in a stupor.

"As you wish, so shall it be," he answered in his mind-speak.

"I don't know what I wish," I replied, "but you're right–it's time to go."

# TAKE ME HOME, JESHUA, TAKE ME HOME
## Chapter Forty-Seven

Elmira and I, now old men, left the sanctuary of the high mountains, going south eastward toward the lands of Yasma, my long ago teacher. Why? I don't know. I planned to go directly to my wife and family, which would have been the opposite direction, but somehow instead I thought I needed to see Yasma, the healer. He was an old man when I was but a boy. I don't know what I was thinking, as I headed towards his village.

Surely, he must have passed on by now, my head told me, but my heart was overriding this logic. Maybe I wanted my body to be healed enough, so I could have more time with my family. It's difficult for me to even remember how decisions were made, for I was losing energy and thinking takes energy. I was in automatic mode, and somehow that auto-mode took me into India.

About our second day, as we were into less mountainous landscape, we could see a shadow in the distance. Elmira saw it first and pointed it out to me. It was something large, standing and swaying back and forth in one spot. He looked at me, puzzled at what this might be.

"If I had enough energy, I would trade places with that hawk soaring on high, and go see what's out there," I said. I didn't even have the energy to mind-speak to the hawk, much less merge with it. The strength I gained in the mountain sanctuary was waning fast. As it takes an ability to shift the thinking vibrations, to go into animal-speak, and I was so depressed, tired and confused, I couldn't do what ordinarily would be easy. So we just walked toward the huge dark shape, drawn to it, because intuitively it called us.

"It is an elephant," I told Elmira, as we got closer and he nodded agreement. It was standing in place, swinging back and forth in a sideways motion, its head held low. "It's mourning something," I said to Elmira, concerned.

When we finally approached the giant animal, we could see this was a domestic elephant, as it wore the head harness of those that served humans. It barely gave us notice as we got closer, just stood there rocking back and forth, its long trunk dangling in the dance-like motion, standing over something.

We tried to approach and see what it might be protecting, but the animal threw its head high, raised and curled its trunk, and trumpeted a warning. It had very long tusks, and it meant to use them if needed. This was clearly a bull elephant, standing guard over something it loved dearly.

Elmira looked at me, to see if I could communicate with the animal. I shook my head 'no.' I had used all the energy I could muster, just getting to this spot. I sat down on the ground, leaned against a large rock and watched the grieving animal. Elmira did the same. We kept an eye on the bundle, lying between the animal's great feet, watching to see if it moved. It didn't. I wondered how such a huge creature could be so graceful upon its enormous legs and feet, as it danced and swayed over this bundle it was protecting, never once stepping on it.

I said, "Whatever is in the bundle, Elmira, must have meant a great deal to this poor elephant. Look at how it weeps." Wet streaks ran down its face and dripped to the ground below, which was damp with the long-flowing stream of sorrow. The place was arid and dry with not much vegetation growing, so wetness was usually quickly absorbed, however, this wet spot was saturated.

"I wonder how long this has been going on," I said to Elmira. He shrugged his shoulders, indicating he certainly had no clue. As I think back, it would have been logical to move on, saving my waning strength to get to my family, but I stayed. I just sat there. Hours later, or maybe it was days, as it's hard to tell, I came to my senses. Elmira was giving me a refreshing drink of water. He must have left and found some source. The elephant was not dancing any longer. It had used its tusks to pile up dirt upon the bundle, which I now knew contained a body. It had stepped away from it and stood looking at me. Being refreshed by the water, I stood up and approached the animal. It didn't seem to threaten me. I carefully touched its face. Petting it gently, I looked into its eye and said, "I know, great one. It's difficult to send off someone you love to the heavens, while you have to stay behind." I was sure it understood my words and knew we were brothers of sorrow.

Physical weakness can drain awareness. This mighty animal was much more aware than I at this point. As I looked over at the now-buried bundle, I saw a hand protruding from the dirt. The old misshapen hand had seen years of work, and this was an old bull elephant, too. It didn't take much thought-energy to put two and two together. They had been partners for a long time. I gently approached the grave. This worried the elephant somewhat, but I didn't sense danger. I very carefully pushed some dirt over the hand. The elephant then knew I didn't plan to desecrate the grave, just help him bury his master, and it relaxed. When I had the hand sufficiently covered, I saw Elmira had the elephant laying down, was touching it here and there, and the great bull was responding.

"Do you know how to handle a domestic elephant, Elmira?" I asked.

He nodded his head 'yes' and motioned for me to approach. He kissed the elephant upon its teary eye, and then motioned me to get upon its back, behind its head. Two huge bumps, as Asian Elephants have, created an indentation behind them, a perfect place for a man to safely sit. I looked at Elmira and said, "If I get up on this animal, then so do you."

Again he nodded 'yes.' We stepped on the leg of the bull, using it as a stepping place, and got into position, me in the front with Elmira behind me. He touched the animal behind the ears, signaling it to rise. The jarring motion of such a huge animal getting to its feet startled me. I was very high up, when this fellow was fully on his feet. I grabbed the halter it wore on its head and hoped for the best. I had seen elephants, but never ridden one before. I thought of little Beeba, the little white donkey who had become a member of the family. Remembering riding upon his back I reflected; I was so big and he was so little that fateful day in Jerusalem and now the situation was reversed. This elephant was huge, even for his species. Funny how the mind works–no sooner had that thought crossed my mind, then thoughts of my family consumed me again. In truth, they were never far from my thinking and yearning. I wondered if Beeba was still alive or had he passed? Donkeys could live into their sixties. Certainly, he was not that old yet, since even I hadn't reached that age. Then, I thought of how I had aged so much faster than my beloved MiryAmah. I was older than she by a good stretch, so she must surely still be strong and hopefully 'alive'. I was glad she didn't have to endure the torture I had; but then again, as soul mates–she being the other part of me–she had endured it all. She was stronger, as all women are, than the men in her life. I thought of the baby on the way, or was it born already, because time was all scrambled up for me. I thought of the other children my beloved wife had gifted me. Men had no idea what strength that took. I surmised, however, it might be a month yet before that babe should emerge, as I rocked with the motion of the moving elephant, and day dreamed–even though I kept hearing 'tomorrow, tomorrow'. That motion can put one in a trance, as deep as walking can. In such a trance, the underlying causes of actions and the awareness of reactions–appropriate or otherwise–could be explored, and my mind drifted on and on. I could see my entire life being played out, from before I emerged into the physical world until now. I could see a door, or portal of light, not far from me. It seemed to be inviting me. Part of me wanted to go through the door; part of me knew it wasn't yet time.

I felt my strength slowly return, as I rode along on this swaying animal. I'm not sure if the elephant was responsible for my feeling better, but it was possible. Here I was sitting, upon its neck, right where the spine connects to the brain. In other words, I was where, according to Yasma, the kundalini[196] (the energy of the physical body) rushed through, from the base of the spine to the crown of the head, overflowing, when allowed to run its proper course. I had spoken of this to my companions many times, saying, "When my cup runneth over, I have more to give." It was energy to which I referred, divine energy, which we all have the ability to bring

---

[196] the energy of the consciousness, that lies at the base of the spine and rises through the chakra vortexes of the body as the entity experiences life in the physical and discovers its divinity

forth. I sometimes relocated myself to sit upon the animal's large head, right on the crown of this huge one and I seemed to feel stronger. I wondered if it was channeling its kundalini energy into me. I got quite comfortable there upon that huge head, and I felt better physically as well. Elmira seemed more energetic, too, and would often get down and walk, or forage for food and drink for us, only to reappear on down the trail later. I never worried about him.

We went on for a day or two like this. Then we saw a group of agitated people on the trail, as we were now on the trade route, a well-worn path. I still yearned to see Yasma and was heading toward his village, but in my mind, I was heading for my beloved MiryAmah, too. I was confused, even as my energy was slightly building. My giant steed stopped near the group of people and lay down, so I could more easily dismount, as usual. Walking over to the group to see what was going on, I found an old woman in much pain, lying on the ground with people surrounding her. She had been run over by a cart loaded with stone, and was crushed, they said. It was quite clear she was a much-loved member of a family group, since they were all in distress as to her situation and didn't want her to be in pain, but couldn't make themselves take her out of pain by helping her die faster.

"Excuse me," I said, as I gently pushed my way to where she lay. The group parted and looked at me like I was an angel. I heard someone mention the glow around me and wondered what that could be. I thought, maybe the dust of the trail was going airborne as I walked forward. I stooped down and looked into the sweetest old face. One could tell from her eyes, she was a wise one, beloved by all she ever gazed upon.

I put my hand on her forehead, went into an automatic mode and said, "Blessed is one so loved as you, dear heart." Her eyes held gratitude as she looked back at me. Then I said, "This isn't your day to die, as those who love you can't bear for you to leave them." Now her brows went up in a questioning manner, and I could see the pain had subsided. So, I went on and said, "Are you willing to stay a little longer for their sake?" She nodded 'yes.' Everyone was watching quietly, their eyes wide and their mouths dropped open. Scanning them, I asked. "Do you want some more time with this woman you love so much?" They immediately answered, all speaking at once, saying 'yes!' even as their minds were saying, 'how could this be?'

I looked down into the hopeful face of the crushed old woman, remembering how Yasma had taught me to find the perfect pattern for the body and bring it back to its natural perfection. "I must touch you, grandmother," I addressed her out of respect, and alerted her to my intent. "Please don't feel offended, for I must put a few of your bones back where they belong. I promise this will not hurt," I reassured her.

"I'm not afraid of pain," she told me. "I have work yet to do within this family, who honors me as grandmother. Anything you do is a blessing, and I trust you, stranger. I think you are really an angel, who has taken mercy on such as me, old and tired but still not quite finished with my work."

I began laying my hands on her as we talked, starting the healing. Beginning with her head, I gently allowed my hands to find the proper pattern of her physical body and to infuse that pattern with an attracting light,[197] which would then pull the body's' components back into its perfection. "I'm not an angel," I said, as my hand lightly slipped across her lovely old face. When I got to her mouth, I gently blew into it. She felt the breath of the Divine. It wasn't just my breath. When one is channeling the Divine, something greater comes through, and I was sharing that essence with her. Her face appeared to grow younger, as she took in the breath. Then I went down each arm, found the pattern and added the attracting light. The body immediately took its proper shape. I spent some time on the heart and chest, since that area was badly crushed, too. As I moved lower to the abdomen, her chest found its full form. It was flattened when I found her; it filled its shape, even as I had already moved on. Then I did likewise, all down through her body, right to the soles of her misshapen feet. Like many who had walked barefoot throughout their lifetime, her feet

---

[197] Light that is divinely perfect for that place and once it is merged perfection is achieved

were gnarled and crooked. I gently rubbed her feet, and they straightened and smoothed.

"Oh!" the old woman uttered. "I have had pain in those poor old feet for so long, I forgot how good toes feel," and she wiggled her toes.

"Arise, woman," I commanded. At this point, the healer had to be commanding. When there has been such extensive injury, the body won't respond to a simple request, in such a state of shock. She looked at me, not sure what to do. So, I said it again, only louder, "Arise, woman, for you are healed."

The denial of shock began to subside. She looked at her hands. They were no longer curled and misshapen. She felt her chest and could feel herself breathing. She looked at her family, who all stood watching. She finally arose and they all went crazy with joy. As they rejoiced, I left. My giant steed was waiting for me to climb aboard again, and I was beginning to feel faint. I barely made it to his side, where Elmira was waiting as well. He helped me board the elephant, and we left. Hearing a child yelling, I turned around. A small girl was running behind us, waving her little arms.

"Hey angel, we love you," she kept saying.

"I'm not an angel, little one," I managed to respond. "I'm just Jeshua ben Joseph and once a child like you. Go enjoy your grandmother, for she is the true angel." The little girl stopped running and waved to us with her entire arm. She understood. I hoped that she would explain to her family, who the angel really was.

It was only a matter of hours, and I was feeling re-energized. We again ran into trouble on the path. This time an ornate carriage was sitting by the path. The carriage had shafts for servants to carry on their shoulders, but the servants were now scurrying about, trying to keep a growing crowd away. This was a much-traveled road, and people were naturally curious, especially if the elite were involved. I could see a great concern for who was inside the carriage. Something was terribly wrong. I stopped, asking what the trouble was. Before anyone could respond to me, an irate man of means dressed in fine clothes and having jewels upon all his fingers, began yelling at me in a rage.

"You aren't wanted here!" he screamed at me and the other onlookers. "Can't a man have some peace in a moment like this?" he yelled, as his face was contorted in anguish and fear.

Ignoring his demand that we leave, I walked over to him, asking again what his trouble might be.

"It is not your business," he yelled in my face.

"That's true, but you're sad and troubled. If there is anything I can do, I'll be glad to help you," I said.

"Get the hell out of here and take these people with you," he yelled so loud, he got a spasm in his side. Striking him hard and fast, the pain diverted his attention. I put my hand on his back, and the spasm went away.

"Give up the anger and you'll give up the pain," I gently said. He just looked at me, as the pain instantly vanished. He had those terrible spasms often–especially when he felt helpless. The relief from the pain calmed him.

I felt he was ready to talk now. "I can help, if you let me," I told him. "It has often been difficult for you in this lifetime to accept help. That has caused you much sorrow. It's time to give up, and open the door to the blessings waiting to visit you. Let me assist you," I bid him.

He thought for a moment, and then said, "Are you a sorcerer?"

"Listen to your heart right now, for it's your love speaking to you," I said. "Your head is too full of worry for power and control. Your head is asking if I am a sorcerer. Your heart knows that I'm not." Then I waited for a moment and said, "If you listen to your head, you will lose that which you love."

"It's my wife," he said. "She is my greatest joy. She has given me four daughters and promised me a son. Now she goes into her birthing early, and I fear the son I was promised will not survive. Worse than that, I fear I shall lose my wife, who I love beyond measure."

"Do you love your daughters?" I asked.

"Of course I do, but a man is not a man, until he has a son," he answered.

I allowed a moment of silence after that statement, then said, "So your wife has blessed you four times with beautiful babies, and you have still felt cheated, because they weren't sons?"

He just looked at me. Then a scream came from the caravan carriage, and he unconsciously grabbed my arm and ran in that direction. One of the servants told him not to enter yet, for a passing mid-wife was tending to the situation.

"If she kills her, I shall do, likewise, to her and her entire family," the angry husband said.

"If your wife dies," I said, "it will be you that killed her." As he looked at me in shock, I went on to say, "Because she has gifted you four times already, and you have felt cheated. If this child is born dead, you have killed it as well, because you have placed too much burden upon this tiny one, even before he comes into your household. Only you can save this baby and its mother. You are about to lose both, because you haven't recognized the gifts God has already sent." I let him think about this and hoped the mid-wife could help the poor woman, for her own sake and for the sake of this ungrateful man.

When he entered the carriage, I followed. The baby was already born dead and his wife so weak, it was clear she wouldn't last long. As the baby boy was handed to him, he put him to his own chest, bloody swaddling and all. Then as an attendant took the baby, he fell upon his weakened wife, begging her forgiveness. He told her of his great love for his daughters, that even without this son, he was totally blessed by the gifts she had already given him. But, he said, he loved her most. If she should go now, he would surely die; without her, he couldn't envision going on alone. It was like a floodgate had opened, and somehow she had the strength to listen, even as she hemorrhaged.

He was so focused on her; he didn't see me gently put my hand to the sacred portal under the blanket covering her. She knew and looked at me for a moment. I just nodded my head, to indicate it was okay. She nodded back, feeling no disrespect or disgrace. It took but a moment for the blood to stop. I withdrew my hand and turned my attention to the small now-blue baby in the attendant's arms. She handed me the infant. Again, intuitively I knew what to do. I gave him the breath of life, gently but steadily sending little puffs of air down into his mouth and nose as my brother had done for my son. Finally, I felt his chest move up and down on its own, and I could see the color returning to the boy. I gently turned the father's face to me. Using the bloody hand, I touched his mouth, leaving a handprint there, and said, "This is the blood of love. Let it bring life. Let that life be gratefully appreciated. Remember, dear man, without this blood neither you, nor any other man would be walking upon the land."

Then he noticed the now-moving baby in my arms. Handing him his son, I said, "Blessed are the grateful, for they recognize the true Divine gifts." I looked at the woman, also gaining strength, and said to her, "Forgive him. He didn't know that his heart doors were closed. Even so, he did know he loved you. Forgive him and live a long and fruitful life." She had silent tears running down her cheeks.

"Who are you?" she asked.

"I am Jeshua, the student of Yasma the healer."

Her attention went to her baby then, who she knew had been dead, but now lived. I quietly left as before, as she reached out for her newborn son.

When I approached the elephant, it took my bloody hand in a grip with its trunk, as if to examine it. It moved my hand to the tears still falling from its eyes, and rubbed the blood from my hand on both its cheeks, dragging me around a bit as it accomplished its intention. It then allowed me up again, kneeling low so I could climb aboard and we were off down the path once more.

The closer we came to Yasma's village, the more I ran into those needing healing: animals, such as a donkey with a broken leg, and even once, the heart of a camel man, who was cruelly treating his charge, hitting it over the head with a big stick. I just leaned down, touching him on the head and said, "Peace be in your heart and have peace in your life." He immediately began to sob. Throwing his club away, he embraced the camel, that at first shied from him expecting to be hurt again. As I looked back over my shoulder, I noticed the animal had sensed the change and was nuzzling his master. I knew a new bond had been linked between them. I found a man full of leprosy, being stoned off the road by people afraid of him. I told him he was beautiful, to go look in the nearest well, then drink of the water and rejoice. His robe fell from his head, and I could see the ugly sores disappearing already. I knew he would be healed, too.

I don't tell you all of this to amaze you or to brag, for that's not my intent. The truth was, as I was nearing the end of my physical life, something was vitally different. The most powerful healing is possible at the emergence, or birth of someone (the healing of hope), and as a person begins the winding down of that sojourn, preparing to leave the plane of the physical (the healing of forgiveness). In the latter case, the soul realizes it will not need the energy much longer and fore-gives of itself (gives of itself before the body departs) this energy to others. This is a divine giving, thus powerfully healing.

I finally arrived at the village of Yasma, but his home was no longer there, nor was he. I asked of him and was told he disappeared long ago, after his student left. I wondered if that was me to whom they were referring. At this news, I felt terrible. I had a need to see Yasma, and I was again too weak from all the healing and traveling, to try scrying or any type of visualization. I wanted so badly to see him, just one more time.

I went to a quiet place, sat down and wept. This time I told Elmira to find water and food for our elephant friend, who made this trip much easier. So, he went in another direction to follow my wishes. A little boy approached, as I sat by a lonely olive tree in this little village and cried great streams of tears. He was very young; maybe around four years old.

"Why do you cry?" he asked, looking at me so compassionately.

"I cry, because I came to see a friend, and he's not here."

"No!" he announced, "you cry for yourself, because you need this friend and feel sorry for yourself."

"You are a wise one," I told him. "He was my teacher. I was hoping he could teach me to heal myself, so I could go home again."

"You can always go home. You don't need to be healed to do that," he said matter-of-factly.

"But I want to be with my family. I'm about to be a father again. All of my children's lives, I haven't been able to be with them." I was pouring my heart out to this little boy, I realized.

"You have been with them always in their hearts. Many parents have children by their sides constantly, but still abandon them in their hearts."

That observation made me feel better, so I asked. "How is it a little boy such as you can be so wise?"

"Weren't you as wise as a small boy?" he asked back.

"They say I was, but the longer I live, the more there is to learn, and I don't feel all that wise now," I replied.

"You were a wise child, and you are a wise man," he said. Then he took my hand, causing a strange comforting feeling to rush through my body. He said, "Not everyone recognizes their wisdom, and not everyone understands that, no matter who helps them, they must heal themselves. I must go," he said and got up to leave.

"Who are you, child?" I asked.

"Yasma," he said, winking at me. Then I noticed he walked the same way my old friend and teacher walked, as he disappeared into a cloud of dust.

The streets were always cloudy and dusty from the crowded traffic. Coming from the opposite direction, I could see Elmira riding upon the elephant, approaching me.

"Did you see that small boy?" I asked Elmira. Elmira looked over his shoulder, and nodded 'yes.' "That is Yasma, or at least that was his name," I said. "Now we can go home," I announced, and saw a huge flash of white light at that statement, then nothing.

The next thing I saw was Elmira upon the elephant, silently riding away, going northward towards his homeland. He was crying in his silent way and so was the elephant. I wondered what made them sad. Then I realized I was looking down on the situation, floating in the air. I wondered what had happened and my attention was immediately taken to a group of people, who were washing my body and putting ointments upon it. I knew I wasn't in it, but I was watching the scene. There were a mixture of people attending to me, one of which was the affluent husband I had encountered on the road, who had saved his own wife and baby with his gratitude. The family of the old grandmother and others were there, as well. They were trying to honor my people's traditions and decided not to burn my body, but rather to encrypt it and send my bones home, wherever that might be. I sensed that a day or so had passed, by this time, since others were joining the group moment by moment. It seemed as if only a split second ago, I was watching little Yasma walk into a cloud of dust and asking Elmira, riding high on the majestic bull elephant, if he saw the boy. I found myself a bit disoriented.

As I watched the events play out, I realized I wasn't alone. I looked behind me and there was my master teacher. He put his hand on my shoulder and said, "Welcome home, lad."

"I didn't want to die," I said, now realizing what had happened.

"You didn't die, you transformed back to your natural state. Your body could no longer hold the energy to keep you miserably contained in that vehicle," he told me.

"You have some things to do before you meet with your council," he said. "Your father will help you tend to them." Then I saw him–my father. I wish I could properly explain how it feels, to be reunited with those who have passed on from the physical before you, but I can't. The love and joy of reunion can only be felt, never properly described. All depression is forgotten. It's such a lonely place in the so-called 'land of the living', as my mother and so many called living in the physical. Yet the challenges of discovering the divinity of yourself and all creation can blind your eyes to seeing the beauty of the opportunity. Seeing my father and teacher lifted the veil of sorrow. Then I saw James as well. He and father took me to MiryAmah and the children.

I arrived just as Joseph, my dear brother, was catching my newborn baby girl. I must tell you that the scene of a birth is beautiful. The spread legs, the blood, and the anticipation–all the drama is beautiful, especially when seen from the spirit realm. Being in the physical is not an easy decision, but its rewards are too great to describe. At each physical birth, there are wondrous divine sounds of rejoicing as the child emerges and literally, angels sing. That was the moment of my reunion with my beloved.

I felt honored, that my brother protected and served my family so well. I looked at James, as I knew he was a guardian angel for them, too. Then I noticed Joseph, helping to swaddle my new daughter. A more beautiful baby couldn't be imagined. All my children were just as beautiful at birth. To see a soul leave the heavenly world and come through the channel of forgetting in service to the Divine, is awesome and every child is born in radiance and beauty. Now, I more completely understood why it is so important that a father catch the emerging child; it's so they can experience this Divine moment. "Is this tomorrow?" I asked James.

"In a way," he answered. "This is Tamara. Her name means there is hope for tomorrow. It also means 'palm tree', the sacred tree that grows even in the desert, and offers hope and shade to those who travel by."

It dawned on me then, what the dreams, visions and confirmations meant. Tomorrow, tomorrow—it meant there is hope for tomorrow. I remembered the palm branches my followers had laid before me, as I entered Jerusalem that fateful Sunday. The palm leaves symbolized the triumph of the faithful. My little girl was surely such a triumph.

I tried to convey my love to my exhausted wife. However, it seemed, the only one who truly knew I was there, was little Tamara, who kept watching me and smiling.

Joseph said to MiryAmah, who was happy for the baby, yet sad because I wasn't there, or so she thought, "See! The child already talks to angels."

I looked at my father and asked, "Why do they keep referring to me as an angel?"

"Because you glow like one, son," he replied.

And with that we returned to my council meeting, which some of you might call the 'last judgment.'

The review of your life is judged by you alone, as the veil of events is lifted. You feel the effect you had on everyone and everything. With the veil of illusion lifted, you see how your life affected everyone and everything with which you interacted. Even the apple you bit into and ingested affected the tree that grew it. So many little things mean so much in the deeper divine scheme of things.

After meeting with my review council, and going over every action and reaction in my physical life–as Jesus ben Joseph, or Jeshua ben Joseph; and also son of Mary; husband to MiryAmah; and father to my little queen, Sarah; my dear sons James and Joshephus, my little Tamara; and also as half-brother to Joseph and brother to James and Simon and sisters, little Jemima, and others through marriage and life's connections–I knew I was

## The Saga-Oracle

blessed beyond the mistakes I had made. The love I had been given, and gave, was most important. Indeed, I was worthy as all God's creation is. I then went back to the galactic council chambers.

I asked their forgiveness for failing on this mission, even as I had just reviewed my life review and knew I did my best. One of the members spoke to me, saying, "You didn't fail, Jeshua. You can't give the divine gift and expect to tell those gifted, what to do with it."

Another council member, a woman from the liquid blue planet, said in her watery voice, "To make mistakes is not to sin. To not have tried, is to sin. To give up, is to sin, when there is still strength to carry on. You are sinless, Jeshua. You never gave up, no matter how your gifts of spirit were received."

"In my soul review, there were many times when I caused pain and suffering from my actions. Isn't that sin?" I asked, still uncertain of my contribution to the project for which I was born.

Another member spoke then. This member reminded me of Elmira. He said, "Intention is the measure. Success or failure of intention doesn't equate to sin. You know that, and you knew that before you took this assignment. We have decided to give you some rest and allow you to keep watch on your family. We will continue this meeting, when MiryAmah joins us. She has some time left yet, in her part of the mission. After that joint council meeting, we will be moving on with your work at a galactic level."

I noticed my master teacher was on the council now. I wondered why I hadn't noticed him before. In this place words don't have to be formed, and he answered the mental question.

"This position was vacated by one who had been given another task to perform for the same Divine Cause. I'm pleased to be invited to be among those working with the shakers and movers of energy that needs attunement and movement," he said. Then he reminded me of our conversation pertaining to how my mission evolved.

629

As I remembered that conversation, I remembered the stages of my mission. First: I spoke to the crowds in parable, because they were mind-controlled and couldn't speak for themselves. They didn't trust their own voices and needed someone to speak for them. That was in the land of my birth, the place the council had determined needed the stimulation of the balancing factors.

"I thought they understood, but even my dearest students got my intentions mixed up," I said, thinking of the apostles and many of the followers, who I thought I had helped comprehend what my true message was.

My old master reminded me, "The concept of duality, as complementing factors, not opposing factors, is simple, but complex within its simplicity. They will understand in time that the duality is 'One.' Change is best coming gradually. If it happens too fast, fear and chaoses get involved," Then he said, "You came to build love, not to feed fear."

He also reminded me that after my crucifixion when I was healed, then traveled and listened and helped those whom I met 'listen to themselves'–which was the best way to help them raise or confirm their awareness–I had woven a web of peace and connection.

"One's own voice," the master said, "is the music of the soul and the most influential sound to the seeker. Listening to what one says is the key to changing that which diminishes them. That's why the second phase of your mission was successful."

Again I didn't feel all that triumphant and said, "But they still wage war against each other and focus on their differences, instead of how they are all divine."

My master teacher had such a penetrating gaze with the deepest dark brown eyes. Even on this council, he kept the look that always pierced me. He was looking right through my soul. I knew he was trying to get me to listen to myself and raise my own awareness of the situation.

"Okay," I said, "I get it. I'm listening to myself and realize that because they are naturally intuitive people and prone to listen to their inner-voices, eventually they will find balance and thus peace, because they will ultimately match their actions to that voice within. When they tell their stories, the voice within comes through. That was why the storytellers were so sacred in their societies."

"You have done well," the master said. Then we came to the final phase of my life, which was helping people 'see' their actions and reactions. He told me, "You helped them see through illusions of power, controlling thoughts and ways."

"I'm not sure how I did that," I replied.

"Through seeing yourself, you helped others see," he told me.

"Didn't you see what taking your last physical strength to heal accomplished?" he asked.

"Healing," I answered, "of the mind, body and soul would be my answer now. At the time I didn't have any intention. I was just moving along within total intuition, and the opportunities kept offering themselves to me."

"Who taught you to heal?" he asked.

"The old man, Yasma," I responded, "Who became a boy again, to teach me more," I added. From this perspective, I could see that, even as I sought my beloved healing teacher, he gave me repeated opportunities to demonstrate and use that which he had taught me.

Another council member, an old woman who had been sitting quietly, appearing as a saga from the faraway land, said, "If you can do this on a planetary level, this planting of fertile seeds in the garden of God, then you can do even more on a universal level, where the planets hold relationship and evolutionary cycles within the grand plan of All That Is, offering a bigger garden. Just as all people are really One Person; so, too, all creation is One Creation. You have much work yet to do," she said. "There are many gardeners, but not all can plant the seeds in the right manner, or at the right time and place."

The entire council nodded to me in dismissal, and said, "Peace be."

Time doesn't exist outside of physicality, as you might think. After I left the council, I near immediately went back to my family. They grew and struggled to survive, like a movie playing at a fast speed, before my eyes. My little queen was greatly loved, yet still feared by those who would wipe out my memory. Eventually, she had to go into hiding. My sons and little Tamara had ups and downs as well in their lives. They became close to Uncle Joseph, who they called 'father' for their own security. They loved Asara as well, which pleased me, for I loved her, too. Her devotion to my beloved and me has never faltered. As they grew and didn't need their mother so much, my beautiful MiryAmah became more and more depressed. She was seldom seen, keeping to herself, often in the caves she had shown me on our last visit. Everyday little Tamara would bring her flowers from her garden to cheer her up. She used to say that I left through the rose garden, and I would return the same way, so she made sure her mother had roses around her always, especially the lovely blue and pink ones that reminded her of our great love. Though she had never met me in the flesh, she knew her parents were lovers, and she was proof of their great passion for each other.

Martha left Tamara to tend the gardens these days, since she was getting elderly, at the time of my spiritual visit to the family, and she was tired, too. She spent most of her time tending her sister, my dear wife, now instead of her beloved roses. She felt shame and responsibility, partly because she didn't recognize the closeness MiryAmah and I felt. However, after all these years, she had finally understood why it was more important MiryAmah had sat at my feet that day of our meeting long ago in their family home, rather than share the burden Martha bore, serving a meal to my followers and me. She realized now, to serve love is the greatest cause, and she was doing just that, by allowing us a time to feast in each other's presence, and that her little sister, Mary, my own MiryAmah, was serving love by our divine reunion. Like so many, she wished she had known then what she knew now, as she had wasted far too much time being judgmental about the situation. So she made it up as best she could, by trying to serve my beloved in her elder years, with total graciousness and gratitude.

As I watched events play out as if in a flash, I could see my wife weakening. I stood behind Martha, who was very concerned for her sister. Then it happened. MiryAmah looked into my eyes. She actually saw me. Her elderly face lit up, and I could see the same passion we always enjoyed upon meeting after a long separation, written all over her lovely face. She dropped the deep pink rose Tamara had brought to her just moments before. She was enjoying the aroma of the rose and the memory of our exchange of roses on our wedding day, when she noticed me. I had given her a rose that looked exactly like the one she held. Her hair was now streaked with gray and hung to the floor. She looked even more beautiful than I remembered. Martha, noticing she was looking past her, asked what she saw.

"I see my beloved here to take me home," she said. I reached for her hand as she stepped out of her body, and we embraced, both no longer frail, perfectly complete. At the same instant, her body just slipped away to the floor. MiryAmah looked at Martha, now holding her lifeless body, then back to me and said, "Martha will follow soon. Take me home, Jeshua. Finally, we can be together; take me home."

*Dedicated in loving memory*

*to Ruthanne,*

*my forever friend.*